FROM
THE
ASHES

MY STORY OF BEING MÉTIS, HOMELESS,
AND FINDING MY WAY

JESSE THISTLE

PUBLISHED BY SIMON & SCHUSTER
NEW YORK   LONDON   TORONTO   SYDNEY   NEW DELHI

SIMON &
SCHUSTER
CANADA

Simon & Schuster Canada
A Division of Simon & Schuster, Inc.
166 King Street East, Suite 300
Toronto, Ontario M5A 1J3

This Simon & Schuster Canada edition August 2019

SIMON & SCHUSTER CANADA and colophon are trademarks of Simon & Schuster, Inc.

For information about special discounts for bulk purchases, please contact Simon &
Schuster Special Sales at 1-800-268-3216 or CustomerService@simonandschuster.ca.

Interior design by Carly Loman

Manufactured in the United States of America

20 19 18

Library and Archives Canada Cataloguing in Publication

Title: From the ashes : my story of being Métis, homeless, and finding my way /
    by Jesse Thistle.
Names: Thistle, Jesse, author.
Identifiers: Canadiana (print) 20190062770 | Canadiana (ebook) 20190062789 |
    ISBN 9781982101213 (softcover) | ISBN 9781982101237 (ebook)
Subjects: LCSH: Thistle, Jesse. | LCSH: Métis—Biography. | LCSH: Cree Indians—
    Canada—Biography. | LCSH: Homeless persons—Canada—Biography. |
    LCSH: Addicts—Canada—Biography. | LCGFT: Autobiographies.
Classification: LCC FC109.1.T45 A3 2019 | DDC 971.004/970092—dc23

ISBN 978-1-9821-0121-3
ISBN 978-1-9821-0123-7 (ebook)

All photographs are courtesy of the author, except as noted.
Portions of this text originally appeared on homelesshub.ca.

This book is dedicated to the families whose loved ones are taken, or disappeared, or lost to them. Those forever watching for their loved one to return home. I watch and wait with you.

It is also dedicated to Indigenous children who grew up with no sense of themselves through projects like the Sixties Scoop, residential schools, adoption, or other such separation from their nuclear family during which they were robbed of their Indigenous identity through no fault of their own.

The pages of this book speak to the damage colonialism can do to Indigenous families, and how, when one's Indigeneity is stripped away, people can make poor choices informed by pain, loneliness, and heartbreak, choices that see them eventually cast upon the streets, in jail, or wandering with no place to be. I dedicate this book to you. I walk with you. I love you. I know the loneliness and frustration you endure.

Lastly, I dedicate this book to my wife, Lucie, who loved me back into the circle. This also goes out to my brothers, Josh, Jerry, and Daniel; my mom and dad; and to my grandparents, who gave me a fighting chance. Our circle is strong; our fire burns; this book is but a torch from the hearth of our clans, and is hopefully enough to light the way for others to follow.

CONTENTS

CONTENTS

CONTENTS

CONTENTS

RECONCILIATION
2008–2017

INDIGENOUS AFFAIRS

at night
alone
when the dope sickness set in
and the begging became too humiliating
I'd wander from the ByWard Market to the Centennial Flame fountain
    on Parliament Hill
looking for respite from my addictions.

ashamed
i sat with my back to the Peace Tower
thrust my hand in the cool fountain water
fishing out the hoard of coins thrown by tourists and passersby.

the RCMP who guarded the fountain
always saw me coming
from way down at the bottom of the Rideau Hill
near the Milestones and Château Laurier
but he never stopped me.

instead he'd sit and wait for me
watch as I shovelled wet change into my pockets.
then, before I got too greedy,
rush out and chase me away.

he always let me escape.

we both understood what was going on

why I was there
stealing from the Centennial Flame.

PROLOGUE

The kingdom of heaven suffers violence, and violent men take it by force.

Matthew 11:12

THE DEAD SILENCE SCREAMED DANGER.

Frenzied squeaks of jail-issued blue deck shoes on sealed cement followed by wet smacks, fast pops, loud cracks, and finally a dull thud confirmed it. A guy lay crumpled on the range floor, our range quartermaster told us. He wasn't conscious. His legs were seized straight, quivering uncontrollably. He had pissed and shit himself.

We didn't need to see it with our own eyes. The unseen, the unknown, in jail is often worse than the seen, the known.

The next day, after cell search, I heard that he had died en route to hospital.

Someone said he'd stolen a bag of chips from another inmate's canteen, but who knew?

Who cared?

It was jail justice. The thief got what he deserved. According to us, according to society. At least that's what I told myself. All I knew for sure was that I didn't know anything and I hadn't seen anything. I'd only heard it, but I wouldn't even tell the guards that much. I had to survive, and the only way you did that was by keeping your mouth shut, turning your head away.

What was I doing here in jail anyway? Why had I put myself in the midst of this filth, this horrible violence?

The answer was simple.

I did it to save my leg—and my life.

LOST AND ALONE

1979–1987

A LITTLE BOY'S DREAM

I had this tiny bag
Had it since my family fell apart
It was red and blue with an Adidas logo on the side
And a golden zipper—the zipper of all zippers!

I had this tiny bag
I took it everywhere with me
When we moved with Dad
Hopped out windows at night
When we ran and ran
On to our next place.

I had this tiny bag
Grandma asked me to unpack it
But I wouldn't do it.
She asked many times after that
But I kept it filled with all my things
Tucked away
Under my bed
Just in case.

I had this tiny bag
It had my old life inside
When I finally got the courage to get rid of it

I left it on my bed
Then jumped out my window
Down two stories
But the grass broke my fall.

"Why did you do that, Baby Boy?" Grandma asked.

"Because I always dream of dying," I said. "And I can't take it to heaven
    with me."

ROAD ALLOWANCE

MY KOKUM NANCY'S PALM FELT leathery in mine as we walked alongside of the train tracks. Stands of poplar swayed and bent in the wind, and she stood still for a second to catch her bearings and watch the flat-bottomed, late-spring clouds slouch by. She mumbled, then began thrusting her gnarled walking stick into the tall brush ahead, spreading it open, looking for flashes of purple or blue. Purple was a clear sign that the pregnant Saskatoon berry bushes were ready to give birth and ease the winter suffering of bears, birds, and humans.

Berries, Kokum said, knew well their role as life-givers, and we had to honour and respect that. We did that by knowing our role as responsible harvesters, picking only what we needed and leaving the rest for our animal kin so they could feed themselves and their young. That was our pact, she said, and if we followed it, they'd never let us down.

My kokum wore brownish-yellow eyeglasses the size of teacup saucers, but her eyes could still see things my three-year-old eyes couldn't. I always tried to search out berry patches before she did, but she always got there first. Always.

As we waded deeper through the rail-side grass and reeds, a vast fleet of mosquitoes and gnats lifted from the ditch floor and enveloped our heads. A few flew into my mouth, choking me. I coughed and batted at the air.

"No, Jesse." Kokum grabbed my arms and held them. "They are our relatives. Never do that!" I'd never seen her angry before, but she was now.

As the black cloud intensified around us, she drew in a deep breath, closed her eyes, and spoke softly in Michif. She pointed to me and our half-full pail of berries, and then to the rat-root plant that protruded out of her dress pocket. Her voice sounded like warm summer air swooshing over the open prairie right before rain comes, and reminded me of when I'd accidentally disturbed the hornet's nest behind the smoke shed. There was no anger in her voice then. The plume of insects hovered mid-air for a second, then flew skyward and dispersed. Just like the hornets had done.

I looked at her in amazement, and my mouth opened but no sound came out. I strained to hear any buzzing, but there was only the call of a loon far in the distance followed by the shuffle of Kokum's moccasins.

"Oh, my silent one," Kokum said. "I just told them we have a job to do." Her brown face cracked into a smile. "I asked them to visit us later, if they must, but for now we need to concentrate." She brushed a few strands of hair from my face and hoisted me over a puddle. "Or maybe they're right, maybe it's quitting time. Let's get back, *chi garçon*; we have enough to make a good bannock."

I loved Kokum's bannock more than anything—even harvesting with her, listening to her stories, or hearing her sing. She made it whenever we visited. We lived in Prince Albert, Saskatchewan, about an hour's drive away from my grandparents'. Their cabin was in Erin Ferry, near Debden, just south of Big River, between the old Highway 1 on one side and the new Highway 55 on the other. The CN Railway cut right up the centre of the road allowance, connecting Debden to Big River and on to the rest of Saskatchewan.

My grandparents' log cabin wasn't like any other place I knew. Mom told us that her dad, Mushoom Jeremie Morrissette, had made it by hand from the surrounding aspen hardwood after our family lost our home-stead in Park Valley, a few kilometres away. It took him one season to fell the trees, strip them of bark, and build it, and another half season to

10

chink in the cracks with mud and moss, waterproof the roof, and make it ready for winter living. Nobody else had a neat house like my kokum and Mushoom, way out in the country in the middle of nowhere, with no water or electricity.

Mushoom said there weren't many people like us anymore, rebels who fended for themselves—maybe a few Arcand relatives down the road, but that was about it. The rest had sold out and got farms or went to the city to find work. He didn't own his land; it belonged to the Queen of England.

"She doesn't mind us being here," Mushoom said. "And it lets me hunt and trap freely and be my own boss, which I like."

He told us stories about how our people once had lived in large communities in handmade houses just like his all over Saskatchewan, living off the land, but that was before the government attacked us and stole our land during the resistance, before our clans fell apart.

I couldn't understand what he was talking about. I tried imagining villages of our people living like he and my kokum did, in their little log house, all squished onto little pieces of land owned by the Queen, and I couldn't. But there were beaver, muskrat, deer, bears, elk, and fish everywhere; forest, streams, and rivers all around to play in; and no neighbours for miles and miles.

"If someone tries to push us around, we just pick up and move somewhere else," Mushoom said. "We live like this to be free, like our ancestors."

I understood that.

When Kokum and I came back from berry picking, Mushoom was standing at the front door of the cabin. The elk-horn buttons that fastened his beige leather vest strained to hold it together over his rounded stomach. Kokum made all of Mushoom's clothes from animals he trapped and materials she traded for in Debden on her monthly visit to town.

"Where are Blanche and Sonny?" Kokum called to him, her brow wrinkling. My parents' car had been in the dirt driveway when we left to go picking, but now there was just my mushoom's plump horse drinking from the trough at the side of the house.

"They went into town. Should be back soon. Fire's ready, though."

Kokum nodded, picked up a pail of rainwater for the washing, and nudged Mushoom aside as she carried it inside. The smell of burnt hardwood licked all around my grandfather's bald head as he bent down to hug me. The press of his fancy vest against my exposed belly felt like thousands of soft pebbles. Blazes of prairie roses, windflowers, big bluestems, hyssops, leadplants, and asters decorated his clothing in beaded patterns that Kokum said were passed down to her from her Michif-Nehiyaw ancestors—mothers to daughters—for over two centuries.

When Mushoom played the fiddle at night, I loved watching moonbeams flickering over his beads—it looked like he was wearing rubies and diamonds all over. And when he tapped his feet to the rhythm of reels he told us were passed down from his grandfather's grandfather, the light lulled me to sleep.

Josh and Jerry were inside the cabin playing on the floor with the wooden toys Mushoom had carved for them while we were out. Jerry's was a captain's sword, and Josh's was a little marionette man that jigged when

Mushoom Jeremie and Kokum Nancy (née Arcand) Morrissette, in their road-allowance home in Erin Ferry, Saskatchewan.

you held the stick that protruded out its back. Mushoom could carve things in five minutes flat. Jerry always got the best toys because Jerry was his favourite grandson, being his namesake and all.

Sometimes Josh and I would get jealous of Jerry. He crawled all over Mushoom's stomach and they both bellowed until tears came out of their eyes. Or Mushoom would take Jerry into the woods to show him his traps and a thing or two about snaring rabbits. He never did that with us. He'd hug us, but it wasn't the same. Jerry even kind of looked like him: stout, thick-legged, and broad across the shoulders. He was like Mushoom, too: powerful, strong-willed, and stubborn.

Josh was tall and thin. Out of all of us, he looked the most "Indian," or at least that's what Mom would say when she brushed his long black hair in the morning. She always took her time with Josh, and I could see that he was her favourite. His skin was much darker than Jerry's and mine, and he looked more like Mom than Dad. Korean or Japanese almost. Everyone was proud of Josh. He was the oldest and smartest and talked the most, and whatever new clothes we got from our aunts and uncles went to him. I'd eventually get them, but not until after Josh and Jerry.

I was much smaller and skinnier than both my brothers and had blond shoulder-length hair. My skin looked like my father's—pinkish cream. People were always saying, "He looks like a little white boy" or "You sure he wasn't switched at the hospital?" Mom said it didn't matter, because I was special. She said that I was the largest of all her babies, a little over ten pounds when I was born in 1976—as long as a carnival hot dog with a huge oblong head—and the doctors were shocked when I came out.

"You didn't make a sound," Mom said. "No screams or whimpers or nothing, just a wet *plop* sound."

I stayed quiet my first three years. The most noise I'd make was a cry or an incomprehensible squeal of excitement.

"Look here," Mushoom said, as he placed me on the floor with my brothers. He pulled a small wooden knife out of his back pocket. It was just little enough for me to grasp. I waved it in front of him, and he jumped back. Jerry charged at me, coming to Mushoom's rescue. Mushoom scooped him up before he could impale me with his wooden sabre.

Heat and the smell of lard radiated from the wood stove. Kokum opened its door to chuck in a few logs, and the muscles on her arms rippled. She was strong. One time a dog almost bit Josh near the road and Kokum threw a cast-iron skillet at it with one flick of her wrist, like a ninja star. The skillet whistled thirty feet in the air and the dog ran into the forest whining and never bugged any of us again.

I watched her as she wiped the dirt off her hands and put rolled-up bannock balls in the skillet. As they hissed and spit into the air, I could hear my parents' car screeching to a stop outside. They were fighting, like always. Mushoom said something to Kokum in Cree. I thought she was going to toss the frying pan, oil and all, out the door at my dad. She just wagged her head, though.

Mom leaned in the front door and announced, "We're going home, boys. Pull your stuff together."

Dad didn't come in. I peeked out the door. Music was blasting from the car, the windows were rolled up, and the inside was flooded with smoke.

"But, Blanche," Kokum said, "we've picked berries for the bannock."

"Can't," Mom said. "Sonny needs to get back. Damn idiot's gotta meet someone. Come, boys, hurry it up."

My mother was just fifteen when she met my father in 1973 at her sister Bernadette's house in Debden, Saskatchewan. According to my aunties, my mother was just about the prettiest Native girl in all northern Saskatchewan—a Michif Audrey Hepburn crossed with Grace Kelly and Hedy Lamarr. Silken black hair down to her waist, jet-black eyes, and a smile like a midnight flame. They said men hovered around her like moths, and that when Dad first laid eyes on her, he tripped all over himself to catch her. He chatted her up, bought her stuff, and fawned over her. He looked like a bumbling fool, my aunties said, all the men did.

But Dad was different. He was an Algonquin-Scot, although my uncles tell me he knew himself as a white man. He wasn't much to look at—chubby around the middle, with a pockmarked face and broken fighter's teeth, and his usual jean outfit was slick with traveller's patina. But there was something charming about him, an ability to talk and a boldness. That apparently came from his rough blue-collar upbringing north of Toronto, where he learned to hustle or perish. He also loved rock music. Deep Purple, Foghat, Jethro Tull, Black Sabbath, Johnny and Edgar Winter—he knew all their songs and more, how they were written and the stories behind their creation.

Mom was stuck in the 1950s, listening to old country music—the Carter Family, Patsy Cline, Hank Williams, Bill Monroe, Don Messer, anyone of the sort. She did know some modern music—Bob Dylan, the Doors, the Guess Who, Joni Mitchell—but she couldn't match my father. My aunties said Mom told them Dad was like a jukebox, with info on all the hottest bands. That made him like a god in northern Saskatchewan,

My mother, Blanche Morrissette, and father, Cyril "Sonny" Thistle, in 1977 in Debden, Saskatchewan.

15

where no one knew anything about rock, or Led Zeppelin, or Jimi Hendrix, or anything.

It made him irresistible, Mom said.

The side of my mom's face was blue. It wasn't that way before she left. And her voice sounded the way I didn't like. Mushoom examined her, and I knew he could see her broken glasses sticking out of her pocket when she went into the back room. He pushed himself up from the table, swore, and reached for his axe.

I thought he was going to kill my dad. Josh, Jerry, and I all started crying.

"Stop, Jeremie," Kokum yelled. She pulled the axe out of his hand and threw it beside the stove. "This is between them," she said, her voice sounding the way it had when she spoke with the mosquitoes.

Mushoom sneered, then stared out the window. Dad didn't notice. I could see him drumming his hands against the steering wheel.

Mom came back with some things. "Sorry, Mom, Dad. Next time we'll stay for bannock." She picked up our toys, then piled us into the car. She was like a whirlwind—we didn't even have a chance to say goodbye. As soon as we were in the car, Dad floored it. The wheels kicked up a cloud of dirt, and I could just see my kokum and mushoom waving to us through it.

HORNET

DAD BURST THROUGH THE APARTMENT door, his dirty-blond mullet in full flight. He was grinning so widely his greasy handlebar moustache splayed out at both ends. In his hands were a coffee tin and a white plastic bag.

"Daddy got paid, boys!" He placed his bounty on the cardboard box that served as our coffee table, then fell backward onto the sofa. A plume of sour dust erupted from the cushions. The tin rattled, and a nickel spilled out over the edge and rolled a foot or two toward us.

When Dad opened his arms for a hug, Josh ran from his usual spot in front of the TV and grabbed his legs. Jerry and I were still watching television—a shark attacking an octopus on *The Undersea World of Jacques Cousteau*. A red cloud of ink filled the ocean water. As the octopus scurried to safety, we joined Josh and hugged Dad.

"I did what you said," Josh said. He still clung to Dad's jeans. "I kept an eye out and made sure no one came in the apartment while you were gone."

Josh was in charge of Jerry and me whenever Dad left us alone to go on a mission. He was five.

"Make sure to feed your brothers," Dad would say. "Don't let no one in. Hide in the vent behind your bed if anyone gets in. And don't turn the light on at night because they'll know you're inside. Got it?" Josh always nodded.

Even four-year-old Jerry was my boss. We were like a little tribe with Josh as our chief, Jerry as second-in-command, and me as the expendable warrior. I had to do the bidding of both. They made me stand on the chair to check the peephole when someone was at the door. They made me fish poo out of the toilet to smear on walls to get even with Dad for leaving us alone. And they always made me climb onto the counter to reach where Dad hid all the best food away in the top cupboard. It was dangerous to climb so high, but I was good, and I was never afraid of heights like Jerry and Josh were. Climbing came naturally, and the distance between me and the floor excited me and made me feel powerful—it was something my brothers couldn't do.

Dad would freak out when he found that we'd eaten his secret food— cans of Spam, peanut butter, loaves of bread, chips, and the odd jar of Cheez Whiz—which he never shared, and I always got the blame because I never talked, even when I played alone with my brothers, and even when I got a licking. Mom used to think I was mute, but I could speak fine, I just chose not to. My words belonged to me, they were the only thing I had that were mine, and I didn't trust anyone enough to share them.

Dad was only gone for a night this time, but in the kitchen, the cupboards only had a few unopened cans of beans and beets he'd gotten from the local food bank a few days before. Empty boxes of crackers and cans piled one on top of another, covering the countertops and cascading out over the stovetop. The fridge had a few half-drunk beer bottles, an old light bulb, and a hardened turnip. Sometimes he'd go away for two or three days and leave us nothing.

"Good boy." Dad rubbed Josh's head, then pushed the three of us off of him. Josh, Jerry, and I fell to the beer-stained carpet, like puppies bucked off their mom's teat, as Dad cradled his bag.

My mother had abandoned my father, my brothers, and me—that was the version of the story we were made to believe by my father's family. But it wasn't the whole picture.

Mom married Dad when she was just seventeen, and my father was twenty-two.

She gave him an ultimatum the day of their wedding: "Quit drinking and running around, or I'll leave you."

He promised her a life of sobriety.

Dad lasted three days before he drank himself into a stupor.

One day he took his anger out on everyone. Josh endured a beating and Mom received it even worse.

Mom had had enough of moving from apartment to apartment, room to room, of my dad wasting all the money and opportunity that came their way. She'd had enough of all the bullshit. She packed our bags while Dad was passed out on the couch, and the four of us moved to Moose Jaw.

Mom went to night school and began working at a local restaurant

My brothers, Jerry (on the left) and Josh (in the middle), and me (on the right) in 1979 in Moose Jaw, Saskatchewan. Our aunt Yvonne, my mother's sister, took this picture.

19

during the day. Life was steady—we stayed in one apartment, slept in beds instead of on piles of laundry, and ate frequent meals, and Mom didn't cry herself to sleep with bruises like before.

One day Dad showed up.

He was healthy, coherent, and his clothes were clean. He charmed his way through the front door, telling Mom he'd found a great job back east with his father, that he wasn't drinking and drugging, and that he'd found an apartment and could afford to keep us boys if she allowed us to go with him. He wasn't trying to get back with her—he knew not to go there.

"I'll return them after a few months. You have my word, Blanche."

I think Mom decided to let us go with Dad because she wasn't thinking straight—she was exhausted—and Dad knew how to sound convincing when he wanted something and could exploit Mom's weaknesses. He had skills from years and years of hustling.

Mom let us go. I could smell the pine scent in her hair as we hugged goodbye on the veranda.

I didn't blame her. Dad could sell the Brooklyn Bridge to New York City officials if he really wanted to, or so people said. He was just that good at lying.

"Look here," Dad said as he broke open the bag and an avalanche of cigarette butts spilled onto the floor. He grabbed my brother's arm and placed him in front of the butts beside the TV. "Jerry, you roll the best. Take my Zig-Zags and do like last time."

Jerry peeled out a rolling paper and set to work ripping open the largest butts onto a sheet of paper. The smell of mouldy smokes filled the apartment. Dad then poured the contents of the tin onto the carpet. The coins were like falling treasure and Dad looked like a pirate, like Captain Hook in the Peter Pan book Mom used to read us before bed.

"Josh, count 'em up," he said. "Jesse knows what pennies are. Just let him pick them out before you get started."

Josh nodded and got my attention. "Like last time, Jesse. Remember?" He held up a penny and told me to dig. I shoved my hand in the pile and began picking out what looked to me like nuggets of gold.

"Dad," Josh said before we got too far. "We haven't eaten since yesterday morning and it's nighttime now. We're hungry. Did you bring anything?"

"Shit. I forgot. Count it up. We'll go to the store and get something after. Promise."

I watched as he pulled a small Baggie filled with white powder out of his jean jacket pocket. He held it up to the light and flicked it, then made his way to the washroom and slammed the door.

Josh sighed and began helping me. My stomach gurgled. He looked over at me. It was Josh's job to feed us. Sometimes he'd leave Jerry and me alone for a while and walk to the convenience store to beg for money to buy food. We'd seen Dad do it and knew how to do it, too. It usually took Josh a couple of hours, but he always came back with chips and pop and other goodies. He was my hero, my chief!

Sometimes, when we got really hungry, Josh even took Jerry and me over to ask for change in front of the hockey arena around the block. It was the best spot because we could buy gigantic hot dogs there. We shared bites. The hot meat burst with such flavour that my jaw would ache up around my ears, and my tongue swam in pools of saliva. Drool would sometimes spill out of my mouth onto my shirt before I even took a bite.

Dad's treasure shimmered in front of the TV. The wildlife program was still playing, and a whale drifted through blue water, calmly scooping mouthfuls of food, as Josh and I rifled through the silver and gold pile, and images of those hot dogs piled high with ketchup and mustard and relish and everything else floated through my head.

I noticed light peeping out of the washroom. Dad must've slammed the door so hard it bounced open a crack. I dropped the gold pennies I had in my hand and crawled over quietly to see what he was doing. Josh trailed behind.

Dad was on the toilet, hunched over with a spoon in one hand, a blue lighter in the other. Red flame licked the bottom of the spoon and bubbles spit droplets into the air. Dad's forehead was wet, sweat dripped onto the tile floor, and that see-through thingy I'd found one day underneath the sofa was by his side.

Dad had told me it was a man-made hornet, and that kids shouldn't play with it because they'd end up getting stung by accident, and the medicine it carried could make young boys so sick they could die. The black stripes on its see-through body looked scary, like the blue-and-black hornets I saw flying in the prairie roses, the kind that stung me when I went to see Kokum Nancy.

Dad picked up the hornet, put it near the spoon, and it sucked the medicine into its belly. Then he wrapped his leather belt around his arm and held one end in his teeth, pulling back with his head like my uncle Paul's dog did whenever we played tug of war. I could see green veins on his arm and hand. He jabbed himself with the hornet and red shot into the hornet's body. I pushed my face right up against the crack trying to get a better look, as bad butterflies swam all through my guts.

It looks just like the red ink that the octopus shot into the ocean right before it escaped the shark, I thought. I wondered if my dad could run away, or if a shark would get him. The softness of Kokum's voice whispered in my ears, as the smell of sweet Saskatoon berries filled my nose. The butterflies flew up my body and out the top of my head.

Dad let go of the belt, moaned, and toppled off the edge of the toilet. I pushed the door open and ran to him. He didn't move, and his eyes were closed. I looked back at Josh. He stood in the arch of the doorway, a dark river spreading down the front of his brown corduroys.

TRASH PANDAS

THE PINK NEON SIGN ON the corner store drooped down to one side and flickered off and on. The light strobed against the window I was standing in front of, staring at the huge ice-cream cone on the advertisement taped against the inside of the glass.

"Jesse, pay attention," Dad said and pushed my shoulder. Blankets of dead leaves swirled alongside the building when the wind picked up, and Dad tucked his head into the collar of his jean jacket. I saw an old man wearing a hat approach from the path over near the grass. Dad headed him off by the corner. I tried to focus.

"Excuse me, sir," Dad said. "I was wondering if you had some spare change? I got three kids, and they haven't eaten today." Dad sounded polite as he motioned over at us, and we stood, hands out, with big eyes, just like Dad taught us. "We'd really appreciate anything."

The man peeled his trench coat open, searched his pockets, and shrugged. "Sorry, fella. Don't have change to spare." He moved past us and entered the store. The entrance bell rang—it was a sound that meant defeat and more begging. I watched through the window as he bought milk and bread. He got some change back. When he came out, I ran over and tugged his leg, trying to make his quarters and dimes jingle in his pocket, to let him know I knew he had change. He kicked me away. "You should be ashamed," he said to my dad.

"Fuck you," Dad fired back and flicked his cigarette in the man's direction. Dad was shivering. Josh sighed, and Jerry wrapped his arms around Josh in a bear hug and squeezed until Josh laughed and begged him to stop. Dad was busy searching the sidewalk and found a half-smoked butt near a trash bin.

"I'm not eating out of there again," Josh said, his eyes focused on my father and the bin. He kicked the wall. "We're not supposed to."

Dad put the butt in his mouth and lifted the lid off the garbage container. "You never know what you'll find."

He was right. A couple of days ago, when Dad had taken off, Josh took Jerry, leaving me in the apartment. I'd watched out of our window and could see Jerry as he made a beeline toward the bin, climbed up, and dove into the pool of black trash bags. He looked like a raccoon. After a few minutes, he emerged clutching some old bread, a couple of packs of cold cuts, and a few dented cans. He tossed them to Josh, but Josh fumbled and dropped them like an outfielder having a bad day. The bread and meat were still good, just a little green around the edges. When we picked that off though, it was as good as new.

"Nothing in here, boys. Pickup was last night." Dad shut the bin lid and pulled his collar up. His cigarette went out. The November wind bit through our clothing, and we huddled together. We'd been out for a few hours and hadn't come up with any change. Everyone seemed to be in a rush or didn't have enough to spare. We always shared what we had, and I didn't understand why people were so mean and wouldn't share with us.

"Listen," Dad said, "I have a plan." He knelt down in front of Jerry and Josh, placing his hands upon their shoulders. "I've done it with Josh before, but we're all here today, so I think it'll work better."

Josh perked up, but Dad didn't even glance at me. I stuck my tongue out.

"Now, now. You're only three, but you can help, too, Jesse." Dad patted my bum. "Josh knows the drill. Just follow behind him and do what he says."

Josh put his arms around Jerry and me and pulled us close. "Just stay beside me and run when I tell you," he whispered. "Go straight back to the apartment and don't follow Dad!"

Dad winked at Josh. "That's right, son."

I was so jealous of Josh.

I held on to Josh's sleeve when we entered the store. Jerry was right beside me ogling the rows of chips and candy. The storekeeper looked down at us but then fixed his eyes on Dad, who walked ahead, leaving us behind. Before I knew it, he was by the milk and pop near the back of the store. His head darted around—down at the floor, over to the chocolate bars, up to the lights—like he didn't know what he was looking for. Inch by inch, Josh nudged us closer and closer to the first aisle near the front door.

I'd never seen Dad move around like that, like a freaked-out squirrel. He looked scared and funny all at once, opening and closing doors. Suddenly, he disappeared. I stood on my tippy toes to see what he was up to.

Smash! A river of milk flowed out from the dairy section. It was followed by the noise of another broken bottle.

"What's going on over there?" the storekeeper shouted as he came out from behind the till and went to investigate.

I was looking in the direction of the milk aisle, trying to catch a glimpse of Dad, but Josh pulled me close, yanked open my drawers, and stuffed in a few bags of chips, a handful of pepperettes, and a loaf of bread. I was shocked, food sticking halfway out of my waistband. Jerry was already at the door ten feet away, holding it open, his pants, too, bulging to the brim with goodies. Josh pulled my shirt and nudged me toward Jerry. I stumbled a few steps before Jerry grabbed my arm and walked me out the front door.

When our shoes touched the sidewalk outside, he pivoted toward the trash bin and dragged me until I almost fell flat on my face. The bell on the door rang as it closed behind us. Josh hurried by with a bunch of gum in one hand, and licorice and more pepperettes in the other. He directed us to a cedar bush a couple of feet behind the bin. We nestled under the cover of the branches and waited for Dad.

When he emerged from the store, he was flailing his arms and arguing with the storekeeper. The storekeeper screamed back, waving around a mop, pointing back into the store. Dad skipped backward a few steps then took off toward the park.

No one noticed us watching through the bush's boughs.

I thought, *This was fun.* I was happy to be working together with everyone. And we now had tons of food.

A FATHER'S LOVE

I dreamed of my birth, all wet from the womb
Blinding light overhead, emergency room

Behind newborn cries, my little hands grasped
"A son!" called the doc, while my tiny lungs gasped

"Oh, happy day," my mother did cry.
"Come, let me hold him," a tear in my dad's eye.

The strength of Father's arms tight around me
He swayed back and forth; his love did surround me

Then, out of nowhere, Dad yanked with a dash
Swung by my legs, he chucked me right in the trash!

"Don't need that." He laughed and slammed down the lid.
He dusted his hands. "Who the fuck needs a kid!?"

THE RED BARON

"**DAD DIDN'T COME HOME AGAIN** last night," Josh said as he jumped off the top bunk, thudding down on the wooden floor. He began rocking the lower bunk. Its rusty springs squeaked with each push. Jerry groaned and pulled the covers over his body, exposing my legs. The chill of the morning air through the holes in my Mighty Mouse PJ bottoms jolted me wide awake. Jerry took up three-quarters of the bottom bunk, which I shared with him, but that was okay, even if I only got the outside sliver of the mattress to sleep on, because his body was warm and soft and reminded me of a teddy bear. I yawned and rubbed my stomach.

"I know," Josh said. "That's why I'm trying to get you up. Dad took off with all the change when he woke up. He said he'd come back with food but hasn't." He shoved the bunk again, this time hard enough to wake Jerry, who let out a fart. He lay on his side, still curled into a ball, his mouth and chin covered in drool. A pool of it drenched the pillow below.

Jerry's crusty eyes blinked open and he looked toward the living room. "Where's Dad?" He sounded angry and annoyed.

"I don't know." Josh threw up his hands. "And we've got no food again."

I could hear Jerry's stomach grumble as he sat up slowly with the blanket tight around his shoulders. It looked like a cape. I watched as the World War I airplanes that decorated its fuzzy surface folded and contorted and collided into one another. I imagined mid-air explosions all across his back. I knew they were fighter planes because Dad told us they were. He said the ones with the black crosses on the tails were Germans, the bad guys, and the ones with the blue, white, and red bull's eyes were the British, the good guys.

I loved the story of the Red Baron and always imagined myself in his three-winged plane shooting down Canadian ace Roy Brown. The Baron's plane was cooler looking than Brown's by a long shot. Both the Baron's red Fokker DR.I triplane and Brown's Sopwith Camel buzzed around Jerry's neck when he stood up and shuffled into the kitchen. He slammed the cupboard doors in frustration and collapsed on the floor crying.

"I'm hungry," he wailed repeatedly.

Josh abandoned me. "Don't cry, Jerry," he said, going to him and rubbing his back. "We're going to go over to the store and get some food, like last week." He looked over at the window I knew faced the convenience store. "With all three of us out there, we'll get all kinds of stuff. It'll be fun."

Josh went to the fridge and grabbed one of the half-drunk beers and gave it to Jerry. "Brown pop. Drink it."

Jerry dropped the blanket and took the bottle with both hands. He

Me, posing for the camera, 1980.

29

scrunched up his face, put the bottle to his lips, tilted his head back, and swallowed.

I pictured him drinking a magic potion. *Jerry is the toughest of us all*, I thought.

"Gross," Jerry let out. He hated brown pops and never drank them when Dad gave them to us, but he knew it would fill him up. He handed the empty back to Josh, who went to place it under the kitchen sink with the others. When he opened the door, cockroaches scurried into the darkest corner of the cupboard.

"We also got this," Josh said as he walked back to the fridge, a glimmer of enthusiasm in his voice. The turnip he pulled from the crisper was as big as his head, and the thump it made when it hit the floor shook our apartment. It sounded like a bomb went off. Josh rolled the clumsy boulder over to the edge of the warplanes, hitting Jerry's foot.

"Dad said we could eat this. I know we tried before, but we gave up too easy," Josh said.

I waddled over to the vegetable wondering how it'd fit in my mouth. Josh pulled a knife out of a drawer and sat down and began to hack at the turnip. Flecks of white and hard yellow the size of pennies flew in all directions as Josh whacked away at it. I put one of the white pieces in my mouth and bit down, but my teeth couldn't meet all the way. I chewed away. It tasted like nothing, but I swallowed anyways. I rubbed my fingers along my bottom teeth—they were covered in a waxy film.

Jerry picked up a yellow piece and chucked it in his mouth. The click of his jaw told me the yellow parts were way harder than the white ones. He folded his arms and spat the piece out onto the ground. "It's worse than brown pops. It's like a rock. I can't eat that."

Josh's blade paused a second as he took a big yellow piece and placed it in his mouth. He tried to look like he was happy eating it, but we could tell it was torture. The muscles on the side of his head flexed and bulged. He spat it out and agreed with Jerry: totally inedible.

There was a loud knock on the door.

Josh gently placed the knife on the ground and put his hands over both our mouths. "Be quiet," he mouthed and made a shush shape with his lips. The battle-scarred turnip rocked back and forth, threatening to give us away.

Another knock assaulted the door.

"Open up," a voiced boomed. "It's the police. We know you boys are in there."

Josh's eyes widened, and he grabbed my shirt and pulled me toward the wall, as if he didn't know what to do or where to go.

Jerry shot up, tossing the blanket on the floor. "Come with me," he said as he launched me and Josh into the bedroom. We skidded over to Jerry's hiding spot, a large air vent in our room that he'd discovered when we first moved in. When he showed it to Dad, he was impressed with how much room there was inside. Jerry told him how he'd used a penny to turn the screws at the corners to take off the grate, and how the shaft went straight twelve feet and then turned right.

"Smart lad," Dad said. He'd tied a string to the back of the grate. "Now, when someone comes—and I mean anyone—you all pile in here and just pull this string. It'll close the vent cover behind you. Got it?"

Jerry nodded and tried it out. The first couple times, the cover went on crooked, or sideways, or not at all. Eventually, though, with enough coaching from Dad, Jerry could pull it closed in a second or two. From the outside, it was hard to see the string or that the screws weren't holding the grate on.

Boom. Boom. Boom.

The knocks at the door turned into what sounded like powerful kicks. It was only a matter of minutes before the door gave way.

"Hurry. They're coming," Jerry said as he pulled the grate off and rammed my head through the vent opening. He kicked my bum to hurry me up. A wall of warm, dry air slammed into my face and arms as I flew down the shaft. Josh was right behind me, pressing his face into my ass. He shoved me farther down the shaft toward the darkness.

31

"Go—go—go," he commanded in a frantic but hushed voice. "Faster, Jesse, crawl faster."

The more we wiggled forward, the more our bodies dented the tin walls. It sounded like thunder all around my head. I began to cry. I looked back and could see Jerry pull the string closed. The grate slapped into place in one shot—perfect, just like Dad taught him. We covered our mouths to silence our breath, dust settling all around us.

Boom. Boom. BOOM!

I could hear the front door burst open and footsteps stampede into the living room. It sounded like the herds of bison stampeding that I'd seen on nature shows.

"Look at this," I heard one man say. "The kitchen is full of trash."

"Hey, look," another called out from the bathroom, his voice echoing off the tiles, "there are rigs and gear in the tub. Check it out."

One voice stood out from the rest. I could tell he was in charge. "Yep. Just like the neighbour described. Dope and children. Find them."

The violent sound of crashing cupboard doors was followed by the clanking of empty beer bottles. "Jesus," a deep voice said from near the kitchen, "they've been hacking up this turnip. They got no food."

I heard them go into Dad's room and then more noise. "Nothing in here but skin magazines."

A pair of black boots appeared in front of the vent, and someone bent down to look under the bed. It was a police officer. I could just see his uniform past Jerry and Josh's bodies. "Nothing in here," he said, as he shone his flashlight into the vent. His voice was higher and younger than the rest. "But the pillow is wet. They must've just left."

"Not possible," the voice in charge said. "The lady next door watched him leave last night at 10:30 and the kids were inside. She saw them herself when she peeked in from the door across the hall. She said they beg for food in front of the store or the arena—we checked both locations, and they weren't there. That means they're still here. Look harder."

"I don't know, Sarge. We checked everywhere. It's a tiny apartment, where else could they be?"

Jerry's arms were shaking as the pair of black boots readjusted in front of the vent. A radio chattered as Josh squirmed. The tin made a muffled knock under his arm.

"Wait a minute," the high voice said. "I think they're in here." The front of the vent shifted as he dug his fingers under the grate and tried to pull.

Jerry gritted his teeth and held it tight with all his might.

"They're in the vent. I can see them! But they've got it locked off somehow." The herd of black boots entered the room as the young officer's eye peered in to get a better look. "Yup." He smiled and put his palm up to the vent holes.

I was shaking, and I could feel Josh was, too.

"It's okay, fellas, nothing to be afraid of."

"Move outta the way," the lead voice barked and the grate was ripped off.

A huge meaty hand with hair on it reached in and pulled Jerry out, then Josh and me, my Mighty Mouse PJs ripping on a screw in the opening.

Jerry and I were shaking and crying. I couldn't speak. The string had rubbed Jerry's palms raw as it was torn from his grasp. Blue-and-red lights flashed against the ceiling of our bedroom.

Dad is going to kill us, I thought. Josh began to cry. He was probably thinking the same thing.

The officer who found us bent down and smiled. "Which one are you?" he asked Josh as he dusted the lint off my brother's shoulder and wiped his tears. Josh just glared at him and kept his mouth shut, the dust on his face now smeared back to his ear.

A kind-looking black woman with a clipboard emerged from behind the young policeman. I could smell her fruity perfume—it made me hungry. She knelt in front of Jerry. "We're going to take you somewhere safe, there's no need to be afraid."

Jerry pushed her away and crossed his arms.

She nodded to the police, and they scooped us up.

As the officer carried me out of the apartment, I looked over his shoulder and saw my blanket sitting on the kitchen floor. It half-covered the turnip and some empty bottles. I could see the edge of the Baron's triplane, and I imagined myself flying it higher and higher into the sky, up near the sun.

THE PACT

THE NICE BLACK LADY AND the young police officer took us to a large red-brick building with lots of windows.

"You boys will be safe here," she said.

She took Jerry by the hand from the squad car. Jerry didn't put up a fight, neither did Josh or I. We walked through a pair of giant steel doors that guarded the front entrance and down a long hall, into a large room with rows and rows of bunk beds. It smelled of bleach.

There were other kids there. They sat on their bunks and checked us out as we walked to three empty beds at the back of the room. Josh and Jerry got bottom beds, I got the top. I noticed two black kids and a few older boys who had dark skin and hair like us. They looked like our Indian cousins in Saskatchewan but different. The covers and sheets of the beds were done up perfectly, corners tucked tight under the mattresses, the pillows flat and smoothed out. I'd seen Mom make a bed that way before, but we'd been with Dad for months and he never did anything like that for us, and he couldn't afford these kinds of pillows.

I was relieved at the order and cleanliness of this new place, whatever it was.

"This is Children's Aid," the black lady told us.

Through the tangle of bedposts I saw a red-headed boy looking at me.

He flashed me a smile and a tiny wave. I ducked down and buried my head in the black lady's leg.

"That's Johnny," she said. "He's a nice boy. No need to be shy."

Jerry and Josh peered over, and the boy again smiled and waved. They stared at him until his hand fell by his side.

The place was way bigger than our apartment or any of the places I'd ever been.

"Where's Dad and when's he coming to get us?" Josh asked.

The black lady just gave us something to eat and then tucked us all in and left, turning the lights out.

I wasn't scared and fell asleep, my belly full. I dreamt about the black lady and wondered what her name was. When I woke in the morning the place buzzed with activity, and we were ushered in lines into a hall where we had oatmeal and bananas. I stuck by my brothers as the other kids checked us out. Josh did all the talking, telling everyone that our dad was away and that we'd be going home as soon as the police found him.

"I used to think that, too," one kid said. "But we're orphans now—don't cha know?"

I didn't know what that meant.

We became good friends with Johnny and the other kids. Jerry said Johnny was like our red-headed brother, that he was part of our tribe, too. Johnny told us that his parents couldn't afford Cheerios one day, had a big fight over it, and then dropped him off here. He said he felt like it was his fault, that he never got the chance to tell his parents that he didn't even like Cheerios and that they'd be okay without cereal.

I was sorry for him. I thought the same about why my mom and dad had left us. I'd been a bad boy and had asked for food too often. We'd eaten Dad's secret food too many times, and he'd probably gotten so mad over it that he'd up and left us. I gave Johnny a hug.

36

After a few days, strange things started happening.

The black lady and other people who worked in the big building started taking kids out of the large room one by one. They asked them all kinds of difficult questions. Doctors examined them for any bugs and sicknesses, checked their hair and tongue, in their underwear, and under their arms—or so we were told by the kids when they returned.

Some were taken out and never came back. That was the scariest. It was like they'd been eaten by monsters. No one knew what happened to them, but the older kids said they were the lucky ones because someone wanted them. I didn't understand that; our mom and dad wanted us, why didn't theirs want them, too?

When they came for Jerry, Josh rushed over and bit the lady on the hand and I ran and kicked her foot as hard as I could. We screamed and screamed, fought and fought, our faces getting redder than fire engines. Johnny joined in, stomping her toe until she let go. We four scurried to the back of the room and nestled in a corner. Josh grabbed hold of our necks and pulled us in close. We locked arms and brought Johnny in, too, holding tight to one another, gnashing our teeth. We did exactly as Dad had directed—protected each other from strangers.

The woman left the room to get help.

"We gotta stick together," Josh said, panting. We all nodded. We made a pact, then and there, to take care of one another no matter what. We squeezed each other with all our might and shut our eyes, sealing the deal.

Five minutes after the pact was struck, a team of workers came in and wrestled Johnny from our circle. We tried fighting back but they held us down and took away our red-headed brother—they were just too strong. We never saw Johnny again.

I thought of him when they came and got us three brothers a few weeks later.

MONSTER RESCUE

"YOU BOYS ARE LUCKY," THE black lady said to me after I'd been checked over by the doctor and placed in the hallway with my brothers. "We've found a foster home that will take all three of you."

Josh stood on defence between the front entrance and the door of the large room. Jerry milled about. He was silent, biting his nails.

"Take us?" Josh asked forcefully. "Where? What about our mom and dad?"

Jerry's face went blank and he stopped pacing. He moved behind Josh, as if to back him up.

What does "foster home" mean? I'd never heard that word before. *Who is going to take us?* I wasn't sure, but I knew my brothers were uneasy.

The lady hesitated, and I could tell she was thinking hard about what she was going to say next.

The doctor came into the hall and handed a clipboard to her. "They're all clear," he said, "but this one's still a little underweight." He pointed to Josh. He looked fine to me.

Josh asked more questions, but we got no answers about our dad or mom. The lady just kept telling us that we were lucky, and that our ride to our new home would be along shortly.

We were cleaned up—teeth brushed, hair combed, shoes tied—and had our belongings packed up. I had the leather Adidas bag Mom had given me before Dad took us from Saskatchewan, and Jerry and Josh had theirs, too. Our names were on them and we always kept them ready just in case we had to run at night—it was a fun game Dad played with us when we moved. The police must've brought them when we first came to the red-brick building, but they forgot to bring our old clothes.

I was glad to hold my bag again; it meant I was going somewhere new. And it was filled with better clothes now, even a brand-new Mighty Mouse T-shirt. I was excited even though I knew my brothers were worried.

We went outside, and an old man drove up and got out of his car.

He said, "Nice to see you, Gladys," to the black lady, and told us his name was Clive. He smelled like old cigars and had grease on his overalls. He was way bigger than Dad, and I thought he was at least a hundred years old, judging by his grey hair and fat belly.

Gladys shook Clive's hand then knelt down and pinched Jerry's cheek. "I'll miss you boys," she said, picking the lint off his yellow-and-brown-striped sweater. "But I'll miss you most, Jerry." I could see he almost burst into tears. They hugged while Clive loaded our bags into the trunk of his car, and with that, we were off.

The car ride to our new house took forever. We drove until nighttime, and I couldn't keep my eyes open. When we pulled up to Clive's place, a woman and girl came out to greet us. They had big smiles and balloons, and a small dog was barking its head off beside them—it was about the size of a beaver and had scraggly brown hair.

"This is my wife, Cynthia," Clive said. "And my daughter, Matilda." Cynthia looked so old to me, like Clive, and Matilda was around the same age as my cousin Suzanne back in Saskatoon—around nine years old. Her hair was curly, down to her shoulders. I could see her braces when she smiled. The dog continued to bark and sniff as we made our way inside.

My memories of the time inside that house are misty. Like a shroud of fog not yet lifted just before dawn. The wild shapes of things black and blue, bleeding into one another. The sunlight not yet strong enough to make out what lurks in the tall azure grass ahead, the line of spruce just out of view at the other end of the meadow.

What I do remember, though, is grease, pressure, that yapping dog, and wishing it would end.

I remember my brother Jerry fighting off the giant wolf that came into our room and floated over our beds and ripped him apart.

Jerry's tiny fists punched up and into the darkness, right before his little body was dug out and broken.

He would put himself between me and the Monster. He would rescue me from whatever it was that had him and Josh squealing in the next room while I cried myself to sleep.

I would turn my head and try to hide from it all, but it always found me.

Jerry and Josh changed after that. They lost their superpowers, they peed the bed every night. But they were still my protectors.

The fragments of that time blend and refract light in a way that blinds me, but I do know that one day the black lady showed up, and that before we left the house, Josh shut the door in the dog's face. Its whining is the last thing I remember from that horrible place.

THE BEAST

WE RACED BY JUTS OF rock and small Jack pines. My eyes tried to keep up with the jagged landscape, but the blurred tracers of green and black just made me feel sick.

My grandparents Cyril and Jackie Thistle looked exactly like they did in the pictures Dad used to show us. Grandpa, who was driving, had a brown moustache like Dad's, but it was trimmed neatly around his upper lip. His hair was slick and parted like Alfalfa's from *Little Rascals*, but not down the middle. Grandma had a grey-black Afro that wobbled with the motion of the van.

She leaned back to offer me a sandwich. I was hungry, so I took it.

Grandpa smiled at me in the rearview mirror. His eyes gleamed like blue sapphires, the light catching them just so through his glasses.

My grandparents didn't say much to us boys on the drive to Toronto, but I could make out that my grandmother was mad at my parents by the way she complained to Grandpa. Her fury at our dad for leaving us alone. Her anger when she talked about our mother. I didn't understand that, though. Dad had talked Mom into letting us go in Moose Jaw. It wasn't her fault the way things ended up.

As Grandma railed on, I realized there was a force in her that was more powerful than that of my grandfather. Grandpa listened and nodded, careful to watch the road, but it was clear Grandma was in charge.

In between sentences, Grandma turned to face me, and, with the taste of ham and cheese thick on my tongue, I could smell the scent of charred wood and tobacco coming from her direction. Somehow, the odour told me I could trust her enough to share my words.

"Thank you for the sandwich, Grandma."

She rubbed my leg. "You're welcome, Baby Boy." She peeled an orange, and I shared it with Jerry and Josh, who fell asleep soon after, but I remained awake, fascinated by Grandma and her campfire smell. I stared at her as she smoked her cigarettes and flicked them in an empty coffee cup she kept between her knees.

I'd later learn from my aunties that Grandma's people came from a place way up in northern Ontario called Timiskaming, and that she was part Native and part white like us boys—Algonquin and Scottish, and that her dad was from a reserve near Notre Dame du Nord in Quebec.

As I examined her features through the cigarette smoke, I recognized that Grandma was a little Indian, but her hair was all curly, not black and straight like my mom's and aunties' out west. Her skin was more tanned than my grandfather's. He had the same tone as a freshly opened cube of Spam—pink through and through—like Dad and me. Not Grandma. She was lighter than Josh, but almost looked the same beige mix as Jerry.

"Look," Grandpa said after hours of driving along what seemed like a never-ending road. We crested a hill and the landscape opened up before us. "That's Toronto—that's where our house is." He lifted his bear paw from the wheel and pointed to a cluster of buildings on the approaching horizon. The toothy jumble of grey concrete in the distance was unlike anything I'd ever seen before. Way bigger than anywhere else I'd ever been.

"You see that needle-looking structure right in the middle?" Grandpa asked. "That's the tallest building in the world—the CN Tower."

I almost fell forward off my seat trying to get a better look.

Grandpa laughed. "We live over there," he said, motioning to a smaller cluster of buildings. "In a place called Brampton. But I'll take you boys to see the tower after we're all settled in."

The houses in Brampton were set in neat little rows, with perfect lawns and freshly paved roads. Everything looked so clean, orderly, and taken care of. Blue jays and robins sang to each other in the treetops; squirrels ran everywhere collecting things; and cats walked, surefooted, along fence tops. There was so much sunlight. It comforted me to see so many parents walking with their kids. I thought of my mom and dad— but in a good way, when we were happy and together.

This new place was so beautiful.

We rounded the corner, pulled into a driveway on the coziest street I ever saw, and Grandpa declared, "We're home."

"Just be careful of Yorkie," Grandma said as we got out and made our way to the front door. "He likes to jump."

Bounding out the door came a beast of a dog. He had brown and black fur with flecks of silver down the sides, and his ears were erect like a German shepherd's. He looked like a wolf and stood as tall as the middle of my chest. His tail wagged so hard that his bum shot from side to side—even while he charged at us. He leapt at me, I fell backward, and he started licking my face until I couldn't breathe. I started to cry.

But Yorkie kept licking, yelping with glee. He was doing his best to welcome us home.

TOUCH OF HOME

"CYRIL," GRANDMA SAID TO GRANDPA. "My catalogues are missing again." Her permed hair bobbed as she lifted the chesterfield cushions. "One of the boys keeps taking them and hiding them all over the house, and I need to order something." She stood, mouth open.

"Maybe they have to order something, too, Jackie." Grandpa smirked at me and returned to his egg-and-bacon breakfast. The fork and knife looked tiny in his elevator-mechanic hands. I peered at my feet, which dangled from the chair next to him. His thumbs were about twice the size of my big toes. My eyes barely rose above the kitchen table. Grandma left to go down to the laundry room. Her slippers slapped against the hard yellow calluses on her heels, like leather against wood.

"What's the verdict, Jesse? Do you have something to order?" Before I could answer, Grandpa delivered a swift karate chop to my leg. "Hiya!"

My knee jerked. I squealed with glee as eggs spilled out of my mouth and down the front of my PJs.

"Grandpa!" I shouted, half shocked, half laughing, ketchup smeared all over my lips and chin. He just winked, looking like Popeye without his corncob pipe. His forearms were bigger than Popeye's for sure.

"Watch it, buddy," he said as he put up his dukes. I put mine up like a little fighting Irishman.

Grandma called upstairs. "Cyril, wait till you see this." I heard her heavy rhino steps, then saw her. She had the missing catalogue in her hand. "I found it behind the toy box. Look." She opened it and held it up. "Just like the last few times it went missing." She placed it in front of my grandfather and pointed. "The women's underwear section is ripped out—the whole section."

"Well, I didn't do it. Must've been one of the boys," he said and laughed. "At least they took the best part."

"Cyril!" Grandma looked disgusted.

I pushed my eggs around to avoid eye contact, but she leaned forward, crossing her arms over the damaged magazine. "Jesse. Do you know who did this?" Her brown-rimmed glasses magnified her eyes. Grandpa turned to face me.

"No, Grandma—"

Yorkie the Wonder Dog, who'd become my most trusted friend and ally, came in and pooped near the fridge, saving me from saying more. Grandpa pushed aside his breakfast, and Grandma ran over as Yorkie scurried away with a guilty-dog smile, his tail tucked between his legs.

"You see what happens when you boys don't walk him enough!" Grandma grabbed a grocery bag from under the kitchen sink and dangled it in my direction. "Come clean it up."

I usually woke up early, and often was the first one up. It was something I'd learned while living with Dad. The first one up and to the cupboards or fridge was the first one to eat. And the first one to eat was often the only one to eat. But this morning at my grandparents' I stayed in bed, cozy in my own room, buried under my blanket, not worried about breakfast. My grandparents had lots of treats, and my instinct to be the first one up was giving way to a desire to sleep in.

I awoke to find Grandma in my room.

"Jesse. Time to get up." She put an armful of clothes on the chest of drawers and began folding sweaters. "Aunt Sherry and Uncle John are coming over and we've got to get you ready."

My aunt Sherry was my grandparents' only daughter, and Grandpa's favourite child by a long shot. She was the youngest and was pretty with long flowing brown hair and beautiful hazel eyes. She always made us the best food when she came over—fried chicken, pasta with salty cheese, and chocolate cake. Uncle John, her husband, was strong like a lumberjack—he cut wood with an axe, beard and all, at their house in the country, and I imagined he was so powerful because of all the delicious foods Aunt Sherry made him.

I cleared the sleep from my eyes and sat up. Yorkie ran in, his tail wagging and tongue hanging out. He jumped on the bed to lick my face, and the sound of crunching echoed throughout the room. *Crunch, crunch, crunch, crunch, crunch.* Everywhere he put his paws on the bed, the sound resonated.

"What the hell?" Grandma said and turned to investigate the strange noise.

Stop moving, dog, I pleaded silently.

Yorkie continued to romp about. Grandma grabbed him by the scruff, threw him off the bed, then reached down and pulled my covers back. I tried raking them back up, but she'd already seen. Strewn all around me were pages and pages of the Sears catalogues. There must've been about seventy-five beautiful young underwear models nestled in my bed.

"It was you," Grandma said. "Why?"

I tried to hide. "I don't know. They . . ."

Grandma pushed the ripped pages aside and sat beside me.

"I like them," I whispered. Yorkie put his paws up on the bed again. "They remind me of my mom. They're beautiful."

Grandma's scents, curves, and soft voice had taken the place of my mother's. But they weren't the same. Mom's body was brown and lean. Grandma's was beige and chubby, with wrinkles and moles all over. I missed holding on to my mother's leg, nuzzling her breast, cuddling against her stomach. I missed feeling the strength her being possessed, the sense of warmth and protection. No matter how hard I squeezed, Grandma just wasn't home.

"Oh, baby," Grandma said and hugged me.

GODZILLA

WHEN I WALKED INTO CLASS the first day of kindergarten, I saw a kid standing alone by the tinker toys and coloured blocks in the corner near Mrs. S.'s desk. He was much shorter than me. His hair was dark brown, cut into a strange kind of bowl cut, and his nose was large and hatchet-shaped.

"My name is Leeroy," the kid said. "I'm a Newfie. My parents come from an island called Newfoundland."

I knew where that was because Grandpa came from Cape Breton. I imagined a land of Newfies with big noses, just like my new friend. I soon found out that he lived on my street, right around the corner from my house. In all, it was around fifty metres from his door to mine.

Leeroy and I got along right from the beginning. We'd jump our bikes off the curbs after school, and he was the only kid on our block who could beat me in a race. But I was tougher and could get the best of him most times—having older brothers gave me an advantage. He took me to cool spots like the gravel pit where we'd catch frogs and crayfish. Jerry would come with us, too, but it was clear Leeroy and I were best friends.

Leeroy had a big sister named Sylvia who was in Grade 2 with my brother Josh. She was twice the size of me and Leeroy.

"We need to watch out for her," Leeroy said. "She's a bully."

There was a wall that separated the kindergarten section from the older kids' playground out back. Whenever Sylvia came into our area, we'd whistle to warn each other, and then take cover behind the bushes. Most times we escaped her wrath, but sometimes she'd catch us by surprise and beat the pulp out of us. Her strength was unreal—like some real-life version of Godzilla, but with dirty-blond hair and a frilly pink dress. Her footsteps seemed to shake the very earth beneath our feet, and her nose was even larger than Leeroy's—when she'd throttle me, I thought it resembled the snout of a T. Rex, roaring and full of dinosaur teeth.

One day, Leeroy and I had had enough. We decided we were going to fire a giant wad of gum into Sylvia's hair at recess. She'd beaten and embarrassed us too many times. The moment the wet gum left the sling and slapped the side of her head, we knew we'd taken it too far.

She reached back and tried pulling it out, but that only made things worse. The gum stuck to her fingers and formed thin strands that blew back with the wind. A whole spiderweb of gum clung to the side of her face and neck. Her hair would have to be cut to get the gum out. Tears filled her eyes and she let out the most monstrous screech I'd ever heard. Her very body seemed to grow larger and larger the louder she yelled. Then she moved with lightning speed, cornered us, and began pummelling us in front of everyone.

Our classmates began screeching, "Save them, Mrs. S., Sylvia is going to murder them," as she tossed us in the air like rag dolls.

It felt like I flew five feet in one direction, Leeroy, four in the other. We knew we'd probably die if we stuck around, so we decided to make a run for it.

The playground was boxed in on one side by the school, and surrounded by fences on the others, and Sylvia blocked the way back toward the main road, so the gravel pit on the other side of the playground seemed like our only option. I signalled to Leeroy with my eyes, he did the same back, and the instant our sneakers hit the ground, we bolted. Sylvia may have been bigger and stronger than us, but we were faster, and we ran like our lives depended on it. When we thought we had a good lead, we turned to see how much earth separated us from the gum-haired Godzilla. She was about a half-kilometre away, screaming, crying, and cursing. For now, we were safe from the beast's clutches. For now, victory was ours.

From then on, Leeroy and I were inseparable.

LEEROY AND THE BROWN POP

LEEROY'S PARENTS BOTH WORKED DAYS, and he stayed in the after-school program until his mom or dad picked him up at 4:30 p.m. Sylvia also stayed after school, and Leeroy didn't like being in an enclosed space for two hours with his big sister and the other kids.

"The class breaks out into wrestling matches," he said, "and I always get the worst of it from Sylvia."

"Come play at my house," I said to him one day. Once 4:20 hit, he could walk back to school for his 4:30 pickup, like he'd never left at all. He jumped at the chance at freedom.

None of the kids usually liked coming to our house to play. Who could blame them? It was like stepping into a time machine. We had blocks of wood to play with; bits of steel my grandpa brought home from his construction job; some old dinky cars; a couple of beat-up hockey sticks from my uncles; and a few beach rocks we'd picked up in Cape Breton on our yearly trips. I knew my grandparents loved us; they just didn't have a lot of money.

We did get some good toys at Christmas, though, from our uncles and aunts, but we always destroyed them in a few days. Josh dismantled them to look inside and see how they were made and never put them back together, and Jerry and I simply abused them.

Down in our basement, I chucked a half-painted red block of wood across the concrete floor at Leeroy, trying to pretend it was Superman. It bounced and stopped dead in its tracks—definitely not Superman. Leeroy let out a sigh. Thirty minutes after reaching my house, I knew he was bored out of his mind. I began searching around for a way to keep us occupied. Then it hit me. I did have something Leeroy didn't have. Something way better than even his mountainous hoard of awesome toys.

"Leeroy," I said, so excited I just about shit myself. "Want to try something?"

"Sure," he said, unenthused.

I walked over to the fridge and yanked on the handle. The seal on the door broke and revealed a massive stack of Labatt 50 beers piled sideways, one on top of the other. They formed an odd pyramid shape that almost touched the bottom of the freezer. There must've been over three feet of them—ninety at least. The brown bodies of the bottles seemed to sweat and gleam in the neon basement light. "Brown pop," I said to Leeroy.

My dad used to give me sips of it when I lived with him in Sudbury, especially when I was crying. I remembered it tasted horrible but I drank it anyway, and the more I drank without complaining, the louder my dad and his friends laughed. They laughed loudest when Dad put me on the counter and I'd piss in the kitchen sink like they did.

Grandpa, too, loved brown pops, and it was my job to bring them to him when he came home from work every night. "Baby Boy!" he'd holler from his purple armchair in the living room. "Gimme a cold one." I would drop whatever I was doing, go grab one from the fridge, and run it upstairs. An empty bottle was always waiting for return by the side of the coffee table. If I was fast enough, and he was in a good mood, he'd give me a karate chop to the leg, then rub my hair. "That's my boy," he'd say through clenched teeth.

"I'm not sure if you've ever tried them," I said to Leeroy, "but my grandpa loves them, my dad does, too. They say it puts hair on your chest."

"Hair?"

"Yeah." I stepped back so Leeroy could look inside the fridge.

"My dad drinks these, too, so does my mom. But not this kind."

I grabbed one and shut the door. The cold glass felt nice. "This metal thing on the wall, that's the opener." Leeroy examined it.

"You just put the cap in at an angle, under the top tooth." I showed him. "Then you press the bottom of the bottle. The lid will come right off. I do it all the time for Grandpa." I could tell by the way he'd been looking at the opener that he'd never opened a bottle himself. When I pressed the bottle toward the wall, it hissed, and the cap fell and danced on the ground by our feet. Before I lost my courage, I hoisted the bottle to my lips and took a big swig. I could tell Leeroy wanted to try it, too. I gulped with all my might and almost vomited. A second later my stomach convulsed, but I said, "Ah," and wiped my mouth with the back of my hand.

"Give it to me," Leeroy demanded. He snatched the bottle. It was clear he wanted to impress me. The swill he took was bigger than mine, and his eyes bulged. He spat it out over the back of the bar. "That's disgusting."

I rescued the bottle from him before he dropped it. The brown pop still felt warm and bubbly inside my guts.

"No! I want to do it!" he yelled and yanked the bottle out of my hand. His chug was even bigger than before. This time he kept it down. *Success.* He smiled and let out a huge burp, and we both giggled.

By the end of the third bottle, I had a pressing urge to pee. I attempted to walk to the washroom, but couldn't see right, and my legs gave out halfway to the stairs. I fell in the middle of the floor and pissed myself where I lay. Leeroy, too, tried taking a few steps, but his legs buckled, and he veered off and slammed headfirst into the bar. He looked like a disoriented cat that tumbles sideways after being spun round and round. As he toppled to the ground, the bottle fell and smashed on the floor. We howled with laughter, our legs and arms writhing.

My grandmother must've heard all the commotion because before I knew it, she was standing over the two of us, hands on her hips. "What in God's name are the two of you up to now?" Her nose sniffed at the air.

We continued giggling, unable to collect ourselves, and totally unafraid. She grabbed my shoulders and hoisted me onto my feet. "Dear Lord, are you drunk, Jesse?" She let go of me. I fell toward her, grabbing her shirt for balance. She had her answer.

"Omm . . . Phurtttt . . . Haazzz . . ." I tried explaining what we'd done but nothing but bafflegab came out. Leeroy was cackling beside us, rolling dangerously close to the broken bottle. Grandma stood him up before he cut himself. She tried to scold us but started laughing until she wheezed, tears rolling out her eyes. I'd never seen her laugh so deeply over something I'd done. It made me feel good.

She got us upstairs and gave us a few drinks of water and some bread, and changed my pants. "Now get outside and walk it off," she said, shooing us away. "Like two miniature drunken sailors, you are."

We eventually fell asleep under a neighbour's tree a few houses down the street. When I woke up, Leeroy was gone.

ROBIN'S EGGS

MY FRIEND BRIAN, WHO LIVED down the street, told me he had a secret one day and that if I kept my mouth shut he'd show me. I promised not to tell a soul, and Brian showed me a robin's nest in his backyard. Every day Brian and his family put seeds beside the nest to feed the mother robin before she went foraging in the afternoon. She would leave at the same time every day—4:30 p.m. on the dot.

I remember looking at the eggs in wonder. There were three of them, and they were so beautiful—bright baby blue, tucked into the yellowed grass and mud of the nest. I imagined the eggs carefully positioned by their mother's feet, protected under her soft feathers, and guarded by her watchful eye.

Brian's mother called him in for dinner. "I'll wait for you and watch over the eggs while you eat," I said. Assured, he left. As soon as he did, I grabbed the eggs, put them in my sock, and ran home. On the way I slipped and fell and broke the eggs. Shocked at what I'd done, I threw the sock in the sewer, then hid in my grandparents' basement.

About a half-hour later Brian and his parents, Mr. and Mrs. T., showed up at our door looking for me. Mr. T. was a police officer but was kind to me and my brothers, and sometimes even played catch with us neighbourhood kids. Mrs. T. was even nicer, always baking up batches of cookies for Brian and me when we played Montezuma's Revenge on his computer—the only high-powered computer on our street.

My grandmother searched the house and found me behind a stack of boxes.

"I'm really sorry," I said when I was confronted about the eggs and told them what I'd done.

Brian cried. He was heartbroken.

"Why did you steal the eggs?" Brian's mother asked.

I broke down into a blubbering mess. The more they asked me, the more I bawled. But I didn't tell them why I did it.

My grandparents gave me the licking of my life, but I didn't break: I still didn't tell them why I stole the eggs.

When I saw Brian the next day at school he wouldn't talk to me.

The truth is, when I saw the three eggs tucked into that nest it reminded me of my brothers and me and our home in Saskatchewan. I thought of how much that mother robin loved those eggs and how well she and Brian's family took care of them, and I got jealous. The eggs had their mother, and my brothers and I didn't anymore. So I took the eggs. I thought that if I had them, in some way I'd have the same love the eggs had, and that would mean that in some way I'd have a mother's love again.

ATTABOY!

AS SOON AS I COULD hold a screwdriver and control a jigsaw—when I was about six years old—Grandpa trained me to use tools.

Grandpa believed in an honest day's work. He told us he was raised by his grandfather, Pappy Peter McKinnon, after his own father, a coal miner, passed from a heart attack. He used to say that if a man didn't have callused hands, he couldn't be trusted and didn't really work. He also said that your word was your worth, something that meant life or death when he grew up during the Depression. Because of his beliefs, I never heard Grandpa lie, never, not even if it hurt him to tell the truth.

"If a man knows how to build," Grandpa said as he wrapped my small hands around the circular saw, "he owns the world. Anything is possible. It's like large-scale Legos, just with sweat and more thinking."

Grandpa steadied the five-by-eight plywood board on the sawhorses, positioned my hips and arms, and continued with his lesson. "I built my own house, once, in Ottawa, just to see if I could do it. Nice house, too. And I had to work one of these saws all the time. After I teach you, you'll know how to do it for life."

Josh cried at first when Grandpa tried to teach him to work the saw, and almost gave up before he gritted his teeth, focused, then ran the blade straight through, winning Grandpa's admiration. Jerry flat-out refused. I assume it was because whenever Grandpa taught us any new skill it meant we'd have to use it to help him on one of his projects. Studding up the basement, ripping plywood for the skirting around the cabin down east, or building a new deck in the backyard, all were things we'd done once he'd trained us on new tools.

When Josh asked him why he made us work so hard, he said it was because his father had died when he was five years old. "That's when I became a man," he'd say. "I didn't have no childhood working in the mines. But growing up without my father made me tough, like a dried piece of salt cod left out in the sun too long. Grandpappy Peter also taught me to work up on Black Point, fishing in the dory. And I ain't letting you boys grow up without some of that hardness. Work was the only thing that pulled me and my mother out of the Depression."

Jerry always rolled his eyes when Grandpa went into his hard-done-by speeches.

As I steadied the saw, which was about the size of my torso, I imagined how hard working the way he did must've been for my grandfather.

"Just hold it straight, level, follow the line, and let the blade do the work. Most importantly, don't be afraid! I'll catch the offcut so the saw doesn't kick when it falls. And if it does buck, for God's sake don't try to grab it, just let it go," Grandpa said. "Got it?"

"Okay, Grandpa." I placed the face of the saw on the board, up against the clamped straight edge, my arms straining to keep it level. Both my brothers were looking on, and I tried my best to hide my fear from everyone. Jerry smirked and made a face. Josh joined in.

"Exactly. Now, press the trigger and let 'er rip. Like Josh did." Grandpa got into position beside me and made sure the extension cord wasn't in the way.

1, 2, 3, I counted in my head then squeezed the trigger tight. I had to fight the urge to close my eyes or run away. The whine and power of the saw frightened me at first, but I waited a second until I was comfortable pushing the machine forward. Grandpa nudged the back of my elbow and the blade moaned and bit into the wood.

"Now, easy does it, Jess. Steady."

The smell of pine filled my nostrils as sawdust kicked down onto my foot and back toward Jerry. I kept my eye on the plywood where the saw met the straight edge. Surprisingly, the saw tugged my hands and lurched forward on its own, but I pulled back against its torque, created some resistance, and kept everything balanced. Soon the blade had run through the length of the wood and the board offcut fell into my grandfather's hands. It looked like a baby delivered into the waiting arms of a doctor. He laughed out loud and his belly shook up and down behind his brown oil-stained overalls.

"That's how it's done. That's my baby boy!"

His eyes beamed with pride as he turned to face Josh and Jerry, who stood cross-armed. Both grimaced at me. I knew I'd get it from both of them later when Grandpa wasn't around. Despite the impending beating, I was proud of myself, even though it was only one piece of lumber.

"Thanks, Poppa," I said, grinning from ear to ear. "I wasn't scared at all."

"I know. Attaboy, Jess. Attaboy."

He reached over to the radio and turned up the George Jones song that crackled across the AM sound waves. He hummed to himself as he examined my cut, then lit a cigarette.

"Listen boys," he said, a plume of Du Maurier smoke swirling around his stubbled face, "I got a secret weapon. No one will have a go-cart racer like ours. Trust me—we'll never lose." He promised us we'd build a go-cart once we learned how to use the saw. He shuffled out onto the driveway, over to the side of his van, and slapped the side panel.

"A man must drive in style, boys, with a clean vehicle. That's his horse. You ever see knights riding around on scrawny, beat-up horses destined for the glue factory? Well, there's a reason for that."

Josh turned to me and said, "What the hell is he talking about? Glue factories didn't exist back when knights were around."

Jerry laughed and said, "He's trying to say that after we're finished with the go-cart we have to wash the van—again," while he pretended he was riding a horse, swinging a cowboy hat above his head, galloping around me and Josh.

Grandpa emerged from the van and caught Jerry making fun of him. "You look like a chubby version of Roy Rogers, galloping around all cock-eyed without a horse or gun."

Josh and I howled, while Jerry stood there stunned.

Grandpa never talked much while he worked, and today was no different while the four of us toiled away on the go-cart. We just kind of nodded and passed each other tools like nurses give surgeons instruments in the operating room—noiseless and quick, no mistakes. I think that's when we were closest, when we were silently working away in the garage, fixing the van, or doing other things. When the job was done, Grandpa cracked a beer, and we all drank Coke.

"It's a fine racer," Grandpa said. The go-cart was all decked out with a real car seat, two-inch-thick chassis, and rope steering, and it rode on "the fastest, most durable wheels known to man!" as he put it. Grandpa had pulled a set of four elevator wheels from the van—they were yellow and small and the same colour and texture as glycerine soap.

I just about pissed myself thinking of beating the pants off the other kids around us in the go-carts they had made with their fathers.

Jerry got the first push down the block. I figured it was because Grandpa felt bad about his comment earlier. Jerry screamed down the street, smiling and laughing, hair waving in the air. We cheered him on from the driveway, and Grandpa took a swig and hollered, "Attaboy, Jerry, attaboy!"

We all lived to hear him say those words.

LITTLE THIEF

"JESSE!" GRANDMA CALLED FROM UPSTAIRS. I could hear from the crinkle of paper and foil that she was searching through an empty pack of cigarettes on the phone stand beside her rocking chair. The terse clinks of her lighter against the side of the ashtray told me she was getting impatient. "Jesse! Hurry up! I need smokes." She broke into a fit of coughing.

Grandma without her smokes was scary. She got aggravated, which usually meant we'd get more chores. The longer she went without nicotine, the more toilets we had to wash, the more carpets we had to vacuum, and the more frequently we had to walk the dog. I ran upstairs.

"Here's the letter. John is working today. You know the kind—Du Maurier Special Mild, the tall silver box, not the short red one. Here's the money, and don't lollygag."

Going to the store was fun. I wasn't allowed to go there usually, only when Grandma sent me. It was far outside my safe terrain, two blocks farther, past the parkette, across the schoolyard, and down the street, where I didn't know anyone. Grandpa would warn me about the older boys who hung around outside the store, saying they were selling drugs and that their minds were warped by heavy metal music. He said they were just like my dad. I wondered about my father: where he was, why he wasn't around, and if he was still mad at me.

Was it my fault he took off? I questioned as I skipped down the street. *Does he miss me like I miss him?*

I rounded the corner and saw the older boys hanging out around the store pay phone, their music blaring on their silver ghetto blaster. I imagined Dad with the same kind of rocker haircut, cut-off jean jacket, and a black Ozzy Osbourne concert shirt.

"Hey, little man," Mitch, the oldest boy, said. "Come here a second, I want to ask you something." The other three boys were passing around a cigarette that smelled like a skunk, and they coughed like my grandma did when she woke up. I wondered how Mitch and his friends could squeeze through the hidden hole in the fence behind where they were standing. I'd seen them do it whenever the police pulled up to the store. My dad had run like that.

I got closer, my hand clutching the ten-dollar bill Grandma had given me. Mitch's aviator glasses glinted and blinded me for a second.

"It's cool, little man, we ain't gonna hurtcha. Relax." Mitch smiled at me. "You here to buy cigarettes for your granny?"

"Y-y-yes," I stammered, my gut churning. I searched to see if Grandpa was anywhere. He'd beat me if he caught me with Mitch and his friends.

Mitch leaned over. "Can you do us a favour?" The other boys suddenly turned and loomed over me. "Can you buy us a pack of cigarettes? John won't sell to us because our parents told him not to, but he'll sell to you because he knows your grandma."

My legs went wobbly. "Um . . . I'm not supposed to talk to you or anything. I'm just here to get her cigarettes. I'll get into trouble."

"No one will know." Mitch thrust a ten-dollar bill into my hand. "Player's king-sized—20s. Now go. I'll be here." Mitch pushed me toward the store and watched as I pulled on the glass door. I hauled away on it until my arm almost came out of its socket, it was so heavy. Each of the boys cracked a sideways smile. I didn't have a choice. They beat guys up if they didn't listen, and I was small. I smiled back and made it in. John was at the counter.

"What is it today, chief?" he said, his tanned face beaming in the dust-filled light. John's hair was curly and cut short. I once heard Grandpa say he was a half-breed like me and my brothers, but our hair and skin didn't look like his. He looked half black and half white to me.

"Here. The silver ones. For my grandma." I slapped down Grandma's letter. John turned around to select a pack from the shelf behind him, and my hand shot toward the shelf of candy bars. I grabbed as many as I could and stuffed them into my underwear—just like Josh and Jerry had taught me. I must've snatched about ten.

John turned back, cocked his head, and asked, "Is that it, chief?"

I almost shit my pants.

"No . . . sir . . . I'd like to buy another pack of cigarettes. Player's King, 20." I reached into my pocket for Mitch's ten. The ruffling noise of candy bar wrappers sounded louder to me than someone crunching up hundreds of newspaper pages. I kept my eyes on his to see if he'd notice.

"Player's?" he asked. "Your grandparents don't smoke those."

"I—I—um . . . My uncle!" I burst out. "They're for my uncle!"

He looked me up and down, then swivelled back to the shelf. I saw my opportunity and my hands darted forward, grasping about five packs of Fun Dip and six packs of Big League Chew and rammed them in my pants. I felt a chocolate bar fall to my ankle. Somehow my pants kept it there.

"I'll give them to you today," John said as he slid the Player's and change across the counter. "But next time I'll need a letter from your uncle, too."

I grinned even though it felt weird and said I'd bring the letter next time, then waddled toward the door. It sounded like I was wearing a diaper.

"Hey, wait!" John called out.

Sweat was pouring from my forehead like water from a faucet.

"Tell your grandpa I say hi. The lottery is up today. He needs to play to win!"

"Okay." I nodded and left. Before the door closed, the chocolate bar down by my ankle dropped out onto the floor. I booted it onto the sidewalk and waited for the door to close behind me. I thought for sure John had seen it, but I walked over to the pay phone to give Mitch the cigarettes, and John just stood behind the counter and watched as the older boys ran up to me. One of them, the one who appeared the slowest and sleepiest of them all, scooped the candy bar off the pavement.

Mitch's gang told me I could keep the change for the work I'd done—about $4.50. I told them John needed a letter next time.

"No problem," Mitch said as he lit a smoke. "This will be our little thing, okay?"

I agreed. Buying cigarettes for the older boys for pocket change sounded great. They were so busy swarming for cigarettes, they didn't even notice that my gotchies were filled with about a half-case of chocolate bars and gum.

When I got home, Grandma wasn't in her rocking chair in front of the veranda door like usual. Something was up. Yorkie barked, and I heard Grandma stampede down three flights of stairs—faster than I'd ever heard her move before. She charged at me. I turned to escape, but she shoved the door closed.

"John called!" she roared like a pissed-off bear, her lips gnarled back so I could see her black cigarette-stained teeth. "His candy bar shelves are bare. He also told me you bought a pack of Player's." She pulled my pants down before I knew what was happening, and my hoard fell onto the floor.

I started crying. She was having none of it and started spanking me.

"Why?" she screamed. "Why. Are. You. Stealing?" She started to weep and hit me even harder.

"I didn't steal, Grandma. Some kids gave these to me, and I stuck them in my pants."

She looked confused. "Now you lie to me on top of it! My God, Jesse. What is going on with you?" She smacked me across the mouth, then pushed me into the corner while she gathered the chocolate bars and gum.

I tried to pull them out of her hands but she was stronger than me. She slapped me again. My cheek was on fire.

"I'm not lying, Grandma. The bad kids outside of the store got me to buy them a pack of cigarettes and gave me this candy! That's what they paid me with." I knew that was something she would understand: *The bad drug-dealing kids—just like her son.* Grandpa always cursed them, and I hoped my lie would sound believable to her.

"They said they'd beat me up if I didn't." To my surprise Grandma stopped. I stared at her. I knew she was weighing the possibility of truth in my gigantic lie.

"I'm sorry, Jesse."

The lie had worked! She thought I'd been bullied. Guilt washed over me—I'd used my dad against her—but I didn't tell her the truth.

"Well, your grandfather will hear about this."

But when Grandpa returned home from work that night, nothing was said. My grandmother, I figured, didn't want to get in trouble, either.

I thought about the feeling of excitement I'd had grabbing the chocolate bars off the shelf when John had turned his back, the feeling of power. Now I had a strange and satisfying feeling of control—control I'd never had before.

I liked it.

SUPREMACY

MY BROTHERS AND I FOUGHT almost every day at school. This was my second time in Grade 2, and fighting probably had something to do with that.

If anyone too big or too strong, from say Grade 4 or 5, picked on me, I'd band together with Leeroy, and we'd annihilate them. We'd chuck rocks, throw baseball bats or whatever, trip people when they weren't looking, or pummel them right in the hallways—whatever it took. Many times, we ended up in detention or in the principal's office together. But Leeroy and I weren't bullies—we didn't go looking for it. We only reacted when we were picked on. And if Leeroy and I couldn't handle it, I'd run to my brothers—by far the strongest kids their age—who could.

We Thistle boys, plus Leeroy, formed a kind of warrior clan that dominated a section of the schoolyard near the portables and the benches. We covered about twenty square metres of terrain, but our domination over this area was contested. There were other tribes of boys, older and younger than us, vying for supremacy, always trying to take our spot. These clans were formed by friends, brothers, cousins, and, if things got intense enough, competing enemies would forge alliances to vanquish common foes.

Otis, Hershel, and the other five black kids in the school formed the strongest clan, but they were more interested in breakdancing and girls and were too old to bother with us second- and third-graders.

Next, there were the two Smith boys and their sister, Tania, along with the rest of the Simmons Street kids. They all played rep hockey, which meant they fought well as a coordinated team. They were quick with their fists and reminded me of professional NHL enforcers.

The Histon crew, on the other hand, was a handful of kids who weren't into sports at all and liked to read the Hardy Boys. James and Doug, two English-descended kids who lived near the fence, were friends with me and Josh. Sometimes, when we needed to duck out from a beat down, they'd invite us over for KD until things cooled off.

The most dangerous kids, however, were the loners. Amongst them was a Vietnamese girl named May, who was the most brutal fighter at our school even though she was tiny. Once, I pissed her off and she just about scratched my eyes out. Even the older kids wouldn't mess with May. She sent scores of tough guys home, crying, to their mothers. But May was sweet if you didn't provoke her, and she never bothered me about my missing parents or called me "Indian."

Our archenemies at school, though, were Ronald and Kurt and their sidekick, Ethan. They didn't need provoking. They'd go out of their way to kick my shins, steal my lunch, push me face down in mud on the way home from school, or embarrass me and my brothers in front of everyone. Ronald, the eldest, was in Josh's Grade 4 class. Kurt was my age but in Jerry's grade, and Ethan was a year younger and in my class. He resembled Beaver Cleaver but had the dastardly personality of Eddie Haskell. Rumour had it that Ronald and Kurt were so tough because they knew karate and had black belts.

When Leeroy and I tried ambushing Ronald and Kurt, they always outsmarted us, leaving us with bloody noses and black eyes. Even my brothers seemed powerless against the duo. You could never catch them off guard or alone. They were strong, tactical, and had backup with Ethan always close by.

Going to school was like entering a battleground full of feral gangs, chanting and scheming and beating the shit out of one another.

I hated every minute of it.

HEART ATTACK

"WHERE'S YOUR MOM AND DAD?" Mando asked. She was a pretty East Indian girl new to the school and my class. She sat in the desk in front of me and when I got frustrated I'd stare at the back of her head—the light played on her shiny black hair whenever she moved and reminded me of my mother's.

I kept my eyes on the dragon I was drawing and thickened the lines until they turned ugly. I wanted to bawl whenever I thought of my parents. My dad hadn't come home from the hospital two years ago like Grandma said would happen over Christmas. All I knew was that he was sick and that he'd be home when he was better. But he didn't show. Grandpa was furious and started spending a lot of time in the garage building and fixing stuff, drinking more brown pop than usual, and yelling at us. I got yelled at the worst, maybe because I looked like Dad the most, but Jerry got hit the most because he stood up to Grandpa.

Maybe he just stayed in the hospital? I reasoned.

Grandma started to eat and sit in front of the TV watching her soaps more. Sometimes the phone would ring in the middle of the night and she'd run downstairs to see who it was. She'd whisper, "Sonny, is that you? Is that you? Please, come home. We love you." She'd say this over and over until Grandpa came downstairs and yanked the receiver from her hand.

Sometimes the phone would ring in the middle of the day and I'd rush to answer it. I'd hear breathing but no words. Grandma usually took the phone from me before I had a chance to ask who it was, but sometimes I was on long enough to ask if it was me who made him run away. The breaths would sometimes turn into what sounded like whimpers, but never words, and never a dial tone. Someone was listening.

Grade 2 was tough on us. Josh had failed it in 1981. Jerry failed it in 1982. And I failed it in 1983. I couldn't concentrate. I kept thinking about Dad. I didn't learn how to read, write, do math, or anything. Mrs. Z., my first Grade 2 teacher, held me back. I hated that Leeroy and all my other friends were a year ahead.

I knew Mando didn't know any of the stuff about my parents, or that I was a failure. My old classmates, on the other hand, did. For a while I used to tell kids at school that my grandparents took care of us to give my mom and dad a break, that they'd come back to get us soon. I stopped when I realized that no one believed us, that our enemies loved watching us squirm. They said our parents had abandoned us because we were ugly Indians who ate from the dump. They'd ask about our missing parents to be dicks and start fights. They'd chant at us with war whoops because Josh told them we once lived in a tipi in Saskatchewan. *Idiot*, I thought.

The tip of my pencil buckled and a shard broke off, hitting Mando's sundress. She brushed it away, and I knew she was waiting for an answer.

"Go away, please," I said.

"Didn't you hear me, Jesse?" she said patiently. "I asked, 'Where are your mom and dad?' I've seen you with your grandma on parent-teacher night, but never your parents. Why?"

"If you really want to know, they're dead, and I'm an orphan," I muttered. But in my head I was yelling, *I don't fucking know where they are*. If Mando were a boy, I would've hauled off and punched her in the mouth right in the middle of class.

Mando's lip quivered as she shifted backward.

The old tipi in the hippie colony near Debden, Saskatchewan. We stayed there one summer with some of Mom's friends before our family fell apart.

I pushed my dragon drawing off the desk and watched it float to the ground.

Mando leaned over. "I'm sorry, Jesse. I didn't know." She grabbed my hand and started crying.

Her hand felt warm on top of mine, and I started crying, too. She squeezed my hand.

There was a nudge against my back.

Then another.

Then another.

"Look at the crybaby crying!"

A finger jabbed into my shoulder. I turned around and saw Ethan, Ronald and Kurt's sidekick. The freckles on his nose looked like someone shit on his face through a screen door. He was laughing and so were some of his buddies.

"Look at Jesse, crying in class. Just like a baby. Boo hoo!" Ethan pushed me and I fell forward into Mando's chair.

"What the hell is wrong with you?" she yelled.

"He's a baby," Ethan teased. "Baby, baby, baby!"

I punched Ethan square in the eye. Spit flew out of my mouth, and my head felt like it was going to explode. I flipped the desk nearest to me into the air, knocking over a few chairs and hitting a couple of people by the blackboard.

"Who's the baby now?" I yelled.

I could see Mrs. C. leaping over about five desks to try to get to us. I grabbed my pencil and lunged at Ethan, aiming for his heart. Mrs. C. tried to push me away, but I kicked and punched her. She had a tough time blocking my shots, and I think Ethan was afraid I'd murder her to get to him, cause he scuttled like a rat to the back of the room.

I couldn't breathe. My chest heaved up and down, my heart was going a thousand beats a minute. I started slamming my fists against my head. Mrs. C. grabbed my arms and placed me in the hallway. Ethan and his cronies were making war whoops as she slammed the door behind us. Mando was at the door trying to say something, but it got lost in the ruckus. Mrs. C. tried to restrain me.

"What happened?" she asked. "Why are you fighting again? Why did you try to stab Ethan?"

I could tell she was shocked. Hell, I was shocked. Ethan was lucky— I'd wanted to kill him. I would have gutted him if it weren't for Mrs. C.

"Answer me!" She put her hand under my chin and forced me to look at her. I squirmed under her gaze. I kept my mouth shut and furrowed my forehead right back at her.

"Answer me. You could have really hurt him!"

I imagined Ethan dead on his back with a pencil jutting skyward out of his chest. I grinned at the thought.

The more Mrs. C. pressed me, the more I dug in. If I was good at anything, it was keeping my mouth shut. I wasn't going to rat, not even on him. Not to her, not to the principal, and certainly not to my grandparents.

NOT A PICTURE IN SIGHT

I LOVED CHRISTMAS.

"I hope I got the new Megatron," I said to Josh as I launched myself down two flights, landing near the base of the tree. Shimmering boxes, bows, and tinsel busted out across the living room floor. The lights flickered and danced, adding to the drama.

After unwrapping half my presents, I realized, to my dismay, that I'd gotten practical items like underwear, socks, or cruddy, oversized long johns. It was, after all, Christmas with my grandparents, and they always bought us grandparent-like things.

For breakfast we had our traditional bologna, bacon, egg, hash brown, pancake, and bannock meal. I ate until I couldn't see.

"My stomach hurts," Jerry complained as he finished, adjusted his PJ bottoms, and belched.

"It's because you drank the corn syrup," Josh said. "Should have left some for the rest of us." We all laughed because it was true.

Even Grandpa was chuckling as he hummed to the Boney M. song that blasted over the old record player. Grandma was at the counter—she was already three-quarters of the way through all her prep work, but she still had lots to go.

I eyed the about fifty pounds of potatoes that needed peeling—a job she always saved for Aunt Sherry—and fired whatever leftovers I had under the table, so Yorkie could partake in the gluttony. My hand was covered in slobber, but it was his way of saying thank you, and I loved the way his tongue tickled my fingers and the *bing* sound his tail made when it banged against the table leg.

At noon, everyone began to arrive—first my aunt Sherry and uncle John; then my dad's brother uncle Ralph and his wife; Uncle Ron, who was my dad's younger brother and best friend; and all my cousins—accumulating until we were packed in like sardines.

The whole comedy roast started with my aunt Sherry's cackle. "The only thing worse than Ralph's turkey farts," she said, adjusting her apron, "are Jesse's butter-tart farts—so creamy. Can you believe a smell like that can come from such a scrawny kid?" The living room quaked with laughter, and the pile of skinned potatoes next to my aunt almost fell over from the commotion.

Each of us took a turn razzing the person next to us, and I swear my aunt turned beet red when Uncle Ron laid into her. As I sat on the couch and watched everyone bellow with laughter, I envisioned my dad at home with us, and it was like the instant I'd opened my eyes that morning, hours before everyone came, before all the jokes.

When I woke up, I'd pictured him arriving at home looking like a gentle yet rugged Marlboro man in a black overcoat, with rosy-red cheeks and a long knitted scarf like Tom Baker's from *Doctor Who*. Grandma watched *Doctor Who* in between reading her Harlequin novels and watching her soaps. She'd been a fan since the early '60s, had seen all the Doctors throughout the years, and thought Tom Baker was the best one of them all. I always figured Dad looked like him for some reason. Maybe I just wanted him to be as smart and brave as Tom Baker, as the Doctor.

I imagined Dad's grand entrance occurring at the perfect time—just as we were unwrapping our treasured gifts. He'd pause in the front alcove, scrape his boots on the doormat, brush gigantic, Hollywood-style snowflakes off his broad shoulders, then look me right in the eye and smile—all without saying a word. I'd throw aside my gifts and rush into his open arms, the presents rendered worthless compared to the prospect of grabbing hold of our long-lost dad.

Or I'd yell, "I'm mad at you!" stopping short in front of him. "You left us with nothing and all alone up in Sudbury!"

I'd kick his foot and try to stay mad, but he'd say, "I'll never leave again, Jesse," his cheeks still cold from the frost. "You have my word on it," talking his way out of it, like usual, giving me all the sweet answers I longed to hear.

I'd collapse into his arms and bury my face in his scarf, smell his cologne, and hold on for an eternity.

That was my Christmas wish, what I'd dreamt of that morning and what I was dreaming of again.

"Wake up, boy," Grandpa said. "You see this mountain of wrapping paper that needs tending?" Only his request for help taking out the trash managed to break me from my imaginings.

I knew Grandma dreamed the same dream that I did. I saw her look at the door even after everyone had arrived. I knew that every year, fuelled by hope, she over-prepared. We watched in awe as she marshalled forth a parade of food—the same way she'd done every year since 1981.

One of my cousins commented first, saying, "This is way too much food, Nana! How are we supposed to eat all this!?"

Grandma didn't answer, but kept the gravy boats and platters floating in. Plates, forks, food, and my relatives mashed together, caught up in the force of it all.

I understood what the flood of food really represented, but didn't have the courage to name it and stop its annual inundation. I sat at the dinner table watching my grandmother out of the corner of my eye. Between laughter and smiles she discreetly and periodically scanned the front door, poised to spring up at the turn of the knob.

I watched my grandfather, too, after dinner, as I played on the floor in front of the tree with my cousins. As usual, he sat glued to his armchair swilling beer, until his speech slurred. I saw him staring at the police awards Uncle Ralph had won and that he kept displayed on the living room wall beside the fireplace.

"See, Ralph," he said, pointing at them, the smell of beer now strong in the room. "That's my boy. That's a *real* Thistle. And you," he fired over at me. "You're an asshole, just like your father. Oh, I know what you've been up to," he said, flicking the snout of his beer with his thumb and making it pop. "I'm watching you, buddy."

I tried to understand what I'd done wrong, but couldn't. I stared up at the wall. It didn't have any pictures of Dad. None. In fact, there weren't any pictures of me or my brothers or my dad anywhere in the whole house.

Grandpa kept glaring at me, and I ran to the washroom looking for a place to hide. He didn't stop as I ran past, but cracked a smile. I slammed the door.

At the end of the day, Grandma collected the extra food and drink she'd laid out, embalmed it in cellophane, and then interred it in the fridge and freezer. I loomed over the unopened presents that lingered under our tree. They were addressed to "Sonny Boy." They stayed under the tree, and the tree remained up for a long time, reminders that something horrible had happened and that Dad wasn't ever going to come home.

We ate the leftovers well into February.

THE FAKE ITALIAN

LEEROY KICKED HIS LEG OVER the blue bin behind the convenience store and disappeared inside. We dove in every other week, and we'd find *Playboy* magazines, old gum, and maybe some candy bars. It was a good little after-school activity that kept us busy.

People thought Leeroy and I were brothers we were together so much, except that I looked like some awkward mix of Italian and something else, and he looked whiter than a bleached bedsheet. Derick, the small Greek kid who lived across the street from my grandparents, was with us and was the darkest kid around—darker than Josh even. I thought I looked like Derick and his father a bit.

"Score," Leeroy called out. He held a porno mag over the edge of the bin and Derick and I cheered.

"Anything else?" Derick asked.

I heard what sounded like boxes shuffle and bags rip followed by Leeroy saying, "We've hit the motherlode!" He tossed out a dusty box of Snickers and climbed out.

"Check the expiry date," I said as I searched the side and found a label: *March 1984*.

"Must be from the backroom or something," Derick said as he examined the label and ripped open the box. He had a bar unwrapped and in his mouth in a matter of seconds. As he tried to gnaw at the brown steel, the skin of the bar cracked and broke.

"That shit's three years old," I said. "Don't break a tooth."

Leeroy stood transfixed near the edge of the bin—he was gawking at the skin mag. He flipped it around and showed us a picture of a naked woman laying down in a desert. She had on feathers and leather buckskins—bits of her costume hung loose and revealed her breasts.

"Your people," he said to me, laughing. I didn't know what to say and picked up a Snickers bar and attempted to snap it in half to see if it was edible. It didn't flex a millimetre. I wasn't putting it in my mouth.

Derick giggled and moved closer to get a better look. He said, "My brother told me about Indians." His mouth was full of chocolate as he looked over at me and tossed his wrapper on the ground. "Said they're all dead."

Leeroy held the magazine up and smiled. "She's not dead." The woman in the pictures was now completely naked but was beside a painted horse and had a spear in her hand.

"It's in that Iron Maiden song," Derick said. "'Run to the Hills.' My brother plays it all the time."

"Yeah," Leeroy added. "My sister, too—I love that song!"

Both broke out into the lyrics, Derick holding his hands in heavy metal devil horns, Leeroy headbanging his mullet. I could make out that the song was about killing Indians and selling them whiskey and destroying the buffalo. The only clear part was the chorus—same as the title. I assumed it meant that the Indians had to run away.

I thought about when Derick's brother, Moses, played that song on the ghetto blaster in front of their house. I heard the name "Cree" in the lyrics and Moses explained to me that it was about when the British Army killed a bunch of Cree Indians on the plains out west and then gave the land to white people.

"You're from out west," Moses said. "Are you a Cree?" I didn't know what to say and wondered if my mom was a Cree for a second.

"No," I blurted out. "We're Italian." The lie came from nowhere, but I thought it might keep me safe or include me somehow. "We have some Indian way back," I went on. "But my skin is dark because we have Italian in us—see." I held my arm to his.

"That's not what Josh said." He gave me a skeptical look.

I thought about my parents and all the questions that burned within me growing up, and the resentment that had taken root. I hated them; I hated myself. I hated explaining to other kids where my parents were and why my skin was darker than theirs. I felt torn between wanting to be Indian and wanting to hide in my lie—kind of how I felt standing there, listening to Derick and Leeroy thrash to that song by the dumpster with the naked woman in the magazine dressed like an Indian.

It would just make life easier, I decided, to tell people I was Italian.

FALLING APART

1988–1996

MY FABRICATED PERSONA

"Life of the party," they said
Whatever they put in front of me, I did.
Lines
Joints
Cups of straight whiskey
Chased down by false manhood

I took bits of all the Gods and mixed them together
Hendrix
Jim Morrison
Conan the Barbarian
Chavez the Native horse thief from Young Guns
And—voilà—an instant Warrior

I drank more than they could
Jumped higher
Ran faster
But nobody told me
That Indians aren't made in Hollywood
And we were never meant to be the good guys

ODDBALL

I COULDN'T READ FOR SHIT and stuttered, so I avoided reading out loud in front of everyone. I didn't understand how I'd graduated Grade 5 without really knowing how to read and write, but there I was, at a new school, in amongst a whole new crop of kids.

Leeroy was in Grade 7 and would walk to school with me every day, so I had the edge over some of the Grade Sixers who, I assumed, didn't know anyone. On our walks we often picked up butts off the ground and pretended we were smoking. We didn't have a lighter or matches because John at the store had stopped selling anything cigarette related to us kids after he found me supplying Mitch a few years back.

Leeroy's sister, Sylvia, however, smoked with her rocker friends, Mitch included. They all had big teased hair—Sylvia's hairsprayed bangs were a three-inch wave cresting on her forehead. Her nose didn't stick out so much anymore, and she'd started getting bumps and curves all over. Her makeup seemed to sparkle, the same dreamy way as the women in Grandma's soap operas, and my vision got blurry whenever I saw her sucking on a cigarette, and words—forget about it. I couldn't form a coherent thought around her.

The first time Leeroy saw me acting like an ass around Sylvia, he said, "I'll rearrange your face if you look at her that way again."

Still, I couldn't help dreaming about her and those cigarettes.

Josh went to the same school and was in Grade 8 with Sylvia, and Jerry was in Grade 7 and had made a whole new batch of friends separate from Josh and me and our street crew. His buddies were now the smart and good kids from neighbourhoods I didn't know. They didn't smoke or drink or cause any trouble that I knew of; they were awkward and read comics. But my brothers still held their ground. I felt safe with them and Leeroy around.

That left me free to explore—girls especially.

One day in October, while waiting to catch a bus for our school field trip to the Royal Ontario Museum, I noticed *her*, up on the hill in front of the arena right beside our school.

She had flaming red hair and a pair of black-and-white British Knights running shoes. I knew her name was Lucie because I'd heard a teacher call it out at an assembly during orientation week. I'd heard classmates say that she was an excellent swimmer and took classes in the swimming club, where all the elite swimmers our age took lessons. She hung out with the cool kids—my friend Brian and some rich kids.

I wasn't like them, though.

I walked around the bottom of the hill, fidgeting with my book bag. I wanted to talk to her, but my brain wasn't working properly, just like when I was around Sylvia. I could tell Lucie didn't even see me, sweating and rehearsing how to say hi. She was gossiping with two other pretty girls I also had weird feelings about. One of them was Kiley. She had long, flowy hair that made my guts do backflips. She had two sisters at the school who were into soccer, just like Kiley.

"They're a family of athlete goddesses," Leeroy said.

The other girl, a strawberry blond named Sarah, was "developed," as Leeroy would say. It drove all us boys nuts. Everyone wanted to dance with her at the seasonal Much Music dances, and when the music started up, she was like a queen bee covered in a beard of adolescent males. I once tried dancing with her but was almost trampled. I spent the rest of the night bopping in the corner all by myself, far from the hormones and chaos.

"Hi," I managed to spit out as I got about halfway up the hill, thirty feet away from the three girls. They didn't hear me. "Hi," I said again, raising the volume a decibel or two. My voice cracked under the strain. I wanted to flee but I pushed on. Still no answer. I thought they were ignoring me.

But Sarah turned and rolled her eyes. "Look, it's that nerd that hangs out with Brian. What does he want?"

Kiley laughed and looked me up and down.

Lucie was silent and scrunched up her face at Sarah.

"Hello, my name is Jesse." I extended my hand. "Is this where the class is supposed to meet to catch the bus for the school field trip?" They giggled. My hand just hung there. *Nice moves.* I squirmed. *Real smooth.*

"Does this look like a bus stop?" Sarah retorted, pushing my hand away. Her flowered sundress looked menacing in the breeze.

I had nothing left to say, no more moves, no courage.

Kiley turned her back and whispered something to Lucie and pinched her nose as if I smelled. Lucie didn't react. I flashed her a smile. She smiled back a little. But I couldn't bear to be there any longer and went to leave.

"Wait," Lucie said, as she reached for my hand and shook it. "My name is Lucie, nice to meet you."

Kiley and Sarah were dumbfounded.

JUST LIKE THE REST OF THEM

"LET'S GO TO THE MALL," I said.

Anything was better than lunch hour at school, even walking two kilometres, and there was a place called Frank's that served the best fries and gravy in the city. After, we could go to the convenience store and play Double Dragon or Time Lord on the arcade machines. Leeroy was pretty good, I sucked ass. Richard was with us. He was a small German kid with a big head who was just as mischievous as Leeroy and me. He'd been in my Grade 6 class the year before, and I'd done something with him I'd never done with Leeroy—I'd skipped school.

At the mall, Leeroy pulled five dollars out of his pocket. Richard had twenty. I, on the other hand, pulled rabbit ears, like usual. When we got to the burger stand the two of them slapped their bills on the counter, ordered "Fly Baby," and laughed.

"Fly Baby" is how Frank called orders of fries and gravy back to his wife, who manned the fry station behind the till. We kids had heard him say that a few times and started saying it ourselves. We thought it was funny. Frank usually gave us our orders without saying a word, then, once we were far enough away, he'd turn to his wife and say something in Korean.

Mrs. N., our home economics teacher, reacted the same way when I made fun of her Japanese accent during class, becoming silent. When

I didn't do my assignments—which happened all the time—it was my way to shut her down. The class loved it every time I deliberately mispronounced something and encouraged me with laughter.

For as long as I could remember, people had teased me about being a half-breed "Indian," and I hated it, but when I acted the same way toward others, nobody ever focused on who I was. Mrs. N. didn't deserve it—no wonder she failed me with the brief report card comment "Frequently unprepared for class."

After Frank handed over the two orders of fries, Richard inhaled his. He didn't share a single bite with me. I was insulted. After all, I was the one who'd asked him along and I expected him to give me at least a couple of fries in return. Leeroy, to my shock, did the exact same thing. He'd never done that before. To make matters worse, just before Leeroy finished up, Richard reached over and grabbed a fry—all dripping with gravy—and chucked it in his mouth. He grinned at me then turned to Leeroy and said, "Those were delicious, eh, buddy?" Both cackled, mouths open, fry matter visible on their tongues. I was furious. I challenged Richard to a fight after school, in the park across the street, where no teachers could interfere. He accepted. I stomped off, leaving the two of them chewing on their shitty fries.

When the school bell rang that afternoon, I bolted to the park. Word had spread quickly that the "crazy Indian" was going to scalp some poor German bastard. A pack of kids followed us across the street and formed a giant circle around Richard and me. Chants of "Go, go, go" filled the air as kids began shoving us closer and closer together. I swung first and hit Richard in the mouth. Stunned, he stood still for a moment, then hurled his book bag at me, missing my head by about a foot. I followed with a straight leg to the gut.

I was winning.

Then he said, "Figures," coughing and holding his ribs. "You're just a dirty Indian, like the rest of them."

Everyone burst into laughter, followed by loud war whoops. The rage that fuelled me drained away. Silence gripped my tongue.

"You'll probably die drinking like they all do."

The crowd shifted from my side to his, and I saw my street friends laughing and pointing at me.

They believed it, too. They all believed it.

THE MOST IMPORTANT THING

IT WAS A SATURDAY. THE summer sun was shining, the lawn mowers were humming, and the bacon was frying. It was all I could smell. I heard my grandfather's flip-flops shuffling against the worn linoleum floor in the kitchen. He was too cheap to replace it. But he was letting me sleep in, which was odd, considering he always got us up at the crack of dawn for chores, or to polish his golf clubs before he went out to the range, now that we were all of working age—thirteen, the same age he told us he'd left home and went picking potatoes in Prince Edward Island.

I heard Jerry sobbing through the wall between our bedrooms. It wasn't his usual, annoying crying. He sounded like a gentle whale plumbing the depths in some uncharted region of the Pacific, calling for a distant herd. I sat up in bed and listened as he went on for what seemed like a million years. I knew something must be wrong and wanted to hug him right through the drywall, but I dared not leave my room. I didn't want to get in trouble or find out that someone had died.

I heard Yorkie pawing at the door. I opened it. He held his head low, like he'd done something bad, and his tail wasn't wagging.

"What is it, boy?" I asked him. "What's going on?" I rustled the top of his head, and the back of his tail raised to quarter mast and batted back and forth.

"Jesus Christ!" Grandpa said after it sounded like he dropped a plate.

Yorkie bolted. Jerry continued to cry. I decided to go down and find out what was going on. I hadn't heard a peep from Grandma and wondered where she was.

When I entered the kitchen, Grandpa was clattering through forks and knives in one of the drawers and swearing.

"Do you want some goddamned eggs?" he barked.

"Sure." I waited, staring at him.

He grabbed a fork and tried to stab out a few pieces of bacon, but he fumbled and the fork fell over the edge of the skillet onto the floor. A strip of bacon teetered on the drawer next to the stove.

"Fuck," he muttered and wiped the stove with a paper towel. "Sit down, boy."

He tossed my breakfast plate on the table and pulled my chair up all in one motion. He looked frail almost, in a way I'd never seen before. To me he was invincible, with his strong, hairy arms and barrel chest. But now he was as he really was—an older, greying man.

"I've already told your brothers, and I don't like beating around the bush, so listen up." He reached over and rubbed my arm. He'd never touched me like that before.

"Your dad was never in the hospital," he said. "He got into trouble robbing some stores, went to jail. When the police found you, you lot were starving and dirty." He tapped his finger against the table like a tiny hammer trying to beat back the past. "Once we heard what went down, me and Grandma went and got you. Sonny got out and was supposed to come home but . . ." Grandpa's voice trailed off for a moment. "I guess he loved drugs and booze more. Fucking asshole." He slammed his fist on the table and his plate fired beans into the air. "Family is the most important thing, Jesse, and if I ever catch you doing drugs I'll disown you."

His face looked harder than I'd ever seen before—like steel, tungsten even. I trembled. Tears began rolling down my cheeks like an ancient levee had broken.

He pulled his hand off my arm.

"None of that," he said. "Men don't cry; you're a man now."

The smell of margarine filled the air as my grandfather slathered his browned square of toast with it and ate it, and I tried not to cry. Then I heard the sound of my grandmother's rocking chair in the next room, moving back and forth, and the sound of her crying.

CANADA GEESE

"THERE'S ONE RIGHT OVER NEAR the portable," Leeroy said as he reached down for a juicy butt. His black-and-white Mötley Crüe concert shirt, a hand-me-down from his sister, was skin-tight against his back. It looked like it'd burst open as he bent over to grab the smoke. Even tighter were his acid-washed jeans, which were rolled up and pinned at the bottom to accentuate his kicks, their tongues hanging out like overgrown dog ears. He looked like Sylvia's rocker friends, but without any style.

I didn't have the wicked threads he did. We wore Bargain Harold's crap Grandma purchased from the sale bin. Black turtlenecks were about as fashionable as I got, and the one I was wearing was covered in mustard from the lunchroom.

"Holy cow!" I said, trying to rub the stain off. "That hasn't even been smoked!" Leeroy held the cigarette up to the sun. The body of it was near perfect, it was just crooked. It had yellow moisture stains, but the Export A logo was intact.

Leeroy pulled a book of matches out of his jeans pocket and dangled them. "Look what I got," he whispered, looking back and forth for Mrs. W. or Mr. G. They were always on patrol and gave any kids they saw hanging around a tough time. We knew we could end up incarcerated in the principal's office.

"I stole them from Sylvia this morning." Leeroy grinned. He peeled open the book of matches to reveal three perfect rows. The cigarette drooped from his lips and begged for a flame. I huddled close to guard against the wind. The ember burned cherry red as he struck the match, lit the butt, and hauled in a breath. He strained to hold the smoke in, and his face turned green. He exhaled and coughed so loud it sounded like a flock of Canada geese erupting from his lungs.

"Here, your turn," he said, still convulsing.

I grabbed the smoke and pictured my grandma and grandpa yelling at me. I took a big drag and pretended to blow smoke at them. I didn't cough like Leeroy, though. I wheezed, dropped the smoke, and fell ass-backward onto the ground. I groped the grass—everything was spinning. I saw black spots dance across the blue sky. Leeroy laughed, a sound that pulled me back into this world.

"You suck." He reached over, plucked the smoke off the gravel where I'd dropped it, took another drag, and handed it back. "Just ease into it, Jess. Like me." He exhaled without coughing, then crossed his arms, oozing style.

I wanted to be as cool as him.

CHEESE SLICES

"WHO THE HELL HAS BEEN into the fridge again?" Grandma hollered. "We aren't rich—you boys know that, right? You'll eat us out of house and home!"

I looked toward the kitchen from the chesterfield and my TV program. I heard Grandma slam the fridge door, and an avalanche of something hitting the floor. All I could see was her hair wagging in the morning light, and the dog's ass bounding up the stairs. Yorkie was never one to miss the prospect of spilled food.

"I dunno," I said, shrugging. "I swear, Grandma. Wasn't me."

"The goddamned cranberry juice is nearly gone, too. I told you boys that's for Grandpa's gout." She held up a bunch of empty cheese wrappers, a near-empty package of hot dogs, and a three-quarters-empty bottle— the remaining red liquid sloshed around, angry.

I wonder how she slammed the fridge door, I thought. *With her foot?*

"I don't know what to do with you boys anymore." She dropped what she was holding and took a drag of her cigarette, smoke licking around her flustered face. I could tell she was trying to remain calm. "Go get your brothers, Jesse."

"Okay, Grandma," I said, with a feeling of dread, even though she sounded defeated, not angry anymore, kind of like everyone in our house since learning the truth about Dad. She nodded and began picking stuff off the floor.

My brothers were wrestling in the backyard; Josh beating the shit out of Jerry like usual. He had Jerry's head in a full nelson, pressing it forward into his collarbone, choking him almost unconscious. It was his signature move—I knew from experience it was impossible to escape.

"Grandma's pissed," I said, trying to catch my breath. Josh let go of Jerry, who fell to the ground clutching his neck, the pinkish colour of life replacing the purple-blue of suffocation.

"What's she on about now?" Josh asked.

"What does it matter?" Jerry shot back, as he got to his feet and made his way to the house. "The dog probably shit inside because we didn't walk him. That's your fault; you're supposed to walk him in the morning."

I bit my nail. "It's more serious than that."

Grandma was sitting on the edge of my grandfather's chair in the living room. On the coffee table were the empty cheese wrappers—a stack of around twenty. Small price tags were taped to the table right next to them.

"See," Grandma began as the three of us walked in, her nicotine-stained index finger pressing down so hard on one of the price tags her fingertip was white. "The wieners here, they cost $2—I buy the good beef kind for your grandfather. He deserves them." She flicked her butt, the ash tumbling into a puke-yellow glass ashtray. "The cheese"—she motioned to the cloudy wrappers—"that's around $3.50. Black Diamond cheddar. Again, only the best for your grandfather." The cherry on her cigarette hissed as she took another drag and moved on to the final exhibit. "And this here, that's cranberry juice, *real* cranberry juice. The doctor told me to buy it to help with your grandfather's gout. He gets it in the knee and big toe and can't work a day without a glass. That costs $5. Together, it all costs $10.50, and I just bought it yesterday. It should've lasted until next Friday when I do my groceries again."

A boa constrictor wrapped tight around my ribs. Jerry rubbed his palms down the front of his jeans.

"But it's gone. Now what am I gonna give him?"

"Wasn't me," Josh blurted, shaking like a Chihuahua with hypothermia as he pushed the bottle toward Jerry.

"Wasn't me, either, Grandma," Jerry said. "I swear!" He kept it together but looked guilty as sin. He shoved the bottle at me, not knowing I'd already been interrogated.

"Jesse already said it wasn't him, either," Grandma said as she tapped the bottle. The tiny echo boomed in my ear drums. "So, I guess you're all lying—again." Her sigh seemed to drain the life out of her. "You boys steal food and lie all the time. This time is no different than the thousands of times before. You came to us like that—broken. But, now, for once, I want a straight answer. Please tell me the truth. Who did this?"

We looked at each other, shrugging and making faces like idiots. Grandma didn't budge. Silence hung heavy around us, resting somewhere between her polyester slacks and the wads of Black Diamond cheese that lay digesting in one of our guts. A smatter of rain misted the sliding doors while we waited for someone to give. Gradually, it turned into a light patter as the wind picked up. I saw a crow perched on the fence looking in at us.

"I can't take it anymore," Grandma finally said, her voice thin and monotone behind a lungful of cigarette smoke. "I want you each to go to your rooms, pack one bag of clothes, and bring it downstairs. I'm taking you to the Children's Aid Society. Your grandfather and I have spoken about this already, and we've tried our best . . ."

Josh's mouth dropped open. Jerry's eyes were wider than Josh's mouth. Me, I felt nothing, or what I can only describe as a yawning chasm of hate—the first time I'd felt it.

"Make sure to take your boots and winter hats. You'll need them. You're old enough now to survive. Go on. Get ready." She shooed us off. "Haven't got all day."

A flash of black caught my eye—the crow had flown off. I went to my room and began packing. I couldn't stop thinking about being hungry when we were kids with my dad, that gnawing ache that haunted me every day, that made me always think we were on the brink of starving, even when we got to my grandparents with their full fridge. I could actually feel that ache in my legs.

Jerry, I knew, felt that hunger most. He'd told me how he always felt like he could never get enough food, even when he was full. It was a force that drove us to steal and lie, to eat until we destroyed every hors d'oeuvre plate at every family function my grandparents took us to. My cousins used to tease us about how we consumed everything in sight. They called us pigs, but it was something we had no control over.

I kept thinking about that hunger as I pulled out my favourite red sweater, my Batman T-shirts, my Blue Jays baseball cap, and four of my favourite jeans from my drawers. I packed them carefully in my Adidas bag, making sure to place pictures of Grandma and Grandpa between the layers. I always wished I'd had pictures of my dad to remember him by and didn't want to forget my grandparents wherever I was going. I also grabbed the old, worn-out Polaroid I had of my mom from off the dresser—one of her wearing a Russian-style fox fur hat—and put it in my back pocket for safekeeping, then made my way down to the front door.

Josh and Jerry were there, bags packed, stone-faced. Yorkie was there, too, whining and turning in circles, tail wagging faster than normal. Grandma was upstairs, we assumed searching the change drawer for taxi fare, slamming things. We didn't wait for her to walk us out. We shut the door and left. The brass door knocker clanged rudely behind us. *Good riddance*, we thought.

Before we hit the end of the driveway, we linked arms and decided to keep going as far as we could, to find homes where we could eat whatever we wanted, where we didn't have to be afraid anymore. Jerry pulled a butter tart out of the side of his suitcase—we had enough to get us to where we were going.

We made it as far as the other side of the mall where Grandma did her shopping, about five kilometres. We sat near a bush and ate the lone tart. As night set in, we got cold and hungry and decided to make our way back home. Jerry and I waited outside the house with our bags, while Josh went inside to take the heat for the missing food and for running away.

DRIVE

ONE DAY, I ASKED MY uncle Ron where Dad went. "I'm sorry, Jess," he said. "I miss him, too, but we don't know."

According to our family, Uncle Ron was the toughest of my uncles. He was like a pro wrestler, stout through the middle, the bridge of his nose was thick, and he had a gold tooth that glinted every time he talked. His body looked like he'd been attacked by wild animals. There were deep gashes, burns, and knife marks all over. The scars on his knees were the deepest—"from a shark attack back in the '70s," he said. Grandma said they were from when he'd broken his legs at work and from when his friend ran him over with a car.

He told me stories about my father, and how they'd get in trouble on the golf course they both worked at as caddies, or fight with neighbourhood boys, or chase girls and terrorize their boyfriends with firecrackers. "I even blew up your grandfather's garage playing with gasoline," he said, adding that Grandpa laid the smack down so hard for that, Ron saw stars for several weeks.

Grandpa and Uncle Ron had a strange relationship. Grandpa tried to keep him out of the house, but always let him back in, I think because he loved him. There were times that Uncle Ron went to jail for months. When he came home, Grandma always hugged him and made him a big meal, and everyone was happy and joking. But when Grandpa got home and saw him, he gave him a tough time. Everyone went silent. Uncle Ron just smiled and didn't say anything. I thought it strange he would allow himself to be treated that way, but I understood why he never quipped off to Grandpa. Respect was important in our home.

When me and my brothers first arrived at our grandparents', it was Uncle Ron who greeted us and made us feel at home. There was something about him. Dogs and kids loved him, but everyone else was scared. My older cousins were terrified of him. They fetched him beers and cigarettes whenever he was around—he'd just motion to the cooler or a pack and they'd run. But I loved him. He lived around the corner from us and he'd come and put me on his shoulders, take me to the park, and swing me on a swing until I laughed so hard I got dizzy. He was a father to me in many ways.

"Come on, Jess," Uncle Ron said, punching his cinder-block fist into my shoulder and bringing me back to the moment. "You wanna come on a delivery downtown tonight? I gotta see a few people on Yonge Street. It'll be fun." He was a flower delivery man and good at his job—he collected money and no one was ever late on a payment. He'd pull up, and men would run into the shops and come out with wads of money. His gold tooth glimmered between his lips, inviting me to join him.

"I guess . . ." I twisted my foot on the ground as if putting out a cigarette, trying to decide if I wanted to feel sorry for myself in my room or go out and cheer up.

"You don't have to look so morose, you know." He punched my arm again, and I struggled to smile through the pain. "I'll be here at four—be ready or else." He winked.

When he screeched into the driveway that afternoon in a red convertible Mustang, I was waiting on the balcony. I had no idea where he'd gotten his new ride, but it was nicer than the beat-up work van he usually drove. I had on a white muscle shirt and a jean jacket with the sleeves ripped off. I thought the frayed strands that dangled over my shoulders made me look tough, like one of the characters from *The Outsiders*. Like Uncle Ron. My fake Ray-Bans added to my persona.

"Get a load of those pipes," Uncle Ron said. I knew he wasn't making fun of my arms, he was trying to make me feel confident. A field of zits covered the whole of my face, and my arms and legs looked like stretched hot dogs as I'd shot up nearly a foot in the past few months. I put on my best bodybuilder pose, curling my fists and biceps inward as hard as I could. It felt good.

"You'll get there, kid," he said as he stood up in the driver's seat and returned my flex with his own double guns. "Just gotta start liftin'." His arms looked like Hulk Hogan's as he rotated his head and kissed the bicep-crest of each arm. They were bigger whenever he returned from jail.

"Now let's ride," he hollered as he sat down, tooted the horn twice, and combed back his hair, looking in the rear-view as if he were a 1950s greaser. "We haven't got all day, Schwarzenegger." I launched myself off the balcony, down ten feet, hopped over the passenger door, and we were off.

A mix of Foghat, Deep Purple, and Steppenwolf blasted out of the car speakers as we drove, announcing to the world that two badasses were in the vicinity. The wind blew through my hair as Uncle Ron drummed on the steering wheel, reminding me of my dad. When we got downtown, people gawked as we went by. I got excited when I saw women looking at us, but they weren't checking me out. Uncle Ron, I knew, caught all the eyes.

"You see that, Jess?" he said as he smiled back at a blond woman coming out of a store. "It's all in how confident you are." He flexed his left arm, twirled a toothpick between his front teeth, then held it erect in the sunlight.

I rolled my eyes.

"Just try it," he said. "Be the rooster." He bobbed his head back and forth to the beat of the music.

"What does that even mean?" I asked, adjusting my vest.

"You know, cock of the walk. Own it; feel the music. Like this." He curled his lip up, revealing his gold tooth; it reminded me of a jailhouse Elvis.

I tried bobbing my head and smiling at the ladies on the sidewalk, just like he told me to. But I knew I was more like a malnourished chicken, and every girl I grooved at stared right through me over to Uncle Ron and his muscles.

He laughed. "Just give it time, it gets easier. I promise."

I laughed back. I was glad to be hanging out with my favourite uncle, making him happy, the sun beaming down on my face.

We stopped in all the cool spots to collect money, eat ice cream and French fries, and listen to street performers. The men we stopped to talk to, though, were terrified, just like my cousins. I'd see the look of relief on their faces in the side mirror as we pulled away. I'd heard that my dad and Ron were in business together years ago and wondered if it was delivering flowers.

Uncle Ron also introduced me to other guys, his friends, as "Sonny's boy," and they all looked like Uncle Ron, muscle-bound and tough, and all of them were super excited to meet me. They had scars and tattoos and toothpicks, and they talked about my dad like he was a legend. The stories washed over me. Not one person had a bad word to say about him—not like Grandpa. It was nice to hear. I'd never been proud to be my father's son before.

On our way out of one of the shops on Yonge Street, we came across a guy bumming change in front of Sam the Record Man. He was thin and looked much older than Uncle Ron, with long, greasy hair and a matted grey-and-brown beard. In front of him were a woollen blanket, a few plastic bags, and a paper coffee cup. Not many people ventured near him, veering close to the storefronts instead and turning their heads. I was compelled to do the same.

Uncle Ron, though, walked right up to him and put a twenty in his cup. The man smiled a toothy smile and said thank you, but Uncle Ron just stared at him. The man looked at him, then over at me. I could tell he was trying to assess what was going on, but then Uncle Ron said, "Don't mention it, brother." Before we rounded the corner to where we were parked, Uncle Ron turned back, but the homeless man was gone.

"I always think," he said, "that it could be Sonny."

BIRDSONG

MRS. R., THE FRENCH TEACHER, walked up to my desk and handed back my report card with its proof of signature. She peered over her glasses at the report card and me, and said, "We need to talk after class."

I could have sworn a black cloud hung low around her calf muscles and knee-length skirt as she turned and walked back to the front of the class. She was stern, powerful, and in control, and the clomp of her high heels thundered through my brain.

Whispers from my classmates came from all directions. My friend Renee, who'd sometimes help me when I didn't understand things, turned around and mouthed, "You're dead meat, Thistle."

I gulped. Mrs. R. wasn't to be trifled with—she screamed in our faces if we did something wrong. In the worst cases, she'd get so mad that she'd cry-yell and make you do consecutive detention for a couple of weeks.

I glanced down at my grade: 35 percent—a big fat F. Worse than F, more like K. The comment beside it read: "Jesse is frequently unprepared for class. A more consistent effort is required." Brutal and bleak. I was two-thirds of the way through the year and sure to fail at this rate.

Aside from taking away our hard-won Nintendo and go-cart and grounding me, I knew Grandpa would whip me so hard I wouldn't be able to sit straight. Like the way he lashed Josh with the red rod—an unbreakable half-inch fiberglass golf flagpole—when Josh had thrown that rock in the park and it ricocheted off the fence and broke that Sikh man's window. It wasn't Josh's fault. I was there—the rock simply bounced, redirected itself off the fence post, then smash! But that didn't matter. A window was shattered, it cost Grandpa $200 to fix it, and Josh had to be punished. The strips Grandpa tore off his backside were purple and puffy, and Josh had to lie on his side while they healed but they still left stripe-like welts. He looked like a zebra.

Grandpa's anger that day wasn't usual—it was the same rage I saw when he warned me about doing drugs after he told me about Dad's disappearance—and it scared me so much that I bawled in my room as Josh received the beating of his life. I lay on my bed and covered my ears with my pillow to hide from the sound of the rod thrashing through the air. In my head, I begged for Josh to cry out, but he kept it together somehow. I knew it was to show he was a man the way Grandpa liked, but that only made things worse. After what sounded like thirty more blows, Josh finally bellowed out in agony. It was a sound so sad it penetrated right to where I was hiding, right through the concrete foundation of our house.

Grandma once told me that Grandpa was that "way" with discipline because his pappy was that "way" with him, and that he got it worse than us. Grandpa was only five when his father died from a heart attack in 1938, and he had to move two hundred kilometres, out to the sticks of Cape Breton, to live with Pappy. There, he'd worked hauling wood, picking rocks, and fishing on the dory like a grown man—he never got to have a childhood like us. I always wondered if that was why Grandpa took us in, because he knew what it was like to have no one, to lose his family.

Whatever the reasons for the way Grandpa was, the scream Josh let out that day sounded like he was being killed, and I questioned how Grandpa's childhood beatings could have been worse.

Mrs. R. rapped the blackboard with her pointer and trained her eyes on me. "Some students"—she cleared her throat—"didn't come with their report card proofs signed by their parents. I've already spoken with most of you, but I'll see those of you who didn't after class."

After class!

I started to chew my thumbnail. I spit a bit out and it landed in the hair of the girl who sat ahead of me, but she didn't notice. The clock hands seemed to beat forward with incredible speed, and each tick sounded like an explosion.

Tick!

I only had four minutes until the bell rang, and I'd have to answer for what I'd done.

Tick!

I stared at the French vocabulary signs that adorned the room, searching for a way out. The stupid French toad with the *à bientôt* word bubble above its head; the picture of that annoying little girl waving *au revoir* to nobody; the huge picture of those bright, obnoxious yellow daffodils that screamed *le printemps*. I imagined them all piled on a bonfire with Mrs. R.'s head roasting on a stick.

TICK!

The minute hand surged forward—two minutes left—reminding me that I was trapped.

Shit!

I knew why Mrs. R. had singled me out. It was in the way she'd looked at me after she'd peered down at my grandmother's signature and handed me back my report card. The edges of my grandma's name were shaky and didn't flow right.

When I'd received my grades before the Christmas break and saw my F, I panicked. I couldn't let my grandparents see how poorly I was doing. It didn't take much to set Grandpa off these days. I didn't want to end up like Josh. I told Leeroy on our walk home, and he told me about a guy in one of his classes who'd forged his parent's signature on a report card and gotten away with it.

The idea sounded plausible—genius even—so I went home and traced over an existing signature Grandma had written on a permission slip for a field trip I'd taken in another class. The practice signatures all looked great. But then I messed up. I only had one report card, one shot, and I failed miserably. When I handed the report card in, I'd done it quickly, tossing it on Mrs. R.'s desk underneath everyone else's report cards, hoping she'd be lazy and would just hand them in that way. But she didn't. She'd checked each one and discovered my crime, and now I had to pay for it.

Ring, ring, ring! The bell went off.

What the hell happened to the time?

As I lurched toward Mrs. R., I straightened my cardigan and kept my eyes down. I somehow thought that if I didn't look at her, I could still hide and maybe everything would be okay. She ushered the class out and paused before shutting the door and asking me to sit in the seat adjacent to her desk. It was known as the hot seat.

"I taught your brothers," she said. "They were good students, Josh especially." She took the forged document from my hands and fingered my sloppy fraud. "I've seen a lot of faked signatures over the years, but this one has to be the worst." Her words were like weights dragging me to the bottom of the ocean.

"You know I have to report you to the principal. He'll contact your grandparents."

I expected her to yell like she always did—cry-yell even—but she didn't. She just kept looking at me. I started squirming.

"This is a very poor start to life. Fraud is a real crime," she continued. "Why did you do this?"

I thought of Josh and the punishments we got. I couldn't breathe.

"You don't know how it is," I said. "You don't know how it is for me." I began to sob.

"How what is?"

I rocked in my chair.

"I can't go home with a report card like this. You don't know what will

106

happen," I couldn't feel my face but I was crying. "It's not his fault. He was raised that way."

Mrs. R. didn't say anything, just sat there, rubbing my back.

I couldn't hear the clock anymore, just Mrs. R.'s soft breath and the sound of a robin singing outside.

JACK HIM

"FUCK *FAMILY TIES*," I GROWLED and changed the channel. I couldn't stand to see Michael J. Fox get hugged by his stupid-looking, bearded father after he'd apologized for taking speed and redeemed himself. If I got caught with even a cigarette I'd be practically tarred, feathered, beaten, and grounded for a year.

"Dude," Leeroy cried. "Now we'll never know what happened. Put it back on!"

"It's bullshit. Bloody Alex P. Keaton." I flicked through a few stations then launched the remote across the room. Bits of brown and green plastic exploded all over the concrete floor. Leeroy let out a goonish laugh, the kind of sound we made when either of us started shit.

I didn't care that my grandparents would be upset. *Fuck them, too*, I thought. *I'll just blame it on Jerry.* Putting it on my brother was a diversion strategy that worked most times. He was a horrible liar; so bad, in fact, that when other people did stuff—stuff he was totally innocent of—and he tried explaining to my grandparents what had happened, he looked guilty just talking. The poor bastard had taken so many of my thrashings I'd lost count.

"We could drink some beer?" I half asked, half offered. I walked over and opened the fridge but saw tumbleweeds. Leeroy searched the empties; nothing there, either. Black-and-white static on the TV rolled and buzzed like a hive of angry bees. The set was stuck on channel 81, the late-Saturday-night porn station, and even if we could hear what was going on, we'd be lucky to see a nipple. It made it difficult to mastur-bate, chasing phantom nipples. I pulled out my pocket knife, stuck it in the broken rotary dial on the left of the screen, and jiggled it. The vise grips we usually used were gone, taken by Josh no doubt in one of his fits of backyard engineering, and my little Swiss Army knife wasn't strong enough. I pulled the plug on the TV with a grunt.

"I think I'm going home," Leeroy said, rubbing his stomach beneath his Maple Leafs jersey. It was hours past dinnertime and we both hadn't eaten. Grandma made fish cakes earlier, but neither of us liked them, so we passed on her offer. It was the only meal I could say no to. I hated the huge raw onions packed into the patties. When I was around five my grandparents caught me one night after I'd stuffed my cheeks until I looked like Dizzy Gillespie and excused myself from the dinner table repeatedly. I was spitting my cargo in the toilet. Grandpa thought it was clever of me—his little puking chipmunk. Grandma wasn't as impressed. They tried to force me to eat them over the years, but I never did.

"Okay, I'll walk you over." I put on my shoes. The smell of fish and oil spilled onto the street as we left. The night air was cool for September. Street lights flickered in the park, surrounded by a blanket of blackness. I kicked a pop can and it rolled over a storm grate and stood motionless at the base of the curb. Leeroy kicked it, sending it up across the boulevard and onto the sidewalk.

As we rounded the corner, we saw Ivan, a blond Polish kid about four years younger than us who lived ten houses down from Leeroy, playing on his front lawn. I thought it was strange that he'd be out at this hour all by himself. To us, he was spoiled beyond belief. He had toys galore, and I often saw him at the convenience store with his dad buying chips and gum and whatever else his little heart desired. His dad usually gave him the leftover change, and sometimes he'd share with me if I was hanging around with my friends. It was hard to see him with his dad, all happy and eating candy, holding hands, and playing hockey together out in front of his house every Saturday. Grandpa never did anything like that with me.

"You thinking what I'm thinking?" I asked as I turned to Leeroy.

"What? No!" The expression on Leeroy's face told me he knew exactly what I was thinking. "That's too much, even for us."

I stopped in the middle of the street and grabbed his arm. "The kid is loaded. We can jack his money and run away. It's dark. He won't know what hit him." My Swiss Army knife burned in my back pocket, begging me to take control of the situation, to follow through so for once I'd have some goddamned lunch money and could buy my own goddamned fries.

"Don't be crazy." Leeroy ripped his arm away. "I live right down the street; I can't." He stood his ground. He wasn't going to cross the line, not now, not tonight, not on his street. Just then Ivan stood up at the end of his lawn and waved over to us.

Leeroy is right, I would get caught, somehow, like everyone gets caught on all the police shows. No one gets away.

"See," Leeroy said with a look of relief, knowing I was backing down. "That's the Jesse I know. Just chill." He smiled at Ivan.

We'd gotten in lots of trouble before, and Leeroy had never put his foot down about anything, but here he was chickening out and telling me what to do. I was humiliated. My knife weighed down the back pocket of my jeans, and I put my hand over it to hide its imprint from the night sky. Leeroy walked backward toward his house and told me he'd see me in the morning on our walk to school. Then he went inside.

I was out there alone with Ivan and my knife.

Without a thought, I walked over to him, thrust my knife in his face, and robbed him. He cried for his dad, then ran into his house when I let him go. I fled into the dark, holding the change I'd ripped from his pockets. I was shocked at what I'd done. I wondered if my grandfather would forgive me like fathers did with their sons on TV.

A NEW FAMILY

THE NIGHT BEFORE CHRISTMAS EVE, Grandma surprised us.

"Your mother moved from Saskatoon to Ottawa," she said. "She's coming to see you tomorrow."

Grandpa grunted and slammed back his chicken and potatoes, barely looking at anyone. Josh, Jerry, and I excused ourselves from the dinner table and retreated to our rooms; it was the first time we'd all left food on our plates before.

I wondered if Mom would still look as beautiful as she did the last time we'd seen her, and I couldn't sleep that night waiting for her. I stared out my window looking at the stars, trying to think of the right words to say, but they all jumbled together. I pictured her laughing face on the surface of the moon, the light of it dimming with each passing cloud. My throat closed as I tried to swallow.

I finally got up and pulled my best Chip & Pepper T-shirt, my nicest black slacks, and my penny loafers out of my closet. I laid all of them on the floor in front of my bed, methodically picked lint off both garments, then applied shoe polish to the loafers until they shined like mirrors. I tried to figure out how I'd comb my hair—down the middle, spiked up, or off to the side. I couldn't decide. I wanted to look good, to show Mom how much I'd grown.

From across the hall the deep rumbles of my grandfather's snores were followed by the squeaky squirrel noises Grandma made to wake him up and keep him from suffocating to death from the sleep apnea he had. They weren't conferencing about me for once, and that made me happy. Often at night, I could hear them talking about me, even though their voices were hushed—as though I was in a different kind of trouble than usual.

Perhaps they know about the things I've done, I'd worry. *Perhaps they're going to take me to the Children's Aid Society after all.*

Finally, morning hit, and Yorkie's bark announced Mom's arrival. I ran downstairs as fast as I could, hair gelled to one side, and flung the door open so hard the door handle punched a hole in the wood paneling. Yorkie was running around in circles behind me.

"Hi, Jesse!" Mom shouted with a huge, beaming smile, her arms stretched out.

She was wearing the Russian hat from my picture tilted to the side. The cold December air froze puffs of breath around her head so they looked like smoke caught amongst the fox fur. Her hair was shorter and browner now, not the black flowy locks I remembered, but she still looked the same to me. Beside her were two gym bags and a little coal-haired boy, around six years old. Mom looked toward a man rummaging in a grey car across the street, who waved over to us, then she turned back to me, waiting for her hug. I had a sudden urge to go and hide in the boot box. The little boy tugged at Mom's leg.

"Hug her, you idiot," I could hear Josh say from behind me. His words snapped me out of my daze. He pushed me aside and embraced Mom. I fell against the wall, my hand finding purchase in the newly created hole. Deep growls of joy emanated from Josh and Mom, warming me somewhat. Josh rubbed the boy's head and introduced himself. The boy said his name was Daniel.

"He's your little brother," Mom said.

A surge of jealousy ran cold up my spine.

Jerry trailed along the hallway leading to the door. Each step was strained and reminded me of when Grandma forced him to walk the dog on Sunday mornings. He had a sneer across his face, and his arms were crossed.

"I can't find my wallet," the man from the car hollered over to Mom. "I think I left it at the gas station near Kingston."

"I have it here in my purse, George," Mom said. "Now get over here and meet my boys!" The man nodded and made his way to us, a small skip in his step. Daniel stuck his hand out to shake mine, but I batted it away and stuck my tongue out at him. Mom didn't see. She was focused on George.

"That's not nice," the man said as he grabbed their luggage and placed it inside the house beside where I was standing. "He's your little brother— my son. His name is Daniel and mine's George. Nice to meet you." He, too, stuck his hand out. I kept mine down by my side.

"It may take some time," Mom said to him as she pushed Daniel and me closer together. We did eventually embrace, but the whole thing seemed wrong. I wanted to bear hug him until he couldn't breathe, crush his ribs, then stomp his tiny head on the driveway right in front of George.

Jerry sighed and went back upstairs without saying hello. I figured he was just as upset as me about Daniel. Josh and Yorkie, however, were wagging their arses like fools at their new friends.

Fucking traitors, I thought. But I forced myself to be nice to Mom and George and helped them with their stuff.

The last time we'd seen Mom was in 1985, when I was ten. She'd bussed out by Greyhound from Saskatchewan—it took her three days to get to Toronto. When she arrived, I'd just stood in the doorway clutching a dream catcher I'd made for her at school, my mouth open. She looked exactly like she did in my faded Polaroid. The photograph was yellowed at the corners and curling inward, but she remained untouched in the centre, standing gracefully in front of some snow-peaked mountains. She looked like a real-life Indian in that photo, one from the movies, not like me and my snotty brothers.

I ran and hid in the boot box, a giant wooden cabinet Grandpa had made beside the downstairs doors, until he yanked me out to say hello. I couldn't muster a sound, just handed her the dream catcher. She laugh-cried and hugged me tight, lost for words herself, holding my gift.

During her visit, Grandma only let us out of her sight a couple of times: once when Mom took us to catch a Saturday matinee of *The Jungle Book*. I thought Grandma was crying as we drove off, but it was hard to tell through the back window of the taxi. The other time was when Grandma went to bed early after dinner one night and we snuck down to the basement to watch TV with Mom. Grandpa saw us tiptoe past his armchair and waved us downstairs like he was landing a plane.

"Go, go," he said, with a grin. He had a soft spot for my mom. He told her she was a good person, that none of it was her fault, and that we'd go back to her once we'd grown up and left home.

Mom was sitting cross-legged on the couch, reading a comic. She had a stack of them she'd brought with her. Josh and I knelt in front of her, while Jerry sat across from us on the wood stove under the window, as silent as ever.

"Josh, I want you to have these before I go back home tomorrow morning." She waved her hand at the comics. "Conan's a fighter like you."

The first time our mother came to visit us at our grandparents', in 1985. I'm on the left; Josh is on the right.

"Cool!" Josh cried out, his eyes lighting up as he rifled through his hoard of newfound treasure.

I strained to imagine my brother wielding a massive broadsword and lopping off the heads of demons, like Conan was doing on the cover of the comic in my mother's hand. Conan's muscles rippled, and his shiny black hair made him look like an Indian, like my uncle Ron, but certainly not like Josh.

Josh splayed the comics across the floor and lost himself in them, turning the pages faster than any human eyes could read.

"And you, Jerry," Mom said, remaining on the couch and respecting the distance between them. "I'll always keep the picture you drew for me. I won't ever fold it or lose it or anything. I promise. Will you do the same with the one I gave you?" The roar of the water heater filled the basement as she waited for an answer. Jerry just shifted his ass around on the stove, then nodded while looking at Josh freaking out.

Mom smiled, then turned to me, and I shifted my knees closer to her.

"And for you, my little pumpkin head, I have something special." She reached down under her ashtray and handed me a glossy photograph. It was of her. Her hair was wet and sticking out all over the place and she was lying on a bed holding a baby.

"That's your younger brother, Daniel," she said.

"What?" the three of us asked in unison.

"You have a brother," she said as she took a drag of her smoke and leaned in close to point to the baby. "I want you to have this picture of us, Jesse." She looked so happy. "I met a kind man a couple of years ago and this is our son. I wanted to tell you before I left and waited for the right moment."

I fell back, the air sucked out of my lungs, but I managed to squeak something out. "I wish we had a sister instead."

Mom looked hurt and confused. I knew she was waiting for me to say something more, but Josh spoke first.

"I think it's wonderful. Now I'll have three younger brothers I can beat up."

115

Mom didn't laugh, nor did Jerry, and I just stared at the picture, wondering how my mom could start over without us, and what Dad would think.

After Mom left, Grandma took us to a drugstore. We were told it was for something called the Kids Identification Sign Up and it was because strangers in our city had murdered and killed children our age and we had to watch out that we weren't stolen from right under our parents' noses.

During the fingerprinting and mug shot process, the workers briefed us on child sexual abuse, stranger danger, street proofing, and how to call the police, and we were told that we should memorize where our home was on a map. Grandma gave them our dental and health records, blood types, and known allergies. I didn't understand much of what I was told, or why I had to promise to keep my eyes out for trouble—trouble that wanted to kill me. I'd never thought about dying or going missing before, and both scenarios scared the shit out of me.

After, Grandpa told us it was because Grandma loved us so much and was trying to protect us.

From what? I thought.

I don't know what I did with that picture Mom gave me. I certainly didn't have it when she, George, and Daniel showed up at our door on Christmas Eve. It was like my memory of it had blacked out.

I had a hard time getting used to seeing myself as a middle brother—it meant I was like goony Jerry all of a sudden, with his middling spot as neither oldest nor youngest. No special responsibilities like Josh had as the oldest to take care of business and teach us younger boys about life or protect us. And Jerry didn't get away with stuff like I did as the youngest because I was too small to understand anything. I was now just an invisible middle child like him.

My grandparents' cottage in Bay St. Lawrence, Cape Breton. We all got to smoke cigars that summer.

The whole time Mom was visiting with Daniel and George, I tried my best to reclaim my status as the "baby boy." I acted younger than I was, purposefully messing up my grammar and asking her to cut my meat at dinner, like she did with Daniel. She ignored me and Grandma swooped in with her mother cape to do it, ruining the whole thing. I showed Mom a photo of when I was five smoking a cigar with Grandpa at the cottage in Nova Scotia—everyone else loved that photo of us, but she barely glanced at it. I tried to remind her that I was the youngest Thistle boy, not Daniel—Daniel was just some latecomer. Turned out he also somehow had our father's name, but he clearly wasn't his son, he was George what-ever-the-fuck's son.

It was all to no avail. Daniel was the centre of her affection—he was her new "baby boy." She let him rest on her lap like an infant in front of everyone, she got him dressed every morning, she made sure he was al-ways with us. I wanted to vomit whenever he was around.

Grandpa, though, was nice during their visit. He went out of his way to make them feel at home, even making George and Daniel baked beans and bannock twice—a record, considering he'd only ever made those staples of the Cape Breton diet for us three times in ten years! He also made them his "special" sugar-glazed apples. "When I was a boy, molten apples were like golden candy," he said. "Everyone lost their minds whenever they got them."

If they're so special, I sneered as Grandpa, Daniel, and George devoured them in front of me in the kitchen, *why don't you stick 'em up your ass.*

Grandpa and George even had a few private heart to hearts in the living room while watching the Leafs play, and I could tell from my vantage point on the stairs that Grandpa was sizing him up. He watched the way George drank his beers, how fast or slow they went down, and if he requested another once the last was done. Grandpa said you could tell a lot about a man by how fast he drinks, how he holds himself during conversation, how he asks for things, and how firmly he shakes your hand. I was sure George had no idea he was under my grandfather's microscope.

Grandma barely spoke with George, Mom, or Daniel. She'd acted the same way when Mom had come before. Just plenty of flybys and quick, probing questions, like, What's going on? Where're you going? Why're you here? What do you want? She was like a patrol helicopter looking for a bank robber. Josh told me it was because she was scared—of what I don't know. Wherever we were with Mom, Grandma was close by, pacing, silent, breathing heavy. She didn't even read any of her Harlequin novels, which was odd considering she did that obsessively any other time. Josh even found her with her ear up to the wall once, listening to our conversations with Mom.

"I'm keeping an eye out for mice," she'd said.

We knew that was bullshit because she kept the house crumb-free and spotless.

One day before New Year's, Mom made me my favourite lunch. Spaghetti and meatballs—she remembered.

"Of course I remember," she said as she placed my plate in front of me. "You're my little pumpkin head." I was happy that I still had a special place in her heart.

Josh and Jerry were outside playing hockey, Grandma was in the living room, the theme to *General Hospital* was blaring, and Daniel and George sat across from me watching Mom serve us.

There was what sounded like an avalanche of two-by-fours outside. Grandpa started swearing. He'd come back from the hardware store with framing wood and I thought maybe I should be outside helping him.

I dug into a meatball and George spoke.

"Look here."

He pulled out a black-and-white picture of a strange man from his wallet. He had on a black robe with a huge cross draped over his shoulder. He was like Friar Tuck from the *Rocket Robin Hood* cartoon: bald on top with a long, unkempt beard. There was a severe look about him. I twirled my noodles around my fork and tried to ignore George and the picture.

"This is Gregory XVII," George said. He yanked a similar photo from the other side of his billfold. Mom placed George's lunch in front of him—I think she was trying to get him to keep quiet.

"He's the real Pope," George went on.

I glanced over at the picture; he didn't look like Pope John Paul II to me.

"A long time ago," George said. "The Catholic Church lost its way. It became decadent and stopped following the true way." Mom's left eyelid twitched.

"That's when Pope Clement XV—the order's first Pope—decided to split from Rome and form the Apostles of Infinite Love out in Quebec, about two hours from where we live in Ottawa."

Daniel sat up straight at his father's words.

"It's nice there," Daniel said, a noodle hanging out of his mouth. "I lived there with the brothers for a few months." He smiled.

Grandma stormed into the room—the strong scent of tobacco trailing behind, which was odd because she was out of smokes. She scowled at George and Mom like a mama bear defending her cub. George stuffed his pictures away. Mom smiled.

"No religion in this house," Grandma barked as she slammed some dishes in the sink. I felt that awesome power in her again, the same as when she got us years before.

I didn't know what to make of George or his picture, but it was creepy.

Mom, George, and Daniel left later that week. I asked Grandma and Grandpa if Mom was okay. They didn't seem too concerned. But Mom and Daniel kind of disappeared after that, no phone calls or anything.

TRADITION

"THIS ONE HERE LOOKS NICE, try it on." Grandma handed me a preppy white button-up shirt to go with the black slacks she'd pulled from the good section of the Hudson's Bay men's department, over near the Polo clothes. The shirt fit slim around my torso and snug around my neck when she buttoned it up. She turned me to look in the mirror, but before she did, she licked her fingers and slicked my eyebrows into place.

Spiffy.

"Well, look at you! My baby boy all grown up and ready for work!"

I fixed my collar and stuck my chin up slightly. I knew this was a special occasion because Grandma usually took me to Bargain Harold's or Zellers, and we'd go to the Skillet Restaurant and eat hot dogs in a basket afterward. Not today, though.

I thought of those Skillet hot dogs as I admired myself, and said, "But, Grandma, these pants and shirt are nearly $200. We can't afford that."

She wagged her head and scoffed. "You better believe we can. When it comes to work you gotta knock 'em dead."

I'd never seen her so excited or generous before, except when it came to Grandpa's work boots and overalls. He always had the best. Even his lunch pail and thermos. Work was important to the Thistles, and Grandma made sure her man looked good and was well-fed when he made our family its money.

Grandpa, too, had acted differently since he'd gone across the street a month ago to talk with our neighbour, Mr. Q . He'd come back whistling, Yorkie by his side, and the dog appeared just as gleeful as he did.

"Good news, Jess," he said with a huge smile. "You've got a job." Mr. Q. was a manager at the produce department at the grocery store in the biggest mall in town, and Grandpa told me I'd start in a few weeks. "You'll be a produce clerk. $3.75 an hour."

He walked past me into the house to announce the good news to Grandma, who was watching a soap opera. She gasped with joy—I could actually hear it through the screen door, from where I was on the driveway. As I pulled out the lawn mower, she waved to me from the balcony. Like those old pictures of when men went off to war on battleships or trains and their women saw them off. I could feel my face flush, and I flashed a smile at her. I knew it looked weird. Grandpa didn't drink that day, and I caught him singing to himself later in the garage as he organized his bits and bobs for his job on Monday.

I examined myself in the mirror. I was now receiving the same treatment as Grandpa, and I smiled. Grandma hiked my pants up, exposing my socks and squaring my nuts in the process. "They fit nice," she said, "but up here, around your waist. I don't want to see you with them hanging low around your ass like you do with your jeans, that godawful rap style."

I thought I looked like Urkel on *Family Matters*, and I grimaced but somehow managed to keep my smile.

Grandma pivoted, grabbing one paisley and one striped tie from the shelf beside me. I covertly pulled my pants back down. *Relief.*

The ties in Grandma's hand weren't the wide-bottomed ones Grandpa wore to the elevator awards once a year that were the worst shades of brown and green, putrid remnants of the 1960s that he refused to replace. The same colours as those hippy flowers on the bath tiles in the upstairs bathroom. No. These ties were royal blue and black, thin at the bottom—actually fashionable.

"Calvin Kleins," she said as she turned them over to show me the labels. She lassoed one around my neck and had it bound up before I could say go, pulling it tight. My eyes bulged in the mirror and she patted my bum. "A lady killer, you are. Tall, dark, and handsome."

I looked at myself in the mirror with doubt. I was tall, but lanky as a daddy-long-legs, and still covered in zits.

But I had just started Grade 9, and Leeroy and I were taking a drama class, and, to our surprise, discovered it was filled with beautiful girls who found us funny. And in one of the photography classes I took, a girl named Heather asked to take my headshot. She had a crush on me, or so I'd heard from classmates.

"Sure," I said. "As long as I get a copy."

She made a bunch of prints and posted them on a wall near the gym—I saw them when I walked past. By the end of the day all the girls at school had stolen them. I knew because they'd been waving them at me in class. I couldn't be angry—I was more flattered than anything.

"No facial hair, though," Grandma said. She rubbed the back of her hand against my cheek and then pinched it hard. I pulled away, rubbing it with my fingers.

"Toughen up, sunshine!" She waved it off like it was nothing. "Native men don't get hair the same as others," she added. "Maybe you'll be lucky and never have to shave, like me." She hiked up her fuchsia slacks, exposing her leg. "It just didn't grow. That's the Algonquin in me."

The thought of never shaving upset me for a brief second. I pictured Grandpa dipping his razor in the sink before work every morning. I loved watching him shave when I was small. Sometimes, he'd lather up my face and we'd shave together. It was serious business. The silence between us was only broken by our laughter when he slapped on aftershave and screamed from the sting.

"Your granddad is as hairy as a Scottish musk ox," Grandma said, as though she could sense what I was thinking. "He hates shaving every day." Not wasting time, she wrangled a black leather belt from over by the till and fastened it around my waist. It fit perfectly, its chrome buckle reflecting light into the mirror. I felt like a millionaire.

"That's it," Grandma said. "That's your uniform."

We stood admiring the ensemble, Grandma holding my shoulders. I loved her so much at that moment—she was a good grandma, I knew that. I leaned over and gave her a big hug. I did look good, in a grown-up kind of way. My new job represented a real step toward adulthood. Most of my friends, like Derick down the street, only had paper routes. But here I was with a real-deal outfit and, soon, a real-deal paycheque. I suddenly felt confident and handsome.

When we got to the front desk to pay, Grandma turned to me.

"Grandma Clara King, my grandmother you met last year that's over one hundred. Her grandpa was a chief factor of the Hudson's Bay Company up on Lake Timiskaming during the fur trade one hundred and fifty years ago. He ran that fort. Our family built this country, Jesse."

The teller scanned the goods, and the total of $374.87 popped up on the register. My heart jumped. Grandma opened her ancient purse and handed over her credit card.

"That's why we shop at the Bay. Tradition is important—remember that."

Grandpa was running the van just by the store entrance. He had "El Paso" by Marty Robbins blasting on the radio when we got in, exhaust fumes flooding around us as we buckled in. Grandma promptly blazed up a Du Maurier and sucked in a massive drag. I coughed, waving my hand in front of my face, but I took in what smoke I could—I needed a cigarette myself. Grandpa leaned over into Grandma's cloud of death, peeking inside the bags.

"What you got there, little lady?" he asked.

"Never you mind, Cyril!" Grandma snapped. She snatched up the receipt, pushing his hairy paws aside, and folding it into the wad of other receipts in her purse. He let out a loud yelp, and they both laughed. "The boy looks like a million bucks."

TROUBLEMAKER

AFTER WORD GOT OUT THAT I had a steady job at the grocery store, my stature at school elevated further.

I had my own cash to buy pizza and cigarettes at a store across the street during lunch, and soon I made friends with older kids at my school and other high schools across the area. I continued to hang with my local street buddies—Brian, Derick, Leeroy—but my new friends drank and slept with younger girls and went to all the best parties. Some weren't in school at all. They had their own apartments, cars, and jobs. We formed a gang. We called ourselves the Bud Boys because Budweiser was our beer and we put Bud beer caps on our baseball hats. The caps helped identify who was who when we brawled at parties or in school parking lots.

By the middle of Grade 10, my grades were plummeting. I was scrapping by with 50s and 60s and still couldn't read or write very well. Math was the only grade I was keeping steady, but even that began to sink after I started skipping class all the time.

I was branded a brash troublemaker by school authorities after the stereo in the drama classroom was lifted in a break-in one Friday night. Leeroy's long arms didn't have any trouble reaching the window into the classroom. I climbed him like a ladder and tossed out the audio equipment. We took it to a Vietnamese kid who was waiting in a townhouse nearby. His cousin bought it for $200. Leeroy and I got $100, and we split that. I was questioned by the police, teacher, and principal, but they didn't have enough evidence to lay any charges.

The authorities threatened to expel me if things didn't turn around, but I didn't give a shit. Grandpa didn't seem interested in me anymore. Sure, he drove me to work here and there, at six a.m. on my weekend shifts, but I expected him to punch me out when he found out about the stereo, and he didn't.

"You're just like your dad," he said instead.

One lunch period near the end of the school year, I wandered over to the Chinese market on the other side of the parking lot where they kept the school buses during the day. I noticed a group of kids out back huddled behind a dumpster, so I decided to check it out.

Balpreet was there—a tough Sikh kid we called Ballpeen because he hit like a ball-peen hammer. I'd known him since Grade 3. He stood in the middle of everyone holding a bottle full of smoke with a backward cigarette sticking out of the bottom. He called me over, and everyone shifted to make room for me.

"Indian," Balpreet said. "You ever smoke hash before?" He held the bottle up in my direction.

"No," I said. "Never."

I looked closer and saw a little brown stone cooking on the end of the cigarette in the bottle. Smoke circled round and round within it and left a cream-coloured stain on the clear plastic side. I thought of Irish coffee.

Balpreet uncorked the lid, pulled the cigarette out, then thrust the bottle full of smoke in my face. "Suck and hold," he said. A wisp of smoke floated up under the bill of his Blue Jays hat. It smelled like burnt earth.

I put the open nozzle to my mouth and sucked as directed. The smoke shot into my lungs.

Raunchy.

I almost coughed it out, but held it for about a minute until my ribs convulsed and I dropped my cigarette, then I spewed a plume of grey air up into the clouds—it was too thin to call it smoke. Still no coughing. A feeling of euphoria hit me, and I wobbled and leaned on the dumpster.

Balpreet said something in Punjabi and laughed. I noticed there was a line of tiny hash balls strewn out on the edge of the dumpster. He cracked a sideways smile and dabbed his cigarette on the next toke then slid it in the bottle. He reminded me of Clint Eastwood after he gunned someone down. I broke out in laughter.

That was my first encounter with drugs.

The next week I was buying a gram of hash from a friend behind the pizza place across from the school when squad cars rolled up. My friend, who had a leg in a cast, crushed the dope on the ground with the end of his crutch and it stuck to the bottom of the rubber tip. The cops searched everywhere—on the roof, in the garbage cans, in our mouths—but couldn't figure out what we'd done with the drugs.

"We know you have some," one cop yelled. "We saw the transaction."

We emerged with only a warning, and my reputation solidified. Older kids, and not just the ones I already hung out with, began showing me respect.

A few months later I was selling acid by the sheet and sniffing speed in the washroom before class every day.

THE STRONGEST BROTHER

JERRY MADE A CHOKER OUT of chicken bones and coloured wooden beads. He was a creative guy and drew things like dragons and elves and played Dungeons & Dragons with his nerd friends at his new high school, an arts school way out in the country. For as long as I could remember, too, he'd been proud of being what he called "Native" and found creative ways to express it. I made fun of him and his friends, but I secretly played D&D with them and always had a blast. They were genuine in a way that my cool friends weren't.

"Look," he said with a big smile. "Isn't it beautiful?"

The bone necklace was kind of alright. I thought it made him look strong and proud.

"It's last night's dinner," I said, deadpan.

"Why do you always do that, Jesse? Why do you shit on our heritage like that?"

I knew he was being sincere. He remembered more of Saskatchewan than I did, and had recently gone on a school trip near Regina and learned stuff about our mother's people and started making pipes out of soapstone, burning herbs, and wearing beads out in public. He started lifting weights after that, taking care of his health, and I even heard a drum bump ever so softly in his room sometimes. He said he was singing

Indian songs. I didn't care. I stole the tobacco he got out west, not concerned about what ceremonial "Indian" uses he had for it.

Heritage be damned, I just wanted a smoke. I looked at him and the necklace.

"Because it looks awful. Why do you and Josh play Indians? Fuck, we're from Brampton and never practiced that stuff. It's embarrassing."

Jerry quietly asked me to leave his bedroom and shut the door as I left. I heard his drum that night, and the next day he wore his choker to school.

I was jealous of Josh when we were little, and I was jealous of Jerry now.

CHOICE

MR. T.'S MUG HAD A blue police emblem on it. He took a sip and placed it on his kitchen table and asked me if I wanted Earl Grey or orange pekoe.

"Doesn't matter," I answered. I wondered why he'd called me over to his house for a chat. He'd never done that before—phoned my grandparents' house and asked me over. I thought maybe Brian was sick. Or worse, that Mr. T. had heard at police headquarters some of the stuff I'd been involved with lately, him being the deputy chief of a police division and all.

He plopped a bag of pekoe in my cup, poured in some boiling water, and then gave it to me. The bag drifted around, releasing a stain that was more brown than orange. He took a seat across from me and slid a stoneware container of sugar my way.

I helped myself.

"Jesse," he began. "I know you're a good kid."

I added another lump to my tea and thought, *Here we go.* I had a hard time not rolling my eyes.

"Since the time you stole our robins' eggs, I knew you had it rough—orphan, no mom and dad." He took a sip and continued: "I grew up without a father; my mother did it all on her own." He pulled a leather photo album that was older than dirt from the counter next to him and opened it. "See here? That's me." He pointed to a picture of a guy around my age doing a layup shot. The picture was black and white, and in it he was clean-cut, thin, and athletic, with hairy legs. The socks and shorts he was wearing were both too high to be fashionable. There were other basketball pictures and a photo of him and a woman he said was his mother outside an old tenement building. She had on a long trench coat, and he told me how she used it to smuggle him into their building as a child because single mothers were looked down upon back then.

"I found basketball and the force," he said and closed the album. "It saved my life."

I poured a bit of milk into my cup and the tea churned in a grey tornado.

"My poor mother," he went on. "She just couldn't show me how to be a man."

I was uneasy hearing Mr. T. speak this way. It was the most any adult had spoken to me in months. I started to respond, but he lifted both hands slightly off the table and said, "Just listen, please," and then planted his elbows down in front of him.

I gave my teacup a turn. I wasn't ready for a lecture.

Brian lit my cigarette with his Zippo and asked me to watch for ashes because they could burn the upholstery of his new car, a used Renault his parents got him for his seventeenth birthday.

"I have something cool to show you," he said as he pulled into the parking lot of the local park. He turned his headlights off, hopped out, and grabbed some beers from the trunk. I got out, and we both sat on a bench.

"See here?" Brian held out one hand. His fingers peeled back to reveal his silver Zippo.

"Yeah. So?"

"And in this hand"—he held up his other hand—"I have the car keys. I want you to pick."

I reached for the beers and yanked one off the rings. "I want one of these. Fuck your lighter and keys." I laughed and pulled the tab and it hissed open. I took a swig and belched.

"No, serious, bro. Pick. It's a lesson I learned at Landmark."

Landmark was a series of empowerment workshops his uncle had gotten him for Christmas the year before. After he'd attended a few sessions, Brian would spout off about how we had to face ourselves, how we had to live our best lives, and how truth was subjective because everyone's truth is true or some shit like that. None of us really paid attention to it.

"Easy, Socrates," I said. "Can't we just drink without all your philosophy bullshit?" I really hoped my comment would diffuse his little life lesson, but he persisted.

"Pick—lighter or keys. There is only one right answer."

"If I must. Keys."

"Why? Explain why."

"What the fuck you mean, explain?"

"Tell me why you chose that over the lighter."

"I don't know. Because I can drive away in it." I took another swig, the beer fizzing in my throat.

"Wrong!" he yelled, sounding like a game-show host. "Pick again."

I was confused but gave it another go.

"Okay, I pick the lighter this time."

"Explain why." Brian flicked the Zippo and twirled it around his knuckles like a leprechaun twirling a gold coin. I snatched it from him.

"Because you said the keys were wrong and I need the light for this blunt." I pulled out the joint I had in my pack of smokes and lit it with the Zippo. I took a big toke, thinking I had the right answer this time.

"No. Wrong again."

"Fuck this game, yo." I took another huge drag and passed the joint over, but Brian declined. He really wanted me to keep guessing, so I did for about ten goes till I had enough of his stupid game.

"I asked you to choose the lighter or the keys. And you rightfully chose one or the other like I asked." He put the lighter and keys on the bench between us and cracked a beer. "And when I asked you to explain why you chose it, you said something about how you'd use it or how it looked—how you could drive it, light it, its colour—anything. That's wrong."

The weed hit me, and I got really interested in what he was saying. "Then? What's the right answer?"

"The right answer is that you chose because you chose. That's it. All the explanations you gave to justify your choice are just excuses your mind made up after the fact."

A gong bonged over my head. I couldn't tell if it was the beer I'd drank and the kush I'd smoked, or the power of his crackerjack philosophy.

"So that's the big reveal?" I said. "I chose it because I chose?"

"Yeah. And when you know that you can just choose to do anything you want."

"Get the fuck outta here," I said. I grabbed another beer, flicked my ash on the grass, and stared up at the stars.

There'd been too many lectures lately, not enough talking with me. But it seemed Mr. T. was determined to give me another.

"Love is an important thing," he said. "And I don't see that in your life too much."

His words lingered around the ceiling fixture and then crept down the walls into my brain. *How dare he.* My fists clenched around my teacup and near scalded under the pressure of my grip.

"I take Brian to basketball, to soccer, to canoe in Algonquin Park, and I help him with his paper route. I do it because I love him. He's my son."

The words dropped like a cold stone in my belly. I remembered all the times Mr. T. had invited me to attend Brian's soccer and basketball games, and how I went out with them on Sundays to deliver newspapers.

He'd always included me throughout the years, bought me snacks at Brian's games when we cheered him on from the sidelines, taught me how to shoot a jumpshot when he taught Brian, showed me how to study for one hour a day, and told me how that added up and made a world of difference in Brian's reading.

I searched my mind for any recollection of my grandfather making time for me like that but couldn't remember anything, except work. There was never any hockey or basketball practice for me or my brothers, no swimming lessons, no canoe trips in the woods, no paper routes, no study time, no interest. We did go to judo for a few months when I was ten, but that was because we got beat up so badly at school, and he rarely stayed to watch us practice. And there were our yearly Cape Breton vacations, but that was mainly about Grandpa, his lobster, and drinking—not us boys.

Then I thought of my father and wanted to run away.

Mr. T. dropped another sugar cube in his tea and slowly stirred.

"For me," he said finally, "it all changed when I realized I had choice. Choice is the human ability to go one way or the other." He opened the album again, but this time to a picture of when he must have been in his thirties, in a police uniform, around when I first met him. His wife was beside him with little Brian in front. He paused a second, then turned until he landed on an older photo of himself in what appeared to be his early twenties taking a shot on a billiards table.

He slammed his finger onto the photo, and I flinched at the force of it. "I was a hustler, Jesse. Was good at it, too. Thought it was all I was worth." He turned the album upright and pushed it toward me, knocking it into my tea. It was a great photo—his hair was greased back, and the bottom of his jeans were rolled up, exposing ankle socks and loafers. He looked cool.

"I had to make a choice," he said. "Live this way"—he flipped to the police pictures—"or this way"—he flipped back to the greaser photo.

"So, how'd you do it?" I asked, truly curious.

"I realized it was all on me and no one could save me—not Mom or anyone. I had to choose to do the work of bettering myself, just like I chose to hustle in pool halls all day. It was that simple." Mr. T. scratched his chin and admired himself in the pool hall shot.

I thought he'd offer me more wisdom, but he offered me more tea.

PREMONITION

"THERE JOSH GOES WITH HIS feather and that shit he keeps burning and waving everywhere," I said to Leeroy and my friends out in the high school smoking pit. Rows of yellow school buses hid us from the view of the teachers who routinely scanned the parking lot for students doing drugs. We blazed about three joints and got away scot-free as always.

"What is it?" Leeroy asked, as he put the roach in his cigarette pack with the rest of the day's smoked roaches.

"Some Indian herbs or something. Sage." I flicked my after-joint cigarette and watched it ricochet off the ground, sending burning ash into the air. I smacked my lips and the taste of cheap cigarettes mingled with the smooth, expensive flavour of Afghan blond hash. "Who the fuck knows, as long as Tonto ain't waving it at me. He's gone Indian. Just like my other brother." I rolled my eyes and popped my jean jacket collar, even as I wondered, *What was it?*

Leeroy laughed and agreed that my brother looked ridiculous.

Later that same week, I was surprised to see Josh come out of the side door of the school. I was skipping off like I always did, but Josh was such a goody two-shoes. Why wasn't he in class like he always was?

"Hey, Josh," I yelled from the smoking pit. "Get to class, you brown-noser!"

Me and my stoner friends giggled as I took another pull of the hash joint. When my toke was finished, I looked up at Josh, but he didn't respond.

"He looks like he's crying," one of the girls, Sarah, said. "Why?"

"What? Josh don't cry. He's a beast," Leeroy said, his eyes bloodshot and nearly closed.

Leeroy was correct, my brother was a beast. He was 240 pounds in Grade 11 and had shattered the long-standing bench-press and leg-press records at our school. He was also one of the biggest and fastest rugby players in the district and struck fear in the hearts of many of his opponents. He could also fight better than anyone at our school if he got pissed off enough, but he had a gentleness about him and only fought when provoked.

"No, seriously, Jesse. He's crying."

Just as Sarah finished saying that, I saw one of the teachers, Mrs. M., burst out the side door. She tried to grab Josh from behind but he collapsed on the ground before she could reach him. I dropped my empty book bag and ran to his side.

"What's wrong, yo? Josh, what's wrong?"

When he looked up I saw his eyes were wide and red.

"I . . . ," he mustered, unable to catch his breath. "You . . ."

"Back up," Mrs. M. said with the force of a lioness. "Something happened in class and he needs air."

I was confused. Had someone died? Had someone said something hurtful to him? Had someone done this?

"I saw . . . I saw you," he said. "I had a vision and . . . It was horr . . ."

A scrum of teachers came out of nowhere and pushed me aside before he could finish his thought. They sat him up and kept anyone—including me—from talking with him. An ambulance came. High off my tree, I soon lost interest and turned my back on him, drifting over to my friends in the smoking pit.

"What the hell happened?" Leeroy asked.

"I don't know. He said something about a vision, like he's a mystic Indian or something."

Leeroy and the gang snickered and talked about the feathers we'd seen Josh with earlier. "You're alright, though, Jesse," Leeroy added.

"Yeah, you're not into that Indian shit. I remember at public school when you used to say you were Italian," someone else said and laughed some more.

I joined in.

BERRIES

IT WAS THE HOUSE PARTY of the century, and in walked a young girl with a Tupperware container.

"Does anyone want muffins?" she asked, her mouth full of braces.

I was sitting by the fireplace sucking on a cigarette and watched the guys in the gang make fun of her. But she persisted, bubbly and friendly, walking around the room. When she offered me a muffin, I took it and just stared at her. Her smile was angelic despite the dental hardware.

As I ate the best blueberry muffin of my life, I was perplexed—by the taste, by our encounter, by everything. There were lots of other girls there, but this odd girl with the muffins captivated me. I mean, who does that? Who brings baked goods to a party with piles of cocaine, weed, and speed? She was like a walking loaf of wholesome Wonder Bread amid a torrent of hard candy. That pure goodness attracted me to her. I followed her into the kitchen and introduced myself and asked for another muffin.

"Sure," she said and gave me the largest one, blueberries popping out all over. The music in the house was pounding louder than a rock concert, and when she handed it to me I had a hard time hearing, but she batted her eyes—they were huge and blue. I almost dropped the muffin.

"Thank you," I said, trying to figure out what she was all about.

"Anytime," she mouthed.

Icebergs cracked and fell away inside me.

A month later we were going steady and were in love. Her name was Karen and she was eighteen, old for those braces.

I was afraid to tell Karen I was half Native at first, but she said, "I think it's wonderful. You should be proud of who you are."

I just about cried.

When Karen took me home to meet her family, I got to talking with her father, and he told me that they were Scottish and Dutch and had settled near Toronto after the Toronto Purchase of 1805 between the British Crown and Mississauga Indians. Their family received a swath of land that they'd farmed ever since. Karen had worked on the family farm since she was young, and she was comfortable doing manual labour. We had that in common.

And when I told Mr. A. about my Scottish side, he asked me all sorts of questions and I could tell he really was interested, just as Karen was, even though I couldn't answer most of them. He was even more interested when I told him about my Native family. He wondered if I was still in touch with anyone. "I read up on history quite a bit, about Canada, the prairies," he said. "And I'm curious: Do you know if your mother's people were Cree or Métis? If they hunted bison? You said they were from Saskatchewan, right?"

"Yes, she's from there, but I wish I knew more, Mr. A.," I said. "She wasn't really around to tell me about that stuff."

The three of us decided to go canoeing one day down the Credit River. It was the end of March and the ice had almost thawed.

I sat at the back of the canoe, Karen in the middle, and Mr. A. was up front.

The river ran fast underneath us, bending wildly down twists and turns. Shelves of ice broke off as our bow slammed headfirst into them—I wasn't good at steering and couldn't get the craft to turn when I wanted it to. There were spots on straightaways where it seemed like I knew what I was doing, but they always gave way to turbulence when we hit a bend. Karen still cheered me on and held on to the sides, laughing and sending up clouds of frozen breath in front of me, but it was hard to deny I was shit at canoeing. Mr. A., though, knew what he was doing and tried to compensate, pulling us forward with his paddle and powerful farmer's arms.

"Watch the corner," I heard him yell as we hurled into a sharp turn. I thrust my paddle into the water and we broadsided the bank. The canoe shifted, Karen's blond hair flew in the wind, and the winter water slammed into my chest.

My ribs ached as I drifted down and down, my arms and legs quickly became heavy and lethargic. I gasped twice and sucked in mouthfuls of water. The heavy cotton and wool of my winter clothing tangled around my body like dead weight as I settled onto the riverbed. I saw a paddle drift by. I screamed for help, releasing a muffled burst of bubbles; then, silence.

I noticed a lock of Karen's hair swaying gently like seaweed as her body writhed above me, the current pulling her downstream in the frozen water. Her movements were slow and getting slower. Her leg kicked, and her boot came loose.

I don't know what came over me then, or how I managed to shift myself. But I ripped off my jacket, kicked off my boots, and swam upward. In a few strokes I was with her. She was already above water, though, gasping for air. She grabbed my arm and pulled me to shore, where we collapsed beside one another.

We shivered and held each other for warmth. She smiled, then her expression froze.

"Where's my father?" she asked.

"I don't know," I said. I raised my head and right away saw him laughing about twenty feet down shore.

"That's how I know you love each other," he shouted and waved. "You didn't even think of dear old dad."

Karen and I went everywhere together.

"You're always with that girl," Leeroy complained. "You're never around anymore."

It was true. We had busy schedules, and spending time with Leeroy interfered with my time with Karen. I worked nights after school, and Karen helped on the farm until I finished at around ten p.m., then she would pick me up in one of her father's old trucks. It smelled like cow shit, but I didn't mind—it was our love shack on wheels.

We'd drive out into the country and talk until dawn, or we'd take off to a rave together and dance until our legs just about fell off. When the beat dropped, and she was grooving right there in front of me, with a huge smile beaming light and love, I was so free and happy.

OPENING UP

THE SIDE DOOR OF KAREN'S truck was open, letting in the cool midnight breeze. We lay side by side on the seat, heads hanging out, staring up at the sky. We were parked out front of my old elementary school, where Leeroy and I had thrown gum in Sylvia's hair. Our friends had wanted to drink and cause pandemonium as usual; we just wanted quiet and each other's company. There was a stillness between us broken only by the rustle of the leaves in the wind.

"Look at that one," I said as I pointed to the North Star. "That's the star Indians used to hunt by; they'd follow it and know where to go." I let the mystic nature of my comment linger in the night air.

"Bullshit," Karen said. She laughed, but I could tell she was halfway convinced.

I took a drag of my cigarette and blew the smoke up and watched it dissipate. The stars grew lighter the longer I stared.

Karen shifted. "Move, you beast, my arm is asleep." She giggled and pushed me over to the gas pedal, right where the scent of cow shit was strongest. I gasped and held my throat, and we both laughed, then wiggled out of the truck.

Once we were settled on a nice spot on the grass next to the playground, Karen said, "Can I ask you something?"

"Sure. Shoot." I wrapped my arm around her shoulder.

"You never talk about why you live with your grandparents." She picked a blade of grass and twirled it.

It was odd for her not to look me in the eye. I searched for the right words. There'd never been boundaries between Karen and me, and I wanted to tell her the truth.

"Sometimes life just tears people from one another. That happened with my family when I was young." I paused and sat up so Karen would look at me, and she did. "Dad had a lot of issues—drugs and violence and other things . . ."

A million years of silence followed. Stars flickered and extinguished one by one, civilizations rose and fell, great pyramids were built and crumbled, yet she kept looking at me. And the wall, a thousand miles high, that I kept between me and the rest of the world didn't exist—not a brick anywhere in sight.

Memories of Josh peeing himself by the bathroom, the hornet by the tub, and the sweet smell of Saskatoon berries along the road allowance with my mushoom and kokum filled my soul. As did the blue bruises along my mother's face. I breathed in and exhaled the rest of my truth.

"My mom had to do what she had to do." I looked up and saw a comet soar by and fall off into the horizon. I thought of Mom standing in front of the mountains in the Polaroid and wondered where she was. "When she left, it all fell apart."

Karen pulled me close.

"I understand," she said. She reached up and knocked off my baseball cap.

I was staying out of trouble for the first time in my life. I stopped stealing and lying, and had saved up lots of cash, around five thousand dollars. I was taking care of my health, too, cutting back on drugs and alcohol.

My grandparents saw the change in me and came to like Karen even more than when they first met her. I would chance to say that they came to love her. They asked her over for dinner every other week, and she always came, blueberry muffins in hand. My grandfather loved those muffins almost as much as I did, and sometimes he'd pick them over Grandma's butter tarts—Grandma didn't like that, but she still had a soft spot for Karen.

Grandpa even sat me down one afternoon and said that if I broke her heart he'd find me and neuter me. "You don't find girls like her every day," he said. "She's special."

I should have listened to the old man.

PRIDE

I CLEARED THE SLEEP OUT of my eyes. It was 5:45 a.m., and Grandpa was driving me to my morning shift at the grocery store. My head pounded, the sour smell of whiskey strong on my breath, the after-effects of a buddy's birthday. It was a reasonable enough occasion to fall off the wagon.

"Grandpa," I announced, "I want to buy a car."

He rolled down his driver-side window and the cold morning air hit my face.

"You will not," he barked.

"But you taught Josh how to drive at sixteen. And I'm nineteen now and you never taught me."

He turned down the Hank Williams song on the radio as we rounded the corner and gunned it. It looked like we entered warp speed as we hit a wall of snowflakes illuminated by the headlights.

"You're wild—always were. You'll kill yourself driving drunk."

I heard the wheels squeal. "But—"

"I said no." He pounded the steering wheel.

I thought the column might break under the force. I kicked my feet and muttered out my window, "I work hard. It's my fucking money." I'd never sworn in front of the old man before, and I recoiled as soon as the words left my mouth.

He slammed on the brakes and the load of tools in the back of the van shifted. "If I ever catch you talking like that again," he said, "I'll snap your neck."

I went to the bank ATM and withdrew the last $2,000 I'd saved. The wad was thick in my hand as I looked at the receipt—*$0*. It was all gone.

Leeroy waited in the car, jungle music pounding, weed smoke pouring out the window. It was our last stop on our way to the rave.

I'd run through my savings in little under two months since the argument with Grandpa, buying everyone drinks, smokes, and endless amounts of drugs. Destroying my future was my way of getting back at the old man.

"Jesse, please," Karen had pleaded. "How are you going to afford college now?"

"College? Are you fucking kidding me—I got kicked out of school last semester."

I never believed post-secondary education was attainable for me, like it was for my friends, whose parents had saved for their education since they were born. Getting kicked out of school and having a car denied me were the final straws.

"Don't talk to me about school, Karen." I hissed. "You're rich—it's different for you." She looked stunned, but I was furious. Leeroy and the other guys never questioned me about my spending. I tried to avoid her after that.

"Wicked," Leeroy said as he opened the passenger-side door of his father's Pontiac 6000. I was waving my cash around like Diamond Jim, the last of the Gilded Age big spenders.

"Let's get there before the line gets too big," I said and hopped in.

I lost Leeroy two hours into the party. I'd picked up a bag of purple Es and a couple ounces of weed from one of my dealers when I first arrived and kept it in my front jean jacket pocket with my roll of money while I tripped about. The Es were so strong I had a difficult time training my eyes on anything for more than a few seconds, so it was inevitable I'd lose him. Every six hours, I dosed another E and puffed another joint hoping Leeroy would show up.

The rhythm of the ragga jungle pounded through me as the night wore on. I danced myself into a deep trance. My throat burned with thirst

Me, nineteen and high on opium.

STEFAN KNIGHT

as sweat poured down my face and neck. I must've drunk ten bottles of water. My sneakers darted nimble on the slick floor, and I grooved with speed like a hummingbird. Shouts and cheers roared with each move, and soon a circle formed around me—women in miniskirts, combat gear, and baseball hats; B-boys and B-girls breakdancing in Adidas tracksuits; dudes with their shirts off pumping their fists in the air; and a horde of other ravers blowing their whistles to the beat. They all looked as high as me. I closed my eyes and kept dancing harder and faster with everyone, the drugs now completely in control of my body and mind.

There was a silence that came over my spirit, followed by what sounded like a gust of wind. The noise of the rave receded into the background, and I heard something emerge from inside my core. My eyes pressed shut, I focused inward on that sound. There was a distant drum—louder, louder, louder still, until it vibrated every molecule in my being. The beautiful cry of Indian drummers rang aloud in every direction—from the north, south, east, west, up, down, over, under, within, and without. I opened my eyes and saw I was dancing alone on the flatness of the great plains. I was dressed in a plume of feathers, deerskins, a bustle, beads, moccasins, a rattle, and tassels. My legs rushed in perfect coordination over top of the grass, pressing and tamping it down, as vast fields undulated before me. The sun hung low as red clouds of dust were kicked up by my feet, filling the air. I danced and danced, moving this way and that, until my thirst for water and the rave seemed but distant memories of a life I once lived.

Only the blinding morning warehouse lights snapped me out of my trance, the music turned to half power, throbbing some mix of break-beats and house. My jacket, my money, my drugs, and most of the rave attendees were gone, and my white muscle shirt had spots of blood the size of cookies on it. There was one girl still dancing next to me, her eyes as wide as some starry universe. The bottoms of her pants were grim and black with cigarette ash and trampled innocence.

"How long have we been dancing?" I asked, disoriented and shaky.

"Two days," she said. Her jaw muscles flexed and clenched as she continued to gyrate, glow sticks dim in both hands. She pointed to the blood stains. "That happened to me once."

I peered inside my shirt and saw that the ends of my nipples were open wounds, like they'd been hit with a belt sander.

"Rubbed them raw against my shirt," she added. "Happens to marathon runners, too."

I never did find Leeroy.

BANANA SPLIT

A WOMAN NAMED SUE SHOWED up at my work one night. "Call me," she mouthed, holding a banana to her ear like she was on the phone.

I was stacking Florida oranges near the lettuce wet case. She put the banana down and pointed to it, then glided toward the cashier to pay for her groceries. I walked over and saw that she had scrawled her number on the side of the banana and had planted a bright red lipstick kiss over top.

That's creative, I thought.

Sue hung around with some of the guys I partied with. She was nice looking, around my age, and had her own car, but I'd never spoken with her before. I placed the banana in my pocket and went to the backroom and got busy with the rest of my work.

I never called.

A few weeks after the banana incident, my buddy Jeff was having a house party, since his father was away on business.

"No girlfriends," he ordered. "Just bring drugs and booze."

"Roger that," I said.

I asked Karen if it was okay for me to go. "It'll give you the chance to hang out with your girlfriends," I said. She was more than happy to do that.

When I got to Jeff's the windows were rattling to a base line so loud I thought they might shatter when the beat dropped. One of my buddies was spinning the turntables, people were grooving in the kitchen and living room, and I saw a few people out back giving each other massages in the hot tub. I could tell everyone was high on coke and E by the size of their pupils and how confident they were in their conversations.

There were a bunch of girls I'd never seen before, but Sue was there. She came over right away.

"Why didn't you call me?"

I didn't know what to say.

"No worries," she said. Her jaw was grinding and I knew it must be from a recently consumed E. She disappeared into the kitchen and re-emerged with a beer and placed it in front of me as I took off my shoes. "My little produce boy." She tapped my bum.

I jumped and smiled awkwardly then moseyed my way over to my friends. Sue melted into the crowd.

By four a.m. I was blitzed off my face and out back trying to cool down. The drugs were super powerful; my skin was goosebumped and sensitive to the touch, and my hair stood on end. I gulped a mouthful of water, poured the rest over my head, and sat down on a garden bench to let the night breeze do its work.

Sue appeared from around the garage and sat next to me. It was clear she was tripping hard, her eyes two pools of India ink. She nudged close and ran her fingers up my spine and through my wet hair, sending shockwaves of pleasure to my toes. Before I knew it, we were upstairs in bed together.

When I emerged from the bedroom, I was ashamed, because I'd betrayed Karen. She was the one person who'd loved and trusted me—the only person I'd ever opened up to. I didn't talk to anyone as I put my shoes on, gathered my things, and caught a taxi back to Brampton.

When I got home, Grandma was up. She handed me a note from Karen, asking me to call so we could have brunch that morning, and asked, "What's wrong, Jesse? You don't look well."

I couldn't look her in the eye. "Nothing," I said, pulling away. I dropped my hoodie and went to call Karen.

She answered, "Hi, baby," her voice so sweet I almost died.

Without a pause, I said, "Karen. It's over. I'm breaking up with you."

There was no noise at first, then a terrible, "No!" She said it over and over, then started saying, "Why, why, why?"

I could hear her crying. I'd never heard someone cry like that before. I swear I heard her heart break right then. I was so ashamed, and I couldn't even tell her why it was over.

I hung up and tried to catch my breath. Grandma cracked the door and came into my bedroom with soft moccasin steps.

"You're making a big mistake," she said. "Karen's a wonderful girl." She shook her head and placed my hoodie on the dresser. A little baggie of coke tumbled out onto the carpet near her feet. I looked down and she gasped. She knew instantly what it was.

"Cyril," she called, panic in her voice. "You better come up."

He rushed upstairs.

When he saw the bag he yelled, "You're just a fucking asshole like Sonny, to shit all over love like that."

I backed up into the corner.

"Pack your things. You can't stay here anymore."

I saw how hurt the old man was and tried to speak.

"But—"

"No. You knew the rules."

I realized then that he'd meant what he'd said all along about drugs.

I remember leaving that night with my stuff in four black garbage bags, frightened of what the future held.

I remember a week later losing my job at the grocery store.

I remember catching a ride out west with one of my buddies.

I remember asking Josh if I could stay with him.

The rest is a blur.

THE STOLEN STREETS

1997–2008

WINDIGO

the long dark winter is ever-consuming
defrost the cold hunger with firewater and skin

meat is scarce on the trap line
but, still, i hunt these alleys.

my fingers claw at the glass
and peel away the label.

i imagine icy northern lakes
abundant with pike
but these fish escape me too.

starvation sets in.
breath freezes
in january's wind.

lost and alone,
wandering.
i swill back the pain; it burns and it belches
rage and despair
leaving only a windigo
who cannibalizes himself.

ADRIFT

LEEROY DROVE DOWN HASTINGS STREET looking for a safe place to park. He'd come out west a few weeks after I did. He just showed up looking all desperate, with no money, just his father's Pontiac 6000. Josh took pity on him and let him crash on his couch until he found a job, but things went south fast—two days fast—as they often did when we were together.

Rain doused the windshield, and the wipers moaned back and forth, the friction hypnotizing me. Grey clouds obstructed the sky above. It had been raining since I'd arrived a month earlier, and I wondered if the city ever saw blue skies or the warmth of the winter sun, or if the mountains that ringed Vancouver were only a myth—I had a hard time believing they were there.

Hordes of homeless junkies slinked down the street, their skin greyer than the clouds and concrete cityscape. They moved like zombies, half-dead, lurching, and hungry. One bag lady pulled down her pants and pissed right there on the side of the road. No one seemed to care, but Leeroy laughed.

"What the fuck?" he said. "Where are we?"

I tried to laugh but a feeling of dread came over me as she lost her balance and fell over in her own urine. A scrum of people congregated on the corner of Main and Hastings—they darted their heads about and

I knew they must be engaged in some sort of drug deal. One of the men yelled and shook his fist, clutching something. His voice was guttural, it sounded torn to shreds, like he'd just drunk a bottle of Drano. His clothes hung off his body, more rags than anything. Another man hollered and the group pounced, arms and legs flailing wildly. The rough-voiced man was consumed by the swarm of violence. I rolled down my window to get a better look and the group scattered, leaving him prostrate on the sidewalk.

"Where the fuck are we is right," I said, squinting to see if he was still breathing. I noticed a pool of blood spreading near his face, a blankness across his eyes. He looked dead, but they all appeared dead in their own way, and the majority of them looked Indian. I'd never seen so many Indians in one spot before, except when I was a kid. I'd also never seen such squalor and despair; in suburban Brampton, places like this didn't exist.

"We've got to pick a spot soon," Leeroy said. "We're gonna blow through all the gas and we ain't got no money left." His left leg was bouncing up and down and he kept glancing in and adjusting the rear-view mirror. I chewed my knuckle down to the flesh. Josh hadn't warned us of any of this when he'd kicked us out.

"I should arrest you both," he'd screamed. He'd come home early one night from his shift and found me and Leeroy smoking pot. "I'm fucking RCMP! What's everyone going to think?" He charged into the room and wheel-kicked my face, sending the joint flying and an explosion of ash and embers into the air. He moved like a black belt after years of tae kwon do. Leeroy cowered beside me on the couch.

It'd never really dawned on me that my older brother was an officer of the law and that I shouldn't be getting high at his place. Even his red Mountie uniform hadn't convinced me. To me he was just Josh—I acted as I always had, stealing his clothes and disrespecting him like the little brother I was. I'd even nicked his badge on occasion and went around telling everyone I was a cop so I could get on public transit free of charge, pick up chicks, and eat complimentary meals at local restaurants after I assured them that I'd protect them personally.

When Josh found out, he wanted to arrest me for impersonating an officer, but I talked my way out of it somehow. But stupid me, I kept pushing the limit. No wonder he went Jackie Chan on me for the pot.

Leeroy pulled into a lot near a river and turned off the car. The engine sputtered, followed by a hiss and a cloud of steam from under the hood. I thought it was the radiator. Leeroy reached into the glovebox and pulled out a map of the Lower Mainland that I'd pinched at a gas station.

"This car isn't in good shape," he said as he spread the map out across the dash. "I borrowed it before my dad had the chance to get it serviced."

"I heard him yell at you when you phoned home last week. He sounded upset that you borrowed it."

Leeroy glared at me. I thought he might hit me, but he furrowed his brow and busied himself with the map.

I kept pressing. "You must've done something pretty serious." I waited for his answer, but he ignored me. He turned over the ignition and it clicked a few times. The interior lights dimmed and flickered, then went black. The car battery was dead, that much I knew. We were stranded.

"Fuck," Leeroy yelled, his voice raising high.

I decided not to enquire further about the trouble he'd fled. "Where are we?" I asked, surveying for street signs. I could make out a couple, plus there was a huge white bridge off to the left. I grabbed the map and searched, trying to pinpoint our locale. Leeroy stared out his window and lit one of our last smokes.

"Here we are," I said. "New Westminster and that's the Fraser River. I think that's the Pattullo Bridge." I glanced over to see Leeroy was crying. He turned his head when he noticed me.

"Yeah," I said, peering out over the river. "At least we found a good spot."

By the third day, food had become a major problem. Every store we went into had floor walkers who followed Leeroy and me whenever we tried to steal even one bag of ramen noodles. We figured it was because of all the addicts who tried to do the same—stores in BC had way better security than out east. I got caught at the Army & Navy and was issued a promise to appear by a policeman, which I tore up the instant I got released.

"We've got to think of something quick," Leeroy said as I emerged. "I'm literally starving."

I examined his face. His eyes were sunken, and the metallic, sweet smell of starvation wafted off his breath. The taste on my tongue told me that I emitted that same odor.

Leeroy's solution was to call home. We ducked into a nearby phone booth, and he went first.

"Hi, Dad," he said. "I need help. I'm homeless in Vancouver and have no food." He sounded pitiful.

I could hear his father's voice booming. Leeroy's shoulders slumped and he hung up. "He told me to figure it out on my own. You try."

I dialled home. It rang a few times before someone picked up.

"You have a collect call from Jesse Thistle," the automatic operator voice said.

The line clicked and my grandmother answered. "Jesse," she said. "Don't ever call here again."

"But, Grandma—"

"No. Your grandfather was clear: you're not welcome."

I couldn't believe what she was saying.

"But I'm starv—"

"You are on your own now—this isn't your home anymore." Her voice was shaky like it was when Yorkie died, and she'd bawled in the kitchen.

I heard my grandfather's gravel yell in the background. "Is that the asshole?"

There was a muffled sound, then his voice blasted in my ear.

"Don't ever call here. Don't ever come here. Don't even think of here. Josh told me what happened—you are not part of this family." He slammed the receiver into the cradle. I slid down the side of the phone booth and hid my face in my knees. Leeroy didn't say a word.

The second week sleeping in the car with no food, I started to panic. Home would never be there again for me, nor would Karen—I still loved her beyond words. The dual losses were like my rudder had snapped off, without warning. I was adrift somewhere in the middle of the ocean and there was no search party coming.

Sleep was impossible. I was overheating, even when I took my clothes off and kept the car windows down in the zero-Celsius winter air. Leeroy complained of the same intense heat.

One of the local street kids told us we were overheating because we were in ketoacidosis—our bodies were too acidic and were digesting themselves, muscles and all.

"You could die from it," he said. And that it was impossible to steal in Vancouver because we looked like "starving crackheads, like all the street people." It didn't help that I was Indian, he added.

The kid's name was Troy. Leeroy got along with him right away and invited him to stay with us in our car. To my dread, Troy slept in the back seat with me, a space already too cramped. Dude smelled like a sewer, and when I complained, he said I smelled even worse. I found that hard to believe.

Troy knew more about the street than we did. He was like Leeroy and never spoke about what he'd done. I knew not to ask. The other good thing he brought was his knowledge of where to sell stuff—clothes, primarily. He had a connection at a local pawnshop. I'd purchased stylish stuff with my produce job money, and piece by piece we sold my clothes and bought food—it lasted maybe three weeks until I had nothing left but one T-shirt I wore, a pair of pants, my sneakers, and a Canada soccer jersey.

Troy introduced us to job agencies and cheque-cashing places, two things I didn't even know existed, and we were always the first, along with the other immigrants and newcomers, at the job agency counter at five a.m. to get general labour jobs. We dug ditches, packed shipping containers, moved furniture, and whatever other shitty hard tasks most Canadians didn't want to do. When we got our cheques—$25 each for eight to ten hours—we'd cash them in.

"To work like a slave only to have the temp agency take half," Leeroy complained, counting out his dough and eating our regular bag of fast food, "then the cheque place gouges us even more. Where's the security?"

"That's how it is for young guys with no education in Canada," Troy said. "They made it this way—our greedy parents. Next, all the jobs will be temp."

We soon learned of a better spot where we could get picked up and toil for the day for better money. The work was much more dangerous—moving heavy cabinets that weighed nearly a thousand pounds each and took four men to move. When Troy lost his grip and one came crashing down on me on a stairway, I quit on the spot. We never did get paid for that job.

We moved on to demolitions of old homes. We got no masks, respirators, or protective gear of any kind. At the end of one day, after weeks ripping down plaster walls at various different places, my chest hurt. I coughed into a tissue and noticed a splash of blood and some yellow stuff that looked like booger cornflakes. The immigrants I worked with said they coughed it, too, said it was from all the asbestos.

"What's asbestos?" I asked. No one told me.

At the end of the three weeks, the job was done, but the employer didn't show up. We didn't get paid.

That was tough. We were trying our hardest, but we were getting ripped off, getting little sleep, rest, or comfort in the car, and we were still wasting away. Soon we gave up getting up for work and just sat in the car.

Leeroy began to cough at night. Troy, too. Greyish phlegm that smelled

163

like dirty honey shot out all over, and they both got a rash that spread up their necks and over their lips and face—red, bumpy, with peeling scales. Leeroy didn't look right. The emaciated skin over his face started to appear translucent, his green veins turned a bluish purple, his eyes pressed way back into his bones till they looked like they rested on the front of his brain. When he smiled his dimples folded into a hundred tiny creases, like he was centuries old and had lived in the desert all his life.

Troy coughed on me a couple times. I never got as sick as they did, but a few weeks later, my hair began falling out in clumps, and so did theirs, like shedding cats in spring. The cap on my front tooth broke off. It took a brittle piece of the bone under my nose with it, leaving me with a grey-and-black jagged-toothed smile. I never realized how important my smile was until then—the loss seemed to suck the joy out of interacting with anyone, more than even the starving situation did. I just couldn't smile without feeling horrible about my already dishevelled appearance.

I stopped smiling altogether.

END OF A FRIENDSHIP

LEEROY AND I WENT OUT begging. Troy had fled the week before, down to the East Side where there were food banks, churches, and shelter beds. But there were also all those zombies and hard drugs, and street people were dying there. We'd decided never to venture down there—we had a difficult enough time staying alive where we were. We'd been homeless for just over four months and were barely hanging on.

We returned to the car defeated, with no money, to find the back window shattered, glass peppered all over my sleeping spot. Night was falling and it was particularly cold for May. The intense heat of ketoacidosis had given way to an intense chill. I cleaned the glass away and tried to go to sleep, but my spine and hips were bending and shattering like layers of ice smashing up on a lake shore. I prayed for morning and the sun to warm me—I waited and waited. When light started appearing on the horizon, I sat up and peered out over the Fraser River. A bunch of logs drifted by, the movement rhythmic and silent as they floated off to their destination.

I looked down at Leeroy, his torso tucked under the steering wheel and legs stretched across the front seats. I knew then that it wasn't my place to stay in the car anymore—I don't know how I knew, but I did. Maybe it was the thought of my mortality that pulled me away, or maybe I didn't know anything other than abandonment, one of the earliest lessons my dad had left me with.

Childhood memories of my times with Leeroy filled me as the sun crested up over the mountains and called for me to let go of our friendship. I'd earned the sunlight, it was mine, and mine alone. I crept out of the car and shut the door gently, careful to not wake him.

As I rounded the corner of the parking lot onto the street, I looked back at the car and saw Leeroy's head appear, turn side to side, then disappear back down. Perhaps he thought I'd gone to the washroom. I said goodbye in my heart and wished him well and then made my way to the Trans-Canada Highway for the long hitchhike back home to Ontario.

ROU GAROUS

I hitchhiked home in early spring.
The mountains, then prairies, swollen lakes, the thickness of forests—all
    was uneventful.
But on the Trans-Canada Highway, somewhere east of the prairies
I was picked up by some farm boys around my age.
They said I looked rough and wanted to feed me, to give me a place to
    rest
So in their car I went.

We drove some distance off the main route
Down some obscure dirt road, far out of the way to an abandoned
    building.
I smelled smoke when I got out; a loon called in the distance.
The driver was kind and asked me to carve my name on a tree.
There were other names carved in too.
"Other hitchhikers," they said. "Others running, trying to get home."

As my blade cut into the trunk, I felt a fist slam into the back of my head.
Stars upon stars; I didn't see it coming.
The one boy tackled me and tried to bring me to the ground.
But my thick skull and strong spirit, they held me up.
I staggered and stumbled, arms outstretched, trying to regain my
    senses.
I ran disoriented into the forest toward where I hoped the highway was.

Warm blood poured out of my head.

It wasn't a fist they'd hit me with, I figured. It must've been a rock or
hammer.

They stalked close behind me through the brush; I ran with all my might.

My chest burning and legs barely under me,

Weakened by months of no food.

I almost gave in.

But my relatives, the trees, saw my trouble.

"Hide within us, nephew," they rustled. "Our leaves will darken their
way."

Their branches bent and covered my passage; they arched over to
save me.

Deeper into the poplars, cedars, and oaks I fled,

A good three miles.

My attackers' footsteps fell silent, their voices trailed off.

In time, I chanced upon good old Highway One.

It felt safe,

Like some mighty river of asphalt that had the current to carry me
home.

I stood there all night with my thumb out, begging to be picked up.

I waved my arms at each passing vehicle but no one stopped.

Or even slowed down.

NEVER THE SAME

"THAT GIRL DANCING NEAR THE base bin is fine," Rex said as he tilted his rum and Coke toward the stage of the nightclub.

I barely had my legs under me, still reeling from the long hitchhike to Toronto and malnutrition. When I got back home, friends commented that I looked like I was dying of starvation. Some were afraid to talk to me. Perhaps they just didn't want to think about how far my addictions had taken me, or that they were headed there, too.

"She fine," I agreed. But my eyes were more interested in Rex's drink than the girl, its ice glistened with each strobe of the lights. House music shook the empty glasses splayed out over the bar, left there by a bartender who, I knew, was too busy doing rails of coke to properly serve customers. Rex had a hell of a time getting his first drink, yelling four or five times before he finally got her attention. My stomach growled, a mixture of hunger and cravings. The memory of the taste of whiskey welled up, reminding me that I had no money and no business being in a club.

"I love this song," Rex said, pumping his hand in the air. The DJ had mixed in the latest track from Chicago—the mecca of house music—and Rex, in his excitement, spilled some of his drink on the man in front of us. Neither noticed. I watched and waited for the ecstasy pill I'd just taken to kick in. I lived for that Chicago sound, an amalgam of gritty four-and-four house beats, old-school funk, and gospel lyrics. No one did it better. No one.

"I'm waiting for my E to kick in," I hollered over to Rex, trying to be heard over top of the throbbing baseline. "Can you buy me a drink?" The beat finally dropped and the crowd went wild, asses gyrating everywhere. "Can you spot me for a drink?" I yelled one more time. Rex didn't hear and continued to thrust his drink in the air, watering the crowd in front of him. I tried again. "Bro!" I yelled and grabbed his arm. "I'm fucking dying over here—I need a drink."

Rex turned to me and said, "You should have said something sooner," his jaw chattering, his pupils wide open. His E had taken effect.

Lucky bastard, I thought. I wondered why I wasn't feeling anything.

"Hey!" he screamed over to the barkeep. "Gimme two rum and Cokes." She heard him right away and fired two tumblers down the bar. Rex dropped a twenty-dollar bill on the bar and she snatched it up without offering change. He handed me my drink.

"Cheers," he said, and we clinked our glasses together and looked out over the crowd of gorgeous women. I again noticed the woman near the base bin—she was beautiful. My belly warmed as the rum settled under my ribs, sending a rush of ecstasy up my spine. A swell of spectacular pins and needles broke over the top of my scalp. My eyelids fluttered, and I braced myself against the bar, waiting for the impeding tsunami of rapture. My knees buckled.

"There he goes," Rex said. His eyes looked like a shark's eyes right before the kill—completely black. I tried to smile back at him but my jaw took on a life of its own, chattering up and down. It was good E—the best kind—the kind that slams into your gut and impregnates you with a cloud of migrating monarchs, fluttering your intestines into a writhing swarm of uncontrollable pleasure.

We'd scored our E earlier from our dealer, a trustworthy guy named Island. He sold primarily to the underground gay clubs on Church Street that always had the best drugs and newest music. My friends had found that out early on, that's how we met Island, and that's how we got high as fuck on $40 Es. Most other dealers sold Es at $10 or $20, but they weren't really methylenedioxymethamphetamine (MDMA), just a mix of cheap crystal meth, caffeine, and maybe a little heroin for euphoric effect. But Island took care of us proper.

"These Es are killer," Rex said. He placed his empty glass on the bar, then rifled through his pockets. I thought he was going to give me another pill, but he pulled out a wad of bills, leafed off $40, and handed it to me. "I know you're broke. I'm just glad you're here, safe. Not hitchhiking across the continent, starving and shit."

I took the money, at a loss for words. I could barely make out Rex's face, the visual vibration was so jarring. "I love you, dude," I said, the words gurgled up out of my throat in a moment of euphoria. I heard them, but hadn't wanted to say them. Sweat poured down my face, dripped off my chin.

"I know that, guy," Rex said as he wiped my face. "We're brothers. One love."

He dapped my hand as the throb of the house music picked up.

We did love each other. It was a camaraderie, a closeness, a fellowship. A connection with the universe that's hard to explain but that happens with E—almost like you turn into Jesus, Gandhi, and Mother Teresa all rolled into one, not a problem in the world, caring for all things at once, a connection you never forget and always yearn for after you've sobered up, and when you mix it with sex, it was even more powerful.

"Listen," Rex said as he grabbed my hand and pulled me back from total ecstasy. "Someone's paged and I gotta go over to Spadina. Meet me there at four a.m." He slapped my cheek to get my attention. I retrained my sights on his face, but had trouble focusing. He was melting, blurring, fading into another dimension. A wall of colours filled my vision: a kaleidoscope of disco-ball refractions. He was somewhere in there.

"Yeah. Got it. Buzz. See you there." I held on to the bar for dear life. His shape was coming in clearer, but still wasn't quite there yet.

"I ordered another drink for you," Rex said before leaving. "It should be along shortly." He winked at the bartender, and she fired another rum and Coke down the bar. It landed in front of me, leaving tracers in its wake. I needed toothpicks to prop my eyes open, and my stomach flipped as the liquid splashed and swirled down.

Was there something different about these E pills, or was it the drink I'd left unattended in my stupor? It was hard to tell. My feet were two hot-air balloons floating high above the Paris fairgrounds, simultaneously lighter than air and heavier than the compressed core of a star for twenty minutes after Rex left. Finding purchase on the ground was nearly impossible. Flashes of black blinded me as I stumbled forward onto the dance floor. I pleaded for help. The other partiers just backed away and shot me expressions of disgust. I stumbled and fell, dropping my drink, the tumbler shattering. My mind was confused, groggy, dark. I thought maybe if I found some coke or speed I might be able to perk up, shake off whatever was happening. I thought I saw Island near the stage and so made my way toward it. I staggered, zigzagging, as far as the base bin where the beautiful girl was dancing, then collapsed.

When I awoke I was on the other side of the club near the washrooms, some forty feet away. The floor was still packed, the music was louder, people were dancing faster, and the bar was closed but decorated with drunk girls giving strip shows, and everyone was way more fucked up. I was still disoriented.

As I pushed myself up the wall off the floor, I noticed that my belt was undone, and my pants were open and hanging off my waist. My underwear was gone. I knew I'd been wearing underwear when I got to the club.

There was a deep pain in my intestines, radiating from my rectum, down across my testicles and penis. I panicked and hobbled over into the washroom and one of the stalls. I wadded up a pad of toilet paper and wiped it across my anus. A dark stain of fresh blood appeared on it. I couldn't believe what I was seeing. I ran my fingers over my bum and discovered that I had what appeared to be hemorrhoids. I tried pushing them in but they hurt more than anything I'd ever experienced—I touched them gently again. I'd never had hemorrhoids before, or whatever these were. I tried to understand what had happened, who was around me before I fell unconscious, why I woke up near the washroom, or why what appeared to be my intestines were hanging out of my bum.

I can't remember how I got home, or even where I actually went—there was nothing but a dense black fog in my memory. I saw nothing but darkness, confusion.

A deep feeling of shame shrouded my soul.

A GUST OF MOLECULES

THE PHONE RINGING PIERCED THE night calm. I rolled off the couch and went into the kitchen to pick it up.

It was Uncle Ralph. "Jesse. Go get Ronald." The urgency in his voice was unnerving.

I ran to Uncle Ron's room, Solomon, my uncle's Rhodesian ridge-back, trotting behind me to investigate the commotion. "Ralph's on the phone," I said as I pushed on Uncle Ron's foot. "Wake up."

He shifted and squinted at the alarm clock—3:40 a.m.—then shot out of bed and into the kitchen.

"What's wrong?" he barked into the receiver. He cleared the sleep from his eyes and waved me away. "Everything okay?"

I moved into the sunroom to eavesdrop but could only hear the static of Ralph's voice and Uncle Ron's "Uh-huh, uh-huh." I stared out the window at the treetops bending in the nighttime wind and hoped the call wasn't about Grandpa or Grandma.

Uncle Ron said, "I'll be right there," and then hung up and bolted out to the car without a word. I watched the car's tail lights disappear into the darkness. I placed a chair next to the window. My adrenaline would keep me awake. Solomon sat by my side.

Uncle Ron had been living in Port Hope with his daughter, who was just sixteen, since she started getting into trouble in Toronto. He figured she'd stay out of trouble out in the country. I thought it was a smart move on his part.

I'd been with them for five months. Uncle Ron got word that I was sleeping at the airport and couch surfing with friends, slipping further into addiction.

The assault at the club left me struggling, grabbing nothing but sand. One never thinks it will happen to them until it does. You are never the same and it's always there.

I had managed to sober up while I'd been in Port Hope with Uncle Ron, somehow, but I was still smoking weed trying to sort through everything that had happened. Uncle Ron represented safety to me, even though I couldn't bring myself to tell him what had happened.

At 7:30 a.m. the next day, Uncle Ron pulled back into the driveway. I was still staring out the window, after downing pot after pot of coffee and smoking cigarette after cigarette. My teeth buzzed like I'd eaten a hive of bees. Uncle Ron slumped over the steering wheel. The car was still running but the car stereo was off—and he always drove with '70s rock blaring.

He finally got out of the car and made his way to the house. I heard the grind of gravel with each step. I poured a cup of coffee and left it on the table. The floorboards creaked as he found his way upstairs and sat down. It appeared he'd been crying, which was odd to me, since he was so powerful, so full of male bravado—I didn't know he could cry.

I was afraid to ask what had happened and went back into the sunroom to my chair by the window. A stand of trees caught my eye, the tops of the birch branches dancing in the wind, the sun tangled up in their rusty leaves. The clink of Uncle Ron's spoon against the sides of his mug sounded out like a chorus of sledgehammers striking railway ties. He cleared his throat and asked me to join him.

"I don't know how to say it," he said, not looking at me, another oddity. I pulled up a chair to the table, as silent as I could be.

"Grandma got a call last night," he began. "From 22 Division in Etobicoke. The police picked up a homeless man last night—he said his name was Ron Thistle—but that's me. The homeless guy knew everything about me—my birthdate, what hospital I was born in, my arrest record, everything about Grandma and Grandpa, my siblings' names and birthdates." Uncle Ron pulled a joint from his pack of smokes and lit it, careful not to singe his hair. He took a moment before he spoke.

"Grandma told them I was out here in Port Hope."

He released a cloud of smoke into the air, then broke into a fit of coughing and handed the spliff my way. We had that between us—weed as a balm to dull the sharp edges of the world, weed as a crutch against addiction. I took a huge draw and held it in, my attention focused on him.

"Mom knew it was Sonny, your dad," he said. "Mother's intuition."

I passed the joint back and waited for him to finish.

"Only Sonny knows all my stuff," he said. His eyes were a little redder now. It was hard to tell if it was the weed.

I watched a tendril of white smoke twist from the head of the blunt. It reminded me of when Uncle Ron took me out on his collections back when I was a kid. I pictured us in his red convertible singing and bopping our heads as he smoked weed—I didn't know then that that was what he was smoking. An image of my dad begging out on Yonge Street came to me. His hands and mind slowed by winter lethargy, his clothes loose and hanging off his wasted body. I thought of Vancouver, of Leeroy's car, of the Fraser River, of sleeping with nowhere to go.

Uncle Ron rolled the end of the joint in the bottom of the glass ashtray, knocking off the excess ash, and handed it back me. It sat idle in my index and middle fingers, digits yellowed from constant use.

"Mom phoned Ralph because he's a cop," Uncle Ron said. "She wanted him to identify the man at 22, but he couldn't leave work, so he called me."

I flicked the joint and watched the ember glow red. I kept looking down, afraid of what Uncle Ron would say next.

He reached over and grabbed my free hand. "They let the guy go before I could get there." His voice wavered.

I could feel my hand going numb.

"The officer said it was because of shift change—they clear the drunks out of the bullpen at five a.m. before the day officers come in. I got there at 5:15. Fifteen minutes too late. I'm so sorry, Jesse."

I tried to follow Uncle Ron's words, but it was as if his lips were moving in slow motion. Dad was gone. He didn't care enough to stay. He didn't want to come back home.

Nothing mattered. It was as if an atomic blast followed. The stand of trees was sucked forward, then blown back with such force they were obliterated. The citizens of Port Hope were vaporized into carbon imprints on the broken cityscape. An old man walking with his cane, a mother holding her baby, a little girl playing in the park—all were transformed into shadows of daily life atomically scorched onto the concrete of sidewalks and roadways, and I was now one of those shadow people. I gazed down at my hand and saw nothing but Uncle Ron grasping a carbon handprint fused onto the table's surface.

It's pointless, I thought, *my destruction is complete*.

The next week I left Port Hope and began drifting again.

SUBURBAN WASTELANDS

MOST OF MY FRIENDS HAD moved on. Brian had gone to university, Leeroy was still out west, Derick was with a new crew, some had moved downtown for jobs. Others just didn't want me around when I got back from Port Hope. I showed up pleading for help and they literally shut the door in my face.

I tripped around for a few months, staying in bus shelters, sleeping in the mall during the day, and staying nights at the top of apartment building staircases. Many times, like a beat-up piece of old driftwood, I washed up on the doorstep of Olive, a church lady who believed in the word of Jesus Christ. Olive was the mother of a friend from high school. She wasn't like the usual hypocrites in church, though, she actually lived it in her daily life. She'd take in youths and make them feel loved, feeding and clothing them, giving them shelter when needed, and she let me in, then tried whittling me into something that resembled a human being. I hated listening to her preach, but she did make the Bible something I could understand.

I couldn't stay at Olive's all the time, though. I discovered that Brampton had emergency shelters. I tried a men's shelter first. It was a converted old fire hall, a rough place that reeked of old feet and broken dreams. The intake worker told me I was too young to stay there. "The women's shelter is safer for you," he said. "Here are a few bus tickets. I'll call so they know you're coming."

When I got to the Sally Ann, I got my own room—small, private, with a bed, dresser, bathroom, and full access to a kitchen—and a fresh change of clothes. I lay on the bed, listening to the creak of the plastic protecting the mattress sounding sweeter than an angel's voice, and thought, *I'm in heaven*. But things didn't stay heavenly for long.

"Who is that *man* making himself a Pop-Tart in the toaster? I don't feel safe with him here!" one lady complained to the frontline staff.

"He's been kicked out of his home," he said. But she kept on. It was clear I was unwanted, so I left.

I begged for money at a strip mall and made my way downtown. I paid the ten- or fifteen-dollar admissions at after-hours raves, clubs, or booze cans, doing drugs and dancing, and ended up sleeping in a corner for a few hours every couple days. New drugs—crystal meth and ketamine—were around, and I started to do and sell both in small batches, gathering enough money to buy food and admission to the next club. They were cheaper than cocaine. I tried to stay away from ketamine, though, because of its sedative effects—the dreaded "K-hole" that left you defenceless and comatose but awake somehow.

The assault was always in the back of my mind.

There was an underground club or rave every day of the week in Toronto, always a place to go to next. There was a whole community of young castaways like me. I liked being around them—they didn't give a shit that I was half Indian, had darker skin, and didn't have a clue who I was or where I was going—and all of us slowly became hooked on meth. I developed sores all over, my nostrils became red and inflamed, and my waistline shrank and shrank. I spent hours picking away at what I believed were bugs burrowing under my skin. It would escalate the longer I was awake—sometimes up to 124 hours at a time. I'd see worms wriggle on my feet, on my forearms, or near my crotch, and I'd scratch at them until my nails ripped the skin open and pulled out my veins. Then I'd repick those scabs, convinced the bugs were still there. My stomach was digesting my intestines. My breath smelled like rotten blood and juicy trash boiled in acid, and it hurt to swallow.

The state of things terrified me, and I took off back to Brampton. I stayed with a buddy for a month, but he had the same problems I had, so I moved on and knocked on Jerry's door. He had an apartment of his own he rented with one of his friends.

"I don't even recognize you," he said when he answered. "What happened?"

"I just can't stop," I said.

I recall him grabbing me and barricading me in his room. I shivered and sweated and thought I was going crazy as the drugs left my system. Every time I tried to leave, he tackled and restrained me and stuck me back in the room and re-bolted the door. Sometimes the door would crack open and a sub sandwich would fly into the middle of the room and land by my feet. I'd eat it and then pass out and have the worst nightmares— zombies eating themselves, the farm boys smashing my skull in, Clive's head exploding in his blue house, Yorkie running backward up the wall like he was possessed by demons.

As I emerged from my chemical haze, there were days when I sat with my ear glued to the wall while Jerry battled with his friends in the living room, negotiating a spot for me to stay on the couch after I sobered up. No one was keen on letting me live there.

When I could, I collected my things in a garbage bag and left.

FAMILY WEDDING

"KEEP SIX," I WHISPERED TO my little brother, Daniel, who stood near the mirror in the Value Village Clothing store in Vancouver. I ducked down and pivoted, blocking the line of sight to the cashier. I grabbed a sports blazer, a pair of black slacks, a white button-up shirt, a belt, a pair of dress shoes, and a skinny black tie and stuffed them in my plastic grocery bag.

"She's coming, she's coming," Daniel said, a note of panic in his voice. I glanced in the mirror and saw a lady in a red employee's smock. She'd been pricing men's shoes two aisles over. I threw the bag under the rack and stood up to greet her. She yanked the bag out, opened it, and threatened to call the police. Daniel and I backpedalled, and then ran out the front door and down the street.

She'd fallen for the ruse. I'd gone in behind Daniel and changed into a suit, tie, and shoes before anyone noticed, then told Daniel to keep an eye out. He had amateur written all over his face. He gawked around like he was doing something wrong, pacing back and forth, while I stuffed the decoy bag full of things—which caught the attention of the store employee who focused on the bag instead of the suit I was wearing. It was an old trick I'd learned.

"How'd you learn to steal like that?" Daniel asked.

"That was nothing." To me, it was just another day at the office. I picked a butt off the ground and lit it. The truth was I didn't know, it just came naturally, kind of like breathing.

It was the first time I'd seen my little brother since he and Mom had disappeared with George years before. When Josh phoned Jerry and invited me to his September wedding, he said we'd put aside our differences and be cordial on his big day, and that he'd pay for my flight out west if I could just get it together long enough to look human. He said it'd be the first time all us brothers would be together again—that it was important I be there.

I jumped at the chance to see my baby brother, and to witness Josh and his fiancée, Margaret, get married. I was lucky to have caught the call—I circled back to Jerry's just to check in or crash periodically—but I was glad I did. I wouldn't have missed the wedding for the world. The suit I'd just nicked was too tight. I bent over and polished my shoes with some spit. They, too, weren't my size. But it would all have to do.

Daniel picked a ball of lint off my blazer and brushed my shoulder. He had features so much like mine, but he was better and healthier looking.

We'd met up earlier that day at the church and got along right away. Mom was there, too, and we'd kissed and all that good stuff, like reunited long-lost mother and son, which is what we were, then I'd pulled Daniel aside.

"Dude, I can't go dressed like this." I pointed at my clothes. They weren't that bad, street garb, just not dressy enough for my brother's wedding. I informed him that I needed a wingman.

Daniel said he'd help right away. I think he wanted to hang out with me. My reputation preceded me, I guessed.

"What happened to you?" I asked him as we headed back to the chapel, fearful that the ass crack in my pants might split wide open. "You and Mom just kind of fell off the map."

"We had to run away."

I could hear the tension in his voice as we crossed the street and picked up the pace.

"There'd be spit flying everywhere," Daniel said about George's fits of rage. "One day, Mom had enough. She pulled me from school and we went to Saskatoon. We left so fast, Mom only had one shoe and I didn't have a coat. I'm sorry we didn't call."

"It's okay, Daniel. I've been messed up. I wouldn't have had much to say."

I sat outside the reception hall for a lot of the night, smoking. The place was crowded with out-of-uniform RCMP officers, Josh's colleagues, and their presence made me jumpy. Grandpa was there, too, and he gave me cut eye so bad I'm sure he was casting a malevolent spell on me. When I tried to speak to him during the photo shoot, he walked away. Jerry told me I was only attending because Josh had gone to bat for me.

I bumped into Grandma on the way to the washroom, though, and she said, "You look good," pinching my cheeks, and slipping a $100 bill in my pocket. "Now smarten up!" It was the only contact we had.

Mom's family was there, as well, my aunts and about seven cousins my age from Saskatchewan. They sat in a section off to the side by themselves but were super friendly, mingling, laughing, drinking, and carrying on—they were the best dancers in the joint—but I didn't really interact with them. Jerry stuck by my side, going inside to dance when a song he liked came on, and we shared bottle after bottle until the world spun around us.

Mom came out to join us about halfway through the festivities.

"Look at you," she said to me, a cigarette in one hand, a glass of red wine in the other. She swayed a little and sat between me and Jerry. Jerry pulled back.

"I hear you're a little troublemaker." She smiled. She was half in the bag, but still very much alert. I wondered if it was her way of mustering up the courage to talk to us. "That's okay," she said. "I still love you no matter what." She hugged me close and the awkwardness fled. It'd been years since we embraced.

"Here," my aunt Cecile said, "a whore's breakfast." She thrust an empty plate with two aspirins on it at me, and then handed me an open beer. I swallowed the pills and took a few chugs to wash them down. I handed back the empty bottle, and she winked and clicked her teeth. A few minutes later the pounding in my head stopped. My hangover was gone.

The smell of eggs and bacon was strong in the kitchen. We'd spent the night after the wedding at my auntie's place. She shuffled around the stove with a cigarette hanging out of her mouth as my other relatives squirmed about, still trying to sleep out on the dining room floor. Their names escaped me, but they all looked familiar. One guy looked like Josh but was slimmer. I recognized my aunt Yvonne, who sat on the couch reading a magazine.

"*Chi garçon, mon bébé*," she said to me, and then a bunch of stuff that sounded French but not quite.

"He doesn't have a clue, *Pedour*," Aunt Cecile said. "He's been gone for *vingt ans*."

"*Mon dieu!*" Aunt Yvonne bellowed. "You can't speak Michif anymore?"

Michif, I thought. *What's that?*

Aunt Cecile said something as my mom came out of the bedroom. She had a big smile on her face, like she'd already consumed Aunt Cecile's special breakfast. She said something back, and my aunties started laughing.

"I spoke Michif?" I asked.

"God, yes." Mom chuckled. "You didn't say a word until you were three, but then we couldn't shut you up!"

Aunt Cecile howled in the kitchen and my mom started to laugh so hard I thought she might pee herself.

One of my cousins sat up and said, "Yeah, and you covered everything in shit when you got upset. Dirty little bugger." Her accent was thicker than Aunt Yvonne's. *"Li Shicock.* Gross!"

Again, the room busted up.

"Never mind them," Mom said. "You were a clean boy. My boy."

"We're just playing," Aunt Yvonne brayed. "It's so good to see you." She got up and squeezed me, and her arms were like powerful bear arms. I hugged back but she was way stronger than me.

Aunt Cecile put a plate of eggs on the counter. "This is mine. All you *chyins* have to fend for yourselves." She laughed and started eating. "But there's tea made." She motioned to the kitchen table, where a teapot squatted on a lace doily.

I sat down and poured myself a cup, and Mom pulled up the chair next to me. It was hard to make eye contact without alcohol coursing through my veins. She was a complete stranger. Her sisters were hovering around like bees pollinating flowers.

"I know you've been all over," she said. She twiddled her thumbs and drew in a deep breath.

There was a jar of jam beside the teapot—"Saskatoons," it read. I focused on that. I thought of Kokum Nancy and her Coke-bottle glasses and her walking stick.

"How would you like to come home with me?"

Aunt Yvonne moved behind me and placed her hands on my shoulders.

"Mom, it's been years . . ." I could hear the tick of the clock and Aunt Cecile's breathing—she sounded like she was having a heart attack.

"It wouldn't have to be forever, Jesse," Aunt Yvonne jumped in. "Just try it out. Saskatoon is a wonderful little city."

"Um . . . I don't think so. I live in Toronto—all my friends are there. Jerry, too."

Aunt Cecile swung open the back door, and I heard something smash.

"There's work and lots of Métis girls for a handsome young man like yourself," Aunt Yvonne said, this time in my ear.

"But my home is Toronto." I felt like I had to defend my point. "I'm sorry." It was like they'd been waiting for me to wake up just to ask me this question. *Did Josh and Jerry set this up to get rid of me?* I started getting angry. I was certain my brothers were behind this.

Mom stood up, called Daniel, grabbed her keys, and marched downstairs. She and Daniel loaded up her car. Daniel asked me to reconsider, and I could tell he was trying to defuse the tension; she was hurt.

I think she really expected me to accept.

CRACK

FOUR OF US WERE HUDDLED around the coffee table in my buddy's Brampton apartment. We poked holes in our pop cans, near the base, the thumbtacks moaning as they bit through the aluminum. The resulting circle of about twenty holes was around the size of a dime. I had mine done in seconds.

"The ash goes on there." My buddy flicked his cigarette so ash covered the holes and flattened the burnt carbon with his thumb, and then waited for us to do the same. Then he pulled a little white rock from his sock and took the plastic wrap off it.

"I've got a chicken here—seven grams." He held up the walnut-sized piece of drywall-looking drug. "Costs a lot, but I'm serving you all free. Just remember to come to me afterward. Enjoy, boys." He broke the piece in quarters and handed one to each of us. "Just watch what I do." He snapped a little fragment off his quarter and placed it on his can, in the centre of the ashes. His fingers shook a little like he was holding a precious jewel. We followed his lead.

I put a particularly large piece on my can.

Ready.

He flicked his lighter and held the open flame over his crack toke and it melted into the ash. It sizzled a bit, like a tiny skillet cooking bacon. He put his mouth to the opening of his pop can and sucked in, gently pulling the flame down. The wet spot where the melted rock was sizzled louder, then collapsed in upon itself. He held in the smoke for a minute and then exhaled. It smelled like burnt cotton candy mixed with fried plastic—sweet but chemical. His chin started wagging and a line of drool rolled over his lip onto the carpet. He tried to speak but a moan came out. The rest of us lit up.

When I released my lungful of crack like a dragon blasting a plume of fire on some medieval castle, the most intense feeling vibrated my brain. I could hear the loudest ringing I've ever heard, like a locomotive train rushing by an inch from my ear. I placed my can down and the void within was filled to overflowing. I felt like a god, superhuman. Like a hundred thousand roman candles were going off in my soul. When that initial high dissipated, I did it again, and again, and again until my little quarter section was gone.

Then I got down on all fours to search the carpet for any remnants that might have fallen.

My buddies did the same.

We kept searching.

I was hooked.

CANADIAN STREETS GREASY WITH INDIGENOUS FAT

The secret history tells us
Once, a blue wolf arose from the soil.
He took as his mate a fallow deer.
There, at the head of the sea
A son was born.

Descendants of that son
Travelled light upon the grasslands
Using speed and surprise.
They learned to own nothing, to adapt to all conditions
And burning dry dung for warmth.

From out of the eastern sunrise, these homeless nomads rode.
On horseback they came,
Setting everything ablaze.
They littered the stolen streets with their bodies
And left them greasy with their own fat.

CAUGHT UP

IT WAS THE TURN OF the millennium, but the day after Y2K was odd—no crash, no power outages, no blood or violence in the streets, no Armageddon. The only thing that seemed out of place was the red University of Nevada, Las Vegas (UNLV) basketball jersey I was wearing. It was new, with the university team's fighting southern rebel mascot in the middle.

I didn't have much these days. I was with Uncle Ron drinking beer at his apartment—he'd moved back in with Jerry after his daughter had graduated high school and had moved back to the city herself. I'd begged him and Jerry for a place to stay after most of my stuff had been stolen from a local shelter, and was lucky they'd agreed. Ron and I were watching *The Saint*, starring Val Kilmer. Random farts from Solomon perfumed the stale air, reminding me that I shouldn't have fed him wet food.

I'd spent the previous night, New Year's Eve, at a friend's party. We drank ourselves into oblivion, singing and wearing those stupid Y2K glasses. As the clock edged close to midnight we congregated in the hot tub and blazed a series of fat joints, then waited for the subsequent hellfire to rip apart our lives. The girl next to me pulled down her bikini top and showed me her breasts—their fleshy presence complemented the celebratory cheers and horns that resounded throughout the house. I grabbed her and gave her a sloppy kiss to welcome in the new millennium. I think she appreciated the distraction because her tongue darted around in my mouth. There was no magic between us—we were just two young people trying to forget about the impending calamity, the emotionless kiss just an available tool of diversion.

After we unhinged our faces, I grabbed my bag of blow and cut two shoelace-sized lines on the edge of the tub. Drugs helped me forget everything I didn't want to think about and made me feel good about myself. I snorted mine first, she followed and then rubbed the leftover residue across her gums with her finger and brayed like a horse. The coke kept us up for another few hours, but there was no sex, even though we did try in the bedroom upstairs—I just couldn't get it up. Hard liquor and blow had that effect on me.

Then the music faded, conversations died out, people bid their farewells, and it was time to go. I thought of her tits as I stumbled home, and was mad at myself for not being a man, for not capitalizing. When I reached Uncle Ron's I was still wired. I leered at myself in the bathroom mirror, and my eyes looked like two piss holes in the snow.

Sleep is impossible tonight, I concluded.

I decided to go farther down the road, to see if anyone was still up over at Olive's, the church lady, where, unknown to her, our crew had our headquarters. When I got there, Olive's son Frank was up watching TV. He told me that the new hang-abouts, Stefan and Mike, two neighbourhood street kids who had no real home like me, had left a few hours before to go out on a "mission."

"What kind of a mission? Deliver drugs, shoplift at the drug store, sell shit—what?"

"I don't know." Frank shrugged.

I could tell he wanted me to leave. I couldn't blame the kid. His house had a revolving door. Olive's Christian mission sometimes left her family crowded in their own home and often without food. Frank, who was just sixteen, had done more mission work, I figured, than many pastors had done over decades in Africa. He was the same as his mom—kind, giving, and open to a fault—even if he wasn't religious. He never raised his voice around any of us, and we'd become good friends.

"Do they have dope?" I asked as I slipped my shoes back on.

"Naw. They smoked it all before they left." Frank got up. "You don't have to go," he grumbled as he shuffled past me to the washroom. "We got PB and J and bread in the cupboard, and you're welcome to it if you want."

If Jesus was like anyone, I believe he was like Frank, but without the Mohawk hairdo, facial piercings, and torn-to-shreds punk attire. But the thought of a sweet sandwich made my stomach turn, the liquor and coke sloshing around all toxic.

"Where's Tim?" I asked. He was Frank's brother. He was eighteen, looked like Alice Cooper when Cooper was young and scary—black eyeliner, black clothes, black hair shaved up the sides—and he was the opposite of his younger sibling. The constant cavalcade of homeless people in the house had hardened him, made him into what can only be described as a pure metal hell spawn who slaughtered daily goodwill by blasting Marilyn Manson and Slipknot over top of the sound of the church organ Olive had in the living room.

I'm sure that eerie mix of gospel hymns and hard-core thrash traumatized me, but Tim's reaction to all the commotion and Christian indoctrination was strange considering that most of the transient guests were *his* friends—teenaged goth misfits from group homes and juvenile detention centres who had been disowned by their families or had fled domestic abuse situations. It left me wondering if it was all some big act Tim put on as a defence against the biblical-level chaos going on around him.

"He's not here," Frank said. The sound of piss echoed in the toilet bowl. "Been gone for a couple of days." I heard the toilet flush, then he returned to his chair to flip through the channels.

I left and went back up the road to Uncle Ron's to catch some sleep.

I awoke around nine a.m. to Solomon licking my face—I was on my makeshift bed in the middle of the sunroom floor and that was his sign he needed a walk. I could hear Uncle Ron and Jerry groaning in their rooms, and a ten-dollar bill magically appeared from under my brother's door.

"Take him out, Jess," Jerry said, his voice as raspy as a desert toad.

"My fucking head's pounding." The place was filled with vodka bottles and ashtrays overflowing with joint roaches. Zig-Zag rolling papers were strewn across the sofa, looking like a trail leading up to a mountain of cigarette butts cascading over the edge of the coffee table.

Must've been one helluva scorcher, I chuckled to myself as I snatched up the money and took the dog out for his shit.

Armed with a little cash for dope, I returned Solomon to the apartment and again made my way down to Olive's. It was eleven a.m. and Mike and Stefan were in the middle of the kitchen throwing dice. Mike dressed like a flashy Puff Daddy crossed with Eminem. He looked Scottish or something, but it was hard to tell. Stefan easily pegged as Italian—olive skin and a Roman nose, and he talked with his hands and said things like "forget about it" and "mangia cake." He was much harder around the edges than anyone in our hood. He dressed like a professional weed dealer and his hair was tied up in a ponytail and was covered in a do-rag, and he had a Yankees hat perched perfectly atop his head. He'd once told me that he'd come to Canada from the United States after he'd gotten into some serious trouble down there. He towered over me and Mike and anyone else at Olive's.

Their friend, Stan, a black kid, was behind the circle of dice players holding the day's winnings. He was born with a club foot and had a severe limp and some cognitive challenges, and it was his job to dish out the round's payout to whoever threw sevens or elevens. Stan was trustworthy and always treated everyone with whatever he had—dope, food, booze, which was rare around us younger street people. I liked Stan, even if I didn't understand what he said half the time, his stutter was so bad.

There were a few other kids I didn't know rifling through the fridge.

"Y-yo, J-Jesse," Stan stuttered. "You-you w-wanna p-play?"

"I can't. I only have ten bucks," I said, "and I want to smoke a dube." I yanked out my lone bill and dangled it mid-air, hoping someone would step up and break open their weed sack and let me have a gram.

Stan smiled. "I'm a-all out-t, b-buddy."

193

Stefan reached into his pocket and hauled out a lean fold of bills. "I'm a-all o-out, bu-buddy." He curled up his arm and held it like a little T. Rex arm, then contorted his face. The room exploded in laugher. Stan froze and stuttered but no words came out. They all sounded like a wild pack of hyenas, and I wanted to fucking punch Stefan in the head.

Stefan peeled back the layers of his billfold, counting out his cash like he was Tony Montana in *Scarface*. He only had around $100, but to us it was like having a fortune, and he knew it.

"We had a good night," he said. He grinned and punched Mike's shoulder.

"Yeah, good night." Mike's voice petered out and he gazed a thousand-mile stare down at the linoleum floor.

Olive's music started up in the next room, so I knew she hadn't gone to church. The sound of her singing psalms cut through the tension. I expected Tim's music to soon drown her out, but he still wasn't home, apparently. I saw Frank get up from the sofa to go into his bedroom, and he waved to me on his way.

"Number one rule," Stefan went on, raising his voice above Olive's melodic petition of David. "Don't rat." The room fell silent.

What Stefan said was true: We were bound by a code—the code of silence. You only talked about what you did with those you did it with—it was better to not know than to know and have a secret that could eventually find its way out. That was our only protection.

Stefan repeated the sentiment slowly, this time running his thumb across his throat. I'd seen lots of guys warn dudes to keep their mouths shut before, but the way Stan cowered made my skin crawl.

One of the kids near the fridge stepped forward to put a glass on the table and fill it with juice. He took a swig and then said, "I got a gram," and flicked a little green baggy my way. It bounced and landed square in front of me. He either didn't care about Stefan and his warning or was too daft to listen.

"Thanks." I opened it, rolled up a pregnant spliff, and invited the room out. Only Stefan, Mike, and Stan accepted and we went out to our spot at the side of the building. Stan trailed behind me. Mike and Stefan shifted from corner to corner, staying in the shadows.

"I don't want to be out here too long," Mike said, ducking behind the cement wall blocking the view of the building next to us. Stefan joined him and kept his eyes on the pathway near the road. Stan and I held our ground out in the open as we blazed up the joint and each took a toke. Sirens in the distance moaned and whined, a familiar sound in the hood. They were much too far away to catch us, but I kept my eyes peeled regardless. Stan took another drag, then passed it off to Stefan. He, then Mike, took a short, almost non-drag then passed it back to me.

"T-that's b-boy d-dem," Stan said, his eyes trained on mine. "L-lots of squad c-cars 'round here l-last night—t-they even had the g-ghetto bird in the air." He made the noise of a helicopter and pretended to duck low. He nudged my arm. "C-careful, J-Jess."

Mike and Stefan fell dead silent watching Stan, then cackled, only softer and more sinister than in the kitchen.

Stan whispered again, so only I could hear. "Be careful."

Mike stopped laughing. "Yo, blood, I see you got some bunk clothes, homeless motherfucker. You like my jersey?" He pointed down to his UNLV shirt, pulling at the bottom to make the team's logo more visible. It was this season's. I couldn't afford something that nice.

"Yeah, dog, it's fresh," I said. "I wish I was dipped out like that, but I'm jus—"

"You can have it," Stefan interrupted, "if you can help us out."

His offer hung in the air as I took another drag.

"Sure," I said, releasing the smoke. "What do you want?"

Stan started shaking his head, his lips pursed shut. Mike walked in front of him.

"Two things," Stefan continued. "We're trying to go out west tonight and know you have connections—can you link us with a place to go? Maybe even a ride?"

I took another puff. Seemed reasonable—ride, place to stay, no problem.

"And we hungry as fuck," Stefan said, rubbing his belly and smiling. "Can you do us a solid and order us a pizza? I ain't no good at it and don't like talking on the phone neither. Plus, we'll give you a whole pizza on your own for doing it."

"Order you pizza? What the fuck is wrong with you?" I laughed and coughed on smoke, the pressure burning my throat and chest. I noticed Stan was gone. He must've slipped in through the side door, didn't even stay to finish the blunt.

"Okay. Give me the jersey right now and I'll do it." As long as I didn't have to do anything sexual or pay out money to get clothed and fed, I was game to do whatever they were asking.

Mike pulled the jersey off and gave it to me and I slipped it on.

"One more thing," Stefan said. "Just ask for the ride—don't say who it's for."

"Whatever," I said as I admired my new dips—it fit snug around my waist and looked crisp as it hung over my frame.

When we got indoors, I got on the phone with my buddy Shawn, a friend I'd hitchhiked and gone to high school with. Shawn said he could hook up a place to stay in Calgary, but that the ride would be harder to find. I knew he was puzzled by my request—I knew how to travel long distance, I knew how to hitchhike, and I already knew people to stay with in Calgary any time. Before I got off the phone, I made a mistake: I let it slip that the ride wasn't for me. But I wasn't clear who it was for.

"That makes a little more sense," Shawn said as he hung up. "I was wondering if you'd banged your head somewhere."

Next, I ordered three large pizzas, and tailored my very own just the way I liked it: ground beef, pepperoni, and extra cheese.

Fucking beautiful.

When the pizza dude arrived, Stefan and Mike told me to tip him extra. I gave him a twenty.

"Thanks, buddy," he said. "Best tip all night!"

I went home to Uncle Ron's thinking it was the simplest work I'd ever done. I was grateful to my new friends that I'd started the new millennium in such a positive way.

"*The Saint*'s a remake, you know," Uncle Ron said as the credits rolled at the end. "I like the original better." He flicked his thumb in his beer and it made a blopping noise, like a stone dropped down a well. Solomon cut another fart. "Jesus," Uncle Ron said, "I'm suffocating over here." The dog lifted his head as if he knew we were talking about him.

Just then the eleven p.m. news flash came across the TV. A cab driver had been murdered, New Year's Eve, near the Gateway Six movie theatre in Brampton. The reporter went on to say that police were looking for two suspects—a tall man with black hair in a ponytail and a shorter man with blond hair, both in their late teens or early twenties.

"If anyone has any information, they are encouraged to contact Peel Police," the reporter said. A picture of the murdered cabbie flashed across the screen, and Uncle Ron went to change the channel.

"No," I said, knocking the remote out of his hand. I stared at the name of the cabbie—Baljinder Singh Rai, 48, father of two.

It was Toronto's first murder of 2000. I swear I heard a helicopter and Stan stammering. Stan lowering his head in silence while Stefan pulled out his roll of bills like a big shot. Everyone in the kitchen laughing. How Stefan and Mike had moved to avoid unwanted attention, watching their angles and lines of sight, like we all did when we shoplifted or ran from the police.

"C-careful, J-Jess," Stan had said.

I stood up, my legs trembled underneath me, and I fell backward onto Uncle Ron.

"What the fuck?" he said. The room started spinning, and I ran to the bathroom to throw up, but I missed the toilet bowl and hit the sides of the sink and tub and got vomit on the front of my shirt.

Uncle Ron ran in. "Jesse. What's going on?"

I wiped my mouth with my shirt then realized it was the jersey—my nice new gift from my nice new friend Mike. I fell back onto my ass, up against

197

the towel rack. The shirt, the pizza, the ride out west, the "mission" from the night before—I fell for everything. I was caught up in something huge.

I didn't even have an alibi for the time of the murder on New Year's—I was with that drunk chick doing blow, trying to score. I'd made all the phone calls, gave the pizza guy the cash, talked with the pizza place and given my name, and had the shirt Mike was likely wearing when the crime was committed.

I vomited again. The small black pubic hair I could see on the bowl's edge seemed immense, the smell of urine dominated my nostrils, nauseating me further, my uncle's breathing behind me sounded like the bellows in a blacksmith's forge. He was scared, I could tell, and the sound of my own blood coursing through my ears thundered louder than a jet engine. I sat down on the tub, clutching the edge. I ripped off the jersey and threw it onto the floor. I wanted to take a shower all of a sudden, but knew nothing could wash off the filth of what they'd done or the trouble I was in.

Uncle Ron looked at the shirt. "What?"

He had no clue.

"They did it," I shouted. "They fucking killed that taxi guy and gave me this shirt!" A stream of tears rolled down my cheeks but I wasn't crying. It was a mix of fear and rage and confusion. I was under a giant's thumb, and it was pressing me further and further through the bathroom floor into hell, crushing every bone in my body.

"Don't you say a word," Uncle Ron said, bending down to me. "Just shut the fuck up. You don't want trouble, if I think you're saying what I think you're saying."

I backed up against the shower wall, shocked. "You don't understand," I said. "I'm involved. I can't shut up."

He shook his head and scrunched up his face like he did when someone fucked around with his money. He was like me—a street person—we weren't supposed to talk. Not now, not ever, no matter the circumstances or the trouble. He was someone who'd done time, was solid, would solve problems at the drop of a hat.

He grabbed my arm and hauled me to my feet. "Snap out of it," he shouted. "You've gotta think." His lunchbox hands squeezed my shoulders. "I love you, Jesse. I'm trying to protect you. Burn the shirt." He picked it up and handed it to me.

I stared at it, wishing the nightmare would end.

He closed my fist around the shirt, holding my hand in his. "Your life's on the line."

I knew what that meant. I ran out of the apartment and down to the dumpster out back, and started gathering paper and sticks. I laid the jersey on my collection of kindling and sprayed the wood pile with the lighter accelerant Jerry kept in the apartment for his Zippo, but just before I struck a match, a sobering thought came to me. I knew Frank had seen me the night before—twice in fact. I'd stopped by Olive's at nine p.m. before I went to the Y2K party, and again at around three a.m. when it was over, and he'd told me that Mike and Stefan had gone out. He was also there, today, right before I got the jersey from Mike, so he would've seen Mike with it on earlier, and then me leaving with it later on after I'd eaten the pizza.

I put my match back in my pocket, rescued the jersey from its funeral pyre, and hightailed it to Olive's. When I got there, I peered through the sliding glass doors. It was dark. I banged on the window a few times but no one answered. Olive's two cats pawed at the glass.

"Frank!" I yelled into the night sky, then at the cats, hoping to conjure him up from thin air. The crickets stopped chirping, though, and a neighbour told me to shut the fuck up. I slumped against the doors, shirt in hand. I considered burning it again. Then a light came on in the kitchen, and I saw a hooded figure shuffling around inside. It was Frank, making himself a peanut butter sandwich. I banged on the glass even harder and held the jersey up against it, finally catching his attention. He made his way to the doors and opened them, wiping crust out of his eyes.

"Dude, fuck. I'm sleeping. Calm your shit." He squinted. "Do you need to crash or something? Come in—but shut the fuck up."

"No, no. It's more serious," I blurted out. "It's about this jersey and Mike and Stefan and the pizza and—"

"Whoa. Slow down. I'm barely awake," he said and rammed a slice of PB and J into his mouth.

"See this?" I shoved the jersey in front of his face. "That's Mike's. I made a few calls and ordered food and they gave it to me for doing them a favour—remember?"

"Yeah, so?"

"You saw him with this on yesterday and earlier today, right?"

"Yeah. Why?"

"They did something terrible," I said and glanced around, scared someone else might hear. "They tried to frame me by giving it to me and making me make phone calls for rides out west and pizza. I need you to be my witness."

Frank's eyes widened.

"The shirt is his, not mine. I'm going to call the cops and explain it all." I put the shirt in Frank's hands and asked him to leave it on the couch or give it back to Mike when he saw him. I could tell he was having a hard time understanding what I was doing, why I'd rat them out.

"Listen," I said. "They killed someone. I don't believe in hurting people like that. Selling dope and stealing is one thing, but murdering is another."

Frank shook his head, threw the jersey on the sofa, and shut the glass doors.

He'd never done that before, closed the door in my face. I wasn't sure he'd help me.

RAT

"I'D LIKE TO REPORT A murder," I said. "The cabbie from yesterday—Baljinder Singh Rai."

The line was silent, then I heard a click and the 911 operator say, "Murder? Where? Be specific."

"Brampton. New Year's Eve. Gateway Six," I said and rubbed the sweat off my free hand onto the arm of the couch. I tried lighting a cigarette but my thumb shook so violently I couldn't strike the wheel to create a spark. I flicked it a few more times—nothing.

"Okay, sir. Where are you?" Her voice sounded firmer, more focused.

I told her the address. I was still at Uncle Ron's place.

"What's your name?"

"Me? I'm Jesse Thistle. Two guys I know did it. Stefan and Mike. I don't know their last names."

She told me to stay on the line. Ten seconds passed, maybe, and I looked around for Uncle Ron. *He must've locked himself in his room*, I thought. *He doesn't want to see me become Judas.* I again tried to light my cigarette, but, again, I failed.

The 911 operator came back on the line. "I've dispatched officers to your location. Do not leave." I heard a chorus of radio chatter in the background, a barrage of police lingo I didn't understand.

Before I knew it, someone was pounding on the door. If it was the police, I had no idea how they'd bypassed lobby security. It'd literally taken them one minute to come—I was still on the phone. I hung up and peered through the peephole and saw two huge men in uniform, although they must've left their jackets in the squad car. Early twenties, their hands hovering over their firearms. My stomach dropped. They weren't fucking around.

This is it. Go time.

I panicked a bit and scanned the apartment for an exit—over near Solomon's bed, then over to Jerry's door, then the sunroom—and considered jumping out the window two stories to the ground below. Running away was my way of dealing with life, my solution when things got hairy, and was something ingrained in me since my days with Dad and travelling with my old Adidas bag. And it always seemed to work. But there was nowhere on Earth I could run to avoid this mega-sized clusterfuck.

"Mr. Thistle. Jesse," a voice thundered. "We know you're in there. We just got a call from dispatch." He hammered on the door so it shook in its frame, and I swear loosened a few marbles in my skull. His radio was going berserk, but I could make out that more officers were en route. I heard sirens screaming outside. They were getting closer and sounded like they were coming from every direction. The idea of a swarm of cops frightened me, but running was impossible now. I opened the door as Uncle Ron came out of his room. His hands were clenched.

One police officer's arms were the size of cement pillars, all veiny and tanned; the left was covered in tribal tattoos. His bulging muscles looked constricted by his tiny blue shirt. His partner was shorter, more refined, with a uniform that actually fit his torso.

The second guy did all the talking.

"Jesse? We've come to escort you to 21 Division. We need your statement."

The elevator doors in the hallway opened and more police appeared.

"Let me get my jacket and shoes," I said, my head spinning.

"No problem. Take your time."

Uncle Ron came up behind me, slipped a pack of smokes in my pocket, and told me to be strong. I can't remember if he said anything to the officers before they ushered me out of the building, but I thought of him the whole ride to the station.

I was surprised at how nice the officers were. They cracked jokes about their jobs and some of the stuff they'd seen earlier that day. They even asked if I was hungry or needed anything before we reached the station.

I blurted out, "Not hungry, but this is like being in a real-life episode of *Law and Order*, eh?" I saw the big guy nudge his partner. He was too stupid to play games, and too stupid to pretend he was my friend.

When we arrived and got out of the car, but before we entered the station, they cuffed me, saying it was for my own safety, and for the safety of the officers inside. The cuffs bit into my wrists as the bigger officer hoisted my arms up behind my back, pushing me forward, parading me past clerical officers toiling at their desks. They acknowledged Mr. Muscles, but none made eye contact with me. It was as if I was a criminal, or some trophy prize they'd dragged home to momma.

The interrogation room had one table with two chairs facing each other. There was a video camera in the corner, and on the desk were two coffees, an empty ashtray, and a pad of paper and a pen.

"Tell us everything you know," the smart officer said. He lit a smoke and pushed the coffee my way. "Don't be afraid." He motioned to his buddy, who unlocked the cuffs, then left us alone. I took a sip of coffee, and the red light on the camera went on.

I told him everything: about the jersey, the pizza, the Y2K party, the drunk girl, the call to Shawn, Frank as my witness to it all—everything. He jotted down things and let me speak freely. At times I felt like he wasn't paying attention. Every so often he'd offer me a new coffee and the big guy would come in and take away the old cup and give me a new one. They did the same with the cigarette butts after I'd smoked—always returning with a fresh new ashtray and a lone cigarette.

"I think we have some evidence," the officer said after a couple hours, as he nodded to the camera, "but not enough to charge anyone." The big officer came back into the room with his own chair and sat beside his partner on the other side of the table. "Did you see any weapons on Mike or Stefan?" the smart one asked.

The steel of the chair was cold against my back as I shifted for comfort. Then it came to me. "I don't know, but Stefan has a big knife. It's about nine inches long with a pearl handle. Serious knife." The two officers turned to face one another.

"Draw it," the big guy said, and tore notes off the pad of paper, leaving a blank page exposed. "As much as you can."

The smart officer bit the nail of his index finger and started shaking his left knee up and down. I glanced and saw that the light on the camera was still on. The lens made me feel like a tiny ant getting roasted under a giant magnifying glass in the sun. I wiped away the sweat drenching my brow and sketched out the knife—a long, sharp blade with a well-formed grip and hilt. The picture was crappy but it conveyed the vital data.

"How do you know he had this knife?" the smart officer asked. His intense stare told me this was the most important piece of information I had to offer. The hum of the neon light above us sounded like a cloud of road-allowance black flies.

"Because I taught him how to scam welfare three weeks ago."

They looked at each other, puzzled.

"Stefan's homeless and Olive was sick of having him around the house eating all the food, so I felt sorry for him and told him to go to the shelter to see the emergency social service worker who cuts cheques. All you need is a rental letter and a phone number."

Both officers leaned in, and I could tell they were having a hard time following.

"They give out $1,000 for start-up if you have that. It's to get you set up in a place with food and clothes—all that shit. But most people just scam it for money and stay at a friend's house. I do it all the time—forge rental documents so I have some money—"

"What does that have to do with the knife?" the smart guy interrupted. He pushed the drawing into the centre of the table, then flicked his butt, blowing smoke up toward the light, where it swirled around the bulb then was sucked up through the ceiling vent.

"When Stefan scammed welfare he bought a knife and some white baseball gloves. I thought it was a waste of money, but, hey, that's what he did. I hear he and Mike are back living at the shelter now. They just go to Olive's during the day."

The officers sat back, and a third, much older, officer came in and said they had what they needed. Then they took all the items out of the room except my chair and the table, and left me sitting there for a couple of hours. After, I was taken down to the holding cells. I got a single cell with an iron waffle bed—the kind they make drunk people sleep on until they sober up.

I awoke to find a perfectly bald detective in a grey suit standing on the other side of the bars. He didn't waste time with introductions, he just opened the door and instructed me to follow him. There were no hand-cuffs this time, but I knew not to fuck around. Out back of the station, there was an armada of black SUVs. A massive black cop was driving the one I got into with the detective. They didn't say a word to each other—not hi, nothing, they didn't even nod to one another.

The black fella scared the shit out of me—he looked like a Navy SEAL, but was dressed in what appeared to me to be a thousand-dollar suit, and was wearing a pair of black sunglasses. His knuckles were scarred, and he had cauliflower ears. I'd seen ears, scars, and knuckles like that before, on professional boxers and rugby players, but never on cops. I tried not to stare at him but he caught me in the rear-view mirror. He turned up the chatter crackling over their walkie-talkies.

With sirens blazing on the lead car, our SUVs blew through a series of red lights—an ominous caravan of justice speeding mercilessly toward its destination. The morning sun didn't penetrate the tinted windows of our vehicle; it spilled in only briefly through the windshield as we turned and drove east a spell before we met another gang of trucks parked behind an abandoned warehouse.

The detective and black guy told me to stay put and jumped out to meet a crew of bigger, even scarier men armed with guns. A few were dressed in black-and-grey-camouflage commando gear, utility belts, and bulletproof vests covered in what looked like ammo magazines. I heard dogs barking in the back of one of their trucks. It was the Peel SWAT and K9 units. They formed a half-circle around the detective, who clapped his hands at every order he gave. The men jumped at his commands, checked their gear, then separated into groups of three and got in six different vehicles.

"The shelter," the black guy said to the detective as he got into the driver's seat. "We're going to apprehend them there." The detective slapped the dashboard. I saw then that he had two handguns—one under his suit jacket under his arm in a holster, and one strapped to his leg—I could see the impression under his pants. He rubbed his hand over his bald head. "After we get them," he said to me, "we're gonna take you up to the Major Crime Unit on Courtney Park. We need more info from you."

"I'll tell you whatever I know," I said, fearful of the power I knew he wielded.

Outside the shelter we saw four homeless men emerge near the smoking pit. The SUVs circled round the building, reminding me of a well-coordinated pack of wolves stalking prey. The sound of truck tires on gravel was the only sound they made; the men in the smoking pit created more noise as they shivered and complained in the cold January dawn.

I heard the black guy unclick the safety on his gun. He motioned to the lead detective, who ordered the others to wait until they had confirmation. The men in the SUV to our right, fifty metres away, were prepping their guns. They stood in position, behind their doors, which were now splayed open for protection. There we waited and waited. Ten minutes went by, until over the radio I heard a voice that said, "Negative on the suspects. Staff says they didn't stay here last night. Stand down." The black cop clicked the safety back on his gun, and before I knew it the pack of SUVs was driving off again.

When we got to the Major Crime Unit building, about a thirty-minute drive from the shelter, I was placed in a room with plush couches and a TV that didn't work. They told me I had to stay there until they appre-hended Mike and Stefan. I asked for a phone call and they denied me. There I languished—for twenty hours.

It was the next evening when they finally came and got me. I'd stretched my shirt up around my head and tucked my arms in for warmth and was sleeping when the bald detective arrived. He seemed happy.

"We got them at three p.m., Jess," he said. "They were at Olive's."

I was relieved at the thought of them getting arrested, but I wasn't happy to hear they'd been at Olive's. I thought of Frank, Tim, and Olive and wondered where they had been when it'd happened. I hoped they weren't home.

The cops never did ask me any more questions. They simply drove me home and told me I'd be okay because they'd protect my status as an informer.

No more than six hours passed before I started hearing that I was a dead man walking.

AFTERMATH

I WAS TERRIFIED THAT I was now in danger, a known informer, but curiosity overcame me. I decided to walk over to Olive's to see what had happened during Mike and Stefan's arrest. I couldn't get any closer than two hundred metres because the area was blocked off by police tape.

Buzzing about were forensics units, police vans, squad cars, sharply suited detectives, and uniformed police officers. There must've been around a dozen people. A few of my street friends stood transfixed, watching the commotion from a distance. They didn't notice me. The investigative team carried out box after box of evidence, and one had Tim's leather jacket in his hand. I imagined lines of determined ants hauling away leaves to their colony-headquarters. Their industry was perfect, inhuman, insidious.

I saw the shattered back window of the apartment, glass strewn all over Olive's porch and out onto the parking lot, where, only two days earlier, Stan had warned me to be careful. The blue-and-red strobe of the squad-car lights refracted off the shards, sending rays of broken colour in every direction, dancing across my eyes, carving the scene into the back of my cranium.

The police must've entered, gangbusters, that way.

Olive, Frank, and Tim were nowhere in sight. I searched for Olive's cats and saw the bald detective arrive in his SUV. He ducked under the yellow tape and entered the apartment through the destroyed glass doors. He, again, seemed to be calling the shots, pointing his finger and making younger cops jump. I looked around for the big black cop but he wasn't there.

I walked closer and caught the attention of one of the neighbourhood street kids who stood watching. "What's going on?" I asked, pretending like I knew nothing. A look of disgust shot across his face.

"Don't chat to me," he said. "You'll get it soon enough, you fucking rat." He spit on the ground, mounted his bike, and flipped me the bird as he rode away.

An old lady nearby said, "What a rude young man."

I had broken a cardinal rule. *The* cardinal rule—omertà, silence above all else. Old friends I'd dealt drugs or gone to raves with wanted nothing to do with me. I was seen as untrustworthy, vile, scum—the worst kind of person.

People lured me to parties or to dark corners of the park with the promise of smoking a joint, then jumped me and beat me up. One tried to knife me in an alley. Another beat my leg with a baseball bat after he'd invited me into his place for a drink; the muscle on my thigh was clobbered so badly it was purple and black halfway up my belly, and it was nearly impossible for me to walk. I was lucky, though, that he never got to my knees—his original target. I surely would've been crippled.

I bumped into a friend at the mall, who I used to sell sheets of acid with a few years before. "I'd have done the same thing," he said when I saw him in front of the Chinese food stand. I was in between meals and he offered me a bowl of stew his mother cooked for lunch. He had it in a container in his knapsack. I ate it, but it tasted funny—bitter, sour, off or something. When I was done he looked me right in the eye and said, "Eat shit and die, motherfucker." I was sick for a couple of weeks afterward. It was the worst retaliation of all—biological warfare, street style.

The people who did talk with me only did so to give me attitude or tell me I wasn't worth the skin I was born in.

All the maltreatment left me wondering if I'd done the right thing, if helping to deliver justice was worth it. I mean, maybe the cops wouldn't have found me with the shirt. Maybe Stefan and Mike would have gotten away with it. Maybe I should've just laid low until things cooled off. Maybe I should've just taken my chances.

When I explained that to Uncle Ron, he assured me that I'd done the right thing. "It takes a lot of balls to do what you did, Jess. Don't doubt it."

I was surprised.

Jerry and Leeroy, too, remained steadfast. Leeroy got back from Vancouver right before the murder.

"What the fuck, guy?" he said when he first saw me. "You just left me out there to die."

"I'm sorry. The logs floated by, there was light on the mountains, we were starving, and I had to go." He crossed his arms, like he wasn't convinced, but we still started hanging out. Things were different, though. We didn't share or trust the way we did before I'd abandoned him, he wouldn't share dope with me as freely, or booze—but he stuck by my side and defended me.

Jerry and Leeroy were spooked by the company I'd gotten myself involved with, though—killers! But they stood with me, my brother and best friend, as everything collapsed around me. They never once told anyone where I was, even though I was sure people offered them rewards for my whereabouts.

Around March a couple of new detectives showed up at Uncle Ron's apartment. They said they were doing follow-up on the investigation. Apparently, they'd been searching for the knife I'd drawn but had come up with nothing. It was a key piece of evidence.

"We even dredged the pond next to the complex where Mike and Stefan ran after they killed the cabbie," one detective said. "We had a team of divers there for a month looking for it, but it wasn't there."

The detectives then told us that post-mortem examinations indicated that Baljinder Singh Rai had sustained massive stab wounds to the face and neck with a sharp object, most likely a knife nine inches in length or longer. Just like I'd drawn. That Rai had evidently picked up two males who matched Stefan and Mike's description at the bus depot in downtown Brampton at ten p.m. on December 31. That he'd then driven them to Gateway Six, just behind the Pizza Hut, where he'd been attacked. They said Rai had held on just long enough to alert staff at the store, before he bled to death.

That turned my stomach. My heart hurt for his two children—I was raised without a father and knew that horrible pain well.

"But Mike and Stefan aren't saying a word," the detective said. "And without the knife, we just can't be sure." His last comment lingered, like a poisonous gas that scorched my lungs, robbing me of breath.

I'm fighting in the trenches on two fronts now. Against the criminals and cops, I thought, because he'd implied the thing I feared most, the reason why they were in the apartment taking Uncle Ron's and Jerry's statements. Why they'd begun canvassing people in my extended family, like Uncle Ralph, who was a Metro copper down at 52 Division. In Ralph's case, they'd asked him for my character profile, and if I was capable of taking another man's life. In Uncle Ron's case, they'd asked for exact times of my movements on December 31, and if I acted strange the next night when we watched *The Saint*. Jerry never did tell me what they asked him; he avoided all my questions.

It also began making sense that they'd held me for twenty-four hours after I'd reported the murder, and that I was denied a phone call the whole time I was in custody. The way they had collected my cigarette butts and coffee cups, one by one, during the initial questioning also pointed to the fact that they'd been collecting my DNA.

I realized I was still a suspect, and had been since the night of the murder. I was a suspect the police couldn't rule out because they'd failed to find the murder weapon, and Mike and Stefan wouldn't squeal on each other. Moreover, I was roughly the same size as Mike, and Leeroy, amazingly, was the exact same height and weight as Stefan. It was well documented, too, that I'd had the shirt the crime was committed in. I wasn't sure if they ever considered Leeroy a suspect, though. I wasn't even sure if it was all in my head, or if any of it was true. Maybe the pressure of everything was beginning to make me see things that weren't grounded in reality.

"Just show up in court and tell the judge what you know," the detective said before he left.

I knew that the expression on my face betrayed me—my mind was fracturing.

"They're the ones charged, Jesse," he said, as if to comfort me. "But a conviction is another matter altogether. We have to look at all possibilities."

I held on to that sliver of hope for justice for two months until it was time for the preliminary hearing. But I questioned myself every day until then. I hid out at Uncle Ron's, and drank and smoked crack until the paranoia forced me to hide under my brother's bed for hours at a time. I wouldn't even take the dog out for his bathroom breaks. My weight dropped and I was afraid to even put garbage in the apartment building's chute, thinking it was the perfect spot for my enemies to ambush me and make me disappear, just like Dad had.

At the end of May, I was called to give evidence for the Crown at the old courthouse on Clarence Street, right in the heart of my old neighbourhood. The courtroom was filled with many of Mike and Stefan's friends—some from around our hood, others I'd never seen before. No one I knew came—not Leeroy nor Jerry nor Uncle Ron. I couldn't blame them. I could swear the people who were there mouthed, "You're dead," to me from the back benches. I tried to ignore them and sat up near the front, a few rows back from the Crown lawyer, where I knew I'd be safe if anything went awry.

Mike and Stefan entered the courtroom and glared at me from the bench behind the bailiff. I stared at them to show I wasn't scared, even though I was shitting bricks. Stefan leered right back. I couldn't turn away and let him win.

When I took the stand, the Crown asked me to run through the details. He paused in between questions and let me think, getting me to note exactly how Stefan got the knife and how I'd helped him scam welfare. To me, the whole thing made sense—I'd been framed, Stefan and Mike were the framers, they were the murderers.

I kept my head up after the Crown finished with me; I sensed it was important to keep an air of confidence. I adjusted my shirt and tie and glanced over and saw that the judge had sketched out a few notes—a couple of words had red underlines.

"Defence," he said, his voice a slab of granite authority. "It's your turn."

The judge peered over his glasses at me, and I held my back straight. I thought it might make him respect me more, but his head just swivelled, detached, unimpressed. He pushed his glasses up with his finger and continued on. I thought he might have secretly given me the middle finger. But the Crown smiled at me as he took his seat.

The defence, however, was having none of it. He walked up to the bench. It was hard to tell if he was angry or happy or what—his face was expressionless. He reminded me of an old west gunslinger at high noon right before a showdown—Johnny Fucking Law. He drew first, interrogating me on where I'd been on December 31.

I was frank. "I can't produce a witness as to where I was that night—I can barely remember where I was or who was at that party, but I didn't kill anyone."

He asked the same question a hundred times over, just in different ways.

I fiddled with my thumbs and thought of my grandma and the time she caught me stealing when I was young.

Finally, I yelled, "And, yes, I am a criminal! Have been since childhood. And, yes, I do drugs. And these are the drugs I do." I proceeded to list over a hundred different kinds of liquids, pills, powders, substances, herbs, plants, moulds, and cacti—every drug that I'd ever done since boyhood. I finished with, "But that doesn't make me someone whose word isn't good!"

The Crown's face had gone ghost white. He was flabbergasted.

Hell, I was flabbergasted. I'd just sunk my own testimony with my honesty. It was totally on the fly. I was an addict, a fucked-up addict. I had to deal with it. End of story.

The defence leaned over to the Crown's desk and whispered loud enough for me to hear, "Solid witness you got there." He turned to Stefan and Mike and grinned. I didn't wait to see their reaction before I again peered over at the judge.

"That's it, Mr. Thistle," he said. "You are relieved." His voice sounded like an ice shelf sheering off into the ocean—kaboom.

My legs wobbled as I slid out of the witness stand and bobbed toward the back doors. The onlookers were confused at what had just happened. Even Stefan, Mike, the lawyers, and the judge had puzzled expressions on their faces. I'd simultaneously given the Crown what it needed to go forward with a trial, while leaving the defence with enough ammunition to call my testimony into question.

As I exited the courtroom, I was approached by an East Indian man around my age.

"Hi, Jesse," he said.

My adrenaline made it hard for me to focus.

"My name is Paul Singh. We were in the same Grade 10 class."

It was difficult to tell, but I did recognize him as the quiet newcomer I'd gone to high school with, a boy who was unsure of his English back then. Paul had no accent at all now.

"Yeah, I remember you," I said, still not fully aware of what I'd just done, or if I'd get attacked outside.

"Baljinder Rai was my uncle." His lip quivered. "I want to thank you for doing what you did—calling the police. I know it wasn't easy." His eyes teared up and he moved in for a hug. I opened my arms like a thistle in bloom, wrapping every leaf around him, thorns outward, keeping us both safe.

"Don't mention it," I said. "I did what I had to do."

He invited me to a celebration of his uncle's life, but I declined.

A few months later, the Crown cut a deal with Mike. There was still no knife. Whatever happened, Mike MacDonald pleaded guilty to manslaughter and got ten years. Stefan Miceli pleaded guilty to second-degree murder and was sentenced to life without chance of parole for thirteen years.

Me, I got a lifetime of people thinking I was a rat. That I could live with, because I knew what really happened—they tried to make me their patsy, and I dealt with it. What other choice did I have as a young Native homeless man? And I knew that the code of the streets was bullshit—everyone cracks, no exceptions.

I never found out if Frank had my back with the jersey, or even if it mattered. When I reconnected with him, I didn't have the heart to ask him about it. I didn't want to put him in the same position I was in.

A BOTTLE FULL OF PILLS

I STARTED SLEEPING ROUGH IN parks, under bushes, on benches in my old neighbourhood—my whole social web was destroyed by the murder case. I went to Olive's new apartment periodically, but she banned me from her couch after a while—something that'd never happened before. I understood—she didn't want me around because of the mayhem I'd been involved in, and she had to protect her family. It became clear, too, that Tim had a score to settle with me.

"Where's my bloody leather jacket?" he'd yell, his fists held aloft ready to strike me. "Ask your friends, the cops, where the fuck my jacket is!" I never did find out why the cops confiscated his jacket or if they returned it later.

I ventured over to Mississauga and began using the Salvation Army shelter there. It was way back in the industrial section of town, at least three hours away by bus from my usual stomping grounds. I stayed for a month but felt isolated so I went back to Brampton. But I still couldn't go back to the Brampton shelter—I'd blown welfare start-up money after the preliminary hearing.

One night, around midnight, drunk and high, I ventured to Leeroy's parents' house. His father and mother had welcomed him home after Vancouver and forgave him—it was like the return of the prodigal son. Sylvia had long since gotten married and started a family of her own, working as a special needs teacher. She'd really come full circle from the Sylvia I remembered in grade school.

I banged on the window. No Leeroy. I pounded on the door and hollered and heard his dog barking. Still no Leeroy. I'd watched him jimmy open his bedroom window in the basement before, so I crawled down into the window well and pushed the glass up and over to the left in spurts. It popped right open. I poked my head in and yelled his name. The dog rushed over, barking. I dropped down into the room, rubbed the dog's head, wandered to the kitchen to make myself a snack, and started watching some TV in his bedroom. The phone rang, which startled me.

Then it hit me. I'd broken into my best friend's house. I'd violated his space, our friendship, his family. It was much worse than me leaving him in Vancouver. I got up, locked the door behind me, and went into his garage and fell asleep on a pile of wood.

When I awoke, Leeroy was standing over me.

"You broke into my house?"

I leaned back against the wall, my leg slipping on a log.

"You crossed the fucking line this time!"

"I'm sorry! I didn't have anywhere to go. I didn't steal anything."

"Fuck, man," he said, but then the expression on his face changed. "You can stay here if you want."

His pity wounded me, made me feel inferior. I told him I was sorry again and scurried away. I slept behind the arena attached to the school where I'd gone to junior high, across the way from where we'd smoked our first cigarettes together.

I felt like Leeroy was avoiding me, like I'd lost my best friend. I figured people would say I was out to rob him blind. Maybe it was payback for Vancouver. Whatever the reasons, without my best friend in my corner, I had nothing.

I was distraught about everything—the case, being a social outcast, being homeless and hopeless. I went to a drugstore and stole a bottle of a hundred acetaminophen tablets and ate them all before I could think better of it. Then I went and sat by the river with my feet in the water, the rush cool against my skin.

My toes numbed as I wiggled them in my shoes. A roar filled my ears—like an approaching hurricane. I checked the treetops and the leaves were still—there was no breeze. Stretched thin and sapped of energy, my vision crowded black at the sides, then formed into deep tunnels. I stood up, but my legs had a hard time holding my weight. I wobbled along the pathway, grabbing branches as I fell down on my knees. I hoisted myself up again using the edge of a garbage bin and attempted to breathe deeply, but no amount of air could fill my lungs—they gurgled and filled with fluid. My heart beat faster than if I'd run a marathon at full sprint. I was dying. I panicked and walked the half-mile it took to get to the hospital.

I glanced in the glass before the emergency department doors slid open and saw myself—deep-set charcoal eyes, plastic-looking skin. I looked like a grey alien.

"I swallowed a bottle of Tylenol," I said to the nurse at the desk. "An hour ago." Without a word, she ran into the back and a team of orderlies came out and put me on a gurney. I gave them Olive's phone number and then my world went white.

My eyes cracked open. I was in a room, strapped onto a bed, with doctors and nurses buzzing around. I heard a beeping, and a sound like Darth Vader next to me. There was a mask strapped over my face, and I called out, "Grandma," but heard nothing. The neon lights above captivated me. The doctors kept running around. I coughed. Breathing was even more laboured now. My head felt thinner, the ringing louder, the wind roaring through me, carrying me away.

A doctor appeared, ripped off the mask, and jammed a tube down my throat. I watched as black fluid crept down the tube and filled my belly, then spilled out of my mouth, down my neck, and all over my blue gown. Then lights. More doctors rushing. And silence.

"Wake up," someone said.

Their breath smelled like onions. Whoever it was peeled my eyes open and a light blinded me. I tried to look away.

"Hello," another said. "Jesse. Mr. Thistle."

I tried to respond but the tube made it hard to speak. Then silence again.

When I finally came to I was in a room with a guard. I was told that was so I wouldn't run away or hurt myself. Apparently, I'd woken up earlier and ripped the tubes right out of my body, undid the straps, and took off. The hospital rang the local police precinct and put out an APB on me—I couldn't remember if the police had brought me back, or if I'd wandered back myself.

"Rest easy," the guard said. "The doctors will be by shortly."

He looked familiar, and told me we'd played together as kids way back in grade school. "We used to scrap, but that school was nuts back then."

I laughed. I remembered him stomping me for playground supremacy. He'd been in one of the rival gangs.

"You've had a rough go of it, eh?" he said.

I broke down.

When the doctor showed up, she informed me that I'd taken a lethal dose of slow-release acetaminophen. "It's one of the hardest overdoses to treat. It releases acetaminophen at a steady rate. We try to treat it with liquid charcoal—which absorbs toxic substances—but you may still have a number of pills lodged in your digestive tract and so are very much at risk. Any more time and your liver would have been destroyed. Did you hear a roaring wind?"

"Yes."

"That's how thin your blood was pumping over your eardrums."

I had to explain to a psychiatrist that I'd meant to end my life, but I now wanted to live.

"Why did you do it?" he asked.

"I destroyed a lifelong friendship, and I don't have anywhere to go. I just can't stop fucking up."

"More common than you know."

He filled in a form, told me I needed rest, and decided to hold me for at least another week. I'd already been under observation for seventy-two hours. I gave the attendants the phone numbers of everyone I knew— Leeroy, my grandparents, Olive, Jerry, and Josh. Only my brothers called to see if I was okay. No one came to see me except a friend of Olive's who'd let me crash on his couch from time to time. He gave me some money, so I could take the bus to Jerry's new place.

SMITTEN

WHEN MY STRENGTH WAS UP after the overdose, I got a job at a local grocery store near Jerry's as a produce clerk, stacking fruit, cutting lettuce, crushing boxes. Josh sent $1,000 to help get me on my feet. "I love you," he said on the phone. "We all do. Just don't kill yourself."

I kept chasing death, though. Each time I got my paycheque, I went out and spent it on comfort for my mind. I started banging needles of crack, melted down with vinegar, with working girls in the train yard at Dufferin and Queen, across from Toronto's Gladstone Hotel. They didn't judge me, and there was an honesty to what they did, like they had the courage to take things all the way. I had respect for that. *There is perfect order in perfect chaos*, I philosophized. We'd shoot up in the abandoned trailer one of the ladies lived in. I brought food from work sometimes, and we'd listen to Charlie Parker or the Velvet Underground or some other brilliant junkie band. They were my friends. My only friends.

One morning while I was stacking apples, my boss, an old Italian guy, glanced down and saw the bruising on my arms and my track marks. "You know, Jess, there's no shame in being sick," he said, but he was polite enough not to say anything outright.

I knew he couldn't complain about my work performance—I worked hard and got the job done, just like Grandpa had trained me to do.

Sometime later I saw a crisis support line number scrawled on the job chalkboard. I called, but the addictions worker told me, "You need three months or more before your employee insurance kicks in." I wasn't surprised. I'd tried accessing treatment before, many times, but the places all had long waiting lists, or needed insurance, or were outpatient only—there was always some kind of restriction. Detox worked, sure—but after that, I'd be left with nowhere to transition to and would relapse. I knew I needed quick isolation to get clean—total, immediate immersion for months and months.

My addictions had become unmanageable. I couldn't escape the horror of being involved with people who'd taken someone's life in such a gruesome way. And I had recurring nightmares of that jersey melting into my body, of being stabbed in the neck, of people lying in wait to ambush me around every corner.

With rent squirted up my veins, I ran away, leaving Jerry and my boss high and dry.

I fled to the Brampton shelter and, to my surprise, met the most beautiful girl. She was just sitting there, surrounded by a pile of plastic bags and suitcases. Her hair was blond and pulled back into a tight ponytail that lifted her eyebrows up, and she was well taken care of.

I went into the washroom to comb my hair and straighten my shirt, and then went over to her.

"I'm Jesse," I said, holding out a cigarette. "You smoke?"

She smiled and took it. Her name was Samantha. She placed her bags near the front office and asked the staff to watch them, then we went outside to the smoking pit.

Straight away I knew she was fearless and powerful, like a lone she-wolf who didn't need help fending for herself. She had no problem talking about how she'd ended up at the shelter—her parents had kicked her out because she was an independent thinker and she'd lost her job at the local gym.

"They're very Christian," she said. "Not me—I love to party."

For two and a half months we tripped around, getting high, staying on people's couches, then decided to combine our welfare start-ups and leave the shelter. We finally got a place and began picking trash to furnish it. She didn't mind, and even brought stuff home herself—an old couch, chairs, a microwave, and a TV.

Uncle Ron saw that we were trying and got me a job building counter-tops. I still took off on paydays trying to numb myself out, but now Samantha blasted stones right by my side—we were like two quarry workers chucking dynamite and smashing crack boulders together.

I ghosted work so often that the owner of the business, Randolph, changed paydays from Thursday to Friday just so I'd make it into work on Friday mornings. I worked my ass off, though, doing the jobs of four men—made sense, I was jacked on cocaine and moved faster than Ben Johnson at the Seoul Olympics.

Randolph ended up firing me, furious because I was so unreliable, but as soon as he axed me, he'd hire me right back—he knew no one could work like me. I was probably fired and rehired over twenty times.

Samantha and I soon lost our place and started moving constantly, gathering household belongings and then jettisoning them like spent rocket-fuel containers whenever we missed rent and entered homeless orbit—we must've moved about thirty times. Everything I pulled in at various temp jobs went to feed our addictions, to keep those nightmares at bay, and we always ended up at another shelter, in another city, or at Jerry's. He always had his door open, and Samantha and I were thankful. But I could tell he was reaching his limit.

In between cheques, food banks, and jobs was the hardest. We'd have no food, no alcohol, no fun, and no hope. I began stealing ground pork and ramen noodles at a market over in Chinatown. I did it at least a dozen times, stuffing my backpack and booking it out the front doors, until one day a security guard stopped me. I broke free and ran but was headed off. Security brought me to the backroom. I shouted and fought, but the security guard restrained me, pushing me to the ground and holding me tight with my arms behind my back. I was sure they'd call the cops, and I'd go to jail on a theft-under-$5,000 charge—the standard Canadian charge for shoplifting. I sat weeping, and when my energy was spent, the owner came in.

"Why you steal from here all the time?" she said with a thick Cantonese accent. "Go steal somewhere else, bad boy."

Bad boy? I thought, thinking that was kind of demeaning and strange. She was right, though. I always chose her store. It was big, and I believed its size concealed me. Obviously not.

"I know the other owners," she said. "They see you, too!" Her neck turned red as she flailed her arms.

"I'm sorry, miss. I—"

"I know you, crackhead."

Her voice made me feel ashamed.

"I see you steal ginseng and steel wool for your pipe." She wagged her finger, a look of disgust upon her face.

How did she know about that, or where I got my gear? I wondered, shocked. *Had she seen me steal it from the local convenience stores? Did she know all the local merchants?*

She pulled up my chin and forced eye contact. "Too skinny," she said, then slapped my cheek, but not with anger. It was like she was sorry for me. "Look at you. Too skinny." She took my backpack and opened it. "You have my pork and noodles." She shook her head.

I felt like an idiot.

She motioned to the security guard and the few employees who were there to leave the room. When we were alone she squatted next to me.

"I was hungry a long time ago, too, you know," she said. "Someone fed me, too."

224

She got up and went over to a skid and grabbed some noodles and yelled something. A man came through a plastic flap door with a big clear grocery bag of ground pork. He handed it to her, looked at me, then left. She stuffed both the noodles and meat into my bag and plopped it into my lap.

"Go now. And don't ever come back." She stood me up, and then shooed me out the back door before I could thank her.

I never stole from there again.

Everywhere else was fair game, though—thieving was the one thing I was good at that Samantha and I could count on. I grabbed her whatever she wanted—meat, alcohol, smokes, the odd article of clothing. I was smitten with her, and it was my selfish way of keeping her by my side.

Maybe I should've just let go and let her be.

THE KING OF SOMALIA

"**GOOD NIGHT, ABDI, YOU CRUSTY** old bastard," I said and rested my head on my pillow. Abdi was a Somali man of about sixty-five. He was my buddy and always slept in the bed next to me at the homeless shelter. Samantha was off on the women's side.

"Hey," I said a minute later. "I've been meaning to ask. You said you were the king of Somalia. Is that true?"

As expected, Abdi's face flushed and his eyes bulged. "Would I lie, peasant? Of course I am the king of Somalia. How dare you question my royal blood?"

Obviously I knew he wasn't Somali royalty. I liked joking with Abdi to get him going, and he'd do the same to me. It was our only form of entertainment in this hospitable yet horrible place.

Life hadn't been good to Abdi. He'd fled Somalia with his family when civil war broke out in the early '90s. Soon after he'd become an alcoholic and his wife had left him for another man. Abdi would reminisce about his homeland, telling me how he used to shepherd massive herds of cattle between Kenya and Somalia, and how he'd sit every night watching the orange-red African sunset. By the way his eyes lit up, I could see it was something he missed dearly. I tried to imagine how hard it must have been for him to be forced out of his homeland, to end up in a homeless shelter in a foreign country that seemingly didn't want him or his problems.

"Hey, Thistle," Abdi said as he leaned over. "You know how I know you're a real streeter like me?"

"Maybe it's the way I drink the last of the Olde English piss water?"

He cringed. "That's just disgusting—dirty Canadian drinking dirty American beer. No, young blood, it's in the way you sleep."

"How do you mean? And why are you watching me while I sleep?"

"I always watch out for you when you sleep, to make sure no one steals your stuff."

I thought about it, and he was right—I watched out for him, too. It was just what friends did in this place.

"Indian, you've had your shoes stolen so many times you sleep with them on. See?" He pulled up his blanket, exposing his grungy, mud-covered black boots, and smiled. "You see those young guys?" Abdi pointed at two men with their shoes placed under their cots. "They're little puppies, down on their luck momentarily. One day, if they're at it long enough, they'll learn like we did: never take your shoes off."

Having no shoes and being homeless was the worst. It could take a day or two to find a new pair that fit from the donation box—and that was if you were lucky. Other times you'd have to leave the shelter shoeless at seven a.m. to go and wait at the chaplain's office until eight a.m. to get a voucher to take to the Sally Ann up the street so they could outfit you with a new pair. Or you had to go without for a few days. Or steal a pair from Zellers and risk your freedom. When you were shoeless in the winter, it was almost unbearable.

I surveyed the shelter beds. Only about a third of the guys had their shoes on.

I'd never noticed, but every night I tied my shoes on with triple, even quadruple, knots, just to give myself a chance of keeping thieves from stealing them right off my feet. Even then, they got them sometimes.

"I guess I do sleep with my shoes on, eh, Abdi?" I said, and laughed.

LIFE AT GUNPOINT

FLIP'S 38 WAS PRESSED HARD into my forehead.

Flip was one of the more aggressive and secretive crack dealers who served the downtown core. He'd been doing it for decades and was a wild card, trigger-happy, too, and even the rival gangs let him chop uncontested. I didn't like going to him—no one did as far as I knew—but he always had good dope, at all hours, and was one of the only choppers who'd exchange goods for crack at a fair price.

I was hoping he'd buy the Gucci bag I'd just stolen from a car with my high school friend Marko, but, in desperation—no one else had dope—I'd disregarded the various rules Flip had put in place to protect himself from crackheads he didn't know.

His number one rule: no new customers.

His number two rule: no new customers, and so on.

I thought our longstanding relationship might supersede the formalities. Marko kept bugging me to sell the bag, and thought maybe our friendship was good enough to get him access to Flip.

"Who is this fool you brought here? I told you not to bring anyone to see me!" Spit and angry breath hissed through Flip's clenched teeth as the hammer cocked into firing position.

"That—that's m-my bu-boy . . . Come on, dog . . . I—I've known you for ye-years." We only wanted to score some dope, and Flip was flipping out.

Just then a cruiser rounded the corner. In an instant Flip rammed his pistol through his belt, pointed his finger at me, mouthed something, and fled down the street toward the Dairy Queen. He was gone before I could process what had happened.

"Man, I'm sorry, guy," Marko said. "I never thought your buddy would react like that. What is his problem?"

I looked at Marko. His astonished words told me that he didn't really understand how close I had come to death.

A week after, the pinkish purple imprint of the gun muzzle, the size and shape of a Life Savers, remained engraved between my eyes.

I never did another run with Marko again.

WE ALL FALL DOWN

THE HALLOWEEN PARTY AT JERRY'S friend's house ran late into the night. I was dressed up as William Wallace from *Braveheart*, half my face blue and with a diaper of fake fur and a plastic sword. Jerry was a Viking with huge horns and a plastic battle-axe, and Samantha was the Pict girl from *King Arthur*, with leather armour and a bow and arrow made from household items. The rest of the partygoers wore costumes ranging from ghosts to Spanish matadors, but a couple of people were just dressed in regular clothes.

One was a beautiful redhead in a tight black sweater. She was the girl from grade school who'd been nice to me on the hill.

"Hi," I said to her. "My name is Jesse. You're Lucie, right?" I stuck my hand out like I had years earlier.

"Yes." She reciprocated like she had years before.

"Do you remember me? I'm Jerry's brother—we were in middle school together." I motioned toward Jerry, who was chatting over near the kitchen.

"No." She grinned, shrugged, and then turned away to talk to a bald guy. Samantha came up with her bow drawn, half-drunk. I disarmed her, and we mingled into the heart of the party, asking people if they had any coke, but I kept looking back. I was enchanted by Lucie, and the fact that she wasn't interested attracted me even more.

After a couple of screwdrivers, I was hit with addiction cravings so bad I ran to the toilet—I needed to take a dump—then I ditched the party and Samantha and went out scouring for a twenty stone. I found plenty, spending our rent money and shoplifting things to generate more cash. Before I knew it, it was around four a.m. I drifted back to the party, but almost everyone had left. One of the last people trailing out told me to get home quick because Samantha was livid. I did my last toke and walked back to Jerry's, which was miles away.

When I got there, I picked the outside lock with my health card. I didn't have my own key—Jerry's rules, even though Samantha and I'd been staying with him for months at his new place in Toronto after we'd fled from Brampton. The inside door to the apartment was locked. It was steel, bolted shut, and impossible to bypass with any of my thieving skills. I banged on it.

"It's me. Open up!"

Nothing. I banged some more. Again nothing. I started kicking the door, the boom echoing through the hallway, and a neighbour stuck his head out his door and said, "Keep it down!"

I kicked the door again. I wondered if Samantha was being faithful to me. Why would she be? I was a terrible provider. I didn't treat her the best. *Maybe she and Jerry are inside having sex. Maybe she's exacting revenge on me for stealing our rent, for smoking it.* Or maybe it was just the copious amounts of crack that was making me paranoid.

I noticed the window down the hall. It was about three feet wide by four feet tall and opened onto the street. I went and stuck my head out of it. Our living room window was about ten feet over to the right. It was open, almost begging me to climb over. I decided to go for it. After all, I'd scaled up the sides of apartment buildings before, and this shimmy between windows was only thirty-five feet above the ground.

Piece of cake.

I charted out my climb. I'd swing from the ledge of the hallway window over to the brick notch between the two windows, where there was a good grip, then swing over to our window and plant my toe, and then pull myself up.

I lowered myself out, swung over, grabbed the notch, then swung over again and grabbed the window ledge.

Perfect so far.

I took a second to collect myself for the pull into the apartment. Scar, Jerry's dog, a pit bull–Rottweiler mix, stuck his head out and started licking my hands.

"Get. Get," I shooed. The fucker was blocking my entrance. He didn't budge. He must have thought I was playing a game or something. A drop of his saliva fell off his tongue and into my eye.

"SCAR, GET!" I blinked to clear my sight. My strength was fading, my fingers slipping. I yelled "get" one more time, desperately, and he finally listened.

I hoisted myself a quarter of the way up and planted my toe against the wall and pushed, but slipped. I was still holding on, but barely, my arms carrying my full weight. I examined the wall closely and noticed a cluster of black cables—rows of them, one over the other, stapled to the bricks. I hadn't seen them in the dark. I mustered my last bit of strength to pull myself up toward the window, planting my toe higher than before—but there was another cluster of cables. My toe slipped. My hands let go.

People who say your life flashes before you when you're about to die are full of shit. What does happen is your world slows down—seconds feel like hours, the sounds all around become clearer, colours and lights become so bright you can see everything—every bug and creepy-crawly thing in existence.

The milliseconds I was falling to my death I thought of a hundred different ways to fall so I wouldn't die. I could try to land square on my feet like I was doing a powerlift, but my face and skull would be ruined as I fell forward into the brick wall with thousands of pounds of force. I could try to do a commando combat roll off to the side but would hit the air conditioner and break my neck. Or I could try to catch the ledge of the windows below. I tried that, but this wasn't *Die Hard*, and I wasn't Bruce Willis.

My last option was to do a break-fall, something I'd learned in judo as a kid—land on my feet, tip backward onto my back, and then slap my arms out straight and let the force ride out my bone structure, out my shoulders, humerus, radius, and ulna, and blow out through the constellation of wrist bones, and finally the fine bones of my hands and digits. That was the only way to stop from smashing my head like a watermelon. Every other scenario ended with brain trauma.

It was my only chance.

When my feet hit the ground, I leaned back. A wave of pressure fired down my arms, followed by two loud cracks that sounded like shotguns. I rolled on the arc of my spine and saw my feet jut above me, and the back of my head lightly hit the sidewalk.

Tink.

The wind knocked completely out of me. I wasn't in pain but tried to scream. Nothing came out. I looked at my hands—they were folded in upon my forearms. I tried to wiggle my fingers. They didn't move. I held up both legs and saw my right heel was in the middle of my shin and my right foot pointed backward. The other foot and my skull were fine.

Scar was looking out the window. He howled.

I managed to pull in a lungful of air and yelled. "Help! Help! I've fallen."

No one came.

I yelled three more times—crickets. I shifted my strategy.

"Fire! There's a fire!"

From every direction people came, in seconds flat. I asked one guy to call my brother and tell him that I needed help.

Moments later, Jerry was downstairs.

"Jerry, I broke my leg and wrists. I need you to call an ambulance."

Jerry just scratched his head, disappeared, and then reappeared with an old set of crutches he had. "Here." He threw the crutches at me. "I don't need this shit. I have work in the morning." He turned and walked away.

In shock, I managed to get up using the crutches and hobbled up three flights of stairs into the apartment. I never wished more that Jerry's building had an elevator. I was still not in any pain, somehow. Samantha came out of our room.

"What's going on?" she said, half asleep, shielding her eyes from the light. She grumbled and swore, I heard the word "asshole," and then she went back to bed.

I grabbed the phone, my hands flopping about, and tapped 911 with the meat of my palm.

The paramedics were confounded that I'd survived. "This isn't Hollywood. Thirty-five feet spells death most times."

The pain was finally hitting, like molten nails driven into my leg, over and over again.

They laid me on the floor and told me not to move because I likely had internal bleeding. "You should have stayed where you fell. You probably have a broken back or neck."

One of them turned to Jerry, who stood watching from the bathroom, and asked, "How did he get up here?"

Jerry was silent.

"I used the crutches," I yelped.

They turned to me, mouths open. They jabbed something in my leg, strapped me to a plank-like stretcher, and carried me down to the ambulance, where they placed me on another softer stretcher.

On the way to the hospital, one guy kept cracking jokes to me even though I was so tired, I just wanted to go to sleep, and then said, "When you get out, you should leave those people. They aren't good."

I felt a slap on my face and saw tubes sticking in my arms and hands. The lights returned to normal, and I felt a sudden warm rush, a fuzzy feeling—I knew it was some kind of opioid. I felt safe.

A doctor appeared by my side as they ran with me down a hall.

"Whaddya call a guy who fell out a building and survived?" He cracked a smile.

"I dunno."

"You. You call him 'you.'"

I laughed, but my back and neck hurt. My foot and wrists pulsed with such sharp pain that the dull ache radiating from my forearms and shins was manageable. The doctor flashed a light in my eyes. I could feel someone cutting my clothes off, and then I was rolled onto my side, and a cold, wet sensation slammed into my asshole. It bloody hurt, sharp with immense pressure like a jagged chili fart scraping my lower intestine.

"You aren't even gonna buy me flowers?" I remarked, as high as Lou Reed in 1967.

The doctor laughed and said he'd take me to dinner when I recovered.

"I like steak."

"You're in good spirits. Just hang in there." He moved the object around inside my anus, then said something to the others around me. There were flashing lights, a giant white machine rotated up and down my body and over my head, and then blackness.

I drifted upon a cloud afterward. Doctors and nurses came in, filled me with fluids, told me I was "lucky" and to "cool it on the morphine drip," got me to sign forms, and then, before I knew it, I was rushed into surgery.

When I awoke in the recovery room, Samantha and Jerry were by my side, apologizing that they hadn't known how serious the fall was.

Samantha cried. I yelled at first, but then forgave them. They didn't know. I was the idiot who'd gone all strung-out-and-drunk Spiderman.

The doctors told me that my fall had shattered my right heel, destroyed my right upper ankle joint, broke my left wrist, and sprained my right wrist. I was told to keep my leg elevated.

The surgeons decided it was best to leave my wrists exposed so I'd be able to walk with crutches. They said they'd fixed my right heel and ankle with a ninety-degree incision on the outside of my right foot—it rode six inches along the back of my ankle and heel, and another six inches along the side of my foot. Two pins protruded out the back of my heel, holding my heel and ankle together.

They sent me home after three days—scabs hadn't even formed.

WESTERN DOOR

SCAR SAT BESIDE ME, NUDGING my arm every few minutes. He was my primary caregiver, along with Samantha. I lay in bed with my leg elevated, just like the doctor had told me to do. World War I documentaries rotated across the black-and-white TV, remnants of Remembrance Day programming. The horrendous 1916 battle at Verdun, with its massive craters and fractured trees, lacerated trenches and knotted barbed wire was the current feature.

This has got to be the worst battle in history per square foot, I thought as the narrator described the sheer number of deaths. It sounded worse than the Somme, and I wondered why we'd focused so much on the latter in grade school.

I gazed down at the tips of my toes. They were red, and the cast on my foot grew tighter and tighter. A strange itching had gnawed at my shin these past few days—I couldn't get to it, not even if I stuck a pencil down the cast. Almost like the itch was several layers below my skin, in the marrow of my leg. A throbbing dull pain radiated up into my buttocks, too, and even the Tylenol 4s I was prescribed couldn't stop it. When Samantha turned me over to clean me, she said that the back of my leg was turning a weird kind of grey, green almost, and was starting to emit an odd sweet smell.

All I could keep down was chicken broth, the nausea was so bad. I thought it was the medication. I'd stopped shitting five days before and was sure I was bunged up from it; I found no relief from the chamomile and senna tea the doctor said would loosen my bowels. Only weed and hash seemed to make me regular and helped with my appetite, but even that wasn't working anymore. The pile of cigarette butts in the ashtray beside me loomed ominously—I wasn't supposed to smoke, the doctor had warned—it'd impede blood flow and increased the chances of infection. But I just couldn't stop cold turkey—I needed something to occupy the time.

I took a handful of T4s before bed. I wanted to sleep all night for once. Scar and Samantha were beside me and I knew Jerry would check up on me every few hours. It felt good to have my older brother watching out for me, despite our growing animosity. I entered the dead zone about thirty minutes after.

My dreams came, as always.

Bombs exploded near my head as I moved down the trench to deliver a vital message, warning our men not to advance. A concussion knocked me into a puddle, and I dropped the letter as soldiers ran past to their deaths. I reached up toward their jackboots to stop them, but my fingers slid off their ankles. One young man looked down at me and startled me. He had dark features, a long braid, and bronze skin. He was an Indian, and looked like me, but different—older, wiser—and I knew somehow he was already dead. He turned and disappeared into an explosion as he went over the top.

The chatter of World War I artillery gave way to the slower, more powerful reports of a nineteenth-century Gatling gun. But the hulking gun sounded more menacing, more real, there were houses burning all around, and children and women were screaming and running into the bush for cover. They were all Native, like me. A handful of Indian men lay beside me in shallow pits dug into the ground, long rifles in hand. We'd pop up periodically and fire down a large prairie slope at redcoat soldiers near the banks of a large river. Our enemies stood in ordered columns and outnumbered us. The man beside me said something to me in a language I'd never heard before but understood, then reached over and took my last bullets. He cocked his rifle and returned our enemies' fire. He looked familiar, like the young man in the trench, and I could tell he was a half-breed like me. He, too, was dead; I somehow knew this.

I looked back out of the pit and suddenly saw myself on the bed at Jerry's apartment. My body was broken, my leg propped up on pillows, Samantha, Jerry, and Scar weren't there anymore. I floated higher above the battle and saw a white church get smaller and smaller on the horizon of the plains, and I knew I was part of this long-ago battle—it was real. I saw my grandparents' house in Brampton, and the house number—eight—appear above the church. The number turned sideways and formed into an infinity symbol on a blue flag. I heard voices on the wind; they told me it was my destiny to be raised under that symbol.

Just then, a great shaft of light from the west broke through the clouds. It was dusk, and the orange light of twilight was fading fast. The guns and cannons fell silent. I saw a vast field before me with mesas and buttes off in the distance, and from the brightest spot of the setting sun a vast herd of horses emerged and ran toward me. I watched their muscles ripple with power, their manes float on the wind as their heads bounded with each stride, and their hooves kicked up a cloud of dust so big it enveloped the whole earth.

A tug, soft at first, then stronger and stronger, pulled me along with the herd as they ran by me and then back again. I was galloping with them, but I was not yet a hooved creature like them. I stared back and saw my broken body on the bed get smaller and smaller, until I could hardly see it. A great sadness came over me. I knew they were taking me home, but that I hadn't yet done what I was destined to do. I tried pulling away, to return to myself, to my body, but the force of the herd was too powerful. I pleaded and cried, and still they pulled me with them.

Just as I was about to cross into the brightest spot of the setting sun, through that western door, I cried out one last time.

"I will do my work, I will change, I will finish it."

Without a sound, the herd pivoted and released me. I watched as they turned into the light, their hooves thundering, then fell behind the great façade of the western door.

As soon as they were gone, my eyes opened. I was with Samantha on the bed. Scar tilted his head, and Jerry burst into the room.

"What the hell is going on?" he asked, his voice shaking. "You were screaming, 'Help, help.'"

"I don't know what happened—I think I have a fever," I said as I looked down and saw my body was covered in sweat.

Samantha slept through it all.

CAST OF HORRORS

WHEN THE DOCTOR'S ASSISTANT CUT away the orange-and-black cast, she gasped. The smell was horrid: like Toronto during a summer garbage strike.

"Excuse me one moment, Mr. Thistle . . . I have to get the doctor," she said and rushed out.

My toes had turned a bluish grey-green and the back of my cast was leaking a swampy crimson, so I'd pushed my post-surgery checkup ahead and was lucky to get a spot. It had been many weeks since my fall. The surgery should have worked. But I couldn't listen to the doctors. It's not like I didn't try to follow their orders. I did. But I was an addict. More important, I didn't have anywhere to live.

I'd been at Jerry's, but after one of my friends stole a neighbour's vintage bicycle, he'd kicked me and Samantha out. He had to do what he had to do. If he'd kept us, he'd have been evicted, and we all would've been homeless. But I figure his place was probably where I caught the infection I likely had—it was full of cat shit and dog piss and hadn't been cleaned properly in years. It was a veritable cesspool.

Samantha and I moved into her parents' house. She got a good job. She was trying to fly straight, but I'd never really been welcome there, as we weren't married and for a bunch of other reasons, so I took off on my own. I thought she could do better without me cramping her style.

When the nurse came back in with the doctor, they both had masks on their faces. My stomach dropped. Their hands were full of instruments, including one that looked like wire cutters, lots of gauze, a kidney-shaped tray, and medical tape. When I finally got the courage to look down at my exposed leg I nearly fainted. There was a black puss-filled blister on the front of my ankle that resembled a giant, deformed pierogi. My foot and lower leg were swollen, green, red, and greyish yellow. When the doctor took the staples out of the incision, the edges of the skin peeled back, exposing fat, muscle, bone, and metallic hardware.

"Not good at all," the doctor said. "The surgery has been a complete failure. Your leg is infected and gangrene is setting in. I'll clean it, cut away the necrotic skin, and trim the bone, but you're at serious risk of losing your leg if you don't take care of yourself."

He gave me something to freeze the area and set to work. Even with the numbing, when his full weight bore down on my leg and I heard a sharp wet pop from the bone clipper, I bellowed, and tears began to stream down my face. As it went on, my field of vision narrowed to pin-points, and my hearing dulled, with the voices around me becoming distant, then inaudible. I vomited, then passed out.

When I woke up my leg was again in a cast. I had on someone else's clothes and a numbness everywhere that smothered my arms and made my legs flop about.

The nurse came in and told me I was free to go but I had to speak to the doctor before I left. She had a prescription for antibiotics, and a suction-pump machine to attach to my leg to improve its circulation, as well as a schedule for an aftercare nurse who was to come and change my wound dressings twice a day. The doctor came in and asked me where I was staying. When I told him I was staying at the shelter, I could see his expression change. I knew it was a shithole of a place to recover in. I'd always been able to hold my own on the streets and in the shelter system, but I had to admit things weren't like before. And I knew I couldn't stay at the hospital.

When the doctor and nurse left me alone a moment, I grabbed the pump and scrip and hobbled out, getting in a cab. The driver kicked me out halfway to my destination when he found out I didn't have the fare.

The first night at the shelter, the pump disappeared. By the third and fourth nights, my prescription was stolen. A week into my stay, the infection was back. Not surprisingly, the nurse never came. When I had the pump and my meds, I could at least feel hopeful, I could at least dream of keeping my leg and walking on my own again. Now I had nothing. I wanted to forget everything. I gave up.

The Personal Needs Allowance (PNA) I got every day at the shelter bought me my morning wake-and-bake hit of crack. That killed the pain in my leg long enough for me to make my way to the nearby drugstore, where I could steal some mouthwash and razors—it was surprising how much crack you could get for a pack of triple razor blades and how stupefied a bottle of mouthwash could make you.

Other homeless people I knew tried to help me. Some gave me free tokes of crack when the pain was unbearable, others shared their liquor. Outreach people who knew me came by and gave me bus tickets, cigarettes, and clean pairs of socks. After they left, I broke down and cried. I couldn't even wear both socks.

After about a week, I realized that I couldn't feel my toes. They were cold and they had changed from greyish blue to waxy black—I hadn't noticed because I'd been too busy feeling sorry for myself. My toenails started to fall away at the slightest tug and the skin sloughed off when I scraped it with my finger.

It was happening: my foot was dying just like the doctor said would happen.

I rushed myself to the hospital again.

The doctor was furious.

"Do you know how sick you've made yourself?" he yelled. The nurse rammed a thermometer in my ear.

I knew I was sick. My upper leg and torso felt like they were on fire and my head had been spinning for over a week.

243

The doctor told me he didn't even have to cut the cast off, he could smell the damage I'd done to myself. "Mr. Thistle, based on your condition during your past visit and your condition today, I regret to inform you that we might have to amputate your leg. The infection is severe, and if it spreads to your brain or heart it will kill you."

His words thundered into my brain. "Like fuck you are!" The words came from somewhere deep within me. They were a knee-jerk reaction to an impossible proposition. They left the room to attend to someone else, and I frantically stumbled off the bed, mounted my crutches, and see-sawed down the hospital corridor, tossing myself out the back door. Before I knew it I was in the dorm room at the shelter. Not wasting any time, I packed what clothes I owned into a plastic bag, collected my PNA, and fled.

I got to the subway and jumped on a train. The ride to the northern part of the city felt like an eternity. I clutched my Pyrex stem the whole way. It was loaded with crack I'd bought before I left the shelter with the hoard of bus tickets I'd got from the outreach workers and my $3.75 PNA. I had about a fifty-piece. I promised myself I wouldn't smoke it until I got to Brampton. I needed to get as far away from the hospital and the threat of my leg being amputated as I could. Where I grew up seemed a safe and logical choice.

Getting on the 77 bus was easy. It was something I used to do all the time. I'd just tell the driver I was homeless and needed to get to a shelter and they'd let me on every time. Now I had a cast—how could anyone say no? I slumped back in a seat, and we were soon cruising along the highway. When the bus started coasting through some of my old stomping grounds, a thought entered my head. We pulled into Bramalea City Centre, the air suspension hissing as the driver lowered the bus for me to get off. I hurried to catch the 1A bus to Four Corners, downtown Brampton.

I had a plan.

TURNING POINT

WHY THE FUCK AM I *wandering in the desert like a wounded animal?* I asked myself as the 1A entered the terminal.

"Last stop!" the driver called out. The bus pulled to a halt, and I stepped off onto the platform and closer to relief. I lit my stem. The sizzle of the stone gave way to a milky stream of smoke that coated the back of my throat. A fire engine howled in my ear, and my heart raced. I found myself striding to a nearby convenience store. I knew what I had to do. It didn't matter that I'd never done anything like it before, or even wanted to. This was beyond wanting. This was need.

Leftover crumbs that resembled bone shards peppered the centre of my palm. With the tips of my fingers I packed them into my pipe and lit it. My leg still hurt, but when I took this last blast, the pain completely subsided. I was ready. I gritted my teeth, opened the door, and walked in.

It's too late to turn back now. There's nowhere left to go.

I swallowed hard and grabbed the first thing in sight—a submarine sandwich wrapped in foil and a small jug of kitty litter. I brought both to the counter and waited until the clerk rang open the register, then made my move.

"Give me all your money or I'll kill you!" I yelled as I pointed my sub sandwich at the clerk. Lettuce and mayo flew everywhere.

The guy looked at me with a half-smirk. "Are you serious, pal?"

A long, awkward silence ensued, or at least it felt that way.

"Of course I'm serious! Give me the cash and hurry the fuck up!"

I could hear my voice rising to a falsetto pitch, but I meant it.

"Look, cowboy, I only have $90—store policy. You can take it; we're insured, so I really don't care. I just want to get home to my family. Understand?"

I understood. He stepped aside. My hand jittered and rifled through the till, firing change and bills all over the place. My other hand squeezed my sandwich through my fist like beef through a meat grinder. Out of the corner of my eye I could see the clerk picking up the phone. I scrambled and tried to bolt out the front door, but missed the handle and slammed headfirst into the glass.

"Ah!" I yelled, clutching my head and dropping even more cash. A goose egg instantly formed. I almost passed out, but kept running.

"You won't get far with that cast on your leg," the clerk hollered as I rounded the corner. "The cops are on their way right now, they'll get you soon enough!"

That was supposed to be the plan: get arrested and go to jail, so I'd get taken care of, so my foot could be fixed, and so my life would be saved. I was desperate. I didn't know what else to do anymore. I felt as though I had nowhere else to go, nowhere else to turn. But as soon as I was out of his sight, I jumped into the store's dumpster and covered myself in trash. I sat there as frozen as a statue for a good four hours until the sounds of the police cruisers, helicopter, and dogs were gone. I was lucky, I guess. The juicy garbage smell must've masked my scent, and the police never even thought to look in the dumpster.

I emerged as smelly as a New York City rat and counted my take: $37.20.

I thought, *This has got to be the worst moment of my life.*

INDESTRUCTIBLE PINK DRESS

I IMAGINED COPS EVERYWHERE—BEHIND TREES, under cars, behind doors, inside toilets, under the fridge, in my coffee. The sheer terror—the constant looking over my shoulder—was maddening. Drugs didn't help, and I couldn't bear the paranoia.

I couldn't go back to Samantha and the little apartment she'd rented for us. I'd cleaned out her bank account, $400, while she was at work one day and blew it all on coke and booze, afraid of withdrawal after my Tylenol 4 prescription ran out and couldn't get it renewed because I'd gone through them too quickly. I wandered around feeling sorry for myself for about a week while my health deteriorated when I should've worried instead about the damage I'd caused Samantha, about how she'd eat and get to work for the next month. We'd gone through a lot of adventures together, living precariously in emergency services, in shitty rooms all over the city, on people's couches, and under constant threat of violence for a long time.

It was the end of our four-year relationship.

I drifted in and out of shelters giving false names and slept on benches and in parks until one night a dive bar let me use the phone and I called the cops and told them I was the guy who'd committed the convenience store robbery in Brampton a few weeks earlier. I knew I'd be safer in jail than wandering around with no place to go. Society, I figured, cares more about criminals than they do about the homeless.

They came and picked me up.

The details of my arrest are sketchy at best. I remember the squad car ride to the station, how the officers were laughing at how bad I smelled, and the relief of knowing I was headed to jail, where I could rest and clean up and get some medical aid.

I also remember the brief statement I made against myself. "I did it," I said. "Now lock me up and throw away the key."

I just wanted a place to hide from the world. More than that, I wanted a place to crawl into and die in, like some wounded dog under a porch somewhere.

They charged me with robbery and shipped me off to the Maplehurst Correctional Complex in Milton to await my first court hearing.

Upon arrival, I was processed, strip-searched, and clothed in an orange jumpsuit, then thrown in the general population bullpen with the other prisoners. I broke a jailhouse rule the instant I was caged—I whistled. Four young guys jumped me from behind and stomped on my head until I was almost unconscious. I'm not sure why they stopped—there wasn't a guard in sight. Maybe they just ran out of energy.

When a guard finally came to take us off to our individual pods, I told him I was suicidal, and that I'd tried to swallow a plastic spoon near the toilet.

"What happened to your face?" he asked with a smirk, spinning his keys on his finger.

"I fell over when I was taking a shit," I replied, my head throbbing. The guys in the bullpen laughed and confirmed my story when he asked for verification.

They pulled me out of gen pop and stuck me in the protective custody holding cells, then processed me out to solitary confinement a few hours later.

I came to realize solitary confinement, or "the hole," usually isn't that bad a place to go while doing a short stretch of time. Sometimes prisoners earned their way there by beating someone senseless or because they wouldn't squeal on their comrades—both commendable things inside. Sometimes those prisoners even got to wear their orange overalls down to the hole, and you could almost see the laurel wreaths on them as the guards paraded them past everyone.

Not me.

I went into solitary confinement because I'd been banged out of general population and then squawked on myself because I was suicidal. From that point on, I was marked as a bitch during my stay at the Milton Hilton, and I was always paranoid someone might find out I'd chirped on Mike and Stefan. To underscore my humiliation and horror, I was outfitted in an indestructible pink dress with no arms or legs—the standard garb given to prisoners on suicide watch. It was made from space-age padded polyester, about eight layers thick, with diamond diagonal stitching and a collar wide enough to jam a pumpkin through, and it felt tougher than a bulletproof Kevlar vest. It was tear-proof, so you couldn't rip it apart and make a braid to hang yourself with. Which I tried to do.

It resembled a loose miniskirt crossed with a tight poncho, and all the guys whistled when the guards walked me down to isolation.

"Shake them fries, baby!" one inmate called.

"She's mine," called another, rattling the Plexiglas on his cell door.

The rest just blew me kisses and made hearts with their hands.

I wasn't ready for this shit.

Inside the hole, there were no blankets, no pillows, no contact, no respect. There was just me, my little pink dress, a blue jail-issue Bible, concrete, my thoughts, and time.

Graffiti was scrawled all over the cinder block walls, lavish script done in the finest dried feces, blood, and pencil someone must've smuggled in in their ass, addressed to God or Satan or other deities I wasn't familiar with. And, of course, there were pictures of giant penises and vaginas everywhere, decorated with old claw marks, broken fingernails, smears of snot, and magnificent pictures of the sun and trees for background effect.

The first few days were excruciating. I entered withdrawal on day two with no medical support—no Librium or Valium or anything. I was getting antibiotics for my foot, because I'd told them about it, but I was too whacked out to mention my addiction. *Just my luck*, I thought as the furies of Hades engulfed and drowned my brown ass in the river Styx.

Breathing was laboured and almost impossible. Vomit and diarrhea fired out of me every forty-five minutes or so. I never got to the toilet in time. My cell looked like it'd been peppered with a strange kind of mud, corn, and peanut shotgun.

My bones sang shrill notes of agonizing pain that vibrated right down to the marrow, shattering and pulverizing my frame into piles of bloody talcum powder. Vivid colonies of maggots burrowed through my flesh and brain and hatched out of my skin into plump flies the size of raisins that clouded the neon light the guards never turned off.

As I lay there convulsing and wishing I would die, the soft voice of my kokum whispered gently in my ear, but her road-allowance song couldn't drive away the insects and demons. She was gone as soon as she came.

I shook.

I vibrated.

I quaked.

The horizon of the cell shifted up and down more violently, I imagined, than the crust of the earth during an earthquake.

If the physical symptoms of alcohol delirium tremens just about killed me, the ever-increasing psychosis of withdrawal from crack broke me into shards of shame and pity and guilt that burned under my forehead like napalm watered with gasoline and lit by a blowtorch. The sharp edges of my memories stabbed into my consciousness, shredding my mind into

250

fragile ribbons of dark introspection. Faces from the past—my grand-mother; Mrs. R., the French teacher; Leeroy; Karen; Ivan, the kid I robbed; Samantha—all came in like razor-edged knives to disembowel me on the altar of long-ago transgressions.

I'm sorry, I'm sorry, I'm sorry, I pleaded, my eyes riveted shut, my tears run dry, my hands held aloft, trying to shield myself from a lifetime of mistakes. Dimensions folded in upon one another with a force that crumpled me in upon myself. I tried in vain to stop the implosion, to gather my intestines from the frozen cell floor, but the walls kept squeezing in and my guts just wouldn't fit back into the empty cavity that was my existence.

I writhed and squirmed, twisted and thrashed, and somewhere in my flailing, the side of my face chanced upon the only thing in the cell—the Bible.

Creator sends me a fucking message now! I sneered, pissed off by the timing.

I snatched it up and hurled it against the wall. It bounced back and landed near my throbbing leg. It lay open to Psalm 32, but the words in the passage ran like black ants in all directions. I kicked it away. It landed near the base of my concrete bed, pages splayed open once again, waiting.

I never read the damned thing.

SOLITARY CONFINEMENT

i dreamt i tread
upon cobblestones
of that ancient city,
Jerusalem.

where once
David betrayed Uriah,
his crown
replaced
by broken bones and sores,
withered in iniquity.

there,
upon marble floors,
he cried out.
met by all he was:
a coyote
languishing in the land of jackals.

selah

SHARING THE LOVE

I FINALLY SOBERED UP, AND within days the infection in my foot began to subside. I couldn't yet defend myself, so they put me in the protective-custody wing, where I could mend.

Lauriston, my cellmate, was a man of seventy from Bermuda. He said he was in for probation violation, but I was skeptical. People in on breach never get more than thirty days, and here he apparently was with two years plus a day. Had he committed some heinous crime? Or had he done just what he said he'd done? Was he just what he said he was? You could never trust other inmates.

I also wondered how he had set up the sugar trade that had made him wealthy in packaged sugars. Each inmate only got one sugar packet on his breakfast tray, one for lunch for our tea, and one for dinner, again for tea, but Lauriston had a pillowcase full of sugar packets, and he consumed at least five of them at each meal. They were a real commodity in jail and could buy food and help make mash liquor from orange peels, water, and bread; along with tobacco and dope, mash was a top jail product.

At mealtimes, the sugars would just pour into our cell.

"Here, Lauriston," said Bucky, the quartermaster—the inmate who gives out and controls the food, the most powerful and respected position on the range, a collection of cells that form a holding area where inmates do the majority of their time.

Lauriston reached both hands through the food port and Bucky dropped a sock full of sugar packages into them.

"Thanks, young blood. I have something for you. Hold up." Lauriston reached down onto his dinner tray and handed Bucky his potatoes.

Bucky dapped his fist on Lauriston's and thanked him for the carbs—much-needed fuel, as Bucky worked out compulsively three hours a day.

"I got you, wisdom. Always."

Bucky smiled and continued distributing the rest of the trays to the other cells down the line.

"You see that, Indian," Lauriston said to me. "Give to the next man and the next man prosper with you."

"It's a nice theory," I snapped, "but how do you know they won't just take your stuff?"

"What are you thinking, fool? Wake up. We are people, too, you know. We give and trust just like all those people on the outside, like all those good people. Know this: all brethren who give to his brethren prosper by his brother, and all those selfish *bloodclaat* that don't, get nothing but fire."

Lauriston was quite angry. It looked like he was going to start swinging. He kissed his teeth and muttered something, then became deadly serious.

"You see me? I'm an old man, I got no family, no drugs, no tobacco, no candy bars—I got nothing. But still my canteen's rammed with goodies and my belly full. These convicts can take anything from me, but I know to give, even in this place. And I trust these guys and they know it. Some of them never been trusted in their whole lives. You know what that's worth in Babylon?"

"I'm sorry, Lauriston. I just . . ." I scurried to the back wall to get ready to defend myself.

"Calm your ass, I'd never hit a cripple. Listen to me—I'm trying to help you. Try it. Give away your food and don't ask for nothing. That means a lot in here. Trust those guys to be good people. But never give it to a *bombaclot* who tries to take it; if that happens, then you beat his ass—life and death."

I agreed to heed his advice and went to bed, all the while thinking about his pile of sugar.

The next morning when Bucky came around, I took my breakfast tray, grabbed my cereal package and bag of milk, and handed it to Bucky.

"Here, take it," I said.

Bucky just glanced at me, put them on his tray, and continued on.

Nothing came back. I waited for an hour, looking over at him while he played cards with the other quartermaster, Priest. He didn't so much as peer up at me.

What a prick, I thought. At lockout, I walked over to the shower, took off my overalls, and was about to get into the stall when Bucky came up to me with Priest and grabbed me.

"What the fuck, you crazy, star?" he said. "You gonna wash your dirty ass in my shower? You never wash your dirty self, star."

Bucky was right, I never showered. I was as afraid of getting an infection in my foot as much as I was afraid of getting raped. Those fears kept me perpetually dirty and stinky. But today I had to shower, my terrible body odour was making it difficult for me and Lauriston to eat in our cell, and I'd forced myself into the stall. I could feel my face turning white at the thought of being beaten, even raped, by Bucky and Priest. I closed my eyes and wished it would end quickly.

"You can't go in there, bomba. Open your eyes. Open them and look at me!" Bucky yelled.

But my eyes remained glued shut, my body stiff as a board.

Bucky shouted again, only louder this time. "Open your *bloodclaat* eyes, star. You can't go in there. Not with your foot wound open like that. Here," Bucky said.

I felt something squishy press against my chest. I opened my eyes a crack, careful to protect them from a fist or finger gouge. Bucky was handing me his black jail sandals.

"You need to wear these to keep your feet off the ground. The bacteria is on the ground; if you step on it, it will get in your wound and you'll lose your foot."

As Bucky said that, Priest grabbed my shoulder and added, "Turn them over. Look. I carved the Star of David on the bottom to protect you against the filth of the place. One, bless."

There it was, the Star of David, engraved on the heel, right where my injured foot would rest.

When I returned to my cell, Lauriston was there, waiting. I told him what had happened.

He just grinned and said, "I told you so."

BIBLES BEHIND BARS

SOON I HAD ALL THE food I could eat, all the sugar I wanted, and all the juice crystals I desired. Moreover, I had all the respect one could hope for inside. The food helped to heal my foot, and in time, when Priest and then Bucky were moved to a supermax prison, I was chosen to take one of the jobs as quartermaster because the guys on the range knew I was fair and that I'd share.

As Lauriston said, "All people who give to those around them prosper by them, and all those selfish *bloodclaats* that don't, get nothing but fire."

I just wish I hadn't had to go to jail to figure that out—that and so much else.

Before Priest was shipped off, he offered me some advice.

"Indian, listen. I've exhausted my appeals. It's over for me."

The look on his face was of utter defeat and worry. It was an expression I hadn't seen on his face since I'd met him sometime earlier.

"It'll be alright, bro," I said. "Just keep to yourself, read, work out, draw . . ."

"I'll try. But shit's crazy down there. At least I'll get conjugal visits after a while . . ." Priest cracked a half smile and his eyes glazed over.

"Anyways, Thistle, listen. You have two official duties in this job: First, you have to make inmates read the rules when they first enter the range and make them shower—people need to be clean. If they don't listen, you have to bang 'em out. You're the first line of defence against disease and nastiness, the guys depend on you. Second, you have to distribute the food fairly, which I know you'll do 'cause Lauriston taught you well."

It was true, Lauriston had taught me the value of sharing and how it maintained order. "Is that it?" I asked, knowing that the quartermaster job was much more complex.

"Of course not. You have to keep the dope and tobacco flowing and you have to pass lighters to other inmates and other ranges. You do that through the cleaners who mop the halls. They come at 8:30 sharp every morning. You pass the lighter to them, they pass it to other inmates, and then they pass it back. It's simple. Here."

Priest handed me the purple lighter I'd seen used many times on our range. I grabbed it and rammed it in my jumpsuit pocket.

"When the screws come to shake down the range," Priest stressed, "it's your job to hoop the lighter. You've got to stick it up your ass, and fast. Don't give me that face, I've had to do it for two years straight! Do you know how many times I've been intimate with that thing?"

The laugh I let out relaxed Priest for the first time in our conversation. I felt happy he could ease up, if only for a second.

"Use soap if you can, slip the lighter up. If not, you're taking the dry hammer—it don't matter, just get it up there. I know it sucks, but the lighter is power. People can't smoke or do dope without it, and they will try to steal it from you. To prevent that, you have to buy protection with food; give it to guys who you want to fight for you—the big guys you work out with. They don't give a shit about you, but they do care where their calories come from, you can bet on that."

"Got it," I said, picturing myself having to repeatedly hoop the lighter during cell raids. "Anything else?"

"Yeah, when new fish come in, you have to take 'em to the toilet and watch 'em take a dump. Remember when I did that with you? There was a reason for that."

The memory of when I first entered the range shot across my mind. Priest met me at the sally port, made me read the rules, told me to shower, then took me to the toilet and watched me. He had his hand over the flusher the whole time. Once I was done, he pushed me aside and took a rolled-up newspaper and stirred the water, breaking up my waste. Then he told me to shower again.

"That's how the drugs come in. Some guys come in with suitcases up their asses and ruin the trade by driving down prices. You can't let that happen. If someone drops a suitcase in the bowl while you're quartermaster, you have to reach in and grab it, bang the guy out, then give the product to Bucky—it's his market. And don't worry about Bucky—he's got an army in here and will sort out any problems if it involves product. Got it? If you follow those rules, you'll be fine."

I assured Priest I understood, but I could see he wanted to tell me something else. I waited patiently until he looked comfortable, then asked, "Is there anything more?"

"Yes," he said intently. "I've seen a lot of guys hurt really bad in here. Some go to the hospital, some die. You see this book right here?" Priest pointed to his blue jail-issue Bible. "This has a lot of power in it and it can tell you things about people."

I tried to piece together what a Bible and people getting killed in jail had in common, while at the same time hoping Priest wasn't going to get all religious on me.

"Lots of people end up here," Priest said. "Some come to jail on remand, some on misdemeanours, some on transfer, some on breach, and some on really serious charges. Many of the fake cats brag about the crimes they've done; they do this to make themselves out to be badder than they really are, to intimidate others. They say they're bank robbers or jewel thieves or murderers but really they got caught with a dime bag of weed in their mother's station wagon at a traffic stop. Whatever they say, remember: braggers get daggers."

Priest paused and looked down at the guys pumping water bag weights at the end of the range; dudes getting their swole on. "But there are others inside who are real criminals, and there's a way to spot them."

"How?" I knew what he was about to say was valuable.

"At night, when you're giving out tea for Jug Up before bed, look at people's bedsides. Look beside the beds of those young punks who brag, then look at the bedside of the quiet guys. You'll see something different."

"What?" the question jumped from my lips before I had a chance to stop it.

"Those in for real crimes, the serious ones, they always have a Bible, Koran, Torah, or some other holy book by their bedsides. Night after night they stay up trying to make it right with God. Don't fuck with guys like that, they'll straight up kill you. The fake criminals, on the other hand, sleep like babies and never keep Bibles by their beds cause they don't need forgiveness cause they ain't done nothing wrong. The real hard nuts can't sleep and can't stop themselves from seeking God. They need forgiveness because they can't accept who or what they've become and what they've done, or accept the life they've made for themselves. It's a hard pill to swallow—to know you're a monster who's done monstrous things. They've got no other comfort than God . . . Somewhere along the line it went bad for them."

I kept a Bible beside my bed, and I asked, "What went bad, Priest?"

"All us criminals start out as normal people just like anyone else, but then things happen in life that tear us apart, that make us into something capable of hurting other people. That's all any of the darkness really is—just love gone bad. We're just broken-hearted people hurt by life."

There were tears in the corners of Priest's eyes. I could see for the first time the good man this muscle-bound criminal must have been once, the man he must have wished he could still be. I felt a deep sorrow knowing that he had no chances left.

The sally-port buzzer blared and the guards came to collect Priest. He composed himself, gathered his pillowcase of belongings, dapped my fist, and said goodbye.

I never saw Priest again. Someone told me that he'd been in for a homicide in a drug deal gone wrong. But I never did find out the details, because that was something he never talked about—except, I assume, in private, between himself and God, at night, with a Bible resting beside his bed.

AUDREY

"I GOT A CAR," SHE said. "We could work together." The gorgeous vanilla scent of her perfume filled my nose, and her deadly smile left me defenceless. I nodded like a moron.

I'd seen her around from time to time at some of the trap houses in the neighbourhood since getting out of jail. She had straight golden-blond hair and grey eyes plastered with mascara. She was a knockout and didn't look like one of us street people. Her cheeks were full, her body well-formed, and she had expensive clothes. She intimidated me at first. Then she introduced herself.

"Hello," she said. "My name's Audrey."

My heart jumped at her East Coast accent.

"What's your name?"

I was too enamoured to form a coherent response.

She twirled her hair on her index finger and giggled.

I was in love.

I learned that she lived around the corner in her own apartment. She was impressed that I fended for myself, begging and stealing, and did it without drug dealing.

"I don't believe in dope dealing," she said. "It's poisoning our kind. Broken-hearted people with nowhere to be in the world."

I related to that. I wondered how she kept her car on the road with such a serious crack addiction, but I never asked. It was none of my business.

One of the working girls who frequented many of the same dope spots wasn't a fan. "She takes away all the business," she said when I'd asked her who Audrey was. "I wish she'd leave some for us."

One day, when I brought in about two hundred dollars of stolen meat I'd pinched from the grocery store, Audrey was sitting in the back room of the trap house, watching the goings-on. I got my standard one-third the retail price for the haul and exchanged it for crack.

"A girl can do a lot with a guy like you, Jesse," Audrey said as she eyed me up and down, then looked at my rock.

We went back to her place that night. I thought we were going to have sex, but we just smoked until the dope ran out, and talked until our jaws hurt, about where she was from and how she wanted out of the life we were both caught up in. I didn't make any moves toward her. I figured she got that all the time—pigs invading her body.

She made up some blankets for me on the couch and said, "Anytime you need a place to crash you're welcome to stay." She covered me up, then went to sleep alone in her bedroom. I dreamt of her the whole night.

The next day we did our first run together.

We hit about twelve grocery stores. I went in with my gym bag, filled it with steaks, shrimp, baby formula, razors, and makeup, until it damn near broke from the weight. She waited outside, her van revving. A couple of times security guards chased me out, but I just hopped in the van and she floored it to our next destination.

The excitement in Audrey's face, the way we cheered and held hands as we sped away, like we'd accomplished something, turned me on. It made my foot feel better, made me feel better about myself, made me feel better about everything. We made a great team. When we cashed out in the evening, we had more dope than we could smoke. I fried up a few steaks, and we had dinner at her place like real people.

Soon, our scams became more complex. The easiest was the water bottle hustle. I'd go into a grocery store and grab two huge water bottles—the ones worth ten bucks when they're returned empty—and carry them out. If I wasn't followed, I'd dump out the water, go back in, and return them. I got twenty dollars for five minutes' work, simple as pie.

If store security did come after me, I'd drop the bottles in the parking lot then rush away. Security had the choice of either chasing me down or staying with the merchandise—they couldn't do both. If they did leave the bottles for someone else to steal, that someone was Audrey. She'd drive behind the action, pick the bottles up, then speed ahead and grab me before I was busted. That was the best scenario, because we'd just return them somewhere else down the road. Again, an easy twenty.

If security stayed with the bottles, Audrey would just drive ahead and pick me up, and we'd try it again somewhere else. In all three scenarios, I always got away safe. It was brilliant. We did it all day.

We hit liquor stores, too. We used what we called our blitzkrieg manoeuvre there, our most daring, but also our most lucrative. We could make upward of $200 or $300 a pop. I'd rush in and grab the first big bottles in sight—maybe five at a time—then I'd make for the front doors and dive headfirst into the van. She'd hit the gas, back door wide open, my legs dangling halfway out. I must've looked like a baseball player stealing second base. Audrey was one hell of a driver, fast and fearless, rubber wheels screeching through red lights and stop signs like she was Steve McQueen on meth. Often, we'd look back at the pack of angry floor walkers standing and screaming, shaking their fists at the van, and we'd yell at the top of our lungs, cheering our victories.

When the liquor stores caught on, we shifted to beer stores. Given the weight and size of beer cases, the runs didn't make as much money, but we still made hundreds of dollars over the course of the day. All of it went to crack.

We got thinner. There was a swagger about us, a strange kind of confidence, like we were rock stars or something. We *were* ghetto rock stars, just not the kind with guitars, and we partied like there was no tomorrow. No matter how much money we got, though, it was never enough. And the excitement was fleeting. Now, looking back on it, we were high, wild, and borderline out of our minds. I can't believe we did what we did. I regret it all.

In a matter of weeks it all fell apart. I was sitting at the end of Audrey's couch drinking a bottle of booze we'd just stolen, waiting for our nightly steaks to grill up. There was a giant pile of crack between us—our day's keep.

"I know you want me," Audrey slurred, drunk off her face. She cozied up to me and put her hand on my lap, sliding it toward my crotch. It felt weird. We'd never been intimate before, even though I'd wanted her since we met.

I sat frozen. She didn't look so hot anymore. It wasn't like she'd changed so much as to not be physically attractive—she was still a bombshell. It's just that I didn't like it when she talked and acted this way, nor did I like what we'd become. I thought we could make a real go of life together, get jobs, clean up, stay out of trouble. I wanted us to be something better and I didn't want to ruin it. It was silly to think this way, because it was clear that we were addict thieves, partners in crime—good at it, too—and that we adored each other and got along great. I just had too many feelings to take advantage of her.

I loaded up the pipe and gave it to her to distract her. She knocked it out of my hand and leaned in for a kiss. I reciprocated. My soul exploded, but it felt wrong. I pulled back.

"I can't," I said. "I think I love you." I reached for her hand. I wanted to explain myself, about how I wanted to wait.

"Don't," she said, sounding hostile. She hoisted herself to the edge of the couch and almost face-planted on the table. Her knee knocked over our little crack mountain and a portion of it tumbled onto the carpet.

I sat speechless. I knew I'd crossed a line.

"Take your half and get out," she said, not looking at me. "I'm done with you." She walked over to the front door and held it open. "Out."

I didn't argue as I collected my belongings and left.

We didn't even say goodbye.

DYNAMITE

THE WICK ON THE STICK of dynamite stuck out of my parka about five inches. I tucked it into my breast pocket as I headed to the dope house.

My crack dealer's name was Green, a gang member from Rexdale, Ontario, and his homies all had colours for names. I assumed they got the idea from *Reservoir Dogs*. Green told his mates that I was dangerous and willing to do anything. He was right. I had no fear of death after Samantha and I broke up and what happened with Audrey and Flip. Everyone was impressed that I'd robbed the convenience store, and that I'd eluded the cops with a cast on my leg. They started calling me "Hot Boy." I hated the moniker, but it gave me a kind of respect, homeless or not.

Piles of snow shimmered in the dusk as I hurried past the mechanic shop. The red stick felt heavy against my chest, like an iron bar. The Oxy-Contin I'd taken three hours earlier was wearing off. My foot was hurting like it'd been crucified with a six-inch railway tie—the staph infection had come back. Cold crept into my ankle and seized the wires holding my foot together. I couldn't run without the aid of pills, and pain could halt my mission.

It doesn't matter, I resolved. *I'm going to get a giant rock from those dealer scum whether I'm high or not.* My jaw muscles flexed and snapped the tooth I'd got fixed in jail. I spit the fragment on the sidewalk and it bounced off into a snowbank. A vision of Vancouver and the car came to me. I wanted revenge for the person they'd turned me into.

I whipped out my crack stem, loaded it with my last twenty-dollar rock, and lit it. I needed that extra push forward. Yellow flames licked the glass and the rock melted, releasing a stream of thick smoke. It sizzled like Rice Krispies covered in milk. A gush of spit poured out of my mouth and thwacked onto the ice below; it froze into a beautiful spiderweb of crystals, making tiny squeaking noises as it formed. In an instant my hearing had sharpened to superhuman levels.

I spun around 360 degrees scanning for the legion of hidden cops I knew tracked my every movement. I saw nothing, but sensed they were close. Once, I'd found a tracking device in my baseball cap—in the button on top. People told me it was just there to hold the hat together, but I didn't believe them. I ripped it off and chucked it into the Etobicoke River to evade capture. These tracking cops, I'd figured out, also sent coded messages to each other using car license-plate numbers. Nine meant they were close; two or five meant they had a lock on my whereabouts and were moving in.

I saw a car with a license plate with a two and a five, and it even slowed down as it passed. I searched around for cover. I contemplated diving into the bush but decided against it. My ears were ringing from the intense crack high, and I almost slipped on the ice and dropped my payload of explosives.

The blast of rock also brought out those Ewok-looking shadow creatures who shot death rays at me with their galactic sorcery. Their chatter drove me nuts; they sounded exactly like they did in *Star Wars*: "*Mechipy chuwa, ah!*" Fuckin' terrifying. They were stealthy creatures, melting in and out of the shadows. They reminded me of those demon shadows in *Ghost* that dragged that Puerto Rican—Willie Lopez—to hell for killing Patrick Swayze after he got hit by that car. I didn't want to end up like him. I lit my pipe again, hoping to rid myself of my paranoia, but an Ewok groaned from the darkness over near the curb.

They're coming for me!

I ran as fast as I could into the middle of the street where the light was strongest. My heart pounded until it hurt. I slapped my face to snap out of it. I slapped it again to remind myself that none of it was real. My arm knocked loose the dynamite and it tumbled down around my waist inside my jacket. I placed it back in my pocket and continued on.

When I got to the dope house, one of Green's men was guarding the door.

"Hot Boy!" he hollered as I approached. He held out his fist and I dapped it. He kept his eyes on my every move. The brown-black hilt of his Glock was exposed in his waistband, his shirt purposefully pulled up, warning people not to fuck around. It didn't faze me.

"Green around?" I smirked back, trying to play it cool. I felt a thunderbolt radiate up my leg. The Oxy had worn off.

"Inside, in the basement." He stood up and reached toward me.

I jumped back. "What the fuck?!" I said, pushing his hands away from my torso. He was going to pat me down. "You know me, dog."

His face hardened, and he put a hand near his pistol. "New policy."

"What do you think? I got a stick of dynamite on me?! Chill." I laughed and nudged his shoulder.

He laughed back. "Wouldn't be surprised." He eyed me one last time, then motioned toward the door with his head. "G'wan in."

My bluff had worked. I dapped his hand and passed.

The house smelled of crack and meth. The walls were caked with a clear layer of resin, enough to get high on if I scraped it off and smoked it. Half the light bulbs were missing or shattered on the floor; the whole place was lit by candles. A dim light radiated from the bowels of the basement. I steadied myself and made my descent.

A few crackheads were in the corner hitting their pipes near the foot of the stairs, and a few tweakers were over near the bathroom smoking broken light bulbs. The door at the back was closed. That was a good sign—it meant the ladies were turning tricks with Johns because there was dope around; no one used that room but them. Green emerged from a door in the hall. He had a sock in his hand—his trademark dope carry-all. It bulged with a load of luscious rocks.

"Crackula, my man," he said to me. "What can I do for you?"

I stood there a second. I felt the explosive press hard against my ribs. Green must have sensed something was up and backed away. I reached into my coat, yanked out the dynamite, and thrust it above my head.

"GIVE ME ALL YOUR FUCKING DOPE OR I'LL LIGHT IT!" I screamed and waved the red cylinder around, my lighter held near the wick, ready to ignite it.

Green's eyes opened wide and all the heads in the room spun around, a look of terror on them. Everyone jostled for shelter, tossing their gear. Green backed up against the wall, almost dropping his plump sock. The gunman at the front door appeared at the top of the stairs and stood there motionless, seemingly stunned. Another emerged from the door where Green had been earlier, gun in hand. He, too, was shitting himself.

"I'LL LIGHT IT—I SWEAR!" I yelled again. I flicked my lighter. A bead of sweat trickled down my forehead, and I wiped it away on the sleeve of my dynamite arm.

Green cracked a smile.

That wasn't the reaction I'd hoped for.

He grabbed the explosive out of my hand. "A fucking road flare?" He laughed and tugged at the wick and it fell onto the floor. He sniffed at the red stick like he was examining a fine cigar. "Doesn't smell like sulphur to me."

Silence fell over the room like a blanket, until I heard the safeties on the guns click. Green stared at me. I was trapped.

I'd picked the flare up near the gravel pit by my old public school. It looked like a stick of dynamite, so I stuck a piece of string in it to make a wick, and hatched a scheme to come to the dope house and threaten maximum carnage to get a rock. I'd gotten the idea from an old story Uncle Ron had told me about when he went into a biker clubhouse with a live grenade to scare the shit out of everyone. It had worked for him, but my plan failed miserably. I waited for Green's men to open fire.

To my surprise, Green giggled. "That's why I like you," he said. "Because you're fucking crazy like me."

He reached into his sock and pulled out a twenty rock. "Here." He placed it in my hand and waved his men off. "Great joke. You had me for a second."

PUSH-UPS

I WAS IN JAIL IN 2007 for assaulting a couple of police officers.

I'd done a huge toke of crack after breaking into a car and was having bad hallucinations and thought the Ewok creatures were coming for me. I ran into the middle of the street hollering that I needed help and was dying and losing my mind.

From a side road, a van flew at me then slammed on its brakes and five huge bearded men jumped out and began chasing me. They looked like bikers. I hobbled as fast as I could, headlong into traffic, cars veering out of the way, horns honking, but the bikers were all larger and faster than I was. They tackled me, but I fought back with all my might until I saw a police cruiser pull up. I knew I'd be safe—the bikers couldn't murder or kidnap me—but they still choked me from behind, and I almost lost consciousness, my arms punching forward until I heard a loud crack and gurgle in my throat.

I was dumped in the back of a paddy wagon, scratching the steel sides and growling, like an injured mountain lion in shackles, and brought to Maplehurst, where I was charged with assault with intent to resist arrest times two, possession of a scheduled substance, break and enter, and theft.

The guys on the range were impressed that I'd fought off so many undercover police—the bikers, as it turned out—and had gone fist-to-cuffs with three uniformed police officers, and in the process re-broke my wrist and fractured my jaw. Truth was, I was just terrified and high and had gone mad, there was no toughness involved.

One.

My arms wobbled as I pushed up. Hands: shoulder-width apart. Feet: together. Body: straight. The latest song from Rihanna blasted across the protective-custody range in the jail in Milton, Ontario. A dank scent of male swamp entered me as I sucked in air for energy.

Two.

The pressure increased in my head as my sternum touched the floor, and my wrist throbbed, but then my arms straightened again. I peered down at myself and saw a rack of bones and a stomach that sucked back toward my spine. My skin was grey and lifeless.

Three.

I gritted my teeth and felt a burn in my triceps as I dipped down and up another time. There was a tightness in my core I hadn't felt for years. These were the first set of push-ups I'd attempted to do since I'd been arrested again.

Four.

I tried with all my might to keep straight but as my nose touched the floor first, my bum shot up in the air. I glanced over at my cellmate, who was drinking his orange crystal drink out of an empty shampoo bottle. A stain of blood near his foot had seeped into the pores of the cement.

Five.

Faintness overtook me. I kept going. My blue jail underwear dangled low, finding the ground before I touched down and hoisted myself up again. The echo of the cell wasn't as bad as the hole, but it still made focusing difficult.

Six.

Halfway down my muscles failed. My arms locked and wouldn't push up anymore. I gave it one more go—they wouldn't budge.

I tucked my legs underneath my bum and pulled myself upright using the side of the steel table. I swayed as my knees buckled and I found myself clinging to the bars of the cell. Last thing I remember was my hands letting go, then the hollow sound of my skull smashing into the pavement.

When I awoke I was in another wing of the jail with an attendant hovering above me.

"You shouldn't be exercising, Mr. Thistle," he said. "Your blood pressure is too low, you're still too emaciated."

"But how am I supposed to defend myself?" I asked. I tried to raise my arms but couldn't. I swallowed and heard a click in my throat.

"I wouldn't worry about that right now." He pulled back the cover revealing my foot. "The disease in here is way more serious than the other inmates."

I wasn't sure if he was talking about my infection or the detention centre.

INCEPTION

I SAW A GUY ON our range at the sally port talking with an older man in a red-and-grey uniform. The geezer wasn't stiff like the guards. He had a peaceful presence about him, but still a hardness about his body language, like he'd been one of us, like he'd done time in the past.

"Who is that?" I asked my cellmate.

"That's the chaplain."

I watched as the inmate gave the chaplain an envelope and took a pile of papers to the back table where he always sat.

When I walked over and asked him what he was doing, he said, "I'm getting my high school. You do that through the chaplain. It's a great way to pass the time."

I observed him for about a week. He was quiet—the mark of a true gent, like Priest said. He never bragged or talked bad or gambled chocolate bars or traded dope—the guy just did his time real classy like. I admired that. I thought maybe I could make a better life for myself in those books, too, like he was trying to do. Or maybe it was silly.

"I'd like to try that out," I said to him one day after I'd finished working out with the water bags. "School. Give it another go."

He lifted his head from his notes.

"But I can't read too good. I dropped out a long time ago. And years of drugs and hard living—well, it's kind of done my head in."

"Nah. It's easy—don't believe those lies." He turned around a piece of paper. "This is my reading assignment. Try reading the first line."

My eyes had trouble focusing, I stumbled and stuttered, and I messed up pronouncing a few words, but I eventually got through it.

"See. Walk in the park. I can help you out if you want."

A week later, I received my first assignment from the chaplain in English. I got help with my reading from other inmates when I needed it and handed in my work the following week. A month later, I got an 85 percent on the final.

Something within me shifted.

Philosophy and world religions classes followed. I got 83 percent in philosophy. World religions was way harder—I didn't finish because I didn't understand all the big words. The local school board, however, recognized my efforts and gave me six maturity credits. Three months into my sentence and I was only two credits short of graduating high school—it was a miracle.

Unbeknownst to me, most of the guys on the range were suspicious. Rumours spread that I was flying kites to the screws, squawking, because cell raids always happened right after I'd handed in my homework or sent a letter to Grandma. After I submitted one of my last assignments, I was confronted in the washroom by a group of inmates.

"Why would you chirp on your brothers?" they asked and slammed me up against the shower wall.

"I'm just trying to finish my schooling," I said, afraid but determined.

They roughed me up some, clocked me in the eye a few times, but eventually stopped, satisfied, I assume, by the fact that I didn't break.

THE MESSENGER

I HAD A VISITOR. I was so excited. No one ever visited me or sent me letters—ever. Grandma didn't even respond. That didn't bother me anymore.

The guard handcuffed me and took me to the visitor's area. I was surprised to see Jerry on the other side of the Plexiglas. Somehow he'd found my hiding spot—again—like he always did. No matter where I ran—to a shelter, jail, or to some far-off random street corner across the country—the fucker kept tabs on me and would track me down. Trying to hide from him was like a souped-up version of that TV show *Mantracker*, except Jerry didn't have a horse or cowboy hat, and I wasn't running and leaping through the bush. This, however, was the first time he'd actually come to see me in jail.

"So, here you are," he said, "hiding like a frightened rat. When is this going to stop?"

"Fuck you," I said. "I'll go back to my cell! You watch!"

"Go then, go back to your hole and die alone, you sad, sad man!"

I wanted to kick the Plexiglas and have it shatter in his pudgy face, blinding him for life.

"I see through your macho bullshit," he said. "Always have. One day I'm going to stop searching, then you'll be fucked."

I fidgeted with my coveralls.

"You put up all these walls to keep people out. Literally—look around.

I just don't have the energy to break them down anymore. No one does. I'm the last—no one else gives a shit anymore. I had to dig really deep to come see you here today. I hate seeing you penned in like some animal, but I forced myself to do it because I have a message."

I looked up at him.

"Grandma is sick. She doesn't have many years left. You living like this is hurting her, and it makes me want to beat you up—seriously. She's been waiting all these years for you to stop living this way. If she dies and you're like this, you'll never recover. I hope you realize that."

I slammed my fists on the counter in front of me and closed my eyes. I didn't know what to do. When I opened them I saw Jerry's hand pressed hard against the Plexiglas. I didn't dare lift my hand to his, but looked up at him.

"See, I knew you were still in there. That's the little brother I remember."

As soon as he said that, the buzzer of the timer went off—our visit was over. As the guard snapped the handcuffs back onto my semi-healed wrists, I turned and saw Jerry's hand still on the glass, his eyes locked onto mine.

A couple weeks later I was released with time served. I felt hopeless—I'd come so close to finishing high school, only to be released right before I could see it through, to be released right back into the life that I knew was slowly killing me. I was in bondage to the dealers, a twenty-four-hour money-generating machine, and the thought of lurching forward, and the pain that shot up my leg with every step in the desert out there, terrified me.

STEAK KNIFE

I WAS STEALING BIKES FROM people's backyards. My dealers took them, thirty dollars a pop, without question. I desperately needed the money to get high. I'd been up for a week solid since being released from jail, and my addictions were worse than ever.

The street I was on in Brampton is gang territory. Crack in Brampton travelled through there before being distributed throughout Peel County. I shouldn't have been jacking bikes there, I knew better. But I was desperate, and my mind wasn't working well. Jail time had softened my begging and thieving skills, too. People just didn't believe my lies anymore. "You're a healthy young man," they'd say. "You should be working."

I spotted a BMX bike, with gold pegs and chrome handle bars, and hauled it over a fence. Before it hit the ground, a group of angry young men confronted me from behind.

"Hot Boy!" one of them hollered. "You know this block's off limits!"

They stripped me of the bike and shoved me into a parking lot. There were five of them. Bandanas flying.

"Now we gotta make an example of you," the smallest one said as he circled behind me to cut off my exit.

A guy in front of me pulled out a steak knife and lunged at me. The knife hit me right in the mouth. I tumbled onto the ground, smashing the back of my head on the concrete. Blood poured down into my throat and I choked, but I swung forward, wildly, punching up at the sky, the instinct to defend myself kicking in.

"Look at him," one guy said. He kicked my ribs repeatedly, pushing me sideways. I felt nothing but heard the dull thuds echo through my body. I saw the knife handle sticking out of my face and covered my head.

I heard laughing, followed by the close whine of sirens and wheels grinding on concrete, and raised my head, saw my attackers running off in all directions like cockroaches as a cop car mounted the curb. I yanked the knife out of my face and tossed it in a bush. A stream of blood gushed onto my shirt—it looked like a massacre. My hands fumbled over my head. The left side of my face was numb. There was a hole above my upper lip. I stuck my finger into it and it slid over my front teeth.

Right down to the bone.

A policewoman ran over. "Who did it?" she asked.

I stayed quiet, fearful that people in the complex nearby were listening.

She helped me to my feet, then put me in her squad car and drove to the hospital.

I was shipped to 21 Division after and charged with theft. Didn't matter. The arrest probably saved my life.

After being attacked by a gang, I was taken to the hospital to get stitches; then the police processed me and shipped me back into custody. The scar is still visible today if you look hard enough.

RANDOM DUDE

"NAME. BIRTHDATE. SOCIAL SECURITY," THE shelter worker rhymed off, thrusting a clipboard at me under the Plexiglas. She looked like she was having a rough day, her hair all frizzed out.

I grabbed the clipboard. "I don't have any ID," I said. "I just got out of jail, and I'm going by bus to Ottawa to rehab tomorrow. The chaplain bought me a ticket." I pushed my Greyhound stub against the glass.

The rehabilitation centre I was going to was Harvest House, a last-chance Christian rehab that took the worst of the worst cases that no other place would touch—I know, I tried calling them all from jail. Given my record, it was my only option. Olive had given me the phone number one day when I called her collect from jail trying to set up a release plan.

"I'm going to be brutally honest with you, Jesse," she said, as I scribbled down the digits. "I've known you forever, and you can't make it another season the way you are. You don't look right anymore. Please call."

Olive was always so optimistic, so hopeful—she believed God could rescue people even in the most wretched of cases—so to hear her talk this way really caught my attention. I phoned Harvest House the instant I got off the phone with her and discovered that they had GED schooling as well as treatment—I could finish what I'd started and graduate high school. Plus, they'd take me right away—no other program would do that. That gave me such hope. When I told the chaplain, he bought me the one-way ticket and gave me a pair of jeans and a shirt, right before the jail gates opened to freedom.

"These don't fit," I said.

"Trust me," he told me when he dropped me off at the shelter. "You'll put on weight."

The electro-haired lady behind the Plexiglas ignored me and my bus ticket, slid a pen through the opening, and started talking with her colleagues.

I filled in the form and passed the clipboard back.

"Jesse Thistle," she said, and I nodded. She buzzed me in and told me to wait near the front to get my toiletries and to finish the intake process.

The shelter was empty, or at least it appeared that way. A few people were playing cards near the doors to the washrooms. A couple were on the phones by the office. I hadn't been to this shelter in months, but had been a regular for years, starting way back in 2001 when they moved it from the old fire hall. I sat down beside an old man with grey hair. His clothes and shoes told me he'd just gotten out of jail or lost his home—they were too nice to be lived-in street gear.

"Did she say you were Thistle?" he asked and motioned with his thumb to the office.

"Yeah." I studied his body language and wondered if I should bolt—thought maybe he could be a friend of Mike and Stefan's.

"Was your dad Sonny by chance? I only ever knew one family of Thistles."

"Cyril Thistle Jr. is my dad."

The man's face changed from hard convict to friendly dog. I noticed a few prison tattoos under his sleeve as he stuck his hand out.

"Name's Rodney. I was a good friend of your pop's."

I took his hand. "I've never met anyone who's known my dad other than my own family. I'm just on my way to Harvest House in Ottawa. I leave tomorrow."

"Been there. Treatment. Not Harvest House."

The tips of his fingers were burnt and swollen. Telltale signs that he suffered from the same addiction I did. Only lighters or crack stems burn like that; that, or maybe he was a mechanic.

Not likely, I deduced. *Working mechanics don't usually stay in homeless shelters.*

"Your dad was a great man. One of the best in Weston back in the day. Too bad what happened."

I nodded. I had no words and just wanted to hear him riff—thought maybe he'd reveal some details I hadn't heard before—but he fell silent.

I finally said, "I wish I knew him." I glanced over to the intake worker, then back, not sure of what was on my new friend's mind. "I grew up at my grandparents'. Last I saw him was when I was three. I've been keeping an eye out for him."

"Keeping an eye out?"

"You know, in case he pops up somewhere. I heard he's homeless. I've been searching all over for years."

He shook his head and sat up. "No one told you? He's gone, son. They got him in '82."

The lady in the booth called my name, but I didn't move.

"Who got him?"

"You better go get signed in," he said. "If you don't, they'll discharge you for wasting their time."

"Who got him?" I asked again before getting up and walking toward the office, glancing back at him the whole way.

He didn't answer.

The worker closed the door behind me, and I sat there the entire time thinking of what he'd said.

When I emerged, he was gone.

THE PROCESS

I DIDN'T GET IT RIGHT the first time in rehab. No one ever does.

I arrived at Harvest House in November 2007 and stayed for three months straight. I didn't really work the twelve steps of Alcoholics Anonymous when I got there, nor did I dig deep in personal development classes to the root of my addictions, like everyone else. I believed I was better than everyone, than the program. I kind of coasted after the initial detox and withdrawal, white-knuckled it, as they say in AA speak. I stayed dry with no cigarettes, sure, but never really achieved sobriety, even though I thought I did. I just repeated the first drugless day for ninety days.

Eventually dreams of liquor and drugs drove me out into a pitch-black February night with my roommate Max, another guy who was lackluster about the program. I was in no shape to face Old Man Winter in Ottawa; I didn't own a jacket or even a sweater. I didn't care. All that mattered was that I was free and that I was going to be high and drunk and that I didn't have to listen to the counsellors yell at me in group therapy while I avoided revealing any of my resentments about Dad or Josh or Grandpa or Jerry, or read the King James Bible, begging God for a forgiveness I knew I didn't deserve.

"Fuck it all! Tonight is mine," I proclaimed. I knew I'd most likely get arrested, so I was going on a tear until my cash ran out and the police caught up with me. "I'm going out in a blaze of glory!"

Max grinned a demonic grin and let out a hellish AC/DC scream, complete with heavy-metal devil horns thrust into the air.

We made it to the fence, and under the cover of darkness, we scrambled over it. My pants tore open as I leapt to freedom, leaving my balls blowing in the freezing wind.

The freedom that first day felt incredible. Like I'd been some cooped-up dog who'd discovered the gate left open.

Frickin' party time!

We arrived at a homeless shelter an hour after we jumped the fence and immediately scored some dope and divided it between us. After the first blast of rock, Max saw an old working girl he'd dated before his stint in rehab. He waved to me, and they disappeared.

I ran to the liquor store, swiped a sixty ouncer of Crown Royal, and slammed it down without even tasting it. Then I went in to steal another to buy a huge chunk of crack. Store security didn't notice me for once with my full cheeks and laundered clothes. My put-togetherness was like a cloak of invisibility.

I went ballistic. I know now that the compulsion to get high had eroded any moral judgment that I had. I was totally out of control. I was doing things like ripping open pay phones, and shoplifting in what felt like every store in the whole Ottawa area—razors, bras, makeup, baby formula, shrimp, whatever the cab drivers in front of Rideau Centre wanted me to steal, I got it for them. They were like my bank account—a twenty-four-hour drive-through cash bar that never closed. I must've been up for fourteen straight days before I finally fell asleep in the parking garage in the market. By then, I knew I was starting to look like some creature, slinking about. And I'd begun to be reduced to begging, worse than I ever was in Brampton, like my addictions had been at the bottom of the Harvest House driveway doing push-ups, getting stronger than before, waiting for me to fuck up.

THE MEANING IS GONE

I RETREATED INTO DARKNESS.

I walked along the boulevard in Ottawa, and the colours of the store-fronts drained down across the sidewalks, faded under the blackened snowbanks, and seeped into the storm grates. Grey on grey, followed by more grey. The city hummed its droning hum, a cacophony of horns and car tires rotating across slick pavement, splashing through puddles. People hustled past me as I limped forward. My bowels loosened and let go, sending a stream of waste down my legs.

I'd held it in the best I could, stopping several times to ask store employees if I could use their washroom, but they'd said, "Sorry, for paying customers only," before ushering me back out into the cold. I shuffled into an alley and attempted to clean myself with a discarded chip bag. After, I asked a restaurant for napkins, and they refused and grimaced. It was impossible to hide my shame.

I steadied myself against a bus stop, pulled out a bottle of Listerine, and took a swig, hoping that the antiseptic would cleanse my spiritual wounds. Mouthwash was the best I could do. Most of the liquor stores had caught me stealing and wouldn't let me in. I heard the LCBO even had pictures of me in their backrooms. When the noxious fluid hit my belly, it torched my intestines but worked its dark magic. I faded into a groggy, chemical drunk, the kind that obliterated existence into fragments, just like I liked.

My digestive system was in tatters. The past few weeks I'd been puking blood mixed with bile, a sour, putrid liquid that burned when it came up. It made eating near impossible, save for a dry slice of toast or some weak chicken broth. The lack of regular meals caused my throat to close up. It hurt in the most ungodly way when I tried to force anything down it. The shelter staff worried. They'd come over and ask me why I wasn't eating. I never answered. It was none of their business and they could fuck off as far as I was concerned. They didn't even know my real name.

A passerby paused and said, "I don't have any money." I hadn't asked. He looked me up and down then glanced at my bottle of Listerine.

"Fuck your money," I said. "Cocksucker." I belched caustic air in his direction then took another swig. It burned as though I'd eaten a forest fire. My stomach contracted, and bile shot onto my shoes and the sidewalk. The rose colour of it used to frighten me, but I didn't care anymore. I wiped my hand across my mouth and started toward the Giant Tiger, where I hoped to steal a new pair of pants. My legs were like wooden stilts underneath my baggy, soiled jeans, knobby knees knocking. It took all the strength I had just to keep steady, my vision wavering. I gave up on my mission after a few laboured steps.

The smell of bread from the bakery on the corner made me think of my grandma and our Christmases in Brampton. There was an ember of that time still alight within me. I inhaled deeply, hoping to set it ablaze. Nothing. The memory passed.

My stomach gurgled, and I searched the ground for lost change and cigarette butts. I found nothing but garbage, more dirty looks, and a bench out in front of a bar. My foot was numb, and I decided to take a rest—I wouldn't be able to fish change from the Centennial Flame fountain on Parliament Hill, either. I'd gotten so used to the pain from my ankle that I routinely forgot about the gaping sore. It'd been over two years since the operation. The hole was the size of a dime, but the flesh around the edge of it was white and shrivelled, like skin submerged in water for too long, and it expelled a green-grey ooze that crusted yellow when it dried. It reeked like the dead. My foot, too, used to frighten me, but now I was indifferent.

A song came on the loudspeaker of the bar. I turned my head to listen, wondering if I recognized it. I didn't. I didn't recognize much anymore—not music, or movies, or anything. Signs blurred into smears of jumbled incomprehension. Faces, too. I was a wild animal, a stray wolf with matted fur covered in filth, one not even a dogcatcher would want to mess with. The world screamed past me. I lived amongst the Ewok shadows; I groaned misery and shifted as they did. I longed to be part of something again, to be known and accepted, to hear my name. No one ever said my name anymore. I never told anyone who I was for fear of being found out. For what? I didn't know. I'd forgotten years ago.

I slumped forward on the bench and held my head in my hands, trying to remember how my name sounded. I spelled it aloud to myself.

"J. E. S. S. E. Jesse."

I smiled, but molten bile bubbled up into my throat, followed by the rude smell of feces, bringing me back to the street. Olive was right, my body was giving out. It wasn't strong enough to endure any more punishment.

SALVATION AND THE SOUP KITCHEN LADY

"HEY YOU!" A VOICE CALLED up to me. "Get down from there."

It was some woman. I paid her no heed on my ascent to the summit of the half-completed building on Rideau Street.

"I said get down, or I'll call the cops."

My bony hand grasped the edge of a roughly finished ledge. My muscles may have atrophied somewhat from addiction and soup-kitchen slop, but I was still as spry as Gollum of Middle-earth looking for his Precious.

"What do you care?" I shot back. "Beat it."

"Why do all these do-gooders keep fucking with me?" I muttered to myself. "Why can't they just mind their own goddamned business?" I hoisted myself up another floor.

"I work over at the Shepherds of Good Hope shelter. I've seen you on the breadlines." The pitch of her voice raised the higher I went.

"So what?" I replied without looking down.

Her efforts were useless. I'd worked out my plan in jail. After I got released, I was going to climb to the top of a construction tower, close my eyes, spread my wings, and float away, crack and alcohol coursing through my brain for courage. I'd had enough. If shuffling around on the streets like a homeless rat on cocaine was bad, a recent stint in jail in the nation's capital was worse. It wasn't like in Maplehurst with Bucky and

Priest—here I got no respect. No one would take my calls—not family, not friends. Rapists and murderers got their calls taken, but not me. And letters—forget about it. I'd wait every day at the front of the range for word from the outside world, and every day I was disappointed.

I shouted down to the woman on the ground. "Listen, lady, I'm just going to go to sleep up here cause it's safer than on ground lev—"

"It's still winter weather and cold as hell. You'll freeze up there."

A gust bit through my H&M hoodie, and I felt weak all of a sudden. "Listen, can you please just leave me be? I just want to be left alone."

"I don't believe you."

I quickened my pace. I didn't want to lose my nerve, so I reached for the next floor. My hand slipped on some ice, and I fell onto my back on the floor below. Writhing, I almost rolled off the edge.

"You almost got what you came for!" she shouted.

Gasping for air, my heart racing, I curled up and covered my ears, trying to hide from both her incessant voice and what had just happened.

"Hey, you know what? I think I do know you. You told me about your grandmother and your brother. You said your name was Jesse or something."

The sound of my own name dropped into my consciousness like a sledgehammer. The tears creeping along the bridge of my nose froze as I thought of my grandma and Jerry—memories that shattered and warmed me at the same time. The woman below was right, I did know her.

I could hear her yelling again.

"You said you missed them and wanted to make them proud. I remember."

I rolled over and peeked over the ledge. Sure enough, it was her, black hair hanging behind her shoulders as she looked up at me.

"Come on now, enough of this nonsense," she said with a big smile. "Get down, and let's get you some soup and socks."

I picked myself up and began my long descent.

When I got to the bottom, she greeted me with a brisk hug. "That was close."

"It sure was," I replied.

RECONCILIATION

2008–2017

FIGHTING THE DARKNESS

once, in a not-too-distant life
i was a different person.

it was a dark time
loveless,
cold,
violent.

a time when I no longer cared about the world,
a world that had taken so much
and left me with nothing.

wîhtikow (monster)

i lived by the criminal's creed:
live for today,
forget the past,
damn the future.

i took what i wanted,
stole what i needed,
and robbed when i could.

dwelling in shadows,

amongst the murderers and thieves,

the highwaymen,

and outlaws.

that is how i can fight the darkness now.

because i once was the darkness,

an apparition,

driven by worst part of the human soul.

a beast lost in resentments.

once, in a not-too-distant life.

DAWN OF THE BRONZE AGE

"WE FOLLOWED A TRAIL OF money from the scene of the crime," the constable told his fellow officers. "Right to where he was smoking crack in front of the Shepherds of Good Hope. Can you believe that?"

It was shamefully true. For my very last crime the cops had literally caught me red-handed. I put up little resistance when they chucked me in the back of the squad car. I'd had enough.

I faced break-and-enter charges and was processed at the Elgin Street police station in a nice part of town I rarely ventured into, except when arrested. Then I was shipped to the Ottawa-Carleton Detention Centre (OCDC).

So there I was, once again, heckling the screws and counting the days and cinder blocks.

Those cinder blocks seemed to follow me wherever I went—the ones found in jails, mental institutions, probation offices, hospitals, detox centres, detention centres, shelters, Sally Anns, welfare offices, court holding cells, police station bullpens. I hated the monotony of doing time, but if I was sick of anything, it was seeing those institutional sixteen-by-eights. I once counted around 180 of them in my cell at the Don Jail in Toronto; around 190 at Maplehurst in Milton, Ontario; and around 160 at OCDC. But the Harvest House rehab centre had over 360 blocks per dorm room; that made it like the Ritz-Carlton to me.

I called Harvest House, dreaming of their abundance of blocks, hoping to get someone to vouch for me in court and bail me out.

The intake worker picked up the phone. "Have you had enough of the life, of the Stone Age, Thistle?"

Employees at Harvest House could be so smug.

"Get me outta here!" I begged. "I'm sick of it all and I'm especially sick of this jail food—reminds me of crappy retirement scraps they feed old people."

"What, you don't like steamed dog food?" He laughed.

Eleven days later, someone from Harvest House came and bailed me out, and I was released directly back into rehab where I could do my dead time before sentencing.

The judge who granted my surety said that if I made the year in rehab, it could serve as my jail time. "But if you skip out, Mr. Thistle, we will

Rehab. I was arrested before I could sell the gold chain to get cash for dope. I can't remember where I got the chain from, but I gave it to my roommate after he achieved three months' sobriety.

find you and send you down to the darkest prison we have because the justice system has had quite enough of your nonsense." The pound of his gavel scared the shit out of me.

A few hours later, I was back at Harvest House shaking and vomiting and praying for mercy. But it was a chance at redemption, and I was grateful for it.

RUNNING ON GLASS

THE LACES ON MY BLUE ASICS were discoloured and frayed, evidence of previous ownership, but they were brand spanking new to me and I loved them for what they were—a second chance.

The shoes had been donated to Harvest House by the local Running Room—all the guys got them when they came to rehab. Some guys mocked them, but they were the ones who relapsed and ended up back in the can within weeks. Those who appreciated them lasted a little longer but still seemed to go back eventually—usually within two or three months.

Harvest House director Gary Wand was a recovering addict like us who had turned to running to get sober some fifteen years earlier when he washed up on the front lawn of Harvest House from Montreal. Everyone at the centre said that he'd been worse off than all of us, and his entry photo, taken the day he arrived at Harvest House, seemed to confirm that. He looked like a real bag of shit in it.

Wand now ran the running program at Harvest House, and had arranged the shoe donations. The concept of running as therapy was brilliant, actually. "The dopamine from running affects the same part of the brain as coke," he said. "Running quells cravings." Lots of guys were in the program, and those who did the ten- or twenty-kilometre runs instead of just running away to smoke cigarettes seemed to fight relapse better.

I wanted what they had. I thought if I ran I might have a chance to stay clean and honour my surety. I had to go all the way this time around, give it my best.

"If Wando can do it, I can do it," I said to myself as I hobbled onto the driveway for the daily five-kilometre jog. The reality of my foot, however, quickly snuffed out my newfound courage, replacing it with doubt and apprehension. It was withered and meatless, bones popping out where flesh should be, and the pins and screws holding my heel together dug into my ankle joint whenever I took a step. I'd never run on it without vast amounts of drugs or alcohol to numb the pain.

"Gary, I'm scared," I said, as the pack gathered. "I don't know if my foot will hold . . ." The grind of pebbles under shoes drowned me out, as everyone began running. I waddled to catch up. I must have looked like a penguin shuffling against the wind on a sheet of ice.

Gary looked back and smiled. "Just go slow. Trust me," he said and turned to join the others.

"Go slow?" I shot back. "Are you fucking kidding me?" No response. "Fuck you!" I yelled. It was no use, everyone had already gone.

I looked down. My damaged foot was longer than the other one, due to the surgery, and the leg it was attached to was atrophied and resembled a sad dollar-store broomstick, the hollow kind that bends if you sweep too hard.

Will it bend and break if I run? I contemplated. *Better that than my foot falling apart.*

I laughed out loud at the image of both gruesome scenarios, even though I felt like crying. Then Grandpa popped into my head. "Get going," I heard him bark in his thick Cape Breton accent. "Get going and stop feeling sorry fer yerself." It had been a long time since I'd thought of the old man, but there he was, kicking my ass again, as always.

I got pissed off and let go and ran. I didn't think about it, I just put one foot in front of the other and went. I tilted and slipped on stones, my leg and foot buckled and shook and wobbled—but they held. I had no push or spring to my gait, burning pain shot up from my ankle to my brain, and the bottom of my foot felt like I was running on broken glass—but it was bearable.

Is this how it feels for babies to walk? I wondered. As soon as that thought ran through my mind, my leg gave out and I tumbled down into a cloud of dust and pebbles.

The dirt in my mouth tasted glorious.

"Holy Christ, I did it!" I exclaimed.

AT LAST

MY HAND SHOOK AS I dialled the number Nicole, the CEO of Harvest House, had given me.

I sat listening to the phone ring. When it clicked, I panicked and hung up. I sat staring at the dial pad. It seemed to get bigger the longer I gazed at it. I dialled again, and again I hung up when I heard an answering click.

I just don't have it in me yet. What do I say to her?

Earlier that day, Nicole had come to my bedside in the dorm room and asked me into her office. She was solemn as I took a seat. I thought I was in trouble for violating a rule—what, I wasn't sure.

"I got an email today," she said. She typed something into her computer. I thought for sure the police were bringing a new charge against me, for something I'd done, from somewhere, some time ago. The long arm of the law was something I always dreaded but had to accept now, in my second attempt at sobriety.

"There's no other way to say this," Nicole said. Her eyes were welling up, but she was smiling.

So not the cops. I was puzzled.

"I'll just let you read it," she said. She turned her screen toward me, and I saw the email.

Hello,

I've been trying to contact my son Jesse Thistle for quite a while and he is never where I'm told he is. I heard he was in Harvest House and I'm sure God had a hand in it. It's a long story, but I haven't talked to Jesse for a long time and I don't know what problems he has anymore. I hope he's not suffering too much. Our family was torn apart a long time ago and I wasn't able to be around Jesse too much, but he always seemed to calm down around me.

Anyway, if he is there, tell him I'm happy he's getting help if he needs it. I love him very much and please just let me know if he is there. If he needs anything, socks, underwear, whatever, let me know and I'll try to send it.

Thank you.
Blanche Morrissette

It was my mom. I couldn't believe it. I held my head low, but my emotions rolled out and down my cheeks onto my lap.

I dialled my mom's number one more time and tried to steady my nerves. Ring—it was picked up straightaway this time.

A shaky, small voice answered, "Hello." It sounded like an old lady, not the mom I remembered from the snowy mountains.

"Mom . . ." was all I could muster before losing my breath. I tried to say more but couldn't.

"Jesse? Is that you?"

302

I'm not sure if I answered her, but we both began crying. Not sobs, more like sweet sucks of air, the silence between us saying more than any words. Finally, she told me that she'd been searching for me for ten years, since just after she saw me in Vancouver at Josh's wedding. In shelters, in the jail system, at places I'd just lived for a spell, in mental health facilities, in detoxes all over Ontario, and at Jerry's.

"You were like a phantom," she said. "I almost caught up to you a couple times, but always just missed you. I'm sorry life has been this way for you. I'm sorry I wasn't there."

I'd forgiven her before the words even left her lips.

The rest of our conversation melted into a drizzle of emotions that fogged my heart in the nicest way. Like a silent summer rain that lightly quenches the prairie after a long drought, or the cloud of droplets that kicks up at the bottom of a waterfall, delicately misting your face. Refreshing and warm, like I'd rediscovered some fragment of home, some lost piece of myself.

It filled me up.

A PLAIN PIECE OF PAPER

A PROFESSOR FROM THE UNIVERSITY of Ottawa who specialized in human relationships was overseeing classes her grad students were giving us Harvest House goons on communication skills, including basic etiquette.

Many of the guys in class mocked the lessons.

"What kind of idiot needs to relearn how to wash their ass," said one.

Another said, "Only total ratchets and baseheads need this."

Maybe I'd been at "the life" longer than they had—over a decade—and had forgotten more than them, but I was determined. And maybe hearing my mom's voice again made me feel like I could do this, made me feel like I could try, gave me that small bit of courage I needed to open my heart once more. I sat in those classes every week. I was embarrassed to admit to the professor, Dr. Jenepher Lennox Terrion, that I needed help with everything—brushing my teeth, combing my hair, dressing myself, washing my clothes. I was really rough around the edges.

Over two months, I relearned everything—I practiced in my dorm room. I looked at myself in the mirror and timed myself while brushing my teeth. I trained myself to look people in the eye and not interrupt them. I shaved with such precision I could run a credit card up my face and not hear it flick.

Perfect.

I spent months working on my reading and writing. When I got to Harvest House, I'd pore over the stack of encyclopedias I got from the rec room every night before bed, forcing the words to make sense. Just like my cellmates did years before, my Harvest House roommates teased me, calling me "Einstein" and "Mr. Spock," and some said it was ridiculous, a crackhead trying to get an education.

"You think people will hire you?" someone said in the slop hall one night. "You're a criminal, junkie piece of shit. You're no better than the rest of us." The table laughed. I wanted to respond, to tell him I had dreams now, but I just took it and kept the bigger picture in mind, kept pressing forward. I took my GED and passed with flying colours. When I received my final report card, I thought of my buddy in jail who'd got me interested in school—I hoped he'd gotten free and found a new life, away from the cinder blocks.

When it was time to graduate the etiquette modules, Dr. Lennox Terrion handed out our certificates as we walked up single file to collect them. She was beaming, and so was I. Some of the guys trashed the certificates as soon as they left the room. But I kept mine. When I got back to the rehab centre, I placed it within a large book to keep the edges from folding or crumpling. It meant the world to me. Every now and again, I'd open the book and just stare at it.

It lit me up to see my name, "Jesse Thistle," alongside "University of Ottawa." I'd done something significant. I'd actually achieved something in my life. I didn't have a driver's license, ID, a proper high school education, a health card, nothing—but here was this completion certificate that had "university" with my name under it!

A PUSH

"HEY, THISTLE . . . GET OUT OF bed, you have a phone call!"

It was 9:30 p.m. and I was already passed out, exhausted from my daily responsibilities at Harvest House. I barely heard Rob's voice when he yelled for me a second time.

"Dude, get up! It sounds important. It's your grandma in Toronto!"

Rob was always the type to be joking or laughing. He was never serious, but he sounded like he was this time. I jumped out of bed and ran to the phone.

"Jesse," whispered Grandma. "I need you."

I hadn't seen her in over four years.

"Where are you, Grandma?"

"Room 525 at William Osler hospital. Come see me."

"But what about Grandpa? I can't come if he's there."

"Just come. It's my time. He'll come around someday, you watch," she said. "He really does love you, you know."

I had betrayed Grandpa and all the good he had taught me and I knew he resented me for it, but I also knew she was right.

"I love you, Grandma. As soon as I get my day pass I'll be there." I hung up. By the end of the next day, I was on a moving truck on my way to Toronto. Randal, my AA sponsor, was my driver. Harvest House let me out on furlough on the condition that he never leave my side.

Grandma's arms were frail and covered with deep purple-black bruises. I tried not to stare, but she caught me looking and pulled the covers over them.

"Don't worry, Jesse," she said. "That'll clear up soon enough."

But I knew the bruises were a sign of the leukemia that was threatening her life and almost broke down.

"You know," she said, "I love science fiction novels. I've already finished the ones everybody brought me and need some more. Could you send me one or two from rehab?"

"Sure," I mustered, immediately thinking of *Doctor Who*. I knew she was trying to distract me. "Anything you want."

She looked at me. She rarely showed her front teeth all the way—one of them was black—but she did now, her face beaming, her smile so warm it could defrost Siberia in January. "Why don't you keep going with the school, baby boy, and give it your all? You were always smart, just a little angry."

I could see the hope ignite in her milky-grey eyes. "Of course I'll keep going," I said.

"Good." She perked up, her grin widening even more. "And university? You don't wanna half-ass it; you've gotta take it all the way."

"Yes, Grandma. Just get better." It wasn't quite a promise, more like words I blurted out to try to comfort her. Anything to make her feel better, to make me feel better, here in this hospital room.

"Good. And don't you worry about me, I'll be fine." She drew me in for a hug from my chair near her bed. "Remember, I'm always with you."

I wrapped my arms around her and could feel how feeble she was, but she squeezed me with all her might. Then all of a sudden she let go and pushed me away. I remembered my first day of kindergarten, right before I met Leeroy. I cried the whole way and didn't want to go in. I was so afraid to let go of Grandma and go to the teacher until Grandma knelt down, looked me right in the eye, and said, "Go on, Jesse, it's okay. Grandma will be here at the end of the day. I promise." She smelled like old cigarettes and perfume as she pushed me toward the teacher.

It was that same push she was giving me now. A push that said, "Go on, make your way in the world. Make me proud."

Two weeks later, she was gone.

THE CLEANEST BACHELOR IN THE WORLD

ON THE DAY MY GRANDMOTHER died, Harvest House took pity on me, I assume, and graduated me. There was no ceremony, no fanfare, no anything. Nicole just came into the dorm room, informed me that I'd completed the first phase of treatment, and told me to pack my things. I was upgraded to a room in reintegration housing, aftercare dwellings adjacent to Harvest House that guys moved into after they'd completed the immersion part of treatment and were transitioning back into the real world.

On my way over, around the boundary fence I'd hopped with Max a year earlier, a gust of wind hit me. It carried a faint smell of burnt hickory and cedar, like a campfire. I wanted to believe it was my grandmother's spirit telling me to keep going. I said a prayer and felt her presence leave this earth, galloping away to the west.

When I got to reintegration, one of the first things I did was start a Facebook account. I didn't even know what Facebook was, but the guys there told me about it and helped me get it set up. Minutes after I signed up, I started getting messages from people I knew from years before—Derick, Brian, Karen, and other neighbourhood friends. They were glad I was still alive—they'd all been searching for me for years, just like Mom.

I heard Leeroy had cleaned up and joined the army and was shipped off to Afghanistan five years before. I was glad he'd straightened out and said a prayer for my old friend. I also heard Stan had gotten a good job and was doing well, and that he often asked if I was okay. He was solid—always was.

I also got a message from Lucie. She was the girl on the hill in middle school who'd been nice to me in front of the popular girls, and she was the red-haired girl at the party the night I'd fallen off Jerry's building and wrecked my foot.

Her message was consoling. She'd heard of my grandmother's passing from Jerry and wanted to make sure I was okay and wouldn't fly off the handle and use again. I thought that it was kind of her to think of me when I needed it most. Her gesture reminded me of Karen—that unconditional kindness, a kindness I hadn't felt for decades.

Intimidated isn't the right word to express how Lucie made me feel as we got to talking—it was more like a mixture of shock and fright, total excitement and extreme pride. I was super pleased with myself for catching the attention of such a respectable woman: she was in university as a mature student, she had her own place, she knew what she wanted out of life, she was more or less sober, she was independent, she didn't need a man to support her or take care of her, and she was beautiful—like some kind of red-headed fire goddess. Me, I was just a recovering addict trying to do right by the world.

Connecting with her, though, I felt like the luckiest guy in the world.

I hadn't talked to a woman so powerful, so bright, and so intelligent in years. I didn't own anything because I'd been on the streets for so long. All I had were words and a desire to impress her.

I wrote her poetry. I'd had corrective surgery on my wrist to fix the break that had never healed properly since the fall from the building, the fight with police, and the thousands of push-ups I did in jail, so I had to do it with one hand. It often took me hours to type one page. I bled for each one. This was one of the first ones I sent:

310

once in a lifetime
two people meet.

not knowing what the universe has designed for them,
they form a bond so strong
that it holds the very fabric of time at a standstill.

this is true love,
it is infinite,
i will always love in this moment forever with you.

now is ours.

Lucie loved the poem. A week after she got it she sent me Michael J. Fox's *Always Looking Up* and *The Alchemist* by Paulo Coelho—books with messages of hope and making the best of our gardens, our lives, even with our shortcomings, that I devoured. I knew it was her way of helping me, of saying it was okay that I was a little broken.

We started to Skype like crazy after that. Before every call, I showered, combed my hair, put on my best hat, my crispest pressed shirt and pants, and my brand-new leather jacket, even clean underwear.

Life on the streets had been horribly dirty. Many times I'd wished I could have had a shower but simply couldn't—I often went for weeks without one. So when I got sober, I collected an abundance of soaps, shampoos, skin creams, face scrubs, toothpastes—I must have had, no exaggeration, about two hundred of each. So many that I filled an entire bookshelf with them and kept them on display in my room at Harvest House behind my computer seat, perfectly lined up.

When Lucie called, I'd sit in front of my wall of soap and shampoo, so she could see that I was clean, so she could see that I was respectable just like her.

I really wanted to impress her.

311

THE OTHER HALF OF THE SOLUTION

MY PROBATION OFFICER, MR. F., came to Harvest House for our last weekly visit. When he sat down, the sun was shining behind him and carried summer warmth onto my face.

"You've done your time, Jesse," he said. "How does it feel?"

"Not sure," I said nonchalantly. The immensity of release was not yet upon me, but I wasn't afraid of freedom for once.

The manila folder he put on the desk that housed my case file was thin, not the usual thick ones I'd had back in Brampton. That alone felt like a major accomplishment. He rifled through it, stamped the last page, and then got me to sign a confirmation of release from the Justice of the Peace.

I was a free man.

"What are your plans when you leave here?"

"That girl in Toronto I told you about, Lucie?" I said. "I'm going to see her."

Mr. F. studied my face for a moment.

"You know, when you first came, I thought you were a long shot," he said. "Wasn't sure if you'd honour your surety bond, thought you'd take off and relapse like the rest of them." He motioned to the long line of clients crowding the hall. "But something was different about you . . ." He tapped the end of his pen against his teeth then went over my activity report.

"You did every chore in the joint—cleaning washrooms, toilets, and showers; kitchen duty; waxing the floors; sold calendars. You mentored the young guys, helped others with reading, academic bridging, ran marathons in the program. You did everything over twelve months without a single violation. That's not normal."

I thought back to my first day at Harvest House the first time around. I was skin and bones, just off the Greyhound bus from Brampton, and as rusty as an iron rivet on the hull of the sunken *Titanic*. I had a real hate for the world, but also a glimmer of hope after hearing news of my dad. It was like that dude in the shelter freed me to move on, made it okay to let go and stop chasing my father's ghost—something that didn't really sink in until I started talking openly in group therapy during my second attempt at rehab. That, and I was desperate—I didn't want to die, which almost happened after I relapsed with Max.

"I guess I just chose to live. And that meant trying my best at everything."

"Come on now." He shook his head like I'd given him the wrong answer. "That's only half the solution."

I didn't know what he meant. I'd put in the work this time. I'd set micro goals and chose to follow through on each one of them, just like Brian and Mr. T. told me was possible years before. I chose to stay sober, pushed myself in therapy, until the minutes turned to days, the days to weeks, and the weeks to months. I'd literally set one- or two-minute goals—*If I can just make it to the next minute*, I thought, *then I might have a chance to live; I might have a chance to be something more than just a struggling crackhead*. I chose, repeatedly, in everything I did until I reached my first three months of sobriety and I thought I'd achieved the impossible—to me it had seemed impossible. My name looked so triumphant on the achievements board: *J. Thistle—90 days*. And now that I'd reached the year and had worked the AA steps properly, I felt I could just keep on choosing a better future forever and ever.

"There's no doubt it took lots of dogged hard work. But don't forget the team of great people behind you, the rehab itself, and the addicts who've struggled and won victories with you these last twelve months—they held you up and gave you the chance to choose better for yourself. They deserve credit, too."

I sat back and thought about what Mr. F. was saying. There was truth in his words, an external factor Brian and Mr. T.'s empowerment philosophy had missed. The support of family and love—Harvest House gave me both; they gave me the opportunity to choose.

"And you, Mr. F. You played a part, too. You got me to write the letter to the convenience store guy I robbed—that helped me move forward in so many ways."

He smiled and slid another paper my way.

"You still have eighteen more months of probation in Toronto. Here's where you report."

I read the form and saw that my new probation office was just down the street from where I fell off the building, on an old corner where I used to use. My gut stirred with crack cravings, but it wasn't enough to send me to the toilet—that was real, tangible progress.

"I hope this Lucie girl will hold you up like everyone here did," Mr. F. said, "and that you remember to keep making the right choices."

I nodded. "I'm sure she will and so will I."

BRAVERY

I WAS MORE AFRAID THAN I'd been in my whole life.

I walked to the oncology ward thinking of what I was going to say, my hands sweaty and heart trembling uncontrollably. I squeezed Lucie's hand like a vise grip.

She smiled. "Have courage, Jesse. Just tell him how you feel."

Afternoon light cascaded through the hall window, shining on her beautiful red hair. It calmed me.

"It's time," she said. "Put pride away."

I nodded. I'd been in Toronto at Lucie's for just two days, but I already knew she was the one. We sat awake both nights discussing my grandfather and how people fight and waste the best years of their lives trying to be right, but that "right" doesn't exist when precious time is spent in such useless ways. She listened to me talk about the void I had within, how I'd tried to fill it with drugs over the years, and how I knew I'd broken my grandfather's heart by hurting myself long after we'd fought in the van over me wanting to buy a car.

"Don't you see?" she said. "You two donkeys just loved each other so much that this fight broke out—and neither of you is willing to admit it's gone on long enough."

She was right. We Thistle men never learned how to express ourselves. We were raised to be tough and unemotional, with the thickness of our calluses and fists the only way we were ever allowed to show how we felt—lessons that went way back to Grandpa's horrible boyhood in Cape Breton—lessons my dad, no doubt, struggled with, too.

The last time I saw my grandfather was at my grandmother's funeral. I'd been granted furlough with my AA sponsor Randal again, a week after she passed, but he left me alone when I walked into the funeral home and up to my grandmother's casket. My grandfather sat with his sisters and my aunts and uncles beside him. He wept softly, as if he was trying to hide his grief, even then. I bent in and kissed my grandmother's face. She had a peaceful smile, almost like Buddha.

When I'd turned to face my grandfather and offer my condolences, he'd wiped his cheeks and barked, "It's too late, asshole. She's gone."

I never felt so sorry for him in all my life—I knew he didn't mean it. I'd used anger myself to hide from emotions I couldn't handle.

I returned to Harvest House. I occasionally worked in the shop making duck decoys or building furniture to sell to support the program, and every time I lifted a drill or held a saw, I thought of the old guy and wished, for just one day, we could work side by side again like we did when I was a boy. That I could hear him say "attaboy" one more time. I missed him so much. I ached to wipe away his tears, to tell him how I really felt.

When we entered his room in the hospital, he was alone with my aunt Sherry, who I hadn't seen in nearly five years. She was holding his hand, tears streaming down her face. She whispered to him, and he looked up at me. I had no words, and neither did he. Soon we were both crying, too.

Finally I said, "I'm sorry, Grandpa."

"I know, Jesse. It's okay." He held his arms out, and we hugged.

I knew he'd heard from the family, Aunt Sherry primarily, of all the things I was doing to better myself, and I knew he knew me better than anyone. I was sure he could look right into my heart and see I really was trying my hardest.

"I'm proud of you," he said and gave me a karate chop on my forearm, like he used to do on my knee when I was a kid, then held my hand. His hands were shaking. He told me that he understood what it was like to be an orphan. "That's why I was always hard on you. To make you strong. Like my granddaddy did with me. That was the only way to protect you. Just keep flying straight or I'll kick your ass." He gave me his trademark Popeye wink.

That was the nearest he'd come to saying he loved me in nearly two decades.

He passed away a month and a half later, six months to the day of my grandmother's passing.

FOLLOW YOUR DREAMS

LUCIE AND I SAT ON the couch in our apartment. My leg rested on the coffee table and shook from pain after a long day of work with Uncle Ron. Fourteen- to sixteen-hour days working again for Randolph installing kitchen countertops had become the norm, and Lucie was always there to help me recover at night—rubbing Swedish bitters on my wound, which had opened back up from the heavy work, binding my leg in special bandages to keep the swelling down, drawing on my shoulders to distract me.

"Ah, watch it," I yelped as she shifted on the couch. "You bumped my foot." I wasn't nice about it, something that was happening as of late—me being snappy and grouchy after work.

"I'm sorry," Lucie said, kissing her hand and placing it on my foot. "I didn't mean to."

I huffed and crossed my arms, making more out of it than I should've. Lucie turned to face me.

"I've kept quiet this last year," she said. "But I'm not going to anymore." She sounded dead serious—she clearly wasn't having it this time. "When I picked you up from Harvest House you had a garbage bag full of donated clothes, a wall of soap, a toothbrush, and tons of shampoo." She paused, her expression even more focused. "But you also had a dream. Remember we'd talk about university, and remember the promise you made to your grandmother?"

I nodded. I knew to drop the act and listen. When we first started talking when I was in rehab, we spent hours on the phone, getting to know one another as I worked nights watching over the new guys. Lucie was at York University, her first year back in school after over ten years of drifting about, and her resolve to give it another go inspired me. We'd talk about her assignments, how she was sacrificing going out with friends to do homework, getting things done on time, with good marks. We were talking about moving in together, too, and how I could do the same once I moved to Toronto. We schemed about how we'd study together, support each other, look over each other's work. We were a lot like each other—late bloomers.

"Remember when I helped you get into academic bridging at the University of Toronto last fall?"

"Yes."

"Well, since you dropped out of bridging to work with your uncle, you haven't been happy. I've watched you day after day come home miserable and limping." She crossed her arms. "I can't watch you break your body anymore—you're not supposed to be a construction worker."

"I'm trying my best!" I said, slamming my hand down. I thought she was insulting the labour that put food on our table and helped pay our rent. I thought she was saying it wasn't good enough.

"You can have a tantrum all you want. I need to be with someone who's living their truth. Because I love you, because I love us, and I know what you're capable of." There was a long pause. "It hurts me so much to watch you keep neglecting your dream."

She reminded me of my grandmother, that power and uncompromising attitude, when she knew she was right. I remembered when we argued over the placement of the TV when I first moved in. I tried to force it onto the stand and hollered when she told me not to because it wouldn't fit. Then I ran out of the house sure that I was right, like I'd learned to do in anger management when I got too worked up.

She didn't chase after me. She waited until I returned an hour later to explain why the TV had to go where it did. She was calm and kind, but firm.

"I understand why you throw fits," she said. "I would, too, after years of having no control over anything." She then said she'd always be there to help me figure out my emotions, even if it was an ugly process.

God, I loved her so much. But I tried to be mad now as she challenged me to face the truth—I'd given up and broken my word to myself, to my grandmother, and to her.

Finally, she said, "You chased the money—I get it, we have to survive—but money will not make you or me happy. Following your heart will."

I thought about it. There was something about the way we'd talked those nights, like we were planting dream seeds in fertile soil, our hopes and desires spigots of water, nurturing a future we both wanted and saw in each other. She gave me the courage to hope and dream, because I saw that in her, and she believed it was possible for both of us. It was contagious.

She was right.

And she trusted and loved me back when I was just a newly recovered criminal, back when it felt like no one else would. I promised myself I'd honour and protect that no matter what. Trying my best in school was part of that.

"Just fill in the line that asks for your major." Lucie's red hair brushed across my arm as she walked me through the York University application process. "What do you want to do?"

I scratched the top of my head. "I like history," I said. "I watch lots of World War I documentaries." I peered down at my callused hands and couldn't picture them writing academic papers. I still doubted my decision—I'd quit installing countertops a few weeks before.

"Good—historian is a great profession." Lucie moved the mouse and clicked a box on the computer and scrolled onto the next screen. She smiled. "Almost done. Now just add in all your personal information here and we're good to go."

She walked away and put the kettle on for tea.

"But—" I said. The application was just halfway finished and it looked like Chinese to me.

"No. You have to do this one on your own."

She wasn't trying to be mean, I knew that.

"I've taught you how to fill in enough forms, my job is done."

I couldn't argue. Since living with her, Lucie had helped me fill in health card forms and taught me how to drive and how to fill in all the car driver insurance forms. She taught me how to email and use the computer halfway decent. She taught me how to make doctor's appointments and fill in the forms at the medical offices. She taught me how to access my debt information and then chart out a plan to pay it all back. She taught me how to open a bank account and how to access credit, and she also taught me how to write properly—she edited most things I wrote and taught me grammar and sentence structure, adding to what I'd already learned in my GED.

Lucie basically taught me how to access society again.

"Okay." I sighed and worked my way through the rest of the application and the Ontario Student Assistance Program forms. She came over occasionally when I got too frustrated, but she was resolute—she made me do it all.

When I pressed return and the forms were submitted, she hugged me.

"You did that." She smiled. "I didn't want to take that away from you."

I felt like I'd climbed a mountain.

THE FINES ARE FINE

WHEN I WAS HOMELESS AND in trouble with the law, I collected fines like boys collect hockey cards. The police slapped fines on me; the courts, too, used to slap fines on me for every missed court appearance; and judges slapped fines on me every time I got convicted. Each fine ranged from $50 to $200. Eventually, my collection added up to over three grand.

The fines had long been a black stain that I believed I could never wash off. They were just there, reminding me I was a criminal who owed a pound of flesh to the state—a pound of flesh I didn't have, would never have. I'd often thought in the past about changing my life, but thinking about those fines would make me give up before I even started. When I got sober, I put the fines aside; mainly because I was struggling just to live. But when I graduated rehab and started working, I began saving with Lucie's guidance, and one day, before I started university, I realized I had over $3,000.

I finally had enough to pay my fines.

I drove to Brampton with Lucie, and we walked into the courthouse together. I licked my thumb, peeled off each fifty-dollar bill, and slapped them down one by one until I'd counted out the full $3,071 in fines.

The teller was gobsmacked and grinned back at me—he knew what paying those fines represented: a break with the past.

FINDING THE COURAGE TO STAND

MY FIRST CLASS AT YORK University was at 8:30 a.m. on September 8, 2011. It was in Canadian History.

"Just remember to breathe," Lucie said to me as I threw my book bag over my shoulder and walked out the door. She waved to me with a tea towel, and I remembered Grandma doing the same when I got my first job at the grocery store. I smiled, but was trembling inside.

I was the first one to arrive, and I found a seat in the front row. I placed my brand-new binders, pens, and paper on my desk in neat rows and readied myself for the lecture. I watched as people trickled in, filling the hall. They were half my age. Everyone—around four hundred people—had laptops, smart phones, or recording devices—only two others that I could see had pen and paper like me.

No one sat beside me, and I fidgeted and tried smiling at some of the kids, but they were more interested in people their age.

Maybe I've made a huge mistake coming here, I worried. *Maybe it was foolish of me to try this.* Me, an ex-con, mid-thirties, barely two years sober, amongst all these glowing young people who had years of education on me, and who still had that bright spot within them that hadn't yet been crushed by the world. I got scared and gathered my things, ready to run away.

Then a memory came to me of when I was in jail and saw the chaplain and started working with him, and then of Professor Lennox Terrion and how I'd relearned everything in rehab.

I wasn't sure why I thought of that when I looked at all the young people with their computers and innocence, but I did. Maybe it was because I was frightened, like when my cellmates tuned me up after I handed in my homework, or maybe it was because I was reaching really deep not to run away, trying to remind myself that I didn't break then, and that I wouldn't break now.

Whatever the reason, I came to the realization that I'd earned my way here and that I had the right to chase my dreams. That even I deserved a second chance.

I thought, *I belong in university, just like everyone else.*

INDIAN TURNED MÉTIS

I STARTED TAKING INDIGENOUS HISTORY classes to figure out who I was and why I saw so many other Natives in all the homeless and justice institutions and out on the streets over the years. I thought I might be able to get some answers in my classes or readings and understand why I had made some poor life choices and keep from relapsing. It was a long shot—but I had to try.

For one of my first assignments, one of my professors, Dr. Victoria Freeman, asked us to look at our family history within the context of Canadian colonization.

Since my grandma in Brampton hardly ever talked about her Native background, I called my mom to ask her questions.

"We're Michif rebel fighters," she said. "Canadians call us Métis."

I recognized that word "Michif" from when we'd all been talking in Aunt Cecile's kitchen after Josh's wedding.

"Your great-grandmother Marianne Ledoux, Mushoom Jeremie's mother, is related to Louis Riel," Mom said. "But talk to your aunt Yvonne, she's the family historian."

When I called Aunt Yvonne the next day and asked her about our involvement with Riel, she could hardly contain herself.

"I've been waiting a very long time for you to get interested in who you are," she said. "A lifetime actually." She asked me to hold on while she turned on her computer to access her genealogy files. "I'm addicted to Ancestry.ca, so if I get a little strung out on the call, just send over the blue bus to take me away." She cackled, and her laughter stirred up a memory of her in our place in Moose Jaw after we ran away from Dad in 1979. She was taking care of us when Mom went off to work and tucking us in. I'd never remembered that before.

"Let's see," she said, and it sounded like she was slurping a drink of some kind. "Ah! Here. The Morrissette family tree. I'll email the link, so you can explore it yourself. If I explain it, you may need to go back to rehab." She cackled again, but I could tell she was serious. "The picture I sent is Chief Mistawasis—a Cree chief. He's your three-times-great-grandfather."

I remembered Derick's brother Moses asking me what I was when I was growing up.

So we are Cree . . .

I checked my email. There, upon my screen, appeared a big black-and-white picture of an old man sitting with other old Indian men. The caption read, "Cree chiefs Ahtahkakoop and Mistawasis." I examined the medals around their necks, and then minimized the image and clicked the link. A huge family tree appeared—hundreds of ancestors with pictures, names, dates, and places of birth beside each box that represented each ancestor. Many had feathered bonnets on, like plains Indians from the movies, others looked like old cowboys, others were just dressed in regular clothes.

"You're Cree and road-allowance Michif, Jesse. You come from a long line of chiefs, political leaders, and resistance fighters." Auntie's voice glowed like fire and lit my curiosity.

I went through the photos faster and faster, trying to drink in the rushing river of information. Those of the Cree chiefs fascinated me most. They were strong and epic in appearance, in their beaded buckskins, feathered headdresses to the ground, and spears in hand, many on horseback and surrounded by warriors. But they looked staged.

Then I saw pictures of my kokum Nancy and mushoom Jeremie and their little shack near the train tracks and felt a lump in my throat—I hadn't seen an image of them in nearly four decades. Below those was a battlefield picture with the heading "Batoche," and underneath it was that blue flag with the infinity symbol I'd seen when I'd had the fever after my operation.

"What is this battle—Batoche? And what's this flag, Auntie?" I asked. Visions of the western door and the horses and the fear I'd felt welled in my chest again, but I fought against it now with my auntie on the line.

"That's where our family fought for our land during the resistance—when Canada attacked us. And that's our flag—the Métis flag."

The reports of Gatling guns thundered in my soul. The face of the Indian I'd been with in the rifle pit in my dream came to me. I searched the family tree and couldn't find him, but I remembered that Iron Maiden song Leeroy and Derick sang near the dumpster.

Could this be part of the same conflict . . . ?

I searched the pictures and saw the same columns of redcoat soldiers near the large river, charging up the same slope of hill, toward that same white church. I couldn't believe what I was seeing. It was real.

I stayed on the phone for a half-hour with Aunt Yvonne and she explained how our people had fought and been pushed off our lands around Batoche, Saskatchewan, after 1885 and were made to squat on public Crown lands on the sides of roads and railways, known as road allowances—land nobody owned or wanted. The Métis weren't taken care of with a treaty like First Nations peoples with reserves, but cast off to wander, unprotected and dispossessed—we were the forgotten people.

The waist-high grass along the old highway in northern Saskatchewan rustled as warm wind blew from the south. I took my camera out and snapped a photo of the now-deteriorating railway line running from Debden up to Big River. Its steel bed snaked up over the crest of the hill then disappeared into the shrubs and thistles; I couldn't trace where Kokum took me berry picking, but knew it was somewhere here. Standing beside me were my mom, Aunt Yvonne, and Dr. Carolyn Podruchny, a York University professor and expert in Métis history.

I'd met Carolyn after Dr. Freeman marked my family history paper.

"This is one of the best papers I've read all year," she said. "I think you need to meet a friend of mine."

Two weeks later, I was at Carolyn's office in York University's History Department, a binder of Aunt Yvonne's and my own genealogy research in hand. Yvonne was right: genealogy was addictive, but in the best possible way.

I learned quickly Carolyn hadn't read my paper, but she wanted to know my family's history. After some explaining, she said she knew exactly who my mother's people were—Arcand, Morrissette, Montour—some of the major Métis resistance fighter clans, bison hunters, and road-allowance families in the northern parkland belt in Saskatchewan.

She agreed to take me on as a student.

"You'll do an independent reading course," she said, adding that she'd hire me as a research assistant on her Social Sciences and Humanities Research Council project, "Tracing Métis History Through Archives," which involved fieldwork at various Métis historical sites in Saskatchewan.

I was thrilled. It meant I would see my mother and our people in our homelands, where I hadn't been since I was three.

Carolyn flew me home in June.

It felt so good to hug my mom after so many years. I don't think I mustered any words in the airport, I let my tears do the talking. We growled like wolves the same way Josh and she did years ago in my grandparents' doorway. Carolyn clapped her hands in excitement.

For two weeks, Carolyn and I, along with my mom and Aunt Yvonne, drove all over the province to interview about a dozen Cree and Métis Elders, visiting historical sites relevant to the 1885 resistance, including Batoche. Many of the Elders told us they'd never shared their history with outsiders before. Given their traumatic history and treatment by the Canadian government, it was understandable.

The road allowance where my kokum and mushoom lived was the last stop on our research trip and my quest back to my identity. The land stretched about an acre back from the old road, right over to the train tracks. I recognized the ash and poplar trees off in the distance, bending and moaning as they arched over the now-derelict property. Mom wandered ahead of us to the old smoker, a small shack where my grandparents used to smoke moose, bear, and deer meat. There was nothing but a few rotten pieces of wood where it once stood.

Aunt Yvonne hiked toward two depressions in the grass and pointed to the ruts. "You can still see where the cars and carts used to drive up, doctor."

I took this photo of my mom (right) and Aunt Yvonne (left) in the Park Valley schoolhouse, about three kilometres from the Morrissette cabin, on the day we visited the road allowance. Mom said she was so happy I was home that she'd dance—and she kept her word.

Carolyn batted at the mosquitoes buzzing around her head as she struggled through the overgrown grass. I limped alongside her, like usual, but energy radiated up my legs—I was stepping on ground I hadn't tread in thirty-seven years—and it was like the road allowance remembered me, the prairie roses all across the property appeared to be smiling at me, welcoming me home, waving their heads this way and that.

Aunt Yvonne motioned her hand over another depression some thirty by sixty feet with small shrubs and trees growing within it—fauna not as tall as the surrounding forest.

"This is where they lived, *ma mère* and *mon père*." She looked at me and her black eyes seemed to hug right around my whole body. Carolyn turned to face me. She, too, had eyes as big as moose tracks in the snow.

I stepped within the depression of the building and fell to my knees.

The smell of lard and my kokum cooking bannock washed over me. I heard kokum singing to the hornets and mosquitoes, lulling them away, as we picked berries. The sweet sound of the Morrissette reels my mushoom played throbbed in my ears, the flicker of moonbeams on his vest danced across my eyes. The faint scent of smoke from my kokum's hearth wafted across the air. I saw my mushoom whittling a toy sword.

I remembered them.

I remembered my mother's people.

I remembered who I was.

IN THE CUSTOM OF THE COUNTRY

LUCIE AND I DIDN'T HAVE a big wedding. We didn't have the money nor did we want the headache. We just went to Toronto City Hall with a handful of our closest family members and friends.

Jerry was there. He was my best man, and he was wearing his finest black shirt, with his hair slicked back.

We didn't talk much, but when he adjusted my tie, he said, "It's been a long road, Jess—time for a new pact, though, eh? She's a wonderful woman," and his voice cracked. Uncle Ron and his daughter were my witnesses. They shed some tears, but he kept a straighter face than she did, the way we Thistle men were trained to do by Grandpa.

Lucie's best friend came, too, along with her boyfriend, a professor at Humber College. He was in charge of the music and was supposed to play "Sweet Disposition" by the Temper Trap after the Justice of the Peace announced we could kiss, but he missed the cue and didn't hit play until a few minutes after everything ended. There were cheers and laughter behind us as we embraced.

Liba, my mother-in-law, sat weeping in the front row. Her smile was so big it filled the whole of Canada.

After the ceremony, we gathered in front of the Jack Layton memorial in Nathan Phillips Square, and everyone drank and clinked together glasses of semi-expensive champagne—I had my bottle of 7Up, ever the teetotaller. My clinks made more of a blopping sound.

We went camping in Killarney Provincial Park for our honeymoon. We brought Luna, a golden Labrador retriever Lucie was dog-sitting for a friend, and got a campsite way at the back of the park. When we arrived near dusk, we saw we had neighbours: a little girl and her father. They were roasting marshmallows and singing. We waved to them, unpacked, got a campfire going, and settled by it, smiling and happy and hopeful of what the future held.

The next morning, we awoke early, walked down to the lakeside, grasped hands, and promised one another that we'd love and support each other and be friends until our last breaths.

Lucie and I were married on August 25, 2012, at Toronto City Hall.

TARA NOELLE BATES

The city hall ceremony had been just a legal formality; the real wedding happened while the two of us were alone in the woods, by the lakeshore, in the misty sunrise. We submerged our hands in the water and the bond was sealed.

In that moment of love, continents joined and the gaping maw within me closed, silent and forever.

Creator and Luna were our only witnesses.

The water ceremony was the way I imagine my ancestors would have married. It was the best wedding we could have asked for.

AMENDS

Today I walked back to where we used to live
Same old fence surrounds,
Same old paint on the windowpanes
This, the place where it all happened.

Guilt pushes me here; I can't live these excuses anymore.
You've long since passed, I know this.

But here I am regardless,
Reaching through time,
Staring at our door
Apologizing for breaking your hearts.

A silent amend you'll never hear.

SIXTEEN LETTERS

WHEN MY AUNT SHERRY DIVIDED my grandparents' estate she discovered an old shoebox, tucked away in the closet, up top, in the hardest to reach spot, with the rest of my grandmother's most precious belongings. Inside it was a stack of old letters from the Ontario Correctional Institute (OCI) in Brampton, where Dad served his last sentence before being released on day parole in December 1982. After that, he vanished forever after getting into a car outside Aunt Sherry's place.

"He just got in and we never saw him again, Jesse," Aunt Sherry said. "I really miss my big brother, too." She cried like she always did.

I was shocked when Aunt Sherry gave the letters to me along with a tiny black prison Bible that OCI sent my grandmother. I didn't know they existed.

"These should go to you," she said. "You're the most like him, lived a life closest to his."

My father's name was scrawled inside the front of the Bible, once in printing, which was scratched out, and then in flourishing cursive script underneath.

I knew what that meant the instant I saw it. The curve of the letters, the gentle pressure on the rounded S and roll of the Ns and T: he was trying to perfect what he'd learned in school and discarded years earlier, he was trying to better himself in his cage.

I'd done the exact same thing in a letter I'd sent to my grandmother when I was practicing my writing in jail years earlier.

I pored over his letters, memorizing every one word for word, and I saw the same effort. He wanted to be a better man, to change and love, and be home for his family, but couldn't for some reason.

My favourite letter was the one addressed directly to me where he talks about Yorkie, my absolute best friend growing up.

"Don't be afraid of the dog—he's a good boy," he assured me.

I was just four years old when he wrote it, and apparently afraid of Yorkie then. In another letter he wrote, "Grandma tells me you have all the women."

I guessed she must have told him about the time I ripped up the catalogue and had the pictures of models strewn beside me under the covers,

One of the letters Dad wrote to me from a corrections facility in 1981. I would have been four years old when he sent it. I didn't see it until I was in my late thirties.

336

and how Yorkie busted me by romping about on the bed. I had a hard time keeping it together reading that one.

Those sixteen letters and the black prison Bible are all I have of my dad—that, and the world of resentments I had to sort through on the streets, then in rehab. But it's more than I ever had, and I was grateful for the journey back to him, even if the old shoebox, some thirty-four years later, was as close as we'd ever get to being father and son.

57 YEARS OF LOVE

ON OCTOBER 14, 2015, I graduated from York University.

As I stood waiting to collect my degree, I smiled at Lucie and her mother, who were sitting in the audience, then patted my left breast pocket, which held my grandmother's picture. I swear the picture glowed over my heart as my name was called, I walked across the convocation stage, shook the chancellor's hand, and accepted my degree.

I'm sure my grandmother was there with me, cheering me on, proud that I had found my way, and that I'd kept the promise I'd made to her.

Grandma never did get to see me sober, or out of trouble with the law. Nor did she ever meet my wonderful wife, Lucie.

Lucie now wears my grandmother's engagement ring, a surprise gift from Aunt Sherry after I told her over dinner one night at her house that I wanted to marry Lucie but mentioned that I couldn't afford a ring on a student budget.

"You can have the most precious ring of all," Aunt Sherry said to me. She got up, went past Uncle John, got her jewel case, and pulled out a dusty box. The two of them were just beaming.

"It's your grandmother's wedding ring—fifty-seven years of love on there—she'd want Lucie to have it, I'm sure."

I like to think Aunt Sherry was right, and that Grandma sent Lucie to take care of me—she's the only woman strong enough to watch over Grandma's wayward, rebellious grandson.

WHEN WALKING IS A PRAYER

MY RIGHT FOOT STILL HURTS over a decade after "the accident." I guess it always will.

Every morning when I place my foot on the ground, a shock of electricity shoots up my leg into my brain like a bolt of lightning striking a rusty country weather vane. That first step is always the most torturous, and the jolt of pain it produces hijacks my cerebral cortex as I try to gain my balance. I hobble toward the bathroom with my hands braced on the apartment walls, my cat, Poppy, slithering between my legs. Sometimes, when I can't face the pain, I simply hop on my left leg, leaving my right leg dangling behind me.

Bone grinding on wire: that is my morning cup of coffee, that is what wakes me up every day, and that is what reminds me that the fall from my brother's apartment window was real—and that I'm lucky to be alive.

The pain also keeps me sober. It reminds me what it was like years ago when addiction and homelessness almost did me in. For that, and those harsh reminders, I am thankful.

The psychological pain, however, is sometimes almost too much to bear.

I have nightmares in which my leg is amputated just below the knee and I'm begging for change on Rideau Street and no one hears me. I dream that a colony of maggots is eating the gangrenous flesh around the incision and my toes are nothing but exposed bone. I dream that I'm scraping the skin off my dying foot like I would scrape soft candle wax off a glass table.

When these nightmares visit me, I feel like I'm drowning in some uncharted region of the icy North Atlantic. I feel helpless and utterly alone—just like I did when I was homeless. Just as I'm about to give up and lose consciousness, I come fully awake, gasping for breath, sweat soaked, and frightened. I am frantic. I cast aside the blankets to catch a glimpse of my foot to see if it's healthy, to see if it's still attached to my shin and knee, to see if all my toes are still there.

Without fail, my foot is always there, waiting for me; toes wiggling and fleshy, assuring me that we've made it, and that the leviathan can never drown us as long as we're together.

Lucie always knows when I've had one of my nightmares. Her method of comfort is always the same: she smiles and tells me it's okay, then she shifts across to my side of the bed, pulls me close, and squeezes me until I fall asleep. When I am lost at sea and drowning, her arms rescue me.

She's also there in the morning when I step down on my foot to receive my morning jolt; however, she's not so understanding then—she almost always shoos me out of the room so she can catch those precious last five minutes of sleep. But when the pain in my foot is too much to bear after a hard day of work, Lucie is there to offer me an arm.

I often wonder how I came to run with my foot the way it is (the doctors told me I'd likely never walk on my own again without medical aid). The truth is, I don't know, but what I do know is that my mangled foot and the pain it brings changed everything. It almost destroyed me, but somehow I survived; it forced me to do something unthinkable to save my life, it forced me to challenge and push myself when I was utterly defeated; it taught me to trust my body, myself, and my wife; and it forces me every day to remember what happened when I gave up and blamed the world for my problems and expected something for nothing.

In these ways, the pain in my foot has been a blessing, and I value each and every step I take. Every step is a gift, every one is sacred, and each, in its own little way, is a prayer for me.

EPILOGUE

I'M HERE IN OTTAWA PRESENTING at a conference on homelessness organized by the Federal Homeless Partnership Strategy, which oversees millions of dollars for emergency homeless services across the country.

My panel is on enumerating homeless people in census surveys called point-in-time counts. I'm also presenting a talk on a preliminary draft of the Definition of Indigenous Homelessness in Canada—I've been working on it at the Canadian Observatory on Homelessness, where I sit as the Resident Scholar on Indigenous Homelessness. But Jesse Donaldson, my boss and co-worker, is my co-presenter, and, truthfully, she carries our presentation—I fumble my words and have trouble reading, just like always.

People have started listening to me lately, though. Apparently, I've become an expert on homelessness and Métis history, and I won the top two doctoral scholarships in the country a month before—the Pierre Elliott Trudeau Foundation Doctoral Scholarship and the Vanier Canada Graduate Scholarship—and I also won the Governor General's Silver Medal for graduating with one of the highest grade point averages in the country— the first student, Indigenous or not, in York University's sixty-year history to do so.

The attention is a bit overwhelming—I just do my work like Grandpa taught me, listen to Lucie's advice, and remember the things Olive told me about being a good human. But people at conferences such as this listen now, instead of batting my hand away. I belong somewhere, finally—in academia, of all places.

People say and know my name now, they remember me when I introduce myself. I'm not just a blur to them. I'm no longer a blur to myself.

After the conference, I'm supposed to go out to dinner with some colleagues, but I pass up on the free meal. Instead, I decide to go for a walk, down Bank Street, along Rideau, past Parliament Hill and the Freedom Tower. I gaze over at the Centennial Flame, where I used to scoop piles of change, its flame of justice forever flickering over crests of our country's provinces and territories. I look for my RCMP friend, but he's not there.

Downtown Ottawa has changed quite a bit since I was here last. There's massive construction, but the Zesty Market on Dalhousie and

Taken the day I gave a lecture at McMaster University in Hamilton, Ontario.

LUCIE THISTLE

344

Rideau is still there, as ghetto as ever. So are the multitudes of shawarma joints that stay open late to feed the hordes of drunk people that spill out onto the block after two a.m. when the bars close. The windows on the one I burgled have long since been repaired.

As I walk up Dalhousie toward the Novotel hotel across from the Mission shelter, I find myself taking off my numerous silver rings and placing them in my pocket. I do the same with my shiny aviator watch and the bracelet Lucie got me for Christmas a few years back. I'm afraid my jewellery might betray me to the local homeless people and make me a prime target for robbery—I would've robbed me back in the day. I also try to hide the rectangular impression of my iPhone in my pocket, but the blasted thing is just too damned big to conceal.

If they rob me, I think, *I'm suing Apple for making such a humongous and unconcealable phone.*

The homeless men who glare at me from out of the Mission's front entrance on Waller Street, however, don't make much of me—they aren't like I was. They aren't interested in me or my huge iPhone. They simply stand and survey the city landscape, glancing at me like I'm some awkward shrub rudely growing out of the sidewalk.

I stand there, the human shrub, trying to find the courage to uproot myself and walk over to see if I know anybody. But my legs won't take me. I just stare in the direction of the Mission and rustle around, wishing I could say hello, but can't.

This place isn't my home anymore, I think. *Maybe it never was.*

After a moment or two I head toward the beer store next to the walkway that leads to the nearby Salvation Army.

As usual, the dealers are in the alley slinging dope to the homeless clientele of the ByWard Market. One is thick and muscular, too thick and muscular to be a long-time regular—just out of jail perhaps, or maybe just a few months shy of drug-induced emaciation. On either side he's flanked by two beautiful but pockmarked working girls.

As I emerge from the alley, the dealer's eyes dart upon me and he jams his hand in his underwear, hiding his dope in the crack of his ass. As he does this, I see him mouth "cop" to his associates. They in turn whistle to other street sentinels. A chorus of whistles echoes into the distance and the dealers and their drugs vaporize into thin air.

They think I'm a cop? I laugh to myself. *I guess I am a burly boy just like those donut-eating mofos.*

It's true. The flesh on my bones in these parts means I'm either that or a lost pedestrian. But even softened by years of luxury and stability, I can still read the street like an open book. I can still see plain as day where the zombies live, where the vampires shift in dark corners, where they sell bones and batwings to the undead, the broken-hearted, and the lost.

As before, I long to go up to the homeless people in front of the Sally Ann, but my legs won't take me. I just stand and watch them from afar smoking their crack and cigarettes, and drinking the beers I assume they must have stolen only moments earlier from the liquor store. It's all so familiar. A man in a wheelchair rolls past me and breaks my trance, reminding me that I have no business watching the homeless consume themselves in this hopeless realm. I gather myself and walk toward the McDonald's. There I spot a guy I knew, but he walks right past me to ask the crowd of people behind me for change.

"Hey," I ask him when he's finished. "Do you remember me?"

"No . . ."

I can tell he's trying to place me. "I stayed at the Mission many years ago—"

He interrupts before I can finish. "Yeah, I remember someone like you. But he was really skinny, and you're fat!"

"That I am," I say and laugh at his honesty. "Life has been good to me these last few years. I'm sober, have a home, a wife, a cat. And you?"

"Oh, you know, same old. I stay on the second floor of the Sheps now. My mind doesn't work so well anymore—they feed me, keep me sorted with clean clothes and bug juice."

I know he means psychotropic medication. I can tell the physical damage the drugs have done to him over the years from the way he can no longer keep himself from fidgeting. His shoes are held together with duct tape and his pants stained with the grime of his thousand-year wanderings in the Ottawa desert. His bloodshot eyes shift about aimlessly, but they still carry the intelligence I remember.

"You used to be my friend, Omar," I say as I shake his hand. "You used to watch my back, give me tokes when I got sick, and we used to joke around and drink beers. Remember?"

"No. Sorry." His eyes break from mine. "I don't remember that. I just remember your face. Nothing comes easy anymore. Sorry, friend."

"No worries. Rest easy, old buddy."

Before he leaves I ask him to take care of himself. He promises he will, but that he needs some change to make it through the night. I give him what I can, then we part ways.

As I sit in my hotel room later, I don't regret missing my dinner meeting with my colleagues. I explored homelessness in a way that would escape them. They could only talk and write about it; I took a walk a stone's throw from my hotel room where I'd lived it.

And I'd said goodbye.

MY SOUL IS STILL HOMELESS

sometimes
in between slumber and consciousness
i sleepwalk.

my mind not yet aware
i shuffle out the front door
the crisp open air and night sky still call me.

at night
in between slumber and consciousness
i sleepwalk.

my soul not yet aware
that my wanderings are over
and I have a home.

MISSING PERSON

HAVE YOU SEEN THIS MAN? Investigators from 22 Division Criminal Investigation Bureau in the Region of Peel, Ontario, are trying to find a missing man, Cyril Thistle, and need your help.

Cyril Thistle, who was born April 3, 1954, disappeared in 1981 in the Region of Peel when he was twenty-six years old. He was last seen by members of his family, and his children have been searching for him for years but have not had any success.

The police note that, "At this time all investigative leads have been exhausted and assistance is being requested from the public."

If you have any information on the whereabouts of Cyril Thistle, please call investigators at the 22 Division Criminal Investigation Bureau at **(905) 453–2121, ext. 2233**. You can also leave information anonymously by calling Peel Crime Stoppers at **1-800-222-TIPS (8477)**, or by visiting **peelcrimestoppers.ca**.

ACKNOWLEDGMENTS

I begin by thanking my wife, Lucie. As always, you are my world, my everything—words fail me when I think how grateful I am to you. Liba, my mother-in-law, you're the best mom-in-law I could ask for, the great teacher of truth in my life. Thank you for letting me make sandwiches out of the *bramborák*. The Suriano family, you likewise love and have given Lucie and me a home; I feel like your son in many ways. Carolyn, you're my great mentor and changed my world in every good way imaginable—I'm infinitely grateful to you. To Thistle and Morrissette family members who shared stories in the crafting of this book—Mom, Dave, Sherry, Jerry, Josh, and Ralph—marcee. Randy and everyone at CASS, you made the academy my home—cheers. Janine, the strongest Kwe I know, along with cousin Cherie: you helped me find my writing legs way back when—thank you. Auntie Maria, you walked me through such beautiful fields of reconnection and are a major factor in all I do. Aunties Nancy and Janet, thank you for the "auntie plan" with Tessa. Tessa, I know I was scared, but you got me to start speaking for the first time in my life, and without you my stories just wouldn't have been told. Nancy, you've always been there, along with Pat, back when the world literally had collapsed on me. The Hockley Crew, Bud Boys, and girls down east, you forged my soul and I think of you often. My Harvest House family and Jenepher, marcee for saving me when I was just an angry wolf. Randolph and Russian

Andre—thanks for employing me over the years; sorry you had to fire me fifty times. Stephen and Allyson and the COH—thank you for believing in me. My last two probation officers—Marta especially—I'm grateful for your light. Jesse Winter, your story changed everything and caught the attention of Adria and Nita at Simon & Schuster—thank you all for seeing value in me. And lastly, I want to thank Laurie, my Jedi master editor who taught me good writing, was patient and kind, and helped me cobble together my life into this memoir—your words and teachings also live upon these pages. Thank you.

A NOTE FROM THE AUTHOR

My memories are memories from my point of view. I have tried my best to remember and relay my life in a meaningful way. But because of my youth and, later, my addictions, I see what happened to me like fragments of light, flickers of a flame, shadows on a wall. And trauma distorts perspectives. I think my mind blocks out a lot, bends time, folds that trauma in on itself so that I can function today.

Much of what I recall is accurate, but my years clouded by drugs and alcohol have left me, at times, an unreliable narrator, so I employed court, probation, and school records in an attempt to help reconstruct the past; and many people who knew me during those turbulent times have helped me fill in the gaps—family and friends, police officers who dealt with me, social workers at rehab centres, shelter workers, probation officers.

Some of the names in the book are real; others aren't.

ABOUT THE AUTHOR

LUCIE THISTLE

JESSE THISTLE is Métis-Cree, from Prince Albert, Saskatchewan. He is an assistant professor in Métis Studies at York University in Toronto. He won a Governor General's Academic Medal in 2016 and is a Pierre Elliott Trudeau Scholar and a Vanier Scholar. He lives in Toronto. Visit **jessethistle.com** and follow him on Twitter at **@michifman**.

Performance Management

by Herman Aguinis, PhD

Performance Management For Dummies®

Published by: **John Wiley & Sons, Inc.,** 111 River Street, Hoboken, NJ 07030-5774, www.wiley.com

Copyright © 2019 by John Wiley & Sons, Inc., Hoboken, New Jersey

Published simultaneously in Canada

Library of Congress Control Number: 2019939296

ISBN 978-1-119-55765-4 (pbk); ISBN 978-1-119-55766-1 (ebk); ISBN 978-1-119-55771-5 (ebk)

10 9 8 7 6 5 4 3 2 1

Contents at a Glance

Table of Contents

Introduction

Performance management is a continuous process of identifying, measuring, and developing the performance of individuals and teams and aligning their performance with the strategic goals of the organization. So performance management is a key tool to transform people's talent and motivation into a strategic business advantage.

But because you are reading this book, you already know that performance management is broken. You hate wasting time dealing with "HR cops" who ask you to fill out useless performance evaluation forms. And you surely hate those dreaded soul-crushing annual performance review meetings. I don't need to tell you, because you already know, that performance management is not even close to living up to its promise of turning human capital into a source of competitive advantage.

Though you may see media headlines proclaiming "Performance Evaluation is Dead" and "The End of Performance Reviews," performance management is not going away. On the contrary, many companies such as GE, Microsoft, Google, Yahoo!, Adobe, and Accenture are transitioning from performance appraisal (once-a-year evaluation and review) to performance management (ongoing evaluation and developmental feedback). In other words, performance management is becoming a normal, routine, built-in, and ever-present aspect of work in 21st-century organizations, particularly considering demographic trends about Gen X and Gen Y employees who are digital natives, demand ongoing feedback, and thrive when given growth opportunities.

So if you want to be a successful manager, you need to be a successful *performance management leader*, which means you need to have the knowledge and skills to manage the performance of your employees. And this is exactly what this book will teach you how to do.

Performance Management For Dummies is a definitive guide on how to design and implement a successful performance management systems. You'll learn how to maximize the benefits of performance management and minimize its pitfalls.

About This Book

Performance Management For Dummies teaches you how to make performance management work for you by connecting individual and team performance with your organization's strategic goals and priorities. This book also teaches you the nuts and bolts of how to define and measure performance in terms of what employees do (behaviors) and the outcome of what they do (results) — both for individual employees as well as teams. And this book also teaches you how to use performance management not just as an evaluation tool but, just as importantly, to help your employees grow and improve on an ongoing basis.

The book also covers how to gather and use data to understand whether the performance management system is working and where fixes may be needed. Overall, the book teaches you how to design and implement a state-of-the-science performance management system.

And if you don't manage employees yet, you can give a copy of this book to your managers because what they learn in this book will help them manage your performance and make your own job a lot more satisfying and rewarding.

The information contained in this book is deliberately accessible and covers everything you need to know about performance management from the basics to the more sophisticated insights that will improve and fine-tune your existing performance management system. As a result, this book is essential reading whether you are new to business, in your first management or HR job, or a seasoned professional seeking some additional nuggets of wisdom to help squeeze just a little more value out of performance management. If you are already familiar with performance management, this book shines some light on the common problems or mistakes people make, so you can rectify any errors that may be impairing your results. Reinventing the wheel is time consuming and costly. Instead, it's better to learn from both the evidence and research accumulated over decades as well as other people's mistakes to make your performance management system work right now. You want to performance management to be a useful and insightful business tool rather than a once-a-year, soul-crushing, and time-wasting exercise.

Consider this book your performance management guide and come back to it often. Try out the ideas and suit your situation in your business. Make it your own and allow performance management to inform your talent-related decisions and support your strategy.

Foolish Assumptions

For this book, I've assumed that you are a participant in performance management in any capacity. This means your performance is evaluated, you evaluate someone else's performance, or you are a member of the HR or related talent management function. Also, I've assumed that your participation in performance management is in the context of a business, government department, or not-for-profit organization seeking to better understand and use performance management.

Icons Used in This Book

All For Dummies books use distinctive icons to draw attention to specific features within a chapter. The icons help you quickly and easily find particular types of information that may be of use to you:

TIP

This icon highlights a practical tip to help you with designing or implementing a performance management practice.

REMEMBER

When you see this icon, I'm highlighting a valuable point that you'll want to remember. It saves you from underlining or using a highlighter pen as you read, but feel free to highlight key points as you go through the book.

EXAMPLE

Nothing makes a point better than a real-life example, so I include illustrations of how many organizations do things in practice. I'm not doing this to impress you but to impress upon you the ideas that I'm trying to get across.

WARNING

Every once in a while, you may want to do one thing when it would actually be better to do the opposite (or to do nothing at all). I call attention to these situations with the Warning icon.

ACTIVE LEARNING

This icon contains an activity, question, exercise, or self-assessment that will help you learn by doing. It will help you make the material more personal and applicable to your organization and specific situation.

Beyond the Book

In addition to the material in this print or e-book you're reading right now, this product also comes with some access-anywhere goodies on the web. Check out the free Cheat Sheet at www.dummies.com for some helpful checklists. Just go to the site and type "*Performance Management For Dummies* cheat sheet" in the Search box.

Also, check out my personal website, where you will find many relevant articles and resources about performance management and talent management in general: www.hermanaguinis.com.

Where to Go from Here

That's entirely up to you. You can read this book in order from Chapter 1 to 21, but you don't have to. Where you start reading depends on how familiar and comfortable you are with performance management already.

In you are new to performance management or are interested in or charged with designing or improving an existing performance management system, then start at the beginning. Otherwise, use the table of contents to find what you are most interested in and jump straight to that section. Whatever reading approach you take, you will find a treasure trove of useful information and evidence-based advice that will allow you to unlock the true potential of performance management to transform people's talent and motivation into a strategic business advantage and make work a more satisfying and rewarding experience.

1

Getting Started with Performance Management

Chapter **1**

Introducing Performance Management

The organizational success equation is quite simple. Organizations that have more and better resources are more successful compared to those that don't. This applies to large corporations, small start-ups, not-for-profits, and to organizations of every size and in every type of industry.

Here's the complicated part. In today's globalized and hyper competitive world, it is relatively easy to gain access to the same resources as your competitors — particularly when it comes to technology and products. For example, most banks offer the same products such as different types of savings accounts and investment opportunities. If a particular bank decides to offer a new product or service, such as an improved mobile phone app, the competitors offer precisely the same product.

But, a key differentiating resource is people. Organizations with engaged, motivated, and talented employees offering outstanding service to customers and coming up with creative ideas pull ahead of the competition, even if the products offered are similar to those offered by the competitors. Performance management is the ideal tool to have this type of workforce.

Why Do You Need Performance Management? To Succeed (of Course)

There are 100s of books on talent management. Why? If you manage your talent right, you create a sustainable competitive advantage.

A performance management system is a key tool to transform people's talent and motivation into a strategic business advantage.

REMEMBER

Performance management is a continuous process of identifying, measuring, and developing the performance of individuals and teams and aligning their performance with the strategic goals of the organization.

Let's take a look at the two main components of the definition of performance management:

>> **Continuous process:** Performance management is ongoing. It involves a never-ending process of setting goals and objectives, observing performance, and giving and receiving ongoing coaching and feedback.

>> **Alignment with strategic goals:** Performance management requires that managers link employees' activities and outputs with the organization's goals. Making this connection helps the organization gain a competitive advantage because performance management creates a direct link between employee and team performance and organizational goals, and makes the employees' contributions to the organization explicit.

Why performance management is alive and well

Because performance management plays such a key rote, many companies, including GE, Microsoft, Google, Yahoo!, Adobe, and Accenture, are going through a similar process of transitioning from a performance appraisal to a performance management system. In other words, they are moving away from a dreaded once-a-year review to ongoing evaluation and feedback.

REMEMBER

Contrary to a trend described in the media with such headlines as "Performance Evaluation is Dead" and "The End of Performance Reviews," the evaluation of performance is not going away. In fact, performance assessment and review are becoming a normal, routine, built-in, and ever-present aspect of work in all types of organizations.

It is not the case that companies are abandoning ratings and performance measurement and evaluation. They are actually implementing performance systems more clearly aligned with best practices, as described in this book, that involve and ongoing evaluation of and conversation about performance.

Many companies are getting rid of the labels "performance evaluation," "performance review," and even "performance management." Instead, they use labels such as "performance achievement," "talent evaluation and advancement," "check-ins," and "employee development." But they still implement performance management, but use new, more fashionable, and perhaps less threatening labels.

REMEMBER

Everyone does performance management one way or another. Results of a survey of about 1,000 HR professionals in Australia showed that 96 percent of companies implement some type of performance management system. And, results of a survey of 278 organizations, about two-thirds of which are multinational corporations from 15 different countries, showed that about 91 percent of organizations implement a formal performance management system.

PERFORMANCE MANAGEMENT PAYS OFF

A study by Development Dimensions International (DDI), a global human resources consulting firm specializing in leadership and selection, showed that performance management pays off. Organizations with formal and systematic performance management systems are 51 percent more likely to perform better than the others financially, and 41 percent more likely to perform better on customer satisfaction, employee retention, and other important metrics.

Performance management systems are a key tool that organizations use to translate business strategy into business results by influencing "financial performance, productivity, product or service quality, customer satisfaction, and employee job satisfaction." 79 percent of the CEOs surveyed in this study said that the performance management system implemented in their organizations drives the "cultural strategies that maximize human assets."

Based on these results, it is not surprising that senior executives of companies listed in the *Sunday Times* list of best employers in the United Kingdom believe that performance management is one of the top two most important HR management priorities in their organizations.

Paraphrasing Mark Twain, I can tell you with certainty that the death of performance has been vastly exaggerated.

Imagining an organization without performance management

Imagine an organization without a performance management system. Not a pretty picture. You cannot do any of the things that are critical for talent management and the success of your organization:

>> Connect the behaviors and results produced by employees to your organization's strategic priorities.

>> Make fair and appropriate administrative decisions such as promotions, salary adjustments, and terminations.

>> Inform employees about how they are doing and provide them with information on specific areas that need improvement.

>> Give employees information on expectations of peers, supervisors, customers, and the organization, and what aspects of work are most important.

>> Give employees information about themselves that can help them individualize their career paths. For example, if they don't know their strengths, they cannot chart a more successful path for their future.

>> Learn who are your high-potential and star performing employees.

>> Anticipate where you will need to hire people and with which particular skill set.

>> Evaluate the effectiveness of HR initiatives. For example, you don't have accurate data on employee performance to evaluate whether employees perform at higher levels after participating in a training program.

Making Performance Management Work in Your Business

Do you want to make sure performance management works in your business? It should be clear by now that performance management is much more than just performance appraisal.

Distinguishing performance management from performance appraisal

Many organizations have what is labeled a "performance management" system. But it actually is a performance *appraisal* system. And performance appraisal is not the same thing as performance management.

A system that involves employee evaluations once a year without an ongoing effort to provide feedback and coaching so that performance can be improved is not a true performance management system. This performance appraisal system is the measurement and description of an employee's strengths and weaknesses. And while performance appraisal is an important component of performance management, it is just a part of a bigger whole because performance management is much more than just performance measurement.

Much like those that focus on performance appraisal only, "performance management" systems that don't make explicit the employee contribution to the organizational goals are not true performance management systems. When you make an explicit link between employee and team performance objectives and the organizational goals also you are establishing a shared understanding about what is to be achieved and how it is to be achieved.

ACTIVE LEARNING

Table 1-1 summarizes main differences between performance management and performance appraisal. Think about the system at your organization. Is it truly performance management, or performance appraisal?

TABLE 1-1

Performance Management versus Performance Appraisal

Performance Management	Performance Appraisal
Driven by the line manager	Driven by the HR function
Strategic business purpose	Mostly administrative purpose
Ongoing feedback	Feedback once a year
Emphasis on past, present, and future	Emphasis mostly on past

Adapting performance management to today's reality

Performance management has a long history and is actually not something new.

Did you know that the Wei dynasty in China, which was in power between the years 220 and 265, implemented a performance evaluation system for government employees? Here's a cool fact: It was a nine-rank system, by which workers were rated based on their performance. A low ranking meant the worker would be fired.

Now, fast forward to nineteenth-century England. The performance of officers in the Royal Navy was rated by their peers.

At approximately the same time, Robert Owen, a Welsh industrialist, set up a large cotton mill in New Lanark (Scotland). By the way, you can still visit it today. He mounted a block of wood on each machine with four sides painted, based on this performance rating system: white was best, then yellow, then blue, and the worst, which was black. At the end of each workday, the marks were recorded, and each worker was evaluated by turning the block to the appropriate side, which would face the aisle. Owen would walk the mill floor daily to see the block color on each machine.

But the nature of work and organizations today is quite different from those in China in the third century and England and Scotland in the nineteenth century. Due to technological advancements, globalization, and demographic changes, we are now in the middle of a new industrial revolution.

Technological changes have occurred on an ongoing basis in the past two centuries. But, the Internet and cloud computing have fundamentally changed the way we work. These advancements give everyone in the organization, at any level and in every functional area, amazing access to information — instantaneously from anywhere. Vast amounts of data, what is often referred to as "Big Data," are collected on an ongoing basis: what employees are doing, what they are producing, with whom they are interacting, and where they are doing what they are doing.

What does this mean for performance management? The old days of paper-and-pencil performance evaluations are mostly gone. So are the old days of static in-house enterprise technology platforms. Instead, performance management can be implemented using dynamic online systems accessed via web and mobile apps.

Get your head in the clouds

The use of cloud computing for performance management is much more than a mere translation of paper evaluation forms to digital format. Cloud computing technology allows supervisors and peers to provide performance evaluations on an ongoing basis and in real time — and employees to receive feedback also on an ongoing basis and in real time. Using cloud computing for performance management allows organizations to update goals and priorities and communicate them also real-time to all employees, thereby allowing them to also update their team and individual goals and priorities. So, the cascading of goals from the organization to its units, and then to individual employees can be implemented successfully across thousands of employees in just a few weeks.

Another advantage of using cloud computing for performance management is that it leads to a clearer understanding of the role of managers in the performance management process. For example, we can quickly learn how often they are communicating with direct reports about their performance. Also, we can quickly learn how often "check-ins" take place.

Zalando, an e-retailer delivering merchandise to about 15 European countries, is taking advantage of technological advancements to improve its performance management system. It put in place an online app that crowdsources performance feedback from meetings, problem-solving sessions, completed projects, launches, and campaigns. Zalando employees can request feedback from their supervisors, peers, and internal customers that lets people provide both positive and more critical comments about each other in a playful and engaging way. An important innovation is that the system then weighs responses by how much exposure the rater has to the ratee. Every time an employee requests feedback, the online app prompts a list of questions that can be answered by moving a slider on the touchscreen of a smartphone or tablet. Clearly, this is very different from a traditional annual performance appraisal, which is currently the target of sharp criticism.

The availability of Big Data is also changing performance management in important ways. For example, about 80 percent of organizations use some type of electronic performance monitoring (EPM). In its early days, EPM included surveillance camera systems and computer and phone monitoring systems. But, today EPM includes wearable technologies and smartphones, including Fitbits and mobile GPS tracking applications.

In today's workplace, every email, instant message, phone call, and mouse-click leaves a digital footprint, all of which can be used as part of a performance management system. But we should not be enamored by the presence of Big Data, and instead, should think about "Smart Data."

Context matters

The availability of online tools allows for the customization of performance management systems such that every step can be customized and tailored to local contexts. For example, consider the case of providing feedback. People from more individualistic cultures, such as the United States, expect to receive feedback and many performance management systems include training for supervisors on how to provide one-on-one feedback in the most effective way. However, in collectivistic cultures, such as China and Guatemala, open discussions about an individual's performance clash with cultural norms about harmony, and the direct report may perceive negative feedback as an embarrassing loss of face.

Successful performance management systems need to consider local norms — including societal and organizational cultural issues.

Adapting performance management for different generations

In the United States and many other Western countries, Baby Boomers, who are people born approximately between 1946 and 1964, are retiring in large number. Members of Generation X, who were born approximately between 1965 and 1976, and Generation Y or Millennials, born approximately between 1977 and 1995, are now entering the workforce in large numbers. This presents a challenge but also an opportunity for performance management systems.

Gen X and Gen Y employees are "digital natives." Also, they are used to immediate feedback — just like when receiving a grade immediately after completing a web-based exam in high school and college. So you need to consider generational differences for the performance management system to be effective. For example, it is important to include "check-in" mechanisms to give managers and direct reports the opportunity to discuss performance issues on an ongoing and real-time basis.

Designing and Implementing a Performance Management System

Performance management is an ongoing process. Unlike performance appraisal, it most certainly doesn't take place just once a year. And it is not "owned" by the HR function. The HR function plays a critical role in terms of offering support and resources such as in-person and online training opportunities and online tools that can be used to measure performance and share feedback.

Performance management must be owned and managed by each unit, and supervisors play a critical role. After all, the principal responsibility of managers is to manage, right?

The components of a performance management system are closely related to each other and the poor implementation of any of them has a negative impact on the performance management system as a whole. The components in the performance management process are shown in Figure 1-1.

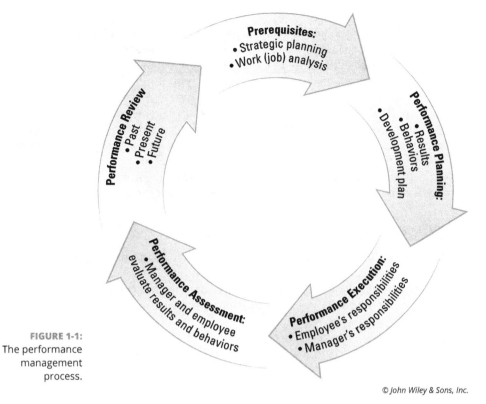

FIGURE 1-1:
The performance management process.

Step 1: Establishing prerequisites

There are two important prerequisites that must exist before the implementation of a successful performance management system. First, there is a need to know the organization's mission and strategic goals. This knowledge, combined with knowledge regarding the mission and strategic goals of their unit, allows employees to make contributions that will have a positive impact on the unit and on the organization as a whole.

Second, there is a need to know the position in question: what tasks need to be done, how they should be done, and what KSAs are needed. Such knowledge is obtained through a work analysis. If you have good information regarding how a job is done, then it is easier to establish key performance indicators for job success.

Strategic planning

The first prerequisite is *strategic planning*, which allows an organization to define its purpose and reasons for existing, where it wants to be in the future, the goals it wants to achieve, and the strategies it will use to attain these goals. Once the goals for the entire organization are established, similar goals cascade downward, with units setting objectives to support the organization's overall mission and objectives. The cascading continues downward until each employee has a set of goals compatible with those of the entire organization. The same process applies to large, small, and medium-size organizations.

WARNING

An important objective of any performance management system is to enhance each employee's contribution to the goals of the organization. If there is a lack of clarity regarding where the organization wants to go, or if the relationship between the organization's mission and strategies and the unit's mission and strategies is not clear, there will be a lack of clarity regarding what each employee needs to do and achieve to help the organization get there.

Work analysis

The second important prerequisite before a performance management system is implemented is to understand the job in question. This is done through what is called a *work analysis:* a process for determining the key components of a particular job, including activities, tasks, products, services, and processes.

REMEMBER

A work analysis is a fundamental prerequisite of any performance management system because without a work analysis, it is difficult to understand what constitutes the required duties for a particular position. If you don't know what an employee is supposed to do on the job, you will not know what needs to be evaluated and how to do so.

As a result of a work analysis, you get information regarding the tasks to be carried out and the knowledge, skills, and abilities (KSAs) required of a particular job:

>> **Knowledge** includes having the information needed to perform the work, but not necessarily having done it earlier.

>> **Skills** refer to required attributes that are usually acquired by having done the work in the past.

>> **Abilities** refers to having the physical, emotional, intellectual, and psychological aptitude to perform the work, though neither having done the job nor having been trained to do the work is required.

The tasks and KSAs needed for jobs are typically presented in the form of a job description, which summarizes the job duties, required KSAs, and working conditions for a particular position.

EXAMPLE

The following job description includes information about what tasks are performed (operation of a specific type of truck). It also includes information about the required knowledge (e.g., manifests, bills of lading), skills (like keeping truck and trailer under control, particularly in difficult weather conditions), and abilities (such as physical and spatial abilities needed to turn narrow corners).

Job Description for Trailer Truck Driver: Civilian Personnel Management Service, U.S. Department of Defense

Operates gasoline- or diesel-powered truck or truck tractor equipped with two or more driving wheels and with four or more forward speed transmissions, which may include two or more gear ranges. These vehicles are coupled to a trailer or semitrailer by use of a turntable (fifth wheel) or pintle (pivot) hook. Drives over public roads to transport materials, merchandise, or equipment. Performs difficult driving tasks such as backing truck to loading platform, turning narrow corners, negotiating narrow passageways, and keeping truck and trailer under control, particularly on wet or icy highways. May assist in loading and unloading truck. May also handle manifest, bills of lading, expense accounts, and other papers pertinent to the shipment.

How do you do a work analysis? Interviews are a very popular work analysis method. During a work analysis interview, the work analyst asks the interviewee to describe what he or she does during a typical day at the job from start to finish. Then, once a list of tasks has been compiled, people doing the job, called *job incumbents,* have an opportunity to review the information and rate each task in terms of frequency and criticality.

To do a work analysis, use the five-point scale anchors shown in Table 1-2.

TABLE 1-2

Scale Anchors for Rating Tasks in a Work Analysis

Frequency	Criticality
0: not performed	0: not critical
1: every few months to yearly	1: low level of criticality
2: every few weeks to monthly	2: below average level of criticality
3: every few days to weekly	3: average level of criticality
4: every few hours to daily	4: above average level of criticality
5: hourly to many times each hour	5: extremely critical

TIP

Rating both frequency and criticality is necessary because some tasks may be performed regularly (such as making coffee several times a day), but may not be very critical.

After you collected the data, multiply the frequency scores by the criticality scores to obtain an overall score for each task.

So, if making coffee receives a frequency score of 4 ("every few hours to daily") and a criticality score of 0 ("not critical"), the overall score would be $4 \times 0 = 0$. Considering frequency scores alone would have given the wrong impression that making coffee is a task that deserves a prominent role in the job description. Overall scores for all tasks can be ranked from highest to lowest to obtain a final list of tasks.

TIP

There are many work analysis questionnaires available online. You can use them for a variety of positions. For example, the state of Delaware uses a work analysis questionnaire available at `www.delawarepersonnel.com/class/forms/jaq/jaq.shtml`. This questionnaire includes 18 multiple choice job content questions. Job content information is assessed through three factors: knowledge and skills, problem solving, and accountability and end results.

You then use the information from a work analysis for writing a job description.

USE O*NET FOR WORK ANALYSIS

No time to do your own work analysis and create your own job descriptions? Do you need a job description for a position for which you have not hired anyone yet? No problem! You can get generic job descriptions from the Occupational Informational Network (O*NET; `www.onetonline.org`). O*NET is a comprehensive database of worker attributes and job characteristics that provides a common language for defining and describing occupations. The information available via O*NET serves as a foundation for a job description. For each job, O*NET gives information on tasks, knowledge, technology skills, knowledge, skills, abilities, work activities, detailed work activities, work context, job zone, education, interests, work styles, work values, and credentials. You can then adapt generic O*NET descriptions to accommodate specific local characteristics of your own organization.

O*NET is a particularly useful resource for small businesses because for most of them, conducting a work analysis may not be feasible simply because there are not sufficient numbers of people in any particular position to collect data from.

TIP

Jobs change. So check job descriptions for accuracy and update them on an ongoing basis.

Why are job descriptions so important for performance management? They provide the *key performance indicators* (i.e., yardsticks) that will be used in measuring performance. These KPIs concern behaviors (i.e., how to perform) or results (i.e., what outcomes should result from performance).

In our truck driver example, a behavioral yardsticks could involve the skill "equipment maintenance." For example, a supervisor may rate the extent to which the employee "performs routine maintenance on equipment and determines when and what kind of maintenance is needed." Regarding results, these KPIs usually fall into one of the following categories: quality, quantity, cost-effectiveness, and timeliness. In the truck driver example, results-oriented KPIs can include number of accidents (or quality) and amount of load transported over a specific period of time (or quantity).

INTEGRATING JOB DESCRIPTIONS INTO THE PERFORMANCE MANAGEMENT SYSTEM AT AllianceHealth DEACONESS HOSPITAL

Take the case of AllianceHealth Deaconess Hospital in Oklahoma City, Oklahoma, which includes a workforce of more than 500 healthcare professionals. AllianceHealth Deaconess Hospital has been able to effectively integrate employees' job descriptions within their performance management system. The need for this integration was reinforced by results from an employee survey showing that employees did not know what they were being evaluated on. So, with the input of employees, the hospital updated each of the 260 job descriptions. Now, each employee's job description is part of the performance review form.

The new forms incorporate tasks and behaviors specific to individual jobs. For example, each nurse is evaluated on "how well they safely, timely, and respectfully administers patient medication and on his or her planning and organization skills." Also, Deaconess Hospital has been able to link each employee's performance to the strategic goals of the organization. That is, all employees are rated on the following core behaviors considered to be of top strategic importance for (1) adaptability, (2) building customer loyalty, (3) building trust, and (4) contributing to team success.

Step 2: Planning performance

Now that you know the organization's strategic goals and have information about the position, the supervisor and the employee formally meet to discuss, and agree upon, what needs to be done and how it should be done. This *performance planning* discussion includes a consideration of both results and behaviors, as well as a development plan.

Performance planning includes the consideration of results and behaviors and the development plan. A discussion of results needs to include key accountabilities (that is, broad areas for which an employee is responsible), specific objectives for each key accountability (such as goals to be reached). A discussion of behaviors needs to include competencies (clusters of knowledge, skills, and abilities). Finally, the development plan includes a description of areas that need improving and goals to be achieved in each area.

Results and key accountabilities

Results refer to the outcomes of what employees do — what employees produce. A consideration of results includes the key *accountabilities,* or broad areas of a job for which the employee is responsible for producing results. This information is typically obtained from the job description.

A discussion of results also includes specific *objectives* that the employee will achieve as part of each accountability. Objectives are specific statements of important and measurable outcomes.

EXAMPLE

Take the job of a university professor. Two key accountabilities are teaching (preparation and delivery of instructional materials to students) and research (creation and dissemination of new knowledge). An objective for teaching could be "to obtain a student evaluation of teaching performance of 3 on a 4-point scale by the end of the academic year." An objective for research could be "to publish two articles in high-quality scholarly refereed journals per year."

Although it is important to measure results, if you only focus on results, you can end up having an incomplete picture of employee performance. For example, for some jobs, it is difficult to establish specific and measurable objectives. For other jobs, employees may have control over how they do their jobs, but not over the results of their behaviors. For example, the sales figures of a salesperson could be affected more by the assigned sales territory than by the salesperson's ability and performance.

Behaviors

Behaviors, or how a job is done, thus constitute an important component of the planning phase. This is probably why results from a survey indicated that in addition to sales figures, salespeople would like to be appraised on such behavioral KPIs as communications skills and product knowledge.

A consideration of behaviors includes discussing competencies, which are measurable clusters of KSAs that are critical in determining how results will be achieved. Examples of competencies are customer service, written or oral communication, creative thinking, and dependability.

EXAMPLE

Returning to the example of the professor, assume that teaching is done online and there are technology-related problems outside of his control (for example, the university does not offer IT support to students who need it), so that the resulting teaching evaluations are lower than stated in the objective. This is an example of a situation in which behaviors should be given more importance than results. In this situation, the evaluation could include competencies such as online communication skills (such as in the chat room) because technology-related problems are outside of the professor's control.

An important step before the review cycle begins is for the supervisor and employee to agree on a development plan. At a minimum, this plan should include identifying areas that need improvement and setting goals to be achieved in each area. Development plans usually include both results and behaviors.

PERFORMANCE PLANNING AT DISCOVER

The Discover credit card was launched in 1986. The company has expanded to over the years to include numerous banking services. Discover is taking several steps to ensure that performance planning and employee development support the organization's business goals. Discover has initiated an approach that addresses the development needs of specific business units by assigning HR professionals to attend business meetings regularly to gain an understanding of what knowledge, skills, and abilities are required. The company asks managers to go through the same curriculum with classroom and online learning opportunities. These managers form discussion groups to talk about what they have learned and how it applies to the challenges of their specific role. Also, part of the strategy includes meeting with employees to agree upon metrics in the performance planning stage, creating an action plan, and following up with evaluations and ratings to determine to what degree the learning experience was successful.

In short, Discover uses the various stages of the performance management process to ensure that employee development is a focus that matches the mission of providing a workplace that supports high performance.

Step 3: Executing performance

After the review cycle begins, the employee strives to produce the results and display the behaviors agreed upon earlier as well as to work on developmental needs.

TIP

The employee has primary responsibility and ownership of this process. Employee participation doesn't begin at the performance execution stage, however. Employees need to have active input in the development of job descriptions and the creation of the rating form.

At the performance execution stage, make sure the following success factors are present:

>> **Commitment to goal achievement.** The employee must be committed to the goals that were set. One way to enhance commitment is to allow the employee to be an active participant in the process of setting the goals.

>> **Check-ins and performance touchpoints.** The employee has performance *touchpoints* with many people inside and outside of the organization on an ongoing basis. So he should not wait until the review cycle is over to solicit performance feedback in the form of check-ins. Also, the employee should not wait until a serious problem develops to ask for coaching. The employee needs to take a proactive role in soliciting performance feedback and coaching from her supervisor. Supervisors and others with whom the employee has performance touchpoints (for example, team members) can provide performance feedback but are generally busy with multiple obligations.

TIP

The burden is on the employee to communicate openly and regularly via ongoing check-ins with her performance touchpoints.

>> **Collecting and sharing performance data.** The employee should provide the supervisor with regular updates on progress toward goal achievement, in terms of both behaviors and results.

>> **Preparing for performance reviews.** The employee should not wait until the end of the review cycle approaches to prepare for the review. On the contrary, the employee should engage in an ongoing and realistic self-appraisal, so immediate corrective action can be taken, if necessary. The usefulness of the self-appraisal process can be enhanced by gathering informal performance information from peers and customers (both internal and external).

Although the employee has primary responsibilities for performance execution, the supervisor also needs to do her share of the work. Supervisors have primary responsibility over the following success factors:

- >> **Observation and documentation;** Supervisors observe and document performance on an ongoing basis. It is important to keep track of examples of both good and poor performance.

- >> **Updates;** As the organization's goals change, update and revise initial accountabilities and objectives (in the case of results) and competencies (in the case of behaviors).

- >> **Feedback;** Supervisors provide feedback on progression toward goals and coaching to improve performance on a regular basis, and certainly before the review cycle is over.

- >> **Resources;** Supervisors provide employees with resources and opportunities to participate in development activities. Thus, they should encourage and sponsor participation in training, classes, and special assignments.

  Supervisors have a responsibility to ensure that the employee has the necessary technology and other resources to perform the job properly.

- >> **Reinforcement;** Supervisors must let employees know that their outstanding performance is noticed by reinforcing effective behaviors and progress toward goals. Also, supervisors should provide feedback regarding negative performance and how to remedy the observed problem. Observation and communication are not sufficient. Performance problems must be diagnosed early, and appropriate steps must be taken as soon as the problem is discovered.

The employee has primary responsibility, but both the employee and the manager are jointly involved in performance execution.

Step 4: Assessing performance

In the assessment phase, both the employee and the manager are responsible for evaluating the extent to which the desired behaviors have been displayed, and whether the desired results have been achieved. Employee involvement in the process increases employee ownership and commitment to the system. Also, it provides important information to be discussed during the performance review.

Although many sources can be used to collect performance information such as supervisors and other team members, in most cases the direct supervisor provides the information. This also includes an evaluation of the extent to which the goals stated in the development plan have been achieved.

PERFORMANCE EXECUTION AT IBM

As an example of how performance execution involves both employees and supervisors, take the case of IBM. IBM recently transitioned from the previous once-a-year "stack ranking" review that compared employees to a more frequent and personalized review focusing on the employee's own goals.

Before deciding on a new performance management system, IBM's HR department asked for employees' inputs through its internal social media site. Employees reported they wanted more frequent feedback and the ability to change their goals as the year progressed. IBM recognized that the fast-paced business environment meant that new things come along, leading to employees experimenting and iterating. This meant that employees are often not working on what they originally proposed at the beginning of the year.

Then a new system was designed that allows employees to set annual goals and short-term milestones. Based on continuous feedback from managers, employees are able to update their goals and milestones throughout the year.

By allowing employees to change and develop their own goals throughout the year, IBM can now avoid irrelevant year-end discussions, and have richer dialogue through frequent check-ins with employees.

REMEMBER

It is important that both the employee and the manager take ownership of the assessment process. The employee evaluates his own performance, and so does the manager. The fact that both parties are involved in the assessment provides good information to be used in the review phase. When both the employee and the supervisor are active participants in the evaluation process, there is a greater likelihood that the information will be used productively in the future.

The inclusion of self-ratings helps emphasize possible discrepancies between self-views and the views that important others (such as supervisors, other team members, customers) have of what employees are doing, how they are doing it, and what results they are producing. It is the discrepancy between these views that is most likely to trigger development efforts, particularly when feedback from the supervisor and others is more negative than are employee self-evaluations.

TIP

Including self-appraisals is also beneficial regarding important additional factors. Self-appraisals can reduce an employee's defensiveness during an appraisal meeting and increase the employee's satisfaction with the performance management system, as well as enhance perceptions of accuracy and fairness, and therefore, acceptance of the system.

PERFORMANCE ASSESSMENT AT GOOGLE

Google is consistently ranked at the top of *Fortune's* 100 best companies to work for. Google uses a 360-degree review process, conducted semiannually. Managers take two things into account when evaluating employees: results (what the employee accomplished) and behaviors (how the employee attained these results). The self-assessment, peer reviews, and manager reviews are based on a five-point scale from 1 = needs improvement to 5 = superb and use the following six key performance indicators:

- Googleyness: Adherence to Google values

- Problem solving: Analytical skills applied to work

- Execution: Delivering great work with great autonomy

- Thought leadership: How much an employee is seen as a reference for a specific area of expertise

- Leadership: Displaying leadership skills such as being proactive and taking the lead on projects

- Presence: The ability to make yourself known in a large organization.

To reduce bias, managers meet and review all employees' ratings together.

In short, Google utilizes its performance assessment process to provide a clear link between each individual and team activity and the strategic objectives of the organization.

Step 5: Reviewing performance

The performance review stage involves the formal meeting between the employee and the manager to review their assessments. This meeting is usually called the *performance review* or *appraisal meeting.*

REMEMBER

Although good performance management systems include ongoing check-ins, the formal appraisal meeting is important because it provides a formal setting in which the employee receives feedback on his performance.

In spite of its importance in performance management, the appraisal meeting is often regarded as the Achilles' heel of the entire process. This is because many managers are uncomfortable providing performance feedback, particularly when performance is deficient. This high level of discomfort, which often translates into anxiety and trying to avoid the appraisal interview, can be mitigated through training those responsible for providing feedback.

Providing effective feedback is extremely important because it leads not only to performance improvement, but also to employee satisfaction with the system. For example, a study published in *Journal of Applied Social Psychology* involving more than 200 teachers in Malaysia, including individuals with distinct Chinese, Malay, and Indian cultural backgrounds, found that when they received effective feedback, they reported greater satisfaction with the performance management system even when they received low performance ratings.

REMEMBER

People are apprehensive about both receiving and giving performance information, and this apprehension reinforces the importance of a formal performance review as part of any performance management system.

In most cases, the appraisal meeting is regarded as a review of the past, that is, what was done (results) and how it was done (behaviors). For example, a survey published in the journal *Employee Relations* including more than 150 organizations in Scotland showed that performance management systems in more than 80 percent of organizations emphasize the past.

The appraisal meeting should also include a discussion of the employee's developmental progress as well as plans for the future. The conversation should include a discussion of goals and development plans that the employee will be expected to achieve over the period before the next formal review session. In addition, a good appraisal meeting includes information on what new compensation and rewards, if any, the employee could receive as a result of her performance.

The appraisal discussion focuses on the past (what has been done and how), the present (what compensation is received or denied as a result), and the future (goals to be attained before the upcoming review session).

As I mention earlier, the discussion about past performance can be challenging, particularly when performance levels have not reached acceptable levels.

The example below includes a script to help you visualize what the first few seconds of an effective appraisal meeting is like.

Script for Effective Performance Review Meeting

Good afternoon, Lucy, please have a seat. As you know, we take performance very seriously and we scheduled our meeting today to talk about the work you have done over the past year. Because we believe in the importance of talking about performance issues, I blocked an hour of my time during which I won't take any phone calls and I also won't be texting or emailing with anyone. I want to be able to focus 100% on our conversation because talking about performance will be helpful to both of us.

There should be no surprises, given that we have been communicating about your performance on an ongoing basis. You have also received feedback not only from me, but also from your peers.

Let's go through this process step by step. First, I would like you to tell me about your own views about your performance during the past year. Specifically, please share with me what are the things you believe you did particularly well and areas in which you think you may have been able to do better. As a second step, I will tell you about the performance evaluation I prepared. As a third step, we will talk about the issues on which you and I agree. As a fourth step, we can talk about issues for which we may have different perspectives. I will explain the reasoning behind my views and I want to hear the reasoning behind yours. In terms of my evaluation of your work, I want to first make sure we agree on what are the specific goals and objectives of your job. Then we will talk about the results you achieved this year and the section on the evaluation form about job skills and competencies. After we talk about that, I will tell you what my overall rating is and why I believe this is an appropriate score.

Ok, let's go ahead and start.

Try to implement the following six recommendations for conducting productive performance reviews:

>> Identify what the employee has done well and poorly by citing specific positive and negative behaviors.

>> Solicit feedback from your employee about these behaviors. Listen for reactions and explanations.

>> Discuss the implications of changing, or not changing, the behaviors. Positive feedback is best, but an employee must be made aware of what will happen if any poor performance continues.

>> Explain to the employee how skills used in past achievements can help him overcome any current performance problems.

>> Agree on an action plan. Encourage the employee to invest in improving his performance by asking questions such as "What ideas do you have for _____ ?" and "What suggestions do you have for _____ ?"

>> Set up a meeting to follow up and agree on the behaviors, actions, and attitudes to be evaluated.

REMEMBER

The performance management process includes a cycle, which starts with establishing prerequisites and ends with conducting the formal performance review. But, the cycle is not over after the formal review. In fact, the process starts all over again.

TIP

Because markets change, customers' preferences and needs change, and products change, there is a need to monitor the prerequisites continuously so that performance planning, and all the subsequent stages, are consistent with the organization's strategic objectives. In the end, one of the main goals of any performance management system is to promote the achievement of organization-wide goals. Obviously, if managers and employees are not aware of what these strategic goals are, it is unlikely that the performance management system will be instrumental in helping accomplish strategic business objectives.

Chapter **2**

Making the Case for Performance Management

6 2 percent of HR executives from Fortune 500 companies say that their per-formance management system serves mostly two purposes: salary decisions and learning about employees' weaknesses and strengths. But performance management can do more, a lot more, for you and your business. It can help you ensure all employees are pulling in the same direction, that rewards and other decisions are fair, it can help you implement organizational changes, and much more. This is especially true if you deploy a state-of-the-science system and everyone in the organization gets something out of it.

In this chapter, you will learn how to use performance management for many useful purposes and discover how to create an excellent system that benefits all members of your organization.

Using Performance Management to Achieve Multiple Purposes

So performance management is mostly used for salary administration, performance feedback, and for learning about employee strengths and weaknesses. Overall, performance management can serve the following six purposes: strategic, administrative, informational, developmental, organizational maintenance, and documentation.

Strategic objectives

Performance management systems help top management achieve strategic business objectives. Performance management links the goals of individuals with the goals of their teams, which in turn are connected with the goals of the entire organization. And even if an individual isn't able to reach his or her goals, the fact that performance management formally and explicitly links them to the team and the organization's goals is very useful in communicating what are the most crucial business strategic initiatives.

Administrative objectives

Performance management is also useful for providing useful information used in making administrative decisions about employees. For example, these include decisions include salary adjustments, promotions, employee retention or termination, recognition of top individual performance, identification of high-potential employees, identification of poor performers, layoffs, and merit increases.

EXAMPLE

The government in Turkey mandates performance management systems in all public organizations in that country. The reason? They serve an important administrative purpose because they aim at preventing favoritism, corruption, and bribery, and send a clear message that administrative decisions should be impartial and based on merit.

Informational objectives

Performance management systems serve an important informational purpose because they are a means to communicate. First, they inform employees about how they are doing and provide them with information on specific areas that need improvement. Second, related to the strategic purpose, they provide information regarding expectations of peers, supervisors, customers, and the organization, and what aspects of work are most important.

Developmental objectives

Overall, performance management helps employees develop and grow because it improves communication, clarifies roles and expectations in terms of career paths, and includes useful feedback.

First, performance management systems serve as an important communication device. One, they inform employees about how they are doing and provide them with information on specific areas that need improvement. Two, related to the strategic purpose, they provide information regarding expectations of peers, supervisors, customers, and the organization, and what aspects of work are most important.

A second aspect of the developmental purpose is that employees receive information about themselves that can help them individualize their career paths. For example, by learning about their strengths, they are better able to chart a more successful path for their future. Thus, the developmental purpose refers to both short-term and long-term aspects of development.

Third, as I mention earlier, feedback is an important component of a well-implemented performance management system. But for feedback to be useful, it needs to be used in a developmental manner. So managers should use feedback to coach employees and improve performance on an ongoing basis. This feedback allows for the identification of strengths and weaknesses as well as the causes for performance deficiencies.

TIP

Feedback is useful only if employees are willing to receive it and the organization takes concrete steps to remedy any deficiencies. You should try to create a "feedback culture" that reflects support for feedback, including feedback that is non-threatening and is focused on behaviors and coaching.

Organizational maintenance objectives

Another purpose of performance management systems is to provide information to be used for several organizational maintenance purposes. First, consider *workforce planning*, which is a set of systems that allows organizations to anticipate and respond to needs emerging within and outside the organization, to determine priorities, and to allocate human resources where they can do the most good.

An important component of any workforce planning effort is the *talent inventory*, which is information on current resources (such as skills, abilities, promotional potential, and assignment histories of current employees). Buying talent is extremely expensive, and top performers know their worth in the market and their value through social media and career sites. In the case of executives, the stock market is a good metric. For example, when Kasper Rosted left his position of CEO at packaged-goods company Henkel to become CEO of Adidas, Adidas gained $1 billion in market cap due to an increase in the share price. Performance management systems are the primary means through which accurate talent inventories can be assembled. Also, these are critical in terms of keeping track of high-potential employees.

Other organizational maintenance purposes served by performance management systems include assessing future training needs, evaluating performance achievements at the organizational level, and evaluating the effectiveness of HR initiatives. For example, accurate data on employee performance can be used to evaluate whether employees perform at higher levels after participating in a training program. This type of evaluation cannot be conducted effectively in the absence of a good performance management system.

USING PERFORMANCE MANAGEMENT TO ACHIEVE MULTIPLE PURPOSES AT SELCO CREDIT UNION

Several companies implement performance management systems that allow them to accomplish the multiple objectives described in this chapter. For an example of one such company, consider the case of SELCO Credit Union in Eugene, Oregon, a not-for-profit consumer cooperative that was established in 1936. SELCO offers many of the same services offered by other banks, including personal checking and savings accounts, loans, and credit cards. Being members of the credit union, however, allows individual members a say in how the credit union is run, something a traditional bank doesn't permit.

Recently, SELCO scrapped an old performance appraisal system and replaced it with a new multipurpose and more effective performance management system. First, the timing of the new system is now aligned with the business cycle, instead of the employee's date of hire, to ensure that business needs are aligned with individual goals. This alignment serves both strategic and informational purposes. Second, managers are given a pool of money that they can work with to award bonuses and raises as needed, which is more effective than the complex set of matrices that had been in place to calculate bonuses. This improved the way in which the system is used for allocating rewards, and therefore, serves an administrative purpose. Third, managers are required to sit down and have regular conversations with their employees about their performance and make note of any problems that arise. This gives the employees a clear sense of areas in which they need improvement and also provides documentation if disciplinary action is needed. This component serves both informational and documentation purposes. Finally, the time that was previously spent filling out complicated matrices and forms is now spent talking with the employees about how they can improve their performance, allowing for progress on an ongoing basis. This serves a developmental purpose.

Documentation objectives

Finally, performance management systems allow you to collect useful information that can be used for several necessary — and sometimes, legally mandated — documentation purposes. Performance management systems allow for the documentation of important administrative decisions, such as terminations and promotions. This information can be especially useful in the case of litigation.

ACTIVE LEARNING

Now think about the performance management system implemented in your organization. Table 2-1 summarizes each of the purposes served by a performance management system. Which of these purposes are being served by the system in your firm? Which are not? What are some of the barriers that prevent achieving some of the six purposes and what can be done about it?

TABLE 2-1 **The Purposes of a Performance Management System**

Purpose	Achieved in your organization?	If not, why not? What can be done about it?
Strategic: To help top management achieve strategic business objectives		
Administrative: To produce valid and useful information for making administrative decisions about employees		
Informational: To inform employees about how they are doing and about the organization's, customers', and supervisors' expectations		
Developmental: To allow managers and peers to provide coaching to their employees		
Organizational maintenance: To create a talent inventory and provide information to be used in workplace planning and allocation of human resources		
Documentation: To collect useful information that can be used for various purposes (e.g., terminations)		

Answering the "What's in It for Me" Question

Slack resources are a luxury few organizations have. So, given the many competing projects implemented at any given time, some organizations are reluctant to implement a performance management system. So, the question is: What is the value added of performance management? And what's in it for me if I put the time and effort necessary? What will be the payoffs?

Convincing top management of performance management's value

The need to align organization and unit priorities with the performance management system is one of the key factors contributing to obtaining the much-needed top management support for the system. A good question that top management is likely to, and frankly, should ask is: "Why is performance management important and even necessary?"

One answer to this question is that performance management is the primary tool that will allow top management to carry out their vision. The performance management system, when aligned with organization and unit priorities, is a critical tool to

>> Allow all employees to understand where the organization stands and where it wants to go

>> Provide tools to employees (for example, motivation and developmental resources) so that their behaviors and results will help the organization achieve its targets

REMEMBER

Fundamentally, the implementation of any performance management system requires that the "What's in it for me?" question be answered convincingly. In the case of top management, the answer to the "What's in it for me?" question is that performance management can serve as a primary tool to realize their vision and achieve strategic objectives.

Building support in the entire organization

Building support for the system doesn't stop with top management, however. All participants in the system need to understand the role they play and also receive a clear answer to the "What's in it for me?" question. Accordingly, communication about the system is key. This includes a clear description of the system's mechanics (for example, how the performance will be defined and measured, when the performance review meetings will take place, and how to handle disagreements between supervisor and employees) and the system's consequences (such as the relationship between performance evaluation and compensation).

WARNING

Not involving people in the process of system design and implementation can create resistance, and the performance management system will end up causing more harm than good.

BUILDING SUPPORT FOR PERFORMANCE MANAGEMENT AT BANKERS LIFE AND CASUALTY

Bankers Life and Casualty, headquartered in Chicago, is an insurance company specializing in insurance for seniors. This is how they built support for their performance management system. When Edward M. Berube was appointed as its president and CEO, he understood that Bankers Life and Casualty was facing important challenges, including new customer demands, the impact of the Internet, outsourcing, and increased competition. So Bankers Life and Casualty engaged in a very aggressive marketing campaign, which included retaining actor Dick Van Dyke as the company spokesperson. In spite of these efforts, however, internal focus groups revealed that employees did not have a clear understanding of how each person could help achieve the organization's strategic objectives, including focusing on the following three key areas: distribution scope, scale, and productivity; home office productivity and unit costs; and product revenue and profitability.

Bankers Life and Casualty realized that it could establish a better link between strategic business objectives and what employees do on a daily basis by improving its performance management system. First, the HR and communications teams spoke candidly with the CEO about his expectations. The CEO responded with overwhelming support, stating that the performance management system would be implemented for every employee on preestablished dates, and that he would hold his team accountable for making this happen. Then, to implement the performance management system, each unit met with its VP. During these meetings, each VP discussed how his or her unit's objectives were linked to the corporate objectives. Next, HR and Communications led discussions surrounding objective setting, giving feedback, and writing development plans. Managers were then given the opportunity to share any feedback, concerns, or questions that they had about the program. During this forum, managers exchanged success stories and offered advice to one another. These success stories were then shared with the CEO. The CEO then shared these stories with those who reported directly to him to strengthen the visibility of his support for the program.

In short, the performance management system at Bankers Life and Casualty helped all employees understand their contributions to the organization's strategic plan. This was a key issue that motivated the CEO to lend unqualified support to the system. This support gave a clear message to the rest of the organization that the performance management system was an important initiative that added value to the entire organization. The support of the CEO and other top executives, combined with a high degree of participation from all employees and their ability to voice concerns and provide feedback regarding the system, was a critical factor in the success of the performance management system at Bankers Life and Casualty.

Realizing the awesome benefits of performance management

President Kennedy famously said, "Ask not what your country can do for you; ask what you can do for your country." Well, in the case of performance management, I will tell you not what you can do for performance management, but what performance management can do for you.

There are many things performance management can do for managers and their direct reports, and the organization. First, this is what performance management can do for employees:

>> **Improved self-insights and development:** Employees develop a better understanding of themselves and of the kind of development activities that are of value to them as they progress through the organization. Participants in the system also gain a better understanding of their particular strengths and weaknesses, which can help them better define future career paths.

>> **Improved self-esteem:** Receiving feedback about one's performance fulfills a basic human need to be recognized and valued at work. This, in turn, increases employees' self-esteem.

>> **Improved motivation:** Receiving feedback about one's performance increases the motivation for future performance. Knowledge about how one is doing and recognition about one's past successes provide the fuel for future accomplishments.

>> **Improved understanding of job requirements:** The job of the person being evaluated is clarified and defined more clearly. In other words, employees gain a better understanding of the behaviors and results required of their specific position. Employees also gain a better understanding of what it takes to be a successful performer.

And this is what performance management can do for managers and your organization:

>> **Improved employee engagement:** Employees who are engaged feel involved, committed, passionate, and empowered. Also, these attitudes and feelings result in behaviors that are innovative, and overall, demonstrate good organizational citizenship and active participation in support of the organization. Employee engagement is an important predictor of organizational performance and success, and consequently, engagement is an important contribution of good performance management systems.

>> **Improved voice behavior:** Voice behavior involves making suggestions for changes and improvements that are innovative, challenge the status quo, are intended to be constructive, and are offered even when others disagree. For example, the performance review meeting can lead to a conversation during which the employee provides suggestions on how to reduce cost or speed up a specific process.

>> **Decreased employee misconduct:** Employee misconduct is an increasingly pervasive phenomenon that has received widespread media coverage. Such misconduct includes accounting irregularities, churning customer accounts, abusing overtime policies, giving inappropriate gifts to clients and potential clients hoping to secure their business, and using company resources for personal purposes. Although some people engage in misconduct compared to others due to individual differences in personality and other attributes, having a good performance management in place provides the appropriate context so that misconduct is clearly defined and labeled as such. Also, performance management can be a detection tool for misconduct before it leads to irreversible negative consequences.

>> **Declines in performance are addressed early on:** Because good performance management systems include ongoing performance measurement, declines in performance can be noticed. This allows for immediate feedback and continuous coaching. When such declines are observed, remedial action can be taken immediately and before the problem becomes so entrenched that it cannot be easily remedied.

>> **Improved employee motivation, commitment, and intentions to stay in the organization:** When employees are satisfied with their organization's performance management system, they are more motivated to perform well, be committed to their organization, and not try to leave the organization. For example, satisfaction with the performance management system makes employees feel that the organization has a great deal of personal meaning for them. In terms of turnover intentions, satisfaction with the performance management system leads employees to report that they will probably not look for a new job in the next year and that they don't often think about quitting their present job.

>> **Improved insights about direct reports:** Direct supervisors and other managers in charge of the appraisal gain new insights into the person being appraised. Gaining new insights into a person's performance helps the manager build a better relationship with that person. Also, supervisors gain a better understanding of each individual's contribution to the organization. This can be useful for direct supervisors, as well as for supervisors once removed.

- » **Improved and more timely differentiation between good and poor performers:** Performance management systems allow for a quicker identification of good and poor performers. This includes identifying star performers — those who produce at levels much higher than the rest. For example, without a good performance management system, it isn't easy to know who are the particular programmers who are producing more and better code.

TIP

Performance management systems help you discover high-potential employees who can be identified as future leaders — also called "HiPos." For example, PepsiCo's performance management system includes what it calls Leadership Assessment and Development (LeAD). A unique aspect of this system is the emphasis on identifying HiPos by measuring specific job and leadership requirement in the future.

- » **Improved understanding of the meaning of performance:** Performance management systems allow managers to communicate to their direct reports their assessments regarding performance. Thus, there is greater accountability in how managers discuss performance expectations and provide feedback. When managers possess these competencies, direct reports receive useful information about how their performance is seen by their supervisor.

- » **More fair and more appropriate administrative actions:** Performance management systems provide valid information about performance that can be used for administrative actions, such as merit increases, promotions, and transfers, as well as terminations. In general, a performance management system helps ensure that rewards are distributed on a fair and credible basis. In turn, such decisions based on a sound performance management system lead to improved interpersonal relationships and enhanced supervisor–direct report trust.

TIP

A good performance management system can help mitigate explicit or implicit emphasis on age as a basis for decisions. This is particularly important given the aging working population in the United States, Europe, and many other countries around the world.

- » **Better protection from lawsuits:** Data collected through performance management systems can help document compliance with regulations (for example, equal treatment of all employees, regardless of sex or ethnic background). When performance management systems are not in place, arbitrary performance evaluations are more likely, resulting in an increased exposure to litigation for the organization.

- » **Organizational change is facilitated:** Performance management systems can be a useful tool to drive organizational change. For example, assume an organization decides to change its culture to give top priority to product quality and customer service. Once this new organizational direction is established, performance management is used to align goals and objectives of the organization with those of individuals to make change possible. Employees are provided training in the necessary skills and are also rewarded for improved performance so that they have both the knowledge and motivation to improve product quality and customer service.

EXAMPLE

IBM used performance management as a tool for organizational change in the 1980s when it wanted to switch focus to customer satisfaction: The performance evaluation of every member in the organization was based, to some extent, on customer satisfaction ratings, regardless of function (i.e., accounting, programming, manufacturing, etc.). For IBM, as well as many other organizations, performance management provides tools and motivation for individuals to change, which, in turn, helps drive organizational change.

What an Ideal Performance Management System Looks Like

All organizations face practical and resource constraints. So the harsh reality is that performance management systems are seldom implemented in an ideal way. For example, there may not be sufficient funds to deliver training to all people involved, supervisors may have biases in how they provide performance ratings, or people may be just too busy to pay attention to a performance management system that seems to require too much time and attention. However, regardless of practical constraints, you should strive to place a check mark next to each of the following characteristics: the more features that are checked, the more likely it will be that the system will live up to its promise and deliver the benefits for employees, managers, and organizations I described in the previous section.

Contextual issues: Making everything fit

The first things you need to think about are the following contextual issues:

>> **Strategic congruence:** The system should be congruent with the unit and organization's strategy. In other words, individual goals must be aligned with unit and organizational goals.

>> **Context congruence:** The system should be congruent with the organization's culture as well as the broader cultural context of the region or country. Consider the example of an organization that has a culture in which communication isn't fluid and hierarchies are rigid. In such organizations, an upward feedback system, in which individuals receive comments on their performance from their direct reports, would be resisted and not very effective.

Regarding broader cultural issues, in countries such as Japan, there is an emphasis on the measurement of both behaviors (how people do the work) and results (the results of people's work), whereas in the United States, results are typically preferred over behaviors. Thus, implementing a results-only system in Japan won't be effective. Specifically, although performance is measured similarly around the world, the interpersonal aspects of the system are adapted and customized to the local culture. For example, performance management systems in the subsidiaries are more likely to differ from those in the headquarters as power distance differences (that is, the degree to which a society accepts hierarchical differences) increase between countries.

>> **Meaningfulness:** The system must be meaningful in several ways:

- The evaluations conducted for each job function must be considered important and relevant.

- Performance assessment must emphasize only those functions that are under the control of the employee. For example, there is no point in letting an employee know she needs to increase the speed of service delivery when the supplier doesn't get the product to her on time.

- Evaluations must take place at regular intervals and at appropriate moments. Because one formal evaluation per year is usually not sufficient, my recommendation is frequent informal reviews.

- The system should provide for the continuing skill development of evaluators.

- The results should be used for important administrative decisions. People will not pay attention to a performance system that has no consequences in terms of outcomes that they value.

EXAMPLE

Consider a comparison of performance management systems in the former East versus former West Germany. In former West German companies, there is a stronger link between the performance management system and administrative decisions such as promotions. This relationship was weaker in former East German companies, and this difference is probably due to the socialist political system in the former German Democratic Republic, which has had a long-lasting effect.

>> **Inclusiveness:** Good systems include input from multiple sources on an ongoing basis. First, the evaluation process must represent the concerns of all the people who will be affected by the outcome. Consequently, employees must participate in the process of creating the system by providing input regarding what behaviors or results will be measured and how. This is particularly important in today's diverse and global organizations, which include individuals from different cultural backgrounds, and this leads to

different views regarding what is performance and how it should be measured. Second, input about employee performance should be gathered from the employees themselves before the performance review meeting.

All participants must be given a voice in the process of designing and implementing the system. Such inclusive systems lead to more successful systems, including less employee resistance, improved performance, and fewer legal challenges.

Practical issues: Striving for effectiveness and fairness

Of course, a system that is not practical, it won't be implemented. So, you need to make sure your system meets the following criteria:

>> **Practicality:** Systems that are too expensive, time-consuming, and convoluted will obviously not be effective. Good, easy-to-use systems (for example, performance data are entered via user-friendly web and mobile apps) are available for managers to help them make decisions. Also, the benefits of using the system (like increased performance and job satisfaction) must be seen as outweighing the costs (such as time, effort, and expense).

>> **Identification of effective and ineffective performance:** The performance management system should provide information that allows for the identification of effective and ineffective performance. That is, the system should allow for distinguishing between effective and ineffective behaviors and results, thereby also allowing for the identification of employees displaying various levels of performance effectiveness.

In terms of making administrative decisions, a system that ranks all levels of performance and all employees similarly is useless.

>> **Acceptability and fairness:** A good system is acceptable and is perceived as fair by all participants.

Perceptions of fairness are subjective and the only way to know if a system is seen as fair is to ask the participants about the system. Perceptions of fairness include four distinct components:

>> You can ask about *distributive justice,* which includes perceptions of the performance evaluation received relative to the work performed, and perceptions of the rewards received relative to the evaluation received, particularly when the system is implemented across countries. For example, differences in perceptions exist in comparing employees from more

individualistic (like the United States) to more collectivistic (like Korea) cultures. If a discrepancy is perceived between work and evaluation or between evaluation and rewards, then the system is seen as unfair.

» You can ask about *procedural justice,* which includes perceptions of the procedures used to determine the ratings as well as the procedures used to link ratings with rewards.

» You can ask about perceptions of *interpersonal justice*, which refers to the quality of the design and implementation of the performance management system. For example, what are employees' perceptions regarding how they are treated by their supervisors during the performance review meeting? Do they feel that supervisors are empathic and helpful?

» You can ask about *informational justice,* which refers to fairness perceptions about performance expectations and goals, feedback received, and the information given to justify administrative decisions. For example, are explanations perceived to be honest, sincere, and logical?

Because a good system is inherently discriminatory, some employees will receive ratings that are lower than those received by other employees. However, you should strive to develop systems that are regarded as fair from the distributive, procedural, interpersonal, and informational perspectives because each type of justice perception leads to different outcomes. For example, a perception that the system isn't fair from a distributive point of view will lead to a poor relationship between employee and supervisor and lowered satisfaction of the employee with the supervisor. On the contrary, a perception that the system is unfair from a procedural point of view leads to decreased employee commitment toward the organization and increased intentions to leave.

TIP

One way to improve all four justice dimensions is to set clear rules that are applied consistently by all supervisors.

Technical issues: Sweating the details

In the end, the system must also meet technical standards to work, including the following:

» **Thoroughness:** The system should be thorough regarding four things:

• All employees should be evaluated (including managers).

• All major job responsibilities should be evaluated (including behaviors and results).

- The evaluation should include performance spanning the entire review period, not just the few weeks or months before the formal review meeting.
- Feedback should be given on positive performance aspects as well as those that are in need of improvement.

» **Specificity:** A good system should be specific: It should provide detailed and concrete guidance to employees about what is expected of them and how they can meet these expectations.

» **Reliability:** A good system should include measures of performance that are consistent and free of error. For example, if two supervisors provided ratings of the same employee and performance dimensions, ratings should be similar.

» **Validity:** The measures of performance should also be valid. Validity refers to the fact that the measures include all relevant performance facets and don't include irrelevant information. In other words, measures are relevant (include all critical performance facets), not deficient (don't leave any important aspects out), and are not contaminated (don't include factors outside of the control of the employee or factors unrelated to performance). In short, measures include what is important and don't assess what isn't important and outside of the control of the employee.

» **Openness:** Good systems have no secrets. First, performance is evaluated frequently and performance feedback is provided on an ongoing basis. Therefore, employees are continually informed of the quality of their performance. Second, the review meeting consists of a two-way communication process during which information is exchanged, not delivered from the supervisor to the employee without his or her input. Third, communications are factual, open, and honest.

» **Correctability:** The process of assigning ratings should minimize subjective aspects; however, it is virtually impossible to create a system that is completely objective because human judgment is an important component of the evaluation process. When employees perceive an error has been made, there should be a mechanism through which this error can be corrected. Establishing an appeals process, through which employees can challenge what may be unjust decisions, is an important aspect of a good performance management system.

» **Standardization:** Good systems are standardized. This means that performance is evaluated consistently across people and time. To achieve this goal, the ongoing training of the individuals in charge of appraisals, usually managers, is a must.

» **Ethicality:** Good systems comply with ethical standards. This means that the supervisor suppresses his or her personal self-interest in providing evaluations. In addition, the supervisor evaluates only performance dimensions for which she has sufficient information, and the privacy of the employee is respected.

ACTIVE LEARNING

A study conducted for Mercer, a global diversified consulting company, showed that the 1,200 workers surveyed stated that they could improve their productivity by an average of 26 percent if they were not held back by a lack of "direction, support, training, and equipment." So implementing a performance management system that includes the characteristics just described will pay off. Successfully implementing a performance management system can give workers the direction and support that they need to improve their productivity.

Table 2-2 lists the characteristics of an ideal performance management system. Think about the performance management system implemented in your organization. Which of the features listed in the table below are included in the system you are considering? How far is your system from the ideal?

TABLE 2-2 **An Ideal Performance Management System**

Ideal Performance Management System Characteristic	Present in Your Organization?	If not, why not? What can be done about it?
Contextual Issues		
Strategic congruence		
Context congruence		
Meaningfulness		
Inclusiveness		
Practical Issues		
Practicality		
Identification of effective and ineffective performance		
Technical Issues		
Thoroughness		
Specificity		
Reliability		
Validity		
Openness		
Correctability		
Standardization		
Ethicality		

Taking Care of Talent Management Functions

Performance management systems serve as important feeders to other human resources and development activities. Performance management is a key component of talent management in organizations. It allows for assessing the current talent and making predictions about future needs both at the individual and organizational levels. Implementing a successful performance management system is a requirement for the successful implementation of many other HR functions, including training and development, workforce planning, and compensation.

Training and development

Consider the relationship between performance management and training and development. Performance management provides information on developmental needs for employees. In the absence of a good performance management system, it isn't clear that organizations will use their training resources in the most efficient way (that is, to train those who most need it in the most critical areas).

EXAMPLE

One organization that is able to link its performance management system to training initiatives is General Electric (GE). GE's performance management system includes over 180,000 salaried employees spread across almost 180 countries. Recently, GE updated its performance management practices, moving from a formal once-a-year performance review to an app-based system that allows managers to provide more immediate feedback and coaching to their employees. The app accepts voice and text inputs, attached documents, and even handwritten notes. Managers can use the app's categories such as "priorities," "touch points," "summary," and "insights," to send short messages (up to 500 characters) to individual team members or groups. For example, a manager can use the app to provide suggestions to employees on areas of developmental needs and where employees may benefit from additional training. Based on these data, the manager, employee, and the HR department can work together to schedule training classes and off-site training opportunities. GE is already seeing the benefits of this direct connection between performance management and training, with some divisions reporting a fivefold increase in employee productivity.

WARNING

Most organizations don't use performance management systems to determine training content and waste an opportunity to use the performance management system as the needs assessment phase of their training efforts. A survey including 218 HR leaders at companies with at least 2,500 employees revealed that there is tight integration between performance management and learning/development activities in only 15.3 percent of the organizations surveyed.

Workforce planning

Performance management also provides key information for workforce planning.

An organization's talent inventory is based on information collected through the performance management system. Development plans provide information on what skills will be acquired in the near future. This information is also used in making recruitment and hiring decisions. Knowledge of an organization's current and future talent is important when deciding what types of skills need to be acquired externally and what types of skills can be found within the organization.

Compensation

There is an obvious relationship between performance management and compensation systems. Compensation and reward decisions are arbitrary in the absence of a good performance management system.

» Becoming a performance
  management leader

» Defining and measuring performance
  and developing employee
  performance

» Assessing performance management
  effectiveness

Chapter **3**

Designing and Implementing Effective Performance Management

One of the very useful purposes of performance management is to connect employee behaviors and results with the organization's strategic goals. If this link is not there, the performance management system becomes a bureaucratic burden and a waste of time rather than something that adds value to the organization.

So it is important that priorities and goals at the organizational level cascade down to the units and eventually all the way down to each individual employee — and for performance management to play an important role in making these connections happen.

For this cascading to take place, you as a manager need to become a performance management leader, which means you need to be an effective coach, make sure performance is defined and measured clearly, and know whether the performance management system is working — and apply fixes where needed. All these tasks are covered in this chapter.

Ensuring Performance Management Delivers Strategic Value

A strategic plan describes what the organization does, its destination, and possible barriers that stand in the way of that destination. It also includes approaches for moving forward.

Key ingredients of a strategic recipe

A strategic plan needs to have the following components:

>> **Mission statement:** the organization's most important reason for its existence. A mission statement gives information on the purpose of the organization and its scope.

>> **Vision statement:** a statement of future aspirations. In other words, the vision statement includes a description of what the organization would like to become in the future — about 5–10 years out.

>> **Objectives:** specific information about how the mission will be implemented. Objectives also provide a good basis for making decisions by keeping the goals in mind.

>> **Strategies:** game plans or how-to procedures to reach the stated objectives. The strategies address issues of growth, survival, turnaround, stability, innovation, talent acquisition, and leadership.

After the organization's mission, vision, objectives, and strategies have been defined, senior management proceeds to meet with department or unit managers, who solicit input from all people within their units to create unit-level mission and vision statements, objectives, and strategies.

REMEMBER

Strategic planning is a tool useful for allocating resources in a way that provides organizations with a competitive advantage because resources are assigned in a more effective and more targeted manner. A strategic plan serves as a blueprint that defines how the organization will allocate its resources in pursuit of its most critical and important objectives.

Making performance management strategic

A critical issue for strategic planning success is to ensure that each unit or department's mission and vision statements, objectives, and strategies are consistent with those at the organizational level.

Then job descriptions, which include information on tasks performed and knowledge, skills, and abilities needed for each position and each employee in the organization, are revised and updated to make sure they are consistent with unit and organizational priorities.

The performance management system defines performance for each individual, and the source of this information is their job descriptions. So if job descriptions are consistent with the strategic plan of the unit and the organization, the way performance is defined and measured is a result of a cascading process of priorities, shown in Figure 3-1.

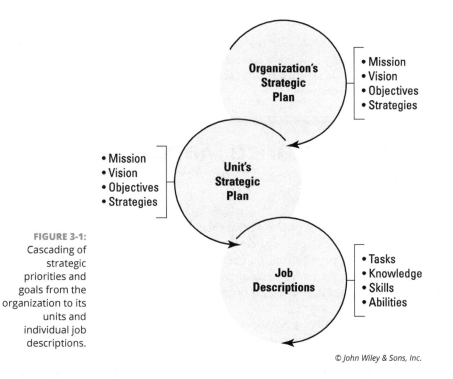

FIGURE 3-1: Cascading of strategic priorities and goals from the organization to its units and individual job descriptions.

© John Wiley & Sons, Inc.

EXAMPLE

KeyBank is a good example of the cascading process shown in Figure 3-1. In the state of Utah, the bank first involved managers at all hierarchical levels to develop an organization mission statement. Next, they developed objectives and strategies that would help achieve KeyBank's mission. The mission statement, objectives, and strategies at the organizational level were used as the foundation for developing the strategies for individual branches. To develop these, senior managers met with branch managers to discuss the organization's objectives and strategies and to explain the importance of adopting similar ones in each branch. Then, each of the branch managers met with their employees to develop branch mission statements and objectives. One important premise in this exercise was that each branch's mission statement and objectives had to be aligned with the corporate mission statement, objectives, and strategies.

After organizational and branch objectives and strategies were aligned, managers and employees reviewed individual job descriptions. That is, each job description was tailored so that individual tasks, duties, and responsibilities were clear and contributed to meeting the department's and the organization's objectives. Involving employees in this process helped them to gain a clear understanding of how their performance affected the branch, and in turn, the organization.

TIP

Even if an employee isn't able to reach individual goals, the fact that performance management formally and explicitly links them to the goals of the unit and the organization goals is very useful in communicating what are the most crucial business strategic initiatives.

Developing Performance Management Leadership Skills

If you manage people, you play a critical role in making sure the cascading of priorities I described in the previous section actually happens. In other words, you need to become a performance management *leader,* meaning that you guide employees so their performance is aligned with the mission, vision, objectives, and strategies of your unit and your organization.

To transition from being a manager to becoming a performance management leader, you must learn a few important skills.

First, you need to be able to serve as a coach. Second, you need to know how to give positive feedback — both positive and negative.

Becoming an effective coach

Coaching is a collaborative, ongoing process in which the manager interacts with direct reports and takes an active role and interest in their performance.

REMEMBER

Good coaches do three things: They direct, motivate, and reward employee behavior.

Coaching happens every day. It is about helping to correct and improve any performance that doesn't meet expectations. But it is also about long-term performance and involves ensuring that each employee's development plan is being achieved.

REMEMBER

Being a coach is similar to serving as a consultant, and for coaching to be successful, you must establish a helping relationship.

Do you want to be an effective coach? Then follow these success factors:

WARNING

>> **Establish a good coaching relationship.** For coaching to work, the relationship between the coach and the employee must be trusting and collaborative. You need to listen to understand. You need to try to walk in the employee's shoes and view the job and organization from his or her perspective. You need to coach with empathy and compassion. Such compassionate coaching will help develop a good relationship with the employee.

>> **Make sure the employee is the source and director of change.** You must understand that the employee is the source of change and self-growth. Accordingly, you need to facilitate the employee's setting the agenda, goals, and direction.

The purpose of coaching is to change employee behavior and set a direction for what the employee will do better in the future. This type of change will not happen if the employee isn't in the driver's seat.

>> **Make sure you understand that the employee is whole and unique.** You must understand that each employee is a unique individual with several job-related and job-unrelated identities (for example, computer network specialist, father, skier) and a unique personal history. You must try to create a whole and complete and rich picture of the employees so that they bring their whole selves to work and are fully engaged. It will be beneficial if you have knowledge of the employee's life and can help the employee connect his life and work experiences in meaningful ways.

>> **Facilitate employee growth.** Your main role is one of facilitation. You must direct the process and help with the content of a developmental plan but not take control of these issues. You need to maintain an *attitude of exploration:* Help expand the employee's awareness of strengths, resources, and challenges. And you need to facilitate goal setting.

You need to understand that coaching isn't something done *to* the employee, but done *with* the employee.

Giving effective feedback

Giving feedback to an employee regarding her progress toward achieving her goals is a key component of the coaching process. Feedback is information about past behavior that you give with the goal of improving future performance.

Feedback includes information about both positive and negative aspects of job performance and lets employees know how well they are doing.

Positive feedback

Although most people are a lot more comfortable giving feedback on good performance than they are on poor performance, you need to follow best practices when you give praise — what is also called positive feedback — so that the feedback is useful in terms of future performance.

Here are some best practices you should implement:

>> **Positive feedback should be sincere and given only when it is deserved.** If you give praise repeatedly and when it isn't deserved, employees are not able to see when a change in direction is needed.

>> **Positive feedback should be about specific behaviors or results.** You should give feedback within context so that employees know what they need to repeat in the future.

>> **In giving positive feedback, you should take your time and act pleased.** Don't rush through the information.

>> **Don't give positive feedback by referring to the absence of the negative.** For example, avoid saying "not bad" or "better than last time." Instead, praise should emphasize the positives and be phrased, for example, as "I like the way you did that" or "I admire how you did that."

Constructive feedback

Constructive feedback includes information that performance has fallen short of expectations. This type of feedback is sometimes referred to as "negative feedback," but I prefer to use "constructive feedback" because this label has a more positive and future-oriented connotation.

The goal of providing constructive feedback is to help employees improve their performance in the future; it isn't to punish, embarrass, or chastise them.

It is not easy to give constructive feedback. Why? Managers fear negative reactions such as employees becoming defensive and even angry. Friendships at work can be damaged.

But not giving constructive feedback when it's due has very negative consequences for the entire organization. Take the following advice from Francie Dalton, founder and president of Columbia, Maryland-based Dalton Alliances, Inc.:

> In organizations where management imposes no consequences for poor performance, high achievers will leave because they don't want to be where mediocrity is tolerated. But mediocre performers will remain because they know they're safe. The entire organizational culture, along with its reputation in the marketplace, can be affected by poor performers.

Constructive feedback is most useful when early coaching has been instrumental in identifying warning signs and the performance problem is still manageable. And constructive feedback is most likely to be accepted when it is given by a source who uses straight talk and not subtle pressure and when it is supported by hard data.

The traditional approach to giving feedback is called weaknesses-based approach:

» Identifying employee weaknesses: deficiencies in terms of their job performance, knowledge, and skills

» Giving negative feedback on what the employees are doing wrong or what the employees did not accomplish

» Asking them ask them to improve their behaviors or results by overcoming their weaknesses

As a more effective alternative, try using a strengths-based approach, which involves:

» Identifying employee strengths in terms of their exceptional job performance

» Asking employees to improve their behaviors or results by making continued or more intensive use of their strengths

In using a strengths-based approach to giving feedback, the key issue is to highlight how strengths can generate success on the job, and this motivates employees to intensify the use of their strengths to produce even more positive behaviors and results.

Here's how to do it:

1. **Start the conversation** with something like, "I want to talk to you about some of the great things that you've been doing lately, as well as areas where you can improve. I'd like this time to be about how I can help you be your very best."

2. Request assistance from the employee in **identifying strength areas** by asking, "In what ways do you feel like you've been standing out?"

3. Identify **how employee strengths,** which are used in some types of behaviors and results, **can be used** in others.

Defining and Measuring Performance

As a performance management leader, you need to help employees define performance and clarify what performance is.

Performance is a combination of two things:

» **Behaviors and actions:** what an employee does

» **Results and products:** the outcomes of an employee's behavior

Do you see the arrows creating a circular motion in Figure 3-2? This means that behaviors & actions affect results & products and vice versa. For example, if an employee puts a lot of time in preparing for an important client presentation (behavior), the client will be pleased (result). In turn, if the client is satisfied (result), this will motivate the employee to allocate sufficient time to client presentations in the future (behavior).

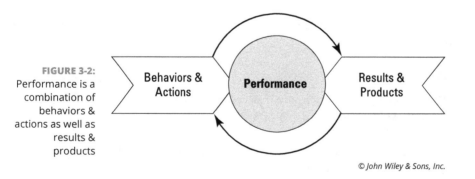

FIGURE 3-2:
Performance is a combination of behaviors & actions as well as results & products

© *John Wiley & Sons, Inc.*

Behaviors & actions and results & products create a virtuous and self-reinforcing cycle that together constitute performance. Effective performance management systems include measures of both behaviors and results.

Measuring performance as behaviors

To measure behaviors, you first cluster them into *competencies.* These are clusters of knowledge, skills, and abilities (KSAs) that are critical in determining how results will be achieved. Examples of competencies are customer service, written or oral communication, creative thinking, and dependability.

Competencies are not directly observable, so you rely on key performance indicators (KPIs), which are observable and measurable behaviors that tell you the extent to which the competency is there or not.

An indicator is a behavior that, if displayed, shows that the competency is present.

Take the case of a professor teaching an online course. An important competency is "communication." This competency is defined as "the set of behaviors that enables a professor to convey information so that students are able to receive it and understand it." For example, one of the KPIs is whether the professor is conveying information during preassigned times and dates. That is, if the professor is not present at the chat room at the prespecified dates and times, no communication is possible.

Another behavioral indicator of the competency communication is whether the responses provided by the professor address the questions asked by the students or whether the answers are only tangential to the questions asked.

Measuring performance as results

To measure results, you first need to answer the following two questions:

>> What are the *key accountabilities* — different areas in which this individual is expected to focus efforts?

Take the position of Training Specialist/Consultant at Target Corporation. Target focuses exclusively on general merchandise retailing, and is the second largest discount store retailer in the United States, behind Walmart. An accountability for this position is "Process leadership": Leads the strategy and direction of assigned processes. Coordinates related projects and directs or manages resources. This is extremely important to the functioning of Target leadership and the ability of executives to meet strategic business goals. If this position is managed improperly, then it will lead to a loss of time and money in training costs and leadership ineffectiveness.

>> Within each accountability, what are the expected *performance objectives* — goals that should be achieved?

Again, for the position of Training Specialist/Consultant at Target, and the accountability Process leadership, examples of objectives are: (a) Establish leadership development processes and training programs within budget and time commitments and (b) Meet budget targets and improve executive leaders' "leadership readiness" scores across organization by 20 percent in the coming fiscal year.

Key accountabilities are broad areas of a job for which the employee is responsible for producing results. Objectives are statements of important and measurable outcomes for each accountability.

Developing Employee Performance

Employee development is a component of a state-of-the-science performance management systems. For employee development to be successful, it has to be a joint activity entered into by both the employee and the manager.

To do so, the first step is to create a personal development plan.

Creating development plans

To be most useful, personal development need to answer the following questions:

>> How can I continually learn and grow in the next year?

>> How can I do better in the future?

>> How can I avoid performance problems faced in the past?

>> Where am I now and where would I like to be in terms of my career path?

Information to be used in designing development plans comes from the performance evaluation form. You can design a development plan based on each of the performance dimensions evaluated. For example, if the performance dimension "communication" is rated as substandard, this area would be included in the development plan.

Do you have a development plan? If not, this is a good time for you to create one. Make sure your plan includes answers to each of the four questions I asked above.

Implementing development plans

The direct supervisor has an important role in the creation and completion of the employee's development plan.

Because of the critical role of the direct supervisor in the employee development process, it is a good idea for the supervisor to have her own development plan as well. This will help the supervisor understand the process from the employee's perspective, anticipate potential roadblocks and pain points, and create a plan in a collaborative fashion.

If you are a manager, make sure you do the following if you want your employees' development plans to be implemented effectively:

>> **Explain** what is required of the employee to reach a required performance level

>> **Refer** to appropriate development activities

>> **Review** and make suggestions about development objectives

>> **Check** on the employee's progress toward development objective achievement

>> **Offer** the opportunity for regular check-ins and reinforcing positive behaviors

TIP

To be successful in implementing each of these five success factors, supervisors themselves need to be motivated to support the employees' completion of their development objectives. For this to happen, supervisors must be held accountable and rewarded for doing a good job of helping their employees develop.

Assessing Performance Management Effectiveness

Is performance management delivering the anticipated, and hoped for, value added? To answer this question, you need to use good measures to monitor and evaluate the system.

You can use both quantitative and qualitative measures that give you very useful information on what is working, what is not, and what needs to be fixed.

Using quantitative measures

You can gather the following types of data to assess your system:

» **Number of people evaluated:** One of the most basic measures is the number of employees who are actually participating in the system. If performance evaluations have not been completed for some employees, you need to find out who they are and why a performance review has not been completed.

» **System satisfaction:** You can distribute a confidential survey to measure the perceptions of the system's users, both raters and ratees. This survey can include questions about satisfaction with equity, usefulness, and accuracy.

» **Overall cost/benefit ratio:** A fairly simple way to address the overall impact of the system is to ask participants to rate the overall cost/benefit ratio for the performance management system. This is a type of bottom-line question that can provide convincing evidence for the overall worth of the system. The cost/benefit ratio question can be asked in reference to an individual (employee or manager), her job, and her organizational unit.

» **Unit-level and organization-level performance:** Another indicator that the system is working well is provided by the measurement of unit- and organization-level performance. Such performance indicators are customer satisfaction with specific units and indicators of the financial performance of the various units or the organization as a whole. You need to be aware that it may take some time for changes in individual and group performance level to be translated into unit- and organization-level results. You should not expect results as soon as the system is implemented; however, you should start to see some tangible results at the unit level a few months after the system is in place.

Using qualitative measures

You can collect the opinions of those involved in your system:

» **Quality of qualitative performance data:** An indicator of quality of the performance data refers to the information provided in the open-ended sections of the appraisal forms. For example, how much did the rater write? What is the relevance of the examples provided?

>> **Quality of follow-up actions:** A good indicator of the quality of the system is whether it leads to important follow-up actions in terms of development activities or improved processes. For example, to what extent follow-up actions involve exclusively the supervisor as opposed to the employee? If this is the case, then the system may not be working as intended because this is an indicator that employees are not sufficiently involved. Also, to what extent have employees learned from their successes and failures and applying those lessons to the future?

>> **Quality of performance discussion meeting:** You can distribute a confidential survey to all employees on a regular basis to gather information about how the supervisor is managing the performance discussion meetings. For example, is the feedback useful? Has the supervisor made resources available so the employees can accomplish the developmental plan objectives? How relevant was the performance review discussion to their job? To what degree have developmental objectives and plans been discussed? To what extent does the supervisor's way of providing feedback encourage direct reports to receive more feedback in the future?

Chapter **4**

Anticipating and Minimizing Negative Consequences

ew organizations use their existing performance management systems in effective ways. And you already know that performance management isn't living up to its promise in terms of turning human capital into a source of competitive advantage. There is big disconnect between what performance management is *supposed to do* in terms of turning human capital into an organization's source of competitive advantage and what it *actually does* in most organizations.

Performance management is usually vilified as an "HR department requirement." In many organizations, performance management means that managers must comply with their HR department's request and fill out tedious, and often useless, evaluation forms. These evaluation forms are often completed only because it is required by the "HR cops." Unfortunately, the only tangible consequence of this type of evaluation process is that managers have to spend time away from their "real" job duties.

EXAMPLE

Consider Sally's situation:

Sally is a sales manager at a pharmaceutical company. The fiscal year will end in one week. She is overwhelmed with end-of-the-year tasks, including reviewing the budget she is likely to be allocated for the following year, responding to customers' phone calls, dealing with vendors, and supervising a group of ten salespeople. It's a very hectic time, probably the most hectic time of the year. She receives a phone call from the Human Resources (HR) department: "Sally, we have not received your performance reviews for your ten direct reports; they are due by the end of the fiscal year." Sally thinks, "Oh, again, those performance reviews. What a waste of my time!" From Sally's point of view, there is no value in filling out those seemingly meaningless forms. She doesn't see her direct reports in action because they are visiting customers most of the time. All that she knows about their performance is based on sales figures, which depend more on the products offered and geographic territory covered than the individual effort and motivation of each salesperson. And based on her own experience, she thinks that little will happen in terms of compensation and rewards, regardless of her ratings. These are lean times in her organization, and salary adjustments are based on seniority rather than on merit. She has less than three days to turn in her forms. What will she do? In the end, she decides to follow the path of least resistance: to please her employees and give everyone the maximum possible rating. In this way, Sally believes the employees will be happy with their ratings and she will not have to deal with complaints or potentially contentious follow-up meetings. Sally fills out the forms in less than 15 minutes and gets back to her "real job."

There is something very wrong with this picture, which unfortunately happens all too frequently in many organizations. I am sure you can relate to Sally's situation. Although Sally's HR department calls this process "performance management," it actually is not.

In Sally's organization, "performance management" is just a useless bureaucratic requirement that wastes everyone's precious time and does more harm than good.

Done right, performance management is a continuous process of identifying, measuring, and developing the performance of individuals and teams and aligning performance with the strategic goals of the organization.

This chapter shows you how to avoid Sally's situation. To do so, you need to anticipate both what can go wrong when you implement performance management and also what can go wrong if you chose to avoid performance management or, more specifically, performance ratings. In addition, you have to create an appeals process and a communication plan.

Anticipating Damage Caused by Flawed Performance Management

What happens when performance management systems don't work as intended, as in the case of Sally's organization? What are some of the negative consequences you can anticipate will result from low-quality and poorly implemented systems? The following sections cover the damage cause to all involved.

Damage caused to employees

Here's what happens to employees when performance management is poorly implemented:

>> **Lowered self-esteem:** Self-esteem is lowered if feedback is provided in an inappropriate and inaccurate way, which in turn creates employee resentment.

>> **Decreased motivation to perform:** Motivation is lowered for many reasons, including the feeling that superior performance isn't translated into meaningful tangibles such as pay increase or intangibles such as personal recognition rewards.

>> **Employee burnout and job dissatisfaction:** When the performance assessment instrument isn't seen as valid and the system isn't perceived as fair, employees feel increased levels of job burnout and job dissatisfaction. As a consequence, employees become increasingly irritated.

Damage caused to managers

Poorly implemented systems don't provide the benefits provided by well-implemented systems, yet they take up managers' time. Such systems are resisted because of competing obligations and allocation of resources (e.g., time). What is sometimes worse, managers simply choose to avoid the system altogether.

Damage caused to relationships

As a consequence of a deficient system, the relationships among the individuals involved are damaged, often permanently.

>> **Emerging biases:** Personal values, biases, and relationships replace organizational standards.

>> **Varying and unfair standards and ratings:** Both standards and individual ratings vary across and within units and are also unfair.

Damage caused to the organization

Organizations certainly suffer in tangible ways from poor performance management:

>> **Increased turnover.** If the process isn't seen as fair, employees become upset and leave the organization. Some will quit, but others will withdraw psychologically. This means that they will be at work physically but not mentally because they will minimize their effort and engage in cyberloafing until they are able to find another job elsewhere.

Turnover is particularly a problem for the case of star performers, who are attracted to organizations that recognize individual contributions.

WARNING

>> **Use of misleading information:** If a standardized system isn't in place, there are multiple opportunities for fabricating information about an employee's performance.

>> **Wasted time and money:** Performance management systems cost money and time. These resources are wasted when systems are poorly designed and implemented.

>> **Unclear ratings system:** Because of poor communication, employees do not know how their ratings are generated or how the ratings translate into rewards.

>> **Increased risk of litigation:** Expensive lawsuits are filed by individuals who feel they have been appraised unfairly.

Learning from Flawed Performance Ratings

Many of the negative consequences I describe in the preceding section are directly related to the issue of performance ratings. For example, ratings are biased, unjustified, inaccurate, and a waste of time and resources; their use can lead to the departure of star performers and even litigation. You can learn a lot from these flawed performance ratings in terms of what is broken with performance management — and hopefully take remedial action.

Performance ratings are often the canary in the coalmine, rather than the problem per se.

What do I mean? Before modern methods became available, coal miners in the early twentieth century used to carry a caged canary with them down into the mine tunnels. When toxic gases such as carbon monoxide were present, the canary would faint, or even die, quickly alerting the miners of imminent danger.

So the canary was not the problem but a sign of the presence of unobserved toxic gases. Similarly, what are the unseen reasons why performance ratings are biased, impractical, and cause more harm than good? What are the "toxic gases" that are producing problems in the ratings?

Here are three reasons why performance ratings are dysfunctional:

>> Ratings are not directly related to an organization's strategic goals.

>> Ratings don't refer to performance dimensions that are under the control of the employee.

>> It takes too long for supervisors to fill out complicated and convoluted evaluation forms.

So when ratings are not working, you need to look under the surface to understand why. Then you can think about how to create a better connection between them and your organization's strategic objectives, performance dimensions that are under the employee's control, and how to gather ratings in a more practical manner.

Why Performance Ratings Are Here to Stay

Biases and other problems with performance ratings have not gone unnoticed. So in the past few years, organizations such as Eli Lilly, Adobe, Microsoft, Accenture, Goldman Sachs, IBM, Morgan Stanley, New York Life, Medtronic, Juniper Networks, and Gap announced that they were going to seriously curtail or even eliminate their use. In fact, surveys results by WorldatWork and Willis Towers Watson Talent Management show that between 8 percent and 14 percent of large corporations in North America have eliminated performance ratings since 2014.

Although the elimination of ratings seems to be the latest fad, performance management without ratings was implemented by GE in the 1960s. In addition to no summary ratings, this system at GE included frequent discussions of performance and an emphasis on mutual goal planning and problem solving. But years later,

GE not only brought ratings back with a vengeance but became famous for the use of former CEO Jack Welch's "vitality curve" in which employees were ranked in the top 20%, middle 70%, or bottom 10% of the performance distribution. Going full circle, GE is now one of the companies reevaluating their use of the annual reviews!

Despite widespread media coverage and hype about many companies "abandoning performance reviews and ratings," many of these companies quickly realized that even if performance ratings are abolished, supervisors evaluate the performance of their direct reports implicitly — and so do peers — even if evaluations forms and ratings are not used. That is, we are always passing judgment about who is doing what at work and how well.

Also, without performance ratings, how are we going to identify, reward, and retain top performers? How will organizations make fair compensation and promotion decisions and deal with possible discrimination lawsuits?

The answer is that performance ratings — good-quality performance ratings — are needed. This is why companies such as Deloitte and many others that tried to eliminate performance ratings are now using ratings again — but they emphasize developmental feedback.

REMEMBER

Clearly, measuring performance isn't easy. However, this isn't a good excuse to abandon ratings. Also, to make sure ratings measure what matters and measure those things well, setting up an appeals process is an important feature to minimize potential negative consequences of performance management.

Setting Up an Appeals Process

Making sure you implement an appeals process is important in gaining employee acceptance for the performance management system and minimizing potential damage. Why? Because it allows employees to understand that if there is a disagreement regarding performance ratings or any resulting decisions, then such disagreements can be resolved in an amicable and nonretaliatory way.

Dealing with judgmental and administrative issues

With an appeals process, employees can question two types of issues: judgmental and administrative.

>> **Judgmental issues** are about the validity of the performance evaluation. For example, an employee may believe that a manager's performance ratings for that employee don't reflect her actual performance.

>> **Administrative issues** are about policies and procedures. For example, an employee may argue that his supervisor did not meet with him as frequently as she did with his coworkers and that the feedback he is receiving about his performance isn't as thorough as that received by his coworkers.

Setting up a three-level appeals process

A good appeals process includes the following three steps:

1. When an appeal is first filed, the HR department serves as a mediator between the employee and the supervisor. An appeal sent to the HR department is usually called a Level 1 appeal. The HR department is in a good position to judge whether policies and procedures have been implemented correctly, and also, has good information about the various jobs, levels of performance expected, and levels of performance of other employees within the unit and organization. The HR department gathers the necessary facts and brings them to the attention of either the rater to encourage reconsideration of the decision that caused the appeal or to the complainant to explain why there have been no biases or violations. In other words, the HR department either suggests corrective action to the supervisor or informs the employee that the decision or procedures were correct.

2. If the rater doesn't believe corrective action should be taken or if the employee doesn't accept the HR decision, and the appeal continues, then the process moves to Level 2. In Level 2, there is an outside arbitrator that usually consists of a panel of peers and managers. The panel reviews the case, asks questions, interviews witnesses, researches precedents, and reviews policy. Then they simply take a vote to make the decision.

3. In many cases, the Level 2 vote represents the final decision. In other cases, the vote is forwarded to a high-level manager (vice president or higher level), who takes the panel's vote into consideration in making the final decision. This is Level 3.

Figure 4-1 will help you visualize these three levels.

ACTIVE LEARNING

Take a close look at Figure 4-1 and think about the appeals process at your organization. From your perspective, how does this process compare to the one summarized in the figure? Is there anything missing that your organization should consider adding?

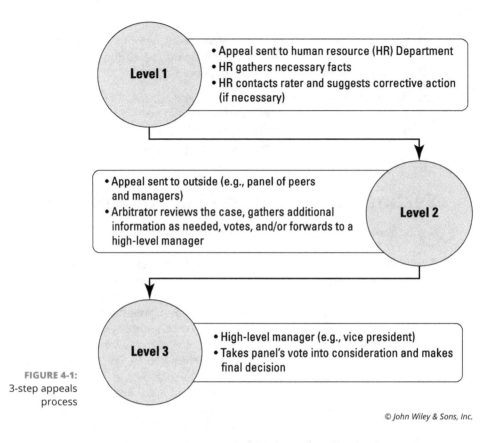

- Level 1
  - Appeal sent to human resource (HR) Department
  - HR gathers necessary facts
  - HR contacts rater and suggests corrective action (if necessary)

- Level 2
  - Appeal sent to outside (e.g., panel of peers and managers)
  - Arbitrator reviews the case, gathers additional information as needed, votes, and/or forwards to a high-level manager

- Level 3
  - High-level manager (e.g., vice president)
  - Takes panel's vote into consideration and makes final decision

FIGURE 4-1: 3-step appeals process

© John Wiley & Sons, Inc.

APPEALS PROCESS AT THE UNIVERSITY OF LETHBRIDGE

What follows is the appeals process at the University of Lethbridge. How does it compare to the process at your own organization? What are some of the features of the process that could be implemented in your organization?

Purpose

The Appeal Process is a means for Employees and Supervisors to resolve disagreements involving the Performance Evaluation process. This Appeal Process doesn't in any way circumvent or prohibit an employee from the invocation of Article 12: Grievance Procedure.

Principles

All appeals:

1. Are to be conducted with diplomacy and impartiality.
2. Aspire to construct and provide the best possible information.
3. Maintain confidentiality and respect for the individual.

Process

If an Employee disagrees with the result of their Performance Evaluation, as conducted by their Supervisor, the Employee may appeal in writing to the Office of Human Resources. A request for appeal must be received within ten (10) Work Days of the date of the Employee's signature on the Performance Evaluation. The deadline for all written appeals is the last work day in June. Late applications shall not be subject to appeal except under extraordinary circumstances as determined by the Associate VP HR and Admin. Submission of an appeal must be with the use of the Performance Evaluation Appeal Form.

Level 1

Following the receipt of an appeal, a member of the Human Resources Department will conduct a confidential investigation, gathering information in discussion with the Employee, the Supervisor, and where necessary other informed parties. A recommendation for resolution will be put forward by HR to the Supervisor and Employee. If an agreement cannot be reached at Level 1 then the appeal will move to Level 2 of the Appeals Process.

Level 2

The appeal will be brought before a Performance Evaluation Committee whose membership shall consist of three (3) AUPE (Alberta Union of Provincial Employees) Representatives, three (3) Representatives of the Board and a Facilitator from Human Resources. The committee members will remain consistent for all appeals relating to the evaluation period except in circumstances where members with a substantial personal or professional relationship with the employee under appeal shall not participate in the review.

The committee will consider the information collected by Human Resources in Level 1, as well as any relevant evidence that may be offered by the Employee and the Supervisor, and may seek out other sources that the committee deems to be of relevance to the appeal. The committee will have five (5) Work Days from the date the committee was convened to review the evidence and then formally issue a ruling.

(continued)

(continued)

Level 3

In the event that an agreement isn't achieved in Level 2, the matter will continue as a grievance commencing at Step 2 of Article 12: Grievance Procedure.

Once a consensus has been reached and signed by all parties involved, at any point in the appeal process, the revised Performance Evaluation will be final and not subject to further appeal. All documentation will be forwarded to the Human Resources department and will remain confidential. The employee may at anytime withdraw the appeal request by writing to the Associate VP HR and Admin who will inform the members of the committee.

Source: www.uleth.ca/hr/performance-management-appeals-process-appeals-form

Setting Up a Communication Plan and Dealing with Resistance to Change

Another thing you can go do make sure you minimize potential damage done by poor performance management is to set up a good communication plan and make sure you deal with resistance to change.

Questions that your communication plan should answer

In general, having more and better knowledge of the performance management system leads to greater employee acceptance and satisfaction and helps you minimize or even prevent possible negative consequences of performance management.

As shown in Figure 4-2, a good communication plan answers the following questions:

>> **What is performance management?** Answering this question involves providing general information about performance management, how performance management systems are implemented in other organizations, and the general goals of performance management systems.

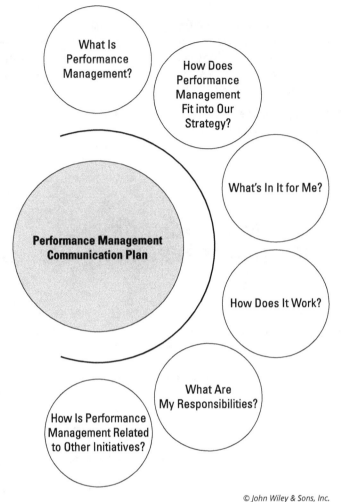

What Is Performance Management?

How Does Performance Management Fit into Our Strategy?

What's In It for Me?

Performance Management Communication Plan

How Does It Work?

What Are My Responsibilities?

How Is Performance Management Related to Other Initiatives?

FIGURE 4-2: Key questions that you should answer with your performance management communication plan.

© John Wiley & Sons, Inc.

>> **How does performance management fit into our strategy?** To answer this question, you should provide information on the relation between performance management and strategic planning. Specifically, information is provided on how the performance management system will help accomplish strategic goals.

>> **What's in it for me?** A good communication plan describes the benefits of implementing performance management for all those involved.

>> **How does it work?** Answering this question entails giving a detailed description of the performance management process and timeline — for example, when meetings will take place, what the purposes of each meeting are, and when decisions about rewards will be made.

>> **What are my responsibilities?** The communication plan should include information on the role and responsibilities of each person involved at each stage of the process. For example, it includes a description of the employees' and supervisors' main responsibilities in the performance management process.

>> **How is performance management related to other initiatives?** The communication plan should include information on the relationship between performance management and other initiatives and systems, such as training, promotion, and succession planning.

PERFORMANCE MANAGEMENT COMMUNICATION PLAN IN U.S. FEDERAL AGENCIES

Here's the performance management communication plan use by U.S. Federal Agencies, specifically for the position of Senior Executive Service (SES). This is a position in several U.S. federal agencies, such as the Department of Justice, Department of Interior, Department of Energy, and Department of Commerce. SES members serve in key leadership positions directly below the top presidential appointees. SES members link the appointees to the rest of the federal government, and they are charged with overseeing various governmental in U.S. federal agencies.

The communication plan that the Department of Justice implemented for this performance management system answers each of the questions included in Figure 4-2:

• **What is performance management?** The plan states the reasons for the department's implementing a performance management system and discusses what it is expected to accomplish. For example, it explains that performance management aims at promoting efficient and effective attainment of the department's mission, program objectives, and strategic planning initiatives, and it also aims at motivating high levels of achievement and accountability. It also includes definitions of several key terms, including performance management system, performance, progress review, rating levels, and annual summary rating.

• **How does performance management fit into our strategy?** The plan includes a list of principles that guide the system, including, "The Department of Justice federal leaders and managers create a climate for excellence by communicating their vision, values and expectations clearly." It goes on to detail all the ways in which leaders in the agency do this. Also, the director of the Office of Personnel Management (OPM) describes how the system would be used to implement key principles, including excellence.

- **What's in it for me?** There is clear information on how the performance management system will help the SES members be more effective leaders so that the department's mission can be achieved.

- **How does it work?** The plan outlines the steps in a performance management process, detailing the managers' responsibilities at each step. For example, it outlines the performance dimensions, the rating categories, and how to assign an overall rating.

- **What are my responsibilities?** The communication plan outlines the responsibilities of the SES members as well as their rating official, the person in charge of rating their performance. The plan emphasizes that leaders must create a culture performing at a high level by continually communicating expectations and rewarding high-achieving performers.

- **How is performance management related to other initiatives?** The communication plan touches briefly on the importance of linking system outcomes to performance-based pay. The importance of training to maximize performance is also considered.

Dealing with cognitive biases

Even if a communication plan answers all or most of the important questions, the fact that the information has been made available doesn't necessarily mean the communication plan will be successful in gaining acceptance.

Why? People resist the performance management system due to cognitive biases. These are "mental filters" that affect what information is taken in and how it is processed.

There are three types of biases that affect the effectiveness of a communication plan, even if yours is an excellent one. Also, these biases are accentuated when people are not willing or interested in change. These biases are:

>> **Selective exposure:** A tendency to expose our minds only to ideas with which we already agree. Those employees who already agree that performance management is a good idea become involved in the communication plan activities, including reading about the system and attending meetings describing how the system works. On the contrary, those who don't see much value in a performance management system choose not to read information about it and not to attend meetings about it.

>> **Selective perception:** A tendency to perceive a piece of information as meaning what we would like it to mean even though the information, as intended by the communicator, means the exact opposite. Someone who believes performance management is about only rewards and punishments incorrectly interprets that receiving formal performance feedback at the end of each quarter translates exclusively into receiving a pay increase or a bonus.

>> **Selective retention:** A tendency to remember only those pieces of information with which we already agree. If an employee perceives his employer as vindictive, that employee won't remember information about how the appeals process works or about other fair and equitable aspects of the system.

Selective exposure, selective perception, and selective retention biases are pervasive and could easily render the communication plan ineffective.

Fortunately, there are several ways to minimize the negative impact of these biases, and therefore, help mitigate potential damage done by performance management:

>> **Involve employees.** Involve employees in the design of the system. People support what they help create. The higher the level of participation is in designing the system, the greater the support for the system will be.

>> **Understand employee needs.** Understand the needs of the employees and identify ways in which these needs can be met through performance management. For example, do they want more feedback? Are they interested in development activities that would eventually lead to a promotion or a different job within the organization?

>> **Strike first.** Create a positive attitude toward the performance system before any negative attitudes and rumors are created. Make communications realistic and don't set up expectations you cannot deliver. Discuss some of the arguments that might be used against the system and provide evidence to counter them.

>> **Provide facts and consequences.** Because of the presence of cognitive biases, facts don't necessarily speak for themselves. Clearly explain facts about the system and also explain what they mean or what the consequences are. Don't let employees draw their own conclusions because they may differ from yours.

>> **Put it in writing.** In Western cultures, written communications are usually more powerful and credible than spoken communications because they can be carefully examined and challenged for accuracy. Create documentation, which is often posted online for everyone to download, describing the system.

>> **Use multiple channels of communication.** Use multiple methods of communication, including face-to-face (especially in the case of small and medium-size organizations) and virtual meetings, email, TED talks, and short

video clips. In other words, allow employees to be exposed repeatedly to the same message delivered using different communication channels. Of course, make sure that all channels convey consistent information.

>> **Use credible communicators.** Use credible sources to communicate the performance management system. In companies where HR department members are perceived as "HR cops" because they continually emphasize what cannot be done as opposed to how one's job can be done better, it is better to use a different department or group. Instead, in such situations, communication should be delivered by people who are trusted and admired within the organization. It also helps if those delivering the communication and endorsing the system are regarded as key and powerful organizational players.

>> **Say it, and then, say it again.** Repeat the information frequently. Because people can absorb only a small amount of information at a time, and may be resistant to change, the information must be repeated frequently.

DEALING WITH COGNITIVE BIASES AND RESISTANCE TO CHANGE AT U.S. DEPARTMENT OF JUSTICE

Let's go back to the Department of Justice communication process I describe earlier in this chapter. That plan attempts to minimize negative biases and gain support for the performance management system. For example, although it is a government agency and the performance management system is a federal mandate, the OPM offered to help managers tailor the systems to their specific agencies. This helps employees become more involved and is also helpful in addressing the specific needs of the employees in the various agencies. The director of the OPM, who is a credible source of information on the performance management system, set a positive tone and even appealed to employees' patriotism by including a message from the United States President, reminding them of the importance of serving the American people.

The communication plan also provides facts and conclusions about the system. For example, it explains the reasoning for realigning the performance management system with the fiscal year, how to carry out this timeline, and the importance of doing so. The communication plan is also posted on the department's website. There are also links to other websites with information about performance management. It isn't clear whether the Department of Justice disseminated the information using other media, such as short video clips. But all in all, the plan implemented by the Department of Justice is a good example of a communication plan that attempts to minimize the detrimental impact of cognitive biases and resistance to change.

2

Designing an Effective Performance Management System

IN THIS PART . . .

Observe and document performance accurately.

Define performance within your organization.

Measure results, competencies, and behaviors in employees.

Collect and use performance data to your advantage.

Develop an accurate ratings system.

Chapter **5**

Delivering Strategic Business Results

Performance management systems receive crucial top management support when the system makes clear contributions to the organizational and unit priorities. Without this support, a performance management system may not even get off the ground. Also, for performance management to be successful, if needs to deliver strategic *value* for the organization. In other words, performance management needs to help the organization reach its strategic objectives.

How, then, are these strategic organizational objectives identified? How does an organization know what the "target" should be, what it is trying to accomplish, and how to do it?

The HR function plays a key role as a strategic partner in helping to answer these questions. The HR function is often vilified as being merely operational and not able to think or act strategically — unfortunately sometimes for good reason. Well, over the past two decades or so, an entire new field of research and practice has emerged, called *strategic human resource management* (SHRM). SHRM is about planning and implementing HR policies and activities with the goal of enabling an organization to achieve its objectives. Performance management is a perfect vehicle to demonstrate the strategic role and contributions of the HR function because it allows for explicit and clear links between what HR is doing and the organization's mission, vision, and objectives. By being involved, and hopefully, leading the rollout of the performance management system, the HR function can serve as an expert internal consultant who deserves and secures a "seat at the table" of the top management team.

TIP

If you work in the HR function and want to make it to the top of your organization, you need to follow in the footsteps of the few Fortune 500 CEOs with an HR background: Samuel R. Allen at John Deere, James C. Smith at Thomson Reuters, Steven L. Newman at Transocean, and Mary Barra at General Motors. What did they do? They served as strategic partners while heading their respective HR units, which is what propelled their trajectory into the very top of their organizations.

Regardless of whether you work in the HR function or you are a manager or employee in any other function in the organization, it's useful for you to learn how to create a strategic plan and link performance management to it. This way, you will ensure that performance management creates value for you and your organization.

Linking Performance Management with Strategic Business Objectives

Strategic planning involves describing the organization's destination, assessing barriers that stand in the way of that destination, and selecting approaches for moving forward. Among other useful outcomes, strategic planning allows for the allocation of resources in a way that provides organizations with a competitive advantage because resources are assigned in a more effective and more targeted manner. Overall, a strategic plan serves as a blueprint that defines how the organization will allocate its resources in pursuit of its most critical and important objectives.

Making sure the strategic plan does what it is supposed to do

The mere presence of a strategic plan doesn't guarantee that this information will be used effectively as part of the performance management system. In fact, countless organizations spend thousands of hours creating strategic plans that are mostly talk and lead to no tangible actions. I am sure you have seen or heard of many organizations that spend too much time and effort crafting their mission and vision statements without undertaking any concrete follow-up actions. The process then ends up being a huge waste of time and a source of frustration and long-lasting cynicism. And this is even worse when there is frequent leadership turnover and a strategic planning process is put into motion over and over again, usually leading to nothing more than reports and updated website content. In those situations, it's typical to hear people say, "Oh no, again! Another CEO and another strategic plan!" For example, a worldwide survey of senior executives from 197 companies with combined sales exceeding $500 million showed that less than 15 percent spent any time evaluating how the previous year's strategic plan affected current performance. The study also found that corporate strategies routinely only deliver between 50 percent and 63 percent of their potential financial performance.

TIP

To make sure that strategy cascades down the organization and leads to concrete actions, you need to make a conscious effort to link the strategic plan with what everyone does in the organization on a daily basis.

Figure 5-1 provides a useful framework for understanding the relationship between an organization's strategic plan, a unit's strategic plan, and job descriptions, which include information on what employees do and what should be measured in the performance management system.

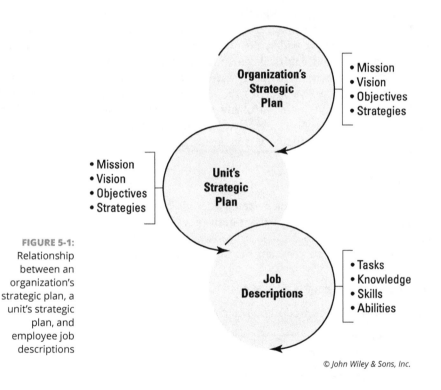

FIGURE 5-1:
Relationship between an organization's strategic plan, a unit's strategic plan, and employee job descriptions

© John Wiley & Sons, Inc.

The organization's strategic plan includes a mission statement and a vision statement, as well as objectives and strategies that will allow for the fulfillment of the mission and vision.

Get the managers involved

The strategies are created with the participation of managers at all levels. The higher the level of involvement, the more likely it is that managers will see the resulting strategies favorably.

As soon as the organizational strategies have been defined, senior management proceeds to meet with department or unit managers, who in turn, solicit input from all people within their units to create unit-level mission and vision statements, objectives, and strategies. A critical issue is to ensure that each unit or department's mission and vision statements, objectives, and strategies are consistent with those at the organizational level. Job descriptions are then revised and updated to make sure they are consistent with unit and organizational priorities. So again, because they are driven by the job descriptions, as a result, the performance management system includes results, behaviors, and development plans for individuals that are consistent with the organizational- and department-level priorities.

Does the process of aligning organizational, unit, and individual priorities actually work in practice? Is it doable? The answer to these questions is "yes," and the benefits of doing so are widely documented. In other words, performance management systems have a critical role in translating strategy into action. In fact, a 2017 study published in *Journal of Accounting and Management* that included 338 organizations in 42 countries found that performance management is the third most important factor affecting the success of a strategic plan. This is particularly true for organizations that operate in rapidly changing environments, regardless of their size, industry, and age.

Keep score

One way to formalize the link between strategic planning and performance management is through the implementation of a *balanced score card*, which involves creating indicators of individual performance along four separate "perspectives" of an organization's success. For the case of a bank, consider the following:

>> **Financial** (cost control, sales growth rate, profit growth rate)

>> **Customer** (service product quality, customer satisfaction, service timing)

>> **Internal process** (information delivery, interaction between employees and clients, standard operation process)

>> **Learning and growth** (corporate image, competitiveness, employee satisfaction)

EXAMPLE

As an example of linking strategy and performance management, let's discuss the case of KeyBank (the primary subsidiary of KeyCorp), which offers financial services and has assets of $134.5 billion. In the state of Utah, KeyBank successfully developed a performance management system that is aligned with the strategic plan of the organization. To do this, the bank first involved managers at all hierarchical levels to develop an organization mission statement. Next, they developed objectives and strategies that would help achieve KeyBank's mission. The mission statement, objectives, and strategies at the organizational level served as the foundation for developing the strategies for individual branches. To develop these strategies, senior managers met with branch managers to discuss the organization's objectives and strategies and to explain the importance of adopting similar ones in each branch. Subsequently, each of the branch managers met with their employees to develop branch mission statements and objectives. One important premise in this exercise was that each branch's mission statement and objectives had to be aligned with the corporate mission statement, objectives, and strategies. After organizational and branch objectives and strategies were aligned, managers and employees reviewed individual job descriptions. That is, each job description was tailored so that individual tasks, duties, and responsibilities were clear and contributed to meeting the department's and the organization's objectives. Involving employees in this process helped them to gain a clear understanding of how their performance affected the branch, and in turn, the organization. Figure 5-2 includes a revised and updated version of Figure 5-1 showing how this was done at KeyBank.

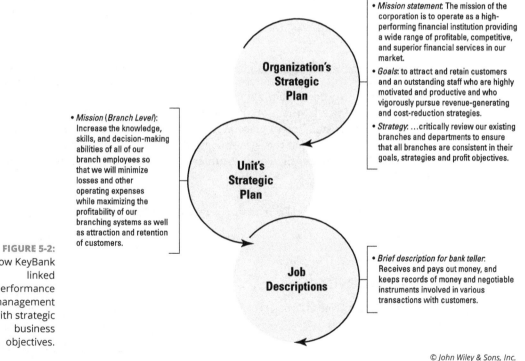

FIGURE 5-2: How KeyBank linked performance management with strategic business objectives.

• *Mission statement*: The mission of the corporation is to operate as a high-performing financial institution providing a wide range of profitable, competitive, and superior financial services in our market.

• *Goals*: to attract and retain customers and an outstanding staff who are highly motivated and productive and who vigorously pursue revenue-generating and cost-reduction strategies.

• *Strategy*: ...critically review our existing branches and departments to ensure that all branches are consistent in their goals, strategies and profit objectives.

Organization's Strategic Plan

• *Mission (Branch Level)*: Increase the knowledge, skills, and decision-making abilities of all of our branch employees so that we will minimize losses and other operating expenses while maximizing the profitability of our branching systems as well as attraction and retention of customers.

Unit's Strategic Plan

Job Descriptions

• *Brief description for bank teller*: Receives and pays out money, and keeps records of money and negotiable instruments involved in various transactions with customers.

© *John Wiley & Sons, Inc.*

Making sure HR does what it is supposed to do

The HR function can and should play a critical role in creating and implementing the strategies that will allow the organization to realize its mission and vision. Specifically, the HR function can make the following contributions:

>> **Communicate knowledge of strategic plan.** The HR function is a good conduit to communicate the various components of the strategic plan (e.g., mission, vision, and objectives) to all the employees.

>> **Outline knowledge, skills, and abilities (KSAs) needed for strategy implementation.** The HR function, through job analyses and the resulting job descriptions, serves as a repository of knowledge regarding what KSAs are needed for a successful implementation of the strategic plan. Thus, the HR function is in a unique situation to provide information about whether the current workforce has the KSAs needed to support the strategic plan, and if not, to offer suggestions about what types of employees should be hired and what types of plans (for example, training and development initiatives) should be put in place to develop the needed KSAs internally.

>> **Propose compensation systems.** The HR function can provide useful information on what type of compensation system should be implemented to motivate employees to support the strategic plan.

In addition to serving as a necessary guide for individual and team performance, knowledge of organization- and unit-level mission and vision provides the HR function with information about how to design the performance management system. Specifically, there are many choices in how the system is designed. For example, the system might place more emphasis on behaviors (processes) than on results (outcomes), or the system might emphasize more short-term criteria (quarterly objectives) than long-term criteria (triennial). Here are some of these choices:

>> **Criteria:** Behavioral criteria versus results criteria

>> **Participation:** Low employee participation vs. high employee participation

>> **Temporal dimension:** Short-term criteria versus long-term criteria

>> **Level of criteria:** Individual criteria versus team/group criteria

>> **System orientation:** Developmental orientation versus administrative orientation

>> **Compensation:** Pay for performance (that is, merit-based) vs. pay for tenure/position

As a result of the strategic planning process, knowledge of the organization and unit vision and mission allows the HR function to serve as an internal consultant and to make informed decisions about performance management design choices. For example, assume an organization is producing a mature product in a fairly stable industry. In this situation, an emphasis on behaviors, rather than results, is preferred because the relationship between processes and outcomes is well known, and the top priority is that employees display reliable and consistent behaviors in making the product. Regardless of the type of criteria used, be it behaviors or results, these must be observable so the person rating the criteria needs to have the ability to observe what is rated and verifiable (that is, there needs to be evidence to confirm the criteria rated).

REMEMBER

To be most useful and impactful, an organization's performance management system must rely on its strategic plan. The job descriptions, which serve as roadmaps for what individuals are supposed to do, how, and what results will be produced must be aligned with the vision, mission, objectives, and strategies of the organization and unit. Organizations can expect greater returns from implementing a performance management system when such alignment is in place. Also, to the extent that the HR function is involved in the design and implementation of the performance management system, it will gain credibility and will be seen as a strategic and valued contributor to the entire organization.

CONNECTING INDIVIDUAL AND FIRM OBJECTIVES AND PERFORMANCE AT DELL

Dell is one of the top players in the personal computer industry through its mode of online direct selling. Dell's main strategic business strategy is to be a low-cost leader in an industry that deals with a product that has now become a commodity. However, in addition to a low-cost strategy, Dell has a customer relationship business strategy of maintaining customer service at a high level, while reducing costs.

Dell's performance management system provides a strong link between individual objectives and organizational performance by including a results component (cost) and a behavioral component (customer service). At Dell, both low cost and high levels of customer service (for both internal and external customers) are important dimensions of the performance management system. Also, the system is strongly linked not only to the strategic objectives (low cost and high levels of customer service), but also to the organization's "winning culture" (which includes achievement of personal and business objectives through its focus on interaction between managers and team members).

Conducting an External and Internal Analysis of Strengths, Weaknesses, Opportunities, and Threats

The first step in conducting a strategic plan is to step back to take in the "big picture." You do this what is called an environmental or *SWOT analysis* (strengths, weaknesses, opportunities, and threats) analysis. An environmental analysis identifies external and internal issues so that you can understand what is going on in the context and industry where your organization operates, enabling you to make decisions about what the performance management system looks like against the backdrop of this broader context.

Analyzing the external environment

How do you conduct an analysis of the external environment? You need to understand what are the opportunities and threats.

>> **Opportunities** are characteristics of the environment that can help your organization succeed. Examples of such opportunities might be markets not currently being served, untapped talent pools, and new technological advances.

>> **Threats** are characteristics of the external environment that can prevent the organization from being successful. Examples of such threats range from economic recession to the launch of innovative products and services on the part of competitors.

A common framework for understanding industry-based threats is the now classic work by Michael E. Porter, called "five-force analysis." These include three forces from horizontal competition (i.e., the threat of substitute products or services, the threat of established rivals, and the threat of new entrants), and two forces from vertical competition (i.e., the bargaining power of suppliers and the bargaining power of customers).

TIP

In addition to the more general five-force analysis proposed by Michael Porter, you need to think about the following more specific factors and how they affect your organization:

>> **Economic:** For example, is there an economic recession on the horizon? Or is the current economic recession likely to end in the near future? How would these economic trends affect our business?

>> **Political/legal:** For example, how will political changes domestically or in the international markets we are planning on entering affect our entry strategy?

- » **Social:** For example, what is the impact of the entry of Millennials in the workforce (and the massive retirement of Baby Boomers)?

- » **Technological:** For example, what technological changes are anticipated in our industry and how will these changes affect how we do business?

- » **Competitors:** For example, how do the strategies and products of our competitors affect our own strategies and products? Can we anticipate our competitors' next move?

- » **Customers:** For example, what do our customers want now, and what will they want in the next five years or so? Can we anticipate such needs?

- » **Suppliers:** For example, what is the relationship with our suppliers now and is it likely to change, and in what way, in the near future?

TIP

Understanding external trends is critical for business of all sizes. But it is particularly challenging for multinational organizations because they are concerned with both domestic and international trends. Monitoring the external environment is so important in the strategic planning of multinational organizations that a survey of U.S. multinational corporations showed that 89 percent of departments responsible for the assessment of the external environment report directly to a member of the board of directors.

ANALYSIS OF THE EXTERNAL ENVIRONMENT AT FRONTIER AIRLINES

Frontier Airlines is an affordable-fare airline headquartered at Denver International Airport, and serving more than 55 cities in the United States, Mexico, the Dominican Republic, and Cuba with approximately 275 daily flights. Frontier started operating in July 1994 when there were two key opportunities in the external environment. First, two major competing airlines (Continental and United, which merged in the year 2012) had downsized their Denver operations and therefore opened up service gaps in several major markets that Frontier filled. Second, the city of Denver replaced the heavily congested Stapleton Airport with the much larger Denver International Airport.

In February 2004, United Airlines, the largest carrier operating out of Denver International Airport, made changes in the environment that resulted in a direct horizontal threat to Frontier: United Airlines launched its own low-fare affiliate. The new affiliate, Ted, was going head-to-head with Frontier. Peter McDonald, then vice president for operations for United Airlines, reported that Ted's cost per available seat mile was in the ballpark of Frontier's 8.3 cents. So what had been an opportunity for Frontier no longer remained one, given the launching of Ted. To make things even worse for Frontier, Southwest Airlines, another low-cost competitor, also entered the Denver market a few years later. Now, Frontier is only the third largest carrier in Denver after United and Southwest.

Analyzing the internal environment

How do you conduct an analysis of the internal environment? You need to think about strengths and weaknesses.

>> **Strengths** are internal characteristics that the organization can use to its advantage. For example, what are the organization's assets and the staff's key skills? Continuing with the Frontier airlines example I mentioned in a nearby sidebar, several key executives from other airlines were recruited, an important strength that was needed, given the emergence of horizontal threats. These executives created a senior management team with long-term experience in the Denver market.

>> **Weaknesses** are internal characteristics that hinder the success of your organization. These could include an obsolete organizational structure that doesn't allow for effective organization across units; the misalignment of organizational-, unit-, individual-level objectives; a talent pool with skills that have become obsolete, given changes in the industry and in technology.

Here are the factors you need to think about in your internal analysis.

>> **Organizational structure:** For example, is the current structure conducive to fast and effective communication?

>> **Organizational culture:** Organizational culture includes the unwritten norms and values espoused by the members of the organization. For example, does the current organizational culture encourage or hinder innovation and entrepreneurial behaviors on the part of middle-level managers? Is there a culture in which new ideas and suggestions are quickly suppressed with the argument that "this has never been done before"?

>> **Politics:** For example, are the various units competing for resources in such a way that any type of cross-unit collaboration is virtually impossible? Or are units open and collaborative in cross-unit projects?

>> **Processes:** For example, are the supply chains working properly? Are all touchpoints with customers working properly? Can customers reach us when they need to and receive a satisfying response when they do?

>> **Size:** For example, is the organization too small or too large? Is it growing too fast? Can it manage growth (or downsizing) effectively?

Table 5-1 below includes a summary list of external and internal trends to be considered when you conduct an environmental analysis.

Think about your current employer and take a look at this table. Where does your organization stand in regard to each of these important external and internal issues? Regarding the external issues, what are some of the opportunities and threats? Regarding the internal issues, what are some of the strengths and weaknesses?

TABLE 5-1

Trends to Consider When Conducting an Environmental Analysis

External Factors	Internal Factors
Driven by the line manager	Driven by HR
Driven by strategic business considerations	Driven by operational/administrative issues
Political/legal	Organizational culture
Social	Politics
Technological	Processes
Competitors	Size
Customers	
Suppliers	

Conducting a gap analysis

Now that you know the external and internal issues facing your organization, you can use information on opportunities, threats, strengths, and weaknesses to do a *gap analysis.*

With a gap analysis, you look at the external environment in relation to the internal environment. Essentially, you pair external opportunities and threats with internal strengths and weaknesses so that you can learn whether or not you are facing a competitive situation as ranked from most to least competitive in the following list:

>> **Opportunity + Strength = Leverage.** The best combination of external and internal factors happens when there is an opportunity in the environment and a matching strength within the organization to take advantage of that opportunity. These are obvious directions that the organization should pursue.

>> **Opportunity + Weakness = Constraint.** In a constraint situation, the external opportunity is present; however, the internal situation isn't conducive to taking advantage of the external opportunity. At IBM (see the nearby sidebar), this situation could have taken place if IBM did not have the internal capabilities to develop software and other products for the network-connected devices and specialized components. The external opportunity would still be there, but, absent the internal capabilities, it would not turn into an advantageous business scenario.

>> **Threat + Strength = Vulnerability.** In this situation, there is an external threat, but this threat can be contained because of the presence of internal strengths. If this had been the case at IBM, the company would not have been able to take advantage of a new situation; nevertheless, existing strengths would have allowed IBM to continue to operate in other areas.

IBM LEVERAGES ITS STRENGTHS

IBM is the world's largest information technology company. IBM has concluded that the personal computer-driven client-server computing models no longer apply and that network-based computing is taking over. IBM's CEO Virginia (Ginni) Rometty said, "Digital is the wires, but digital intelligence, or artificial intelligence as some people call it, is about much more than that. This next decade is about how you combine those and become a cognitive business. It's the dawn of a new era."

So IBM shifted the focus to servers, databases, and software for transaction and data management. Also, IBM recognized the upsurge of network-connected devices, including smartphones and tablets. To take advantage of this external opportunity, IBM now focuses its resources on supporting network systems, developing software for the network-connected devices, and manufacturing specialized components.

These are the types of products that IBM offers today: cloud, cognitive, data and analytics, internet of things, it infrastructure, mobile, and security. This is a long way from IBM's first products involving clocks and cash registers! IBM built up its software capabilities through internal development and outside acquisitions. In short, IBM developed a leverage factor by identifying internal strengths that matched external opportunities, which in turn leads to a successful business model.

>> **Threat + Weakness = Problem.** In the worst scenario, there is an external threat and an accompanying internal weakness. For example, in the 1980s, IBM refused to adapt to the demands of the emerging microcomputer market (today's personal systems including desktops, laptops, and notebooks). IBM did not have the internal capability to address customers' needs for personal systems, and instead, continued to focus on its internal strength: the mainframe computer. IBM's poor performance in the early 1990s was a direct consequence of this problem situation: The external threat (increasing demand for personal systems and dwindling demand for mainframe computers) was met with an internal weakness (lack of ability to shift internal focus from the mainframe to the personal systems and devices).

Creating and Understanding Your Organization's Mission and Vision

Now that you understand your organization's leverage, constraints, vulnerabilities, and problems, you need to understand who you are as an organization and what you do. This information will then be included in the organization's mission statement.

Creating your mission

The mission statement summarizes the organization's most important reason for its existence. Mission statements provide information on the purpose of the organization and its scope. They need to answer the following questions:

>> Why does the organization exist?

>> What is the scope of the organization's activities?

>> Who are the customers served?

>> What are the products or services offered?

Creating your vision

An organization's vision is a statement of future aspirations. In other words, the vision statement includes a description of what the organization would like to become in the future — about 5 to 10 years out.

MISSION STATEMENT AT COCA-COLA

This is the mission statement for the Coca-Cola Company:

- To refresh the world in mind, body, and spirit.
- To inspire moments of optimism and happiness through our brands and actions.
- To create value and make a difference.

Presumably, Coca-Cola's mission statement was preceded by an environmental analysis examining external and internal trends. I don't have information on this, but what I do know is that this mission statement provides some information regarding the four questions noted in this chapter.

Based on this mission statement, we have information about why the company exists ("to refresh the world") and the scope of the organization's activities ("to inspire moments of optimism and happiness, create value, and make a difference"). The mission statement doesn't, however, include information about who are the customers served. Also, there is no information about specific products (for example, Fanta, Sprite, Minute Maid, Powerade, Dasani, Fresca). More specific and detailed information would be needed if Coca-Cola's mission statement is to be used by its various units to create their own mission statements. More detailed information is also needed if both the organization and unit mission statements are to be used as input for individual job descriptions, which will, in turn, be used for managing individual and team performance. State-of-the-science mission statements include the following components:

- Basic product or service to be offered (does what?)
- Primary markets or customer groups to be served (to whom?)
- Unique benefits and advantages of products or services (with what benefits?)
- Technology to be used in production or delivery
- Fundamental concern for survival through growth and profitability

TIP

You create your vision statement typically after the mission statement because you first need to know who you are and your purpose before you can figure out who you want to be in the future.

Mission and vision statements are often combined, and therefore, in many cases, it is difficult to differentiate one from the other. In such cases, the vision statement usually includes two components: *a core ideology,* which is referred to as the mission, and an *envisioned future,* which is what is referred to as the vision per se. The core ideology contains the core purpose and core values of an organization, and the envisioned future specifies long-term objectives and a picture of what the organization aspires to in the long term.

Are you interested in creating a powerful, useful, and state-of-the-art vision statement? Then your vision statement needs to have the following characteristics:

>> **Brief:** A vision statement should be brief so that employees can remember it.

>> **Verifiable:** A good vision statement should be able to stand the reality test.

>> **Bound by a timeline:** A good vision statement specifies a timeline for the fulfillment of various aspirations.

>> **Current:** Outdated vision statements are not useful. Vision statements should be updated on an ongoing basis, ideally as soon as the old vision is fulfilled.

>> **Focused:** A good vision statement isn't a laundry list of aspirations, but rather, focuses on just a few (perhaps not more than three or four) aspects of an organization's performance that are important to future success.

>> **Understandable:** Vision statements need to be written in a clear and straightforward manner so that they are understood by all employees.

>> **Inspiring:** Good vision statements make employees feel good about their organization's direction and motivate them to help achieve the vision.

>> **A stretch:** Consider Microsoft's vision statement in the 1980s of "putting a computer on every desk and in every home," which was the vision when CEO Bill Gates started the MS-DOS operating system. This vision statement was such a stretch that it was considered ludicrous at a time when the mainframe computer still reigned supreme and the first personal computers were being made and sold. But that vision became a reality. Two decades later, Microsoft revised its vision as follows: "putting a computer in every car and every pocket." Once again, this vision has now become a reality — in the form of car dashboards and smartphones.

MISSION AND VISION STATEMENTS AT SPECTRUM BRANDS

Spectrum Brands provides an example of combining mission and vision into one statement. Spectrum Brands is a global consumer products company and a leading supplier of batteries, kitchen appliances, shaving and grooming products, personal care products, pet supplies, and home and garden products. Spectrum Brands' combined mission and vision statement is the following:

Spectrum Brands is a rapidly growing, global, diversified, market-driven consumer products company.

- We will continue to grow our company through a combination of strategic acquisitions and organic growth.

- We will strengthen our brands and generate growth through emphasis on brand strategy/marketing and innovative product technology, design and packaging.

- We will leverage IT infrastructure, distribution channels, purchasing power and operational structure globally to continue to drive efficiencies and reduce costs.

- We will profitably expand distribution in all served markets.

This statement includes components of a mission statement (i.e., "a rapidly growing, global, diversified, market-driven consumer products company") as well as components of a vision statement (e.g., "will strengthen our brands and generate growth through emphasis on brand strategy/marketing and innovative product technology, design and packaging"). Thus, this statement combines the present (i.e., who the company is, what it does) with the future (i.e., aspirations).

Setting Up Objectives and Strategies Based on Your Mission and Vision

Ok, now you know your organization's external opportunities and threats. You also know the internal strengths and weaknesses. And you have your mission and vision.

So you now can realistically establish objectives that will further your mission. The purpose of setting such objectives is to formalize statements about what your organization hopes to achieve in the medium- to long-range period (that is, within the next three to five years). Also, once you set objectives, you need to know what strategies you will implement to reach them.

Setting up objectives

Objectives provide more specific information regarding how the mission will be implemented. Objectives also provide a good basis for making decisions by keeping the desired outcomes in mind.

Objectives provide the basis for how to define and measure performance because they allow for a comparison of what needs to be achieved versus what each unit, group, and individual is achieving. Also, objectives can also be a source of motivation and provide employees with a more tangible target for which to strive.

Matthew S. Levatich, president and CEO of Harley-Davidson, Inc. (the motorcycle manufacturer) since May 2015, said that a major objective is to

> ". . .deliver those customer-growth objectives, not chassis-growth objectives. It sounds kind of trite: We're not really in the business of manufacturing motorcycles. We're in the business of building customers. When I joined [in 1994], we had made 86,000 motorcycles the prior year. Compare that to the peak in 2006 at about 350,000. It's less today, but we're working hard to get that volume back up. But the emphasis has shifted from making motorcycles to what I would say is identifying and finding customers — with product, with distribution, with everything we do at the company."

Operationally speaking, this means that Harley-Davidson is trying to achieve the following:

» **Lead in every market.** Harley-Davidson plans to achieve the leadership position in the 601cc motorcycle segment. As the company's CEO Matt Levatich put it, "This isn't just about competing, but winning."

» **Grow sales at a faster rate.** Harley-Davidson plans to grow its retail sales in the United States as well as internationally at a faster pace. In the next five years, the company plans to add 150–200 dealers globally to achieve this objective.

» **Grow earnings faster than revenues.** Harley-Davidson has stated an objective of growing its revenues over the next five years. It is also aiming at growing its earnings faster than its revenues through 2020.

These objectives provide a clear direction for Harley-Davidson. In fact, they provide useful information to guide unit-level objectives as well as individual and team performance. The entire organization has a clear sense of focus because all members know that there are clear objectives in terms of market presence, growth, sales, earnings, and financial performance.

Setting up strategies

So you now know what our organization is all about (mission), what it wants to be in the future (vision), and what it needs to do to get there (objectives).

What remains is a discussion of how to fulfill the mission and vision and how to achieve the objectives. This is done by creating strategies, which are descriptions of game plans or how-to procedures to reach the stated objectives. The strategies could address issues of growth, survival, turnaround, stability, innovation, talent acquisition, and leadership, among others.

Did you know that there is an entire field of study called "strategic management studies" devoted to the development and implementation of strategies? In fact, Deloitte, Boston Consulting Group, Bain & Company, KPMG, and Accenture offer consulting services in the domain of business strategy. Also, there are hundreds of books written on this topic. To give you a brief overview of some possibilities, consider the following strategies, out of many, that could be implemented:

>> **Operations:** Addressing issues about the global economic environment in terms of market, capital, interest rates, labor costs, taxes, regulations, and available infrastructure

>> **Competitiveness:** Operating at optimum levels of productivity and efficiency: continuous benchmarking, use of statistical tools for process optimization, total quality model, gathering data on customer expectations and experiences

>> **Optimal use of resources:** Optimization of global collaboration with suppliers, parts standardization and reduction, and flexible manufacturing and services

>> **Global corporate culture:** Respecting cultural values of different regions, constant training at all levels, policies of respect and recognition to individuals, and selecting highly qualified employees

>> **Research and development:** Ongoing initiatives aimed at innovation and creativity

Linking Your Organization's and Unit's Strategic Plans with Job Descriptions

As shown in Figure 5-1 earlier in this chapter, the organization's strategic plan has a direct impact on the units' strategic plans. Similarly, the vision statement, objectives, and strategies of the various units need to be congruent with the overall organizational vision, objectives, and strategies.

Linking the strategy of the organization and its units

The congruence between the mission of the organization and its various units is important, regardless of the type of industry and the size of the organization. High-performing organizations have a clear alignment in the mission and vision of the overall and unit-level mission and vision statements.

Going back to the example of Microsoft, see the example below including a job announcement describing the position of Performance Solutions Group Manager in Microsoft's training and education unit.

EXAMPLE

Consider the case of Microsoft Corporation and how the organization's mission statement is linked to one particular unit — Training and Education.

Microsoft's Mission

Our mission is to empower every person and every organization on the planet to achieve more.

What we value

- **Innovation:** Learn about innovations from our computer science research organization. With more than 1,000 researchers in our labs, it's one of the largest in the world.

- **Diversity and inclusion:** Explore how we maximize every person's contribution — from our employees to our customers — so that the way we innovate naturally includes diverse thought.

- **Corporate social responsibility:** See how we work to be a responsible partner to those who place their trust in us, conducting business in a way that is inclusive, transparent, and respectful of human rights.

- **Philanthropies:** Find out how we empower people by investing technology, money, employee talent, and the company's voice in programs that promote digital inclusion.

- **Environment:** Discover how we lead the way in sustainability and use our technologies to minimize the impact of our operations and products.

- **Trustworthy computing:** Check out how we deliver secure, private, and reliable computing experiences based on sound business practices.

Now, consider the mission statement Microsoft's Training and Education unit:

> With the charter to enable Microsoft engineering workgroups to realize their full potential for innovation and performance through world-class learning strategies, Microsoft Training and Education (MSTE) provides performance support strategies to support the overall corporation's software engineering efforts. Our efforts include the design, development, and delivery of learning programs, on-line information, and resources for Microsoft employees. MSTE's integrated suite of technical offerings supports our objective of having a significant impact on Microsoft's business. We promote best practices, cross-group communication, Microsoft expertise and Industry expertise.

As you can see, the mission of the training and education unit regarding the realization of people's full potential for innovation and performance is consistent with the overall mission to empower every person, which plays a central role. Of course, MSTE's mission is more focused on issues specifically relevant to the training and education function. But the link between the two mission statements is obvious.

REMEMBER

The organization's strategic plan, including the mission, vision, objectives, and strategies, cascades down to all organizational levels. Thus, each division, branch, department, or unit also creates its own strategic plan, which should be consistent with the organization's overall plan.

Linking the organization and units with job descriptions

Continuing with the sequence of components shown in Figure 5-1, job descriptions also need to be congruent with the organization and unit mission, vision, objectives, and strategies.

Job descriptions are important because they serve as a roadmap for what individuals are supposed to do, how, and what results will be produced. So, if job descriptions are consistent with the organization and unit mission, vision, objectives, and strategies, results produced by individuals and teams will contribute to the success of their units and organization as a whole.

TIP

Job descriptions are particularly important for new employees because they set clear expectations from day one.

EXAMPLE

After the strategic plan is completed, it is useful to update the existing job descriptions to make sure employees are focusing on the things that matter the most for the organization. Take this example from Microsoft:

Job Description for Performance Solutions Group Manager in Microsoft's Training and Education Unit

As the Performance Solutions Group Manager, you will be accountable for developing and delivering on a portal strategy that touches over 20,000 employees worldwide and involves a complex data delivery system. Additionally, the person is responsible for defining the cutting-edge tool suite used by the team to develop and maintain the portal, the content housed by the group, and all e-learning solutions. Key initiatives include redesigning the Engineering Excellence Guide within the next 6 months and evolving it over the next 18 months to 3 years to become the industry-leading performance support site. Key challenges include maintaining and managing the cutting-edge tool suite used by the team and driving a clear vision for an industry-leading portal and content delivery plan. Qualifications for this position are a minimum of five years of senior management experience, preferably in knowledge management, e-learning, or Web-based product development roles; ability to think strategically and exercise sound business judgment on behalf of Microsoft; excellent leadership, communication, interpersonal, and organizational skills; firsthand experience delivering/shipping Web-based learning and content management solutions; proven record of successful team management; and ability to work well independently and under pressure, while being flexible and adaptable to rapid change. Knowledge of performance support and training procedures and processes is preferred. With the charter to enable Microsoft engineering workgroups to realize their full potential for innovation and performance through world-class learning strategies, Microsoft Training and Education (MSTE) provides performance support strategies to support the overall corporation's software engineering efforts. Our efforts include the design, development, and delivery of learning programs, online information, and resources for Microsoft employees. MSTE's integrated suite of technical offerings supports our objective of having a significant impact on Microsoft's business. We promote best practices, cross-group communication, Microsoft expertise and Industry expertise.

This job description makes the link between the individual position and MSTE quite clear. First, the description includes MSTE's mission statement so that individuals become aware of how their specific role fits within the overall mission of the department. Second, the job description includes language to the effect that the work must lead to an "industry leading" product, which is consistent not only with MSTE's mission, but also with Microsoft's overall mission. Third, in the needed qualifications section, there is a clear overlap between those needed for this specific position and those mentioned in MSTE's as well as in Microsoft's overall mission. In short, the person working as performance solutions group manager has a clear sense not only of her position, but also of how behaviors and expected results are consistent with expectations about MSTE and Microsoft in general.

REMEMBER

The tasks and knowledge, skills, and abilities (KSAs) included in individual job descriptions must be congruent with the organization's and unit's strategic plans. Job descriptions should include activities that, if executed well, will help execute the mission and vision.

WARNING

Job descriptions that are detached from strategic priorities will lead to performance evaluations focused on behaviors and results that are not central to an organization's success, and the performance management system will be seen as irrelevant and a big waste of time by managers and employee alike.

Chapter **6**

Becoming a Performance Management Leader

Performance management systems don't help employees develop and improve their performance if managers don't guide and facilitate the employee development process. To do so, if you are a manager, you must learn several important skills to become a performance management *leader*.

What do performance managers do? They serve as coaches. They observe and document performance accurately. And they give both positive feedback (including praise) and constructive feedback (also referred to as negative feedback).

Are you ready to learn how to do each of these things and become a performance management leader? Ok, let's do it.

Becoming an Effective Coach

Coaching is a collaborative and ongoing process in which the manager interacts with direct reports and takes an active role and interest in their performance.

Good coaches do three things: They direct, they motivate, and they reward employee behavior.

Coaching is a day-to-day and ongoing function that involves observing performance, complimenting good work, and helping to correct and improve any performance that doesn't meet expectations. Coaching is also concerned with long-term performance and involves ensuring that each employee's development plan is achieved.

Effective coaches establish a helping and trusting relationship, and this is particularly important when the supervisor and direct report don't share similar cultural backgrounds, as is often the case with expatriates or when implementing global performance management systems.

Of course, coaching isn't beneficial to large organizations only. In fact, it's particularly important in small and medium-sized enterprises (SMEs) as well. A study conducted in the United Kingdom involving more than 1,200 SME managers over a three-year period showed that coaching training was seen as a very positive experience. Also, for some of the SME managers, coaching training was seen as a "life changing experience."

Four guiding principles of effective coaches

There are four guiding principles you need to follow to become an effective coach:

>> **A good coaching relationship is essential.** For coaching to work, the relationship between the coach and the employee must be trusting and collaborative. As noted by industrial and organizational psychology Professors Farr and Jacobs from Penn State University, the "collective trust" of all those involved in the process is necessary. You must listen in order to understand. In other words, the coach needs to try to walk in the employee's shoes and view the job and organization from his or her perspective. Overall, you need to coach with empathy and compassion.

Establishing a good relationship with your employees and being a compassionate coach has an important benefit for you as a coach: It's an antidote to the chronic stress experienced by many managers. Why? The experience of compassion elicits responses within the human body that arouse the parasympathetic nervous system (PSNS), which can help mitigate stress.

>> **The employee is the source and director of change.** You must understand that the employee is the source of change and self-growth. After all, the purpose of coaching is to change employee behavior and set a direction for

what the employee will do better in the future. This type of change will not happen if the employee isn't in the driver's seat. Accordingly, you need to facilitate the employee's setting the agenda, goals, and direction.

>> **The employee is whole and unique.** You must understand that each employee is a unique individual with several job-related and job-unrelated identities such as customer service rep, father, avid football fan, and a unique personal history. The coach must try to create a whole and complete and rich picture of the employee so that employees bring their whole selves to work and are fully engaged. It will be beneficial if you have knowledge of the employee's life and can help the employee connect his life and work experiences in meaningful ways.

>> **The coach is the facilitator of the employee's growth.** Your main role is one of facilitation. You must direct the process and help with the content of a developmental plan. You must resist the temptation to take control. Keep an *attitude of exploration*: Help expand the employee's awareness of strengths, resources, and challenges, and also help with goal setting.

You need to understand that coaching isn't something done *to* the employee, but done *with* the employee.

Based on the four guiding principles, it's evident that coaching requires quite a bit of effort from the managers. But when done right, you can become a true performance management leader and your organization is able to create a healthy "coaching culture."

Seven behaviors of effective coaches

Given the available empirical evidence, coaching helps turn feedback into results. For this to happen, you need to engage in the following specific behaviors:

>> **Establish development objectives.** You work jointly with the employees in creating the development plan and its objectives.

>> **Communicate effectively.** You maintain regular and clear communication with employees about their performance, including both behaviors and results.

>> **Motivate employees.** You must reward positive performance. When you do it, employees are motivated to repeat the same level of positive performance in the future.

>> **Document performance.** You observe employee behaviors and results. You gather evidence about instances of good and poor performance.

>> **Give feedback.** You measure employee performance and progress toward goals. You praise good performance and point out instances of substandard performance. You also help employees avoid poor performance in the future.

>> **Diagnose performance problems and performance decline.** You must listen to employees and gather information to determine whether performance deficiencies and declines in performance are the result of a lack of knowledge and skills, abilities, or motivation or whether they stem from situational and contextual factors beyond the control of the employee. Diagnosing performance problems is important because such a diagnosis dictates whether the course of action should be, for example, providing the employee with resources so she can acquire more knowledge and skills, or addressing contextual issues that are beyond the control of the employee (for example, the employee is usually late in delivering the product because he receives information too late).

>> **Develop employees.** You provide financial support and resources for employee development (for example, funding training, allowing time away from the job for developmental activities). By helping employees plan for the future and by giving challenging assignments, you help employees learn new things.

Not all coaches follow the four guiding principles or engage in the seven behaviors I just described. But managers who do become performance management leaders. In fact, some have become legendary, as is the case of Jack Welch, whom I discuss in a nearby sidebar.

JACK WELCH: LEGENDARY PERFORMANCE MANAGEMENT LEADER

Jack Welch was an extremely dedicated performance management leader when he was CEO of General Electric (GE). To get involved with his employees, Welch spoke during a class held at a three-week developmental course for GE's high-potential managers. Over the course of his career, he attended more than 750 of these classes, engaging over 15,000 GE managers and executives. During these presentations, he expected to answer hard questions and he communicated honestly and candidly with his employees. Also, he invited all the participants to talk with him after the course concluded. In addition to attending these sessions, he held meetings with his top 500 executives every January.

Although Welch did not engage in formal coaching, he used the opportunities to communicate his expectations and receive feedback from the various business groups at GE. Welch also conducted formal performance reviews in which he engaged in several of the seven behaviors, including establishing developmental objectives, motivating employees, documenting performance, giving feedback, and diagnosing performance problems. He set performance targets and monitored them throughout the year. Each year, the operating heads of GE's 12 businesses received individual, two-page, handwritten notes about their performance. Welch attached the previous year's comments to the new reviews with comments in the margin about the progress made by the individual managers toward his goal or the work that he or she still needed to do to reach the goal. Then he distributed bonuses and reiterated the goals for the upcoming year. This process cascaded throughout the organization, as other operating heads engaged in the same performance review discussions with their direct reports.

Another example of Welch's coaching behaviors occurred after he had heard customer complaints about a specific product. Welch charged the manager of the division with improving the productivity of that product fourfold. The manager sent Welch detailed weekly reports over the course of the next four years. Welch would send the reports back every three or four weeks, with comments congratulating successes or pointing out areas in which the manager needed to improve. The manager stated that the fact that the CEO took the time to read his reports each week and send back comments motivated him to reach the lofty goal that Welch had set for him.

In addition to this, Jack Welch took the time to recognize hourly workers and managers who impressed him. For example, after one high-ranking leader turned down a promotion and transfer because he did not want his daughter to change schools, Welch sent him a personal note stating that he admired the man for many reasons and he appreciated his decision to put his family first. The employee explained later that this incident proved that Welch cared about him both as a person and as an employee.

What do we learn from this case? Jack Welch was a legendary performance management leader who developed his employees by setting expectations, communicating clearly, documenting and diagnosing performance, motivating and rewarding his employees, and taking an interest in their personal development. In fact, he followed the principles and engaged in virtually all four guiding principles and seven behaviors I cover in this chapter.

Understanding your coaching style

Your personality and behavioral preferences influence your coaching style. There are four main coaching styles: driver, persuader, amiable, and analyzer.

>> You can adopt a **driving style** in which you tell your employee being coached what to do. Assume that you want to provide guidance regarding how to deal with a customer. In this situation, the preference for a driver is to say to the employee, "You must talk to the customer in this way." Such coaches are assertive, speak quickly and often firmly, usually talk about tasks and facts, are not very expressive, and expose a narrow range of personal feelings to others.

>> Coaches can use a **persuading style** in which they try to sell what they want the employee to do. Someone who is a persuader would try to explain to the employee why it's beneficial for the organization, as well as for the employee himself, to talk to a customer in a specific way. Like drivers, persuaders are assertive, but they tend to use expansive body gestures, talk more about people and relationships, and expose others to a broad range of personal feelings.

>> Other coaches may adopt an **amiable style** and want everyone to be happy. Such coaches are likely to be more subjective than objective and direct employees to talk to customers in a certain way because it "feels" like the right thing to do or because the employee feels it's the right way to do it. Such coaches tend not to be very assertive and to speak deliberately and pause often, seldom interrupt others, and make many conditional statements.

>> Coaches may have a preference for an **analyzing style** in which they are logical and systematic and then follow rules and procedures when providing a recommendation. To use the same example, such analyzer coaches may tell employees to talk to a customer in a specific way "because this is what the manual says." Analyzers are therefore not very assertive, but like drivers, are likely to talk about tasks and facts rather than personal feelings.

TIP

No style is necessarily superior to the others. Performance management leadership involves sometimes providing direction, sometimes persuading employees how to do things a certain way, sometimes showing empathy and creating positive effects, and sometimes paying close attention to established rules and procedures.

WARNING

If you adopt only one of the coaching styles, and never the others, you will not be able to help employees develop and grow. Ineffective coaches stick to one style only and cannot adapt to using any of the other styles. On the other hand, adaptive coaches, who are able to adjust their style according to an employee's needs, are most effective.

Observing and Documenting Performance

If you think that observing and documenting performance is easy, think again. Why? You have three type of constraints going against you:

>> **Time constraints:** Managers and peers are too busy to gather and document information about an employee's progress toward his developmental goals. So, too much time may elapse between the assignment of the activity and when there is a check on the employee's progress.

>> **Situational constraints:** Many managers are often unable to observe employees as they engage in developmental activities and don't have firsthand knowledge about their performance. For example, managers don't observe the extent to which an employee enrolled in an online course is an active participant and contributor or a passive learner. In this context, it's appropriate to gather performance data from peers or others who are able to observe performance directly.

>> **Activity constraints:** When the developmental activity is highly unstructured, such as an employee reading a book, the manager has to wait until the activity is completed to assess whether the activity has been beneficial.

How can you address these constraints and make sure that you will be able to observe and evaluate an employee's performance regarding developmental activities, which is critical you to become a performance management leader? See the nearby sidebar for a description of how this is done at Hallmark.

You also need to understand the forces that motivate managers to invest time and effort, or not, in the development of their employees. Clearly, some managers will be more motivated than others to help their direct reports because they may be "givers" rather than "takers." In other words, there are individual differences in how different people behave toward others.

TRAINING MANAGERS TO BECOME PERFORMANCE MANAGEMENT LEADERS AT HALLMARK

Hallmark sought to help managers become performance management leaders. To do this, it initiated a coaching training program that has been well received and viewed as a strategic benefit to the company. U.S.-based Hallmark is a retailer and wholesaler of greeting cards, stationery, flowers, and gifts, with operations in the United States and Great Britain. The training aimed at improving skill on how to increase two-way communication, with a greater frequency of communication and increased interaction of managers with employees. Training sessions included self-assessment, small group role-playing, and viewing video clips to enhance understanding of the role of communication. Engagement training focused on gaining the trust of employees as well as their involvement and ownership in business outcomes. Follow-up resources were also made available for managers to continue to improve their leadership competency. Following the training in this area, managers gave positive feedback, and employee surveys have shown that employee engagement has increased at all levels of the organization.

In spite of differences in how people tend to behave naturally, it's important that managers see a direct connection between their efforts to develop people around them and outcomes for themselves.

TIP

What does the manager gain if her employee's developmental activities are supervised appropriately? What does the manager gain if she becomes a performance management leader? You need to be able to answer these questions convincingly if you hope managers in your organization will become performance management leaders.

Why documenting performance is so important

I cannot overemphasize the importance of documenting an employee's progress toward the achievement of developmental goals. Similarly, it's critical to document employee performance in general. Why is this so important for performance management leaders to do so? Consider the following reasons:

>> **Minimize memory errors.** Observing and evaluating developmental activities, and performance in general, is a complex cognitive task. Thus, documentation helps prevent memory-related errors.

>> **Eliminated mystery and create trust.** When documentation exists to support evaluations, there is no mystery regarding the outcomes. This, in turn, promotes trust and acceptance of decisions based on the evaluation provided.

>> **Plan for the future.** Documenting developmental activities and their outcomes enables discussion about specific facts instead of assumptions and hearsay. An examination of these facts permits better planning of developmental activities for the future.

>> **Provide legal protection.** Specific laws prohibit discrimination against members of various classes (such as gender or religion) in how developmental activities are allocated. For example, it's prohibited to provide male employees with better developmental opportunities than female employees. So keeping accurate records of what developmental activities employees have completed and with what degree of success, as well as performance in general, provides a good line of defense in case of litigation based on discrimination or wrongful termination.

FAILED PERFORMANCE DOCUMENTATION AT WESTERN ELECTRIC CO.

It's important to keep thorough performance documentation and take actions consistent with this documentation. To illustrate this point, let's take a look at the outcomes of a legal case involving Western Electric Co. John E. Cleverly, an employee at Western Electric Co., was discharged after 14 years of good service. Western Electric was found guilty of age discrimination, and Cleverly was awarded back pay because the documentation indicated that Cleverly had been given adequate performance ratings and increases to his salary over a course of 14 years. Upon his discharge, six months before his pension vested, Cleverly was informed that one reason for his discharge was to make room for younger employees.

As illustrated by this example, you should take the issue of documenting performance seriously. In this case, the documentation available indicated the employee had a valid claim. In other cases, documentation could be used to discount charges of discrimination. If Cleverly had alleged age discrimination, but the company could show that his performance was declining over time, then the company could have won the case.

Documenting performance accurately

What can performance management leaders do to document performance regarding developmental activities, and performance in general, in a useful and constructive way? Here are seven success factors:

- **Be specific.** Document specific events and outcomes. Avoid making general statements, such as "He's lazy." Provide specific examples to illustrate your point, for example, "He turns in reports after deadlines at least once a month."

- **Use adjectives and adverbs sparingly.** The use of evaluative adjectives (e.g., good, poor) and adverbs (e.g., speedily, sometimes) lead to ambiguous interpretations. In addition, it's not be clear whether the level of achievement has been average or outstanding.

- **Balance positives with negatives.** Document instances of both good and poor performance. Don't focus only on the positives or only on the negatives.

- **Focus on job-related information.** Focus on information that is job-related, and specifically, related to the developmental activities and goals at hand.

>> **Be comprehensive.** Include information on performance regarding all developmental goals and activities and cover the entire review period as opposed to a shorter time period. Also, document the performance of all employees, not just those who are not achieving their developmental goals.

>> **Standardize procedures.** Use the same method and format to document information for all employees.

>> **Describe observable behavior and results.** Phrase your notes in behavioral and results terms and avoid statements that would imply subjective judgment or prejudice.

Obviously, not all managers do a good job of documenting performance about the accomplishment of developmental goals or performance in general. Do you? Think about the last time you evaluated someone else's performance. Which of the seven success factors do you think you may have left out?

Giving Feedback Effectively

Giving feedback to an employee regarding her progress toward achieving her goals is a key component of the coaching process. Keep in mind that feedback is information about past behavior that is given with the goal of improving future performance.

Although "back" is part of feedback, giving feedback has both a past and a future component. This is why, when done properly, I prefer to use the label "feedforward."

Feedback includes information about both positive and negative aspects of job performance and lets employees know how well they are doing.

Making sure feedback serves a purpose

Feedback is important in the context of performance regarding development activities and goals. However, feedback goes beyond that because it information about performance in general. Although feedback isn't a magic bullet for performance improvement, it serves several important purposes:

>> **Helps build confidence and self-efficacy:** Praising good performance builds employee confidence about future performance. It also lets employees know that their manager cares about them. Also, praising good performance

enhances self-efficacy: An employee's belief that she will succeed in specific situations or accomplish a task.

TIP

Self-efficacy isn't the actual probability that the employee will succeed, but an employee's subjective belief that she will. Self-efficacy is critical because if an employee doesn't believe he has a good chance of improving his performance, he isn't likely to even try.

>> **Develops competence:** Communicating clearly about what has been done right and how to do the work correctly is valuable information that helps employees become more competent and improve their performance. Also, communicating clearly about what hasn't been done right and explaining what to do the next time provides useful information so that past mistakes are not repeated.

>> **Enhances engagement:** Receiving feedback and discussing performance issues allow employees to understand their roles in the unit and organization as a whole. This, in turn, helps employees become more engaged in the unit and the organization.

WARNING

The mere presence of feedback, even if it's delivered correctly, doesn't necessarily mean that all these purposes will be fulfilled. For example, a review of 131 studies that examined the effects of feedback on performance concluded that 38 percent of the feedback programs reviewed had a negative effect on performance. In other words, in many cases, the implementation of feedback led to lower performance levels! This can happen when, for example, feedback doesn't include useful information or isn't delivered in the right way.

Avoiding the very high cost of NOT providing feedback

Sure, giving feedback takes time and effort. But consider the very high cost of not providing feedback:

>> Organizations deprive employees of a chance to improve their performance.

>> Organizations are stuck with chronic poor performance because employees did not recognize any performance problems and felt justified in continuing to perform at substandard levels.

>> Employees develop inaccurate perceptions of how their performance is regarded by others.

Making sure feedback is beneficial

Given that, overall, feedback systems can be beneficial, what can you do to make the most of them? These are the success factors:

>> **Timeliness:** Deliver feedback as close to the performance event as possible. For feedback to be most meaningful, give it immediately after the event.

>> **Frequency:** Provide feedback on an ongoing basis — daily, if possible. Because performance improvement is an ongoing activity, feedback about performance is also given on an ongoing basis.

>> **Specificity:** Include specific work behaviors, results, and the situation in which these behaviors and results were observed. Feedback isn't about the employee and how the employee "is" but about behaviors and results and situations in which these behaviors and results occurred.

>> **Verifiability:** Use information that is verifiable and accurate. Don't base it on inferences or rumors. If you use information that is verifiable, feedback will be more accurate and more readily accepted.

>> **Consistency:** Make feedback consistent. In other words, information about specific aspects of performance should not vary unpredictably between overwhelming praise and harsh criticism.

>> **Privacy:** Give feedback in a place and at a time that prevent any potential embarrassment. This applies to both criticism and praise.

>> **Consequences:** Include contextual information that allows the employee to understand the importance and consequences of the behaviors and results in question.

EXAMPLE

Take the situation that an employee becomes frustrated and behaves inappropriately with an angry customer and the customer's complaint is not addressed satisfactorily. Feedback should explain the impact of these behaviors (such as behaving inappropriately) and results for the organization (for example, the customer's problem was not resolved, the customer was upset, and the customer was not likely to give repeat business to the organization).

>> **Description first, evaluation second:** Focus first on describing behaviors and results rather than on evaluating and judging behaviors and results. It is better first to report what has been observed, and once there is agreement about what happened, to evaluate what has been observed.

WARNING

If evaluation takes place first, employees may become defensive and reject the feedback.

>> **Performance continuum:** Describe performance as a continuum, going from less to more in the case of good performance, and from more to less in the case of poor performance. In other words, include information on how to display good performance behaviors more often and poor performance behaviors less often.

TIP

Performance is a matter of degree, and even the worst performer is likely to show nuggets of good performance that can be described as a starting point for a discussion on how to improve performance.

>> **Pattern identification:** Feedback is most useful if it's about a pattern of poor performance, rather than isolated events or mistakes. Identifying a pattern of poor performance also allows for a better understanding of the causes leading to poor performance.

>> **Confidence in the employee:** Include a statement that the manager has confidence that the employee will be able to improve her performance. It's important for the employee to hear this from the manager, and this enhances employee self-efficacy. This reinforces the idea that feedback is about performance and not the performer.

WARNING

Say that you have confidence in the employee only you really believe the employee can improve his performance. In the case of a chronic poor performance, this type of information could be used out of context later if the employee is fired.

>> **Advice and idea generation:** Feedback can include advice given by the supervisor about how to improve performance. In addition, however, the employee should play an active role in generating ideas about how to improve performance in the future.

An example of effective feedback

EXAMPLE

Alexandra, a supervisor, has observed a specific performance event and provides feedback to her direct report. Alexandra is the manager of a small retail store with approximately five employees. With a small staff, Alexandra looks for coaching opportunities on a weekly basis. Alexandra is working with Caleb today, and she has just witnessed him complete a customer sale. Caleb did not follow several steps, however, that should be included at each sale, and because the store is now empty, Alexandra decides it's a perfect opportunity for a coaching session.

ALEXANDRA: Hey, Caleb, that was great the way that you just assisted that customer in finding her correct size in the jeans. Thanks for taking the extra time to help her.

CALEB: Thanks, Alexandra, not a problem.

ALEXANDRA: I would like to go over the sales transaction with you.

CALEB: Sure.

ALEXANDRA: After you helped the woman find her jeans, you promptly brought her over and rang her up. That was a good sale because those jeans were a full-priced item; however, you didn't complete all of the tasks associated with closing a sale. In the training last week, we discussed the importance of adding on additional sales, entering the customer's personal contact information in our system, and letting them know about upcoming sales.

CALEB: Yes, I just remembered us talking about that. When customers seem in a hurry, I feel bad about asking them additional questions.

ALEXANDRA: That's a very valid concern. Can we think of ways to increase the efficiency of adding these few steps into the sales transaction process so that you feel comfortable performing them in the future? I would like to help you do that because increasing the number of items you sell during each transaction could help you win the upcoming sales contests.

CALEB: That would be great. I would really like some new ideas about talking to customers.

ALEXANDRA: No problem. I know that you are a very capable salesperson. You have great customer service skills, and I think that you can improve your sales and possibly win one of the upcoming contests.

Alexandra and Caleb then generate ideas about how to improve Caleb's performance.

In this vignette, Alexandra demonstrated several of the suggestions to enhance the positive effects of feedback. She was specific about the behaviors and results, the information was verifiable, and it was timely because the behavior had just occurred. Also, because Alexandra communicates her expectations on a weekly basis, the information she provides is consistent. Finally, she described the behavior first, and then, evaluated its effectiveness; she communicated confidence in Caleb and she offered to help him generate ideas about how to improve his effectiveness.

On the other hand, Alexandra left out several important success factors while coaching Caleb. First, she did not communicate the consequences of his behavior, for example, that his failure to follow the procedures could hurt sales for the entire store. Although the vignette doesn't describe the idea generation portion of the feedback session, Alexandra did not describe behaviors that Caleb could use to improve his performance. Finally, Alexandra did not communicate to Caleb whether this behavior was a one-time incident or whether it was a pattern that was affecting his overall work performance.

Overall, if Alexandra continues to look for coaching opportunities with her employees, her relationship with her employees and their performance in the store will continue to improve. To be more effective as a performance management leader, however, she needs to work on communicating the patterns of behavior that result in poor performance and the consequences of continued poor performance.

ACTIVE LEARNING

Do you agree with these conclusions? What are the missing success factors in the interaction between Alexandra and Caleb? What would you have done differently if you were in Alexandra's shoes?

Giving praise

Effective feedback includes information about both good and poor performance. Although most people are a lot more comfortable giving feedback on good performance than they are on poor performance, you need to follow certain guidelines when giving praise:

>> Praise should be **sincere** and given only when it's deserved. If praise is given repeatedly and when it isn't deserved, employees are not able to see when a change in direction is needed.

>> Praise should be about **specific behaviors** or results and be given within context so that employees know what they need to repeat in the future. For example, a manager can say the following:

> Naomi, thanks for providing such excellent service to our client. Your efforts helped us renew our contract with them for another two years. It's these types of behaviors and results that our group needs to achieve our goal for this year. And, this is exactly what our company is all about: providing outstanding customer service.

>> In giving praise, **take your time and act pleased,** rather than rush through the information, looking embarrassed. Finally, avoid giving praise by referring to the absence of the negative like, for example, "not bad" or "better than last time." Instead, praise should emphasize the positives and be phrased, for example, as "I like the way you did that" or "I admire how you did that."

An example of effective praise

EXAMPLE

Consider the following vignette, which illustrates how a manager might give praise to her employee.

After the successful completion of a three-month project at a large telecommunications company, Hannah, the manager, wants to congratulate Jacob on a job well done. Hannah calls Jacob into her office one day after the project is completed.

> HANNAH: Thanks for stopping by, Jacob, and thank you for all of your hard work over the past three months. I know that I might not have congratulated you on every milestone you reached along the way, but I wanted to take the time to congratulate you now. Your organizational skills and ability to interact successfully with multiple departments led to the successful completion of the project on time and within budget.
>
> JACOB: Thanks, Hannah. I have really been putting extra effort into completing this project on time.
>
> HANNAH: It shows, Jacob, and I appreciate all of your hard work and dedication to this team and our department. Thanks again and congratulations on a great end to a long three months.

In this vignette, Hannah delivered praise to Jacob successfully and followed the recommendations I described earlier. She was sincere and made sure not to praise Jacob too often, so that when she did praise him, it was meaningful. She described how Jacob's organizational and project management skills led to the successful completion of the project. And, Hannah took her time in delivering the praise and made sure that Jacob took the praise seriously.

Giving constructive feedback

Constructive feedback includes information that performance has fallen short of what is expected. This type of feedback is sometimes called "negative feedback," but I use constructive feedback because this label has a more positive and future-oriented connotation.

REMEMBER

The goal of constructive feedback is to help employees improve their performance in the future. It isn't to punish, embarrass, or chastise them.

But we all know that managers are usually not very comfortable providing constructive feedback. These are the reasons why:

>> **Negative reactions and consequences:** I understand that you, as a manager, are possibly concerned that employees will react negatively. Negative reactions can include being defensive and even becoming angry at the information received. In addition, you may fear that the working relationship, or even friendship, with their direct reports may be affected adversely and that giving constructive feedback can introduce elements of mistrust and annoyance.

>> **Negative experiences in the past:** You possibly received constructive feedback at some point in your career and have experienced firsthand how feelings can be hurt. Receiving constructive feedback can be painful and upsetting, and managers don't want to put their direct reports in such a situation.

>> **Playing "God":** You may be reluctant to play the role of an all-knowing, judgmental God. You may feel that giving constructive feedback puts you in that position.

>> **Need for irrefutable and conclusive evidence:** You may not want to provide constructive feedback until after they have been able to gather irrefutable and conclusive evidence about a performance problem. Because this task may be perceived as too onerous, some managers choose to skip giving constructive feedback altogether.

Avoiding the dreaded feedback gap

If you avoid giving constructive feedback and employees avoid seeking it, the result is a *feedback gap:* Managers and employees mutually instigate and reinforce lack of communication, which creates a vacuum of meaningful exchanges about poor performance.

Eventually, the manager gives the employee the message that performance is adequate. But when performance problems exist, they become more and more intense over time. For example, clients may be so dissatisfied with the service they are receiving that they eventually choose to close their accounts and work instead with the competition. At that time, it becomes impossible for you to overlook the performance problem, and you will have no choice but to deliver the feedback. At this stage of the process, however, feedback is delivered too late, it's often punitive, and unhelpful.

Highlighting strengths

Constructive feedback is most useful when early coaching has been instrumental in identifying warning signs and the performance problem is still manageable. And constructive feedback is most likely to be accepted when it's given by a source who uses straight talk and not subtle pressure and when it's supported by hard data.

The traditional, also called *weaknesses-based approach,* involves identifying employee weaknesses: deficiencies in terms of their job performance, knowledge, and skills. Then you provide negative feedback on what the employees are doing wrong or what the employees did not accomplish. Finally, you ask them to improve their behaviors or results by overcoming their weaknesses.

In contrast, a better option is to use a *strengths-based approach,* which involves identifying employee strengths in terms of their exceptional job performance and asking them to improve their behaviors or results by making continued or more intensive use of their strengths.

The key feature of a strengths-based approach is to highlight how strengths can generate success on the job, and this motivates employees to intensify the use of their strengths to produce even more positive behaviors and results.

How is this done? First, the conversation can start with something like:

> I want to talk to you about some of the great things that you've been doing lately, as well as areas where you can improve. I'd like this time to be about how I can help you be your very best.

The supervisor can request assistance from the employee in identifying strength areas by asking:

> In what ways do you feel like you've been standing out?

Then the last step involves identifying how employee strengths, which are used in some types of behaviors and results, can be used in others.

Giving feedback to Millennials, Post Millennials, and Baby Boomers

A management theory called *socioemotional selectivity theory* (SST) says that younger individuals, because they are closer to the beginning of their life cycles, anchor the concept of time as time since birth. In their minds, time is mostly open-ended. So because of this particular time orientation, Millennials and Post-Millennials (that is, Generation Z) tend to have work-related goals that are clearly future-oriented: knowledge acquisition, career planning, and the development of ability and skills that will pay off in the future. We call these *utility goals.*

In contrast, Baby Boomers and now many Gen-Xers anchor the concept of time as time left in their careers and in life in general and see time as more limited. They tend to have work-related goals that are more present-oriented: regulating their emotions to be positive and the pursuit of positive social relationships at work. We call these *social awareness goals.*

Performance management leaders are aware of the needs and feedback orientations and reactions of their employees. So they modify the type of feedback so that it is most useful, given individual needs and orientations.

ACTIVE
LEARNING

How can you determine whether your feedback orientation is consistent with other members of your generation? To help you ponder on this issue, answer the following questions using a five-point scale, ranging from strongly disagree to strongly agree.

Then compare your scores with those of a coworker, classmate, or family member who is a member of a different generation:

Utility goals:

1. Feedback contributes to my success at work.
2. To develop my skills at work, I rely on feedback.
3. Feedback is critical for improving performance.
4. Feedback from supervisors can help me advance in a company.
5. I find that feedback is critical for reaching my goals.

Social awareness goals:

1. I try to be aware of what other people think of me.
2. Using feedback, I am more aware of what people think of me.
3. Feedback helps me manage the impression I make on others.
4. Feedback lets me know how I am perceived by others.
5. I rely on feedback to help me make a good impression.

These questions are part of the **Feedback Orientation Scale** (http://journals. sagepub.com/doi/abs/10.1177/0149206310373145?journalCode=joma0).

CHAPTER 6 Becoming a Performance Management Leader   119

Chapter **7**

Defining Performance

n this chapter, I begin with a question that may seem simple, but it isn't: What exactly is performance?

Answering this question is absolutely key if you want to implement a successful performance management system. If you don't have a good answer, you will not know how to measure performance.

Performance Is All about Behaviors and Results

Performance is a combination of two things:

» **Behaviors and actions:** What an employee does

» **Results and products:** The outcomes of an employee's behavior

Both of these components are important and they influence each other, as shown in Figure 7-1.

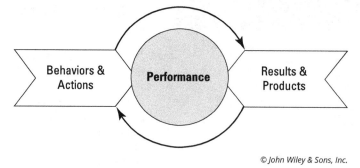

© John Wiley & Sons, Inc.

FIGURE 7-1:
Performance
is a combination
of behaviors &
actions and
results &
products

EXAMPLE

If an employee allocates a sufficient amount of efficient time to preparing for an important client presentation (behavior), the client will be pleased (result). In turn, if the client is satisfied (result), this will serve as a motivating factor for continuing to allocate sufficient time to client presentations in the future (behavior). So behaviors and results create a virtuous and self-reinforcing cycle that together constitute performance.

There are two characteristics of the behaviors and results we label "performance":

>> **Performance is evaluative,** which means that it can be judged as negative, neutral, or positive for individual and organizational effectiveness. In other words, the value of these behaviors and results can vary depending on the extent to which they make a contribution toward the accomplishment of individual, unit, and organizational goals.

>> **Performance is multidimensional,** which means that there are many different types of behaviors and results that have the capacity to advance (or hinder) organizational goals.

Defining performance as behaviors

Think of a set of behaviors that can be grouped under the general label "contribution to effectiveness of others in the work unit." This set of behaviors can be defined as follows:

Works with others within and outside the unit in a manner that improves their effectiveness; shares information and resources; develops effective working relationships; builds consensus; constructively manages conflict.

Contribution to the effectiveness of others in the work unit could be measured by using a scale that includes anchors demonstrating various levels of competence. For example, anchors could be words and phrases such as "outstanding," "significantly exceeds standards," "fully meets standards," "doesn't fully meet standards," and "unacceptable."

This example shows the evaluative nature of performance because this set of behaviors is judged as positive, neutral, or negative. Also, this example illustrates the multidimensional nature of performance because there are several behaviors that, combined, affect the overall perceived contribution that an employee makes to the effectiveness of others in the work unit. In other words, you would be missing important information if you only considered, for example, "shares information and resources" and did not consider the additional behaviors listed earlier.

Defining performance as results

As an example of results, take the case of a salesperson whose job consists of visiting clients to offer them new products or services. The salesperson's supervisor is back in the home office and doesn't have an opportunity to observe the salesperson's behaviors firsthand.

In this case, sales volume can be used as a performance measure. In other words, the supervisor makes the assumption that if the salesperson is able to produce high sales figures, then she is probably engaging in the right behaviors.

Causes for Excellent and Poor Performance

Why do some people perform better than others? What factors cause an employee to perform at a certain level?

As shown in Figure 7-2, a combination of three factors allows some people to perform at higher levels than others:

>> **Abilities and other traits:** These include such things as cognitive abilities (that is, intelligence), personality, stable motivational dispositions, and physical characteristics and abilities. Also, knowledge and skills include job-related knowledge and skills, attitudes, and changeable motivational states.

>> **Knowledge and skills:** These can be divided into *declarative knowledge*, which is information about facts and things, including information regarding a given task's requirements, labels, principles, and goals; and *procedural knowledge*, which is a combination of knowing what to do and how to do it and includes cognitive, physical, perceptual, motor, and interpersonal skills.

>> **Contextual issues:** These include HR policies and procedures (for example, compensation system), managerial and peer leadership, organizational and national culture, issues about time and timing of performance, and resources and opportunities given to employees to perform.

As show in Figure 7-2, the three factors have an additive relationship, which means that two employees can achieve the same level of performance by having different levels of each of the three factors. For example, one employee can be more motivated and spend more hours at work, whereas another can work fewer hours, but have higher levels of skill. Yet, both show a similar level of performance.

WARNING

If any of the three causes of performance is very low, then overall performance won't be satisfactory, no matter how high the other two factors are.

EXAMPLE

Take the case of Jane, a sales associate who works in a national clothing retail chain. Jane has excellent declarative knowledge regarding the merchandise. In particular, she knows the names of all the brands; the prices for all products; sizing charts for clothes for women, men, and children; and sales promotions.

So her declarative knowledge is very high. Jane is also intelligent and physically able to conduct all the necessary tasks — both considered important traits for the job. However, her interactions with customers are not so good (that is, procedural knowledge regarding interpersonal skills). She doesn't pay much attention to them because she is busy restocking clothes on shelves and hangers. She doesn't greet customers and is also not good at providing answers to their questions.

Her overall performance, therefore, is poor because although she has the declarative knowledge necessary to do the job, as well as cognitive and physical traits, she lacks procedural knowledge. In short, it is necessary to have at least some level of each of the determinants of performance.

How individual differences affect performance

An important difference between abilities/traits and knowledge and skills is that knowledge and skills are more malleable — meaning that they are easier to change. In general, individual differences that cause different levels of performance and are less malleable are called traits. For example, intelligence and personality are considered traits because they are fairly stable.

Regarding personality traits, the following are called the Big Five:

>> **Extroversion:** Being sociable, gregarious, assertive, talkative, and active (the opposite of extroversion is introversion)

>> **Neuroticism:** Being anxious, depressed, angry, embarrassed, emotional, worried, and insecure (the opposite of neuroticism is emotional stability)

>> **Agreeableness:** Being curious, flexible, trusting, good-natured, cooperative, forgiving, and tolerant

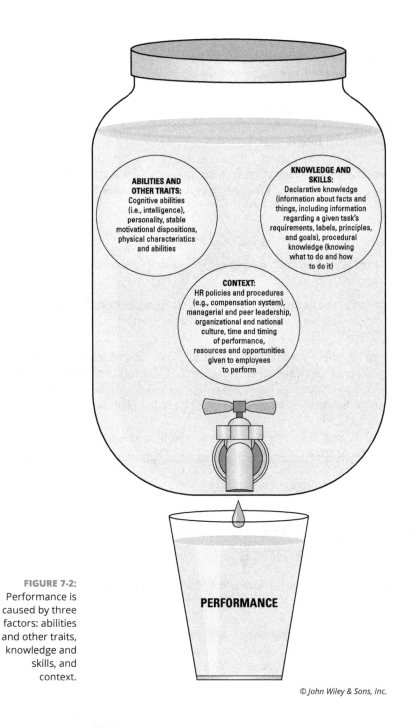

FIGURE 7-2:
Performance is caused by three factors: abilities and other traits, knowledge and skills, and context.

>> **Conscientiousness:** Being dependable (that is, being careful, thorough, responsible, and organized), as well as hardworking, achievement-oriented, and persevering

>> **Openness to experience:** Being imaginative, cultured, curious, original, broad-minded, intelligent, and artistically sensitive

REMEMBER

Individual differences that cause performance and are easier to change (that is, more malleable) are called *states*. This can be done through a training program or other organizational interventions.

Clearly, people vary in terms of their motivation, which is characterized by how much energy and effort they allocate. Specifically, consider the following three choices:

>> **Choice to expend effort:** "I will go to work today."

>> **Choice of level of effort:** "I will put in my best effort at work" versus "I will not try very hard."

>> **Choice to persist in the expenditure of that level of effort:** "I will give up after a little while" versus "I will persist no matter what."

The first two are more malleable and therefore considered state motivation. For example, you could influence an employee's choice regarding whether she shows up at work — and on time — using HR policies regarding absenteeism and tardiness. You could influence the second choice by setting clear goals.

But the third is less malleable and a more stable individual trait rather than a state. This type of trait motivation is considered a fairly stable personality trait, called *achievement motivation,* and is a facet of conscientiousness — one of the Big Five personality traits I mention earlier.

How knowledge and skills affect performance

What can you do to improve your own knowledge and skills and therefore improve your performance?

Let's think about those individuals who have achieved the top level of performance in their fields. Think about Tiger Woods as a golf player, Beyoncé as a singer and songwriter, Bill Gates as Microsoft's founder, Magnus Carlsen as a chess player, Thomas Edison as an inventor, Marie Curie as a physicist and chemist, and Socrates as a philosopher. How did they achieve such excellence? What made these individuals' performance so extraordinary? How were they able to improve their performance constantly even when others would believe they had reached a plateau and could not possibly improve their performance?

What these individuals have in common is that they devoted a large number of hours to *deliberate practice.* Deliberate practice is different from regular practice and from simply working many hours a week.

EXAMPLE

Professor K. Anders Ericsson of Florida State University gives the following example: "Simply hitting a bucket of balls isn't deliberate practice, which is why most golfers don't get better. Hitting an eight-iron 300 times with a goal of leaving the ball within 20 feet of the pin 80 percent of the time, continually observing results and making appropriate adjustments, and doing that for hours every day — that's deliberate practice."

Top performers in all fields engage in deliberate practice consistently, daily, including weekends. The famous pianist Vladimir Horowitz was quoted as saying: "If I don't practice for a day, I know it; if I don't practice for two days, my wife knows it; if I don't practice for three days, the world knows it."

Deliberate practice involves the following five steps:

1. Approach performance with the goal of getting better and better.

2. As you are performing, focus on what is happening and why you are doing things the way you do.

3. Once your task is finished, seek performance feedback from expert sources, and the more sources, the better.

4. Build mental models of your job, your situation, and your organization.

5. Repeat steps 1–4 continually and on an ongoing basis.

ACTIVE LEARNING

Think about a particular task at which you would like to do better. This could job-related, a hobby (for example, music, sports, cooking, playing poker), or even family-related (for example, be a better father, mother, son, daughter, or sibling). Now, create a deliberate practice program for yourself. Who are the experts from whom you could solicit feedback? How often would you practice? For how long? What would be some of your specific goals you would like to achieve, and by when?

How context affects performance

The third major cause of performance is *context* because performance is also determined by what is happening around the employee.

For example, HR policies and practices can have an important impact of employee performance. Take the case of IBM. In December 2016, Ginni Rometty, IBM's CEO, said that over the next four years, the company would invest $1 billion in training and development in the United States. In contrast to IBM, working for a company with an HR function that doesn't offer much in terms of training means that, sooner or later, performance will suffer as skills become obsolete.

As a second example, an organizational culture that doesn't promote excellence will also have negative consequences on performance. Take the case of a compensation system that includes paying everyone the same, regardless of employee performance. Why would such a system motivate employees to do better?

As a third example, time and the timing of performance is another contextual factor that also plays a role. Typical performance refers to the average level of an employee's performance, whereas maximum performance refers to the peak level of performance an employee can achieve.

TIP

Employees perform at maximum levels when they understand they are being evaluated, when they accept instructions to maximize performance on the task, and when the task is of short duration.

A key issue is that the relationship between typical (what employees will do) and maximum (what employees could do) performance is very weak. What this means is that measuring performance during short time intervals is assessing maximum, and not typical, performance. Most organizations are more interested in what employees will do on a regular basis rather than what they could do during the short period of time when they are observed and evaluated. In short, the time and timing of performance observation and measurement also affect the observed levels of performance.

EFFECTS OF CONTEXT ON PERFORMANCE AT WORLDCOM

Remember WorldCom? It's a good example of a detrimental effect of context on performance.

WorldCom was the second largest long-distance company in the United States before it collapsed in 2002. One of the reasons for its collapse was its "cult-like corporate culture" around a charismatic leader, former basketball coach Bernie Ebbers. Ebbers exercised unquestioned authority and demanded unquestioned loyalty from employees. Within this context, it was difficult, if not impossible, for employees to do anything different from what they were told — even if this meant doing things that were clearly unethical. This was an important contextual factor that affected the performance of all employees at WorldCom, regardless of their levels of abilities and traits as well as knowledge and skills.

Resources and opportunities to perform are also important contextual issues. We all know that there is a harsh reality in organizations that involves some employees receiving less resources and opportunities than others. For example, within the same firm, some consultants have more opportunities to work with important clients than others. This issue is quite obvious in sports: There is a limited amount of playing time during each game. So some athletes have more playing time than others. In both of these cases, although employees have the same levels of abilities and other traits as well as knowledge and skills, differential levels of opportunities will have a direct impact on their performance.

Anticipating performance problems

Because you now know that performance is affected by the combined effect of three different factors, you can use this knowledge to anticipate performance problems.

So, you need to find information that will allow to to understand whether the source of a performance problem is abilities and other traits, knowledge and skills, contextual issues, or some combination of these three factors.

For example, if an employee lacks procedural knowledge (knowing what to do and how to do it) but you believe the source of the problem is declarative knowledge (information about facts and things), you may give the employee a manual with facts and figures about products so he can acquire the knowledge that is presumably lacking. But, unfortunately this would be a waste of time and resources for you, your employee, and the organization.

Remember the case of Jane I described earlier in this chapter? Her performance problem was caused by lack of procedural knowledge, and not lack of declarative knowledge. In other words, her overall performance was poor because although she had the declarative knowledge necessary to do the job, as well as cognitive and physical traits, she lacks procedural knowledge. This is why to help her improve her performance, what you need to do is improve her procedural knowledge — information about facts and things, including information regarding a given task's requirements, labels, principles, and goals. Improving her procedural knowledge would know change things much.

TIP

Because performance management systems are used for measuring performance, they are also excellent tools to understand the source of any performance deficiencies.

Another issue regarding the identification of performance problems relates to what is called *ownership,* or what Jocko Willink, retired United States Navy SEAL and former commander in the Battle of Ramadi in Iraq, calls extreme ownership.

Willink served in SEAL Task Unit Bruiser, the most highly decorated Special Operations unit from the war in Iraq. They faced tremendous difficulties along the way, including being involved in a "blue-on-blue": friendly fire fratricide, which is the worst thing that could happen. One American soldier was wounded, an Iraqi soldier was dead, and others were seriously wounded. This incident led to asking very difficult questions, and the most critical one was this: "Who was responsible for this debacle?" Willink says that the very first step is to take ownership of poor performance, no matter how painful this process may be.

What Willink learned in war can be extrapolated to other contexts: Acknowledging that we have performed under par is never easy. It hurts our egos. It hurts our self-esteem. But these are short-term effects only. Unless we engage in this process, it will be very difficult to address any type of performance problem. Willink said that he "had to take complete ownership of what went wrong. That is what a leader does — even if it means getting fired."

REMEMBER

When addressing and anticipating performance problems, you first need to identify whether abilities and other traits, knowledge and skills (declarative and procedural knowledge), or context are hampering performance, and then, help the employee improve the specific factors that are causing poor performance.

ACTIVE LEARNING

Think about the last time when you or a coworker showed a level of performance that was not considered adequate. What were the causes of this substandard level of performance: lack of traits, knowledge and skills, or contextual issues? Which were the two most important factors? What is the evidence that led you to this conclusion?

Focusing on Four Different Performance Dimensions

I mentioned earlier that performance is multidimensional, meaning that you need to consider many different types of behaviors and results to understand performance.

There are four types or dimensions of performance: task performance, contextual performance (also called prosocial or organizational citizenship performance), counterproductive performance, and adaptive performance. A good performance management system should include key performance indicators (KPIs), or observable measures, for each of these types.

Task and contextual performance

Contextual and task performance must be considered separately because they don't necessarily occur in tandem. An employee can be highly proficient at her task, but be an underperformer regarding contextual performance.

Task performance involves

>> Activities that transform raw materials into the goods and services that are produced by the organization

>> Activities that help with the transformation process by replenishing the supply of raw materials; distributing its finished products; or providing important planning, coordination, supervising, or staff functions that enable the organization to function effectively and efficiently

Contextual performance involves behaviors that contribute to the organization's effectiveness by providing a good environment in which task performance can occur. Contextual performance includes behaviors such as the following:

>> Persisting with enthusiasm and exerting extra effort as necessary to complete one's own task activities successfully (for example, being punctual and rarely absent, expending extra effort on the job)

>> Volunteering to carry out task activities that are not formally part of the job (for example, suggesting organizational improvements, making constructive suggestions)

>> Helping and cooperating with others (for example, assisting and helping coworkers and customers)

>> Following organizational rules and procedures (for example, following orders and regulations, showing respect for authority, complying with organizational values and policies)

>> Endorsing, supporting, and defending organizational objectives (for example, organizational loyalty, representing the organization favorably to outsiders)

Both task and contextual performance are important dimensions to take into account in performance management systems. Imagine what would happen to an organization in which all employees are outstanding regarding task performance but don't perform well regarding contextual performance. What if a colleague whose cubicle is next to yours needs to take a restroom break and asks you to answer the phone if it rings, because an important client will call at any moment? What if you said, "That isn't MY job"?

TASK AND CONTEXTUAL PERFORMANCE AT SPRINT

Sprint is a communications services company serving 59.7 million connections. Sprint is widely recognized for developing, engineering, and deploying innovative technologies. At Sprint, all employees are evaluated and development plans are created through the use of five core dimensions: acting with integrity, focusing on the customer, delivering results, building relationships, and demonstrating leadership. The dimensions are used not only for business strategy and objectives but also as a template for what successful performance looks like at the company. These dimensions include the consideration of both task and contextual performance, and employees in the evaluation and development process are asked to write behavioral examples of how they have performed on each dimension.

For example, the delivering results dimension clearly links to performing specific tasks of one's job. Each employee has certain tasks to complete on a regular basis to keep the business moving. On the other hand, the company is concerned about how the work gets done and contributing to a good work environment that allows for greater effectiveness. This is apparent through the dimensions that look at how employees develop relationships with others and act with integrity in their day-to-day functioning. In summary, Sprint has recognized the importance of considering both task and contextual components of a job in its performance management system. Employees are evaluated not only on results but also on how they are achieved through working with others.

CONTEXTUAL PERFORMANCE AT TRW AUTOMOTIVE

TRW Automotive Holdings Corp. designs, manufactures, and sells automotive systems and components to automotive original equipment manufacturers. The company was founded in 1904, is based in Livonia, Michigan, and has approximately 67,000 employees.

With increasing market pressures and sluggish growth, the company wanted to become more performance driven, experiment in new markets, and offer greater value to its shareholders. To do so, the senior management team developed what they labeled the "key behaviors." These behaviors are communicated throughout the company and have a prominent role in the performance management process. The majority of these key behaviors actually focus on contextual performance. Specifically, the TRW behaviors emphasize many of the elements of contextual performance, including teamwork and trust.

REMEMBER

Many organizations now realize that there is a need to focus on both task and contextual performance because organizations cannot function properly without a minimum dose of positive contextual behaviors on the part of all employees.

Key differences between task and contextual performance

Table 7-1 summarizes the main differences between task and contextual performance. First, task performance varies across jobs. For example, the tasks performed by an HR manager are different from those performed by a line manager. Also, the tasks performed by a senior HR manager are more strategic in nature compared with those performed by an entry-level HR analyst, which are more operational in nature.

On the other hand, contextual performance is fairly similar across functional and hierarchical levels. All employees, regardless of job title, function, and responsibilities, are equally responsible for volunteering to carry out task activities that are not formally part of the job. Second, task performance is role prescribed, meaning that task performance is usually included in one's job description. In contrast, contextual performance behaviors are usually not role prescribed, but are typically expected without making them explicit. Finally, task performance is influenced mainly by abilities and skills (for example, cognitive, physical), whereas contextual performance is influenced mainly by personality (for example, conscientiousness, agreeableness).

TABLE 7-1   **Key Differences between Task and Contextual Performance**

Task Performance	Contextual Performance
Varies across jobs	Fairly similar across jobs
Role prescribed	Not role prescribed
Antecedents: abilities and skills	Antecedent: personality

There are many pressing reasons why both task and contextual performance dimensions should be included in a performance management system:

>> **Global competition** is raising the levels of effort required of employees. Thus, whereas it sufficed in the past to have a workforce that was competent in task performance, today's globalized world and accompanying competitive forces make it imperative that the workforce also engages in positive contextual

performance. It is difficult to compete if an organization employs a workforce that doesn't engage in contextual behaviors.

>> Related to the issue of global competition is the **need to offer outstanding customer service.** Contextual performance behaviors can make a profound impact on customer satisfaction. Imagine what a big difference it makes, from a customer perspective, when an employee puts in extra effort to satisfy a customer's needs.

>> Many organizations are forming employees into **teams.** Although some teams are not be permanent because they are created to complete specific short-term tasks, the reality of today's world of work is that teams are here to stay. Interpersonal cooperation is a key determinant of team effectiveness. Thus, contextual performance becomes particularly relevant for teamwork.

>> Including both task and contextual performance in the performance management system provides an additional benefit: **Employees being rated are more satisfied with the system and also believe the system is more fair** if contextual performance is measured in addition to task performance. It seems that employees are aware that contextual performance is important in affecting organizational effectiveness, and therefore, believe that these types of behaviors should be included in a performance management system in addition to the more traditional task performance.

>> When supervisors evaluate performance, **it is difficult for them to ignore the contextual performance dimension,** even though the evaluation form they are using does not include any specific questions about contextual performance. Consequently, since contextual performance has an impact on ratings of overall performance even when only task performance is measured, it makes sense to include contextual performance more explicitly.

Counterproductive performance

Counterproductive performance involves behaviors and results that are voluntary and that violate organizational norms and threaten the well-being of the organization, its members, or both.

It may seem that counterproductive performance is simply the opposite of contextual performance, but it isn't. Specifically, the same employee can engage in both contextual and counterproductive performance. Some KPIs of counterproductive performance include the following:

>> Exaggerating hours worked

>> Falsifying a receipt to get reimbursed for more money than was spent on business expenses

- » Starting negative rumors about the company

- » Gossiping about coworkers

- » Covering up one's mistakes

- » Competing with coworkers in an unproductive way

- » Gossiping about one's supervisor

- » Staying out of sight to avoid work

- » Blaming one's coworkers for one's mistakes

- » Intentionally working slowly or carelessly

- » Being intoxicated during working hours

- » Seeking revenge on coworkers

- » Cyberloafing

- » Presenting colleagues' ideas as if they were one's own

COUNTERPRODUCTIVE PERFORMANCE AT ENRON

Remember the corporate scandal of Enron, which led to the bankruptcy of the Enron Corporation? This was a large American energy company based in Houston, Texas, and the "Enron scandal" was the largest bankruptcy reorganization in American history, as well as the biggest audit failure. A book by McLean and Elkind, based on hundreds of interviews and details from personal calendars, performance reviews, emails, and other documents, showed that one of the primary reasons for the company's collapse was widespread counterproductive performance. In fact, Enron executives were described as "supersmart." For example, its former CEO, Jeffrey Keith "Jeff" Skilling, and many other top executives, had earned their MBAs from top-ranked business schools such as Harvard Business School and The University of Texas. But a performance management system that included not only task performance but also counterproductive performance could have detected unethical behaviors and accounting practices before they became widespread and led to the collapse of the entire company — including a loss of 99.5 percent of its market value in a year. Not surprisingly, when he became dean of the Harvard Business School a few years after Enron's collapse, Professor Nitin Nohria posed the core question for the school: "Are we educating people who have the competence and character to exercise leadership in business?"

Adaptive performance

Adaptive performance is the fourth dimension of performance and is related to an individual's adaptability to changes — be it in the organization and its goals, in the requirements of the job, or the overall work context.

Given the rapid pace of technology and other factors that are constantly changing the nature of work and organizations, adaptive performance is becoming an increasingly important performance dimension. For example, an organization may change its strategic priorities, merge or be acquired, and have more or less resources. The way employees react to and anticipate these changes is, therefore, an important performance component.

There are several KPIs of adaptive performance. Consider the following eight:

>> **Handling emergencies or crisis situations:** To what extent can employees react with appropriate and proper urgency in dangerous or emergency situations; quickly analyze options for dealing with danger or crises; maintain emotional control and objectivity while staying focused on the situation at hand; and step up to take action and handle danger or emergencies?

>> **Handling work stress:** To what extent can employees remain composed and cool when faced with difficult circumstances or a highly demanding workload or schedule; not overreact to unexpected news or situations; and manage frustration well by directing effort to constructive solutions rather than blaming others?

>> **Solving problems creatively:** To what extent can employees use unique types of analyses to generate new, innovative ideas in complex areas; turn problems upside down and inside out to find fresh, new approaches; integrate seemingly unrelated information to develop creative solutions; and entertain wide-ranging possibilities others may miss?

>> **Dealing with uncertain and unpredictable work situations:** To what extent can employees take effective action without knowing all the facts at hand; change gears in response to unpredictable or unexpected events; adjust plans, goals, actions, or priorities to deal with changing situations; not need things to be black and white; and refuse to be paralyzed by uncertainty or ambiguity?

>> **Learning work tasks, technologies, and procedures:** To what extent can employees demonstrate enthusiasm for learning new approaches and technologies; do what is necessary to keep knowledge and skills current; learn new methods; adjust to new work processes and procedures, and anticipate changes in the work demands; and search for and participate in assignments or training that will prepare them for these changes?

>> **Demonstrating interpersonal adaptability:** To what extent can employees be flexible and open-minded when dealing with others; listen to and consider others' viewpoints and opinions and alter their own opinion when it is appropriate to do so; be open and accepting of negative or developmental feedback regarding work; and work well and develop effective relationships with people with diverse personalities?

>> **Demonstrating cultural adaptability:** To what extent can employees take action to learn about and understand the climate, orientation, needs, and values of other groups, organizations, or cultures; integrate well into and be comfortable with different values, customs, and cultures; and understand the implications of one's actions and adjust their approach to maintain positive relationships with other groups, organizations, and cultures?

>> **Demonstrating physically oriented adaptability:** To what extent can employees adjust to challenging environmental states such as extreme heat, humidity, cold, or dirt; accommodate frequent physical pressure to complete strenuous or demanding tasks and adjust weight and muscular strength; and become proficient in performing physical tasks as necessary for the job?

When to Define Performance as Behaviors or Results and Why

Remember that performance involves both results and behaviors (as shown back in Figure 7-1). So good systems need to define performance in terms of both.

Having said that, there are situations when it is better to emphasize one or the other.

When to define performance as behaviors

The behavior approach emphasizes what employees do on the job and doesn't consider the outcomes or products resulting from their behaviors. This is basically a process-oriented approach that emphasizes how an employee does the job and not what is produced.

The behavior approach is most appropriate when

>> **The link between behaviors and results isn't obvious.** Sometimes, the relation between behaviors and the desired outcomes isn't clear. In some

cases, the desired result is not achieved in spite of the fact that the right behaviors are in place. For example, a salesperson is not be able to close a deal because of a downturn in the economy. In other cases, results are achieved in spite of the absence of the correct behaviors. For example, a pilot may not check all the items in the preflight checklist, but the flight is nevertheless be successful (take off and land safely and on time). When the link between behaviors and results isn't always obvious, it is beneficial to focus on behaviors, as opposed to outcomes.

» **Outcomes occur in the distant future.** When the desired results will not be seen for months, or even years, the measurement of behaviors is beneficial.

» **Poor results are due to causes beyond the performer's control.** When the results of an employee's performance are beyond the employee's control, it makes sense to emphasize the measurement of behaviors. For example, consider a situation involving two assembly line workers, one of them working the day shift, and the other, the night shift. When the assembly line gets stuck because of technical problems, the employee working during the day receives immediate technical assistance, so the assembly line is back in motion in less than 5 minutes. By contrast, the employee working the night shift has very little technical support, and, therefore, when the assembly line breaks down, it takes about 45 minutes for it to be up and running again. If you measured results, you would conclude that the performance of the day-shift employee is far superior to that of the night-shift employee, but this would be an incorrect conclusion. Both employees may be equally competent and do the job equally well. The results produced by these employees are uneven because they depend on the amount and quality of technical assistance they receive when the assembly line is stuck.

A popular type of behavior approach used mostly for managerial positions is called *competency modeling.* In a nutshell, competencies are clusters of knowledge, skills, and abilities (KSAs) that together determine how results are achieved. As such, competencies are not directly observable, but you can measure them by assessing behavioral indicators. For example, to measure the competency "leadership," you can measure the behaviors that a manager uses in mentoring and developing her direct reports. For an example of competency modeling, see sidebar describing how it's done at Dollar General.

When to define performance as results

The results approach emphasizes the outcomes produced by the employees. It doesn't consider how employees do the job. This is basically a bottom-line approach that isn't concerned about employee behaviors and processes but instead focuses on what is produced (for example, sales, number of accounts acquired, time spent with clients on the telephone, number of errors).

DEFINING PERFORMANCE AS BEHAVIORS AT NASA

Take the case of NASA's Mars Exploration Rover Mission program. NASA launched the exploration rover Spirit on June 10, 2003, which landed on Mars on January 3, 2004, after traveling 487 million kilometers (302.6 million miles). Its twin, the exploration rover, Opportunity, was launched on July 7, 2003, and landed on the opposite side of Mars on January 24, 2004.

From launch to landing, this mission took about six months to complete. In this circumstance, it is certainly appropriate to assess the performance of the engineers involved in the mission by measuring their behaviors in short intervals during this six-month period, rather than waiting until the final result (successful or unsuccessful landing) is observed.

Now, NASA has the goal of sending humans to the Red Planet in the 2030s. That journey is already well under way. But we will have to wait more than 10 years until we are able to evaluate performance based on results. So a behavior approach is appropriate in this case.

DEFINING PERFORMANCE AS BEHAVIORS AND USING COMPETENCY MODELING AT DOLLAR GENERAL

Dollar General emphasizes a behavior approach to defining performance. Tennessee-based Dollar General operates about 13,000 stores in 43 states in the United States.

As part of the performance management system, Dollar General has identified behaviors that serve as indicators to underlying competencies. These behaviors are reviewed and used to encourage certain outcomes and provide feedback and rewards to staff members. For example, the company management sought to improve attendance among employees. In order to encourage employees to arrive at work on time, a system was developed to group employees into teams who earn points. A wall chart was created displaying a racetrack, and each team was given a car that would be moved forward by the number of points earned each day. After a certain number of laps around the track, employees on the teams with the most points would be given a choice about how to celebrate.

The program was successful within the first two weeks and increased attendance significantly. In summary, Dollar General's performance management system includes the use of a behavior approach to measuring performance.

The results approach is most appropriate when

>> **Workers are skilled in the needed behaviors.** An emphasis on results is appropriate when workers have the necessary abilities, knowledge, and skills to do the work. In such situations, workers know what specific behaviors are needed to achieve the desired results, and they are also sufficiently skilled to know what to do to correct any process-related problems when the desired results are not obtained. Consider the example of a professional basketball player. A free throw is an unhindered shot made from the foul line and is given to one team to penalize the other team for committing a foul. Free throw shooting can make the difference between winning and losing in a close basketball game. Professional players know that there is really no secret to becoming a great free throw shooter: just hours and hours of dedicated practice besides actual basketball play (much like the discussion earlier in this chapter about deliberate practice). In assessing the performance of professional basketball players, the free throw shooting percentage is a key results-oriented performance indicator because most players have the skills to do it well. It's just a matter of assessing whether they do it or not.

DEFINING PERFORMANCE AS RESULTS AT L BRANDS

L Brands Inc., which used to be known as Limited Brands and The Limited, is a retailer that owns the brands Victoria's Secret, Bath & Body Works, PINK, La Senza, and Henri Bendel. L Brands operates more than 3,000 company-owned specialty stores and employs more than 88,000 associates, who produced combined sales of $12.6 billion. L Brands aims to foster an entrepreneurial culture for its managers; therefore, managers who thrive in the company have a history of delivering impressive business results. They decided to design a new performance management system that is now used uniformly by all L Brands companies. With the involvement of outside consultants and employees, L Brands developed a performance management system wherein managers are measured on business results, including total sales, market share, and expense/sale growth ratio, as well as leadership competencies that are tailored to L Brands. A few of these competencies include developing a fashion sense, financial acumen, and entrepreneurial drive.

Overall, L Brands has been pleased with the new system because it helps align individual goals with business strategy and results. Raters like the new system because behavioral anchors help define the competencies, which make ratings more straightforward. Finally, employees comment that they appreciate the new focus on how results are achieved as opposed to the earlier focus on what is achieved (such as sales).

>> **Behaviors and results are obviously related.** In some situations, certain results can be obtained only if a worker engages in certain specific behaviors. This is the case of jobs involving repetitive tasks such as assembly line work or newspaper delivery. Take the case of a person delivering newspapers. Performance can be measured adopting a results approach: whether the newspaper is delivered to every customer within a particular time frame. For the employee to obtain this result, she needs to pick up the papers at a specific time and use the most effective delivery route. If these behaviors are not present, the paper will not be delivered on time.

>> **Results show consistent improvement over time.** When results improve consistently over time, it is an indication that workers are aware of the behaviors needed to complete the job successfully. In these situations, it is appropriate to adopt a results approach to assessing performance.

>> **There are many ways to do the job right.** When there are different ways in which one can do the tasks required for a job, a results approach is appropriate. An emphasis on results can be beneficial because it could encourage employees to achieve the desired outcomes in creative and innovative ways.

Let me emphasize again that these approaches are not mutually exclusive. Measuring both behavior and results is the approach adopted by most organizations.

DEFINING PERFORMANCE AS BEHAVIORS AT BASECAMP

Basecamp is a web and mobile project management company that generates more than $25 million in revenue with only 52 employees. It was recognized in *Forbes's* 2017 Small Giant List as being among the top 25 small businesses in the United States. Since it was founded in 1999, it has lost only four employees.

The company divides its work into six-week work cycles containing one or two "big batch projects" and four to eight "small batch projects" that take anywhere from a day to two weeks to complete.

As founder and CEO Jason Fried explains, "We don't measure efficiency, compare actuals versus estimates. We have six weeks to get something done. However, a team decides to get it done during that time is up to them."

In summary, Basecamp utilizes a performance management system focusing on outcomes or results in order to motivate employees and bring about business results. The company looks at what is produced in the work rather than at behaviors or how the job gets done.

» Determining performance
accountabilities and objectives

» Choosing a measurement system
congruent with your organization
and industry

Chapter **8**

Measuring Performance as Results

As the saying goes, the devil is in the details. So the way in which we measure performance is absolutely critical in terms of the effectiveness of a performance management system.

This chapter covers how to measure performance as results, which are the outcomes of what people do. I will also explain when and why it makes the most sense to measure performance as results. And I will also explain when and why you need to also understand organizational culture, industry trends, and your organization's leadership when choosing how to measure performance.

REMEMBER

Performance management systems include measures of both results and behaviors.

Measuring Performance as Results

To measure results, you first need to answer the following two questions:

» What are the *key accountabilities*, or areas in which this individual is expected to focus efforts?

» For each accountability, what are the expected *performance objectives*?

MEASURING RESULTS AT KRAFT HEINZ, HEWLETT-PACKARD, GOOGLE, LinkedIn, AND ZYNGA

Organizations that implement a management by objectives (MBO) philosophy are likely to implement results-based performance management systems that include objectives. For example, as part of Kraft Heinz's MBO system, employees' personal goals are publically displayed on their desks, while top executives' goals, including those of the CEO, are posted on the wall. The goals are data-driven, measurable, and linked to other employees' goals, to encourage teamwork as well as the company's values of ownership and transparency.

Several other companies have also made MBOs an integral part of their performance management systems. For example, Bill Packard, one of the founders of the computer company Hewlett-Packard (HP), said that no operating policy contributed more to HP's success than MBOs. Google uses MBOs to set "stretch" goals and asks that employees achieve 65 percent of these seemingly unachievable goals. Business networking site LinkedIn uses MBOs to set three to five objectives for the quarter that are difficult to achieve, and then uses weekly meetings to monitor progress made toward achieving the objectives. Zynga, maker of the popular computer game FarmVille, uses MBOs to encourage focus and urgency by asking employees to set three objectives each week and attempt to achieve at least two out of the three, and then tracking how they performed.

Nevertheless, overall, an emphasis on objectives is likely to allow employees to translate organizational goals into individual goals, which is a key goal of MBO philosophies.

REMEMBER

Key accountabilities are broad areas of a job for which the employee is responsible for producing results. A discussion of results also includes specific objectives that the employee will achieve as part of each accountability. Objectives are statements of important and measurable outcomes.

Determining accountabilities and their importance

To determine accountabilities, you first need to collect information about the job. The primary sources are existing job descriptions, such as the announcement that is used to recruit for the position, as well as the unit's and organization's priorities. The job description gives you information on the tasks performed. You can group tasks included in the job description into clusters, based on their degree of relatedness. Each of these task clusters or accountabilities is a broad area of the job for which the employee is responsible for producing results.

After the accountabilities have been identified, you need to determine the importance of each. To understand this issue, you need to answer the following key questions:

>> What percentage of the employee's time is spent performing each accountability?

>> If the accountability were performed inadequately, would there be a significant impact on the work unit's mission?

>> Is there a significant consequence of error? For example, could inadequate performance of the accountability contribute to the injury or death of the employee or others, serious property damage, or loss of time and money?

Determining accountabilities may, at first, seem like a daunting task. But, actually, this is not too difficult.

I think an example will be helpful to show this. Take the position of Training Specialist/Consultant — Leadership & Team Development for Target Corporation. Target focuses exclusively on general merchandise retailing and is the second largest discount store retailer in the United States, behind Walmart. A brief summary of the job description is the following:

Identifies the training and development needs of Target Corporation's work force (in collaboration with partners), with primary emphasis on exempt team members. Designs and delivers training and development workshops and programs and maintains an ongoing evaluation of the effectiveness of those programs. Assumes leadership and strategic responsibility for assigned processes. May supervise the non-exempt staff.

Based on the job description and additional information found on Target's web page regarding the company's strategic priorities, a list of the accountabilities, consequences of performing them inadequately, consequences of making errors, and percentage of time spent in each follows:

>> **Process leadership:** Leads the strategy and direction of assigned processes. Coordinates related projects and directs or manages resources. This is extremely important to the functioning of Target leadership and the ability of executives to meet strategic business goals. If this position is managed improperly, then it will lead to a loss of time and money in training costs and leadership ineffectiveness. (40 percent of time).

>> **Supervision of nonexempt staff:** Supervises nonexempt staff working in the unit. This is relatively important to the functioning of the work unit. If nonexempt staff members are supervised improperly, then the development of the

employees and the ability to meet business targets will be compromised. (10 percent of time)

>> **Coaching:** Conducts one-on-one executive coaching with managers and executives. This is extremely important to the development of internal leaders. If managers and executives are not coached to improve their performance, there is a loss of time and money associated with their poor performance as well as the cost of replacing them, if necessary. (20 percent of time)

>> **Team-building consultation:** Assists company leaders in designing and delivering their own team-building sessions and other interventions. This is relatively important to the success of teams at Target. Mismanagement of this function will result in teams not meeting their full potential and wasting time and resources on conducting team sessions. (10 percent of time)

>> **Assessment instrument feedback:** Delivers feedback based on scores obtained on assessment instruments of skills, ability, personality, and other individual characteristics. This is relatively important to the development of leaders. If assessment is incorrect, it could derail leader development. (10 percent of time)

>> **Product improvement:** Continuously seeks and implements opportunities to use technology to increase the effectiveness of leadership and team development programs. This is important to the effectiveness of training delivery and could result in significant gains in efficiencies of the systems if carried out effectively. (10 percent of time)

Determining objectives

After you have the list of accountabilities, the next step is to determine specific objectives. Objectives are statements of an important and measurable outcome that, when accomplished, will help ensure success for the accountability.

The purpose of establishing objectives is to identify a limited number of highly important results that, when achieved, will have a dramatic impact on the overall success of the organization. After objectives are set, employees should receive feedback on their progress toward attaining the objectives. Also, rewards should be allocated to those employees who have reached their objectives.

Objectives are clearly important because they help employees guide their efforts toward a specific target. But to be most useful, objectives must have the following characteristics:

>> **Specific and clear:** Objectives must be easy to understand. In addition, they must be verifiable and measurable — for example, a directive: "Cut travel cost by 20 percent."

>> **Challenging:** Objectives need to be challenging but not impossible to achieve. They must be a stretch, but employees should feel that the objective is reachable.

>> **Agreed upon:** To be most effective, objectives need to result from an agreement between the manager and the employee. Employees need an opportunity to participate in setting objectives. Participation in the process increases objective aspirations and acceptance, and it decreases objective resistance.

>> **Significant:** Objectives must be important to the organization. Employees must believe that if the objective is achieved, it will have a critical impact on the overall success of the organization. In addition, achieving the objective should give the employee a feeling of congruence between the employee's performance and the goals of the organization. This, in turn, is likely to enhance feelings of value to the organization.

>> **Prioritized:** Not all objectives are created equal; therefore, objectives should be prioritized and tackled one by one.

>> **Bound by time:** Good objectives have deadlines and mileposts. Objectives lacking a time dimension are likely to be neglected.

>> **Achievable:** Good objectives are doable; that is, employees should have sufficient skills and training to achieve them. If they don't, then the organization should make resources available so that the necessary skills are learned and technology is made available to achieve the goals.

>> **Fully communicated:** In addition to the manager and employee in question, the other organizational members who may be affected by the objectives need to be aware of them.

>> **Flexible:** Good objectives are not immutable. They can, and likely will, change based on changes in the work or business environment.

>> **Limited in number:** Too many objectives may become impossible to achieve, but too few may not make a sufficient contribution to the organization. Objectives must be limited in number. Between five and ten objectives per review period is a manageable number, but this can change, based on the position and organization in question.

Taking into account the characteristics of useful objectives, let's go back to the position of position Training Specialist/Consultant—Leadership & Team Development at Target Corporation. Here are examples of possible objectives per accountability:

>> **Process leadership:** Establish leadership development processes and training programs within budget and time commitments. Meet budget targets and improve executive leaders' "leadership readiness" scores across organization by 20 percent in the coming fiscal year.

>> **Supervision of nonexempt staff:** Receive acceptable managerial effectiveness rating scores from your nonexempt staff in the coming fiscal year.

>> **Coaching:** Improve the managerial effectiveness scores of executive coaching clients in the coming fiscal year.

>> **Team-building consultation:** Deliver necessary team-training sessions throughout the year within budget and with an acceptable satisfaction rating (as measured by the follow-up survey that is sent to every team) for team-training sessions in the coming fiscal year.

>> **Assessment instrument feedback:** Deliver assessment feedback with an acceptable approval rating from your coaching clients in the coming fiscal year.

>> **Product improvement:** Improve satisfaction with training delivery in the coming fiscal year by receiving acceptable scores while staying on budget.

SMART GOALS AT MICROSOFT

Many organizations set goals following the guidelines that I describe in this chapter. For example, Microsoft Corporation has a long history of using individual goals in its performance management system. The goals at Microsoft are described by the acronym SMART: specific, measurable, achievable, results-based, and time-specific.

Research based on more than 1,000 empirical studies has demonstrated that setting goals that are specific and challenging leads to higher performance than setting an easy or vague goal, such as "I will do my best."

Why does setting goals work? There are four main reasons why goal setting leads to better performance. First, setting a goal establishes a clear priority and clear focus over other less important tasks. Second, a specific and difficult goal increases effort over and above an easy, vague, or nonexistent goal. Third, setting goals improves persistence because there is a clear target in sight. Finally, and perhaps the most critical reason, a specific and difficult goal forces people to create and implement specific strategies, such as how to allocate time and resources, to reach the goal.

Now compare the objectives listed above with the characteristics of useful objectives. Do these objectives comply with each of the ten characteristics of good objectives? Which objectives could be improved? How, specifically?

Choosing a Measurement System Congruent with Context

In addition to practically and usefulness, context plays an important role in how to measure performance.

Reasons for measuring performance as results or behaviors have to do with the nature of the job and the nature of work. However, there are also contextual factors that play an important role in how performance is measured and these are related to the culture of the organization, characteristics of the industry, and the strategic direction chosen by the organization's leadership.

Considering the role of organizational culture

First, consider the role of organizational culture. In some organizations, the culture is highly competitive, and there is a win-lose mentality such that employees know that to succeed and receive the rewards they want, they need to be concerned about themselves first and others last. In those organizations, it is unlikely that the performance management system will include measures of contextual performance such as competencies regarding cooperation and working with others.

As a second example, the culture in some firms is such that employees know, although this will not be found in the "employee manual," that they are not rewarded for establishing long-term relationships with customers. Rather, the name of the game is to get as much out of customers as possible. In fact, many financial advisors working for investment banks are fully aware that pushing the products of their own banks (for example, mutual funds) to clients is seen favorably because this helps their organization's bottom line. So a performance management system in an organization such as this one is likely to include measures of results in the form of sales volume. Because of this situation, as noted by *The Wall Street Journal* in an article by Michael Wursthorn from January 6, 2017, many of the largest brokerage firms in the United States are now trying to shrug off "their lingering boiler room images and sales-driven cultures, which have contributed to their loss of market share to independent peers the past several years."

In the recent Wells Fargo scandal, employees created as many as 2.1 million phony deposit and credit cards accounts, and branch managers were told that they "would end up working for McDonald's" if they missed sales quotas.

Considering the role of industry trends

Another contextual factor that affects choices in terms of performance measurement is the issue of industry trends. To continue with the financial brokerage industry, an important change is that consumers are starting to recognize that investment "advisors" actually have a conflict of interest when they recommend their bank's own products. Accordingly, many firms are changing their performance management systems, and specifically, the way in which they measure performance.

EXAMPLE

Early in 2017, Merrill Lynch, which has $2 trillion in client assets, abandoned the traditional model in which employees' performance is measured based on the amount of charges to customers on each transaction in a retirement account. Rather, performance is no longer measured based on revenue generated from the number of transactions, and customers are charged a flat fee based on a percentage of a portfolio's asset. This change in how performance is now measured was a direct result of changes in the industry.

Considering the role of leadership

Leadership also plays an important role in how performance is measured. At Merrill Lynch, Andy Sieg, head of Merrill Lynch Wealth Management, sees the recent change in the way performance is measured as a critical strategic move. In fact, he hopes that this change in how the performance of financial advisors is measured "will help raise the level of trust in our industry because clients are going to be assured that when it comes to their retirement savings, there's no one's interest that is being put in front of the interest of a client."

Chapter **9**

Measuring Performance as Behaviors

As the saying goes, the devil is in the details. So the way in which we measure performance is absolutely critical in terms of the effectiveness of a performance management system.

This chapter is about how to measure performance as behaviors, which is what employees do. I will also explain when and why it makes most sense to measure performance as behaviors.

REMEMBER

Performance management systems include measures of *both* results and behaviors.

Measuring Competencies

To measure behaviors, we first cluster them into competencies. These are measurable clusters of knowledge, skills, and abilities (KSAs) that are critical in determining how results will be achieved. Examples of competencies are customer service, written or oral communication, creative thinking, and dependability.

Measuring two types of competencies

There are two main types of competencies.

>> *Differentiating competencies* are those that allow you to distinguish between average and superior performers.

>> *Threshold competencies* are those that everyone needs to display to do the job to a minimally adequate standard.

For example, for the position Information Technology (IT) Project Manager, a differentiating competency is process management. Process management is defined as "managing project activities." For the same position, a threshold competency is change management. The change management competency includes knowledge of behavioral sciences, operational and relational skills, and sensitivity to motivators. Therefore, for an IT project manager to be truly effective, she has to possess process management and change management competencies.

EXAMPLE

Competencies should be defined in behavioral terms. Take the case of a professor teaching an online course. An important competency is "communication." This competency is defined as the set of behaviors that enables a professor to convey information so that students are able to receive it and understand it. For example, one such behavior might be whether the professor is conveying information during preassigned times and dates. That is, if the professor is not present at the chat room at the prespecified dates and times, no communication is possible.

To understand the extent to which an employee possesses a competency, we measure *key performance indicators* — or KPI for short.

Each indicator is an observable behavior that gives us information regarding the competency in question. In other words, we don't measure the competency directly, but we measure indicators that tell us whether the competency is present or not.

Figure 9-1 shows the relationship between a competency and its indicators. A competency can have several indicators, and Figure 9-1 shows a competency with five indicators. An indicator is a behavior that, if displayed, suggests that the competency is present. In the example of the competency "communication" for a professor teaching an online course, one indicator is whether the professor shows up at the chat room at the preestablished dates and times. Another behavioral indicator of this competency could be whether the responses provided by the professor address the questions asked by the students or whether the answers are only tangential to the questions asked.

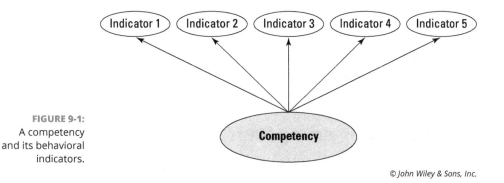

© John Wiley & Sons, Inc.

FIGURE 9-1:
A competency
and its behavioral
indicators.

As another example, consider the two competencies that define good leadership: consideration and initiation structure. Consideration is the degree to which the leader looks after the well-being of his followers. Initiating structure is the degree to which the leader lays out task responsibilities. Here are five indicators whose presence would indicate the existence of the consideration competency:

» Supports direct reports' projects

» Asks about the well-being of employees' lives outside of work

MEASURING COMPETENCIES AT XEROX CAPITAL SERVICES

At Xerox Capital Services (XCS), identifying leadership competencies was the first step in a successful leadership development program. XCS is jointly owned by the Xerox Corporation and General Electric. The company offers financing, risk analysis, credit approval, order processing, billing, and collection services. It employs 1,800 people in the United States and generates an estimated $146.5 million in annual revenue.

A leadership development program at XCS was focused on high-potential future leaders that were currently in premanagement roles. An important step in developing training sessions was to identify the key competencies of leaders in the organization. This process involved senior managers giving their opinions about what was most critical for leadership success in the company. After a clearly defined list of 12 competencies was identified, a curriculum was developed that included readings and a specific course each week on each topic.

In summary, XCS provides an example of the importance of identifying competencies and how the competencies can be used within the context of a performance management system.

>> Encourages direct reports to reach their established goals

>> Gets to know employees personally

>> Shows respect for employees' work and personal lives

Describing competencies

To be most useful, a description of competencies must include the following components:

>> Definition of competency

>> Description of specific behavioral indicators that can be observed when someone demonstrates a competency effectively

>> Description of specific behaviors that are likely to occur when someone doesn't demonstrate a competency effectively (what a competency is not)

>> List of suggestions for developing the competency in question

Using the competency "consideration," let's discuss the four essential elements in describing a competency. I define consideration like this: It is the degree to which a leader shows concern and respect for followers, looks out for their welfare, and expresses appreciation and support. Next, I list five indicators or behaviors that can be observed when a leader is exhibiting consideration leadership. Leaders who don't show consideration may speak with direct reports only regarding task assignments, repeatedly keep employees late with no consideration of social lives, take no interest in an employee's career goals, and assign tasks based only on current expertise. Finally, how do leaders develop the consideration competency? One suggestion would be to ask employees, on a regular basis, how their lives outside of work are going. This may lead to knowledge about an employee's family and interests outside of work.

REMEMBER

Compared to the measurement of results, the measurement of competencies is intrinsically judgmental. In other words, competencies are measured using data provided by individuals who make a judgment regarding the extent to which the competency is present. So the behaviors displayed by the employees are observed and judged by raters such as the direct supervisor, peers, customers, the employee himself, and direct reports (for the case of managers). These possible raters constitute different performance touchpoints and are complementary sources of performance information.

Two types of systems are used to evaluate competencies: comparative systems and absolute systems. Comparative systems base the measurement on comparing employees with one other. Absolute systems base the measurement on comparing employees with a prespecified performance standard.

Table 9-1 lists the possible comparative and absolute systems that could be used. The next few sections in this chapter discuss how to implement each of these systems, and I also point out some advantages and disadvantages of each.

TABLE 9-1 **Comparative and Absolute Systems to Measure Performance as Behaviors**

Comparative	Absolute
Simple rank order	Essays
Alternation rank order	Behavior checklists
Paired comparisons	Graphic rating scales
Relative percentile	
Forced distribution	

Measuring Behaviors Using Comparative Systems

Comparative systems of measuring behaviors imply that employees are evaluated relative to one other. You can consider the options discussed in the following sections.

Rank order

If a rank order system is used, employees are simply ranked from best performer to worst performer.

Alternation rank order

In an alternation rank order procedure, the result is a list of all employees. Then raters selects the best performer (#1), then the worst performer (#n), the second best (#2), the second worst (#n–1), and so forth, alternating from the top to the bottom of the list until all employees have been ranked.

Paired comparisons

Paired comparisons is the third type of comparative system. In contrast to the simple and alternation rank order procedures, this system makes explicit comparisons between all pairs of employees to be evaluated. In other words, raters systematically compare the performance of each employee against the performance of all other employees. The number of pairs of employees to be compared is computed by n(n–1)/2, where n is the number of employees to be evaluated. If a rater needs to evaluate the performance of 8 employees, she would have to make [8(8–1)]/2 = 28 comparisons. The rater's job is to choose the better of each pair, and each individual's rank is determined by counting the number of times he was rated as better.

Relative percentile

The fourth type of comparison method is the relative percentile method. This type of measurement system asks raters to consider all employees at the same time and to estimate the relative performance of each by using a 100-point scale. The 50-point mark on this scale (50th percentile) suggests the location of an average employee — about 50 percent of employees are better performers and about 50 percent of employees are worse performers than this individual. Relative percentile methods may include one such scale for each competency and also include one scale on which raters evaluate the overall performance of all employees.

Figure 9-2 includes an example of a relative percentile method scale to measure the competency "communication." In this illustration, the rater has placed Heather at roughly the 95th percentile, meaning that Heather's performance regarding communication is higher than 95 percent of other employees. On the other hand, Don has been placed around the 48th percentile, meaning that about 52 percent of employees are performing better than him.

FIGURE 9-2:
Example of
relative percentile
method scale.

Forced distribution

A fifth comparison method is called forced distribution. In this type of system, employees are classified according to an approximately normal distribution — a curve that looks like a bell and has approximately the same number of performers to the right and the left of the mean or average score (that is, the center of the distribution). For example, 20 percent of employees must be classified as exceeding expectations, 70 percent must be classified as meeting expectations, and 10 percent must be classified as not meeting expectations.

FORCED DISTRIBUTION SYSTEM AT GENERAL ELECTRIC

General Electric (GE) is one of the most frequently cited companies to have used a comparative rating system with a forced distribution. In recent years, the rigid system of requiring managers to place employees into three groups (top 20 percent, middle 70 percent, and bottom 10 percent) has been revised to allow more flexibility. While the normal distribution is still referenced as a guideline, the rigid 20/70/10 split has been removed, and work groups are now able to have more "A players" or "no bottom 10s."

The company did not view the forced distribution system of the past as a match for fostering a more innovative culture in which taking risks and failure are part of the business culture. As a result, the company has begun evaluating employees relative to certain traits, including one's ability to act in an innovative manner or have an external business focus. In summary, GE's performance management system and revisions to the system provide an example of how decisions about how to measure performance need to consider the ramifications and resulting behaviors that are encouraged or discouraged. The consideration of culture and overall business strategy is also crucial in determining how to measure performance.

More recently, GE has revised its measurement system again. Specifically, GE has moved from a formal "once-a-year" performance review to an app-based system. Using this system allows managers to provide feedback and coaching on a more frequent basis to their employees. Performance management tasks such as recognizing employee contributions, identifying areas of concern, and offering developmental opportunities can now be offered in near real-time, rather than waiting until the annual performance appraisal. Also, performance appraisal meetings are themselves more productive as there are few surprises. Rather than using an exclusively backward-looking system, the new system is also forward-looking and focuses on development by guiding, coaching, and providing feedback to employees that helps them on their path to achieving their goals. These changes at GE reflect a shift from a performance appraisal system focused on ratings to a performance management system involving a constant and ongoing evaluation of performance.

General Electric (GE) is one organization that adopted a forced distribution system under the leadership of former CEO Jack Welch. This forced distribution system was called the "vitality curve." In Welch's view, forced ranking enables managers to "take care of your very best, make sure the valued middle is cared for, and weed out the weakest." GE's success in implementing a forced ranking system is cited as the model by many of the 20 percent of U.S. companies that have adopted it in the past three decades. At GE each year, 10 percent of managers used to be assigned the "C" grade, and if they did not improve, they were asked to leave the company. Want to learn more about this topic? See the nearby sidebar describing the evolution of forced distribution systems at Cargill and Adobe.

Cargill, Adobe, and many other companies are going through a similar process of transitioning from a performance appraisal (the dreaded once-a-year evaluation and review) to a performance management system (ongoing evaluation and feedback). Also, you may have noticed quite a bit of popular business press hype about the "demise of performance evaluation and measurement."

However, contrary to the way this trend is usually described with such headlines as "Performance Evaluation is Dead" and "The End of Performance Reviews," the evaluation of performance is not going away. In fact, it is becoming a normal, routine, built-in, and ever-present aspect of work in 21st century organizations. So to paraphrase Mark Twain, the death of performance management has been vastly exaggerated.

Considering Advantages and Disadvantages of Comparative Systems

These are clear advantages to using comparative measurement methods:

>> These types of measurement procedures are usually easy to explain.

>> Decisions resulting from these types of systems are fairly straightforward: It is easy to see which employees are where in the distributions.

>> They tend to control several biases and errors made by those rating performance better than do those in absolute systems. Such errors include leniency (giving high scores to most employees), severity (giving low scores to most employees), and central tendency (not giving any above-expectations or below-expectations ratings).

>> They are particularly beneficial for jobs that are very autonomous (where employees perform their duties without much interdependence).

>> Individuals high in cognitive abilities are more attracted to organizations that have forced distribution systems because they expect to perform well and benefit directly from this type of system. Also, to them, it is an important signal that the organization values high achievement.

On the other hand, there are also disadvantages associated with the use of comparative systems, which may explain why a 2017 study published in the *International Journal of Selection and Assessment* reported that only about 17 percent of HR executives report that their companies use these types of systems exclusively. The disadvantages are as follows:

>> Employees usually are compared only in terms of a single overall category. Employees are not compared based on individual behaviors or even individual competencies, but instead, they are compared based on an overall assessment of performance. As a consequence, the resulting rankings are not sufficiently specific so that employees can receive useful feedback. In addition, these rankings may be subject to legal challenge.

>> Because the resulting data are based on rankings and not on actual scores, there is no information about the relative distance between employees. All we know is that employee A received a higher score than employee B, but we don't know if this difference is, for example, similar to the difference between employee B and employee C.

EXAMPLE

Some of these disadvantages were experienced by Microsoft and were noticed by Lisa E. Brummel, former vice president for HR. She noted that by using a forced distribution system, "people were beginning to feel like their placement in one of the buckets was a larger part of the evaluation than the work the person actually did." Similarly, a posting on an anonymous Microsoft employees' blog called *MiniMicrosoft* read as follows: "I LOVE this company, but I hate the Curve."

Anticipating problems caused by forced distributions

Many of the criticisms about against forced distribution systems, and comparative systems in general, are about performance ratings. After all, ratings are often the building blocks for making employee comparisons.

Also, although many of the criticisms may seem directed at comparative rating systems, they are actually about how the system is designed and used. For example, criticisms involve saying that forced distributions are biased, unjustified, inaccurate, and may even lead to litigation. But much like performance ratings, the problem is often not the forced distribution per se, but what is measured, how it is measured, the extent to which employees participate in the process, and consequences associated with the resulting ratings.

WARNING

Forced distribution systems that are perceived as being unfair and even cruel are signs that the performance management system is broken. For example, it is likely that there is no clear explanation of how ratings were produced. Also, it is likely that employees not rated at the top of the distribution feel that their contributions are not valued by their organizations.

DITCHING PERFORMANCE RATINGS AT CARGILL AND ADOBE? NOT REALLY

Many organizations that initially ditched forced distributions and even ratings altogether are using them again, although they use different labels and terms to refer to them. For example, Cargill introduced its "Everyday Performance Management" system, designed to incorporate daily encouragement and feedback into on-the-job conversations. Managers offer performance evaluations and feedback on an ongoing basis. As another example, consider Adobe, which is one of the most frequently discussed cases regarding its performance management system because the company reported it was able to reduce voluntary employee turnover by about 30 percent after introducing a frequent "check-in program." Again, performance is evaluated on an ongoing basis.

As noted by Adobe's Senior Vice President for People and Places, Donna Morris, the new system "requires executives and managers to have regular tough discussions with employees who are struggling with performance issues rather than putting them off until the next performance review cycle comes around."

So as mentioned earlier, contrary to what one may conclude based on reading the popular business press, it is not the case that companies are abandoning distributions and ratings. They are actually implementing performance systems more clearly aligned with best practices, as described in this book, that involve a constant and ongoing evaluation of performance! These and many other companies may have eliminated the labels "performance evaluation," "performance review," and even "performance management." Instead, they use labels such as "performance achievement," "check-ins," and "employee development." But at the end of the day, they are implementing performance management using new labels.

Understanding the shape of the performance distribution and producing star performers

The use of a forced distribution system implies that performance scores are forced to fit under a particular distribution shape. As mentioned earlier, companies such as GE, Yahoo!, and many others have used the bell-shaped distribution for decades. And today, it is used in many colleges and universities as part of the student grading system.

Think about the following: If the distribution of performance is truly bell-shaped, this means that the majority of employees are grouped toward the center (that is, are average), and there is a very small minority of individuals who are very poor and very good performers, as shown in Figure 9-3. Also, if you use a bell curve to assign ratings, you ration the number of top performers. For example, if you use a five-point scale, many companies would tell managers that "no more than 10 percent of the direct reports get the highest rating of 5." But what if this is an outstanding unit that had an excellent applicant pool, recruited the best among the best, and then offered training and development opportunities resulting in even better performance? Why should you limit the highest ratings to just the top 10 percent if you have, say, 40 percent as star performers?

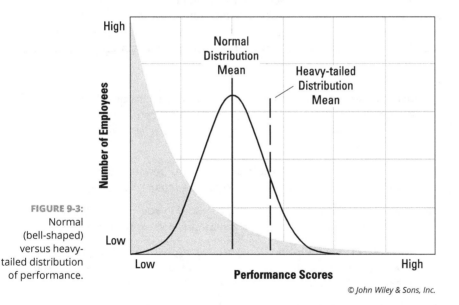

FIGURE 9-3: Normal (bell-shaped) versus heavy-tailed distribution of performance.

© John Wiley & Sons, Inc.

My colleagues, doctoral students, and I have done research on this issue during the past 10 years and collected data on more than 800,000 workers, including researchers in 52 scientific fields: actors, actresses, directors, choreographers, and lighting specialists in the movie and TV industries; fiction and nonfiction writers; musicians; professional and collegiate athletes in football, baseball, basketball, cricket, swimming, track and field, skiing, tennis, and other sports (individual and team sports); and other types of workers, including bank tellers, call center employees, grocery checkers, electrical fixture assemblers, and wirers. The result was consistent over and over again: Performance scores are not distributed following a normal curve, but a heavy-tailed distribution.

As shown in Figure 9-3, there is a critical difference between these two types of distributions. Under a heavy-tailed distribution, we expect to see many "star performers" (those very far to the right of the mean or average). However, under a normal distribution, the presence of such extreme scores is considered an anomaly. Also, Figure 9-3 shows that performance (the area under the curves) is such that under a heavy-tailed distribution, differences between the top and average performers are much greater under a heavy-tailed compared to normal distribution.

What does all of this mean for performance management and your understanding of star performers? And by star performers, I'm talking about those individuals who not only do well in terms of their individual performance, but more importantly, have a large positive influence on numerous key outcomes, such as firm survival, retention of clients, new product development, and many other indicators of organizational performance. How can an organization produce more star performers? You can do the following:

>> **Identify, and if possible, eliminate situational constraints** (that is, ceiling constraints) faced by workers to allow for the emergence of star performers. For example, what are the resources needed to facilitate the emergence of stars?

>> **Allow star performers to rotate across teams** because this widens their network and takes full advantage of knowledge transfer to rising stars.

>> **Make sure sufficient resources are invested in star performers** who are making clear contributions to an organization's core strategic objectives.

>> **Take care of star retention** by paying attention to their developmental network (for example, employment opportunities for significant others and long-term contracting with a star's subordinates).

>> **In times of financial challenges and budget cuts, pay special attention to star performers** because once they leave, an organization's recovery will be very difficult. In fact, star departure can create a downward spiral of

production when average and even mediocre performers deliberately replace stars with inferior workers.

>> **Star performers should be given preferential treatment,** but these perks should be clearly articulated to all workers and applied fairly. In other words, anyone can receive those perks if they achieve high levels of performance. Consider the following analogy. If a large proportion of your company sales come from just 30 percent of your customers, you would be thinking about making sure these customers are happy and how to treat them better. Also, you would probably call them to thank them and even offer to treat them to a very nice lunch or dinner. Similarly, if a minority of employees is responsible for a disproportionately large amount of results, you should talk to them and find ways to treat them better so they stay within the organization.

>> **Invest a disproportionate amount of resources into stars,** which will likely generate greater overall performance and create positive gain spirals.

WARNING

The easiest way to not produce star performers is to use non-performance-based incentives, encourage limited pay dispersion, and implement longevity-based promotion decisions because they emphasize homogeneity of employee performance.

Measuring Behaviors Using Absolute Systems

In absolute systems, raters provide evaluations of an employee's performance without making direct reference to other employees. In the simplest absolute system, a rater writes an essay describing each employee's strengths and weaknesses and makes suggestions for improvement.

Essays

One advantage of the essay system is that raters have the potential to provide detailed feedback to employees regarding their performance. On the contrary, essays are almost totally unstructured, so some raters may choose to be more detailed than others. Some raters may be better at writing essays than others. Because of this variability, comparisons across individuals, groups, or units are virtually impossible because essays written by different raters, and even by the same rater regarding different employees, may address different aspects of an employee's performance. Finally, essays don't provide any quantitative information, making it difficult to use them in some personnel decisions (such as allocation of rewards).

Behavior checklists

A second type of absolute system involves a behavior checklist, which consists of a form listing behavioral statements that are indicators of the various competencies to be measured. The rater's task is to indicate ("check") statements that describe the employee being rated. When this type of measurement system is in place, raters are not so much evaluators as they are "reporters" of employee behavior. Because it is likely that all behaviors rated are present to some extent, behavior checklists usually include a description of the behavior in question (for example, "the employee arrives at work on time"), followed by several response categories, such as "always," "very often," "fairly often," "occasionally," and "never." The rater simply checks the response category she feels best describes the employee. Each response category is weighted — for example, from 5 ("always") to 1 ("never") if the statement describes desirable behavior such as arriving at work on time. Then an overall score for each employee is computed by adding the weights of the responses that were checked for each item. Figure 9-4 includes an example of an item from a form using a behavior checklist measurement approach.

FIGURE 9-4: Example of behavior checklist item.

1	2	3	4	5
Never	Sometimes	Often	Fairly often	Always

© John Wiley & Sons, Inc.

Anchors for behavior checklists

How do you select response categories for behavior checklist scales? Often, this decision is fairly arbitrary and equal intervals between scale points are simply assumed. For example, in Figure 9-4, you would assume that the distance between "never" and "sometimes" is the same as the distance between "fairly often" and "always" (that is, 1 point in each case). However, great care must be taken in how the anchors are selected.

Table 9-2 includes anchors that you can use for scales involving frequency, and Table 9-3 has anchors for scales of amount.

Tables 9-2 and 9-3 include anchors to be used in both seven-point and five-point scales. For most systems, a five-point scale should be sufficient to capture an employee's performance on the behavior being rated. One advantage of using five-point scales is that they are less complex than seven-point scales. Also, five-point scales are superior to three-point scales because they are more likely to motivate performance improvement because employees believe it is more doable to move up one level on a five-point scale than it is on a three-point scale.

TABLE 9-2

Anchors for Behavior Checklists of Frequency

7-Point Scale	5-Point Scale
Always	Always
Constantly	Very often
Often	Fairly often
Fairly often	Occasionally
Sometimes	Never
Once in a while	
Never	

TABLE 9-3

Anchors for Behavior Checklists of Amount

7-Point Scale	5-Point Scale
All	All
An extraordinary amount of	An extreme amount of
A great amount of	Quite a bit of
Quite a bit of	Some
A moderate amount of	None
Somewhat	
None	

Table 9-4 includes anchors that can be used in scales involving agreement, and Table 9-5 includes anchors for scales about evaluation. These tables include 13 anchors that you can use for each of these types of scales.

In creating scales, you must choose anchors that are approximately equally spaced based on the anchors included in Tables 9-4 and 9-5. So if you were to create a five-point scale of evaluation using the information provided in Table 9-4, one possible set of anchors might be the following:

1. Terrible
2. Unsatisfactory

3. Decent
4. Good
5. Excellent

TABLE 9-4   ## Anchors for Behavior Checklists of Evaluation

Anchor	Rating
Terrible	1.6
Bad	3.3
Inferior	3.6
Poor	3.8
Unsatisfactory	3.9
Mediocre	5.3
Passable	5.5
Decent	6.0
Fair	6.1
Average	6.4
Satisfactory	6.9
Good	7.5
Excellent	9.6

Source: Adapted from http://psycnet.apa.org/record/1974-32365-001

TABLE 9-5   ## Anchors for Behavior Checklists of Agreement

Anchor	Rating
Slightly	2.5
A little	2.7
Mildly	4.1
Somewhat	4.4
In part	4.7
Halfway	4.8

Anchor	Rating
Tend to	5.3
Inclined to	5.4
Moderately	5.4
Generally	6.8
Pretty much	7.0
On the whole	7.4
Very much	9.1

Source: Adapted from http://psycnet.apa.org/record/1974-32365-001

In this set of anchors, the distance between all pairs of adjacent anchors ranges from 1.5 to 2.3 points. Note, however, that the use of the anchor "terrible" has a very negative connotation, so you may want to use a less negative anchor, such as "bad" or "inferior." In this case, you would choose an anchor that is closer to the next one ("unsatisfactory") than you may want, but using the new anchor may lead to less defensive and overall negative reactions on the part of employees who receive this rating.

REMEMBER

Behavior checklists are easy to use and to understand. But it is difficult to extract detailed and useful feedback from the numerical rating provided. Overall, however, the practical advantages of checklists explain their popularity.

Critical incidents

Every job includes some critical behaviors that make a crucial difference between doing a job effectively and doing it ineffectively. The critical incidents measurement approach involves gathering reports of situations in which employees exhibited behaviors that were especially effective or ineffective in accomplishing their jobs. The recorded critical incidents provide a starting point for assessing performance. For example, consider the following incident as recorded by a high school principal regarding the performance of Tom Jones, the head of the disability services office:

> A sophomore with learning disabilities was experiencing difficulty in writing. Her parents wanted an iPad for her. Tom Jones ordered an iPad and it was delivered to the student's teacher. No training was provided to the child, her teacher, or her parents. The iPad was never used.

This recorded incident is actually the synthesis of a series of incidents:

1. A problem was detected (a student with a special need was identified).

2. Corrective action was taken (the iPad was ordered).

3. Corrective action was initially positive (the iPad was delivered).

4. Corrective action was subsequently deficient (the iPad was not used because of the lack of training).

When critical incidents are collected, this measurement method allows raters to focus on actual job behavior, rather than on vaguely defined traits. On the contrary, collecting critical incidents is very time-consuming. As is the case with essays, it is difficult to attach a score quantifying the impact of the incident (either positive or negative). A revised version of the critical incidents technique involves summarizing critical incidents and giving them to raters in the form of scales (for example, behavior checklist). One example following up on the critical incident involving Tom Jones might be the following:

Addresses learning needs of special-needs students efficiently				
Strongly Agree	Agree	Undecided	Disagree	Strongly Disagree

A second variation of the critical incidents technique is the approach adopted in the performance management system at the city of Irving, Texas. First, the city identified core competencies and classified them as core values, skill group competencies, or performance essentials. Then the team in charge of implementing the system wrote dozens of examples of different levels of performance on each competency — from ineffective to highly effective. In other words, this team was in charge of compiling critical incidents illustrating various performance levels for each competency. Then managers used this list by simply circling the behavior that best described each of the employees in the work unit.

As an example, take the competency Adaptability/Flexibility. For this competency, critical incidents were used to illustrate various performance levels:

Completely Ineffective	Somewhat Ineffective	Effective	Highly Effective	Exceptional
Able to focus on only one task at a time	Easily distracted from work assignments/ activities	Handles a variety of work assignments/ activities with few difficulties	Handles a variety of work assignments/ activities concurrently	Easily juggles a large number of assignments and activities
Avoids or attempts to undermine changes	Complains about necessary changes	Accepts reasons for change	Understands and responds to reasons for change	Encourages and instructs others about the benefits of change
Refuses to adopt changed policies	Makes only those changes with which they agree	Adapts to changing circumstances and attitudes of others	Adapts to changes and develops job aids to assist others	Welcomes change and looks for new opportunities it provides
Considers only own opinion when seeking solution	Occasionally listens to others but supports own solutions	Listens to others and seeks solutions acceptable to all	Ensures that everyone's thoughts and opinions are considered in reaching a solution	Actively seeks input in addition to recognized sources and facilitates implementation of solution

A third variation of the critical incidents technique is the use of behaviorally anchored rating scales (BARS), which I describe next, as one of several types of graphic rating scales.

Using a graphic rating scale system

The graphic rating scale is a popular tool used to measure performance. The aim of graphic rating scales is to ensure that the response categories (ratings of behavior) are clearly defined, that interpretation of the rating by an outside party is clear, and that the rater and the employee understand the rating. An example of a graphic rating scale used to rate the performance of a project manager is the following:

> Project management awareness is the knowledge of project management planning, updating status, working within budget, and delivering project on time and within budget. Rate _____'s project management awareness using the following scale:

1	2	3	4	5
Unaware or not interested	Needs additional training	Aware of responsibilities	Excellent knowledge and performance of skills	Superior performance of skill; ability to train others

BARS (behaviorally anchored rating scales) use graphic rating scales that employ critical incidents as anchors. BARS improve on the graphic rating scales by first having a group of employees identify all the important dimensions of a job. Then another group of employees generates critical incidents illustrating low, average, and high skills of performance for each dimension. A third group of employees and supervisors takes each dimension and the accompanying definitions and a randomized list of critical incidents. They must match the critical incidents with the correct dimensions. Finally, a group of judges assigns a scale value to each incident. Consider the following BARS for measuring job knowledge:

Job Knowledge: The amount of job-related knowledge and skills that an employee possesses.

5	Exceptional: Employee consistently displays high level of job knowledge in all areas of his or her job. Other employees go to this person for training.
4	Advanced: Shows high levels of job knowledge in most areas of his or her job. Consistently completes all normal tasks. Employee continues searching for more job knowledge, and may seek guidance in some areas.
3	Competent: Employee shows an average level of job knowledge in all areas of the job. May need assistance completing difficult tasks.
2	Improvement Needed: Does not consistently meet deadlines or complete tasks required for this job. Does not attempt to acquire new skills or knowledge to improve performance.
1	Major Improvement Needed: Typically performs tasks incorrectly or not at all. Employee has no appreciation for improving his or her performance.

See the following BARS which measures "Knowledge of Accounting and Auditing Standards/Theory," which is one of ten performance dimensions identified as important for auditors:

Knowledge of Accounting and Auditing Standards/Theory: Technical foundation, application of knowledge on the job, ability to identify problem areas and weigh theory versus practice.

3	High-Point Performance: Displays very strong technical foundation, able to proficiently apply knowledge on the job, willingly researches areas, able to identify problems, can weigh theory vs. practice considerations.
2	Mid-Point Performance: Can resolve normal accounting issues, has adequate technical foundation and skills, application requires some refinement, has some problems in weighing theory vs. practice, can identify major problem areas.
1	Low-Point Performance: Displays weak accounting knowledge and/or technical ability to apply knowledge to situations/issues on an engagement, has difficulty in identifying problems and/or weighing factors of theory vs. practice.

For graphic rating scales to be most useful and accurate, they must include the following features:

>> The meaning of each response category is clear.

>> The individual who is interpreting the ratings (for example, a human resources manager) can tell clearly what response was intended.

>> The performance dimension being rated is defined clearly for the rater.

Compare the two examples of BARS shown earlier. Which is better regarding each of these three features? How would you revise and improve these BARS?

There are several types of methods for measuring performance. They differ in terms of practicality (some take more time and effort to be developed than others), usefulness for administrative purposes (some are less useful than others because they don't provide a clear quantification of performance), and usefulness for users (some are less useful than others in terms of the feedback they produce that allows employees to improve performance in the future). Practicality and usefulness are key considerations in choosing one type of measurement procedure over another.

Chapter **10**

Using Performance Management Analytics

Performance management cannot exist without *performance analytics.* What is this, exactly? It's the collection of performance data, usually in the form of performance ratings. And performance ratings are collected from all relevant performance touchpoints, which include supervisors, peers, direct reports, self, and customers, as well as employee performance monitoring systems that are involved in collecting Big Data (that is, lots of data about what employees do and produce on an ongoing basis).

But what type of data should you collect from each performance touchpoint? How should you use electronic performance monitoring effectively? How can you collect performance data that are fair and accurate? How can you make sure raters don't intentionally distort their evaluations? This chapter deals with these questions and many other issues about performance analytics, including how to collect performance data and from what sources.

The Jury Is Out: All Firms Collect Performance Data

I am sure you are aware that the issue of performance ratings is hotly debated. Although many companies such as Adobe, Microsoft, Eli Lilly, and The Gap have announced that they are "abandoning performance ratings," they actually engage in various forms of performance analytics and continue to collect and compile performance data. But instead of using the term "performance ratings," they use labels such as "judgments," "achievement metrics," and "expectations." In other words, managers and employees continue to gather and compline data about performance, and those data are used to make administrative decisions about employees and evaluations of employees' on-the-job behaviors and results.

EXAMPLE

Juniper is an example of a company that has supposedly "abandoned" performance ratings. Juniper is based in California and develops and markets networking products such as routers, switches, and network security software. Juniper uses the label "J Players" to refer to the performance of employees who meet expectations against four performance elements. Also, the performance of employees is calibrated based on relative contribution. Similarly, other companies use different labels in their performance analytics efforts, such as "don't have it," "have it," or "knock it out of the park." In addition, companies continue to ask managers about their recommendations regarding who should receive a pay increase or bonus, and of what size, based on employee performance — regardless of whether they call this a "rating" or not.

Why all organizations collect performance data

The fact is that in organizations, evaluations about performance are made all the time — explicitly or implicitly — because, simply put, an organization cannot be successful in accomplishing its goals if the performance of its employees is not measured in some way. Performance analytics is also critical for managing individual and team performance. Absent performance analytics, how can an organization understand if its employees are making progress? How can an organization make decisions about promotions and compensations? How can an organization that wants to create a "personal growth and development culture" offer meaningful development and coaching opportunities absent knowledge about who is doing what — and how? And even if they don't say it openly, managers and peers form impressions and evaluate the performance of people around them on a daily basis — even if these evaluations are not written down or said out loud. The fact is that judgments and evaluations of performance are part of organizational life.

PERFORMANCE MANAGEMENT "WITHOUT RATINGS" AT THE GAP? NOT REALLY . . .

The Gap, Inc., is one of the companies frequently talked about as being the leader in implementing a performance management system "without ratings." Gap, Inc. is an American worldwide clothing store that includes renowned brands such as Gap, Banana Republic, Old Navy, Athleta, Intermix, and Weddington Way. In 2014, the company decided to revamp its performance management system to "eliminate performance ratings." Its new system is called GPS, which stands for grow, perform, and succeed (not coincidentally, Gap's New York Stock Exchange stock symbol is also GPS).

GPS includes many of the features of best-in-kind performance management systems described throughout this book. For example, performance management doesn't take place once a year; instead it is a yearlong process that involves monthly "touch base" sessions between supervisors and direct reports. Also, each employee has a limited yet meaningful number of eight goals and this includes not only what has been achieved but also how — which are measured as behaviors and competencies. Goals are updated throughout the year and are closely linked to company goals. For example, the touch base sessions involve answering the question of whether an employee's performance is "demonstrating the values of the company."

How about performance ratings? Rob Ollander-Krane, Senior Director, Organization Performance Effectiveness, said that "With the removal of ratings, employees are no longer awarded a grade at the end of the year." So how do managers make decisions about compensation and development needs? Can these decisions be made fairly and accurately without performance ratings? Is it really true that the system is ratingless? Well, not really.

As noted by Ollander-Krane, managers "are not giving an A, B, or C, but they still need to rank their employees. They still need to say here's my number one employee, here's my number two, here's my number three — and to allocate their merit and bonus pot accordingly." How about documentation? Ollander-Krane said that "We've had a new CEO and CHRO since we introduced GPS, and they have questioned whether we need to have a bit more of a written record of employee performance."

The lesson? It is simply not possible to implement a performance management system that doesn't include measures of performance — regardless of whether those measures are called ratings, rankings, grades, scores, achievement metrics, or anything else. As the saying goes, if it looks like a duck, swims like a duck, and quacks like a duck, then it probably is a duck. This applies quite well to metrics used by many companies that have seemingly abandoned "performance ratings." Ratings are still very much part of their process in one way or another.

So this chapter includes useful information and guidelines so your performance analytics practices become systematic, transparent, and effective.

Setting the evaluation period

In collecting performance data, the first question you should answer is: How long should the appraisal period be? In other words, what period of time should be included in the evaluation?

Most organizations typically conduct a formal annual review. However, others choose to conduct semiannual or even quarterly formal reviews. Conducting only an annual review is usually not sufficient for most employees to discuss performance issues in a formal setting. In particular, Millennials value more frequent feedback about how they are doing.

My recommendation is that you conduct formal sit-down semiannual or quarterly reviews.

EXAMPLE

Colorado-based Hamilton Standard Commercial Aircraft uses a semiannual review system. Twice per year, the company performs a modified 360-degree appraisal, meaning that performance information is collected from performance touch-points from all around (hence, the "360-degree" label). This type of system allows individuals to receive feedback and adjust goals or objectives, if necessary, in preparation for the more in-depth annual review.

EXAMPLE

Synygy, Inc., a Philadelphia-based compensation software and services company, has formal quarterly reviews. Each quarter, employees receive a summary of comments and specific examples from coworkers about how they are performing.

When is the best time to complete formal sit-down reviews? You have two choices:

>> **The appraisal form could be completed on or around the annual anniversary date.** In the case of semiannual reviews, the first review would be six months before the annual anniversary date, and the second review would be on or around the annual anniversary date. The biggest advantage of this choice is that the supervisor does not have to fill out all employees' forms at the same time. The disadvantage of this choice is that because results are not tied to a common cycle for all employees, resulting rewards cannot be tied to the fiscal year.

>> **The second choice is to complete the appraisal forms toward the end of the fiscal year.** In the case of a system including semiannual reviews, one review would be completed halfway through the fiscal year and the other one toward the end of the fiscal year. Adopting this approach leads to the completion of the appraisal form for all employees at about the same time,

which facilitates cross-employee comparisons as well as the distribution of rewards. Another advantage is that individual goal setting can be more easily tied to corporate goal setting because most companies align their goal cycle with their fiscal year. This helps employees synchronize their work and objectives with those of their unit and organization. But what about the additional work imposed on the supervisors who need to evaluate all employees at once during a short period of time? If there is ongoing communication between the supervisor and the employee about performance issues throughout the year, completing appraisal forms should not uncover any major surprises and filling out the appraisal form does not create a major time burden for the supervisors.

Including Critical Components in Effective Performance Appraisal Forms

Information on performance is collected formally by using forms, which are most often administered online.

Saying goodbye to paper performance evaluation forms

The availability of apps and off-the-shelf software to collect performance data has produced a veritable revolution. So performance data are collected real-time using web and mobile apps, and the information can easily be shared, also real-time. In this way, other team members, supervisors, direct reports, and also the HR function have access to the same data.

TIP

Using online forms is very useful because as changes take place in the organization (such as a new strategic direction) or job in question (for example, new tasks), forms need to be revised and updated, and this can be done fast and efficiently by keeping them online.

Nine critical components of effective evaluation forms

These are the critical components of useful performance evaluation forms:

>> **Basic employee information:** This section of the form includes basic employee information such as job title, division, department and other work

group information, employee ID number, and pay grade or salary classification. In addition, forms usually include the dates of the evaluation period, the number of months and years the rater has supervised or worked with the employee, an employee's starting date with the company and starting date in the current job, the reason for appraisal, current salary and position in range, and the date of the next scheduled formal evaluation.

» **Accountabilities and objectives:** If the organization adopts a results approach to defining and measuring performance, this section of the form includes the name and description of each accountability (that is, broad areas of a job for which the employee is responsible for producing results), objectives agreed upon by manager and employee, and the extent to which the objectives have been achieved. In many instances, the objectives are weighted in terms of importance, which facilitates the calculation of an overall performance score. Finally, this section also includes a subsection describing conditions under which performance was achieved, which helps explain why performance achieved the high or low level described. For example, a supervisor has the opportunity to describe specific circumstances surrounding performance during the review period, including a tough economy, the introduction of a new line of products, and so forth.

» **Competencies and behavioral indicators:** If the organization adopts a behavior approach (that is, what employees do), this section of the form includes a definition of the competencies to be assessed (clusters of knowledge, skills, and abilities that are critical in determining how results will be achieved) together with their behavioral indicators.

» **Major achievements and contributions:** Some forms include a section in which a rater is asked to list the two or three major accomplishments of the individual being rated during the review period. These could refer to results, behaviors, or both.

» **Developmental achievements:** This section of the form includes information about the extent to which the developmental goals set for the review period have been achieved. For example, this information can include a summary of activities, such as workshops attended and online courses taken, as well as results, such as a description of new skills learned. You can document evidence of having learned new skills by, for example, obtaining a professional certification or designations (for example, human resource management certifications, information systems certifications). Although some organizations include developmental achievements in the appraisal form, others choose to include them in a separate form. For example, Sun Microsystems (now part of Oracle) separates these forms. Some organizations don't include development content as part of the appraisal form because it is often difficult for employees to focus constructively on development if they have received a less-than-ideal performance review.

» **Developmental needs, plans, and goals:** This section of the form is future-oriented and includes information about specific goals and timetables in terms of employee development. As I note earlier, some organizations choose to create a separate development form and don't include this information as part of the performance appraisal form.

» **Multiple performance touchpoints:** Some forms include sections to be completed by different raters involved in different types of performance touchpoints, such as customers with whom the employee interacts. Those involved in performance touchpoints are people who have firsthand knowledge of and are affected by the employee's performance. In most cases, input is collected by using forms separate from the main appraisal because not all sources of performance information are in the position to rate the same performance dimensions. For example, an employee is rated on the competency "teamwork" by peers and on the competency "reliability" by customers. I include a more detailed discussion of the use of information derived from different performance touchpoints later in this chapter.

» **Employee comments:** This section includes reactions and comments provided by the employee being rated. In addition to allowing formal employee input, which improves the perceived fairness of the system, the inclusion of this section helps with legal issues because it documents that the employee has had an opportunity to participate in the evaluation process.

» **Signatures:** The final section includes a section in which the employee being rated, the rater, and the rater's supervisor provide their signatures to show they have seen and discussed the content of the form. The HR function also provides approval of the content of the form.

Evaluating the components of a sample evaluation form

Let's go over an example and you can see the extent to which it includes all the critical components I list above — and how they can be improved. That is, to what extent these forms lack some of the critical components that should be included?

Please see the form in Figure 10-1. This is a fairly generic form that can be used for almost any position in pretty much any company. Let's evaluate this form in relation to the critical components.

PERFORMANCE REVIEW FORM

Employee Name: [   ]

Title: [   ]

Manager: [   ]

Date of Appraisal Meeting: [   ]

Employee Performance Reviews improve employee performance and development by encouraging communication, establishing performance expectations, identifying developmental needs, and setting goals to improve performance. Performance reviews also provide an ongoing record of employee performance, which is helpful for both the supervisor and employee.

Use the form below to list examples of outstanding performance or achievements as well as areas of performance that need improvement. Please provide open comments on your employee's performance. Complete each section and list examples of performance where applicable.

❒ Job description/key responsibilities/required tasks:

[   ]

❒ Note expected accomplishments vs. actual accomplishments:

[   ]

❒ List the areas where the employee developed in ways enabling him or her to take on additional responsibilities or be eligible for high-profile assignments:

[   ]

❑   Areas of development for upcoming quarter (i.e., communication skills, teamwork, project management skills, budgeting experience, etc.):

[blank box]

❑   Goals for upcoming quarter (Please list S.M.A.R.T. goals):

[blank box]

Please circle the number below that best describes the employee's performance in the following areas:

Areas of concentration	Did not meet expectations	Achieved most expectations	Achieved expectations	Achieved expectations and exceeded on a few	Significantly exceeded expectations
Teamwork	1	2	3	4	5
Leadership	1	2	3	4	5
Business acumen	1	2	3	4	5
Customer service	1	2	3	4	5
Project management	1	2	3	4	5

Average Performance Score	

Employee Use Only:

Please provide comments and examples of behaviors to describe your performance in the past quarter.

[blank box]

FIGURE 10-1:
Example of generic performance review form.

Manager Signature: _____   Date : ☐ / ☐ / ☐

Employee Signature: _____   Date : ☐ / ☐ / ☐

First, the form asks for the employee's basic information. Second, while the form asks the manager to list the expected versus the actual accountabilities, it doesn't include objectives. Third, the form includes five competencies including team-work and leadership, but it doesn't include a definition of those competencies nor does it list the indicators to look for to determine whether the employee has mastered the relevant competencies. The form does include space to list major developmental achievements, developmental needs, and employee comments. The form doesn't include information regarding different performance touchpoints and it seems that the supervisor is the only source of performance data. So to summarize, Table 10-1 shows which of the components are present:

TABLE 10-1   **Critical Components Present in Generic Performance Review Form in Figure 10-1**

Critical Component	Present?
Basic employee information	✓
Accountabilities and objectives	
Competencies and indicators	
Major achievements and contributions	✓
Development achievements	✓
Development needs, plans, and goals	✓
Multiple performance touchpoints	
Employee comments	✓
Signatures	✓

WARNING

Many forms seem to be complete and thorough, but they are not. So before using an appraisal forms, make sure that all their necessary components are present.

Including Critical Characteristics to Make Evaluation Forms Effective

There is no such thing as a universally correct appraisal form that can be used for all purposes and in all organizations. In some cases, a form emphasizes competencies (i.e., necessary knowledge and skills needed to do the job). This would be the case if the system adopted a behavior approach (i.e., what an employee does) as opposed to a results approach to measure performance. In others, the form emphasizes developmental issues. In such cases, the form would be used for developmental purposes only and not for administrative purposes. In yet other cases, there is a very short form used for weekly check-ins and a separate and more comprehensive form used for a quarterly, semiannual, or even annual review.

Eight critical characteristics of effective evaluation forms

In spite of the large variability in terms of format, components, and length, there are eight desirable features that make appraisal forms particularly effective for all types of jobs and hierarchical positions in the organization:

>> **Simplicity:** Forms must be easy to understand, easy to administer, quick to complete, clear, and concise. If forms are too long, convoluted, and complicated, the performance assessment process will not be effective or may not even happen at all.

>> **Relevancy:** Good forms include information related directly to the tasks and responsibilities of the job; otherwise, they will be regarded as an administrative burden and not as a tool for performance improvement.

>> **Descriptiveness:** Good forms require that the raters provide evidence of performance regardless of the performance level. The form should be sufficiently descriptive that an outside party (for example, supervisor's supervisor or HR department) has a clear understanding of the performance information conveyed.

>> **Adaptability:** Good forms allow managers in different functions and departments to adapt them to their particular needs and situations. Also, this feature allows for changes over time to reflect changes in the nature of work and an organization's strategic direction. This feature also encourages widespread use of the form.

>> **Comprehensiveness:** Good forms include all the major areas of performance for a particular position for the entire review period.

>> **Definitional clarity:** Desirable competencies (and behavioral indicators) and results are clearly defined for all raters so that everyone evaluates the same attributes. This feature enhances the consistency of ratings across raters and levels of the organization.

>> **Communication:** The meaning of each of the components of the form must be clearly and successfully communicated to all people participating in the evaluation process. This enhances acceptance of the system and motivation to participate in it, both as rater and ratee.

>> **Time orientation:** Good forms help clarify expectations about performance. They address not only the past but also the future.

Evaluating the characteristics of a sample evaluation form

Let's go back to the generic form in Figure 10-1. How good is this form if you compare it against the eight characteristics I just listed?

First, it is simple because it is easy to understand and clear. The fact that it includes an essay format implies that it would take a little more time to complete, but the number of essays is kept to a minimum. The form is also relevant, but only if the supervisor enters the correct job description and actual accountabilities. This form can be extremely descriptive owing to its narrative nature. The form encourages the manager to give examples of relevant behavior. Next, the first portion of the form is also adaptable, perhaps too adaptable; it would be hard to compare performance across employees because the manager can adapt and change the content of the form to each employee. This form is comprehensive, but again, only if the manager lists all the expected accountabilities. This form doesn't have definitional clarity. Because the competencies listed are not clearly defined, ratings will be inconsistent across raters. Next, this form can be communicated across the organization. Manager acceptance will be hard to gain, however, because of the amount of detail required by the essay answers. Finally, the form is time-oriented. It asks for past and future performance expectations and goals. In short, Table 10-2 summarizes which of the desirable features are present in this form:

TABLE 10-2   **Critical Characteristics Present in Generic Performance Review Form in Figure 10-1**

Critical Component	Present?
Simplicity	✓
Relevancy	✓
Descriptiveness	
Adaptability	✓
Comprehensiveness	✓
Definitional clarity	
Communication	✓
Time orientation	✓

Computing Overall Performance Score

After performance data have been gathered for each employee, there is usually a need to compute an overall performance score, which is particularly necessary for making administrative decisions such as the allocation of rewards. Computing overall performance scores is also useful in determining whether employees, and groups of employees, are improving their performance over time. This is a critical aspect and advantage of approaching performance management with a performance analytics mindset: You use performance data collected on an ongoing basis to create useful and meaningful insights that help individuals grow and develop, and data serve the purpose of improving individual and team performance in terms of both behaviors and results.

Using judgmental and mechanical procedures to compute overall score

You can use two main strategies to obtain an overall performance score for each employee: judgmental and mechanical. The judgmental procedure consists of considering every aspect of performance, and then arriving at a defensible summary. This holistic procedure relies on the ability of the rater to arrive at a fair and accurate overall score. The mechanical procedure consists of first considering the scores assigned to each section of the appraisal form, and then combining them up to obtain an overall score. When adding scores from each section, weights are typically used based on the relative importance of each performance dimension measured.

Let's go over the performance evaluation form shown in Figure 10-2, which is used to evaluate the performance of sales associates at a supermarket chain. (It's adapted from `www.workforce.com/2003/03/27/buschs-performance-evaluations`.) This form includes the hypothetical ratings obtained by a sales associate on just two competencies and just two key results (the complete form probably includes more than four performance dimensions). You can see that in the Competencies section, each competency is weighted according to its value to the organization. Specifically, Follow-Through/Dependability is given a weight of 0.7, whereas Decision Making/Creative Problem-Solving is given a weight of 0.3. For the competency Follow-Through/Dependability, Patricia Carmello obtained a score of 4 for the first half of the review period and a score of 3 for the second half of the review period; consequently, the scores for this competency are $4 \times 0.7 = 2.8$ for the first half and $3 \times 0.7 = 2.1$ for the second half of the review period. Adding up the scores obtained for the first and second halves in each competency leads to a total of 3.7 points for the first half and 2.7 for the second half of the review period.

PERFORMANCE EVALUATION FORM

For use by Store Director; Co-Director; Meat, Seafood, Produce, Deli/Bakery, Floral and Grocery Managers

Name	Patricia Carmello	Review Period	2018	
Position	Sales Associate	Store	#25	
Evaluator	James Garcia	Date	12/15/18	

Competencies: Please rate the Associate on the following competencies. Determine the point total and multiply by the weight factor to achieve the point total for the competencies.

Follow-Through/Dependability		Points:		1st	2nd	Wgt	Pts	Pts
				4	3	0.7	2.8	2.1
4	3	2	1					
Work is completed correctly and on time without supervision. Anticipates needs Extremely organized.	Work is usually completed correctly and on a timely basis with some supervision. Very organized.	Work is completed as assigned and results can usually be relied upon with normal supervision. Organized.	Work can seldom be relied upon. Often fails to complete tasks correctly. Unorganized.					

Comments:

Decision Making/Creative Problem Solving		Points:		1st	2nd	Wgt	Pts	Pts
				3	2	0.3	0.9	0.6
4	3	2	1					
Anticipates, recognizes, and confronts problems with extraordinary skill. Perseveres until solution is reached. Extremely innovative and takes risks.	Defines and addresses problems well. Typically reaches useful solutions and decisions are sound. Innovative, with above-average risk taking.	Acknowledges and attempts to solve most problems when presented. Usually comes to conclusions on solving basic issues. Little innovation and sometimes takes risks.	Has difficulty recognizing problems and making decisions. Always needs guidance. No innovation and never takes risks.					

Comments:

Total Score for Competencies Section	3.7	2.7

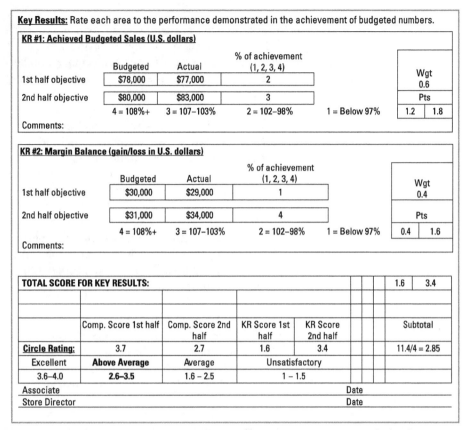

Key Results: Rate each area to the performance demonstrated in the achievement of budgeted numbers.

KR #1: Achieved Budgeted Sales (U.S. dollars)

	Budgeted	Actual	% of achievement (1, 2, 3, 4)		Wgt 0.6
1st half objective	$78,000	$77,000	2		
2nd half objective	$80,000	$83,000	3		Pts
	4 = 108%+	3 = 107–103%	2 = 102–98%	1 = Below 97%	1.2 | 1.8

Comments:

KR #2: Margin Balance (gain/loss in U.S. dollars)

	Budgeted	Actual	% of achievement (1, 2, 3, 4)		Wgt 0.4
1st half objective	$30,000	$29,000	1		
2nd half objective	$31,000	$34,000	4		Pts
	4 = 108%+	3 = 107–103%	2 = 102–98%	1 = Below 97%	0.4 | 1.6

Comments:

TOTAL SCORE FOR KEY RESULTS:							1.6	3.4
	Comp. Score 1st half	Comp. Score 2nd half	KR Score 1st half	KR Score 2nd half			Subtotal	
Circle Rating:	3.7	2.7	1.6	3.4			11.4/4 = 2.85	
Excellent	**Above Average**	Average	Unsatisfactory					
3.6–4.0	**2.6–3.5**	1.6 – 2.5	1 – 1.5					
Associate					Date			
Store Director					Date			

FIGURE 10-2: Performance appraisal form in grocery retailer.

© John Wiley & Sons, Inc.

The form also indicates that the key results have different weights. Specifically, KR #1 has a weight of 0.6, whereas KR #2 has a weight of 0.4. Consider KR #1. The objective for the first half was to achieve a sales figure of $78,000. The actual sales figure achieved by Patricia was $77,000, representing a 98.71-percent achievement, which is a score of 2. Multiplying this score times the weight of 0.6 yields 1.2 points for the first half of the review period. Similarly, for the second half, the goal was $80,000 and Patricia surpassed it by achieving a figure of $83,000, which represents a score of 3 (103.75-percent achievement); therefore, the score for the second half is 3 × 0.6 = 1.8. Finally, the form shows that the total score for the first half for all key results combined is 1.6, whereas the score for the second half is 3.4. These scores were computed by simply adding the scores obtained in each half.

Finally, the form shows the scores obtained for the competencies and the key results in each of the two halves of the review period. To obtain the overall performance score, you simply take an average of these four numbers: $(3.7 + 2.7 + 1.6 + 3.4)/4 = 2.85$. This puts Patricia in the 2.6–3.5 range, which represents a qualification of "above average."

Now, suppose that you don't follow a mechanical procedure to compute overall performance score, and instead, use a judgmental method. That is, suppose raters have no information on weights. How would James Garcia, Patricia's supervisor, compute the overall performance score? One possibility is that he might give equal weights to all competencies and would therefore consider that Follow-Through/Dependability is as important as Decision Making/Creative Problem-Solving. This would lead to different scores compared to using weights of 0.7 and 0.3. Or as an alternative, the supervisor has his own ideas about what performance dimensions should be given more weight, and he decides to ignore how the work is done (that is, behaviors), and instead, he assigns an overall score based primarily on the key results (such as sales and margin balance).

The use of weights allows the supervisor to come to an objective and clear overall performance score for each employee. As this example illustrates, the use of clearly specified weights allows the supervisor to obtain a verifiable score for each employee. Thus, the supervisor and the employees can be sure that the overall performance rating is reflective of the employee's performance in each category.

REMEMBER

Which strategy is best, judgmental or mechanical? In most cases, the mechanical method is superior to the judgmental method. A supervisor is more likely to introduce her own biases in computing the overall performance score when no clear rules exist regarding the relative importance of the various performance dimensions and there is no direction on how to combine the various performance dimensions in calculating the overall score. As far as the computation of overall scores goes, the mechanical method is superior to the judgmental method.

TIP

You will notice that the form included in Figure 10-2 has sections labeled "comments." These open-ended sections are common in most appraisal forms. However, this information is typically not used effectively. If raters are not given any training or general instructions on what to write, comments can range from none at all to very detailed descriptions of what employees have done (past orientation) and very detailed descriptions of what employees should do (future orientation). So make sure you first establish the goals of the information that raters are asked to include in these open-ended sections and then offer raters training on how to do that in a systematic and standardized fashion across ratees.

Using Multiple Performance Touchpoints

Usually the supervisor is the main source of performance information. This is the case in many organizations because the supervisor usually observes employees directly and has good knowledge about performance standards.

But there are multiple performance touchpoints, which are all the relevant sources that have firsthand knowledge of the employee's performance: direct supervisors, peers, direct reports, self, and customers. And of course, there is also Big Data collected using electronic performance monitoring systems.

Using supervisors

An advantage of using supervisors to collect performance information is that they are usually in the best position to evaluate performance in relation to strategic organizational goals. Also, supervisors are often those making decisions about rewards associated with performance evaluation.

So supervisors are often the most important source of performance information because they are knowledgeable about strategic issues, understand performance, and are usually in charge of managing employee performance.

EXAMPLE

In some cultural contexts, supervisors are seen as the exclusive source due to the pervasiveness of hierarchical organizational structures. For example, a survey of 74 HR directors in Jordan revealed that in every one of these organizations, the supervisor had almost an exclusive input in terms of providing performance information; 95 percent of respondents reported that peers had no input; 82 percent reported that employees had no input; and 90 percent reported that customers had no input either.

Although supervisors are usually the most important — and sometimes, only — source of performance information, other sources should be considered as well. For some jobs, such as teaching, law enforcement, or sales, supervisors are not performance touchpoints because they don't observe direct reports' performance on a regular basis. Also, performance evaluations given by the supervisor can be biased because the supervisor evaluates performance based on whether the ratee is contributing to goals valued by the supervisor as opposed to goals valued by the organization as a whole. For example, a supervisor provides high performance ratings to employees who help the supervisor advance his career aspirations within the company as opposed to those who engage in behaviors conducive to helping achieve organizational strategic goals.

Using peers

Many organizations use performance evaluations provided by peers. Take, for example, the system implemented at a large international financial services bank with which I am familiar but whose name needs to remain anonymous. Through acquisitions, the bank has been growing rapidly and has as its strategic goal the consolidation of its offices. Change management is extremely important to the successful implementation of this consolidation. The company is therefore revising how it assesses the competency "teamwork" at the senior and middle management levels, with the belief that successful teamwork is crucial to change management initiatives. Specifically, one-third of the score for this competency is determined by ratings provided by peers.

EXAMPLE

The Australian National University Medical School recently introduced a system in which students rate their peers in terms of personal and professional performance. Students begin to provide anonymous ratings online at the end of their first year in medical school. The system allows students to share their assessment of their peers and provides faculty with early-warning signs to assist students who are not performing up to personal or professional standards.

EXAMPLE

Although the use of peers as a source of performance data is often described as a "breakthrough" or "new" feature in many performance management systems, they have been around for quite some time. For example, in the 1940s and 1950s, they were called "buddy ratings" and were used to select military leaders in the United States.

Peer evaluations suffer from three problems, however.

> **First, such evaluations are not be readily accepted when employees believe there is friendship bias at work.** In other words, if an employee believes that ratings provided by his peers will be lower than those provided for another employee because the other employee has more friends than he does, then performance evaluations will not be taken seriously. In this situation, it is not likely that the employee will use the feedback received to improve his performance.

> **A second problem with peer evaluations is that peers are less discriminating among performance dimensions compared to supervisors.** In other words, if one is rated high on one dimension, one is also likely to be rated high on all the other dimensions, even though the performance dimensions rated are not be related to one another and require very different knowledge, skills, and abilities. This is what is called the *halo effect.*

>> **Finally, peer evaluations are affected by what is called context effects.** For example, consider the situation in which peers evaluate communication behaviors. The salience of such behaviors will be affected by context: These behaviors are much more salient when there is a conflict as compared to routine daily work. The resulting peer evaluations can thus be quite different based on whether the peer providing the rating is thinking about one specific situation versus another one, or communication behaviors across situations in general.

WARNING

Given the known weaknesses of peer evaluations, it would not be wise to use them as the sole source of performance information. Peer evaluations can be part of the system, but information should also be obtained from additional sources involved in performance touchpoints.

Using direct reports

Direct reports are a good source of information about the performance of their managers. For example, direct reports are in a good position to evaluate leadership competencies, including delegation, organization, and communication. In addition, direct reports are asked to rate their manager's ability to:

>> Remove barriers that employees face

>> Shield employees from politics, and

>> Raise employees' competence

TIP

Direct reports hesitate to provide upward feedback if put on the spot; however, if managers take the time to involve employees in the process by soliciting their input, employees will give honest feedback.

Many organizations take upward feedback very seriously because it provides tangible benefits — especially long-term benefits — as demonstrated by the results of a study in a Korean public institution with about 2,500 employees that engages in research, development, tests, and evaluation. Managers received upward feedback once per year during a period of seven years. Then the data were analyzed based on whether managers were classified as low, medium, or high-performers. Results showed that those in the low-performing group benefited the most. Also, there were additional benefits of using upward feedback for administrative, rather than developmental, purposes because performance improvements were even more noticeable.

Here's an example of a company that you probably know well because its products are seen everywhere: computer giant Dell. Dell employs over 100,000 individuals worldwide. At Dell, all employees rate their supervisors, including Michael Dell himself, who is currently chairman and CEO, every six months, using "Tell Dell" surveys. Michael Dell said, "If you are a manager and you're not addressing [employee] issues, you're not going to get compensation. And if you consistently score in the bottom rungs of the surveys, we're going to look at you and say 'Maybe this isn't the right job for you.'"

Performance information provided by direct reports is more accurate when the resulting ratings are to be used for developmental purposes, rather than administrative purposes. When evaluation data are intended for administrative purposes (that is, whether the manager should be promoted), direct reports are likely to inflate their ratings. Most likely, this is because direct reports fear retaliation if they provide low performance scores. Confidentiality is key if direct reports are to be used as a useful and valid source of performance information.

Using employees themselves

Self-appraisals are an important component of any performance management system. They have become particularly prominent, given the increasingly popular view regarding the need to shift from performance appraisal to performance management.

If the only focus is appraisal, collecting data from supervisors might do the job. However, if you want to implement a state-of-the-science performance management system that serves as a tool for continuously identifying, measuring, and developing the performance of individuals and teams, it is crucial to include self-evaluations as well.

When employees are given the opportunity to participate in the performance management process, their acceptance of the resulting decision will increase and their defensiveness during the appraisal interview will decrease. Another advantage of self-appraisals is that the employee is in a good position to keep track of activities during the review period, whereas a supervisor may have to keep track of the performance of several employees.

On the contrary, self-appraisals should not be used as the sole source of information in making administrative decisions because they are more lenient and biased than are ratings provided by other sources, such as a direct supervisor. This may explain why only 16 percent of HR managers report that their organizations include self-appraisals as part of their performance management systems.

Fortunately, self-ratings tend to be less lenient when they are used for developmental as opposed to administrative purposes.

The following suggestions will improve the quality of self-appraisals:

>> **Use comparative as opposed to absolute measurement systems.** For example, instead of asking individuals to rate themselves using a scale ranging from "poor" to "excellent," provide a relative scale that allows them to compare their performance with that of others (for example, "below average," "average," "above average").

>> **Allow employees to practice their self-rating skills.** Provide multiple opportunities for self-appraisal because the skill of self-evaluation improves with practice.

>> **Assure confidentiality.** Provide reassurance that performance information collected from oneself will not be disseminated and shared with anyone other than the direct supervisor and other relevant parties (for example, members of the same work group).

>> **Emphasize the future.** The development plan section of the form should receive substantial attention. The employee should indicate his plans for future development and accomplishments.

Using customers

Customers provide yet another source of performance information because they participate in performance touchpoints in many types of industries, occupations, and jobs. Although collecting information from customers can be costly and time-consuming, performance information provided by customers is particularly useful for jobs that require a high degree of interaction with the public. Also, performance information can also be collected from internal customers. For example, line managers could provide performance data regarding their HR representative.

Although the clients served may not have full knowledge of the organization's strategic direction, they can nevertheless provide useful performance data.

Using electronic performance monitoring

Many companies are now using electronic performance monitoring (EPM) to collect performance data. In the past, EPM included surveillance camera systems and computer and phone monitoring systems. Now, EPM includes wearable technologies and smartphones, including Fitbits and mobile GPS tracking applications.

USING CUSTOMERS TO COLLECT PERFORMANCE DATA AT FEDEX

Take the case of Federal Express, which has revised its performance management system to include measures of customer service. FedEx, which employs 400,000 people, has a total income of about $1.82 billion and ships more than 13 million packages every business day. Also, it has been ranked as one of Fortune's "100 Best Places to Work For."

The company uses a six-item customer-satisfaction survey, which is evaluated by a representative sample of the employee's customers at the end of the year. As a result of adding customer input and customer-developed goals to the performance review process, employees are more focused on meeting customer expectations.

FedEx already uses external customer input in evaluating performance, but organizations in other industries have some catching up to do. For example, a study examining appraisal forms used to evaluate account executives in the largest advertising agencies in the United States found that much more emphasis is placed on internal than on external customers. Specifically, external client feedback was measured in only 12 percent of the agencies studied. About 27 percent of agencies don't evaluate the contributions that account executives make to client relationships and to growing the client's business. In a yet more recent study involving those in charge of the HR function, only 8 percent reported that clients and customers provide performance evaluations of employees. In short, many companies might benefit from assessing the performance of employees — including managers — from the perspective not only of internal but also external customers.

REMEMBER

In the contemporary workplace, every email, instant message, phone call, and mouse click leaves a digital footprint, all of which can be used as data to be included in the performance management system.

EPM sparked a lot of enthusiasm about the availability of *Big Data*, a generic label used to describe large repositories of data. So Big Data is just a fancy label for "a lot of data." The availability of Big Data related to the behavior of people in organizations has led to the emergence of "people analytics," "HR analytics," "talent analytics," and "workforce analytics." Essentially, these are different labels used to describe how to collect and analyze Big Data.

TIP

The key issue in terms of collecting, compiling, and analyzing performance data is not Big Data but *Smart Data*, and that's because "a lot of data" is not necessarily the same as "accurate and useful data."

An analytics mindset means that you collect, compile, and analyze data with the goal of gaining insights that can be used to enhance individual, team, and organizational performance, as well as individual well-being. Having a lot of data doesn't mean you have good data. You should not be enamored by the presence of Big Data, and instead, should think about the criteria that make data useful and accurate. For example, is the information related to the position in question; are the issues measured specific, concrete, meaningful, and under the control of the employee? From the perspective of employees, is EPM considered useful, or a nuisance and an invasion of privacy?

The motto "garbage in–garbage out" is particularly relevant in the domain of Big Data and performance analytics.

When implemented well, EPM can lead to very useful data. For example, it can used to collect information on the various dimensions of performance I discuss in previous chapters, including task performance (productivity) and counterproductive performance such as cyberloafing (which is spending time on the Internet engaging in non-work behaviors such as online shopping or gaming).

Take tracking software such as WorkIQ and Desk Time, which allows companies to condense real-time employee behavior data into weekly or quarterly reports that are emailed directly to the employees, outlining how they used their computer time throughout the week. Also, mobile tracking systems collect useful time-oriented data to help employees engage in safer behaviors. This is precisely what semi-truck company Ryder implemented recently: A driver-facing camera docks a satellite-based monitoring system to record both positive and negative personal driver behaviors, such as speeding, safe turning, abrupt braking, and authorized and unauthorized stops.

But EPM certainly has challenges, as was learned the hard way by Intermex, a money transferring company based in the United States. For example, EPM can result in feelings of invasion of privacy, perceptions of unfairness, decreased job satisfaction and organizational commitment, and even increased counterproductive performance — just the opposite of what EPM is trying to achieve.

Clearly, EPM and Big Data are becoming more and more prominent in organizational life as we continue to see technological advancements. So given that EPM is part of most firms, make sure you follow these recommendations to ensure EPM will lead to positive results:

>> **Be transparent.** Employees need to know that they are being monitored. In fact, employee reactions will be affected by their perceptions of justice and the most negative reactions to EPM come from employees who don't

know whether they are being monitored, why they are being monitored, or how they are being monitored.

» **Be aware of all potential employee reactions.** Even when perceived as fair, EPM can be perceived as invasive. Also, employees respond differently to two types of EPM because they target different aspects of the employee. First, *passive monitoring* typically concerns artifacts of employee behavior, such as emails and number of phone calls. Second, *active monitoring* involves evaluating real-time location (GPS, surveillance cameras), computer (time spent on computer), or Internet use (website tracking). Consider making sure you do the following to minimize negative reactions:

- If there is a choice, use the least invasive technique possible.

- Make sure employees understand the reasoning behind the decision and have an opportunity to voice their opinions and concerns.

- Make sure employees understand the details of the monitoring system (for example, what information is collected and stored and how is it used).

» **Use EPM for learning and development.** Employees are more likely to accept EPM when it is used for learning and development purposes. For example, in the case of Ryder I mention earlier, it would be important to use the resulting data in subsequent training programs teaching drivers how to improve their safe-turning skills.

» **Restrict EPM to job-related behaviors and behaviors.** As in the case of Intermex, EPM can blur the boundaries between work and personal life. Make sure that data collected are job-related.

Chapter **11**

Minimizing Rating Distortion

I f you collect data from multiple touchpoints such as supervisors, peers, and customers, it is possible that the ratings won't be consistent: Some sources may tell you the employee is doing better than others in certain performance dimensions.

Is this a problem? Could it be that all performance touchpoints are somewhat accurate? When and why could it be that some of the sources of data are biased? And what can you do about it?

Clearly, these are critical issues because performance ratings need to be accurate for the performance management system to be fair and effective.

Dealing with Disagreements across Performance Touchpoints

When you collect performance information from more than one source, there will be some overlap in the dimensions you are measuring. For example, a manager's peers and direct supervisor may rate him on the same competency "communication."

In addition to the overlapping dimensions across sources, each source is likely to evaluate performance dimensions that are unique to each source. For example, direct reports may evaluate "delegation," but this competency may not be included on the evaluation form used by the supervisor.

Once you know which competencies and objectives will be measured for a particular position, you need to decide which source of information will be used to measure them.

It is important that employees take an active role in deciding which sources will rate which dimensions. Active participation in the process will enhance acceptance of results and perceptions that the system is fair.

Why disagreements across performance touchpoints is not always a problem

When the same performance dimension is evaluated across sources, you should not necessarily expect ratings to be similar. In other words, different sources disagreeing about an employee's performance is not necessarily a problem.

The rating an employee receives may come from different organizational levels. These are raters in different hierarchical positions and observe different facets of the employee's performance, and this can happen even if they are evaluating the same general competency such as "communication."

For example, an employee may be able to communicate very well with his superior but not very well with his direct reports.

Dealing with disagreements when giving feedback

In terms of feedback, there is no need to come up with one overall and consistent conclusion regarding the employee's performance. But it is important for the employee to learn how her performance was rated by each of the sources that were used. This is the crux of what are called *360-degree feedback systems:* Performance data are collected from "all around" the employee. When feedback is broken down by source, the employee can place particular attention and effort on the different performance touchpoints.

If disagreements are found, you need to make decisions about the relative importance of the rating provided by each touchpoint. For example, is it equally important to please external and internal customers? Is communication an equally important competency regarding direct reports and peers? Answering these questions can lead to assigning differential weights to the scores provided by the different sources in computing the overall performance score used for administrative purposes.

Minimizing Intentional Rating Distortion

Regardless of who rates performance, it is often the case that performance ratings are intentionally distorted or inaccurate.

WARNING

When ratings are distorted, employees feel they are treated unfairly, and the organization is more prone to litigation.

When performance ratings are distorted, the performance management system not only fails to result in desired outcomes but also leads to very negative consequences for employees and the organization. To prevent these negative outcomes, you need to understand why raters are likely to provide distorted ratings and what to do about it.

Understanding rater motivation

Raters have two main motivations: (1) the motivation to provide accurate ratings and (2) the motivation to distort ratings. When you combine these two reasons, you have what is called a *model of rater motivation*:

>> **The motivation to provide accurate ratings** is caused by whether the rater expects positive and negative consequences of accurate ratings and by whether the probability of receiving these rewards and punishments will be high if accurate ratings are provided.

>> **The motivation to distort ratings** is caused by whether the rater expects any positive and negative consequences of rating distortion and by the probability of experiencing such consequences if ratings are indeed distorted.

Think about a supervisor and her motivation to provide accurate ratings. What will the supervisor gain if ratings are accurate? What will she lose? Will her own performance be rated higher and will she receive any rewards if this happens? Will the relationship with her direct reports suffer? The answers to these questions tell you whether this supervisor is likely to be motivated to provide accurate ratings.

Similarly, are there any positive and negative consequences associated with rating distortion? What is the probability that this will indeed happen? The answers to these questions will determine the supervisor's motivation to distort ratings.

There are *motivational barriers* that prevent raters from providing accurate performance information. Raters are motivated to distort performance information and provide inflated or deflated ratings. Rating inflation is called *leniency error* (when raters assign high lenient ratings to most or all employees) and deflation is called *severity error* (when raters assign low ratings to most or all employees).

WARNING

Some supervisors may not even be trying to measure performance accurately. Instead, they use performance ratings for other goals that are unrelated, and often run completely counter, to what a good performance management system is trying to accomplish.

Why raters inflate ratings

Some supervisors are motivated to provide inflated ratings in order to . . .

>> **Maximize merit raise and rewards.** A supervisor wants to get the highest possible reward for her employees and she knows this will happen if she provides the highest possible performance ratings.

>> **Encourage employees.** A supervisor believes that employees' motivation will be increased if they receive high performance ratings.

>> **Avoid creating a written record.** A supervisor doesn't want to leave a "paper trail" regarding an employee's poor performance because such documentation may eventually lead to negative consequences for the employee. This situation can happen if the supervisor and employee have developed a friendship.

>> **Avoid confrontation with employees.** A supervisor feels uncomfortable providing negative feedback. So to avoid a possible confrontation with the employee, he decides to take what may seem like a less painful path and gives inflated performance ratings.

>> **Promote undesired employees out of unit.** A supervisor believes that if an employee receives very high ratings, he may be promoted out of the unit. The supervisor sees this as an effective way to get rid of disliked employees.

>> **Make the manager look good in the eyes of his own supervisor.** A supervisor believes that if everyone receives very high performance ratings, she will be considered an effective unit leader. Also, when the performance ratings for the manager himself depend on the performance of his direct reports, managers are likely to inflate their direct reports' ratings.

Again, you can understand each of the reasons for a supervisor's choosing to inflate ratings using the model of rater motivation (that is, motivation to provide accurate ratings versus motivation to provide distorted ratings).

For example, looking good in the eyes of one's own supervisor is a positive consequence of providing inflated ratings. Avoiding a possible confrontation with an employee is also a positive consequence of providing inflated ratings. So given these anticipated positive consequences of rating inflation, the supervisor will choose to provide distorted instead of accurate ratings.

Why raters deflate ratings

Supervisors are also motivated to provide ratings that are artificially deflated in order to . . .

>> **Shock an employee.** A supervisor believes that giving an employee a "shock treatment" and providing deflated performance ratings will jolt the employee, demonstrating that there is a problem.

>> **Teach a rebellious employee a lesson.** A supervisor wishes to punish an employee or force an employee to cooperate with the supervisor and believes that the best way to do this is to give deflated performance ratings.

>> **Send a message to the employee that he should consider leaving.** A supervisor lacking communication skills may wish to convey the idea that an employee should leave the unit or organization. Providing deflated performance ratings is a way to send this message.

>> **Build a strongly documented, written record of poor performance.** A supervisor wishes to get rid of a particular employee and decides that the best way to do this is to create a paper trail of substandard performance.

You can also understand the psychological mechanisms underlying the decision to provide deflated ratings using the model of rater motivation.

For example, if shocking employees and building strongly documented records about employees are considered to be positive consequences of rating deflation, it is likely that the supervisor will choose to provide distorted ratings.

WARNING

Performance ratings can be filled with emotional overtones and hidden political and personal agendas that are driven by the goals and motivation of the person providing the rating and do not reflect an employee's performance.

If raters are not motivated to provide accurate ratings, they will use the performance management system to achieve political and other goals, such as rewarding allies and punishing enemies or competitors, instead of using it as a tool to improve employee, and ultimately, organizational performance.

WARNING

Performance measurement doesn't take place in a vacuum but in an organizational context with written and unwritten norms. One such norm could be that performance ratings are not expected to be accurate.

Increasing accountability in performance ratings

What can you do to motivate raters to provide accurate ratings? If a supervisor is able to see the advantages of a well-implemented performance management system, as opposed to one dominated by office politics, he will be motivated to help the system succeed. Also, if a supervisor believes there is accountability in the system, and ratings that are overly lenient are likely to be easily discovered, resulting in an embarrassing situation for the supervisor, leniency is also likely to be minimized.

TIP

Because of the many reasons that exist to provide inaccurate ratings, the key is to provide incentives so that raters will be convinced that they have more to gain by providing accurate ratings than they do by providing inaccurate ratings.

You can minimize rating distortion by increasing accountability. It works like this:

>> **Have raters justify their ratings.** Ratings are more accurate when raters justify their ratings to someone with authority, such as their own supervisors.

>> **Have the raters justify their ratings in a face-to-face meeting.** Ratings are also more accurate when the rating justifications are offered in a face-to-face meeting, compared to justifications offered in writing only.

TIP

A supervisor asks himself, "What's in it for me if I provide accurate ratings versus inflated or deflated ratings?" Make sure you design the performance management system in such a way that the benefits of providing accurate ratings outweigh the benefits of providing inaccurate ratings. This includes measuring the performance of the supervisor in how he is implementing performance management within his unit and communicating that performance management is a key part of a supervisor's job.

Minimizing Unintentional Rating Distortion

Although there are many reasons why raters distort ratings intentionally, there are reasons why they do so unintentionally. The previous sections in this chapter described how to minimize intentional rating distortion.

Now let's discuss how to minimize unintentional distortion. In a nutshell, you do this by implementing training programs, and their goal is to help raters observe, record, and measure performance more accurately.

Designing rater error training

The goal of *rater error training* (RET) is to make raters aware of typical rating errors and help them develop strategies to minimize or even eliminate those errors. Implementing RET should increase rating accuracy by making raters aware of the unintentional errors they are likely to make.

RET programs include definitions of the most typical errors and a description of causes for those errors. These programs also show raters examples of common errors and review suggestions on how to avoid making errors. This is done by showing video vignettes designed to elicit rating errors and asking trainees to fill out appraisal forms regarding the situations they observed on the video clips. Then a comparison is made between the ratings provided by the trainees and the correct ratings. The trainer then explains why the errors took place, which specific errors were made, and ways to minimize these errors in the future.

RET does not guarantee increased accuracy, but raters do become aware of the possible errors they can make. Because, however, many of the errors are unintentional, simple awareness of the errors does not mean that errors will not be made. Nevertheless, it may be useful to expose raters to the range of possible errors, which are covered in the following sections.

Similar to me error

Similarity leads to liking, so we like and favor those who are similar to us. So raters are more likely to give higher performance ratings to those employees who are perceived to be more similar to them in terms of attitudes, preferences, personality, and demographic variables, including race and gender.

Contrast error

Contrast error occurs when raters compare individuals with one another, instead of against predetermined standards. For example, when a rater evaluates an individual of only average performance, the rating may actually be higher than deserved if the other individuals rated by the same rater had substandard performance levels. So the average performer is seen much better in comparison to the others. This error occurs when raters complete multiple appraisal forms at the same time because in these situations, it is difficult to ignore the ratings given to other employees.

Halo error

Raters do not distinguish between the different aspects of performance. If an employee gets a high score on one dimension, she also receives a high score on all other dimensions, even though performance may not be even across all dimensions. This error is typically caused by the rater's assigning performance ratings based on an overall impression about the employee instead of evaluating each performance dimension independently.

EXAMPLE

If an employee has a perfect attendance record, then the rater may give her a high mark on dedication and productivity. The perfect attendance record, however, may be caused by the fact that the employee has large loan payments to make and cannot afford to miss work, not because the employee is actually an excellent overall performer. In other words, being present at work is not the same as being a productive employee.

Primacy error

Performance evaluation is affected by information collected during the initial phases of the review period. For example, in rating communication skills, the rater gives more weight to incidents involving communication that took place toward the beginning of the review period, as opposed to incidents taking place at all other times.

Recency error

Performance evaluation is influenced by information gathered during the last portion of the review period. This is the opposite of the primacy error: Raters are more heavily influenced by behaviors taking place toward the end of the review period instead of giving equal importance and paying attention to incidents occurring throughout the entire review period.

Negativity error

Raters place more weight on negative information than on positive or neutral information. The negativity error explains why most people have a tendency to remember negative rather than positive news that they read online or watch on television.

EXAMPLE

A rater observes one negative interaction between the employee and a customer and several positive interactions in which customers' expectations were surpassed. The rater then focuses on the one negative incident in rating the "customer service" dimension.

First impression error

Raters make an initial favorable or unfavorable judgment about an employee and then ignore subsequent information that does not support the initial impression. This type of error can be confounded with the "similar to me error" because first impressions are likely to be based on the degree of similarity: The more similar the person is to the rater, the more positive the first impression will be.

Spillover error

Scores from previous review periods unjustly influence current ratings. For example, a rater makes the assumption that an employee who was an excellent performer in the previous period ought to be an excellent performer during the current period also, and provides performance ratings consistent with this belief.

Stereotype error

A rater has an oversimplified view of individuals, based on group membership. That is, a rater may have a belief that certain groups of employees (for example, women) are unassertive in their communication style. In rating women, therefore, he may automatically describe communication as being "unassertive" without actually having any behavioral evidence to support the rating. This type of error can also result in consistently lower performance ratings for members of certain groups. For example, a study including an identical sample of black and white workers found that white raters gave higher ratings to white workers relative to black workers than did black raters. In other words, if a white worker is rated, then it does not really matter whether the rater is black or white; however, if a black worker is rated, the rater's ethnicity matters because this worker is likely to receive a higher rating from a black rater than from a white rater.

WARNING

This type of error can also lead to biased evaluations of performance when an individual violates stereotypical norms by working in an occupation that does not fit the stereotype (for example, a woman who works assembling airplane parts).

Attribution error

A rater attributes poor performance to an employee's dispositional tendencies (for example, personality, abilities) instead of features of the situation (for example, malfunctioning equipment). In other words, different raters may place different relative importance on the environment in which the employee works in making performance evaluations. If raters make incorrect inferences about the employees' dispositions and ignore situational characteristics, actions taken to improve performance may fail because the same situational constraints may still be present (for example, obsolete equipment).

Designing frame of reference training

RET exposes raters to the different errors and their causes; however, being aware of unintentional errors does not mean that raters will no longer make these errors. Awareness is certainly a good first step, but you need to go further if you want to minimize unintentional errors. One fruitful possibility is the implementation of a frame of reference training.

Frame of reference (FOR) training helps improve rater accuracy by familiarizing raters with the various performance dimensions that are measured. The goal of FOR is to give raters skills so that they can minimize unintentional errors and provide accurate ratings on each performance dimension by developing a common mental picture.

FOR training programs include a discussion of the job description for the individuals being rated and the duties involved. Raters are then familiarized with the performance dimensions to be rated by reviewing the definition for each dimension and discussing examples of good, average, and poor performance. Raters are then asked to use the appraisal forms to rate fictitious employees, usually shown in video practice vignettes. The trainees are also asked to write a justification for the ratings. Finally, the trainer informs trainees of the correct ratings for each dimension and the reasons for such ratings and discusses differences between the correct ratings and those provided by the trainees.

Effective FOR training programs include the following formal steps:

1. Raters are told that they will evaluate the performance of three employees on three separate performance dimensions.

2. Raters are given an appraisal form and instructed to read it as the trainer reads aloud the definition for each of the dimensions and the scale anchors.

3. The trainer discusses different employee behaviors that illustrate different performance levels for each rating scale included in the form. The goal is to create a common mental picture among raters so that they will agree on the appropriate performance dimension and effectiveness level for different behaviors.

4. Participants are shown a video clip of a practice vignette, including behaviors related to the performance dimensions being rated, and are asked to evaluate the employee's performance using the scales provided.

5. Ratings provided by each participant are shared with the rest of the group and discussed. The trainer seeks to identify which behaviors participants used to decide on their assigned ratings and to clarify any discrepancies among the ratings.

6. The trainer provides feedback to participants, explaining why the employee should receive a certain rating (target score) on each dimension, and shows discrepancies between the target score and the score given by each trainee.

FRAME OF REFERENCE TRAINING AT THE CANADIAN MILITARY

This is how the Canadian military uses FOR training. First, the training program includes a session regarding the importance of performance management systems in the military. In the next session, raters are told that they will be evaluating the performance of four direct reports. They are given the appraisal form to be used and information on each of the scales included in the form. As the trainer reads through each of the scales, trainees are encouraged to ask questions. At the same time, the trainer gives examples of behaviors associated with each level of performance. The trainer thus makes sure that the trainees come to a common FOR concerning what behaviors constitute the different levels of performance.

Participants are shown a video clip of a soldier and are asked to evaluate the performance using the appraisal form explained earlier. Next, the ratings are discussed as a group, focusing on the behaviors exhibited in the video clip and the ratings that would be most appropriate in each case. This process is repeated several times. Finally, the participants are given three more samples of behavior to rate, as displayed by three hypothetical soldiers, and they receive feedback on how well they evaluated each soldier.

REMEMBER

FOR training can take quite a bit of time and effort to develop and administer, but it is well worth it. As a consequence of implementing this type of training, raters not only are more likely to provide consistent and more accurate ratings, but they are also more likely to help employees design effective development plans. This result occurs because sharing a common view of what constitutes good performance allows supervisors to provide employees with better guidelines that will allow them to reach such performance levels.

Designing behavioral observation training

Behavioral observation (BO) training is the third type of program implemented to minimize unintentional rating errors. BO training focuses on how raters observe, store, recall, and use information about performance. Fundamentally, this type of training improves raters' skills at observing performance.

For example, one type of BO training involves showing raters how to use notes or diaries. These observational aids help raters record a preestablished number of behaviors on each performance dimension. These aids also help raters increase the sample of incidents observed and recorded during a specific time period. Also, an aid such as a diary is an effective way to standardize the observation of behavior and record of critical incidents throughout the review period. And it serves as a memory aid when filling out evaluation forms.

TIP

Memory aids are helpful because ratings based on memory alone, without notes or diaries, are likely to be distorted due to factors of social context (for example, friendship bias) and time (such as duration of supervisor–direct report relationship).

BEHAVIORAL OBSERVATION TRAINING AT THE CANADIAN MILITARY

The Canadian military has found that a combination of FOR and BO training works best. Earlier, I described how the Canadian military uses FOR training. In addition to FOR training, there are sessions on the importance of BO and common errors, including first impression, stereotypes, and halo effects. Finally, the participants are trained on the importance of keeping diaries and taking notes on their direct reports throughout the year. Furthermore, the trainer explains the criteria for each performance dimension and provides written descriptions of the different levels of performance. Trainees are given a chance to practice keeping a diary while watching the video clips used in the FOR training section of the training program. After watching each video clip, participants are given tips on note-taking and recording behaviors as well as the resulting outcomes.

3

Implementing Performance Management Effectively

Chapter **12**

Creating and Implementing Personal Development Plans

E mployee development is a key result of state-of-the-science performance management systems. For employee development to be successful, it has to be a joint activity entered into by both the employee and the manager.

This chapter addresses how to use a performance management system to help you develop and improve your own performance and that of others. To do so, the first step is to create a personal development plan.

Creating Personal Development Plans

Personal development plans specify courses of action you can take to improve your performance. Also, achieving the goals stated in the development plan allows you to keep abreast of changes in your profession. Such plans highlight your strengths and the areas in need of development, and they include actions to improve in areas of weaknesses and further develop areas in which you are already strong.

Using development plans to answer four key career questions

To be most useful, personal development needs to answer the following questions:

>> How can I continually learn and grow in the next year?

>> How can I do better in the future?

>> How can I avoid performance problems faced in the past?

>> Where am I now and where would I like to be in terms of my career path?

You can create a development plan for every job, ranging from entry level to the executive suite. No matter how high up the position within the organization and how complex the nature of the job in question, there is always room for improvement.

Information to be used in designing development plans comes from the performance evaluation form. Specifically, a development plan can be designed based on each of the performance dimensions evaluated. For example, if the performance dimension "communication" is rated as substandard, this area would be included in the development plan.

Using development plans to improve your short- and long-term career goals

Development plans focus on the short term and on specific roles and positions. But they can also focus on the knowledge and skills needed for more long-term career aspirations and career development.

Good development plans also focus on developing career competencies, including the following three sets of competencies:

>> **Reflective career competencies:** Being aware of your career and combining personal reflections with your professional career. The two competencies that comprise this dimension are *reflection on motivation,* which refers to reflecting on values, passions, and motivations with regard to your career; and *reflection on qualities,* which refers to reflection on strengths, shortcomings, and skills with regard to your career.

>> **Communicative career competencies:** Being able to effectively communicate with others to improve your chances of career success. The two competencies are *networking,* which refers to the awareness of the presence and

professional value of your network and the ability to expand this network for career-related purposes; and *self-profiling,* which refers to presenting and communicating your personal knowledge, abilities, and skills to individuals inside and outside the organization.

>> **Behavioral career competencies:** Being able to shape your career by taking action and being proactive. The two specific competencies are *work exploration,* which refers to actively exploring and searching for work-related and career-related opportunities inside and outside the organization; and *career control,* which refers to actively influencing learning processes and work processes related to your career by setting goals and planning how to reach these goals.

ACTIVE LEARNING

Now pause for a few minutes and give yourself some time to think about these three sets of career competencies. Where do you stand regarding reflective (reflection on motivation and reflection on qualities), communicative (network and self-profiling), and behavioral (work exploration and career control) competencies? What are your strongest and your weakest competencies? Which ones should you be working on to improve your future career prospects?

In addition to improved short-term performance and career path clarity, the inclusion of development plans, and in more general terms, identifying employee strengths and weaknesses as part of the performance management system have another important benefit: Employees will be more satisfied with the performance management system. For example, a study including 137 employees at a production equipment facility in the southern United States showed that the greater the extent to which employees believed that the system was being used for development purposes, the more satisfied they were with the system.

On the other hand, perceptions of the extent to which the system was used for evaluative purposes did not relate to employee satisfaction with the system. In other words, using the system for evaluative purposes did not relate to employee satisfaction, but using the system for development purposes had a positive relationship with satisfaction.

This is precisely the reason why so many companies, such as The Gap, Ely Lilly, Microsoft, and Accenture, emphasize that their performance management systems have a strong focus on employee development. For an example, see the sidebar "Development Plans at General Mills."

DEVELOPMENT PLANS AT GENERAL MILLS

At General Mills (an international foods company), individual development plans (IDPs) are promoted strongly throughout the company. The formally written IDPs are completed annually, but the expectation is for ongoing conversations with managers and employees, focusing not only on competencies that are well developed and those that are in need of improvement, but also on the employee's career aspirations.

General Mills hosts speakers, offers web-based learning tools, and holds workshops for employees and managers to get the most out of IDPs. Some of these sessions are specifically tailored to different kinds of positions within the company with different needs in the development process. Also, the IDP is kept separate from the annual performance evaluation. In short, General Mills is an example of a company that has made a strong commitment to the growth and learning of all employees as part of its performance management system.

Using development plans for succession planning

Here's another important benefit of personal development plans: They allow organizations to gather information that can be used for succession planning purposes.

For example, based on individual career aspirations, an organization is able to identify employees who may be interested and able to serve in leadership positions in the future.

REMEMBER

Many "high-potential" programs are essentially based on combining employees' current performance and future aspirations with the organization's future talent needs. Thus, development plans serve an important strategic role in helping an organization address future possible talent gaps.

Setting your development plan objectives

The overall objective of a development plan is to encourage continuous learning, performance improvement, and personal growth. Also, development plans have other, more specific objectives:

>> Improve performance in current position. A good development plan helps you meet performance standards. So a development plan includes suggested courses of action to address each of the performance dimensions that are deficient. This is an important point, given that, for example, surveys have shown that about 25 percent of federal employees and between 11 percent and 16 percent of private sector employees in the United States are not performing up to standards.

>> Sustain performance in current position. A good development plan provides tools so that you can continue to meet and exceed expectations regarding your current position. Thus, the plan includes suggestions about how to continue to meet and exceed expectations for each of the performance dimensions included in the performance evaluation form.

>> Prepare employees for advancement. A good development plan includes advice and courses of action that should be taken so that you will be able to take advantage of future opportunities and career advancement. For example, a good plan specifies which new competencies should be learned to help with career advancement.

>> Enrich the employee's work experience. Even if career opportunities within the organization are not readily available, a good plan provides employees with growth opportunities and opportunities to learn new skills. These opportunities provide employees with a more challenging work experience, even if the new skills learned are not a formal part of their jobs. Such opportunities can make jobs more attractive and serve as a powerful employee retention tool. In addition, the new skills can be useful in case of lateral transfers within the organization.

As an example, take the employee development plan used for staff at Texas A&M University in College Station, Texas. Because the development plan is a formal component of the university's performance management system, the development plan is included within the performance evaluation form. The evaluation form used by Texas A&M first lists the six objectives of the performance management system:

1. Provide employees with feedback to improve or maintain job performance.

2. Outline areas for employee development.

3. Set standards for the next review period.

4. Recognize job-related accomplishments.

5. Enhance communication and working relationships.

6. Identify job performance deficiencies (any factor that "doesn't meet expectations") and report to the next level of supervisory responsibility.

Based on objective 2, the employee development plan is an important component of the performance management system. The inclusion of this objective upfront sets the tone for the development process by helping managers understand that this is an important issue.

After the sections in the form in which the manager rates employee performance, the form includes this:

SECTION B: PROFESSIONAL DEVELOPMENT PLAN

Please list professional development activities to be completed and resources needed to support these activities, if applicable

Professional Development Needs	Resources/Support Needed	Time Frame

Including this information after performance ratings allows the manager and employee to focus on development areas identified as weaknesses in the performance review process. In this way, the development plans created for employees at Texas A&M are directly related to performance dimensions important for the unit and the overall organization. Also, including the development plan at the end of the review and after setting annual performance goals allows employees to determine whether there are areas they need to develop in order to attain the specified goals.

Setting the content of your development plan

What does a development plan look like? Good plans include a description of specific steps to be taken and specific objectives to reach. In other words, what is the new skill or knowledge that will be acquired and how will this occur? This includes information on the resources and strategies that will be used to achieve the objectives.

For example, will the employee learn the skill from a coworker through on-the-job training? Will the company reimburse the employee for expenses associated with taking an online course?

The plan's objectives should include not only the end product, such as the new skill to be learned, but also the completion date and what evidence will be gathered to know whether the new skill has indeed been acquired.

For example, in the case of an online course, the objective could state that it will be completed by July 23, 2019, and the employee is expected to receive a grade of B+ or better.

Objectives included in the development plans should be practical, specific, time-oriented, linked to a standard, and developed jointly by the supervisor and the employee.

An additional important feature of development plans is that it should keep the needs of both the organization and the employee in mind. As I mention earlier, state-of-the-science development plans are used strategically to connect the organization's future talent needs with an employee's performance and aspirations. So the choice of what specific skills or performance areas will be improved is influenced by the needs of the organization, especially when the organization is investing substantial resources in the plan. And the plan created is influenced by the needs of the employee.

The supervisor and the employee need to agree on what development or new skills will help enrich the employee's work experience, as well as help accomplish organizational goals now or in the near future.

As an example, take again the content of the development plan at Texas A&M. First, employees are directed to a website that includes examples of possible development activities. This list includes workshops; certifications; local, state, and national conferences; on-the-job training; and other activities. This information presents employees and managers with various options they can use to achieve the development objectives. Second, the form includes space so that each development need is paired with a description of resources or support needed and a time frame for completion.

For example, the development plan for an administrative assistant in the business school may look like this:

SECTION B: PROFESSIONAL DEVELOPMENT PLAN

Please list professional development activities to be completed and resources needed to support these activities, if applicable

Professional Development Needs	Resources/Support Needed	Time Frame
1. Knowledge of Excel (spreadsheet program)	Reimbursement for online course	Course to be completed by August 1, 2019
2. Customer service skills in dealing with students and faculty	Reimbursement for one-day workshop. Time to receive on-the-job training from administrative assistant in communications department	Workshop to be completed by October 15, 2019 On-the-job training to be completed by November 8, 2019

Overall, the Texas A&M plan includes all the required components. There is a description of development objectives, activities that will be conducted to reach these objectives, and dates of completion.

One important piece seems to be missing, however. The plan doesn't include specifics of how the accomplishment of each objective will be measured. How will the supervisor know if the administrative assistant has a good working knowledge of Excel after he has completed the online course? How will the supervisor know if the administrative assistant's customer service skills have improved after he has attended the workshop and has undergone on-the-job training?

The Excel training could be measured by the administrative assistant's performance in the course or by examining answers to questions about knowledge of Excel that faculty and others giving Excel assignments to the administrative assistant answer in filling out appraisal forms. Regarding customer service skills, the accomplishment of the objective might be measured by gathering data from those customers served by the administrative assistant (that is, faculty and students).

Setting the activities of a development plan

Clearly, development activities are dependent on an organization's strategic goals and objectives and also on resources that may or may not be available. For example, a large organization may have a training and development unit, have sufficient resources to offer in-house courses, or pay for an employee to take a course somewhere else, such as a local university. Many small business don't have such resources.

These are the ways through which employees can reach the objectives stated in their development plans:

>> **On-the-job training:** Employees are paired with a peer or supervisor who designs a formal on-the-job training course. The design of these "minitraining programs" includes how many hours a day or week training will take place and specific learning objectives.

>> **Courses:** Some large organizations like McDonald's, Motorola, Capgemini, and Ernst & Young offer in-house courses given at their own corporate universities. Other organizations provide tuition reimbursement. Given the proliferation of online courses, there is a wide variety of options from which to choose.

>> **Self-guided studying:** Employees can read books, watch video presentations, and study other materials on their own.

TIP

It is important that an objective be set regarding what will be read and within what time frame, as well as what measures will be used to assess whether learning has taken place.

>> **Mentoring:** Many organizations have mentoring programs. Mentoring is a developmental process that consists of a one-on-one relationship between a senior (mentor) and junior (protégé) employee. Mentors serve as role models and teach protégés what it takes to succeed in the organization. In more specific terms, mentors can help protégés gain targeted skills.

TIP

For mentoring programs to be successful, it is best to allow the mentor and protégé to choose each other, rather than arbitrarily assigning who will be mentoring whom.

>> **Attending a conference or trade show:** Another way to acquire required knowledge and skills is to sponsor an employee's attendance at a conference or trade show. It is useful to require that the employee provide a written report and deliver a brief presentation upon returning from the conference. In this way, it is easier to assess what has been learned. Also, the knowledge gained can be shared with other employees.

WARNING

As is true for most development activities, attending a conference or trade show has to be directly linked to an employee's development plan and also an organization's needs. This principle clearly applies to attending off-site conferences and trade shows, given that this development activity is particularly prone to abuse.

>> **Mixing with the best:** A development activity particularly targeting entrepreneurs and high-level executives involves the "Genius Network," a by-application-only network whose participants pay $100,000 to attend three meetings per year. This network connects high-achieving entrepreneurs, industry innovators, and best-selling authors, and their goal is to help them grow their business tenfold.

>> **Getting a degree:** Some organizations provide tuition reimbursement benefits for their employees to obtain additional degrees or certifications. For example, the organization can sponsor an employee's MBA program or an employee's taking specialized courses with the goal of earning a certification designation (for example, Certified Novell Administrator, Professional in Human Resources). In most cases, employees commit to continuing the relationship with their employer for a prespecified amount of time after completing the degree. If the employee leaves the organization before this time frame, she may have to reimburse the organization for the cost of her education.

EXAMPLE

The firm Boston Consulting Group (BCG) sponsors "BCG MBA Fellows," which is a scholarship program that includes not only a tuition reimbursement, but also individual mentorship by senior BCG consultants. To be eligible for this program, a BCG employee must work for the company for at least two years and then be enrolled in a full-time MBA program approved by BCG. This is a development activity that serves an important strategic purpose for BCG because it helps build the talent pool for its succession-planning needs, given that it has more than 80 offices in 48 countries and more than 14,000 employees.

>> **Job rotation:** Another way to gain necessary skills is to be assigned to a different job on a temporary basis. This is the model followed in the medical profession in which residents have to rotate across specialty areas for several months. For example, residents may be required to rotate across the various emergency medicine services for a 19-month period.

>> **Temporary assignments:** A less systematic rotation system includes the opportunity to work on a challenging temporary assignment. This assignment allows employees to gain specific skills within a limited time frame.

>> **Membership or leadership role in professional, trade, or nonprofit organizations:** Some employers sponsor membership in professional, trade, or nonprofit organizations. These organizations distribute publications to its members and hold informal and formal meetings in which employees have an opportunity to learn about best practices and other useful information for their jobs. Also, presentation, communication, planning, and other skills can

be learned while serving in a leadership role in a volunteer organization outside of work (such as a local charity, church, or synagogue).

ACTIVE LEARNING

Please go over this list of activities I just described one more time. Based on your own preferences and learning style, which of these activities do you believe would be most beneficial to you? Please rank these activities in terms of your preference. Does the organization you work for now offer any of these opportunities? If not, to what extent is this a factor that would motivate you to look for a job elsewhere, where more of these development activities would be made available to you?

See an example of a development plan in Figure 12-1. The development plan can be part of the evaluation form, or it can be included in a separate form.

The form included in Figure 12-1 shows that you have several choices in terms of development activities. The form includes space so that information can be inserted regarding what activities take place when, what the objectives are, and whether the objective has been met or not.

Many of the activities I listed above are relevant for employees at all levels. However, some such as the "mixing with the best" activity pertain specifically to high-level managers. In fact, the issue of managerial development is very important on its own because it is directly related to succession planning, as discussed earlier. For example, employees who aspire to secure managerial positions should evaluate all development activities to understand which ones would be most beneficial to achieve this particular career goal.

ACTIVE LEARNING

Consider your future career expectations and development needs. Then, fill out the form included in Figure 12-1, assuming your current or future employer will be willing to provide any development opportunities of your choosing. What does your plan look like? What did you discover about what you would like to learn in the future? What does this information tell you about your level of aspirations and future prospects for your career advancement?

Facilitating Employee Development

The direct supervisor has an important role in the creation and completion of the employee's development plan. Because of the critical role of the direct supervisor in the employee development process, it is a good idea for the supervisor to have her own development plan as well. This will help the supervisor understand the process from the employee's perspective, anticipate potential roadblocks and defensive attitudes, and create a plan in a collaborative fashion.

| Update Date:
Name:
Job Title/Job Code:
Department:
Primary Reviewer:
Education:
Prior Training:
Job History:
Career Goals:
    Next 1 year
    Next 2 years
    Next 3 years
    Next 5 years | | | | | | | |

Developmental Options OJT (on-the-job) Training	Description	Type of Development	When	How Long	Completed Hours (This Quarter)	Comments—Approximate Cost—Other	Objectives/Evaluation
Classes	Current Quarter						
Conferences							
On-line							
Self-study							
Job rotation	Next Quarter						
Videos							
Books							
Temporary assignment							
Mentorship	Current +2						
Other (specify)							
	Current +3						

FIGURE 12-1: Example of a development plan.

Performing five functions in the development process

In terms of the specific role of the supervisor, consider the following five functions if you want to facilitate the development of your employees:

>> **Explain** what is required of the employee to reach a required performance level. A useful tool for this function is the feedforward interview.

>> **Refer** to appropriate development activities. The supervisor has a primary role in referring to appropriate development activities that can assist the employee in achieving her goals. For example, this includes helping the employee select a mentor, appropriate study resources, courses, and so forth.

>> **Review** and make suggestions about development objectives. Specifically, the supervisor helps assure the goals are achievable, specific, and doable.

>> **Check** on the employee's progress toward development objective achievement. For example, the supervisor can remind the employee of due dates and revise goals, if needed.

>> **Offer** the opportunity for regular check-ins and reinforcing positive behaviors. The supervisor needs to provide reinforcements so the employee is motivated to achieve the development goals. Reinforcements can be extrinsic and include rewards such as bonuses and additional benefits, but reinforcements can also include the assignment of more challenging and interesting work that takes advantage of the new skills learned.

Using the feedforward interview

You need to explain what is required for the employee to achieve the desired performance level, including the steps that an employee must take to improve performance. You need to provide this information together with the probability of success if the employee completes the suggested steps. A good tool that supervisors can use to accomplish this goal is to use the *feedforward interview* (FFI).

REMEMBER

The goal of the FFI is to understand the types of behaviors and skills that individuals have that allow them to perform well and to think about ways to use these same behaviors and skills in other contexts to make further improvements in the future.

The FFI includes a meeting between the supervisor and employee and involves the following three steps:

Step 1: Eliciting a success story

The supervisor sets the stage as follows:

> All of us have both negative and positive experiences at work. I would like to meet with you to discuss some positives aspects only and see how we can learn from those experiences about things that work well.

Then the supervisor can ask this question:

> Could you please tell me about a story about an event or experience at work during which you felt at your best, full of life and in flow, and you were content even before the results of your actions were known?

It is important that the story be very specific about an actual incident and not a general statement about

> In general, these are the things I do at work. . . .

So the story must be situated within a specific context. After the supervisor hears the story, she can summarize it for the employee to hear it, and then the supervisor can ask whether any information is missing or anything else should be added to the story. A follow-up question is

> Would you be happy to experience a similar process again?

If the answer is yes, then the subsequent questions attempt to go deeper into the details of the story. If the story is associated with mixed feelings and is not completely positive, then you need to elicit a different story.

Step 2: Uncover the underlying success factors

The second step involves understanding the factors that led to the successful story. For example, the supervisor can ask

> What were some of the things you did or did not do, such as your specific personal strengths and capabilities that made this success story possible?

and

> What were the conditions that made this success story possible?

In a way, you are playing the role of a detective trying to discover what are the personal and contextual factors that led to success, including the role that the work environment (for example, technology) and others (for example, customers, peers) played in the story.

Step 3: Extrapolating the past into the future

The third step involves asking questions that will lead to an employee's ability to replicate the conditions that led to success in the past into the future. So the supervisor can first note that

> The conditions you have just described seem to be your personal code for reaching [insert the key achievement in the story such as happiness at work, optimal performance, outstanding leadership, etc.].

Then, follow up with questions such as the following:

> Think about your current actions, priorities, and plans for the near future (for example, next week, month, or quarter) and tell me how you think you may be able to replicate these conditions to be able to achieve the same level of [insert satisfaction, achievement, performance, etc.] as you did before.

EXAMPLE

An experiment involving all 25 managers in the sales and customer service units of a business equipment firm in Canada showed that the FFI works. The managers and their direct reports were randomly assigned to one of two experimental conditions, the feedforward interview or traditional feedback. Results showed that compared to traditional feedback, the FFI increased performance four months later. So the effects of the FFI are relatively enduring. Also, the training required to teach managers how to use the FFI is fairly short. In this particular experiment, it took just 2.5 hours to train 13 managers, which helped shift the role of the manager from a critic of an employee's past performance to someone who supports what an employee will do in the future.

Motivating supervisors to facilitate employee development

To be successful in performing the five functions I describe earlier in this chapter, supervisors themselves need to be motivated to support the employees' completion of their development objectives. For this to happen, supervisors must be held accountable and rewarded for doing a good job of helping their employees develop.

REMEMBER

Direct supervisors play a crucial role in the success of the development plan because they are directly involved in the assessment of accomplishments and monitor progress toward reaching development objectives. Also, they must be highly committed to the development of their employees and motivated to help their employees fulfill their career aspirations. To do so, supervisors must be evaluated based on how well they manage the development process for their employees.

KLA-Tencor Corporation is one of the world's top-ten developers and manufacturers of inspection and measurement equipment for the semiconductor and nanoeletronics industries. At KLA-Tencor, between 10 percent and 30 percent of supervisors' bonus pay is directly tied to employee development, which is measured in terms of employee training and certification levels. Managers are given at least quarterly updates on the status of their staff development. In addition, employees themselves are rewarded for engaging in development activities. In fact, only employees with up-to-date training and certification levels are eligible for bonuses. Thus, employee development is successful at KLA-Tencor because both employees and managers are directly rewarded for employee development. After several years of implementing these practices, employee development has become the norm and is part of the KLA-Tencor's culture.

THE ROLE OF DIRECT SUPERVISOR IN DEVELOPMENT PLANS AT DIAGEO

Diageo makes and distributes alcoholic beverages that include well-known brands such as Smirnoff, Johnnie Walker, Baileys, and Guinness. Diageo sells its products in more than 180 countries and has offices in about 80. The company has recognized the value of employee development and expects supervisors to play an important role in the development of their direct reports. Specifically, the company's career development program includes a formal review and goal setting along with regular meetings to keep development fresh in the minds of employees.

The supervisor facilitates the process in several ways. The supervisor helps identify specific development goals that are aligned with the employee's career aspirations. Monthly meetings, referred to as "call overs," are held to review progress toward goals and to adjust goals as necessary. Also, the supervisor helps provide a means for development and reaching goals by ensuring employees receive training, course work, or by studying material on relevant topics.

Another strategy includes giving employees assignments outside of their current position responsibilities, such as leading a project to practice skills the employee has learned in the development process. In short, Diageo has recognized the critical role that managers should play in the employee development process. This involvement benefits the individual employee's growth and also aids in aligning employee skills and actions with the strategic goals of the organization as a whole.

Using Multisource Feedback Systems in Implementing Development Plans

An important tool for implementing development plans is a multisource feedback system. Although these systems are called using different labels such as 360-degree systems, multirater, multisource, full circle, or 450 feedback, the basic principle is the same: You gather the most useful information about employee's development needs when you use multiple sources of information.

REMEMBER

The multisource feedback system has become a preferred tool for helping employees, particularly those in supervisory roles, improve performance by gathering information on their performance from different sources.

As I mentioned, multisource feedback systems are usually called "360-degree" systems because information is gathered from sources all around the employee. Specifically, information on what performance dimensions could be improved is gathered from superiors, peers, customers, and direct reports. This information is usually collected anonymously to minimize rating inflation due to conflicts of interest.

Employees also rate themselves on the various performance dimensions and compare self-perceptions with the information provided by others.

A nice product of multisource feedback systems is a gap analysis: areas for which there are large discrepancies between self-perceptions and the perceptions of others. A multisource feedback system report usually includes information on dimensions for which there is agreement that further development is needed. This information is used to create a development plan, as described earlier in the chapter.

TIP

A multisource feedback system is most helpful when it is used for development purposes only and not for administrative purposes. People will be more honest if they know the information will be used to help people improve and not to punish or to reward them. However, it is possible to implement such systems successfully for administrative purposes after they have been in place for some time — usually, two years or so.

Feedback reports usually include graphs showing the areas in which employees' perceptions differ the most from the perceptions of other sources of performance data. They can also show average scores, across sources of information, so that the areas that need improvement are readily identified. The resulting report is usually made available to the employee and his supervisor so that both have an opportunity to review it before meeting to create a development plan.

A trend adopted by many vendors that offer online multisource feedback systems is to offer a bundle of systems, including multisource feedback together with learning management, compensation, and even recruiting and succession planning. These integrative applications, usually called "talent management" systems, allow organizations to manage data about employees in a systematic and coordinated way. These integrative software applications allow organizations to create an inventory of their human capital and better understand their strengths and weaknesses at the organizational level. For example, an organization that uses such applications is quickly able to deploy project teams with the appropriate mix of skills and experience after doing a quick search in the database.

TIP

An advantage of these integrative apps is that performance management can be more easily linked to recruiting, compensation, training, and succession planning. In other words, the system can keep track of an employee's development needs and how these needs have been addressed (for example, via training) over time.

Maximizing benefits of multisource feedback systems

Organizations and individuals can gain several advantages as a consequence of implementing a multisource feedback system. These include the following:

>> **Decreased possibility of biases:** Because these systems include information from more than one source, there is a decreased possibility of biases in the identification of employees' weaknesses.

>> **Increased awareness of expectations:** Employees become aware of others' expectations about their performance. This includes not only the supervisor's expectations but also the expectations of other managers, peers, direct reports, and customers.

>> **Increased commitment to improve:** By using multisource feedback systems, information about performance is no longer a private matter. Thus, employees become aware of what others think about their performance, which increases their commitment to improve in the future.

>> **Improved self-perceptions of performance:** Employees' distorted views of their own performance are likely to change as a result of the feedback received from other sources. In other words, it is difficult to continue to have distorted views of your own performance in the presence of overwhelming evidence that these perceptions may not be correct.

>> **Improved performance:** Although receiving information about your performance is not sufficient cause to improve, it is certainly a very important step. Thus, having information on your performance, if paired with a good development plan, will lead to performance improvement.

>> **Reduced "undiscussables" and defensiveness:** Multisource feedback systems provide an excellent opportunity to coworkers, superiors, and direct reports to give information about performance in an anonymous and nonthreatening way. Many supervisors feel uncomfortable when they have to give negative feedback and some issues become "undiscussables." But a multisource system makes providing such feedback easier. Also, from the perspective of employees, it is harder to ignore and become defensive regarding the accuracy of feedback when it originates from multiple sources.

>> **Employees enabled to take control of their careers:** By receiving detailed and constructive feedback on weaknesses and strengths in various areas, employees can gain a realistic assessment of where they can go with their careers.

ACTIVE LEARNING

Please reread the preceding list of benefits. Now, think about an organization for which you have worked that implemented some type of multisource feedback system. If you cannot think of one, talk to friends or family members and ask them about a system they have experienced. Then consider the preceding list of potential benefits. Which of these benefits were not actually realized by the system? Why not?

Minimizing risks of multisource feedback systems

There are some risks and potential pitfalls in implementing multisource feedback systems and you need to think about how to minimize them:

>> Negative feedback can hurt an employee's feelings, particularly if those giving the feedback don't offer their comments in a constructive way.

>> Multisource feedback systems lead to positive results only if individuals feel comfortable with the system and believe they are rated honestly and treated fairly. User acceptance is an important determinant of the system's success.

>> When very few raters are providing the information, say, two or three, it may be easy for the employee being rated to identify who the raters are. When anonymity is compromised, raters are more likely to distort the information they provide.

>> Raters can become overloaded with forms to fill out because they need to provide information on so many people (peers, superiors, and direct reports).

>> Implementing a multisource feedback system should not be a one-time-only event. The system should be in place and data collected over time on an ongoing basis. The implementation of ongoing multisource feedback systems is sometimes labeled a 720-degree feedback system, referring to the fact that

the collection of multisource data takes place at least twice. In short, administering the system only once will not be as beneficial as administering the system repeatedly.

WARNING

Multisource feedback systems are not necessarily beneficial for all individuals and all organizations. For example, individuals who are high on self-efficacy (that is, they believe they can perform any task) are more likely to improve their performance based on feedback received from peers compared to individuals low on self-efficacy. Also, the effect of receiving feedback from multiple sources is most beneficial for individuals who perceive there is a need to change their behavior, react positively to feedback, believe change is feasible, set appropriate goals to improve their performance, and take concrete actions that lead to performance improvement.

Deciding whether a multisource feedback systems will work in your organization

Multisource systems work best in organizations that have cultures that support open and honest feedback. Also, these systems work best in organizations that have a participatory, as opposed to authoritarian, leadership style in which giving and receiving feedback is the norm and is regarded as valuable.

EXAMPLE

Take the case of the Patent Office of the United Kingdom. This organization is characterized by a hierarchical structure, typical of many civil service organizations, as opposed to a flat structure, where employees are involved and teamwork is the norm. The implementation of a multisource feedback system did not lead to the anticipated positive results, and there was a mismatch of expectations between what the board members wanted (better working relations and a culture change) and what the employees wanted (individual improvement). Also, managers did not show a good understanding of the behaviors they were expected to display, and their performance did not show improvement. Overall, the multisource feedback system was not sufficiently linked to other HR systems and policies.

Answering the following questions allows you to learn whether implementing a multisource system would be beneficial in your organization:

>> Are decisions about rewards and promotion fairly free of favoritism?

>> Do decisions take into account the input of those affected by such decisions?

>> Do people from across departments usually cooperate with each other and help each other?

>> Is there little or no fear of speaking up?

>> Do people believe that their peers and direct reports can provide valuable information about their performance?

>> Are employees trusted to get the job done?

>> Do people want to improve their performance?

TIP

The successful implementation of a multisource feedback system depends on the culture of the organization and the work context. If the answer to most of these questions is "yes," the implementation of a multisource feedback system will likely be successful and lead to performance improvement.

Implementing a state-of-the-science multisource feedback system

There are several things that you can do to maximize the chance that the system will work properly. Successful systems share these characteristics:

>> **Anonymity:** Feedback is anonymous and confidential. When this is the case, raters provide honest information about performance, particularly when direct reports are providing information about superiors.

>> **Observation of employee performance:** Only those with good knowledge and firsthand experience with the person being rated should participate in the process. There is no point in asking for performance feedback from people who are not able to observe performance directly.

>> **Feedback interpretation:** Allow the person being rated to discuss the feedback received with those genuinely interested in the employee's development. In most cases, feedback is discussed with the direct supervisor. In other cases, the discussion can involve a representative of the HR department, a superior, or peer to whom the person doesn't report directly.

>> **Follow-up:** The information gathered has little value if there is no follow-up action. Once feedback is received, it is essential that a development plan is created right away.

>> **Used for developmental purposes only (at least initially):** When multi-source feedback systems are used for administrative purposes such as promotions and compensation, raters may distort the information provided. Make it clear that the purpose of the system is developmental, and developmental only. Initially, the information collected should not be used for making reward allocations or any other administrative decisions. However, you can use the system for administrative purposes after it has been in place for some time — approximately two years or so.

>> **Avoidance of rater fatigue:** Rater fatigue can be avoided if individuals are not asked to rate too many people at the same time. For example, you can stagger data collection so that not all surveys are distributed at the same time.

>> **Emphasis on behaviors:** Although systems can include feedback on both behaviors and results, it is better to emphasize behaviors. Focusing on behaviors can lead to the identification of concrete actions that the person being rated can take to improve performance.

>> **Raters go beyond ratings:** In addition to providing scores on the various dimensions, raters should provide written descriptive feedback that gives detailed and constructive comments on how to improve performance. It is helpful if this information also includes specific examples that help support the ratings and recommendations.

>> **Raters are trained:** As in the case of providing evaluations for administrative purposes, raters should be trained. Mainly, this includes skills to discriminate good from poor performance and how to provide feedback in a constructive manner.

ACTIVE LEARNING

Given this list, consider the case of AAH Pharmaceuticals I describe in the nearby sidebar. Based on this information, which characteristics are present? Which are absent?

MULTISOURCE FEEDBACK AT AAH PHARMACEUTICALS

AAH Pharmaceuticals (AAH) uses a multisource feedback system that includes several characteristics of a good system. The company is a wholesaler of pharmaceuticals and provides medical products and services in the UK. AAH, with the help of professional consultants, found the multisource feedback system to be very useful. To help ease potential employee concerns, AAH clearly outlined for employees that development planning and feedback were the only goals, and information would not be used for any other purpose. Employees were also given the option of sharing information with their supervisors. The system included gathering performance data from several sources through an automated online system of surveys, ensuring that information was anonymous and confidential.

After the results were obtained, participants attended a one-day meeting about the results away from the office that included one-on-one interpretation and discussion with the consultant to initiate a development plan. Six-month follow-up meetings were held to review progress toward development objectives. AAH found the process to be successful with a first group of managers who went through the process and made plans for a broad rollout of the program for more employees to take advantage of development opportunities.

Chapter **13**

Conducting Effective Review, Disciplinary, and Termination Meetings

I f you are a manager, you have a tough job: You need to judge and coach at the same time. In other words, if you are a manager, you serve as a judge by evaluating performance and allocating rewards. But you also serve as a coach by helping employees solve performance problems, identify performance weaknesses, and design developmental plans that will be instrumental in future career development. And supervisors often feel uncomfortable because they need to convey bad news, which may cause employees to react negatively. In other words, there is a concern that managing performance unavoidably leads to negative surprises.

This chapter teaches you how to be effective in three types of performance meetings: review, disciplinary, and termination.

Conducting Effective Review Meetings

Performance review discussions serve three important purposes:

>> **These discussions allow employees to improve their performance** by identifying performance problems and solutions for overcoming them.

>> **They help build a good relationship** between the supervisor and the employee because the supervisor shows that she cares about the employee's ongoing growth and development and that she is willing to invest resources, including time, in helping the employee improve.

>> **Performance management leaders use review discussions as *stay interviews.*** Stay interviews focus on finding out what makes employees stay in the organization and help managers create strategies to enhance employee engagements and retain star performers.

Setting up review meetings

Because performance management leaders play these paradoxical roles, it's usually helpful to separate the various meetings related to performance. Separating the meetings also minimizes the possibility of negative surprises. Also, when meetings are separated, it's easier to separate the discussion of rewards from the discussion about future career development, which allows employees to give their full attention to each issue, one at a time.

Performance management systems can involve as many as six formal meetings. Each of these sessions should be seen as a work meeting with specific goal, including the following:

>> **System inauguration:** A discussion of how the system works and the identification of the requirements and responsibilities resting primarily on the employee and on the supervisor. This discussion includes the role of self-appraisal and the dates when the employee and supervisor will meet formally to discuss performance issues.

TIP

This meeting is particularly important for new employees, who should be introduced to the performance management system as soon as they become members of the organization.

>> **Self-appraisal:** This meeting involves the employee's assessment of herself. This meeting is informational in nature, and at this point, the supervisor doesn't pass judgment on how the employee regards her own performance. This meeting provides an opportunity for the employee to describe how she

sees her own performance during the review period. It is helpful if the employee is given the same form to be filled out later by the supervisor so that she can provide self-ratings using the same dimensions that will be used by the supervisor.

>> **Classical performance review:** During this meeting, you discuss employee performance, including both the perspective of the supervisor and the employee. Most performance management systems include this type of meeting only. No other formal meetings to discuss performance are usually scheduled. This meeting is mainly past-oriented and typically doesn't focus on what performance should look like in the future.

>> **Merit/salary review:** During this meeting, you discuss what, if any, compensation changes will result as a consequence of the period's performance. It is useful to separate the discussion of rewards from the discussion of performance so that the employee can focus on performance first, and then, on rewards. If these meetings are not separated, employees may not be very attentive during the discussion of performance and are likely to feel it is merely the price they must pay to move on to the part of the meeting that really matters: the discussion about rewards. Although these meetings are separate, supervisors should explain clearly the link between the employee's performance, discussed in detail in a previous meeting, and the rewards given. Rewards are not likely to carry their true weight if they are not linked directly to performance.

>> **Developmental plan:** In this meeting, you discuss the employee's development needs and what steps will be taken so that performance will be improved during the following period. This meeting also includes information about what types of resources will be provided to the employee to facilitate the development of any required new skills.

>> **Objective setting:** This meeting involves includes setting goals, both behavioral and results-oriented, regarding the following review period. At this point, the employee has received very clear feedback about her performance during the past review period, knows what rewards will be allocated (if any), understands developmental needs and goals, and knows about resources available to help in the process of acquiring any required skills.

Although six types of meetings are possible, not all six take place as separate meetings. For example, the self-appraisal, classical performance review, merit/salary review, development plan, and objective setting meetings may all take place during one umbrella meeting, labeled "performance review meeting."

TIP

As I noted above, it's better to separate the various types of information discussed so that the employee and supervisor focus on each of the components separately.

Implementing an optimal sequence for review meetings

Regardless of the specific type of meeting, there are several steps that performance management leaders take before the meeting takes place:

1. **Give at least a two-week advance notice** to the employee to inform her of the purpose of the meeting and enable her to prepare for it.

2. **Block out sufficient time** for the meeting and arrange to meet in a private location without interruptions.

Taking these two steps sends a clear message that the meeting is important and that, consequently, performance management is important.

As I mentioned earlier, most organizations merge several meetings into one labeled "performance review meeting." The optimal sequence of events for such a meeting is the following:

1. **Explain the purpose of the meeting.** Include a description of the purpose of the meeting and the topics to be discussed.

2. **Conduct self-appraisal.** Ask the employee to summarize her accomplishments during the review period. This is more easily accomplished when the employee is given the appraisal form to be used by the supervisor before the meeting. This portion of the meeting allows the employee to provide her perspective regarding performance. The role of the supervisor is to listen to what the employee has to say and to summarize what he hears. This isn't an appropriate time for the supervisor to disagree with what the employee says.

3. **Share performance data and explain rationale.** Explain the rating you provided for each performance dimension and the reasons that led to each score. It's more effective to start with a discussion of the performance dimensions for which there is agreement between the employee's self-appraisal and the supervisor's appraisal. This reduces tension and demonstrates to the employee that there is common ground and that the meeting isn't confrontational. Also, it's better to start with a discussion of the performance dimensions for which the scores are highest. Then move on to the dimensions for which the scores are lower.

TIP

For areas for which there is disagreement between self- and supervisor ratings, the supervisor must take great care in discussing the reason for his rating and provide specific examples and evidence to support the score given. At this point, make an effort to resolve discrepancies and take extra care with sensitive areas.

Provide the employee with the opportunity to explain her viewpoint thoroughly. This is a very useful discussion because it leads to clarifying performance expectations. For dimensions for which the score is low, have a discussion about possible causes. For example, are the reasons related to lack of knowledge, lack of motivation, or contextual factors beyond the control of the employee?

1. **Discuss development.** After the supervisor and employee have agreed on the scores given to each performance dimension, discuss the development plan. At this point, the supervisor and the employee should discuss and agree on the developmental steps that will be taken to improve performance in the future.

2. **Ask employee to summarize.** Next, the employee summarizes, in her own words, the main conclusions of the meeting: What performance dimensions are satisfactory, which need improvement, and how improvement will be achieved. This is an important component of the meeting because it gives the supervisor an opportunity to determine whether he and the employee are on the same page.

3. **Discuss rewards.** The next step during the meeting includes discussing the relationship between performance and any reward allocation. The supervisor should explain the rules used to allocate rewards and how the employee would be able to reach higher reward levels as a consequence of future performance improvement.

4. **Hold follow-up meeting.** Before the meeting is over, schedule the next performance-related formal meeting. The employee needs to understand that there will be a formal follow-up and that performance management isn't just about meeting with the supervisor once a year. Usually, the next meeting will take place just a few weeks later to review whether the developmental plan is being implemented effectively.

5. **Discuss approval and appeals process.** The supervisor asks the employee to sign the form to attest that the evaluation has been discussed with him. This is also an opportunity for the employee to add any comments or additional information she would like to see included on the form. In addition, if disagreements about ratings have not been resolved, the supervisor should remind the employee of the appeals process.

6. **Conduct final recap.** Finally, use the "past-present-future model." In other words, the supervisor summarizes what happened during the review period in terms of performance levels in the various dimensions, reviews how rewards will change based on this level of performance, and sums up what the employee will need to do in the next year to maintain and enhance performance.

TIP

If you are dealing with a top performer, use the final recap meeting as a *stay interview* by asking these type of questions:

>> Have you ever thought about leaving our team?

>> How can I best support you?

>> What do you want to learn here?

>> What can you learn here that will make you feel good when you go home every day?

Although stay interviews will not ensure that a star employee will never move, they can be very useful in identifying the factors that matter most to a firm's or team's most impactful contributors.

Dealing with employee defensiveness

Performance review discussions often don't serve their intended purposes because employees are defensive and many supervisors don't know how to deal with this attitude because they lack the necessary skills to conduct an effective performance review.

How can you tell when an employee is being defensive? Typically, there are two patterns of behavior that will show you this.

>> **Fight response:** Blaming others for performance deficiencies, staring mutely at the supervisor, and other, more aggressive responses, such as raising her voice or even pounding the desk.

>> **Flight response:** Looking away, turning away, speaking softly, continually changing the subject, or quickly agreeing with what the supervisor is saying without basing the agreement on a thoughtful and thorough discussion about the issues being discussed.

When employees have a fight-or-flight response during the performance review discussion, it's unlikely that the meeting will lead to improved performance in the future.

But there are several things you can do:

>> **Establish and maintain rapport.** You can establish rapport by choosing a meeting place that is private and by preventing interruptions from taking place. Also, the supervisor should emphasize two-way communication and put the employee at ease as quickly as possible.

>> **Be empathetic.** Try to put yourself in the shoes of the employee. Make an effort to understand why the employee has performed at a certain level during the review period. This includes not making attributions that any employee success was caused by outside forces (for example, a good economy) or that employee failures were caused by inside forces (for example, employee incompetence).

>> **Be open-minded.** If the employee presents a different point of view, be open-minded and discuss it directly and openly. There is a possibility that the employee provides information that is relevant and of which you are not aware. If this is the case, ask for specific evidence.

>> **Watch for verbal and nonverbal cues.** Try to read verbal and nonverbal signals from the employee to determine whether further clarification is necessary. Be attentive to the employee's emotions and react accordingly.

TIP

If the employee becomes defensive, the supervisor should stop talking and allow the employee to express her point of view regarding the issue being discussed.

>> **Encourage participation.** The employee needs to have her own conversational space to speak and express her views. Try not to dominate the meeting. Instead, listen without interrupting and avoid confrontation and argument.

Despite these suggestions, defensiveness is unavoidable in some situations. If you are facing one of those, you need to recognize it.

Rather than ignoring the defensive attitude, deal with the situation head on:

1. **Let the employee vent and acknowledge the employee's feelings.** You want to pause to accept the employee's feelings.

2. **Ask the employee for additional information and clarification.** If the situation is reaching a point where communication becomes impossible, the supervisor may want to suggest suspending the meeting until a later time. For example, you can say the following:

   I understand that you are angry, and that you believe you have been treated unfairly. It's important that I understand your perspective, but it's difficult for me to absorb the information when you are so upset. This is an important matter. Let's take a break and get back together at 3:00 p.m. to continue our discussion.

WARNING

If the relationship between the supervisor and the employee isn't good, the performance review meeting will expose these issues in a blatant and often painful way.

HANNAH DEALS WITH SOFIA'S DEFENSIVENESS

In this vignette, Hannah is the manager at a large accounting firm, and Sofia is one of the employees on her team. She chooses a conference room with privacy that is away from the other offices.

HANNAH: Hi, Sofia. I wanted to meet with you today to discuss your performance appraisal for this quarter. At any time, please offer your input and ask questions if you have any.

SOFIA: OK.

HANNAH: You did meet two important objectives that we set this quarter: sales and customer service. Thanks for your hard work.

SOFIA: No problem.

HANNAH: You did miss three of the other objectives.

SOFIA: What? I worked as hard as I could! It wasn't my fault that the other people on the team did not carry their weight.

HANNAH: Sofia, I am not here to blame anyone or to attack you. I want to generate some ideas on what we can do to ensure that you meet your objectives and receive your bonus next quarter.

SOFIA (sitting back with crossed arms): I told you I worked as hard as I could.

HANNAH: I know that you worked hard, Sofia, and I know how hard it is to balance all of the objectives that we have in our department. When I first started, I had a hard time meeting all of the objectives as well.

SOFIA: It is hard and I try my best.

HANNAH: Sofia, can you think of anything that we can work on together that would help you meet the last three objectives? Is there any additional training or resources that you need?

SOFIA: I am having a hard time prioritizing all of my daily tasks. There is a class offered online on prioritizing, but I feel I am too busy to take it.

HANNAH: That is good that you think the class will help. Take the class online, which will not disrupt your work schedule, and I will go to all of your meetings and follow up with clients as needed.

SOFIA: Thanks, Hannah. I really appreciate your help.

How did Hannah do? My take on this is that she did a good job. Hannah was empathetic, she picked up on Sofia's nonverbal behavior, she had Sofia offer her input, she held the meeting in a comfortable, private location, and she emphasized that the meeting was to work on future performance and not to punish Sofia. In the end, she was able to address Sofia's defensiveness and turned a meeting that could have gone very poorly into a productive exchange of information and ideas. What do you think? What would you have done better or differently if you were in Hannah's shoes?

Making the Tough Calls: Disciplinary Process and Organizational Exit

This section is about making some tough calls. In some cases, an employee may not respond to the feedback provided and may not make any improvements in terms of performance.

Offering decision-making leave

Giving bad news is never an easy process. But in such cases, there is one intermediate step that can be taken before the employee enters a formal disciplinary process, which involves a verbal warning, a written warning, and may lead to termination. The employee can be given a once-in-a-career *decision-making leave.*

This is a "day of contemplation" that is paid and allows the employee to stay home and decide whether working in this organization is what he or she really wants to do. This practice is based on adult learning theory, which holds individuals responsible for their actions.

Unlike a formal disciplinary action, the decision-making leave doesn't affect employee pay. As noted by Tim Field, principal of a consulting firm in Los Angeles, California, "This element of holding people accountable without negatively impacting their personnel file or payroll tends to catch people off guard, because problem employees, like problem children, are often expecting negative attention for their bad behavior."

How can the decision to grant an employee a decision-making leave be communicated? Assuming this is a company policy and there is senior management support, you can communicate the leave as follows in this example scenario:

> Hailey, as you know, you and I have met on several occasions to talk about your performance. In spite of these feedback sessions, I see that you are still having some difficulties with important tasks and projects. Consistent with my observations, I have received comments from some of your peers related to some performance deficiencies they have also noticed. I think that issuing a written warning would be counterproductive, as I am concerned that it may decrease your motivation and do more harm than good. Instead, what I am going to do is to put you on what we call a "decision-making leave" for a day. This is a type of intervention that has worked very well with other individuals in your same position in the past.

> I want you to know that this is a once-in-a-career benefit that you should use to your advantage, and I decided to do this because I truly believe that you are capable of improving your performance.

> It works like this: I am going to ask you to not come to the office tomorrow, but you will be paid for that day, so you don't have to worry about your paycheck being affected. While you are away from the office tomorrow, I want you to give serious thought to whether you really want to work in this company. You and I will meet when you return to the office the day after tomorrow, and I will ask you to tell me whether you'd rather resign and look for work elsewhere. I will understand and will be fully supportive if that is your decision. On the other hand, if when we meet, you tell me you want to keep your job here, then I will give you an additional assignment on which I want you to work while you are away from the office tomorrow. Recall that you are being paid for the day, so here is what I want you to do. Please prepare a one-page letter addressed to me, convincing me that you assume full and total responsibility for the performance issues we discussed during our feedback sessions. You will have to provide clear and specific arguments as well as describe a specific set of actions you will take to convince me that you will address the problems. I will keep the letter in a safe place, but I am not planning on including it in your personnel file for now. To be clear, however, this letter is a personal commitment from you to me and our agreement is that if you don't stick to the terms of your letter, you will essentially fire yourself.

> This is a very important moment for you and also for me, and it could be a turning point in your career development. Now that I have explained the process, I would like to hear any questions or comments you may have about this decision-making leave day that you will be taking tomorrow.

Using a decision-making leave as part of the performance management system can be a powerful tool to give problem employees an opportunity to improve their performance. However, if this tool doesn't lead to the desired outcomes, then the employee doesn't have to enter into a disciplinary process. A demotion or transfer may be a more appropriate action when there is evidence that the employee is actually trying to overcome the performance deficiencies but isn't able to do so.

However, termination is the appropriate action when performance doesn't improve and the employee continues to make the same mistakes or fails to meet standards. Also, termination is the appropriate course of action when an employee engages in serious violations of policies, laws, or regulations such as theft, fraud, falsifying documents, and related serious offences.

Avoiding five common pitfalls in the disciplinary process

The disciplinary process should not come as a surprise to the employee or supervisor if there is a good performance management system in place. After all, there should be ongoing check-ins and plenty of opportunities for the employee to overcome performance problems. And there should be opportunities for the supervisor to offer support and feedback.

However, when a disciplinary process seems to be the only recourse, it's important to follow a set of steps so as not to fall into legal problems. Also, all employees, even those who are terminated, deserve to be treated with respect and dignity. Nevertheless, even if there is a top-notch performance management system in place, there are several pitfalls that you need to try to avoid and specific actions you can take to do so, which are the following:

Pitfall 1: Acceptance of poor performance

Many supervisors may just want to ignore poor performance, hoping that the problem will go away. Unfortunately, in most cases, the performance problems escalate and become worse over time.

Solution: Don't ignore the problem. Addressing it as soon as possible can not only avoid negative consequences for the employee in question, peers, and customers, but it also help put the employee back in track in terms of his career objectives.

Pitfall 2: Failure to get the message through

The poor performing employee argues that she did not know the problem was serious or that it existed at all.

Solution: In the decision-making leave described earlier, make sure to be very specific about the performance problem and the consequences of not addressing it effectively. Make sure you document the action plan and that you have secured the employee's agreement regarding the plan.

Pitfall 3: Performance standards are "unrealistic" or "unfair"

The employee may argue that performance standards and expectations are unrealistic or unfair.

Solution: Remind the employee that his performance standards are similar to others holding the same position. Also, remind the employee that performance standards have been developed over time with the participation of the employee in question and share with him documentation regarding past review meetings, including past appraisal forms with the employee signature on them.

Pitfall 4: Negative affective reactions

The employee responds emotionally, ranging from tears to shouts and even threats of violence. This, in turn, creates an emotional response on the part of the supervisor.

Solution: Don't let emotional reactions derail you from your mission and role as a performance management leader, which is to describe the nature of the problem, what needs to be done, and consequences of not doing so. If the employee is crying, do offer compassion and give him some space to compose himself. You can give the employee some time and resume the meeting a few minutes later, or a rescheduling of the meeting at a later time may be a good alternative. If the employee reaction involves a threat or suggests possible violence, call security immediately. If such threats do take place, report them to the human resources (HR) department.

Pitfall 5: Failure to consult HR

There are hundreds of wrongful termination cases that have cost millions of dollars to organizations that have not followed the appropriate termination procedures.

Solution: If you are planning on implementing a disciplinary or termination process, consult with your HR department regarding legal requirements. For the most part, if you have a good performance management system in place, you have all necessary steps in place. However, consulting with HR is a good idea to ensure you are following all appropriate steps.

Dealing with terminations

Avoiding the five pitfalls I just described minimizes the possibility of problems during the formal disciplinary process. If the performance goals are not reached, there will be a need for a termination meeting. This meeting is, of course, extremely unpleasant for all involved, to say the least. However, it's the right and fair thing to do at this stage.

Do the following to make sure the termination meeting is respectful, fair, and effective — as less unpleasant as possible for you and the employee:

1. **Be respectful.** Treat the terminated employee with respect and dignity. Keep the information about the termination confidential, although it's likely others will learn about it in subsequent days.

2. **Get right to the point.** The less said, the better. You can start by saying, "There is no easy way to say this," and then summarize the performance problems, actions taken to try to overcome these problems, outcomes of these actions, and the decision about termination that you have reached.

3. **Let the employee grieve.** It's important to let the employee grieve because it's likely that there will be a sense of loss. Show empathy with phrases such as "I know this is sad for you" and "Go ahead and take a moment. When you're ready, we'll continue."

4. **Wish the employee well.** The purpose of the meeting isn't to rehash every single reason why you are letting the employee go and every single instance of poor performance. Instead, use the meeting to wish the person well in her next job and endeavors and tell her that she will be missed.

5. **Send the employee to HR.** Let the employee know that she needs to go to HR to receive information on benefits, including vacation pay, and also to receive information on legal rights. If you are working in a small business, seek outside legal counsel regarding the information to give to the terminated employee.

6. **Have the employee leave immediately.** Keeping the terminated employee on-site can lead to gossip and conflict, and disgruntled employees may engage in sabotage.

7. **Have the termination meeting at the end of the day.** It's better to conduct the termination meeting at the end of the day so that the employee can leave the office along with everyone else and there are fewer people around.

IN THIS CHAPTER

» Understanding how teams work

» Designing and implementing
performance management
for teams

» Connecting team performance
management with team rewards

Chapter **14**

Implementing Team Performance Management

Surveys by Deloitte and other consulting firms show that more than 90 percent of companies believe that organizations should be redesigned by including a team component. So it is impossible to think of an organization that doesn't organize its functions at least, in part, based on teams. Why is this happening? Teams are critical for decentralizing authority, improving communication, and creating more customer-centric organizations. The use of teams is not an industry-based phenomenon. It is happening everywhere: IT, consulting, health care, and the military.

EXAMPLE

The U.S. military's hierarchical command and control structure hindered operational success during the early stages of the Iraq war. Consequently, retired U.S. Army General Stanley McChrystal, who served as Commander of U.S. Forces in Afghanistan, decentralized authority to empowered teams. In his view, a team-based approach led to greater dynamism and flexibility and enabled officers to quickly move from their administrative positions to mission-oriented projects for a set purpose, knowing that they would once again have a home to return to within the larger organizational structure after the mission was completed. This type of organization structure, which consisted of a "network of teams," is now becoming popular in nonmilitary organizations in all industries.

Clearly, then, you need to learn how to make sure teams, and not just individuals, are part of performance management.

Not All Teams Are Created Equal

Examples of teams range from a group of top managers working together face-to-face on an ongoing basis with the goal of achieving corporate goals to a group of programmers in India and the United States writing programming codes that eventually will be put together as one software program.

Teams don't have to be permanent, and team members don't have to be in the same location. In fact, members don't need to have ever met in person to be on the same team. As long as they work together, need each other, and share common goals, they are considered to be members of the same team.

Many organizations are structured around teams, including teams called autonomous work groups. When autonomous work groups are in place, members have the authority to manage their own tasks and interpersonal processes as they carry out their work.

Reasons why teams exist in all organizations

Why are teams so popular? Here are a few reasons:

>> **Businesses are facing increased pressures and global competition.** Using teams is one way to address these challenges because teams can include members from different parts of the world.

>> **Due to rapid changes in the environment, organizations need to be prepared to adapt and change quickly.** Using teams provides greater flexibility because individuals can be rotated in and out of teams, based on particular needs.

>> **Products and services are becoming very complex, requiring many people contributing their diverse talents to the same project.** Teams are able to respond more quickly and more effectively to changes than can individuals working alone.

>> **Many organizations have gone through downsizing and restructuring, which has led them to become flatter and has reduced the number of hierarchical levels.** A team-based structure is more congruent to these changes compared to traditional hierarchical structures.

Team-based organizations are not necessarily better. Although many organizations choose to structure themselves around autonomous work teams and teams in general, team-based organizations don't necessarily outperform organizations that are not structured around teams.

Team performance doesn't always fulfill its promise. So it is important for performance management systems to go beyond focusing on individual performance and, following the definition of performance management, to also aim at identifying, measuring, and developing the performance of teams and aligning their performance with the strategic goals of the organization.

A good performance management system should target not only individual performance but also an individual's contribution to the performance of his or her teams and the performance of teams as a whole.

An organization that includes any type of teams will benefit from managing the performance of both individuals and teams.

Designing a State-of-the Science System

Including team performance as part of a performance management system is an extension of a system that focuses on individual performance. You are still trying to design and implement the best possible system. Specifically, the system should be . . .

>> **Congruent with strategy:** There is a clear link between team and organizational goals.

>> **Congruent with context:** The system is consistent with norms based on the culture of the organization and the region and country in which the organization is located.

>> **Thorough:** All teams are evaluated, and you include all relevant performance dimensions.

>> **Practical:** The system doesn't require excessive time and resources.

>> **Meaningful:** There are important consequences.

>> **Specific:** There is a concrete team improvement agenda.

>> **Able to identify effective and ineffective performance:** You are able to distinguish teams at different performance levels.

>> **Reliable:** The measurement of performance is consistent.

>> **Valid:** The measures of performance measure important and relevant aspects of performance and not things unrelated to performance.

>> **Acceptable and fair:** People participating in the system believe the processes and outcomes are just.

>> **Inclusive:** There is input from multiple sources on an ongoing basis.

>> **Open:** There is transparency and there are no secrets.

>> **Correctable:** There are mechanisms so that errors can be corrected.

>> **Standardized:** Performance is evaluated consistently across teams and time.

>> **Ethical:** The system complies with ethical standards.

Anticipating dangers of poorly designed systems

You should also anticipate what can go wrong if there is a poorly implemented system. These are some of the bad things that happen in those situations:

>> **Lowered self-esteem:** Self-esteem is lowered if feedback is provided in an inappropriate and inaccurate way.

>> **Increased turnover:** If the process is not seen as fair, employees may become upset and leave the organization.

>> **Damaged relationships:** The relationship among the individuals involved may be damaged, often permanently.

>> **Decreased motivation to perform:** Motivation is lowered for many reasons, including the feeling that superior performance is not translated into meaningful tangible or intangible rewards.

>> **Employee burnout and job dissatisfaction:** When the performance assessment instrument is not seen as valid and the system is not perceived as fair, employees feel increased levels of job burnout and job dissatisfaction.

>> **Use of misleading information:** If a standardized system is not in place, there are multiple opportunities for fabricating information about a team's performance.

>> **Wasted time and money:** Performance management systems cost money and quite a bit of time, and these resources are wasted when systems are poorly designed and implemented.

>> **Emerging biases:** Personal values, biases, and relationships are likely to replace organizational standards.

- » **Unclear ratings system:** Because of poor communication, teams don't know how their ratings are generated and how the ratings are translated into rewards.

- » **Varying and unfair standards and ratings:** Both standards and individual ratings vary across teams, which can be unfair.

- » **Unjustified demands on team leaders and team members' resources:** Poorly implemented systems don't provide the benefits provided by well implemented systems, yet they take up people's time.

- » **Increased risk of litigation:** Expensive lawsuits may be filed by people who feel they have been appraised unfairly.

Setting necessary conditions for an effective system

These are the conditions that are necessary for team performance management to lead to improved team performance:

- » **The processes involved in the performance of the team are relatively unconstrained by other requirements of the task or the organization.** The organization should not constrain the amount of effort and skill that the team members can invest in a particular team-based project. An example of a constraint may be individual and team goals that compete against each other.

- » **The team is designed well and the organizational context supports team performance.** In other words, there are elements in the organization that support team performance. (For example, reward systems, training systems, resources are made available to the team; the team has an opportunity to perform.)

- » **Performance feedback focuses on team processes that are under the control of team members.** There is no point in providing feedback on aspects of performance that are beyond the control of the team.

Implementing a system for virtual teams

In a 1974 television interview, science fiction author Arthur C. Clarke predicted what the world would look like at the beginning of the 21st century. One of his many extraordinarily accurate predictions was about a "a console . . . . in a compact form . . . with a screen . . . through which he can talk" that people would have in their homes or offices. "Any businessman [sic], any executive, could live almost anywhere on Earth and still do his business through a device like this and this is a wonderful thing." Wow.

Regardless of the particular type of team, the reality of today's organizations, which are immersed in a global and highly competitive environment, dictates that many teams are virtual in nature. In other words, armed with laptops and smartphones, team members work from anywhere and at any time.

REMEMBER

Virtual teams have become very popular. For example, in a CareerBuilder survey involving 1,700 knowledge workers, 79 percent reported working always or frequently as part of virtual teams. And results of a 2014 survey of business leaders at the Global Leadership Summit showed that about 60 percent of them predict that more than half of their entire workforce will work remotely by 2020.

From an organization's practical and resource-based standpoint, it seems that the use of virtual teams has many benefits:

>> Virtual teams allow organizations to save money on travel expenses.

>> From the employee point of view, personal and professional disruptions due to travel are minimized.

>> Virtual teams also include individuals who live locally but telecommute — an important benefit for employees with various personal and family needs who may want to minimize commuting time.

This type of work arrangement is very attractive to Millennials. And it also allows organizations to reduce the size of their brick-and-mortar offices, which can lead to substantial savings, particularly in highly populated urban areas with high leasing costs.

However, managing the performance of virtual teams also has its own unique challenges. For example, many virtual teams, precisely because of a lack of face-to-face interactions, sometimes become "invisible" in organizations, and therefore, lack clear performance standards and even an identity as a team. Feeling that one is a member of the team and trusting other team members are important determinants of team performance, but these factors may not be present in virtual teams.

WARNING

Only about 20 percent of organizations offer training on how employees can improve their performance within the context of virtual teams. In addition, although team members may communicate using Skype and other videoconferencing technology, they usually communicate less frequently compared to members of nonvirtual teams. And this lower degree of communication often makes it difficult for team members to understand what is going on in the group. This is a particularly challenging issue when a team conflict needs to be addressed or when a controversial decision, such as charting a particular course of action, needs to be made.

A state-of-the-science performance management system can address the afore-mentioned challenges posed by virtual teams. How?

1. Create team charters, which are similar to job descriptions but for teams rather than individuals.

2. Have regular check-ins that help members stay connected and also lead to improved cooperation and conflict management tactics.

3. Implement team performance review meetings, which provide structure and increase team effectiveness. In addition, team developmental activities including intercultural skills, teamwork, and technology usage also lead to improved team performance.

TEAM PERFORMANCE MANAGEMENT AT MySQL

MySQL, (pronounced "My S-Q-L"), based in Cupertino, California, produces and develops database servers, software, and related tools. MySQL is the world's most popular open source database. The company employs more than 300 people spread across 25 countries, and 70 percent of the employees work from home. Employees in some cases have never met anyone they work with in person. This work arrangement requires a different approach to managing team performance as compared to the traditional office where face-to-face meetings and contact are the norm.

Technology enables a different approach to performance management. The company uses an Internet Relay Chat, which employees sign onto regularly to hold real-time meetings. Also, a software system called Worklog was developed by the company specifically to allow employees to mark off tasks when they have been accomplished. The company's method for evaluation and feedback are also adapted for virtual teams. Output and results produced are the focus of measuring productivity. There is not a strict chain of command in the MySQL work environment. Colleagues often seek out advice or ask questions to coworkers electronically, and all employees help manage individual and team performance by evaluating one another. Performance is also evaluated based on required weekly reports of accomplishments and by keeping track of employee involvement through conference calls and frequency of electronic communications, such as chat sessions and emails.

In short, MySQL has adapted to a virtual work environment by using technology that enables some unique strategies to be used for managing the performance of both individuals and teams.

The reality of work today is that virtual teams are here to stay. This highlights the importance of implementing performance management systems that include a team component. Not doing so is likely to result in more negative than positive outcomes resulting from the work of virtual teams. For an example, see the nearby sidebar on MySQL's attempts to reap the benefits and minimize potential pitfalls associated with virtual teams.

Accountability as a key purpose of team performance management

In the specific case of a system concerned with team performance, a key purpose is to make all team members accountable and to motivate them to have a stake in team performance.

WARNING

Many organizations have become more team-based, but they have not changed their performance management systems to accommodate this new organizational reality, which presents a unique challenge. If the organization is based on teams, but performance is still measured and rewarded at the individual level, team performance will suffer. In fact, some of the existing individual rewards may motivate people not to contribute to team performance, and instead, to focus on individual performance only.

Organizations that choose to include a team component in their performance management system must answer the following questions:

>> **How do we assess relative individual contribution?** How do we know the extent to which particular individuals have contributed to team results? How much has one member contributed in relation to the other members? Are there any slackers or free riders on the team? Is everyone contributing to the same extent, or are some members covering up for the lack of contribution of others?

>> **How do we balance individual and team performance?** How can we motivate team members so that they support a collective mission and collective goals? In addition, how do we motivate team members to be accountable and responsible individually? In other words, how do we achieve a good balance between measuring and rewarding individual performance in relation to team performance?

>> **How do we identify individual and team measures of performance?** How can we identify measures of performance that indicate individual performance versus measures of performance that indicate team performance? Where does individual performance end and team performance begin? Finally, based on these measures, how do we allocate rewards to individuals versus teams?

A study including interviews with 102 working adults in Hong Kong and another 96 in the Pearl River Delta (cities of Chung-shan, Quang-zhou, and Zhu-hai) showed organizations are faced with these challenging questions. For example, results revealed that about 38 percent of individuals participated in systems based on individual performance only, whereas about 34 percent participated in systems that included both individual and team components, and about 25 percent of respondents participated in systems that included a team component only.

Implementing a State-of-the-Science System

Although the questions I asked in the previous section may seem difficult to address, designing a performance management system that includes team performance is not difficult if you follow the following six team performance management principles:

>> **Make sure your team is really a team.** As I described earlier, there are different types of teams. Before a team component is introduced in the performance management system, you need to make sure the organization does have actual teams.

>> **Invest in performance management analytics.** Measuring team performance, as is the case with measuring individual performance, takes time and effort. You must be ready to make this investment for the measures to yield useful data.

>> **Define measurement goals clearly.** Defining how the data will be used (for example, administrative versus developmental purposes, or both) is a decision that you need to make before you design measures of team performance. As is the case with individual-level analytics, there are different variables that must be taken into account in relationship to the measures' purpose (for example, what will be the sources of data, how data will be collected, and so forth).

>> **Use a multimethod and multisource approach to measurement.** The measurement of team performance is complex. So you need multiple methods and sources of data.

>> **Focus on process as well as results.** Behavioral and process-oriented measures as well as results and outcomes are as useful for team performance management systems as for individuals. Thus, you need to give serious consideration to how both types of measures will be used within the context

of managing team performance. In other words, you should measure the results that teams produce and also how they achieve those results.

» **Measure long-term changes.** Although short-term processes and results are easier to measure, you need to also consider long-term measures of performance. You need to sample team performance over a variety of contexts and also over time.

Figure 14-1 shows the basic components of the team performance management process.

In the rest of this chapter, I will cover how to include a team component in a performance management system. In doing so, I discuss how organizations can address each of the questions I asked earlier.

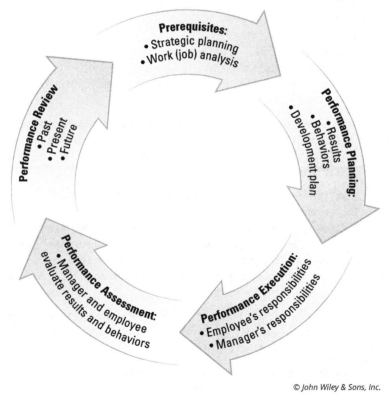

FIGURE 14-1. The components of the team performance management process.

© John Wiley & Sons, Inc.

Step 1: Establishing prerequisites

The first component of the team performance management process involves two prerequisites:

>> **You need to have good knowledge of the organization's mission.** This prerequisite is present regardless of whether there is an emphasis on team performance. This knowledge, combined with knowledge regarding the mission of the team's unit, allows employees and teams to make contributions that will have a positive impact on the unit and organization as a whole.

>> **You need to have good knowledge of the job in question.** In the case of individual jobs, a job analysis is conducted to determine the key components of a particular job: what tasks need to be done, how they are to be done, and what knowledge, skills, and abilities (KSAs) are needed to do them. Similarly, if you have good information about what a team is supposed to do and how, then it is easier to establish criteria and measures for team success.

Job descriptions summarize the job duties, needed KSAs, and working conditions for a particular position. In the case of teams, job descriptions take the form of what are called team charters. Much like job descriptions, team charters can be very detailed and refer to the team activities.

Team charters differ from job descriptions in that they also include information on within-team processes such as communication. Overall, good team charters include the following components:

>> **Strategic alignment:** How does the team's work support and relate to unit and organizational goals?

>> **Team purpose:** What is the team's reason for being?

>> **Team objectives, goals, and priorities:** What are the team's primary objectives and how are they prioritized?

>> **Key stakeholders:** Who are the key stakeholders who have an interest in the team's work?

>> **Team customers:** Who are the team's internal and external customers?

>> **Team leader and sponsor:** Who is the team leader and who is its champion (that is, a team supporter who is not a member of the team and has decision-making power in the organization)?

>> **Team member roles and responsibilities:** Who are the team members and what are their respective roles and responsibilities?

- **» Team member time commitments:** What time commitments are expected of all team members?

- **» Team communication plan:** What are the communication rules for the team? How often will you communicate, and what forms will communication take?

- **» Team ground rules:** What rules will the team adopt about interactions among team members, such as how to conduct meetings?

- **» In/out of scope elements:** What tasks and functions are in scope for the team, and which ones are out of scope?

- **» Key deliverables:** What are the team's key deliverables or tangible work products?

- **» Performance analytics:** How will we measure team success?

In addition to considering the team's charter, you still need to identify KSAs that will allow individuals to make a positive contribution to the team. These include not only KSAs related directly to the task at hand, such as a programmer who needs to have knowledge of a particular programming language. These are usually in each employee's job description. Rather, I'm talking about KSAs that are especially conducive to team performance. Examples include the following:

- **» Communication:** Giving and receiving constructive feedback, listening, and sharing information and ideas

- **» Decision making:** Helping the team make decisions

- **» Collaboration:** Dealing with conflict effectively, committing to the team and its goals, valuing the diversity and experience of other team members, and sharing accountability

- **» Team leadership:** Taking on the role of team leader, including knowing how to extract the best out of the team

- **» Self-control:** Keeping emotions under control and not displaying negative actions even when faced with opposition or even hostility from others

EXAMPLE

The University of California at San Diego (UCSD), like many other universities around the world, is structured around academic and administrative units called departments. Each of these departments can be considered a team. In terms of the prerequisites component, individual departments at UCSD develop a mission statement that is clearly related to the overall university's mission. This process allows each member of the team to become knowledgeable regarding the university's overall mission. After the department's mission is established, individual job descriptions are discussed and directly linked to both the mission of the university and the mission of the department. Job descriptions include KSAs needed for both individual and department performance.

Step 2: Performance planning

The second component of the performance management process shown in Figure 14-1 involves performance planning. Performance planning includes the consideration of results and behavior. In addition, performance planning involves the creation of a developmental plan. Each of these issues needs to be considered at the team level: results expected of the team, behaviors and process expected, and developmental objectives to be achieved by the team and its members.

A discussion of results must include key team accountabilities, specific objectives for each key accountability (goals to be reached), and performance standards (what constitutes acceptable and unacceptable levels of performance). A discussion of behaviors needs to include competencies (clusters of KSAs).

Finally, the developmental plan includes a description of areas that need improving and goals to be achieved in each area. The plan includes not only goals for the team as a whole but also developmental objectives for individual performance that will benefit team performance. For example, the team may have as its goal improvement of its internal decision-making processes, and some team members may have the individual goal to improve listening skills, which would help to improve the team's decision-making processes.

Try to follow the following recommendations to facilitate and accelerate team learning and development:

>> **Facilitate adaptive learning.** As part of the team developmental plan, encourage team members to try new behaviors. Also, as the team completes work or a specific project, you can review changes made in processes to understand what worked and what did not.

>> **Facilitate generative learning.** Give teams information about best practices implemented by other teams in the same organization or even in other organizations. Give teams time to practice new skills until they become habitual.

>> **Facilitate transformative learning.** Encourage teams to experiment with new ways of working together, including a discussion of feelings of uncertainty when facing change. Invite members from other teams to participate in discussions about performance or even to work as team members temporarily as a way of importing innovation and change into the team.

EXAMPLE

Duke University in Durham, North Carolina, considers performance planning to be the foundation of its performance management system, which creates the groundwork for what the supervisor and the team expect of the individual throughout the performance year. The process at Duke consists of two parts: understanding the behaviors that are expected, and defining the job results that are expected.

Step 3: Performance execution

The third component of the performance management process involves performance execution. Autonomous teams are solely responsible for performance execution; however, when a team has a supervisor or team leader, then both the team and the supervisor share responsibilities for performance execution. For example, team members need to be committed to goal achievement and should take a proactive role in seeking feedback from one another as well as from the team leader (if there is one).

REMEMBER

The burden is on the team to communicate openly and regularly with its supervisor.

Also, team members are responsible for being prepared for the performance review by conducting regular and realistic peer assessments and check-ins. In this way, team members have solid information regarding their performance as perceived by other team members before they meet the team leader.

REMEMBER

The team leader also has important responsibilities, including observing and documenting team performance and the relative contribution of the team members, updating the team on any changes in the goals of the organization, and providing resources and reinforcement so that team members will be motivated to succeed.

TEAM PERFORMANCE MANAGEMENT AT WHATABURGER

Related to team performance execution, team performance management can be fun. For example, let me tell you about Whataburger, a Texas-based fast-food chain of about 800 restaurants in the southern United States and in Mexico. The company holds an event called the "Whataburger Games" twice per year, during which managers, cooks, dishwashers, servers, and busboys compete in events testing their team skills against others in the company. The top prize winners receive $5,000 in cash.

The company believes that many benefits result from holding the games twice per year. According to management, the goals of the games are to emphasize operating procedures, to improve skills, to enhance teamwork, to reduce turnover, and to enhance the overall performance of the restaurants. The finals of the competition are held in conjunction with the managers' convention, where winners are formally recognized before corporate owners and executives, along with peers and management, in a ceremony awarding medals and cash prizes. In summary, the leadership at Whataburger has identified a friendly and fun competition as part of the overall performance management system that aims to contribute to improved team performance and the success of the company.

Building and leading high-performing teams requires specific KSAs:

>> Trust is a critical issue in most organizational contexts, but trust is especially important in virtual teams. Specifically, team members have to trust their leaders, but also their peers, and the entire organization to be most effective.

>> Team leaders also need to help establish a motivating vision and goals for the team.

>> Team leaders need to be able to provide helpful feedback to the entire team, as well as individual team members.

Step 4: Performance assessment

The fourth component of the performance management process is performance assessment.

All team members must evaluate one another's performance as well as the overall performance of the team. Peer evaluations are a key component of the assessment stage because they lead to higher levels of workload sharing, cooperation, and performance. Also, team coordination and feedback improve when peers monitor the performance of all other members in the team. This in turn leads to the recognition of errors and to taking subsequent actions to correct these errors quickly. Also, the team leader evaluates the performance of each team member as well as the team as a whole. Finally, members from other teams may also evaluate the performance of the team, which would apply only if members of other teams have firsthand experience with the performance of the team in question.

TIP

Peer evaluations can also include team members nominating someone else as the review period's most valuable performer (MVP).

Involvement of each team member in the performance assessment process increases the members' ownership and commitment to the system. Self-appraisals also provide important information to be discussed during the performance review. In the absence of self-appraisals, it is often not clear to team leaders whether the team and its members have a real understanding of what is expected of them.

In short, you need to assess three types of performance:

>> Individual performance based on task performance, which refers to the specific activities required by one's individual job, such as a programmer's ability to write quality code.

>> Individual performance based on contextual performance, which refers to specific activities that contribute to team performance, such as team members cooperating with each other.

>> Team performance as a whole.

REMEMBER

Although the saying goes, "There is no 'I' in team," it just isn't true because teams consist of individuals with their individual motivation, needs, and talents. The system should include a good combination of both "me" and "we" considerations.

How can you assess the "we" side of performance? As in the case of measures of individual performance, measures of team performance should include both results and behaviors.

Make sure you measure team performance as a whole using these performance dimensions:

>> **Effectiveness:** The degree to which results satisfy team customers and stakeholders, including both internal and external customers. Results could be the same as those that are measured to evaluate individual performance, which includes measures of quality, quantity, cost, and time.

>> **Efficiency:** The degree to which internal team processes support the achievement of results, team growth, and team member satisfaction, which includes measures of communication, coordination, collaboration, and decision making.

>> **Learning and growth:** The degree to which the team is able to learn new skills and improve performance over time. Specific measures are innovation, documented learning, best practices, and process improvements.

>> **Team member satisfaction:** The degree to which team members are satisfied with their team membership. Measures include team members' perceptions regarding the extent to which teamwork contributes to their growth and personal well-being.

TIP

In total, don't include more than about 15 measures of overall team performance; otherwise, team members may spend too much time collecting information and monitoring their activities and insufficient time actually working on their assigned tasks.

TIP

One more tip: When the team has a meeting to assess its own overall performance, include a person from outside the team as part of the performance discussion. This addition helps team members be more objective in their evaluation.

Step 5: Performance review

The fifth component of the performance management process is the performance review, which takes place when the team members meet with the team leader or manager.

TIP

In organizations that are structured around autonomous teams, there may not be a supervisor or manager. In that case, a team leader or representative would meet with a performance review board, which includes representatives from all teams.

At least two meetings are needed:

>> **The team leader meets with all members of the team together.** The focus of this meeting is to discuss the overall team performance, including results achieved by the team as a whole. Information for this meeting comes from

team members evaluating their collective performance, other teams evaluating the team in question, and the supervisor's evaluation.

>> **The team leader meets each team member individually.** The focus of this meeting is to discuss how the individual's behaviors contributed to team performance. Information for this meeting comes from individuals evaluating their own performance, peer ratings of the individual's performance, and the supervisor's evaluation. Recall the discussion in Chapter 6 regarding giving praise and constructive feedback (including the use of a strengths-based approach to giving feedback).

REMEMBER

Both meetings emphasize the past, the present, and the future. The past involves a discussion of performance during the review period. The present involves any changes in compensation, depending on results obtained. The future involves a discussion about goals and developmental plans the team and its members will be expected to achieve during the next review period. Discuss specific KSAs that would be important for a particular team member to develop further in the future.

In the particular case of virtual teams, a study involving more than 400 professionals showed that these two KSAs are related to virtual team member performance:

>> **Leading and deciding:** Making clear decisions, taking responsibility, motivating other team members, acting on own initiative, working autonomously, and setting clear goals for other team members.

>> **Analyzing and interpreting:** Using communication media effectively, communicating in writing understandably and in a structured way, working in a solution-oriented way, analyzing data effectively, effectively learning to use new technologies, gaining an understanding of others' tasks, working effectively with computers and digital media, and showing analytical skills.

ACTIVE LEARNING

Now pause for a moment to reflect on these two team competencies, which are particularly relevant for virtual teams. Which of the behaviors involved in each of the competencies are your strengths? Which your weaknesses? Given the inevitability of virtual teams in your career progression, what steps could you take to improve your proficiency regarding each of your weaknesses?

REMEMBER

An important issue in team performance management is that in addition to individual performance, the system includes individual performance as it affects the functioning of the team, as well as the performance of the team as a whole.

USING PERFORMANCE MANAGEMENT TO TURN "B PLAYERS" INTO A WINNING TEAM

What can team leaders do to turn "B players" into a winning team? In 2004, Greece, which was an underdog by a long shot, won the European Championship, one of the most competitive soccer tournaments in the world. Greece was considered a peripheral team with mostly unknown players. But they defeated favorites France and Portugal and lifted the trophy. This victory made Greece the first team to defeat both the holders (France) and the hosts (Portugal) in the same tournament. The odds that Greece would win had been estimated at 1 out of 150! But they won. Why? The following four performance management factors were key:

- **Vision** is the performance planning component of the performance management system. There needs to be a good idea of future goals. In addition, there should be a clear strategy on how to achieve them. In other words, what are the specific results and behaviors expected of team members and the team as a whole?

- **Performance analytics** is the performance assessment component of the performance management system. Team leaders can make better decisions if they have accurate and fair performance data — from multiple sources.

- **Feedback** is an essential ingredient of the performance review component of the performance management system. In the context of team performance management, this involves information on individuals and also information on the team as a whole.

- **Morale** requires the collective engagement of the entire team. When all the components of a state-of-the-science performance management system are in place, the natural result is that team members share common goals, are motivated to achieve those common goals, and have the necessary resources to do so. When team members feel that they are part of something bigger than each individual, they work together and are able to achieve great things. This means that cooperation is valued more than competition, and the team — as a whole — is on a journey of continuous improvement. To be able to enhance a team's morale, it is important for team members to also see that the leader is committed to the team, and not just using the team as a springboard of his next career move.

Connecting team performance management with team rewards

Organizations that implement performance management systems that include team performance must redesign their rewards system to reward team performance.

Teams of workers in the production line at Motorola's plant in Tianjin, China, receive additional compensation if they keep the percentage of errors under a prespecified threshold.

A recent study investigated the effects of implementing a pay-for-performance system at the team level with top management teams at a global information technology company. The teams included seven or eight members. Each of the teams had team-level performance goals, which were specific but differed from team to team. Rewards were allocated based on organizational performance goals (25 percent), team-level goals (50 percent), and individual-level goals (25 percent). Similarly, at Apple and Google, team performance assessment and rewards are part of the formal review process.

Organizations can reward team performance in ways similar to those in which they reward individual performance. For example, take the case of Phelps Dodge Mining Company. The company implemented a team-based reward system involving more than 4,200 employees in six locations throughout North America. The company moved from being unionized to being nonunionized, and a key strategic objective was to help employees move away from working for an hourly wage to understanding how to work as a salaried workforce. To accomplish this goal, team performance was measured and rewarded accordingly. For example, a team goal in a truck maintenance shop was to shorten the time that trucks were off-line for maintenance. Goals were set through the active participation of all team members, and employees are given additional compensation, depending on whether they accomplish team-based goals.

An organization can have a variable pay system in which an individual is eligible for a bonus if his or her team achieves specific results. This reward would be in addition to any performance-based rewards allocated according to individual performance (either task performance or contextual performance). The amount of the bonus could also be controlled by the team: Teams that are able to generate savings that result from controlling cost and improving efficiency may see some of this money come back in the form of bonuses. In this case, the rewards are called self-funded. In other cases, the bonus can come from a company-wide pool that varies each year, based on overall organizational performance.

Team-based rewards are effective if they are implemented following similar principles as those used for individual rewards. For example, all teams should be eligible, and rewards should be visible, contingent, and reversible. Do these team-based reward systems work? In one study, team performance-based pay motivated teams to spend 22 percent more time on the task at hand, which led to improved performance.

A study consisting of a review of 30 separate investigations concluded that team rewards are more potent in smaller compared to larger teams. The reason? In smaller teams, it is easier for everyone to see everyone else's effort, motivation, and performance. Also, studies have provided evidence in support of team-based contingent pay plans.

But similar to the case of individual rewards, in implementing team rewards, you need to be aware of the factors that make rewards fail. For example, rewards given to team members based on the extent to which they cooperate with each other are likely to enhance accuracy, but not necessarily speed. If the goal of the reward is to motivate employees to work faster, giving rewards for cooperation may be yet another example of what former chief learning officer for Goldman Sachs, Steve Kerr, called the "folly of rewarding A while hoping for B."

Chapter **15**

Evaluating Your System

Before the performance management system is rolled out, it is a good idea to test a version of the entire system so that adjustments and revisions can be made as needed. You don't want to roll out a performance management system that has a major flaw, right?

Also, after the system is in place, you will find it useful to collect data to see what is working and what is not. You can use this information to make fixes where needed.

Pilot Testing the Performance Management System

In the pilot test of the system, you implement the system in its entirety from beginning to end, including all the steps that would be included if the system is fully implemented. In other words, meetings take place between supervisor and employee, performance data are gathered, developmental plans are designed, and feedback is provided.

TIP

The most important aspect of the pilot test is that all participants maintain records, noting any difficulties they encounter, ranging from problems with the appraisal form to how performance is measured to the quality and usefulness of feedback received.

The pilot test allows for the identification and early correction of any flaws before the system is implemented throughout the organization.

Reasons for doing a pilot test

The pilot test allows you to gain information from the perspective of the system's users on how well the system works, to learn about any difficulties and unforeseen obstacles, to collect recommendations on how to improve all aspects of the system, and to understand personal reactions to it.

Also, conducting a pilot test is yet another way to achieve early acceptance from a group of people, those involved in the pilot test, who can then act as champions for the performance management system.

Participants in the pilot test can help you "sell" the performance management system to the rest of the organization. In this way, the system is not seen as owned by the HR function, but by the entire organization.

A final reason for conducting a pilot test is that end users are likely to have a higher system acceptance rate, knowing that stakeholders in the company had a say in its design, rather than feeling that the system was created by the HR department alone.

Don't assume that the performance management system will necessarily be executed as planned or that it will produce the anticipated results.

Selecting the pilot test group

In larger organizations, it's important to select the right group of employees for the pilot test. In choosing this group, you need to understand that the managers who will be participating should be willing to invest the resources, including time, needed to do the pilot test.

The pilot test group should be made up of managers who are flexible and willing to try new things. Also, make sure managers receive a realistic preview about what the system looks like before they decide whether to participate in the pilot test.

In selecting the group, make sure the group is sufficiently large and representative of the entire organization so that reactions from the group will be generalizable to the rest of the organization. So in selecting the group, select jobs that are similar to those throughout the company, and the group selected is not an exception in either a positive or a negative way. In other words, the group should not be regarded as particularly unique in terms of its productivity or anything else.

PILOT TESTING THE PERFORMANCE MANAGEMENT SYSTEM AT THE WASHINGTON STATE PATROL

The Washington State Patrol (WPS) realized that several changes were occurring, just as similar changes were occurring in patrol departments in other states. This prompted the revision of its performance management system. WSP established a committee to develop the new appraisals. Before implementing the system, the state patrol pilot tested it in two districts. First, the committee prepared a training module that included a pre-appraisal work group meeting. In this meeting, employees discussed their roles and expectations surrounding the performance management system and applied those discussions to a common goal. The training also focused on how new developments in the patrol led to new elements in the performance management system. The trainers encouraged the participants to ask questions regarding the shift to the new approach. The trainers then used the feedback received in these sessions to fix specific operational issues before introducing the training to the entire agency.

After the appraisal process was fine-tuned, it was submitted for the approval of the troopers' and sergeants' associations. A select number of individuals across the districts received "train the trainer" training. Finally, the system was instituted agency-wide. Each of these steps allowed the Washington State Patrol to identify potential barriers that could have prevented the system from being successful.

EXAMPLE

The Gap, Inc., chose to pilot test its revamped performance management system in a representative store because it is a self-contained business unit.

REMEMBER

Pilot tests provide crucial information to be used in improving the system before it is actually put in place. Pilot testing the system provides huge savings and identifies potential problems before they become irreversible and the credibility of the system is ruined permanently.

Ongoing Monitoring and Evaluation of the Performance Management System

When the testing period is over and the performance management system has been implemented organization-wide, it is important to use clear measurements to monitor and evaluate that things are working as expected.

How do you evaluate the system's effectiveness? How do you evaluate the extent to which the system is being implemented as planned, and how do you evaluate the extent to which it is producing the intended results?

What to measure

Evaluation data should include reactions to the system and assessments of the system's operational and technical requirements.

For example, you can administer a confidential survey to all employees, asking about perceptions and attitudes regarding the system. This survey can be administered during the initial stages of implementation and then at the end of the first review cycle to find out if there have been any changes.

Also, regarding the system's results, you can measure performance ratings over time to see what positive effects the implementation of the system is having.

Finally, you can also interview key stakeholders, including managers and employees who have been involved in developing and implementing the performance management system.

EVALUATING THE PERFORMANCE MANAGEMENT SYSTEM IN THE U.S. FEDERAL GOVERNMENT

The U.S. federal government takes the evaluation of performance management systems very seriously. For example, several laws have been passed and bills are being prepared that mandate federal agencies to develop a strategic plan, a performance plan, and a performance report.

Although these initiatives concern agencies and not individuals, ultimately, the performance of any agency depends on the performance of the individuals working in that agency. The net result of such laws as the Government Performance and Results Act is an increase in accountability and funding allocation based on performance. Thus, federal agencies are required to evaluate the relative efficiency of their various management techniques, including performance management systems.

How to measure

These are good measures you can use on a regular basis to monitor and evaluate the system:

>> **Number of people evaluated:** One of the most basic measures is the number of employees who are actually participating in the system. If performance evaluations have not been completed for some employees, you need to find out who they are and why a performance review has not been completed.

>> **Quality of qualitative performance data:** An indicator of quality of the performance data refers to the information provided in the open-ended sections of the appraisal forms. For example, how much did the rater write? What is the relevance of the examples provided?

>> **Quality of follow-up actions:** A good indicator of the quality of the system is whether it leads to important follow-up actions about development activities and improved processes. For example, to what extent follow-up actions involve exclusively the supervisor as opposed to the employee? If this is the case, then the system is not working as intended because employees are not sufficiently involved. Also, to what extent have employees learned from their successes and failures and applied those lessons to the future?

>> **Quality of performance discussion meeting:** You can distribute a confidential survey to all employees on a regular basis to gather information about how the supervisor is managing the performance discussion meetings. For example, is the feedback useful? Has the supervisor made resources available so the employee can accomplish the developmental plan objectives? How relevant was the performance review discussion to one's job? To what degree have developmental objectives and plans been discussed? To what extent does the supervisor's way of providing feedback encourage direct reports to receive more feedback in the future?

>> **System satisfaction:** You can also distribute a confidential survey to measure the perceptions of the system's users, both raters and ratees. This survey can include questions about satisfaction with equity, usefulness, and accuracy.

>> **Overall cost/benefit ratio:** A fairly simple way to address the overall impact of the system is to ask participants to rate the overall cost/benefit ratio for the performance management system. This is a type of bottom-line question that can provide convincing evidence for the overall worth of the system. The cost/benefit ratio question can be asked in reference to an individual (employee or manager), the job, and the organizational unit.

>> **Unit-level and organization-level performance:** Another indicator that the system is working well is provided by the measurement of unit- and organization-level performance. Such performance indicators might be customer satisfaction with specific units and indicators of the financial

performance of the various units or the organization as a whole. It may take some time for changes in individual and group performance level to be translated into unit- and organization-level results.

TIP

Don't expect results as soon as the system is implemented; however, you will start to see some tangible results at the unit level a few months after the system is in place.

EVALUATING THE PERFORMANCE MANAGEMENT SYSTEM AT THE WASHINGTON STATE PATROL

In a sidebar earlier in this chapter, I discuss pilot testing the performance management system at the Washington State Patrol. Let's take a look at how this organization evaluated effectiveness after the system was implemented.

The patrol has several measures in place for continual monitoring and evaluation. Before all employees were reviewed using the system, they were surveyed regarding their satisfaction with the new system. This input was then used to further improve the appraisal process. In addition, the patrol uses the results of a biyearly citizen's survey conducted by Washington State University. The results of this survey are used to determine whether the state patrol's customers are satisfied with its performance, and the data are also used to adjust and reprioritize performance objectives. In addition, the data are used to measure division-level performance, one indicator of the success of the performance management process.

The Washington State Patrol collects other types of data as well. For example, every six months, division managers give presentations regarding performance management to their peers and to several executives. Initially, the meetings focused on efforts to implement the new performance management system and increase quality, but this will change as new issues arise. The presentation is 30–40 minutes long, followed by 20–30 minutes of questions from peers and executives.

The feedback from these presentations is used to measure how well the system is being implemented, and feedback on the success of the meetings will be used to make any necessary changes to the system. The Washington State Patrol may also want to consider measuring how many people are participating in the system. The patrol would also benefit from assessing whether the new system is distinguishing high- from low-level performers and from ascertaining the overall cost/benefit ratio of implementing the system.

4

Connecting Performance Management with Rewards and the Law

IN THIS PART . . .

Connect performance management to financial and nonfinancial rewards.

Set up an effective pay system.

Implement performance management systems that are legal and fair.

Chapter **16**

Offering Financial and Nonfinancial Rewards

One of the purposes of performance management is to make administrative decisions about employees. And of those, decisions about rewards, which used to be labeled "compensation and benefits," are the most meaningful consequences of a performance management system for many employees.

Clearly, most people are interested in their personal growth and development. But pay is often at the top of the list in terms of people's needs — although they may rarely admit it openly. Also, from the perspective of organizations, compensation shapes the culture because it sends a very clear message about what behaviors and results are more or less valued.

In this chapter, I cover the two main types of rewards: financial (also called "tangible") and nonfinancial (also called "intangible"). These are the basic ingredients of a reward systems. Also, you learn about how to connect performance management to different types of rewards.

Not All Rewards Are Created Equal

Until a few years ago, the terms "compensation" and "compensation and benefits" were used commonly. But more recently, these labels have been replaced with "rewards" and "total rewards." A reward system is the set of processes for distributing both financial and nonfinancial rewards as part of an employment relationship.

Financial rewards

An employee's *financial rewards* include cash compensation (base pay, cost-of-living and merit pay, short-term incentives, and long-term incentives) and benefits (income protection, work–life focus, tuition reimbursement, and allowances).

Nonfinancial rewards

Employees also receive *nonfinancial rewards,* which include recognition and status, employment security, challenging work, learning opportunities, and work-life focus, among others.

REMEMBER

Not all types of rewards are directly related to performance management because not all types of rewards are allocated based on performance. For example, some allocations are based exclusively on seniority.

Different Types of Financial Rewards

There are six different types of financial rewards: base pay, cost-of-living adjustments and contingent pay, short-term incentives, long-term incentives, income protection, and allowances.

Base pay

The *base pay,* which usually includes a range of values, focuses on the position and duties performed, rather than an individual's contribution. Thus, the base pay is usually the same for all employees performing similar duties and ignores differences across employees. However, differences within the base pay range may exist based on such variables as experience and differential performance.

Employees in most professional and managerial jobs (also called "salaried employees") are *exempt employees.* On the other hand, *nonexempt employees* receive their pay calculated on an hourly wage.

REMEMBER

In the United States, there is a difference between wage and salary. Salary is base cash compensation received by employees who are exempt from regulations of the Fair Labor Standards Act, and in most cases, cannot receive overtime pay.

Cost-of-living adjustments and contingent pay

Cost-of-living adjustments (COLA) imply the same percentage increase for all employees, regardless of their individual performance. COLA are given to combat the effects of inflation to preserve the employees' buying power.

EXAMPLE

In 2017, in the United States, organizations that implemented COLA used a 3-percent pay increase. In 1980, it was 14.3 percent, whereas in 2013 it was only 1.5 percent. You can get year-by-year COLA percentages from the Social Security Administration (www.ssa.gov/OACT/COLA/colaseries.html).

Contingent pay, sometimes referred to as *merit pay,* is given as an addition to the base pay based on past performance. As I will describe later in more detail, contingent pay means that the amount of additional compensation depends on an employee's level of performance.

For example, the top 20 percent of employees in the performance score distribution may receive a 10 percent annual increase, whereas employees in the middle 70 percent of the distribution may receive a 4% increase, and employees in the bottom 10 percent may receive no increase at all.

Short-term incentives

Similar to contingent pay, *short-term incentives* are based on past performance. But incentives are not added to the base pay and are only temporary pay adjustments based on the review period (for example, quarterly or annual). Incentives are one-time payments and are sometimes called *variable pay.* A second difference between incentives and contingent pay is that incentives are known in advance.

EXAMPLE

A salesperson in a pharmaceutical company knows that if she meets her sales quota, she will receive a $6,000 bonus at the end of the quarter. She also knows that if she exceeds her sales quota by 10 percent, her bonus will be $12,000. By contrast, in the case of contingent pay, in most cases, the specific value of the reward is not known in advance.

SHORT-TERM INCENTIVES FOR PHYSICIANS IN COLORADO

Short-term incentives were put to use in a reward program in Colorado Springs, Colorado. Eight health care providers and three insurance companies teamed up with the nonprofit Colorado Business Group on Health to pay physicians cash awards per patient for providing diabetes care that results in positive outcomes for patients. Doctors in the program received the additional pay as an incentive without an increase in base salary.

The program required doctors to work closely with patients and focus on preventative medicine, including education, goal setting, and follow-up meetings. Physical indicators, such as blood pressure, blood sugar, and cholesterol, are measured against goals to determine whether successful outcomes are being achieved. The goals of the program were to provide better disease control for the patient and to cut down on expensive future treatments, such as emergency room visits and inpatient stays in the hospital. Additional savings were expected through reduced medical claims and health insurance premiums paid by employers.

In short, the health providers and insurers used short-term incentives as part of the performance management systems with the goal of motivating physicians to focus on treatments that will enhance the overall health and well-being of the patient in an ongoing manner.

Long-term incentives

Whereas short-term incentives usually involve an attempt to motivate performance in the short term (such as the quarter or year) and involve cash bonuses or specific prizes (for example, two extra days off), *long-term incentives* attempt to influence future performance over a longer period of time. Typically, they involve stock ownership or options to buy stocks at a preestablished and profitable price.

REMEMBER

The rationale for long-term incentives is that employees will be personally invested in the organization's success, and this investment is expected to translate into a sustained high level of performance.

Both short-term and long-term incentives are quite popular. For example, surveys involving several hundred reward and HR practitioners across the public, private, and voluntary sectors by the Chartered Institute of Personnel and Development conducted over the past few years showed that between 50 percent and 65 percent of their organizations offer performance-based rewards. As we will discuss later in this chapter, some organizations such as Google are taking this idea to the limit and offer "big pay for big performance."

Income protection

Income protection programs serve as a backup to employees' salaries in the event that an employee is sick, disabled, or no longer able to work.

Other types of benefits under the income protection rubric include medical insurance, pension plans, and savings plans. These are optional benefits provided by organizations, but they are becoming increasingly important and often guide an applicant's decision to accept a job offer.

Allowances

Benefits in some countries and organizations include allowances covering housing and transportation. These kinds of allowances are typical for expatriate personnel and are also popular for high-level managers throughout the world. In South Africa, for example, it is common for a transportation allowance to include one of the following choices:

>> The employer provides a car and the employee has the right to use it both privately and for business.

>> The employer provides a car allowance, more correctly referred to as a travel allowance, which means reimbursing the employee for the business use of the employee's personal car.

INCOME PROTECTION IN THE U.S. AND CANADA

In the United States, employers pay 50 percent of an employee's total contribution to Social Security so that income is protected for family members in case of an employee's death or a disability that prevents the employee from doing substantial work for one year and for an employee when he or she reaches retirement age. For example, a 40-year-old employee earning an annual salary of $90,000, and expected to continue to earn that salary until retirement age, would receive about $1,739 a month if he retired at age 62 (in 2039), about $2,509 a month if he retired at age 67 (in 2044), and about $3,133 if he retired at age 70 (in 2047). (All of these figures are in 2017 dollars without calculating inflation.)

Canadian organizations pay into a fund that provides income protection in the case of a disability. For example, the University of Alberta offers a monthly income of 70 percent of salary to employees who become severely disabled.

Other allowances can include smartphones and their monthly charges, club and gym fees, discount loans, and mortgage subsidies.

TIP

These allowances are clearly a benefit for employees, and some of them directly or indirectly also produce a benefit for the employer. For example, providing smartphones means that employees are reachable via phone, text, and email pretty much at all times. Similarly, if employees take advantage of a gym fee allowance, they are likely to stay healthier, which in turn may lead to less health-related expenses for the organization.

Different Types of Nonfinancial Rewards

There are two types of nonfinancial rewards: relational and work-life focus.

Relational

Relational rewards are about the relationship between the employee and the organization. Some examples of nonfinancial rewards are

>> Recognition and status

>> Employment security

>> Challenging work

>> Opportunities to learn

>> Opportunities to form personal relationships at work (including friendships and romances)

EXAMPLE

Sun Microsystems, which has been purchased by Oracle, allows employees to enroll in SunU, which is Sun's own online education tool. SunU encapsulates a mix of traditional classroom courses with online classes that can be accessed anywhere in the world at any time. Sun offers its employees enormous scope for development and career progression, and there is a commitment to ensuring that all employees are given the opportunity to develop professionally. The new knowledge and skills acquired by employees can help them not only to further their careers within Sun, but also, to take this knowledge with them if they seek employment elsewhere. Thus, some types of relational rewards can be long lasting.

Work-life focus

Work–life focus rewards include programs that help employees achieve a better balance between work and nonwork activities. These include time away from work such as vacation time, services to meet specific needs such as counseling and financial planning, time off for volunteering, and flexible work schedules such as telecommuting and nonpaid time off.

EXAMPLE

Sun Microsystems actively promotes an equal balance between work and home life and closes its Broomfield, Colorado, campus from late December through early January every year. This benefit (vacation time for all employees in addition to individual yearly vacation time) is part of Sun's culture. Sun believes in a work hard–play hard attitude, as is evidenced by CEO Scott McNealy's motto: "Kick butt and have fun."

Many Silicon Valley companies, including Google, Apple, Asana, and Facebook, have become famous for offering work-life focus benefits, which also include free on-site gourmet cafeterias, auto insurance, free dry cleaning, concerts, on-site yoga classes, and concierge services that help employees plan vacations and even buy tickets for sporting events.

Does this mean that Google and other Silicon Valley companies are overly generous with their employees? Maybe not. This is a strategic and well thought-out reward policy because, as noted by Gerry Ledford, Senior Research Scientist at the Center for Effective Organizations in Los Angeles, "An employee who never has to leave the workplace to eat, shower, exercise, run errands, or sleep is an employee who can work extraordinarily hours — and is expected to do so."

TIP

A benefit of work-life focus policies is that some programs are designed specifically to attract and retain Millennials, who typically place greater importance on work-life balance, compared to Baby Boomers.

EXAMPLE

PricewaterhouseCoopers makes annual contributions toward employees' student loan repayment, and IBM, GE, and Accenture help nursing mothers by providing materials and funds to ship breast milk home when they are traveling on a work-related assignments.

Linking Performance Management with Different Types of Rewards

Table 16-1 includes a list of rewards, together with their degree of dependency on the performance management system.

TABLE 16-1

Different Types of Rewards and Their Dependency on the Performance Management System

Reward	Degree of Dependency
Cost-of-living adjustment	Low
Income protection	Low
Work-life focus	Moderate
Allowances	Moderate
Relational rewards	Moderate
Base pay	Moderate
Contingent pay	High
Short-term incentives	High
Long-term incentives	High

Rewards with low dependency on performance management

As an example of the low end of the dependency continuum, cost-of-living adjustment has a low degree of dependency on the performance management system, meaning that the system has no impact on this type of reward. In other words, all employees receive this type of reward, regardless of their performance.

Rewards with high dependency on performance management

On the other end, short-term incentives have a high degree of dependency, meaning that the performance management system dictates who receives these incentives and who doesn't.

Long-term incentives (for example, profit sharing and stock options) also have a high degree of dependency. Although this type of incentive is not specifically tied to individual performance, it does depend on performance measured at the team, unit, or even organizational levels.

Rewards with moderate dependency on performance management

Between the high and low end, we find some rewards with a moderate degree of dependency on the performance management system, such as base pay, a type of reward that may or may not be influenced by the system.

ACTIVE LEARNING

Think about the performance management system of your current employer. Based on Table 16-1, try to think about the various types of financial and nonfinancial rewards allocated in your organization. To what extent is each of these rewards dependent on the organization's performance management system? Does the organization emphasize rewards that are related to performance or not? What does this tell you about the culture of your organization?

Chapter **17**

Setting Up an Effective Pay System

Pay is very important to most people, but this chapter teaches you that "throwing more money" at people not always improves performance. And this strategy may actually motivate employees to behave badly.

Also, you learn when and why you should implement a traditional versus a contingent (known as pay-for-performance) pay plan. Importantly, you will also discover pitfalls you should avoid when you implement contingent pay plans.

Setting Up Traditional and Contingent Pay Plans

A *traditional* approach in implementing reward systems is to reward employees for the positions they fill as indicated by their job descriptions and not necessarily by how they do their work. In other words, employees are rewarded for filling a specific slot in the organizational hierarchy.

Traditional pay plans

In traditional pay systems, your job directly determines pay and indirectly determines benefits and incentives received. Typically, there is a pay range that determines minimum, midpoint, and maximum rates for each job.

For example, a university may have five ranks for professors who have just been hired, with the following base pay:

1. Instructor (pay range: $50,000–$65,000)

2. Senior instructor (pay range: $60,000–$75,000)

3. Assistant professor (pay range: $80,000–$110,000)

4. Associate professor (pay range: $105,000–$125,000)

5. Professor (pay range: $120,000–$160,000)

In a traditional reward system, each of these positions would have a minimum, midpoint, and maximum base salary. For assistant professors, the minimum is $80,000 per year, the midpoint is $95,000, and the maximum is $110,000. Salary increases at the end of the year would be determined by seniority or by a percentage of a professor's base salary (and the same percentage would be used for all people holding the same position). Rewards would not be based on teaching quality, as indicated by student teaching ratings, or research productivity, as indicated by the number and quality of publications.

If an assistant professor's base salary is $110,000, she cannot realize an increase in her salary unless she is promoted to associate professor because $110,000 is the maximum possible salary for this job title.

REMEMBER

In traditional reward systems, the type of position and seniority are the determinants of salary and salary increases, not performance. In such reward systems, there is a very weak or no relationship between performance management and rewards.

The traditional system is quite common. In South Korea, as is the case in other collectivistic cultures (including, for example, China), employees tend to avoid confrontation for fear of losing face. Thus, supervisors may be reluctant to give employees unsatisfactory performance ratings or ratings based on individual performance because this would single out individuals. Instead, systems that measure and reward team performance are more effective in collectivistic cultures. It is possible, however, to move away from more traditional systems based mainly on seniority by establishing clear links between performance management and other functions such as training. If you clearly establish such links, employees are more likely to see the benefits of the performance management system and believe that the system is fair.

Contingent pay plans

Contingent pay (CP), also called *pay-for-performance*, means that individuals are rewarded based on how well they perform on the job. Thus, employees receive increases in pay based wholly or partly on job performance. These increases can either be added to an employee's base salary or can be a one-time bonus.

Originally, CP plans were used only for top management. Gradually, the use of CP plans extended to sales jobs. Now, CP plans are pretty much everywhere.

For example, as of 2001, about 70 percent of workers in the United States have been employed by organizations implementing some type of variable play plan, and many of these organizations tie variable pay (for example, bonus, commission, cash award, lump sum) directly to performance. A remarkable change in the past two decades has been a steady decrease in base pay and an increase in different types of variable pay.

REMEMBER

Rewards are increasingly influenced by performance, which highlights the increased importance and having a good performance management system that yields useful and fair information for making decisions about the allocation of rewards.

Let's go back to the example of salaries for university professors. When a CP plan is implemented, pay raises are determined in part or wholly based on performance. For example, two assistant professors may be hired at the same time at the same base salary level (for example, $75,000). If one of them outperforms the other, year after year for several years, then eventually, the better performing assistant professor could make $110,000, which is a higher level of pay than most associate professors make. This is because every year, this assistant professor receives a substantial salary increase, part of which may be added to the base salary, based on her outstanding teaching and research performance. On the other hand, the other assistant professor may still be making the same amount, or close to the same amount, that he was making when he was first hired.

Under a traditional pay plan, an assistant professor would not receive a higher salary than most associate professors. Under such a plan, the assistant professor would have to be promoted to associate professor before she could receive a salary of $110,000, which is outside the traditional range for assistant professors.

Implementing Contingent Pay Plans

Why are organizations using CP plans? One reason is given by results of a survey of Fortune 500 companies, which showed that performance management systems are more effective when results are directly tied to the reward system.

When the performance management system has a direct relationship with the reward system, performance measurement and performance improvement are taken more seriously.

When a CP plan is implemented, organizations need to make clear what is expected of employees, what specific behaviors or results will be rewarded, and how employees can achieve these behaviors or results. This, in and of itself, serves as an important communication tool because supervisors and employees are better able to understand what really matters.

The benefits of CP plans

CP plans force organizations to define effective performance more clearly and to determine what factors are likely to lead to effective performance. Also, high-achieving performers are attracted to organizations that reward high-level performance, and high-level performers are typically in favor of CP plans. This tendency is called the *sorting effect:* Star performers are likely to be attracted to and remain within organizations that have implemented CP plans.

TIP

An organization's ability to retain its star performers is obviously crucial if an organization wants to win the talent war and have a people-based competitive advantage.

EXAMPLE

An article published in the *Journal of Business* described a study at a glass installation company that found that productivity improved by 44 percent when the compensation system was changed from salaries to individual incentives. A closer look at the data showed that about 50 percent of the productivity improvement was due to the current employees being more productive, whereas the other 50-percent improvement was due to less productive employees quitting and the organization's ability to attract and recruit more productive workers.

REMEMBER

Contingent pay plans serve as a good tool to recruit and retain star performers as a result of the sorting effect, which in turn, leads to greater overall productivity.

Hicks Waldron, former CEO of cosmetics giant Avon, in an eloquent statement, explained why CP plans are so popular: "It took me 30 years to figure out that people don't do what you ask them to do; they do what you pay them to do."

How about organizations that are struggling financially? Can they still implement CP plans? Can they afford to give performance-based rewards to their employees? The answer is "yes" to both questions.

TIP

Making sure that top performers are rewarded appropriately keeps them motivated and prevent them from leaving the organization in difficult times. It is these top performers who are the organization's hope for recovery in the future. In fact, giving rewards to poor performers means that these rewards are taken away from high-level performers.

REMEMBER

CP plans improve employee motivation to accomplish goals that match organizational needs. CP plans have the potential to help people change behavior and improve performance.

For example, assume an organization is trying hard to improve customer satisfaction. Some units in this organization decide to implement a CP plan that awards cash to employees who improve their customer satisfaction ratings. By contrast, other units continue with a traditional pay plan in which there is no clear tie between performance levels and rewards. Who do you think will perform better — employees under the CP plan or those under the traditional plan? Well, if all other things are equal, it is likely that employees under the CP plan will improve the service they offer to customers. In fact, a review of several studies by Professor Edwin Locke from the University of Maryland concluded that using individual pay incentives increased productivity by an average of 30 percent.

REMEMBER

Contingent pay plans and pay in general should not be regarded as the Holy Grail of employee performance. Pay only affects the motivation aspect of performance. If an employee is not performing well, pay may not solve the problem if poor performance results from a lack of knowledge as opposed to lack of motivation.

Reasons why contingent pay plans fail

In spite of the overall positive impact of CP plans, we should be aware that not all CP plans work as intended. In fact, several recent corporate scandals, including the one at Wells Fargo, are directly related to the implementation of CP plans.

Why is it that some CP plans don't succeed and produce results that are so opposite to what they intend to do? The following sections offer some answers.

A poor performance management system is in place

What happens when a CP plan is paired with a poorly designed, poorly implemented performance management system, one that includes biased ratings and the measurement of unrelated performance dimensions? This situation leads some employees to challenge the CP plan legally.

PROBLEMS CAUSED BY CONTINGENT PAY AT WELLS FARGO

At Wells Fargo, retail bank employees had specific rewards associated with specific performance targets, such as selling eight banking products per household. Wells Fargo's retail banking unit is critical because it has about 40 million customers.

What did this type of CP plan unwittingly motivate Wells Fargo employees to do? Many employees secretly opened phony bank and credit accounts without customers' knowledge! Bank employees opened over 2.1 million deposit accounts that may not have been authorized.

From the employees' perspective, the CP plan was quite straightforward. To receive rewards associated with the CP plan, employees knew what to do exactly: They moved funds from customers' existing accounts into newly created ones, such as credit card accounts (often without clients' authorization or even knowledge). Then customers were charged for insufficient funds or overdraft fees due to lack of funds in their original accounts, which resulted in monetary rewards for employees.

About 14,000 of those accounts incurred over $400,000 in fees, including annual fees, interest charges, and overdraft protection fees. What was the result for Wells Fargo? It faced the largest penalty since the Consumer Financial Protection Bureau was founded in 2011. The bank agreed to pay $185 million in fines along with $5 million to refund customers. The company's latest estimate of the total cost of litigation losses is about $2 billion. Also, Wells Fargo had perennially been ranked as one of *Fortune's* most admired companies, and it had been ranked number 25 in 2016. But it did not even make the list in 2017. Also, Harris Poll's 2017 survey of corporate reputations showed that it plunged to the 99th place among the "most visible companies," above only Takata, the company whose defective airbags have been linked to 11 deaths.

The scope of the Wells Fargo scandal is truly shocking, but it demonstrates the motivational power of CP plans — even to motivate people to do things clearly not in the interest of customers, the organization, or themselves. In fact, 5,300 Wells Fargo employees have been fired due to this scandal. But the blame should not be put entirely on employees because the performance management system played a critical role. At Wells Fargo, branch managers were told that they "would end up working for McDonald's" if they missed sales quotas.

WARNING

Rewarding behaviors and results that are not job-related will cause good performers to leave the organization. If that's not bad enough, those who stay are not likely to be motivated to perform well.

There is the folly of rewarding A while hoping for B

What happens when the system rewards results and behaviors that are not those that will help the organization succeed, such as what happened in Wells Fargo? Employees engage in these often counterproductive behaviors when that is what will earn them the desired rewards. One example is the hope that executives will focus on long-term growth and environmental responsibility when, in fact, they are rewarded based on quarterly earnings. Given this situation, what are these executives likely to do? Will they think in the long term, or quarter by quarter?

A second example is an organization that would like its employees to be more entrepreneurial and innovative, but it doesn't reward employees who think creatively. What are employees likely to do? Will they be innovative and risk not getting rewards, or will they continue to do things the old way?

A third example is an organization that would like employees to focus on team-work and a one-for-all spirit, but it rewards employees based on individual results. This happens in many professional sports teams. What are professional athletes likely to do? Will they pass the ball, or will they try to score themselves as often as possible to improve their own individual statistics?

Rewards are not considered significant

What happens when a CP plan includes pay increases and other rewards that are so small that they don't differentiate between outstanding and poor performers? For example, what happens when the top performers receive a 5-percent pay increase and an average performer receives a 3-percent or 4-percent pay increase? In this context, rewards are not really performance-based rewards, and they don't make an impact. The message sent to employees is that performance is not some-thing worth being rewarded.

WHY CONTINGENT PAY FAILED AT GREEN GIANT

Green Giant, which is part of the General Mills global food conglomerate, implemented a bonus plan that rewarded employees for removing insects from vegetables.

What was the result regarding performance? Initially, managers were pleased because employees were finding and removing a substantially higher number of insects. The initial enthusiasm disappeared, however, when managers found out that employees were bringing insects from home, putting them into vegetables, and removing them to get the bonus!

TIP

For rewards to be meaningful, they need to be significant in the eyes of the employees. Usually, an increase of approximately 12 to 15 percent of one's salary is regarded as a meaningful reward and would motivate people to do things they would not do otherwise.

Managers are not accountable

What happens when managers are not accountable for how they handle the performance and the performance evaluation of their employees? They are likely to inflate ratings so that employees receive what the manager thinks are appropriate rewards. Similarly, employees set goals that are easily attainable so that performance ratings lead to the highest possible level of reward.

WARNING

When managers are not held accountable, rewards may become the driver for the performance evaluation, instead of the performance evaluation being the driver for the rewards.

Selecting a Contingent Pay Plan

If your organization wishes to implement a CP plan, what should the plan look like? Based on the discussion of different forms of compensation earlier in this chapter, what considerations should you take into account in choosing, for example, among offering employees group incentives, profit sharing, or individual sales commissions? What is the appropriate mix of incentives at the organization, team, and individual levels?

A critical issue to consider is that of *organizational culture*. An organization's culture is defined by its unwritten rules and procedures. For example, is the organization fundamentally built around individual performance, or is teamwork the norm? Is the organization one in which high-level performers are regarded as role models who should be emulated, or are they viewed as a threat to upper management? Are you happy with the current culture, or do you wish to change it? CP plans are powerful tools that help solidify the current culture, and they can also be used to create a new type of culture. There should be a careful consideration of the culture of the organization before a specific type of CP plan is selected.

Traditional versus involvement cultures

Consider the types of systems that can be implemented in cultures that we can label *traditional* versus *involvement* cultures. Traditional cultures are characterized by top-down decision making, vertical communication, and clearly defined jobs. What type of plan should be implemented in organizations with this type of culture? An effective choice would be a plan that rewards specific and observable measures of performance, where that performance is clearly defined and directly linked to pay. Examples of such CP systems are the following:

>> **Individual incentives: (1) Piece rate.** Employees are paid based on the number of units produced or repaired. This system is usually implemented in manufacturing environments. In service organizations, this could involve the number of calls made or the number of clients, or potential clients, contacted. This system is usually implemented in call centers. **(2) Sales commissions.** Employees are paid based on a percentage of sales. This system is usually implemented in car dealerships.

>> **Group incentives:** Employees are paid based on extra group production based on result-oriented measures (for example, sales volume for the group). This system is implemented frequently in the retail industry.

An *involvement* culture is different from traditional culture. Organizations with involvement cultures are characterized by shared decision making, lateral communications, and loosely defined roles. Examples of systems that work well in organizations with involvement cultures are the following:

>> **Individual incentives: Skill-based pay.** Employees are paid based on whether they acquire new knowledge and skills that are beneficial to the organization. This type of system is usually implemented in knowledge-based organizations such as software development companies. A Compensation Programs and Practices survey conducted by WorldatWork showed that about 70 percent of private sector firms used skill acquisition as a yardstick for employees' base pay increase.

>> **Group, unit, and organizational incentives: Profit sharing.** Employees are paid based on the performance of a group (for example, team, unit, or entire organization) and on whether the group has exceeded a specific financial goal. This type of system is implemented in many large law firms.

Strategic direction

In addition to the organization's culture, an important consideration in selecting a CP plan is the organization's strategic direction. Strategy is not only a key element in designing the performance management system, but it is also a key element in designing a CP plan. Table 17-1 includes a selected list of strategic objectives and CP plans that are most conducive to achieving each objective.

TABLE 17-1 **Which Contingent Pay Plan to Use Depending on Your Strategic Business Objective**

Strategic Business Objective	Contingent Pay Plan
Employee development	Skill-based pay
Customer service	Competency-based pay and gain sharing
Individual productivity	Piece rate and sales commissions
Team productivity	Gain sharing and team incentives
Teamwork	Team sales commissions, gain sharing, and competency-based pay
Overall profit	Executive pay, profit or stock sharing

Based on Table 17-1, if employee development is a key strategic priority, rewards should emphasize new skills acquired. If customer service is a priority, then rewards should emphasize competencies related to customer service and gain sharing. Gain sharing links individual and group pay to an organization's overall profitability: the greater the organization's overall profit, the greater the rewards given to individuals and teams in the organization. In this case, gain sharing would be based on whether customer service ratings improve during the review period.

If the major goal of the CP plan is to increase the organization's overall profit, choices include executive pay and profit or stock sharing. Executive pay includes cash bonuses that are given in response to successful organizational performance. Usually, however, executive pay includes company stock to ensure that executives' activities are consistent with the shareholders' interests and to encourage executives to tend to the long-term performance of the organization. This is also called profit sharing, although profit sharing is usually short-term and focused on organizational goals while stock sharing and executive pay are more long-term.

Stock sharing has caught media attention in recent years. In this type of plan, stock is distributed as a reward, or executives are given the option to buy company stock at a reduced rate per share.

WARNING

Stock sharing has led many executives to attempt to maximize their personal wealth by inflating the price of their personal stock, often through fraudulent means, and selling their stock before the public is aware of the situation. This happened at Enron and WorldCom, where thousands of investors lost their retirement funds.

Take the example of Google, described in a nearby sidebar. Some argue that Google can only employ the strategy of "big pay" because it has so much money. But this is not accurate. Google, like all other companies, has a limited amount of money to be allocated to employee compensation — albeit the total pool is larger than other companies. As noted by Google's former VP for People Operations Laszlo Bock, "The only way to stay within budget is to give smaller rewards to the poorer performers, or even the average ones. That won't feel good initially, but take comfort in knowing that you've now giving your best people a reason to stay with you, and everyone else a reason to aim higher."

REMEMBER

Google's policy of big pay for big performance works because it is based on empirical evidence. A review of 146 studies involving more than 30,000 people published in the *Journal of Occupational and Organizational Psychology* showed that when rewards are distributed equitably (that is, based on performance), performance improves compared to a distribution based on the principle of equality (that is, similar salaries for people in similar positions).

What pay can and cannot do about improving performance

Is pay the main motivating factor driving people? For most of the 20th century, the belief was that people go to work to collect a paycheck and money was the main, or even the sole, motivator.

In the 21st century, however, we now recognize that pay is not everything. For most people, money is an important motivator because it supplies many things from basic needs (such as food and shelter) to providing higher education for one's children and a means for retirement.

FAIRNESS, NOT EQUALITY: BIG PAY FOR BIG PERFORMANCE AT GOOGLE

At Google, contingent pay has been a part of the company's approach to compensation for many years. Google has long ago realized that the best people are increasingly discoverable and mobile. Just a few years ago, performance information on individual employees was very difficult to come by. But social media websites such as LinkedIn make this information quite obvious. Many companies use systems labeled "internal equity," which involves restricting pay so that top performers are not paid much more than average performers. In contrast, Google's approach emphasizes "fairness" over "equality." Specifically, Google's definition of fairness is not to pay everyone the same, but that pay is commensurate with contribution.

As noted by Google's former VP of People Operations Laszlo Bock, there are situations where "two people doing the same work can have a hundred times difference in their impact and in their rewards. For example, there have been situations where one person received a stock award of $10,000 and another working in the same area received $1,000,000. . . . The range for rewards at almost any level can easily vary by 300 to 500 percent. . . . We have many cases where people at more junior levels make far more than average performers at more senior levels. It's a natural result of having greater impact, and a compensation system that recognizes that impact."

But people seek more than just a paycheck when they go to work. People want to work in an environment of trust and respect, where they can have fun and develop relationships with others, and do meaningful and interesting work. People also want to balance their work and home lives, and this is particularly salient for Millennials.

A survey by the online job-searching site CareerBuilder.com showed that 42 percent of working fathers say they are willing to see a reduction in their pay if this means having a better balance between work and home. In addition, people look for learning and developmental opportunities that may lead to better career opportunities in the future.

Pay is just one element in a set of management practices that can either improve or reduce employee commitment and satisfaction, teamwork, and performance. It is true that people do work for money, and an organization's pay level and pay structure affect productivity. On the other hand, people also seek meaning in their lives and need leisure time to pursue nonwork interests.

Organizations that believe that money is all that motivates people are basically bribing their employees and will eventually pay a high price in a lack of employee loyalty and commitment.

A reward is something that increases the frequency of an employee action. In other words, when an employee is given a reward, you expect to increase the chances that specific results and behaviors will be repeated or that the employee will engage in new behaviors and produce better results.

If pay raises are not producing this result, because they are not meaningful or are given arbitrarily, then you should not view them as rewards.

What can organizations do to ensure that actions intended to be rewards are actually regarded as rewards? What can they do to make rewards work? Consider the eight recommendations detailed in the following sections.

Define and measure performance first, then allocate rewards

Before you allocate rewards, there must be a good performance management system in place that (1) defines performance and performance expectations, and (2) measures performance well.

In many cases, organizations believe that they have a rewards problem when in fact, the problem is with the definition and measurement of performance.

Use only rewards that are available

If the organization doesn't have financial rewards available, then employee expectations should be adjusted accordingly, and the focus should be on nonfinancial rewards. It makes no sense to discuss pay raises as an important component of a CP plan if existing budget constraints mean meager raises.

Make sure that all employees are eligible

In many organizations, top executives receive profit sharing, stock options, executive life and liability insurance, invitations to meetings in attractive locations, and permission to fly first-class. Are these benefits truly rewards as I have defined them here? Do these incentives enhance motivation? In general, they seem to do so because they motivate lower-level employees to strive to become executives. However, what would happen if these types of incentives were extended to the lower ranks of an organization? What if nonexecutive members of organizations were also eligible for such rewards based on their performance level? By making more employees eligible for the potential reward, there is a greater chance that more employees will strive to become top performers.

Make rewards visible

Rewards should be visible to those who receive them. Rewards should also be visible to others along with information about what needs to happen for an employee to receive the reward in the future. This recommendation applies to both financial and nonfinancial rewards. Nonfinancial rewards in particular are usually more effective if they are made public.

Make rewards contingent

Rewards should be tied to performance directly and exclusively. Imagine that an outsider is asked to guess the salary levels for various employees in an organization. Assume that she can ask the following questions: What do people do (for example, administrative assistant, mailroom clerk, VP for HR)? How long have they done it? How well have they done it? If information based on the "How well?" question is not the most useful in guessing what salaries are, then the organization is not making rewards contingent on performance. This is the case in many organizations in which what people do and how long they have done it are far better predictors of their salaries than how well they perform.

EXAMPLE

In many countries around the world, including Eritrea in Africa, all employees receive one month's extra salary as a noncontingent reward each year. In other words, employees receive pay for a "13th month."

WARNING

When rewards are not contingent on performance, organizations can alienate their best workers, precisely those who make the greatest contributions and can easily find employment elsewhere.

Make rewards timely

Rewards should be given soon after the occurrence of the result or behavior being rewarded. Experimental psychologists know that if a mouse in a cage pulls a lever and a lump of sugar appears 10 months later (on the mouse's anniversary date), no learning will take place. This is why many organizations implement on-the-spot rewards. These spot bonuses don't have to be cash awards. They can be theater tickets, a prime parking space, or anything else that targets an employee's specific needs.

TIP

How do you know what type of reward to give? The answer is simple: Get to know your employees and watch what they do and how they spend their time when they have a chance to choose. If this doesn't work, you can simply ask them.

EXAMPLE

At Lake Federal Bank in Hamburg, Indiana, the president has an annual budget that he can use to give relatively small, spur-of-the-moment gifts to employees who are performing well.

Make rewards reversible

Increasing an employee's base pay creates an annuity for the employee's tenure with the organization. If mistakes are made in the allocation of increases in base salary (especially upward), they are usually irreversible and can be very costly over time. This is why variable pay, which is not added to an employee's base salary, has become an attractive option for many organizations.

REMEMBER

Variable pay is consistent with the recommendations that rewards be contingent and reversible. If high-quality performance occurs again, then the employee receives the additional compensation again. If high-quality performance doesn't occur, then the additional compensation is not given.

Turning recognition and other nonfinancial incentives into rewards

Similar to financial incentives, praise and recognition for a job well done, without a monetary value attached, can be a powerful reward if such praise and recognition enhance the chances that specific results and behaviors will be repeated.

Similarly, praise and recognition should not be considered rewards if they don't motivate employees to perform well in the future. Unfortunately, many organizations underestimate the impact of nonfinancial rewards, including the following:

>> Formal commendations and awards

>> Favorable mention in company publications

>> Private, informal recognition for jobs well done

>> Public recognition, including praise, certificates of accomplishment, and letters of appreciation

>> Status indicators, such as a new and enhanced job title, larger work area, improved office decoration, promotion, ability to supervise more people, and newer or more equipment

>> Time, such as taking a longer break, leaving work earlier, and getting time off with or without pay

>> A more challenging work environment, responsibility, and freedom

>> Sabbaticals such as paid time off work to devote to job-related growth and development activities, such as learning new skills or traveling abroad

One advantage of nonfinancial rewards is that they are typically allocated following the recommendations I provide in this chapter for making rewards work in general. That is, nonfinancial rewards are usually available (there is an unlimited supply of recognition); all employees are usually eligible; and nonfinancial rewards are visible and contingent, usually timely, and certainly reversible.

But do they work? Yes! For a good example, see the sidebar about nonfinancial rewards at the SAS Institute.

REMEMBER

The concept of a reward is broader than just pay. Of course, money allows people to do great many things, and people do incredible things to get more and more out of it. For rewards to be effective, however, they must motivate employees to become, or continue to be, excellent performers.

TIP

If an organization is trying to solve performance problems by focusing on money only, one result is expected for sure: The organization will spend a lot of money. It is not always clear that anything will change unless rewards are given taking into account the eight recommendations described earlier and listed here:

>> Define and measure performance first and then allocate rewards.

>> Use only rewards that are available.

>> Make sure all employees are eligible.

>> Make rewards visible.

>> Make rewards contingent.

>> Make rewards timely.

>> Make rewards reversible.

>> Use recognition and other nonfinancial rewards.

Take the case of Graniterock described in a nearby sidebar. This particular company uses both financial and nonfinancial rewards. Consider this company in the context of the eight recommendations.

ACTIVE LEARNING

Think about your current job. How are rewards allocated? Which of the eight recommendations listed above were followed in the process of allocating rewards? Based on this, how effective are the rewards that are given? Do they help improve your and other employees' motivation and performance?

FINANCIAL AND NONFINANCIAL REWARDS AT GRANITEROCK

Graniterock uses several strategies to recognize and reward performance. Graniterock provides materials to the construction industry, including asphalt, concrete, and building materials. The U.S.-based company employs 750 people and its core purpose is to "provide a place where inspired people can do their best work — building great projects, producing quality materials, and developing enduring customer relationships."

The company uses both financial and nonfinancial incentives. Employees earn bonus pay of as much as $1,000 for specific performance achievements that require an effort that goes "above and beyond" normal job expectations. Several nonfinancial incentives are also used, such as sending a letter from the president along with cash rewards. The company holds regular events called "recognition days," where employees give presentations before the CEO, executive management, and coworkers about improvements they have made on the job. This gives employees the chance to receive credit in a highly visible manner, directly from others in the company. As part of an emphasis on improvement, employees continually seek out better ways of handling processes, and about a third of all company processes are changed each year as a result. The company publishes stories about special efforts in a weekly newsletter. Supervisors also use rewards on a day-to-day and less formal basis, such as providing lunch to a group of employees who are putting forth a strong effort on a large job pouring concrete.

In short, Graniterock uses both financial and nonfinancial rewards to motivate employees and to reinforce a culture that values constant improvement and innovation in the workplace.

Chapter **18**

Staying on the Right Side of the Law

Performance management systems that are fair and acceptable to employees are typically also legally sound.

A basic principle that guides the design of a fair system is that procedures are standardized and that the same procedures are used with all employees. In other words, when the rules and procedures are known by everyone and they are applied in the same way to everyone, the system is likely to be regarded as a fair one. This is also the basic principle that underlies the implementation of performance management systems that are lawful.

This chapter covers how to implement a lawful performance management system.

Implementing the Golden Rule

Legislation and court cases in the United States, Canada, the United Kingdom, and many other countries around the world show that the discriminatory effects of a performance management system can be minimized by applying this golden rule:

> Treat everyone in exactly the same way, regardless of sex, ethnicity, and other demographic characteristics that are unrelated to job performance.

This golden rule also applies to international employers — multinational organizations that implement their performance management systems across countries around the world.

Implementing the golden rule around the world

Given China's increasing global importance and economic power, it is interesting to consider how recent legislation is affecting performance management and reward systems in firms in China.

The Chinese government has recognized that performance management systems contribute to firm productivity and also to the competitiveness of China in the global arena. So the Chinese government is accelerating economic reforms related to performance management, such as giving employers more rights to terminate employees. These changes have led to what can be considered very innovative performance management practices in many Chinese companies.

EXAMPLE

Chinese software developers Ufida, Shanda, and Natease adopt practices that are quite consistent with those used by U.S. firms. Ufida uses performance information to determine as much as 25 percent of annual salaries, and Shanda has a company-wide performance management system with clearly specified standards: Employees are evaluated twice a year; there is a multisource feedback system; and bonuses are awarded based on performance ratings.

When the golden rule breaks down

In spite of an increased global awareness regarding legal issues regarding performance management, the golden rule is not applied as often as it should be.

WARNING

There has been a 100-percent increase in the number of employment discrimination cases filed in the United States from 1995 to 2005, and many of these cases have involved issues around the design and implementation of the performance management system.

In 2016, the United States Equal Employment Opportunity Commission received 91,503 charges claiming discrimination based on race, age, national origin, religion, color, retaliation, disability, equal pay, and GINA (Genetic Information Nondiscrimination Act), which is discrimination against employees based on genetic information.

For an organization to minimize legal exposure regarding performance management, it is important to follow the specific principles I describe next.

Six Legal Principles Affecting Performance Management

There are six important principles that often come into play in the case of litigation related to the implementation of a performance management system: employment at will, negligence, defamation, misrepresentation, adverse impact, and illegal discrimination.

Employment at will

In employment at will, the employer or employee can end the employment relationship at any time. This type of employment relationship gives employers considerable latitude in determining whether, when, and how to measure and reward performance. Thus, an employer could potentially end the employment relationship without documenting any performance problems.

There are two exceptions regarding an organization's ability to terminate an employee under these circumstances:

» There may be an implied contract derived from conversations with others in the organization or from information found in the company's documentation (for example, employee handbook) indicating that employees would be terminated for just cause only.

» Decisions about terminating an employee should consider a potential violation of public policy.

Negligence

Many organizations outline a performance management system in their employee manual, employment contract, or other documents. When the system is described in such documents and not implemented as described, legal problems arise.

For example, there may be a description of how frequently appraisals take place, or how frequently supervisors and employees are to meet formally to discuss performance issues. If an employee receives what she believes is an unfair performance evaluation and the system has not been implemented as was expected, she may be able to challenge the system based on negligence on the part of the organization.

NEGLIGENCE AT SCRANTON SCHOOL DISTRICT

In 2015, Gwendolyn Damiano, who was a principal in the Scranton, Pennsylvania, school district, was dismissed by the school district due to "unsatisfactory performance." Ms. Damiano claimed that there was negligence in her dismissal because the decision did not properly take into account the performance standards outlined by the district.

In its defense, the school district claimed that Ms. Damiano's performance was below par with regard to teacher evaluations and student discipline. For example, the district argued that she had left standardized tests in her office without locking them in a cabinet. Also, regarding teacher evaluations, the district argued that she did not observe teachers' performance for the required number of times per year.

However, the court found that the performance management system did not clearly specify a method for conducting such teacher evaluations, nor the number of evaluations to be conducted. In addition, the court also noted that the district did not implement its own policies regarding student disciplinary procedures consistently. Accordingly, the court ruled that the district had been negligent in the manner in which it used its performance management system, and therefore, Ms. Damiano should be reinstated to her position of principal — with full back pay.

Defamation

Defamation is the disclosure of untrue, unfavorable performance information that damages an employee's reputation.

An employee can argue that the organization defamed her if the employer states false and libelous information during the course of the performance evaluation, or negligently or intentionally communicates these statements to a third party, such as a potential future employer, thus subjecting the employee to harm or loss of reputation.

The definition of defamation includes the disclosure of untrue information. Defamation can take place when an employee is evaluated based on behaviors that are irrelevant and not job-related, when an evaluator doesn't include information that would explain or justify poor performance, or when an evaluator revises a prior evaluation in an attempt to justify subsequent adverse action taken against the employee.

REMEMBER

Defamation doesn't exist when information regarding poor performance is clearly documented.

DEFAMATION AT BARTON HEALTHCARE SYSTEMS

Susan Reese filed a suit against Barton Healthcare Systems, alleging that the company committed defamation against her by using unrelated information, such as the fact that Ms. Reese taught dance on the weekends, as factors that were included in her performance evaluation.

The court decided that the appraisal forms used in the performance management process by Barton Healthcare systems (for example, Disciplinary Notices) did rely on unrelated information. Moreover, the court found that the company used disparaging language in referring to Ms. Reese as "pole dancer."

Misrepresentation

Whereas defamation is about disclosing untrue unfavorable information, misrepresentation is about disclosing untrue favorable performance, and this information causes risk or harm to others.

When a past employer provides a glowing recommendation for a former employee who was actually terminated because of poor performance, that employer is guilty of misrepresentation.

MISREPRESENTATION AT A MIDDLE SCHOOL IN CALIFORNIA

Consider this case decided by the Supreme Court of California. Randi W., a 13-year-old female student enrolled in a middle school, accused her school vice-principal, Robert Gadams, of sexual molestation. Gadams had received glowing letters of recommendation from other school districts (his former employers), who had recommended him without reservation. For example, one letter of recommendation stated, "I wouldn't hesitate to recommend [the vice-principal] for any position!" However, the former employers knew that Gadams had performance problems that included hugging female students and making sexual overtures to them. In fact, he had been pressured to resign because of such behavior.

The Supreme Court of California ruled that employers can be held liable for negligent misrepresentation or fraud when an employer fails to use reasonable care in recommending former employees without disclosing material information that has a bearing on their performance.

Adverse impact/unintentional discrimination

Adverse impact, also called unintentional discrimination, occurs when the performance management system has an unintentional impact on a protected class, such as sex or race.

REMEMBER

Contrary to a common misconception that "class" refers to ethnic minorities or women only, adverse impact also happens when, for example, men receive consistently lower performance ratings than women. In other words, a protected class is a group of people with a common characteristic who are legally protected from discrimination on the basis of that characteristic.

So if a group of white men consistently receives lower performance scores, then there is adverse impact because these individuals share the same characteristic (male) of a class that is protected (that is, sex).

Illegal discrimination/disparate treatment

Illegal discrimination, also called disparate treatment, means that raters assign scores differentially to various employees based on factors that are not performance related, such as race, nationality, color, or ethnic and national origin. As a consequence of such ratings, some employees receive more training, feedback, or rewards than others.

ADVERSE IMPACT AT A FIRE DEPARTMENT

As an example where adverse impact exists against women, consider the position of firefighter, and more specifically, the performance dimension of physical strength.

If members of a protected class receive consistently lower performance ratings, then the employer must be able to demonstrate that the performance dimension measured is an important part of the job. In this case, the fire department should demonstrate that physical strength is a key KSA for the job of firefighter, and based on the argument of business necessity, an appropriate measure should be included as part of the performance evaluation, and every employee should be evaluated in the same fashion. As a precautionary measure, you should gather data on an ongoing basis regarding performance scores obtained by members of various groups, broken down by the categories indicated by the law (for example, sex or ethnicity). A periodic review of these data can help detect the presence of adverse impact, and the organization can take corrective action if necessary.

Illegal discrimination is usually referred to as disparate treatment because employees claim they were intentionally treated differently because of their sex, race, ethnicity, national origin, age, disability status, or other status protected under the law.

The majority of legal cases involving performance management systems involve a claim of disparate treatment. What can an employee do if, for example, she feels she was given unfairly low performance scores and skipped over for promotion because she is a woman?

To make such a claim, an employee can present direct evidence of discrimination, such as a supervisor making sexist comments that may have influenced the performance management process. Alternatively, she needs to provide evidence regarding the following issues:

» She is a member of a protected class.

» She suffered an adverse employment decision as a result of a performance evaluation (was skipped over for promotion).

» She should not have been skipped over for promotion because her performance level deserved the promotion.

» The promotion was not given to anyone, or it was given to an employee who is not a member of the same protected class (that is, another woman).

If an employee provides this kind of evidence, the employer must articulate a legitimate and nondiscriminatory reason for not having given the promotion to this female employee. Usually, this involves a reason that is clearly performance related.

TIP

This is the point at which employers benefit from having designed and implemented a system that is used consistently with all employees — what I refer to as the golden rule. Such a system is legally defensible, and any decisions that resulted from the system, such as promotion decisions, are also defensible.

WARNING

Let's distinguish *illegal* discrimination from *legal* discrimination. A good performance management system is able to discriminate among employees based on their level of performance, and this is legal discrimination. In fact, a system that doesn't do this is not very useful. But a good performance management system doesn't discriminate illegally. Illegal discrimination is based on variables that should not usually be related to performance, such as sex, national origin, ethnicity, and sexual orientation.

ILLEGAL DISCRIMINATION AT SAFEWAY

Michael Chapman filed suit against the supermarket Safeway for illegal age discrimination. Mr. Chapman had received positive performance reviews and promotions during his more than 30 years with the supermarket. Then, after a labor dispute between the union representing store employees (including managers) and Safeway, Mr. Chapman's performance evaluations were considerably lower; he was subject to previously undisclosed performance standards; and the company began selectively applying performance standards.

The court determined that Safeway had engaged in illegal discrimination based on age to try to "force out" long-serving and older employees and replace them with younger staff, whom they could pay less, by arbitrarily applying performance standards.

Laws Affecting Performance Management

In the past few decades, several countries have passed laws prohibiting discrimination based on race, color, religion, sex (including pregnancy, gender identity, and sexual orientation), national origin, age (40 or older), disability, and genetic information.

These are the laws that have been passed in the United States and are enforced by the United States Equal Employment Opportunity Commission:

>> **Equal Pay Act of 1963:** Prohibits sex discrimination in the payment of wages.

>> **Title VII of the Civil Rights Act of 1964 (as amended by the Equal Employment Opportunity Act of 1972):** Prohibits discrimination on the basis of race, color, religion, sex, or national origin.

>> **Age Discrimination in Employment Act of 1967 (as amended in 1986):** Prohibits discrimination on the basis of age.

>> **The Pregnancy Discrimination Act of 1978:** Makes it illegal to discriminate against a woman because of pregnancy, childbirth, or a medical condition related to pregnancy or childbirth.

>> **Americans with Disabilities Act of 1990:** Makes it illegal to discriminate against people with disabilities.

>> **Sections 102 and 103 of the Civil Rights Act of 1991:** Among other things, this law amends Title VII and the ADA to permit jury trials and compensatory and punitive damage awards in intentional discrimination cases.

>> **Genetic Information Nondiscrimination Act of 2008 (GINA):** Makes it illegal to discriminate against employees because of genetic information. This includes information about an individual's genetic tests and the genetic tests of an individual's family members, as well as information about any disease, disorder, or condition of an individual's family members.

Laws affecting performance management around the world

Do you need to know what laws affect performance management in other countries? Similar laws exist in numerous countries around the world, including Canada, Australia, Germany, and Spain, among many others.

A study published in the journal *Industrial and Organizational Psychology* compared laws and regulations across 22 countries and found that the majority of countries have laws similar to the ones I describe earlier for the United States.

>> **In Canada,** there is the Canadian Human Rights Code of 1985, Section 15 of the Charter of Rights and Freedoms (1982), Federal Employment Equity Act (2004), Federal Contractors Program, and Pay equity legislation (federal and some provinces).

>> **In Australia,** there is The Crimes Act (1914), Racial Discrimination Act (1975), Sex Discrimination Act (1984), Human Rights and Equal Opportunity Commission Act 1986, Disability Discrimination Act (1992), Workplace Relations Act (1996), Equal Opportunity for Women in the Workplace Act (1999), and Age Discrimination Act (2004).

>> **In Germany,** there is the Allgemeines Gleichbehandlungsgesetz: General Equal Opportunity Law (last modified in April 2013), which covers all stages of the employment relationship, including definition of payment, performance appraisal, promotion, and dismissal.

>> **In Spain,** there is the Spanish Constitution (1978), Law of Worker's Statute (1980 and 2005), Organic Law for Effective Equality between Women and Men (2007), and the Law of Basic Statute of Public Employee (2005).

REMEMBER

These laws aim at forcing organizations to implement performance management systems that are applied consistently to all employees, regardless of demographic characteristics. Although these laws are not enforced to the same degree throughout the world, their collective goal is that performance management systems focus on job-related factors and not personal, individual characteristics that are unrelated to job performance.

Lawful performance management in global organizations

One question that is particularly pertinent to organizations that operate across borders is the extent to which laws from the company's headquarters apply to performance management systems in the subsidiaries.

In the specific case of applying U.S. laws, there are four questions that you need to ask:

>> What is the work geographic location?

>> What is the employer status (for example, U.S.-based firm or not)?

>> What is the employee status (for example, U.S. citizenship status)?

>> Are there international law defenses (that is, international treaties)?

Let's answer these questions about four different scenarios:

>> We may assume that U.S. laws apply to non-U.S. firms working in the United States. But U.S. employment discrimination laws don't apply to jobs located inside the United States when the employer is a foreign entity exempted by a treaty.

>> U.S. employment discrimination laws also don't apply to jobs located outside the United States when the employer is a foreign entity, even though the employee is a U.S. citizen.

>> U.S. laws apply to jobs located outside the United States when the employer is a U.S. entity and the employee is a U.S. citizen, if compliance with U.S. laws would not violate foreign laws.

>> U.S. laws apply to jobs located outside the United States when the employer is a U.S. entity and the employee is a U.S. citizen (assuming that compliance with U.S. laws doesn't violate foreign laws).

Putting it all together: A legally defensible performance management system

The following list, adapted from the chapter "Current legal issues in performance appraisal" by S. B. Malos (in the book *Performance Appraisal: State of the Art in Practice*, published by Jossey Bass) gives you a summary of the seven features of legally defensible performance management systems:

>> Performance dimensions (including behaviors and results) and standards are clearly defined and explained to the employee, are job-related, and are within the control of the employee.

» Procedures are standardized and uniform for all employees within a job group.

» Employees are given timely information on performance deficiencies and opportunities to correct them.

» Employees are given a voice in the review process and are treated with courtesy and civility throughout the process.

» The performance management system includes a formal appeals process.

» Performance information is gathered from multiple, diverse, and unbiased raters.

» The system includes thorough and consistent documentation, including specific examples of performance based on firsthand knowledge.

When you think about it, designing a system that is legally defensible is not a difficult goal to achieve, and it is a natural consequence of following the best-practice recommendations I offered in this book. You will see that the preceding list summarizes many of the practices about system design and implementation that I discussed throughout this book.

Two researchers from the United States reviewed 295 different U.S. circuit court decisions regarding litigation involving performance management systems. The goal of their study was to understand the factors carrying the most weight in the decisions reached by the court. They investigated various features of the performance management systems that were challenged in court, including many of the characteristics I just listed.

What was their conclusion? They found that systems that emphasized the measurement of job-related performance dimensions, provided written instructions to raters, and allowed employees to review appraisal results were more likely to withstand legal challenge. Overall, these researchers concluded that the employees' perceptions of whether the system was fair and whether they were given due process were the most salient issues considered by the courts.

This conclusion reinforces the recommendation offered throughout this book: It is important to allow employees to participate in the design and implementation of the system because employee participation leads to the design of systems viewed as fair.

REMEMBER

Fairness and lawfulness don't necessarily go hand in hand. But systems that are fair are less likely to be challenged on legal grounds.

5

The Part of Tens

Chapter **19**

Ten Reasons for Implementing Effective Performance Management

There are hundreds of reasons why your organization should have a state-of-the-science performance management system. If you need to convince others or even yourself about this need, you must consider these ten reasons first.

Six Useful Purposes

Performance management provides the following functions within organizations:

» It helps top management achieve strategic business objectives because they link the goals of individuals with the goals of their teams, which in turn are connected with the goals of the entire organization.

>> It helps your organization in making administrative decisions about employees such as salary adjustments, promotions, employee retention or termination, recognition of top individual performance, identification of high-potential employees, identification of poor performers, layoffs, and merit increases.

>> It helps your organization communicate the expectations of peers, supervisors, customers, and the organization, and it also conveys what aspects of work are most important.

>> It helps employees reach development objectives because it improves communication, clarifies roles and expectations in terms of career paths, and includes useful feedback.

>> It helps organizations with maintenance because it provides information used in forecasting talent needs for the future, including workforce and succession planning.

>> It helps organizations document information that can be used for several necessary — and sometimes, legally mandated — purposes. This documentation is helpful for important administrative decisions, such as terminations and promotions.

Self-Insights, Development, Motivation, and Self-Esteem

Performance management helps employees develop a better understanding of themselves and of the kind of development activities that are of value to them as they progress through the organization. Participants in the system also gain a better understanding of their particular strengths and weaknesses, which can help them better define future career paths.

Also, receiving feedback about one's performance increases the motivation for future performance. Knowledge about how one is doing and recognition about one's past successes provide the fuel for future accomplishments.

Better Understanding of Job Requirement

The job of the person being evaluated is clarified and defined more clearly when a performance management system is implemented. In other words, employees gain a better understanding of the behaviors and results required of their specific position. Employees also gain a better understanding of what it takes to be a successful performer.

More Employee Engagement and Voice Behavior

Performance management improves employee engagement because they know what they are doing and why, which results in employees being more involved, committed, passionate, and empowered. Also, these attitudes and feelings result in behaviors that are innovative, and overall, demonstrate good organizational citizenship and active participation in support of the organization. The performance review meeting can lead to a conversation during which the employee provides suggestions on how to reduce cost or speed up a specific process, which is called *voice behavior*. Voice behavior involves making suggestions for changes and improvements that are innovative, challenge the status quo, are intended to be constructive, and are offered even when others disagree.

Improved Commitment and Decreased Turnover

When employees are satisfied with their organization's performance management system, they are more committed to their organization and won't try to leave. Satisfaction with the performance management system makes employees feel that the organization has a great deal of personal meaning for them. In terms of turnover intentions, satisfaction with the performance management system leads employees to report that they will probably not look for a new job in the next year and that they don't often think about quitting their present job.

Early Detection of Performance Declines and Less Employee Misconduct

Because good performance management systems include ongoing performance measurement, declines in performance can be noticed, which allows for immediate feedback and continuous coaching. When such declines are observed, remedial action can be taken immediately and before the problem becomes so entrenched that it cannot be easily remedied. Having good performance management in place provides the appropriate context so that misconduct is clearly defined and labeled as such. Also, performance management can be a detection tool for misconduct before it leads to irreversible negative consequences.

Differentiation between Good and Poor Performers

Performance management systems allow for a quicker identification of good and poor performers. This system includes identifying star performers — those who produce at levels much higher than the rest. For example, without a good performance management system, it isn't easy to know who are the particular programmers in your company producing more and better code. Also, direct supervisors and other managers in charge of the appraisal gain new insights into the person being evaluated. Gaining new insights into a person's performance helps the manager build a better relationship with that person. Also, supervisors gain a better understanding of each individual's contribution to the organization. This information can be useful for direct supervisors as well as for supervisors once removed.

Common Understanding of What Is Good Performance

Performance management systems allow managers to communicate to their direct reports their assessments regarding performance. In other words, there is greater accountability in how managers discuss performance expectations and provide feedback. When managers possess these competencies, direct reports receive useful information about how their performance is seen by their supervisor.

More Fair and Legally Defensible Administrative Decisions

Performance management systems yield valid information about performance that can be used for administrative actions, such as merit increases, promotions, and transfers, as well as terminations. In general, a performance management system helps ensure that rewards are distributed on a fair and credible basis. In turn, such decisions based on a sound performance management system lead to improved interpersonal relationships and enhanced supervisor–direct report trust. Also, data collected through performance management systems helps document compliance with regulations (for example, equal treatment of all employees, regardless of sex or ethnic background). When performance management systems are not in place, arbitrary performance evaluations are likely, resulting in an increased exposure to litigation for the organization.

Easier Organizational Change

Performance management systems are a useful tool to drive organizational change.

For example, assume an organization decides to change its culture to give top priority to product quality and customer service. Once this new organizational direction is established, performance management is used to align goals and objectives of the organization with those of individuals to make change possible. Employees are provided training in the necessary skills and are also rewarded for improved performance so that they have both the knowledge and motivation to improve product quality and customer service.

Chapter **20**

Ten Key Factors for Delivering Outstanding Results

Want to make sure the performance management system works as intended and delivers excellent results? Then you need to ensure the system has these ten key factors.

Congruence with Strategy and Context

Make sure the system is congruent with the unit and organization's strategy. In other words, align individual goals with unit and organizational goals. Also, make the system is congruent with the organization's culture as well as the broader cultural context of the region or country.

If an organization has a culture in which hierarchies are rigid, an upward feedback system, in which individuals receive comments on their performance from their direct reports, will be resisted and not very effective.

Regarding broader cultural issues, in countries such as Japan, there is an emphasis on the measurement of both behaviors (how people do the work) and results (the results of people's work), whereas in the United States, results are typically preferred over behaviors. Thus, implementing a results-only system in Japan won't be effective.

Thoroughness and Inclusiveness

Do these four tasks to make the system thorough:

>> Evaluate all employees (including managers).

>> Evaluated all major job responsibilities (including behaviors and results).

>> Evaluate performance over the entire review period, not just the few weeks or months before the formal review meeting.

>> Give feedback on positive performance aspects as well as those that are in need of improvement.

Also, in terms of inclusiveness, include input from multiple sources on an ongoing basis. The evaluation process must represent the concerns of all the people who will be affected by the outcome. Employees must participate in the process of creating the system by providing input regarding what behaviors or results will be measured and how.

Meaningfulness

Make the system must be meaningful in five ways:

>> Make sure the standards and evaluations conducted for each job function are important and relevant.

>> Assess performance only for functions that are under the control of the employee.

>> Conduct evaluations at regular intervals and at appropriate moments.

>> Provide continuing skill development of evaluators.

>> Use results for important administrative decisions.

Practicality

Systems that are too expensive, time-consuming, and convoluted will obviously not be effective. Make sure good, easy-to-use systems (for example, performance data are entered via user-friendly web and mobile apps) are available for managers to help them make decisions. Also, the benefits of using the system (like increased performance and job satisfaction) must be seen as outweighing the costs (such as time, effort, expense).

Reliability, Validity, and Specificity

Regarding reliability, the system should include measures of performance that are consistent and free of error. If two supervisors provide ratings of the same employee and performance dimensions, ratings should be similar.

Also, the measures of performance should be valid. Validity refers to the fact that the measures include all relevant performance facets and don't include irrelevant information. In other words, measures are relevant (include all critical performance facets), not deficient (don't leave any important aspects out), and are not contaminated (don't include factors outside of the control of the employee or factors unrelated to performance). Measures include what is important and don't assess what isn't important and outside of the control of the employee.

And the system should be specific: It should provide detailed and concrete guidance to employees about what is expected of them and how they can meet these expectations.

Identification of Effective and Ineffective Performance

The performance management system should provide information that allows for the identification of effective and ineffective performance. So the system should allow for distinguishing between effective and ineffective behaviors and results, thereby also allowing for the identification of employees displaying various levels of performance effectiveness.

Standardization and Thoroughness

The system should be standardized, which means that performance is evaluated consistently across people and time. To achieve this goal, the ongoing training of the individuals in charge of appraisals, usually managers, is a must.

Openness

The system should have no secrets:

>> Evaluate performance frequently and give feedback on an ongoing basis. Employees know how well they are doing at all times.

>> Turn the review meeting into a two-way communication process during which information is exchanged, not delivered from the supervisor to the employee without his or her input.

>> Make standards clear and communicate them on an ongoing basis.

>> Make communications factual, open, and honest.

Correctability

The process of assigning ratings should minimize subjective aspects. However, it is virtually impossible to create a system that is completely objective because human judgment is an important component of the evaluation process. When employees perceive an error has been made, there should be a mechanism through which this error can be corrected.

Establishing an appeals process, through which employees can challenge what may be unjust decisions, is an important aspect of a good performance management system.

Acceptability, Fairness, and Ethicality

The system should be acceptable and perceived as fair by all participants. Because perceptions of fairness are subjective and the only way to know if a system is seen as fair is to ask the participants about the system.

Perceptions of fairness include four aspects:

>> **Distributive justice:** Perceptions of the performance evaluation received relative to the work performed, and perceptions of the rewards received relative to the evaluation received, particularly when the system is implemented across countries

>> **Procedural justice:** Perceptions of the procedures used to determine the ratings as well as the procedures used to link ratings with rewards

>> **Interpersonal justice:** Quality of the design and implementation of the performance management system

>> **Informational justice:** Perceptions about performance expectations and goals, feedback received, and the information given to justify administrative decisions

Regarding ethicality, the system should comply with ethical standards, which means that the supervisor suppresses his or her personal self-interest in providing evaluations. In addition, the supervisor evaluates only performance dimensions for which she has sufficient information, and the privacy of the employee is respected.

Chapter **21**

Ten Tips for Becoming a Great Performance Management Leader

f you manage people, you must learn several important skills to become a performance management leader. This chapter describes the ten skills that are most important.

Become an Effective Coach

To become an effective coach, do the following seven things:

>> Establish development objectives.

>> Communicate effectively.

>> Motivate employees.

>> Document performance.

- » Give feedback.
- » Diagnose performance problems and performance decline.
- » Develop employees.

Develop a Good Coaching Relationship and Facilitate Employee Growth

A good coaching relationship is essential. The relationship between the coach and the employee must be trusting and collaborative.

You must listen in order to understand. In other words, the coach needs to try to walk in the employee's shoes and view the job and organization from his or her perspective. Coach with empathy and compassion. Such compassionate coaching will help develop a good relationship with the employee.

Your main role is one of facilitation. You must direct the process and help with the content (for example, a developmental plan) but not take control of these issues. You need to maintain an attitude of exploration; help expand the employee's awareness of strengths, resources, and challenges; and facilitate goal setting.

Understand Your Own Coaching Style

Learn which is your preferred coaching style:

- » **Driving style:** You tell your employee being coached what to do.
- » **Persuading style:** You sell what you want the employee to do.
- » **Amiable style:** You want everyone to be happy.
- » **Analyzing style:** You offer logical and systematic analysis and then follow rules and procedures when providing a recommendation.

Here's the catch: No style is necessarily superior to the others. Performance management leadership involves sometimes providing direction, sometimes persuading employees how to do things a certain way, sometimes showing empathy and creating positive effects, and sometimes paying close attention to established rules and procedures.

Make the Employee the Director of Change

You must understand that the employee is the source of change and self-growth. After all, the purpose of coaching is to change employee behavior and set a direction for what the employee will do better in the future.

This type of change does not happen if the employee isn't in the driver's seat. So allow the employee to set the agenda, goals, and direction.

Learn How to Evaluate Performance Accurately

Performance management leaders are experts at observing and evaluating performance. To do so, they participate in three types of training programs:

>> **Rater error training (RET):** Increases rating accuracy by making raters aware of the unintentional errors they are likely to make. RET programs include definitions of the most typical errors and a description of possible causes for those errors.

>> **Frame of reference (FOR):** Helps improve rater accuracy by familiarizing raters with the various performance dimensions to be assessed. The overall goal is to give raters skills so that they can minimize unintentional errors and provide accurate ratings on each performance dimension by developing a common FOR.

>> **Behavioral observation (BO):** Focuses on how raters observe, store, recall, and use information about performance. This type of training improves raters' skills at observing performance.

Document Performance Accurately

Document performance accurately by following seven recommendations:

>> Be specific.

>> Use adjectives and adverbs sparingly.

>> Balance positives with negatives.

>> Focus on job-related information.

>> Be comprehensive.

>> Standardize procedures.

>> Describe observable behavior and results.

Give Feedback Effectively

Effective feedback has the following seven qualities:

>> **Timeliness:** Give feedback as close to the performance event as possible.

>> **Frequency:** Feedback should be provided on an ongoing basis.

>> **Specificity:** Give feedback about specific work behaviors, results, and the situation in which these behaviors and results were observed.

>> **Privacy:** Give feedback in a place and at a time that prevent any potential embarrassment.

>> **Consequences:** Feedback should include contextual information that allows the employee to understand the importance and consequences of the behaviors and results in question.

>> **Description first, evaluation second:** Focus on describing behaviors and results first and then evaluating them.

>> **Advice and idea generation:** Feedback can include advice given by the supervisor about how to improve performance.

Conduct Effective Performance Review Meetings

Use the following nine steps to have good meetings:

1. Explain the purpose of the meeting.
2. Conduct self-appraisal.
3. Share performance data and explain rationale.
4. Discuss development.
5. Ask employee to summarize.

6. Discuss rewards.

7. Hold follow-up meeting.

8. Discuss approval and appeals process.

9. Conduct final recap.

Be Fair and Direct in the Disciplinary Process

When a disciplinary process seems to be the only recourse, treat employees with respect and dignity. This is what performance management leaders do to avoid common pitfalls:

» Don't ignore performance problems and address them as possible.

» Be very specific about the performance problem and the consequences of not addressing it effectively.

» Don't let emotional reactions derail you from your mission and role as a performance management leader, which is to describe the nature of the problem, what needs to be done, and consequences of not doing so.

» If you are planning on implementing a disciplinary or termination process, consult with your HR department regarding legal requirements.

Be Fair and Direct in the Termination Process

This is what performance management leaders do when they face a termination situation:

» Be respectful.

» Get right to the point.

» Let the employee grieve.

» Wish the employee well.

» Send the employee to HR.

» Have the employee leave immediately.

» Have the termination meeting at the end of the day.

Index

most valuable performers (MVPs), 261

motivation, 36–37, 320
  achievement motivation, 126
  coaching, 103
  damage avoidance and control, 63
  performance measurement and definition, 126
  rating distortion, 199, 200
  reflection on motivation, 212
  team performance management, 250

motivational barriers, 200

multiple performance touchpoints, 189–196
  customers, 193–194
  direct reports, 191–192
  electronic performance monitoring, 193–196
    Big Data and Smart Data, 194–195
    job-related behaviors, 196
    learning and development, 196
    passive versus active monitoring, 196
    potential employee reactions, 196
    tracking software, 195
    transparency, 195–196
  employee self-appraisals, 192–193
  peers, 190–191
  rating distortion, 197–208
    disagreements across touchpoints, 197–199
    intentional, 199–202
    unintentional, 202–208
  supervisors, 189

multisource feedback systems (360-degree feedback systems), 198, 227–232
  advantages of, 228–229
    decreased possibility of biases, 228

employees enabled to take control of their careers, 229
    improved performance, 228
    improved self-perceptions of performance, 228
    increased awareness of expectations, 228
    increased commitment to improve, 228
    reduced "undiscussables" and defensiveness, 229
  characteristics of, 231–232
    anonymity, 231
    avoidance of rater fatigue, 231
    development instead of administrative purposes, 231
    emphasis on behaviors, 232
    feedback interpretation, 231
    follow-up, 231
    going beyond ratings, 232
    observation of employee performance, 231
    rater training, 232
  for development versus administrative purposes, 227
  feedback reports, 227
  fit with organization, 230–231
  gap analysis, 227
  online system bundles, 228
  risks of, 229–230

MVPs (most valuable performers), 261

MySQL, 253

N

NASA, 139
negativity error, 205
negligence, 308–309
neuroticism, 125
Newman, Steven L., 80
Nohria, Nitin, 135
nonexempt employees, 279

nonfinancial rewards, 282–284
  defined, 278
  types of, 282
    relational rewards, 282, 284
    work-life focus rewards, 283, 284

O

Occupational Informational Network (O*NET), 18
Ollander-Krane, Rob, 175
ongoing system evaluation, 271–274
  how to measure, 273–274
    number of people evaluated, 273
    overall cost/benefit ratio, 273
    quality of follow-up actions, 273
    quality of performance discussion meeting, 273
    quality of qualitative performance data, 273
    system satisfaction, 273
    unit-level and organization-level performance, 273–274
  what to measure, 272
online resources
  appraisal form, 185
  author's website, 5
  Cheat Sheet (companion to book), 4
  cost-of-living adjustments, 279
  Feedback Orientation Scale, 119
  generic job descriptions, 18
  work analysis questionnaires, 18
openness, 43, 328
  to experience, 126
  team performance management, 250
Oracle, 282
Organic Law for Effective Equality between Women and Men of 2007, 314

strengths, weaknesses, opportunities, and threats analysis. *See* SWOT analysis

strengths-based approach to feedback, 53–54, 118

succession planning, 214

Sun Microsystems, 282–283

supervisors and managers. *See also* performance management leaders

contingent pay, 294

damage avoidance and control, 63

involvement in strategic planning, 81

multiple performance touchpoints, 189

personal development plans, 221–226

feedforward interviews, 223–225

functions in process, 221

motivating supervisors in, 225–226

SWOT (strengths, weaknesses, opportunities, and threats) analysis, 86–89

of external environment, 86–87

factors to consider, 89

five-force analysis, 86–87

opportunities, 86

threats, 86

gap analysis, 89–91

of internal environment, 88–89

factors to consider, 88–89

strengths, 88

weaknesses, 88

Synygy, Inc., 176

T

talent inventory, 31

talent management, 45–46

compensation, 46

training and development, 45

workforce planning, 46

Target Corporation, 55–56, 145–146, 148

task performance, 131–134

contextual versus, 133–134

defined, 131

team performance management, 247–267

accountability, 254–255

caveats, 249

characteristics of, 249–250

ability to identify effective and ineffective performance, 249

acceptability, 250

congruence with context, 249

congruence with strategy, 249

correctability, 250

ethicality, 250

fairness, 250

inclusiveness, 250

meaningfulness, 249

openness, 250

practicality, 249

reliability, 249

specificity, 249

standardization, 250

thoroughness, 249

validity, 250

components of, 256–264

performance assessment (step 4), 261–262

performance execution (step 3), 260–261

performance planning (step 2), 259

performance reviews (appraisal meetings) (step 5), 263–264

prerequisite establishment (step 1), 257–258

conditions for, 251

dangers of poorly-designed systems, 250–251

burnout and job dissatisfaction, 250

damaged relationships, 250

decreased motivation, 250

emerging biases, 250

increased risk of litigation, 251

increased turnover, 250

lowered self-esteem, 250

misleading information, 250

unclear ratings, 251

unjustified demands on resources, 251

varying and unfair standards and ratings, 251

wasted time and money, 250

principles of, 255–256

actual teams, 255

clearly defined goals, 255

focus on process and results, 255–256

long-term changes, 255–256

multimethod and multisource approach, 255

performance management analytics, 255

reasons for, 248

team rewards, 265–267

types of teams, 248

virtual teams, 251–254

benefits of, 252

challenges of, 252–253

Ted airlines, 87

termination meetings, 244–245, 335

Texas A&M University, 215–218

Thomson Reuters, 80

thoroughness, 42–43, 326, 328

feedback, 43

team performance management, 249

About the Author

Herman Aguinis, PhD, is the Avram Tucker Distinguished Scholar and Professor of Management at The George Washington University School of Business in Washington, DC. He has been elected for the five-year presidency track of the Academy of Management, the world's oldest, largest, and most prestigious professional organization for management professors.

His research, teaching, and consulting activities focus on the acquisition and deployment of talent in organizations. He has written 9 books, about 160 articles in peer-reviewed journals, and delivered more than 400 presentations in all seven continents except for Antarctica.

Dr. Aguinis's research has placed him as one of the most influential and prolific contemporary management professors. A November 2018 study ranked him among the 96 most influential business and economics researchers in the world. He has received many awards, including the Losey Award by the Society for Human Resource Management Foundation for lifetime achievement in human resource research, Academy of Management Research Methods Division Distinguished Career Award for lifetime contributions, and Academy of Management Practice Theme Committee Scholar Practice Impact Award recognizing outstanding impact on policy making and managerial and organizational practices.

Dr. Aguinis has consulted with organizations in the U.S., Europe, and Latin America, including Accenture, the City of San Francisco Police Department, Kronos, Sears Holdings Corp., TCI-AT&T, U.S. Department of State, and the United Nations, among others. Also, his research has been referred to in court cases at the U.S. Supreme Court and U.S. District Court levels and has been featured by *The Economist, The Wall Street Journal, Forbes, Business Week,* National Public Radio, *USA Today, The Seattle Times, The Chicago Tribune, The Denver Post, HR Magazine,* Univision, and many other outlets.

Download his latest articles from www.hermanaguinis.com and follow him on Twitter at @HermanAguinis and on LinkedIn, where you will find information about his latest public appearances and publications.

Dedication

I dedicate this book to the love of my life, my soul mate, and my best friend: my wife Heidi.

Author's Acknowledgments

I want to thank students, colleagues, and organizations with which I have worked on performance management and talent management projects over the past 25 years. Although I hope you will understand that I cannot thank all of you individually, you know that I am thanking you personally — each of you. All of our experiences and interactions were helpful in allowing me to produce this book.

I also want to thank the team at Wiley for their tremendous dedication and professionalism. In particular, I thank Tracy Boggier, who was a champion for this project from day one, and Tim Gallan for his expert editorial work.

Publisher's Acknowledgments

Acquisitions Editor: Tracy Boggier
Project Editor: Tim Gallan
Technical Reviewer: Anthony Santero

Production Editor: Mohammed Zafar Ali
Cover Image: © alphaspirit / Shutterstock

CPSIA information can be obtained
at www.ICGtesting.com
Printed in the USA
LVHW102028210120
644302LV00008B/232